DATE DUE

FEB 2 1 2017		
AUG 0 9 2017		

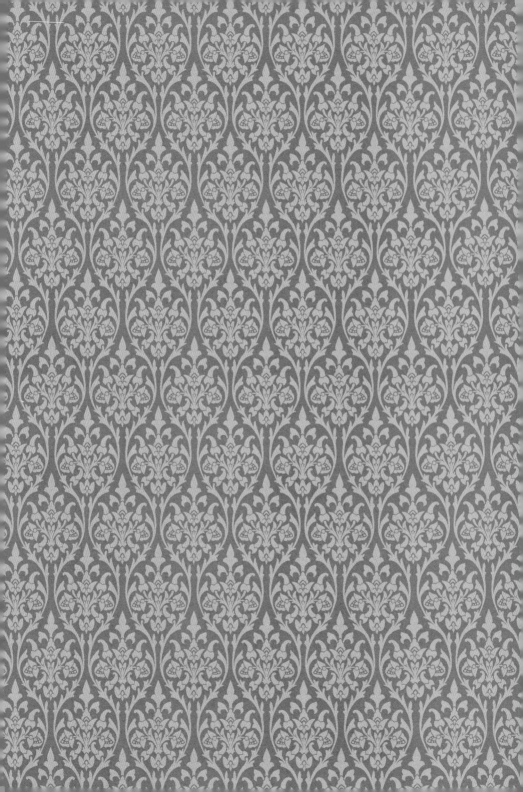

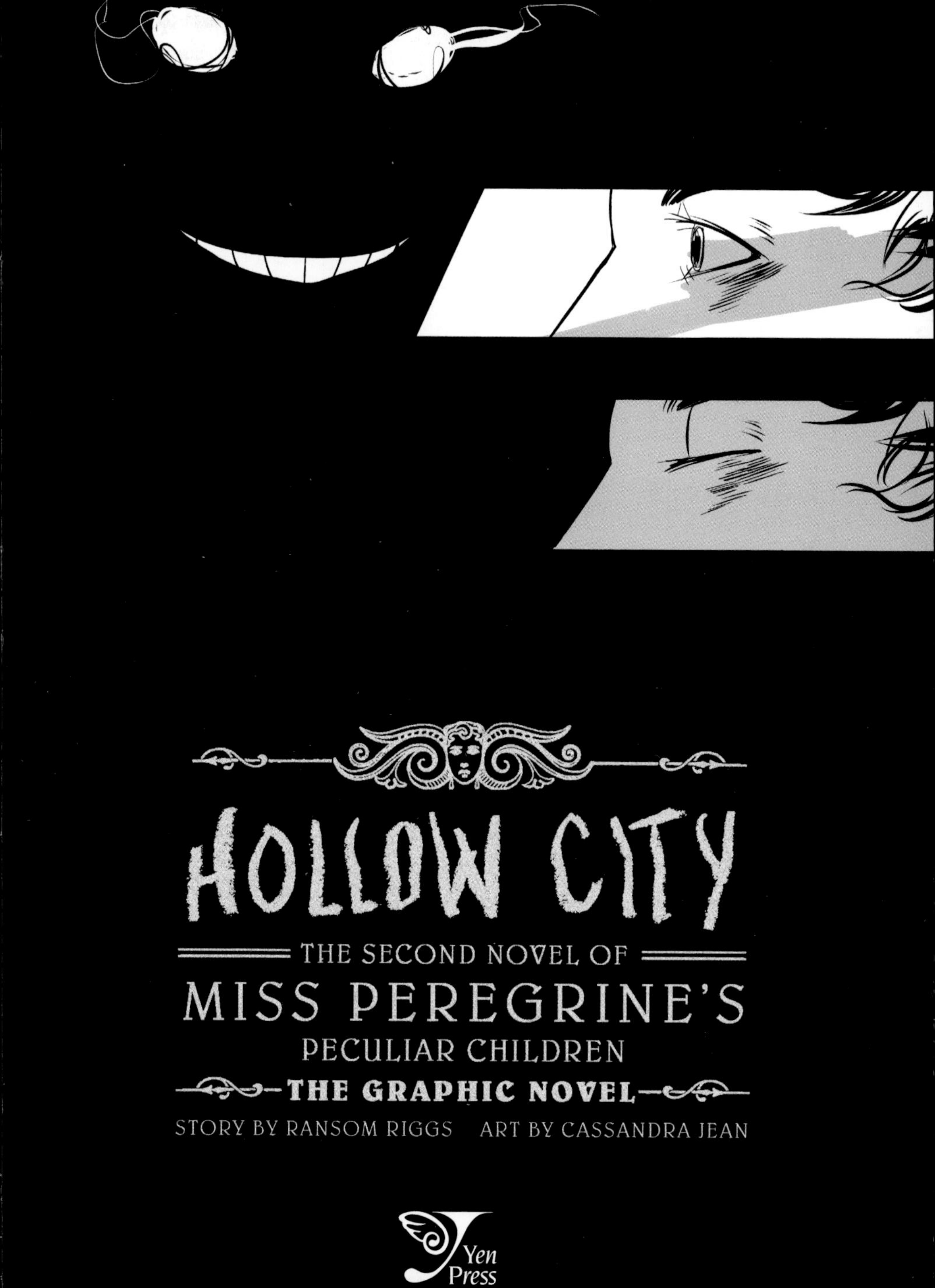

HOLLOW CITY

THE SECOND NOVEL OF

MISS PEREGRINE'S PECULIAR CHILDREN

THE GRAPHIC NOVEL

STORY BY RANSOM RIGGS ART BY CASSANDRA JEAN

Yen Press

HOLLOW CITY, THE SECOND NOVEL OF MISS PEREGRINE'S PECULIAR
CHILDREN: THE GRAPHIC NOVEL

Adaption and Illustration: Cassandra Jean
Lettering: JuYoun Lee & Stephanie Lee

HOLLOW CITY, THE SECOND NOVEL OF MISS PEREGRINE'S PECULIAR
CHILDREN: THE GRAPHIC NOVEL
Text copyright © 2014 Ransom Riggs
Illustrations © 2016 by Yen Press, LLC

Yen Press
1290 Avenue of the Americas
New York, NY 10104
Visit us at yenpress.com
facebook.com/yenpress
twitter.com/yenpress
yenpress.tumblr.com

First Edition: July 2016

Yen Press is an imprint of Yen Press, LLC.
The Yen Press name and logo are trademarks of Yen Press, LLC.

Library of Congress Control Number: 2015952157

ISBN: 978-0-316-30679-9

10 9 8 7 6 5 4 3 2 1

WOR

Printed in the United States of America

CHAPTER ONE

WE WERE TEN CHILDREN AND ONE BIRD IN THREE SMALL AND UNSTEADY BOATS, ROWING WITH QUIET INTENSITY STRAIGHT OUT TO SEA.

WE ROWED OUT THROUGH THE HARBOR, PAST BOBBING BOATS WEEPING RUST FROM THEIR SEAMS, PAST THE OLD LIGHTHOUSE WHICH ONLY LAST NIGHT HAD BEEN THE SCENE OF SO MANY TRAUMAS.

OUR GOAL, THE RUTTED COAST OF MAINLAND WALES, WAS SOMEWHERE BEFORE US BUT ONLY DIMLY VISIBLE, AN INKY SMUDGE SQUATTING ALONG THE FAR HORIZON.

WE ROWED IN SHIFTS, THOUGH I FELT SO STRONG THAT FOR NEARLY AN HOUR I REFUSED TO GIVE THE OARS UP.

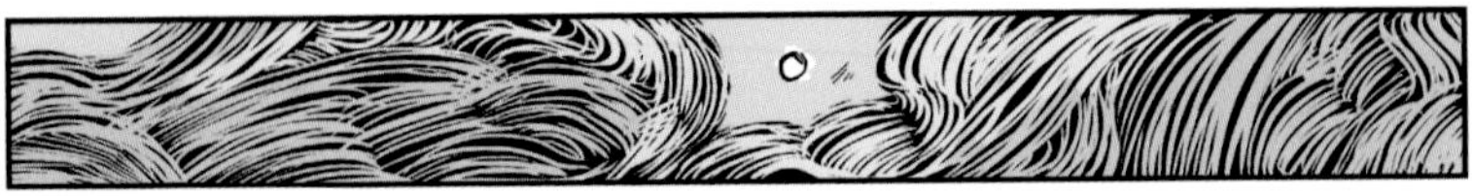

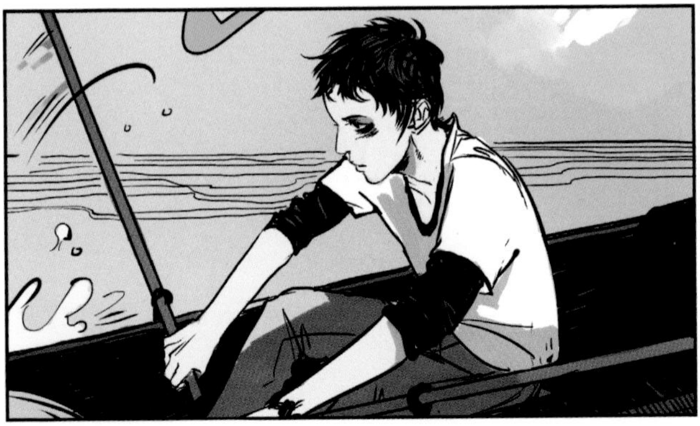

THOSE OF US WHO WORRIED ABOUT SUCH THINGS ASSUMED THE WIGHTS WERE NEARBY, SOMEWHERE BELOW US IN THAT SUBMARINE. IF THEY DIDN'T ALREADY KNOW WE'D FLED THE ISLAND, THEY'D FIND OUT SOON ENOUGH.

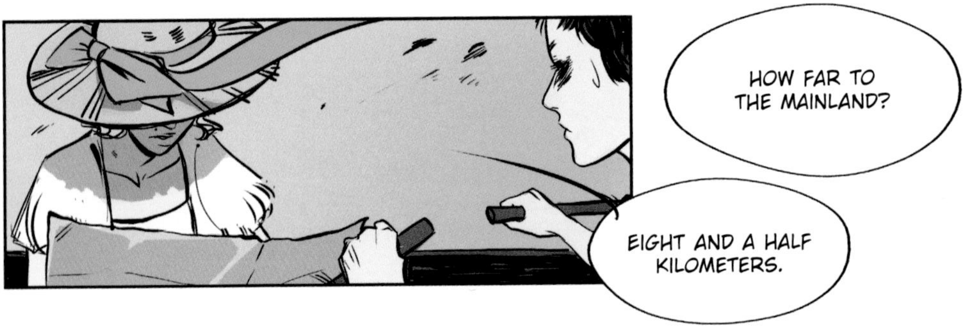
HOW FAR TO THE MAINLAND?
EIGHT AND A HALF KILOMETERS.

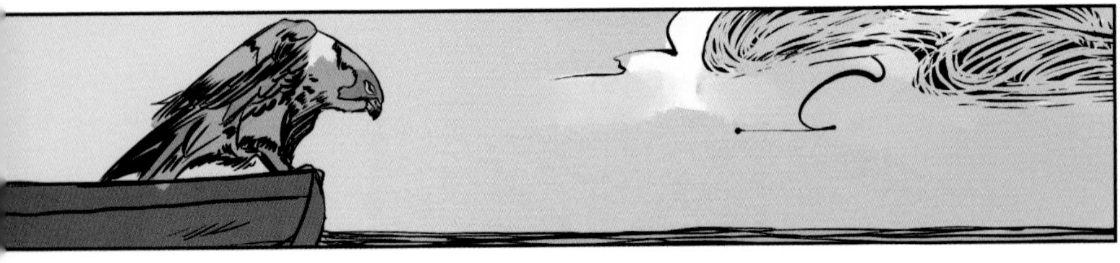

THEY HADN'T GONE TO SUCH LENGTHS TO KIDNAP MISS PEREGRINE ONLY TO GIVE UP AFTER ONE FAILED ATTEMPT. IT MIGHT HAVE BEEN TOO DANGEROUS FOR THE SUBMARINE TO SURFACE IN BROAD DAYLIGHT, BUT COME NIGHTFALL, WE'D BE EASY PREY.

SO WE ROWED, OUR ONLY HOPE THAT WE COULD REACH THE MAINLAND BEFORE NIGHTFALL REACHED US.

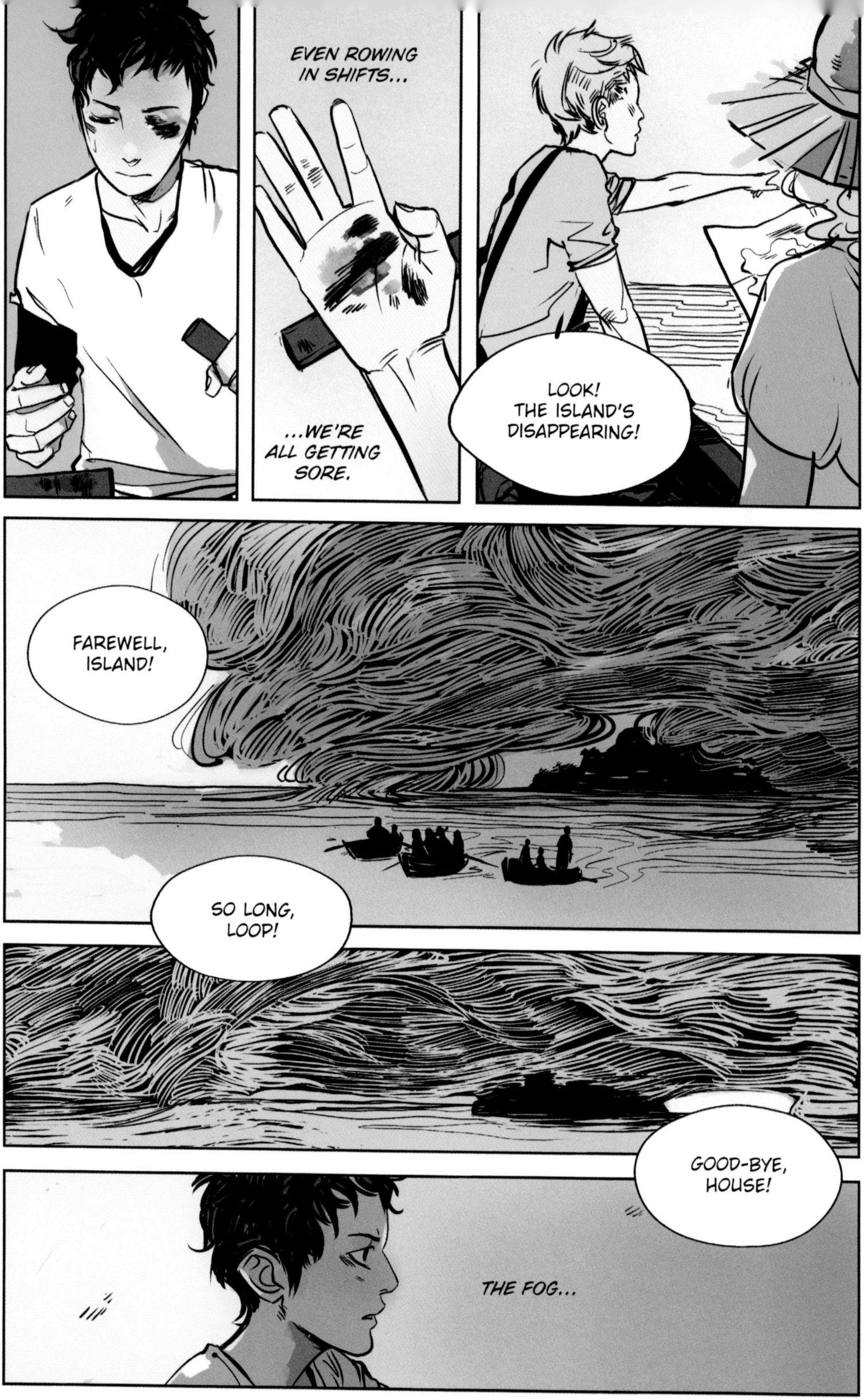
EVEN ROWING IN SHIFTS...
...WE'RE ALL GETTING SORE.
LOOK! THE ISLAND'S DISAPPEARING!
FAREWELL, ISLAND!
SO LONG, LOOP!
GOOD-BYE, HOUSE!
THE FOG...

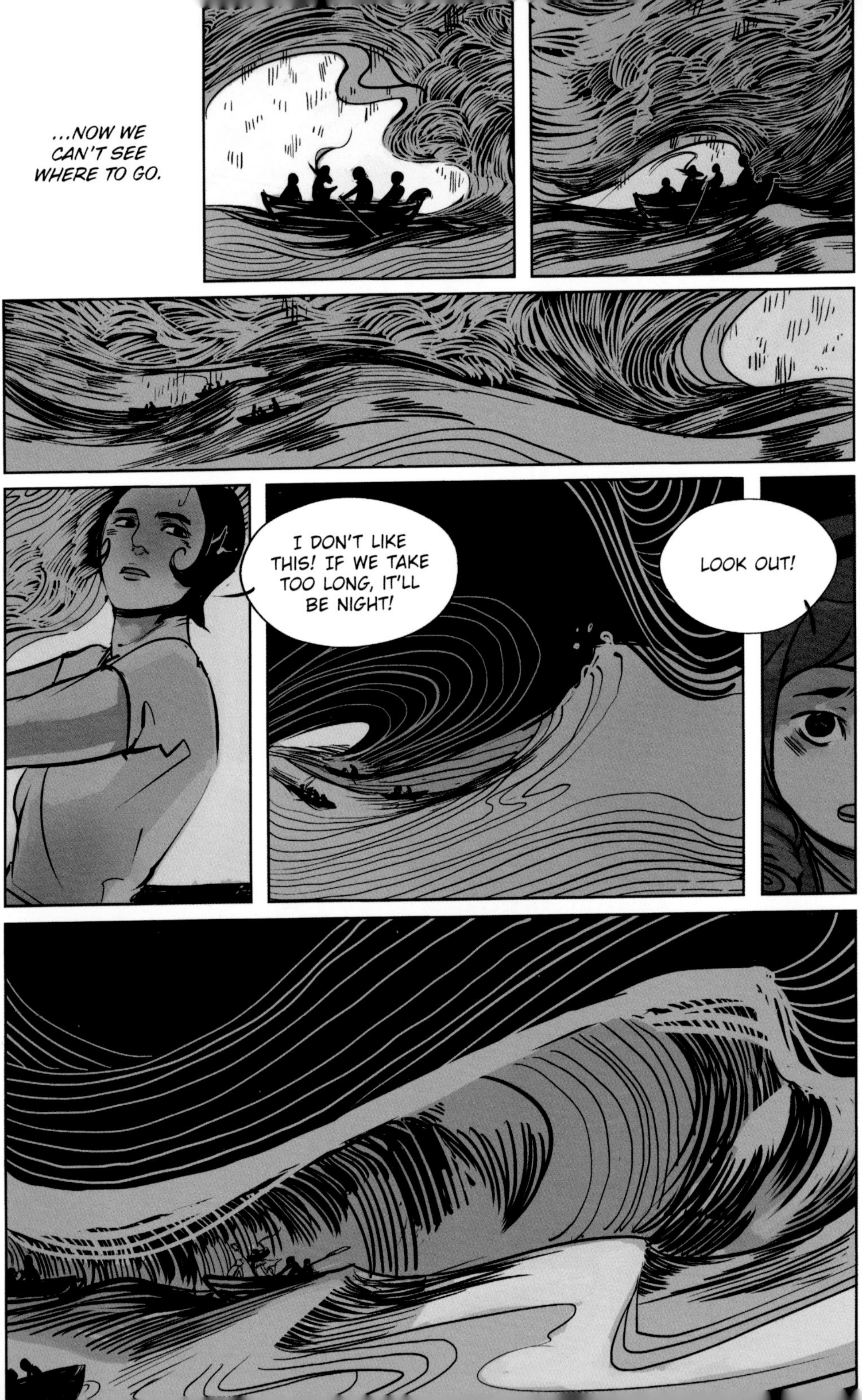
...NOW WE CAN'T SEE WHERE TO GO.
I DON'T LIKE THIS! IF WE TAKE TOO LONG, IT'LL BE NIGHT!
LOOK OUT!

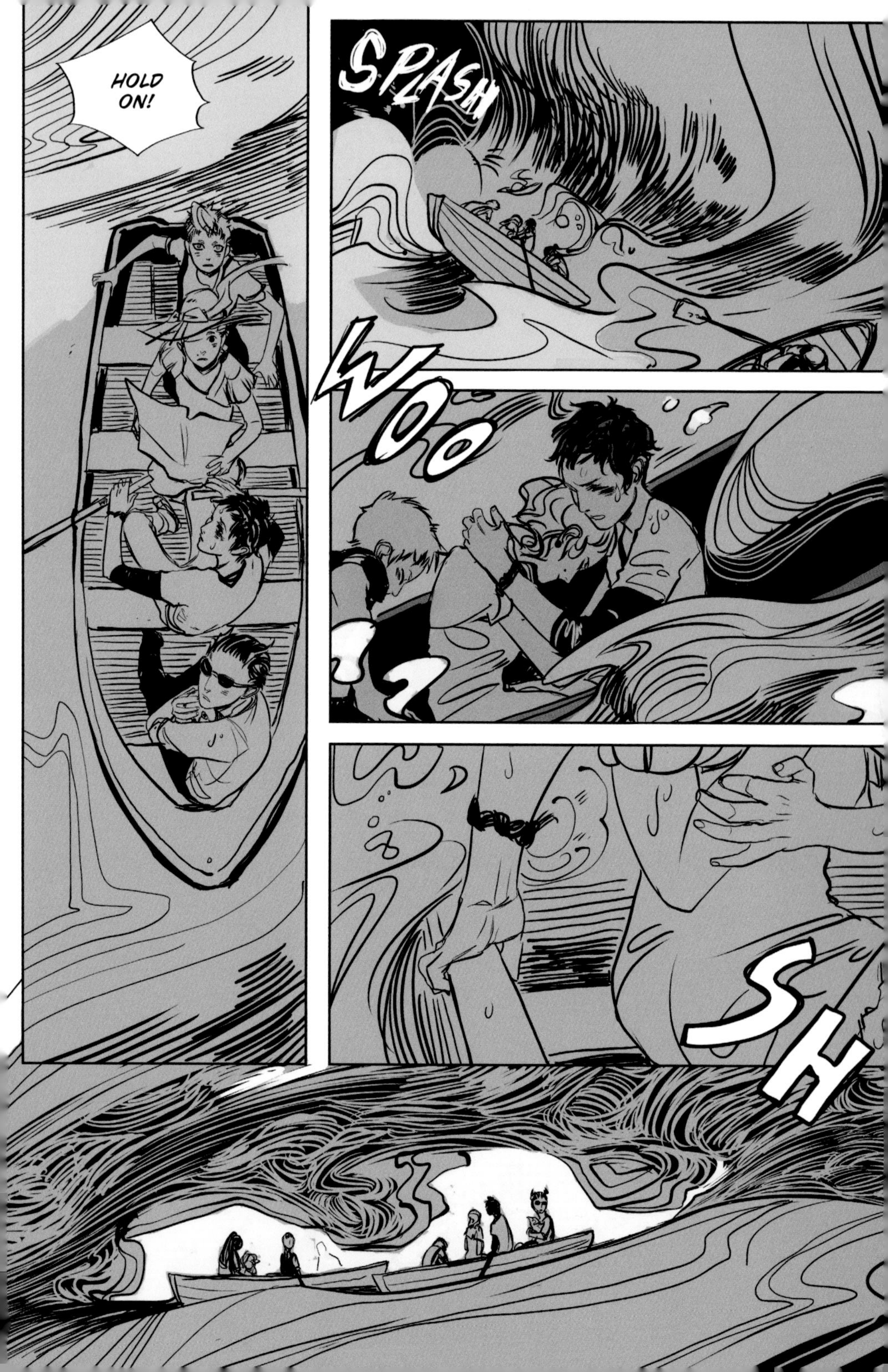
HOLD ON!
SPLASH
WOOO
SH

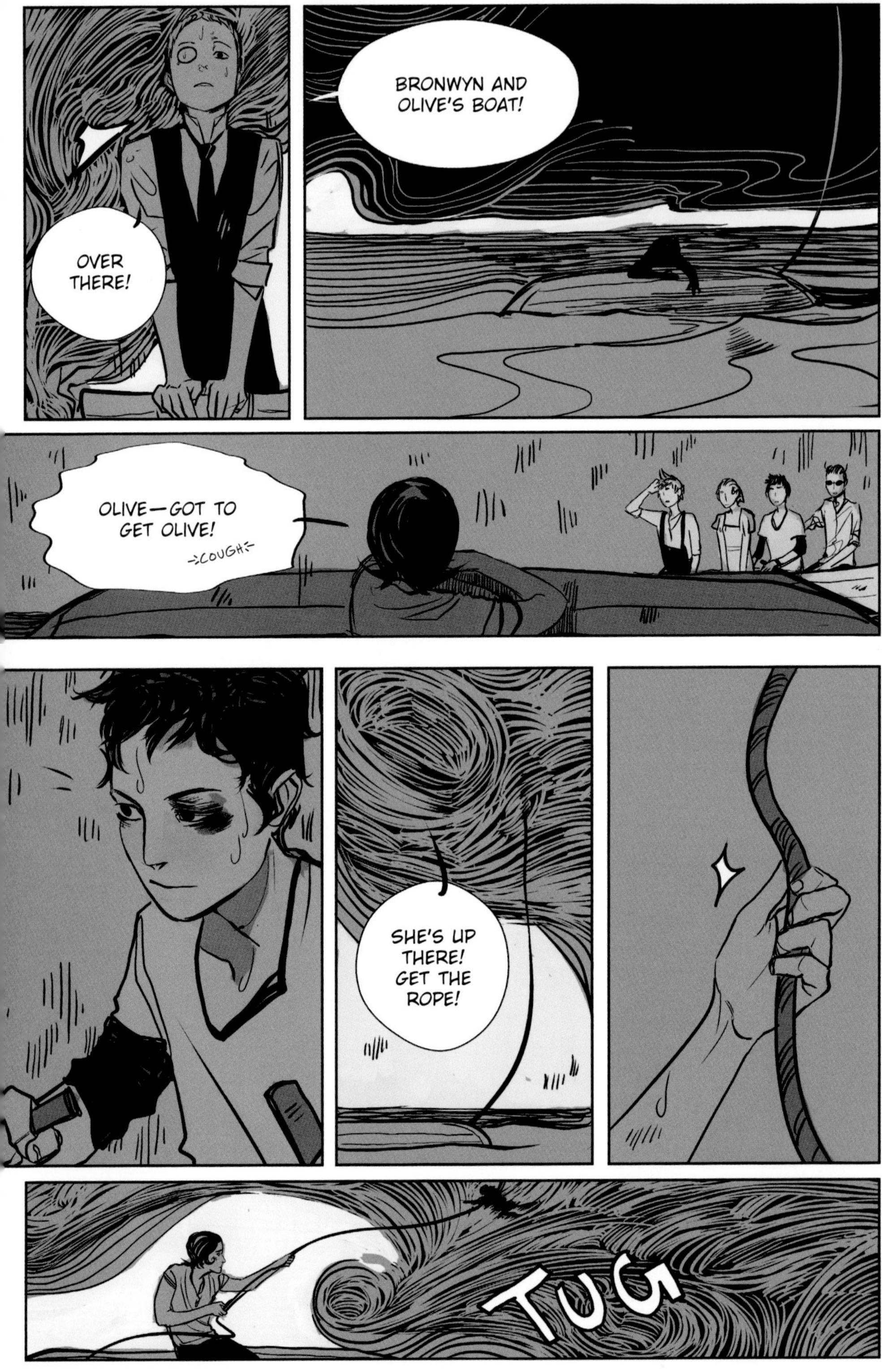
OVER THERE!
BRONWYN AND OLIVE'S BOAT!
OLIVE—GOT TO GET OLIVE!
COUGH
SHE'S UP THERE! GET THE ROPE!
TUG

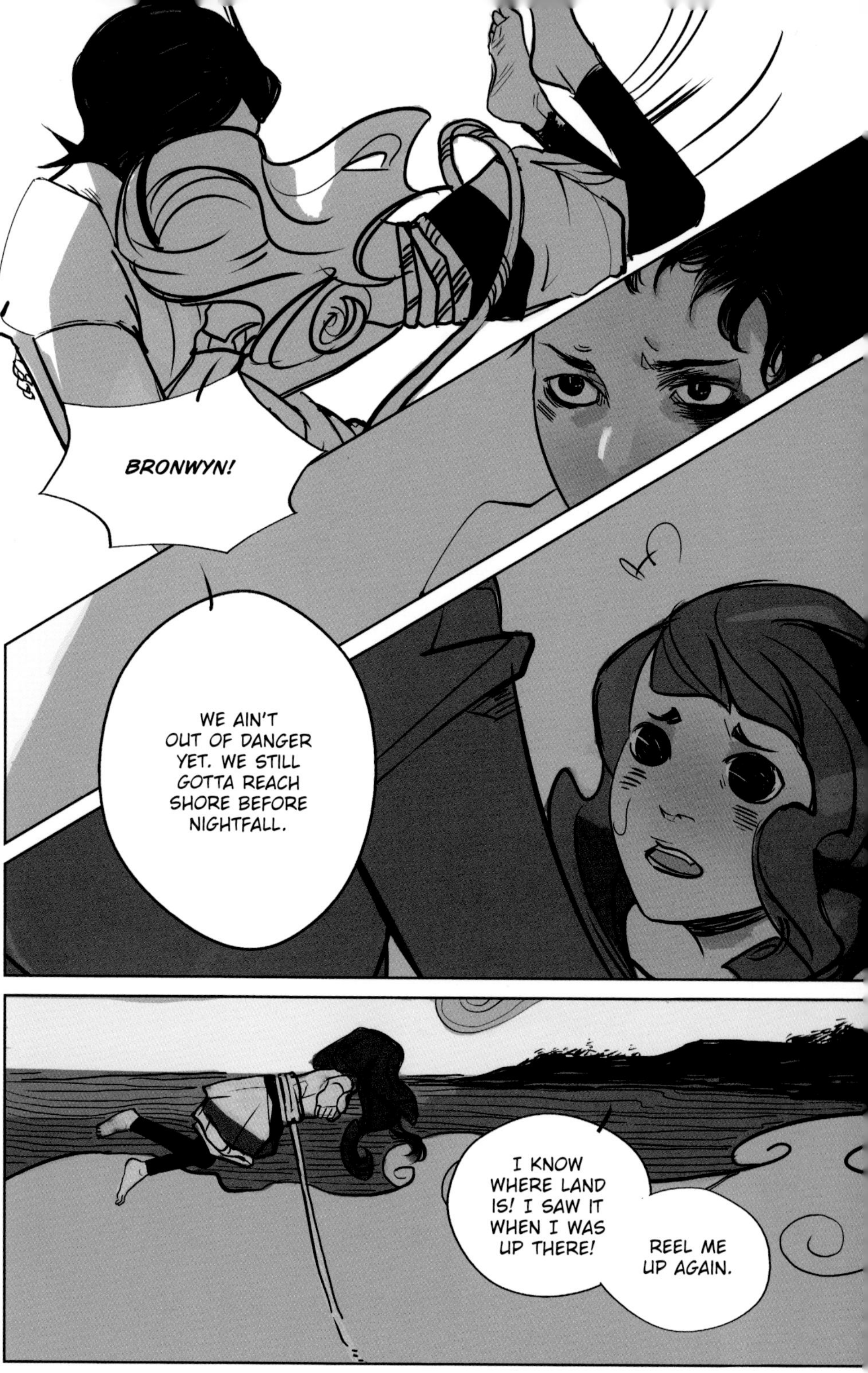
BRONWYN!
WE AIN'T OUT OF DANGER YET. WE STILL GOTTA REACH SHORE BEFORE NIGHTFALL.
I KNOW WHERE LAND IS! I SAW IT WHEN I WAS UP THERE!
REEL ME UP AGAIN.

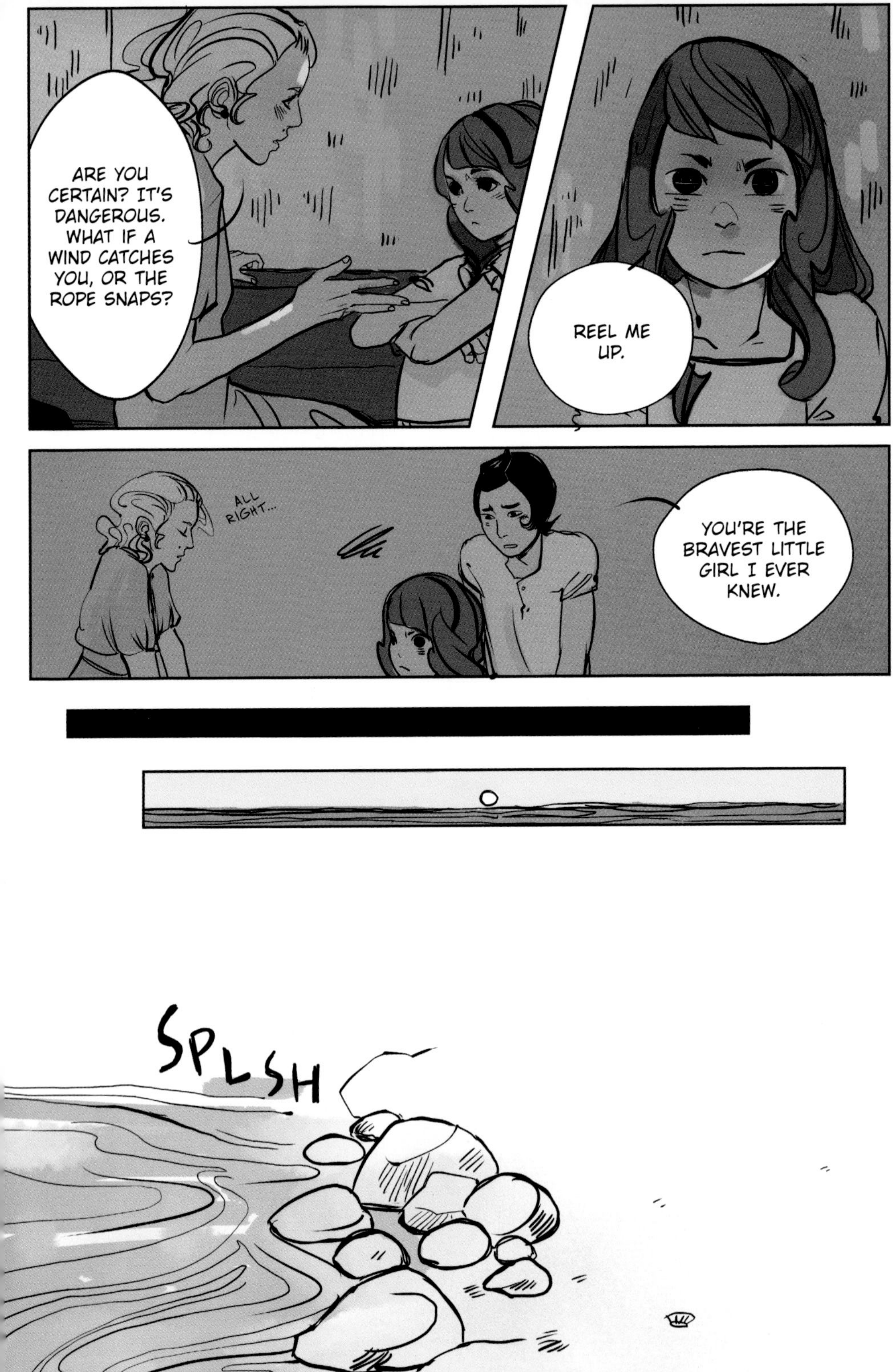
ARE YOU CERTAIN? IT'S DANGEROUS. WHAT IF A WIND CATCHES YOU, OR THE ROPE SNAPS?
REEL ME UP.
ALL RIGHT...
YOU'RE THE BRAVEST LITTLE GIRL I EVER KNEW.
SPLSH

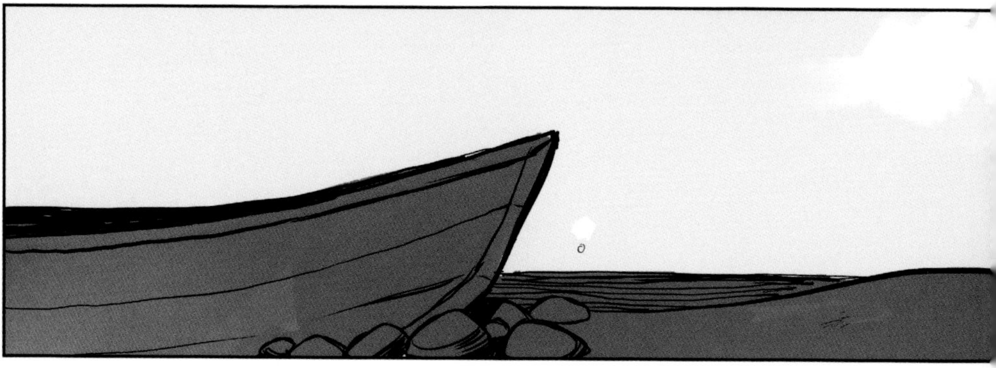

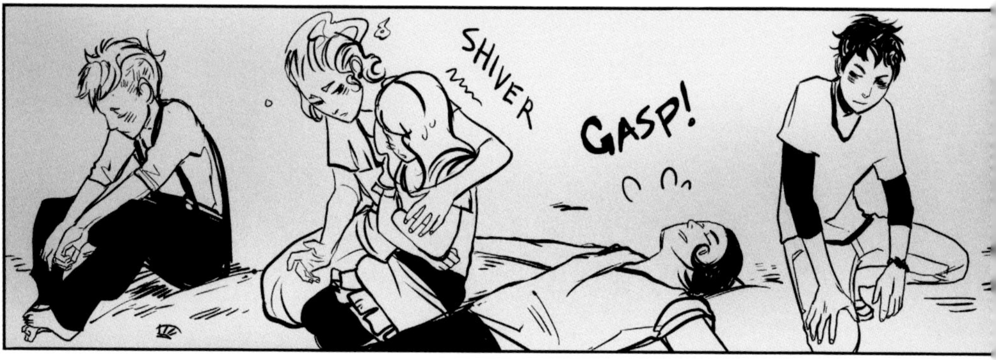
SHIVER
GASP!

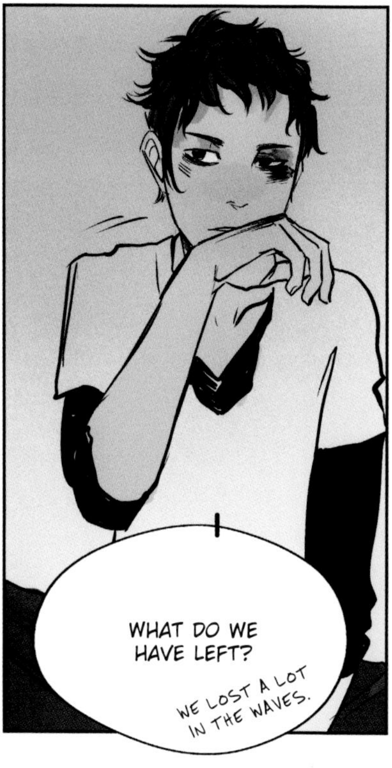
WHAT DO WE HAVE LEFT?
WE LOST A LOT IN THE WAVES.

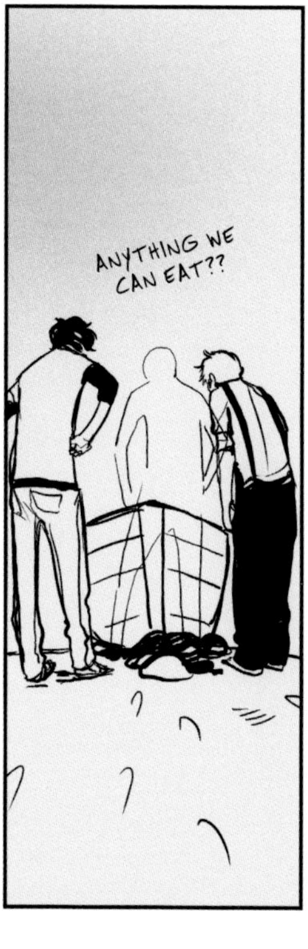
ANYTHING WE CAN EAT??

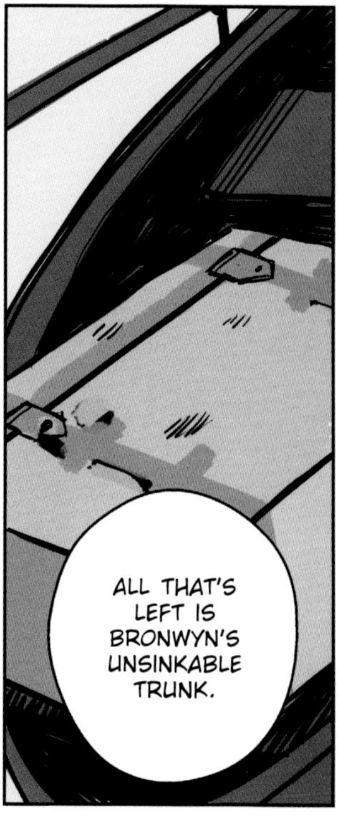
ALL THAT'S LEFT IS BRONWYN'S UNSINKABLE TRUNK.

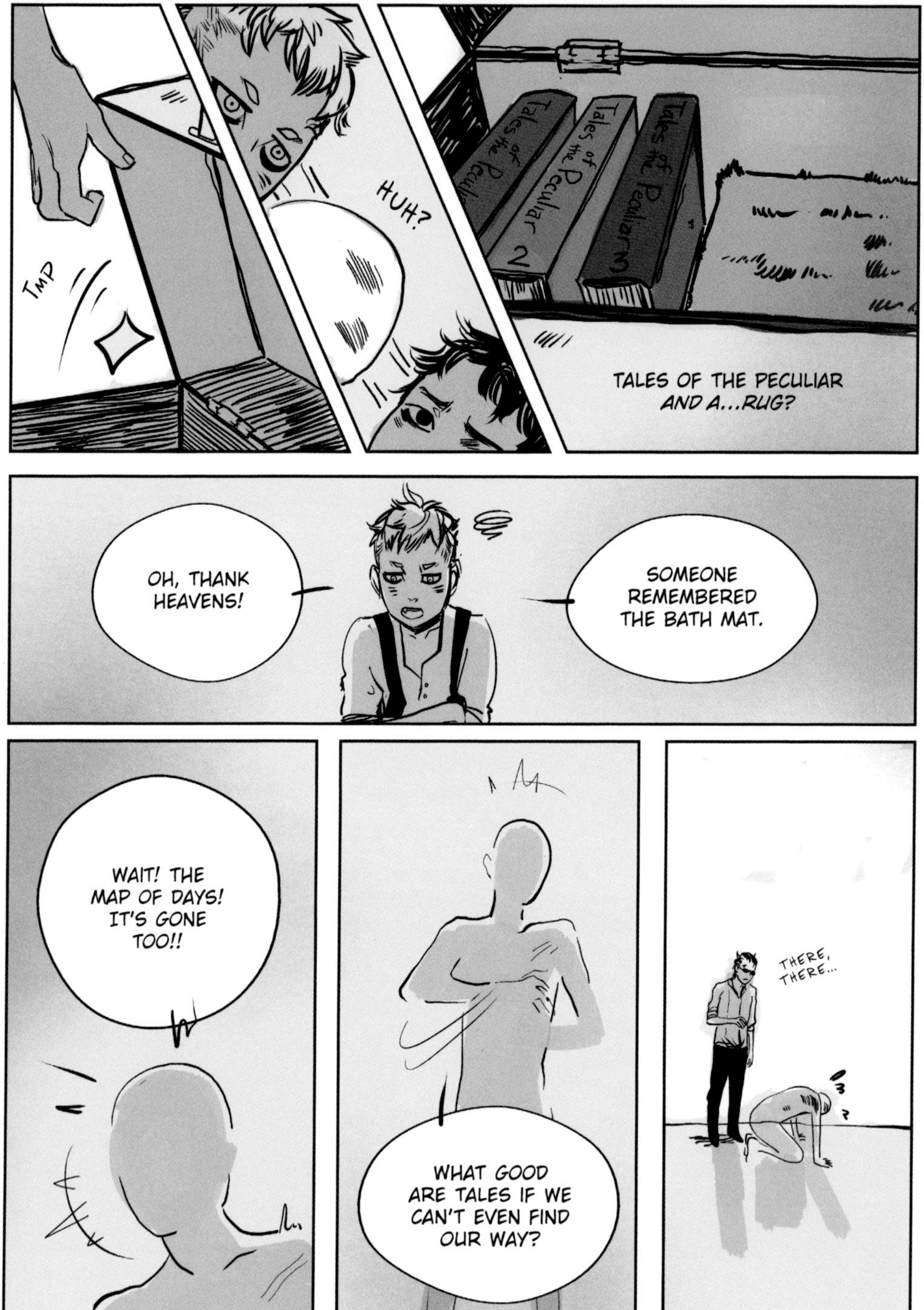
TMP
HUH?
Tales of the Peculiar 2
Tales of the Peculiar
TALES OF THE PECULIAR AND A...RUG?
OH, THANK HEAVENS!
SOMEONE REMEMBERED THE BATH MAT.
WAIT! THE MAP OF DAYS! IT'S GONE TOO!!
WHAT GOOD ARE TALES IF WE CAN'T EVEN FIND OUR WAY?
THERE, THERE...

FIND OUR WAY TO WHERE? I REALIZED THAT I HAD HEARD THE CHILDREN TALK ABOUT REACHING THE MAINLAND, BUT WE NEVER DISCUSSED WHAT TO DO ONCE WE GOT THERE.

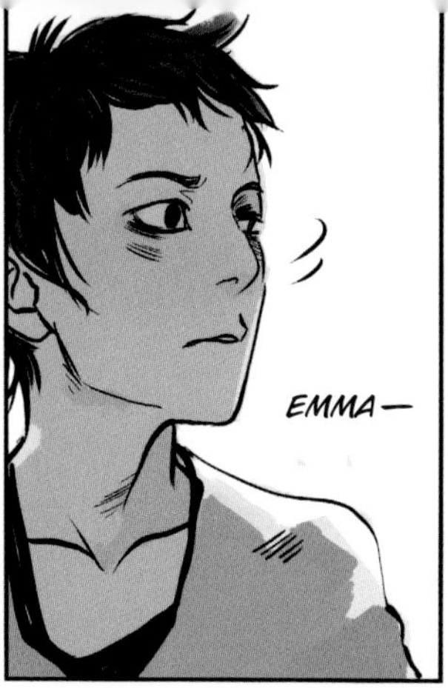
EMMA—

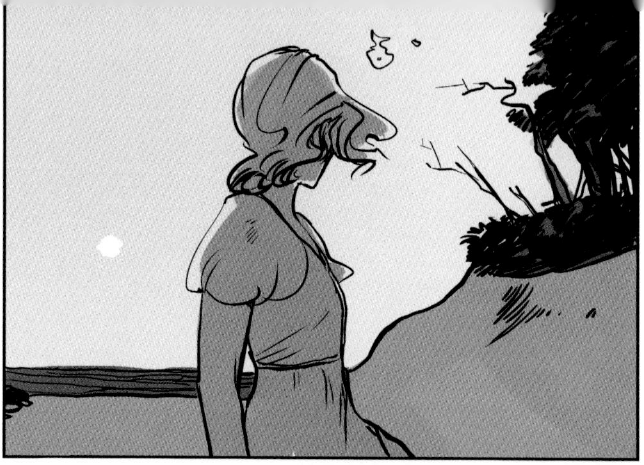

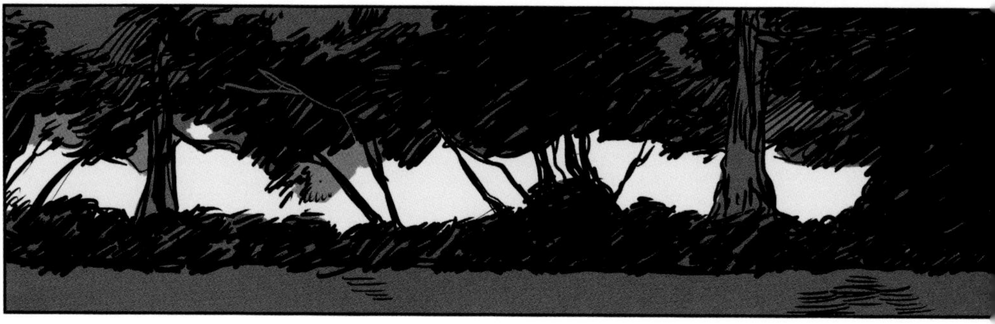

NOTHING BUT WILDERNESS. THERE'S NO TELLING HOW FAR WE'VE STRAYED OFF COURSE.

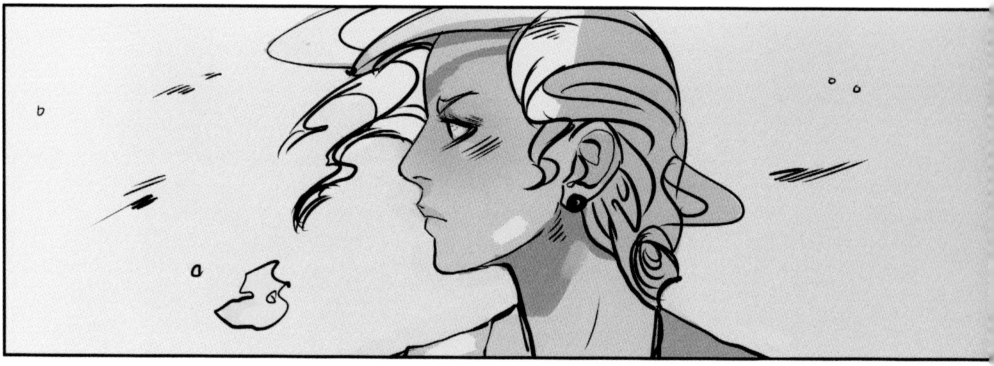

BUT...WE DON'T REALLY NEED A MAP.

OR A SIGNPOST.

OR ANYTHING ELSE.

WE NEED MISS PEREGRINE. WHOLE AND HEALTHY.

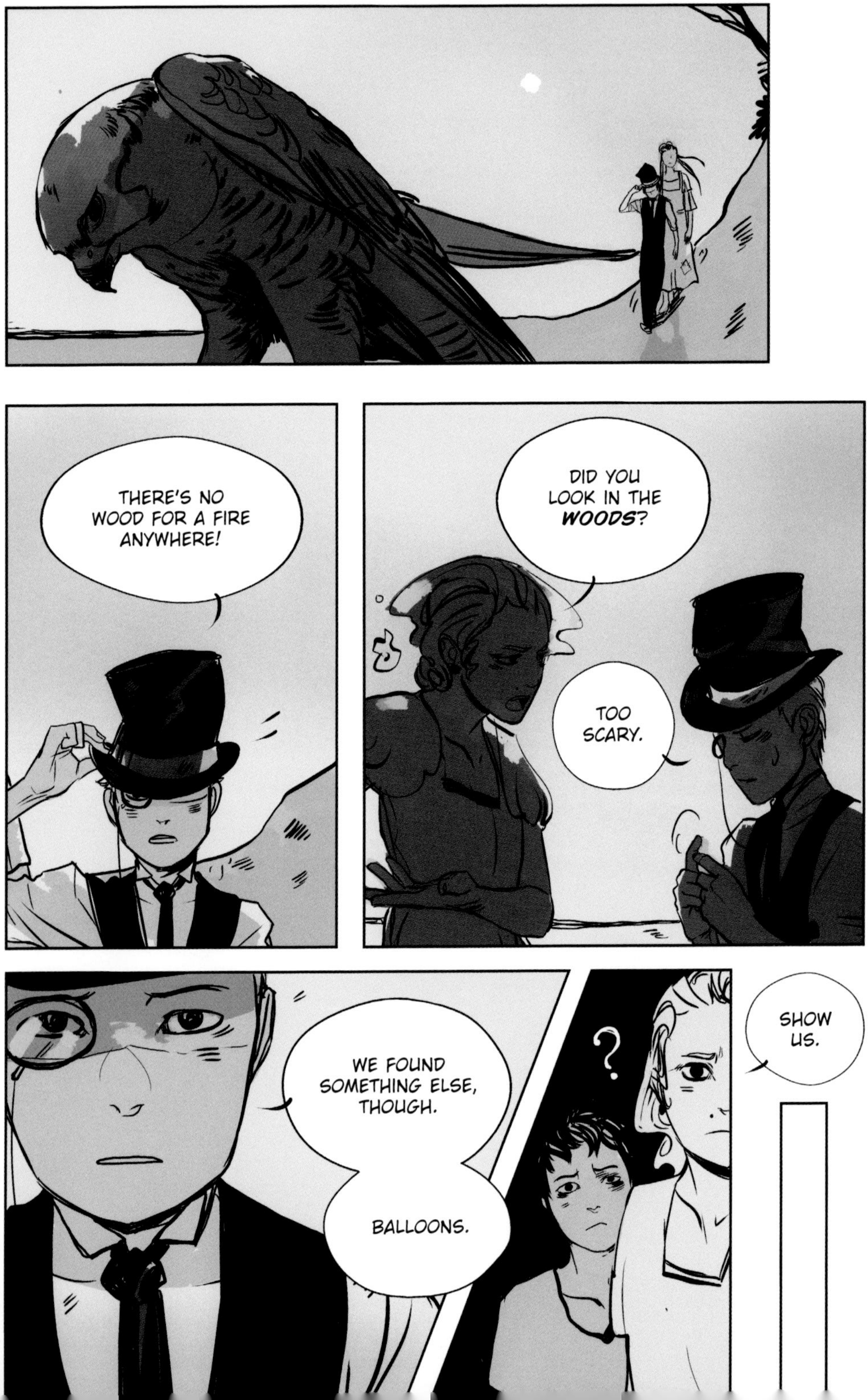
THERE'S NO WOOD FOR A FIRE ANYWHERE!
DID YOU LOOK IN THE **WOODS**?
TOO SCARY.
WE FOUND SOMETHING ELSE, THOUGH.
BALLOONS.
SHOW US.

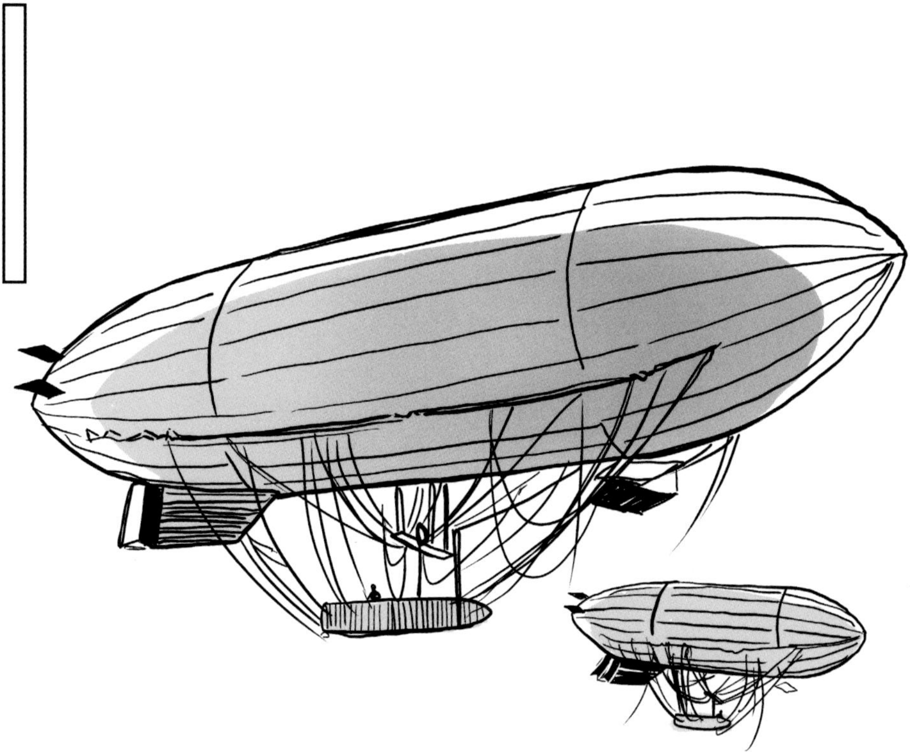

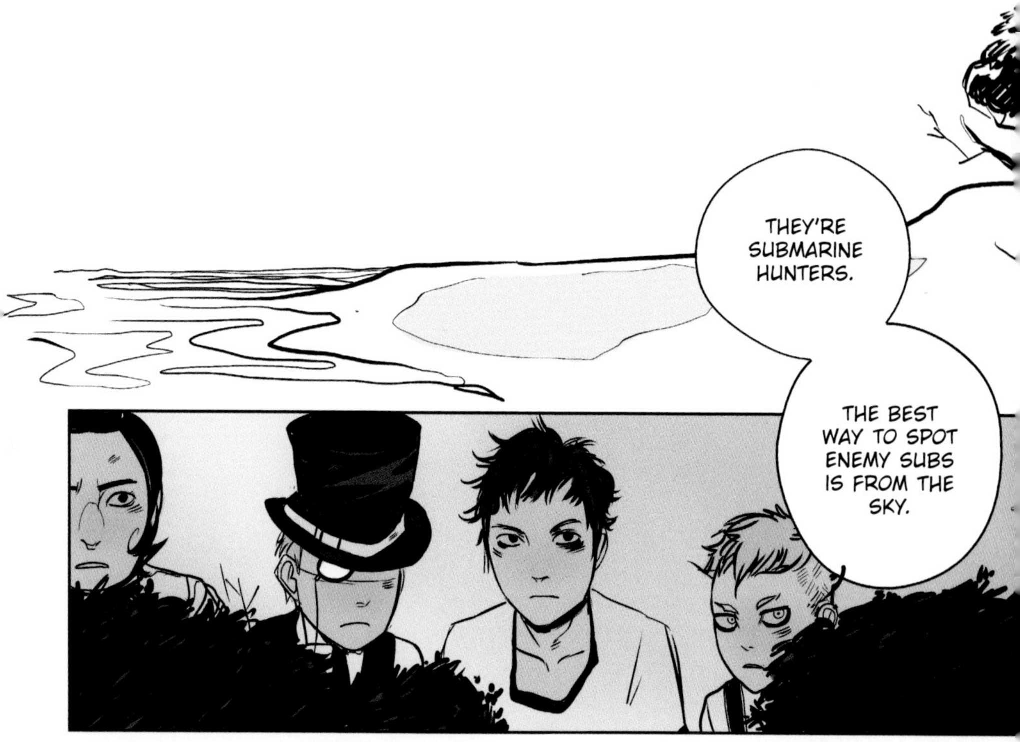
THEY'RE SUBMARINE HUNTERS.
THE BEST WAY TO SPOT ENEMY SUBS IS FROM THE SKY.

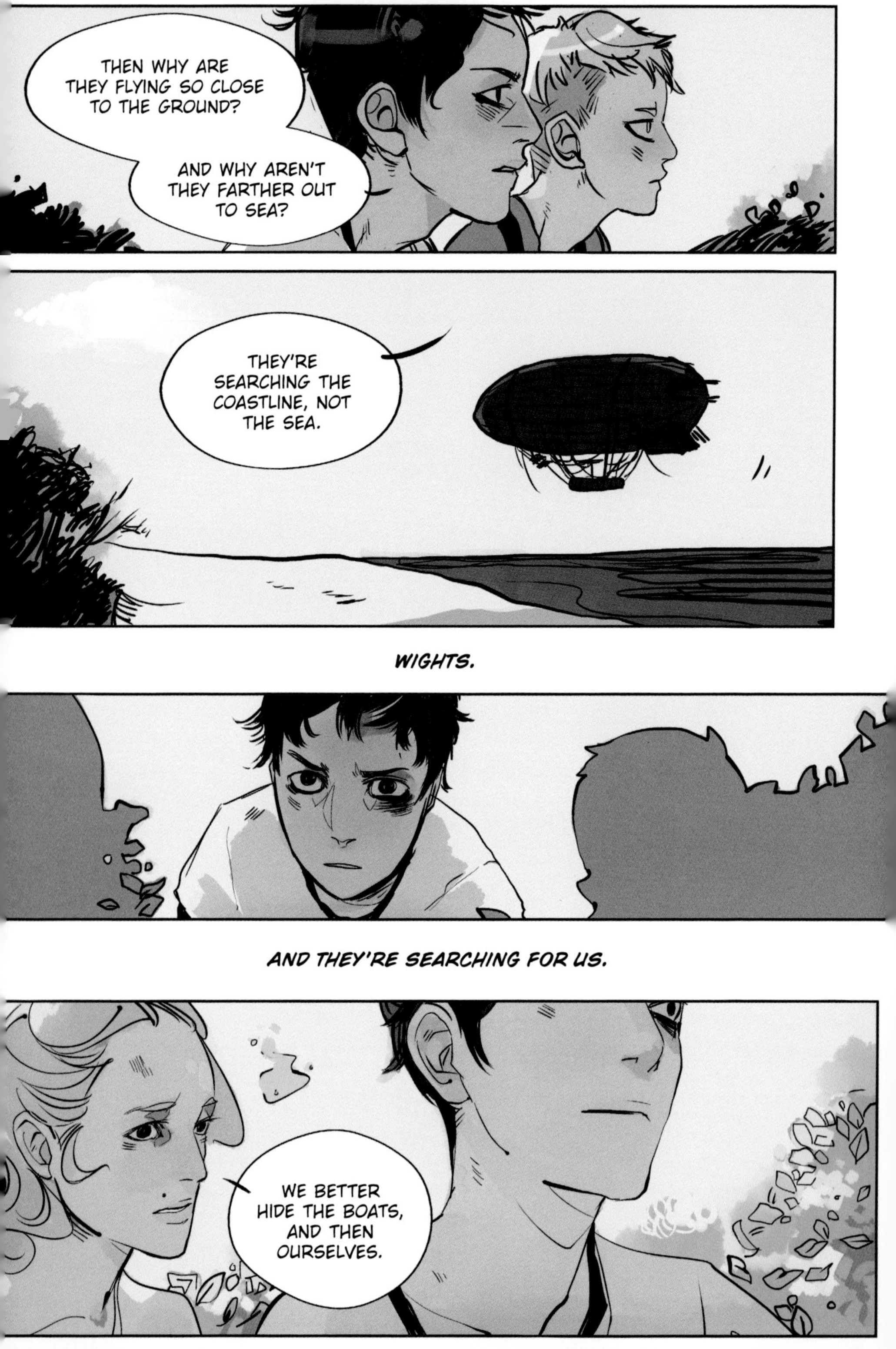
THEN WHY ARE THEY FLYING SO CLOSE TO THE GROUND?
AND WHY AREN'T THEY FARTHER OUT TO SEA?
THEY'RE SEARCHING THE COASTLINE, NOT THE SEA.
WIGHTS.
AND THEY'RE SEARCHING FOR US.
WE BETTER HIDE THE BOATS, AND THEN OURSELVES.

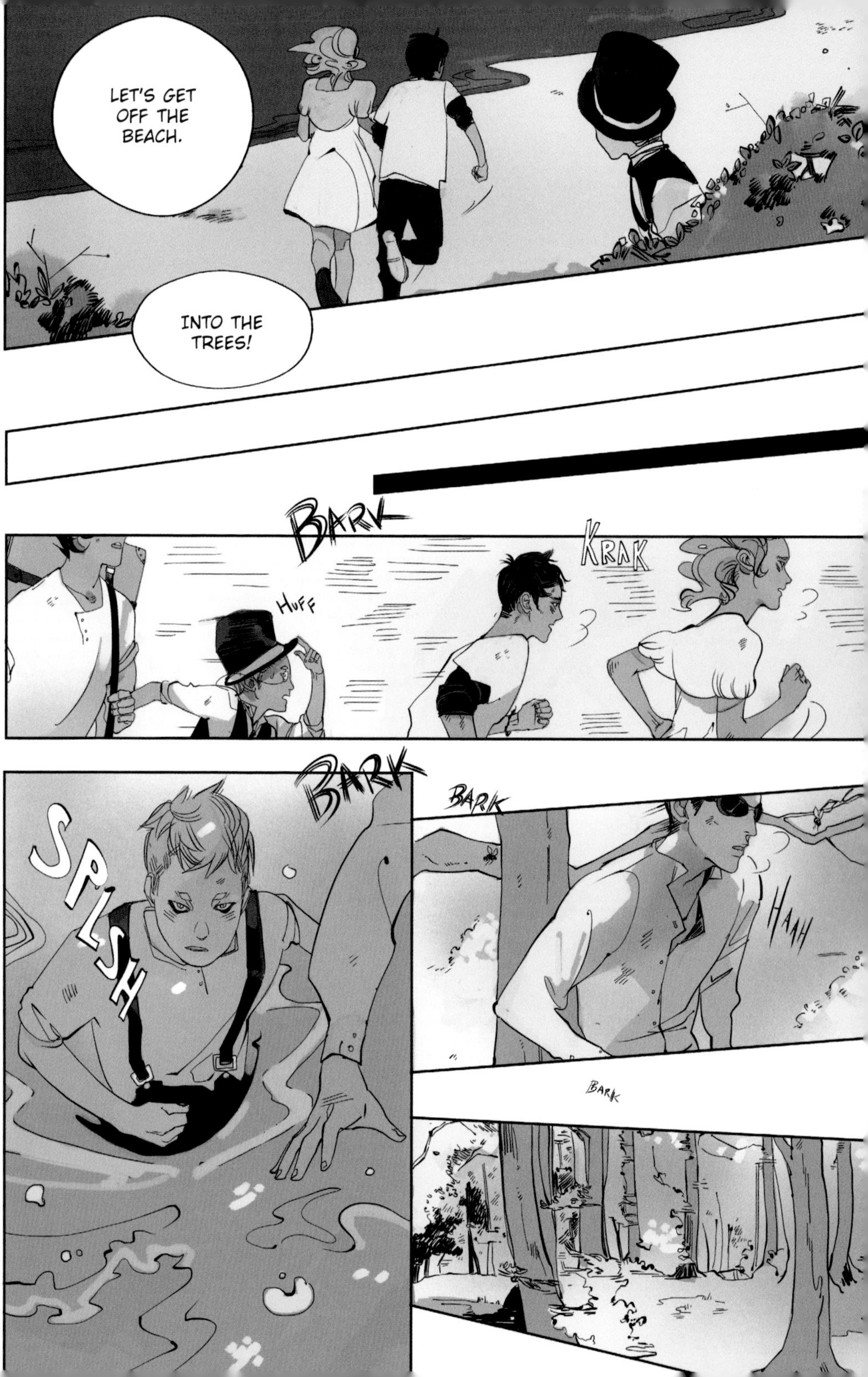
LET'S GET OFF THE BEACH.
INTO THE TREES!
BARK
KRAK
HUFF
SPLSH
BARK
BARK
HAAH
BARK

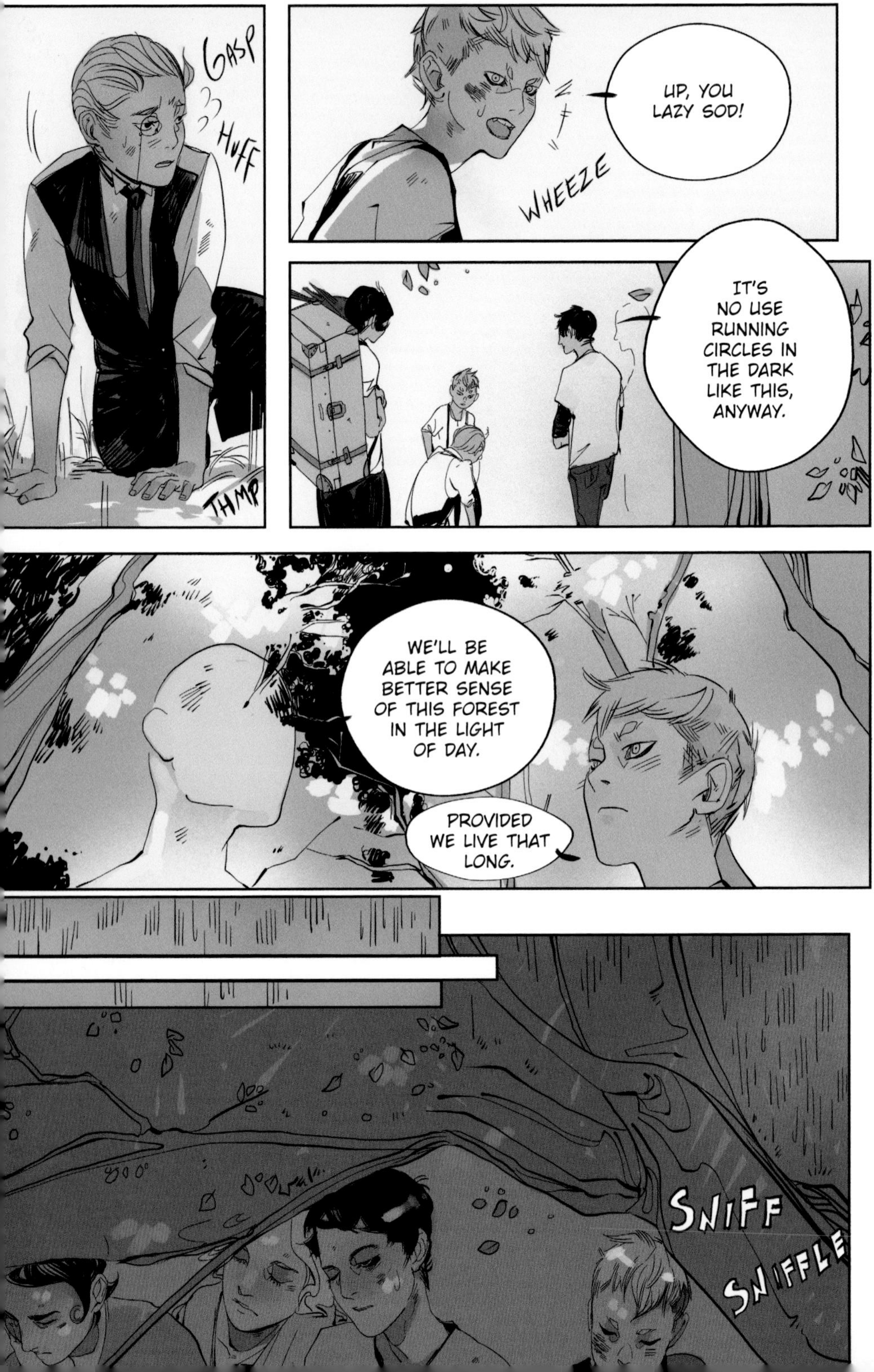
GASP
HUFF
THMP
UP, YOU LAZY SOD!
WHEEZE
IT'S NO USE RUNNING CIRCLES IN THE DARK LIKE THIS, ANYWAY.
WE'LL BE ABLE TO MAKE BETTER SENSE OF THIS FOREST IN THE LIGHT OF DAY.
PROVIDED WE LIVE THAT LONG.
SNIFF
SNIFFLE

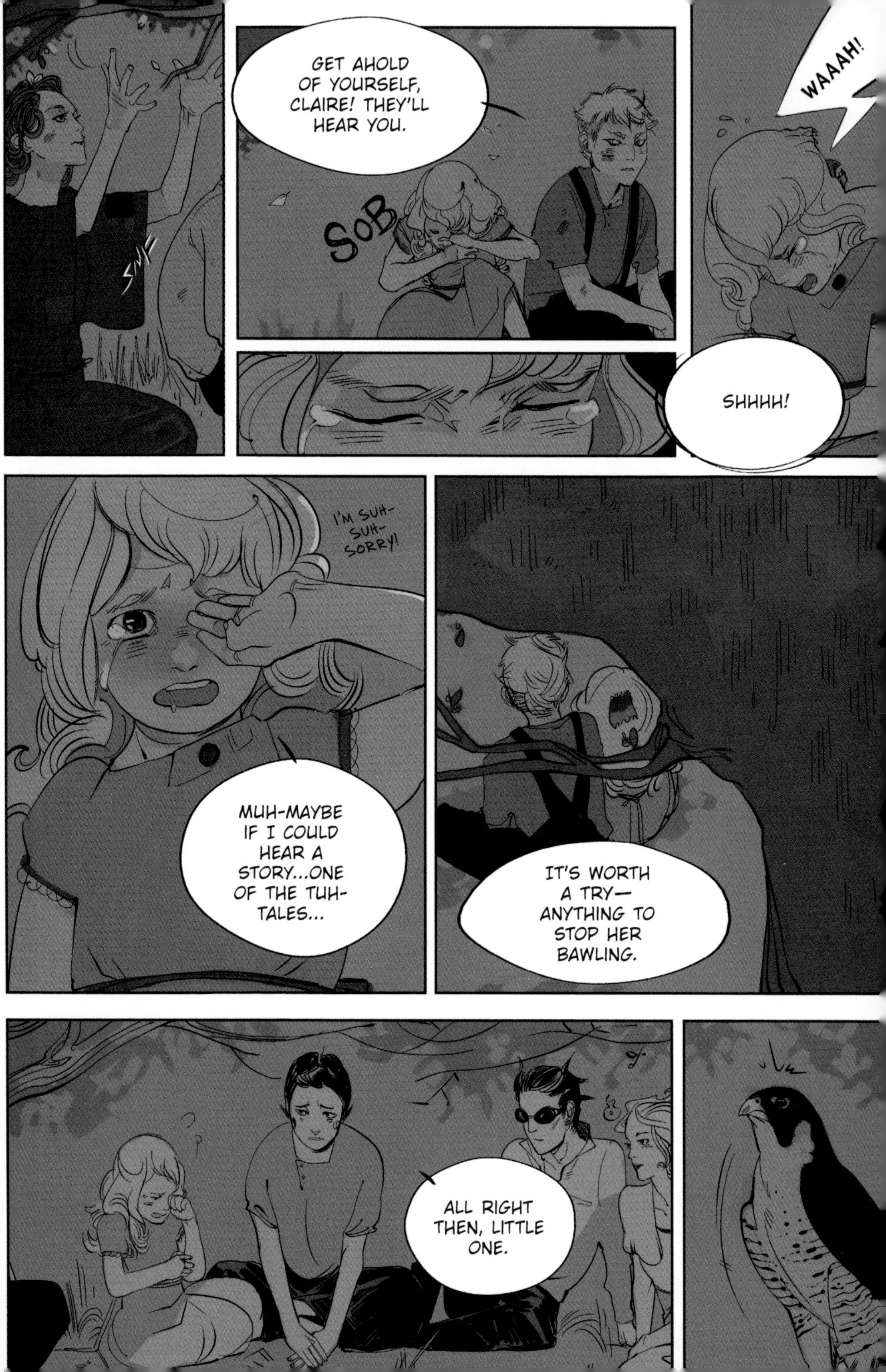
SNIF
GET AHOLD OF YOURSELF, CLAIRE! THEY'LL HEAR YOU.
SOB
WAAAH!
SHHHH!
I'M SUH-SUH-SORRY!
MUH-MAYBE IF I COULD HEAR A STORY...ONE OF THE TUH-TALES...
IT'S WORTH A TRY— ANYTHING TO STOP HER BAWLING.
ALL RIGHT THEN, LITTLE ONE.

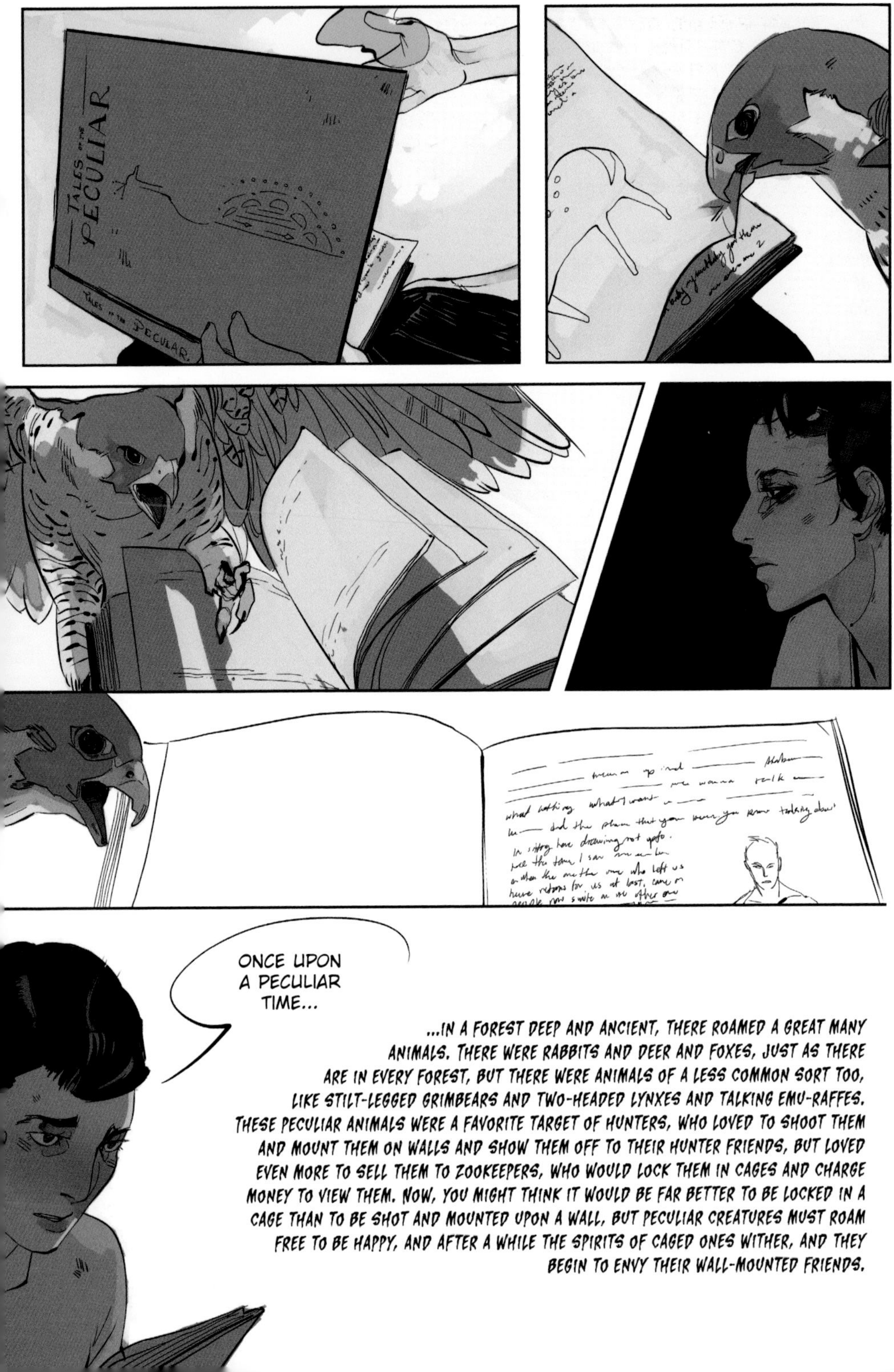
TALES OF THE PECULIAR
ONCE UPON A PECULIAR TIME...
...IN A FOREST DEEP AND ANCIENT, THERE ROAMED A GREAT MANY ANIMALS. THERE WERE RABBITS AND DEER AND FOXES, JUST AS THERE ARE IN EVERY FOREST, BUT THERE WERE ANIMALS OF A LESS COMMON SORT TOO, LIKE STILT-LEGGED GRIMBEARS AND TWO-HEADED LYNXES AND TALKING EMU-RAFFES. THESE PECULIAR ANIMALS WERE A FAVORITE TARGET OF HUNTERS, WHO LOVED TO SHOOT THEM AND MOUNT THEM ON WALLS AND SHOW THEM OFF TO THEIR HUNTER FRIENDS, BUT LOVED EVEN MORE TO SELL THEM TO ZOOKEEPERS, WHO WOULD LOCK THEM IN CAGES AND CHARGE MONEY TO VIEW THEM. NOW, YOU MIGHT THINK IT WOULD BE FAR BETTER TO BE LOCKED IN A CAGE THAN TO BE SHOT AND MOUNTED UPON A WALL, BUT PECULIAR CREATURES MUST ROAM FREE TO BE HAPPY, AND AFTER A WHILE THE SPIRITS OF CAGED ONES WITHER, AND THEY BEGIN TO ENVY THEIR WALL-MOUNTED FRIENDS.

NOW, THIS WAS AN AGE WHEN GIANTS STILL ROAMED THE EARTH, AS THEY DID IN THE LONG-AGO *ALDINN* TIMES, THOUGH THEY WERE FEW IN NUMBER AND DIMINISHING. AND IT JUST SO HAPPENED THAT ONE OF THESE GIANTS LIVED NEAR THE FOREST, AND HE WAS VERY KIND AND SPOKE VERY SOFTLY AND ATE ONLY PLANTS AND HIS NAME WAS CUTHBERT. ONE DAY, CUTHBERT CAME INTO THE FOREST TO GATHER BERRIES, AND THERE SAW A HUNTER HUNTING AN EMU-RAFFE. BEING THE KINDLY GIANT THAT HE WAS, CUTHBERT PICKED UP THE LITTLE 'RAFFE BY THE SCRUFF OF ITS LONG NECK, AND BY STANDING UP TO HIS FULL HEIGHT, ON TIPTOE, WHICH HE RARELY DID BECAUSE IT MADE ALL HIS OLD BONES CRACKLE, CUTHBERT WAS ABLE TO REACH UP VERY HIGH AND DEPOSIT THE EMU-RAFFE ON A MOUNTAINTOP, WELL OUT OF DANGER. THEN, JUST FOR GOOD MEASURE, HE SQUASHED THE HUNTER TO JELLY BETWEEN HIS TOES.

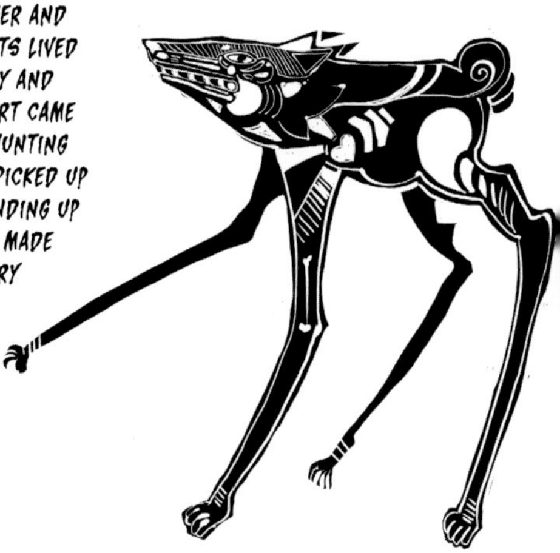

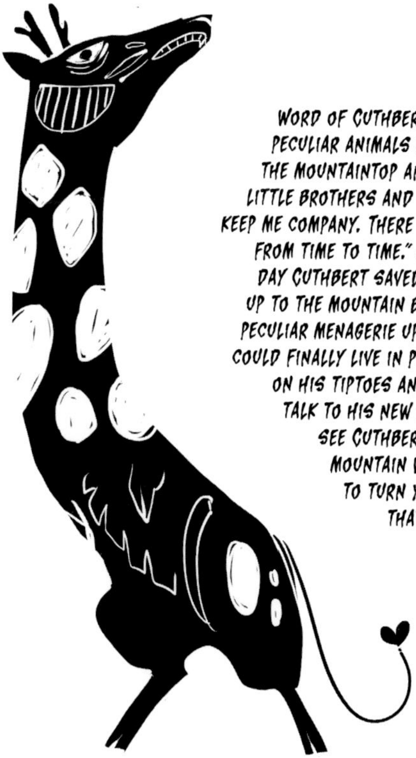

WORD OF CUTHBERT'S KINDNESS SPREAD THROUGHOUT THE FOREST, AND SOON PECULIAR ANIMALS WERE COMING TO HIM EVERY DAY, ASKING TO BE LIFTED UP TO THE MOUNTAINTOP AND OUT OF DANGER. AND CUTHBERT SAID, "I'LL PROTECT YOU, LITTLE BROTHERS AND SISTERS. ALL I ASK IN RETURN IS THAT YOU TALK TO ME AND KEEP ME COMPANY. THERE AREN'T MANY GIANTS LEFT IN THE WORLD, AND I GET LONELY FROM TIME TO TIME." AND THEY SAID, "OF COURSE, CUTHBERT, WE WILL." SO EVERY DAY CUTHBERT SAVED MORE PECULIAR ANIMALS FROM THE HUNTERS, LIFTING THEM UP TO THE MOUNTAIN BY THE SCRUFFS OF THEIR NECKS, UNTIL THERE WAS A WHOLE PECULIAR MENAGERIE UP THERE. AND THE ANIMALS WERE HAPPY THERE BECAUSE THEY COULD FINALLY LIVE IN PEACE, AND CUTHBERT WAS HAPPY TOO, BECAUSE IF HE STOOD ON HIS TIPTOES AND RESTED HIS CHIN ON THE TOP OF THE MOUNTAIN HE COULD TALK TO HIS NEW FRIENDS ALL HE LIKED. THEN ONE MORNING A WITCH CAME TO SEE CUTHBERT. HE WAS BATHING IN A LITTLE LAKE IN THE SHADOW OF THE MOUNTAIN WHEN SHE SAID TO HIM, "I'M TERRIBLY SORRY, BUT I'VE GOT TO TURN YOU INTO STONE NOW." "WHY WOULD YOU DO SOMETHING LIKE THAT?" ASKED THE GIANT. "I'M VERY KINDLY. A HELPING SORT OF GIANT." AND SHE SAID, "I WAS HIRED BY THE FAMILY OF THE HUNTER YOU SQUASHED."

"AH," HE REPLIED. "FORGOT ABOUT HIM." "I'M TERRIBLY SORRY," THE WITCH SAID AGAIN, AND THEN SHE WAVED A BIRCH BRANCH AT HIM AND POOR CUTHBERT TURNED TO STONE. ALL OF THE SUDDEN, CUTHBERT BECAME VERY HEAVY—SO HEAVY THAT HE BEGAN TO SINK INTO THE LAKE. HE SANK AND SANK AND DIDN'T STOP SINKING UNTIL HE WAS COVERED IN WATER ALL THE WAY UP TO HIS NECK. HIS ANIMAL FRIENDS SAW WHAT WAS HAPPENING, AND THOUGH THEY FELT TERRIBLE ABOUT IT, THEY DECIDED THEY COULD DO NOTHING TO HELP HIM. "I KNOW YOU CAN'T SAVE ME," CUTHBERT SHOUTED UP TO HIS FRIENDS, "BUT AT LEAST COME AND TALK TO ME! I'M STUCK DOWN HERE, AND SO VERY LONELY!"

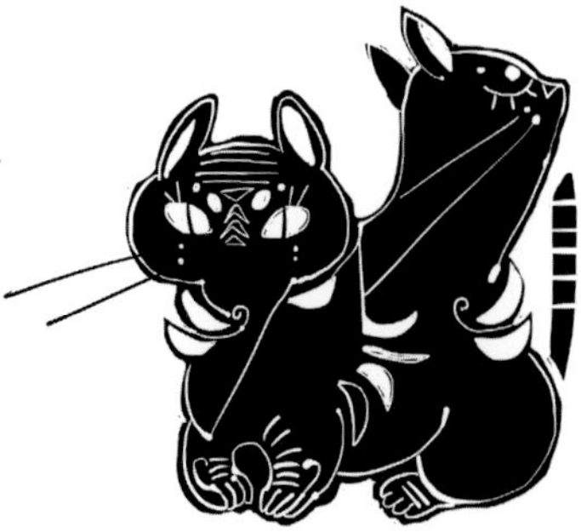

"BUT IF WE COME DOWN THERE, THE HUNTERS WILL SHOOT US!" THEY CALLED BACK. CUTHBERT KNEW THEY WERE RIGHT, BUT STILL HE PLEADED WITH THEM. "TALK TO ME!" HE CRIED. "PLEASE COME AND TALK TO ME!" THE ANIMALS TRIED SINGING AND SHOUTING TO POOR CUTHBERT FROM THE SAFETY OF THEIR MOUNTAINTOP, BUT THEY WERE TOO DISTANT AND THEIR VOICES TOO SMALL, SO THAT EVEN TO CUTHBERT AND HIS GIANT EARS THEY SOUNDED QUIETER THAN THE WHISPER OF LEAVES IN THE WIND. "TALK TO ME!" HE BEGGED. "COME AND TALK TO ME!" BUT THEY NEVER DID. AND HE WAS STILL CRYING WHEN HIS THROAT TURNED TO STONE LIKE THE REST OF HIM.

THE END.

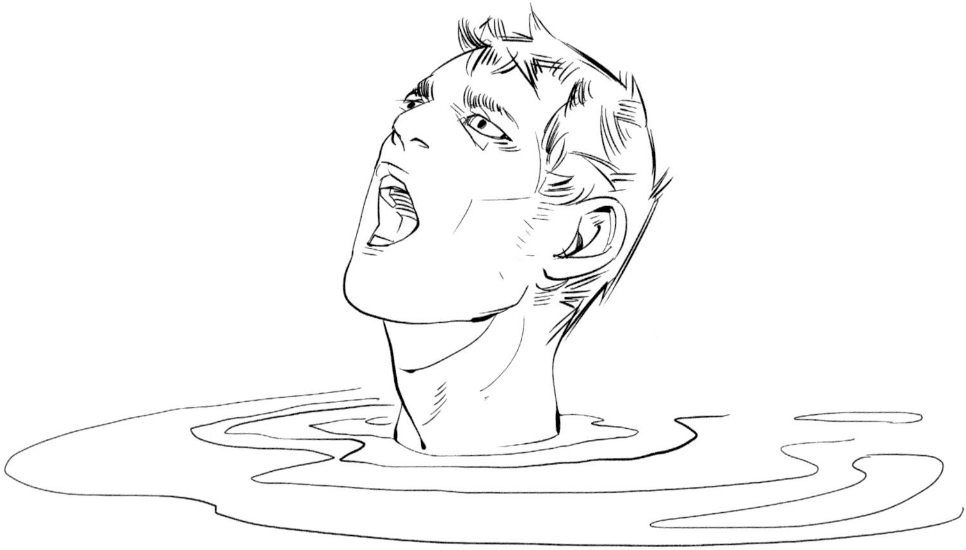

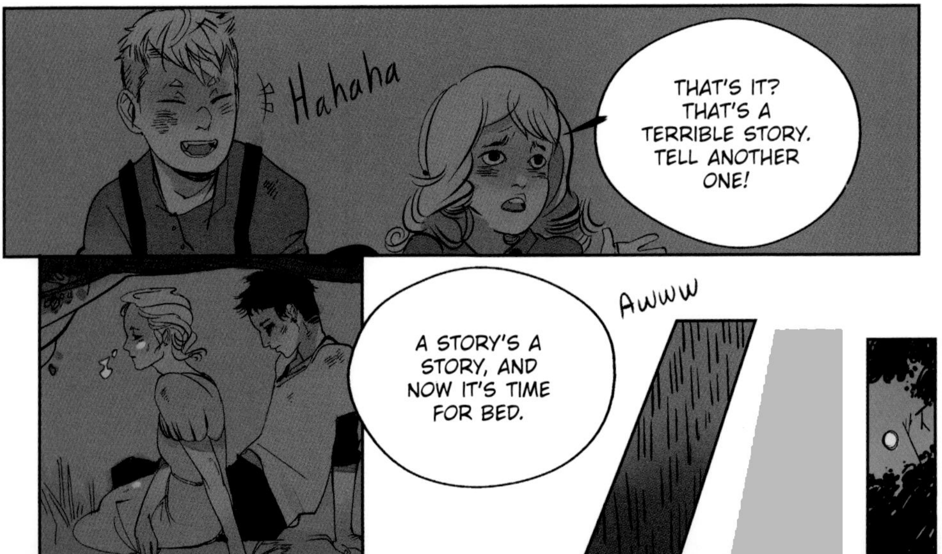
Hahaha
THAT'S IT? THAT'S A TERRIBLE STORY. TELL ANOTHER ONE!
A STORY'S A STORY, AND NOW IT'S TIME FOR BED.
Awww

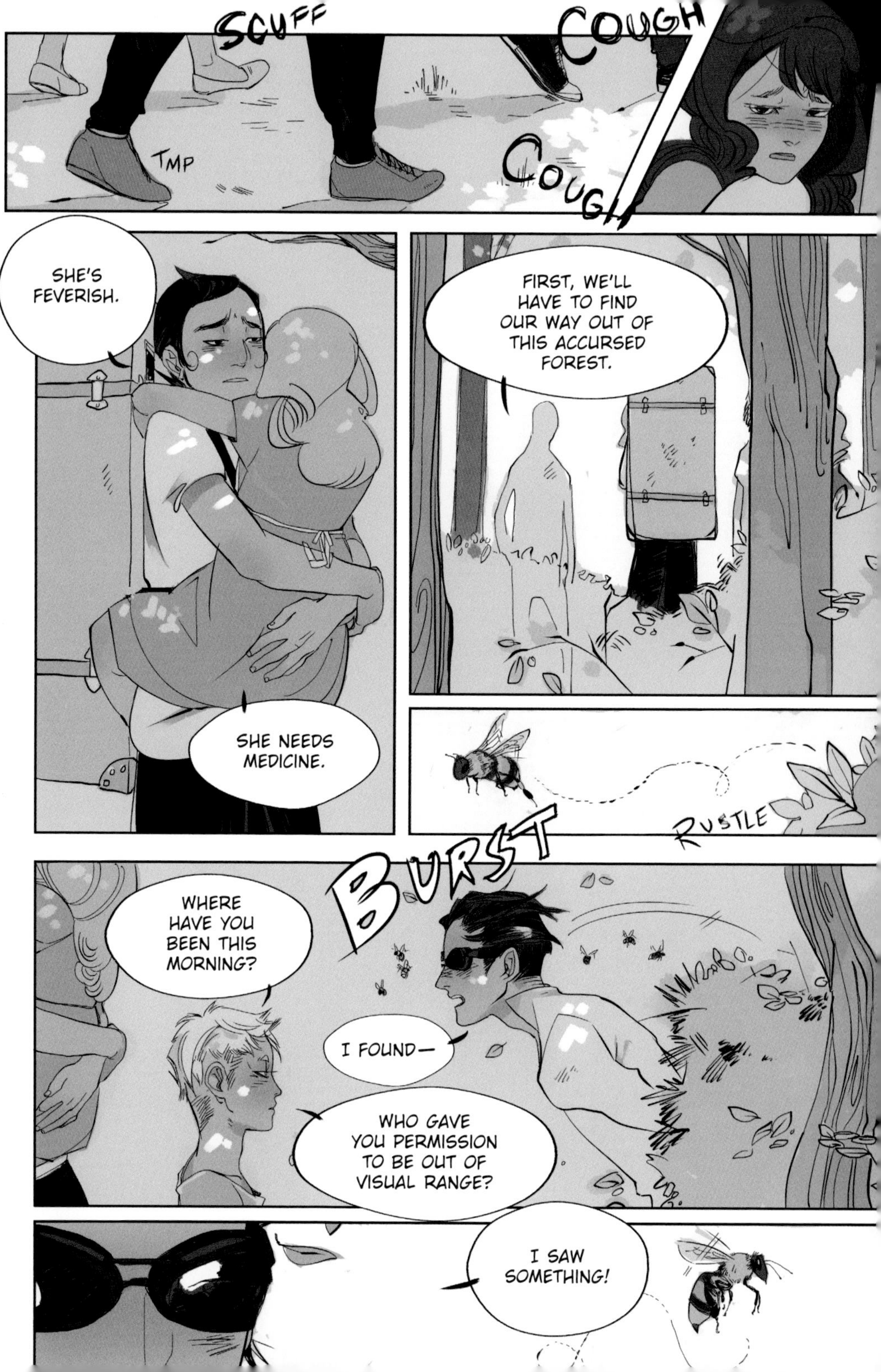
SCUFF
TMP
COUGH
COUGH
SHE'S FEVERISH.
SHE NEEDS MEDICINE.
FIRST, WE'LL HAVE TO FIND OUR WAY OUT OF THIS ACCURSED FOREST.
RUSTLE
BURST
WHERE HAVE YOU BEEN THIS MORNING?
I FOUND—
WHO GAVE YOU PERMISSION TO BE OUT OF VISUAL RANGE?
I SAW SOMETHING!

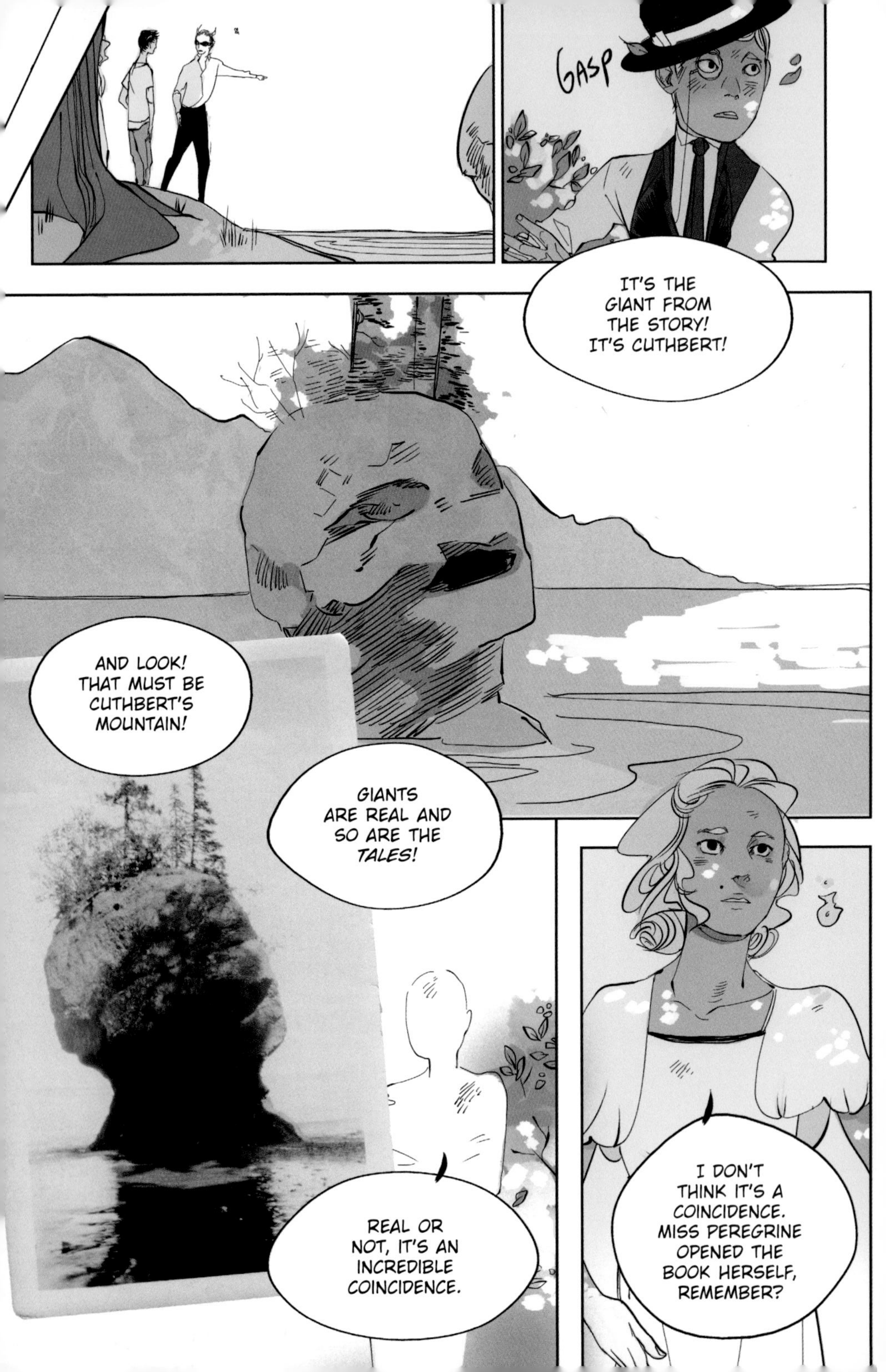
GASP
IT'S THE GIANT FROM THE STORY! IT'S CUTHBERT!
AND LOOK! THAT MUST BE CUTHBERT'S MOUNTAIN!
GIANTS ARE REAL AND SO ARE THE *TALES!*
REAL OR NOT, IT'S AN INCREDIBLE COINCIDENCE.
I DON'T THINK IT'S A COINCIDENCE. MISS PEREGRINE OPENED THE BOOK HERSELF, REMEMBER?

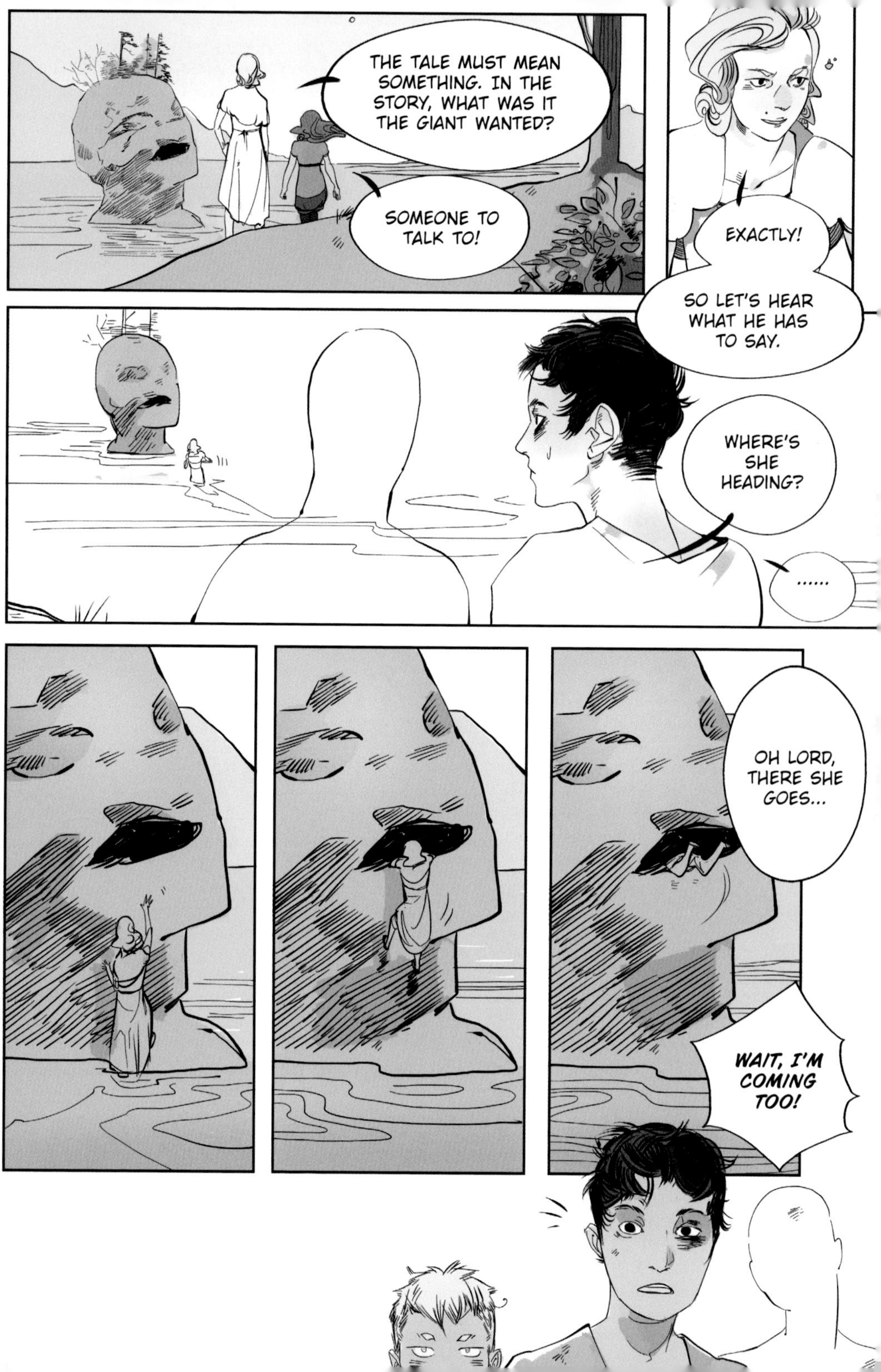
THE TALE MUST MEAN SOMETHING. IN THE STORY, WHAT WAS IT THE GIANT WANTED?
SOMEONE TO TALK TO!
EXACTLY!
SO LET'S HEAR WHAT HE HAS TO SAY.
WHERE'S SHE HEADING?
......
OH LORD, THERE SHE GOES...
WAIT, I'M COMING TOO!

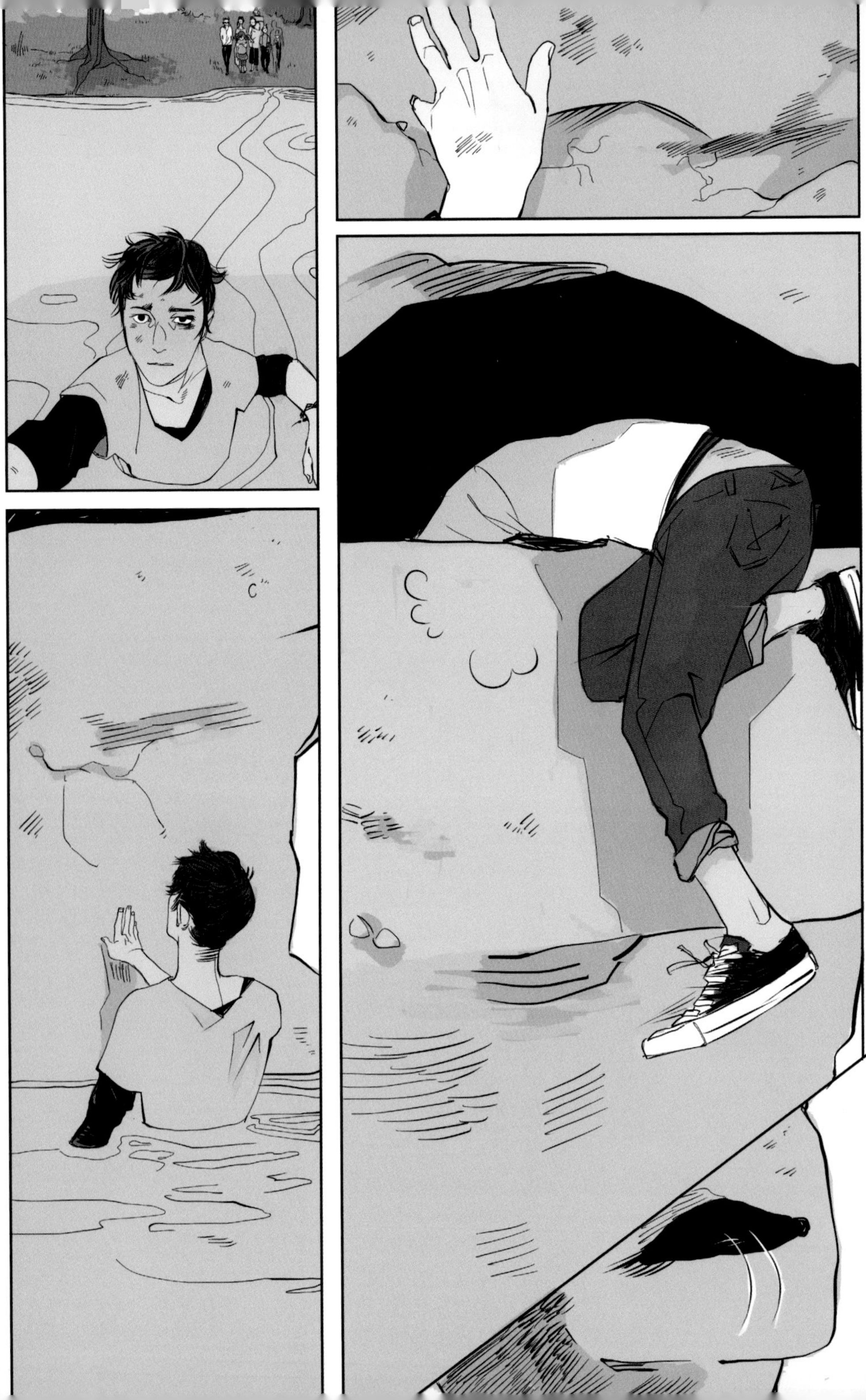

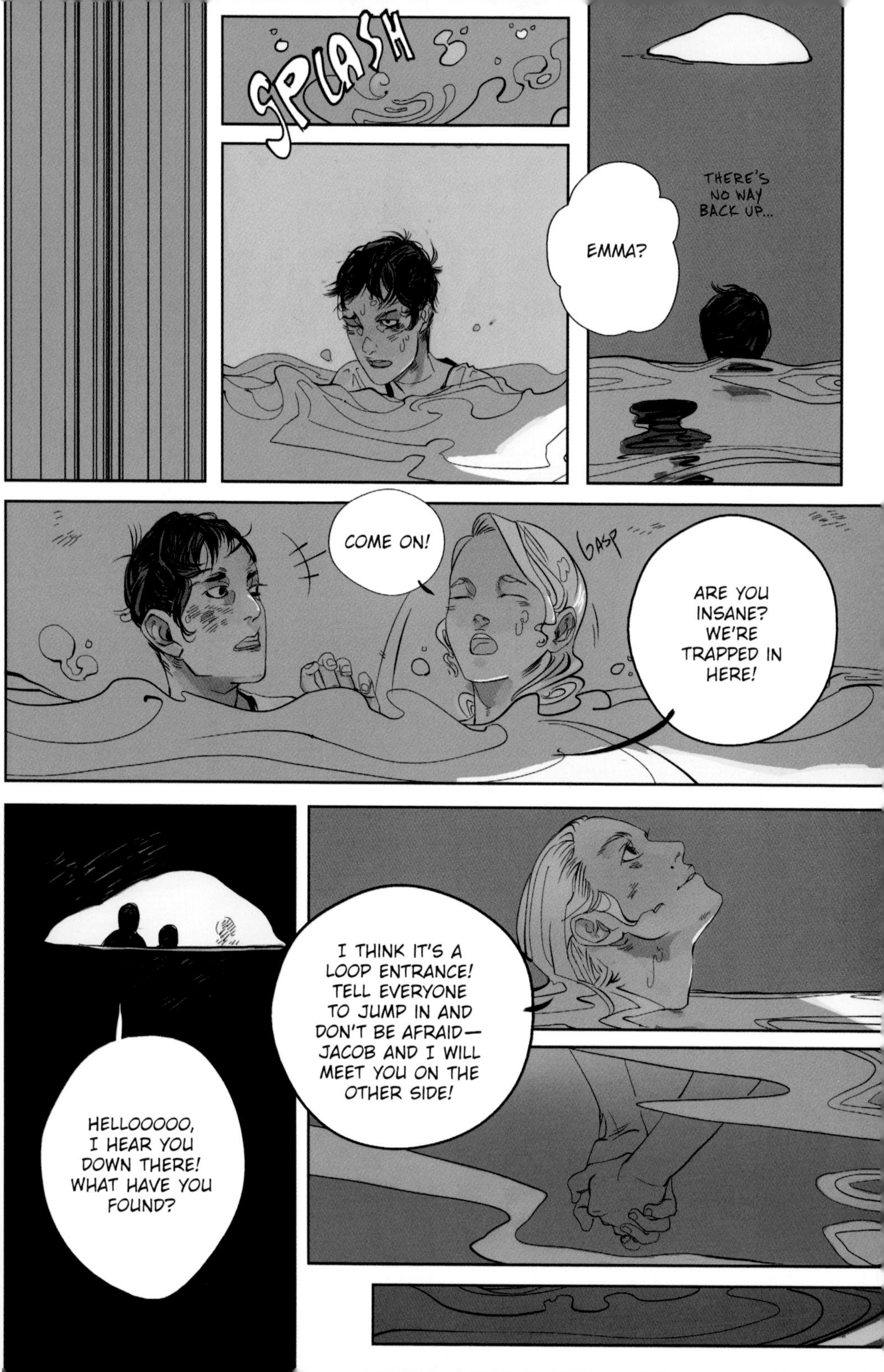
SPLASH
EMMA?
THERE'S NO WAY BACK UP...
COME ON!
GASP
ARE YOU INSANE? WE'RE TRAPPED IN HERE!
HELLOOOOO, I HEAR YOU DOWN THERE! WHAT HAVE YOU FOUND?
I THINK IT'S A LOOP ENTRANCE! TELL EVERYONE TO JUMP IN AND DON'T BE AFRAID—JACOB AND I WILL MEET YOU ON THE OTHER SIDE!

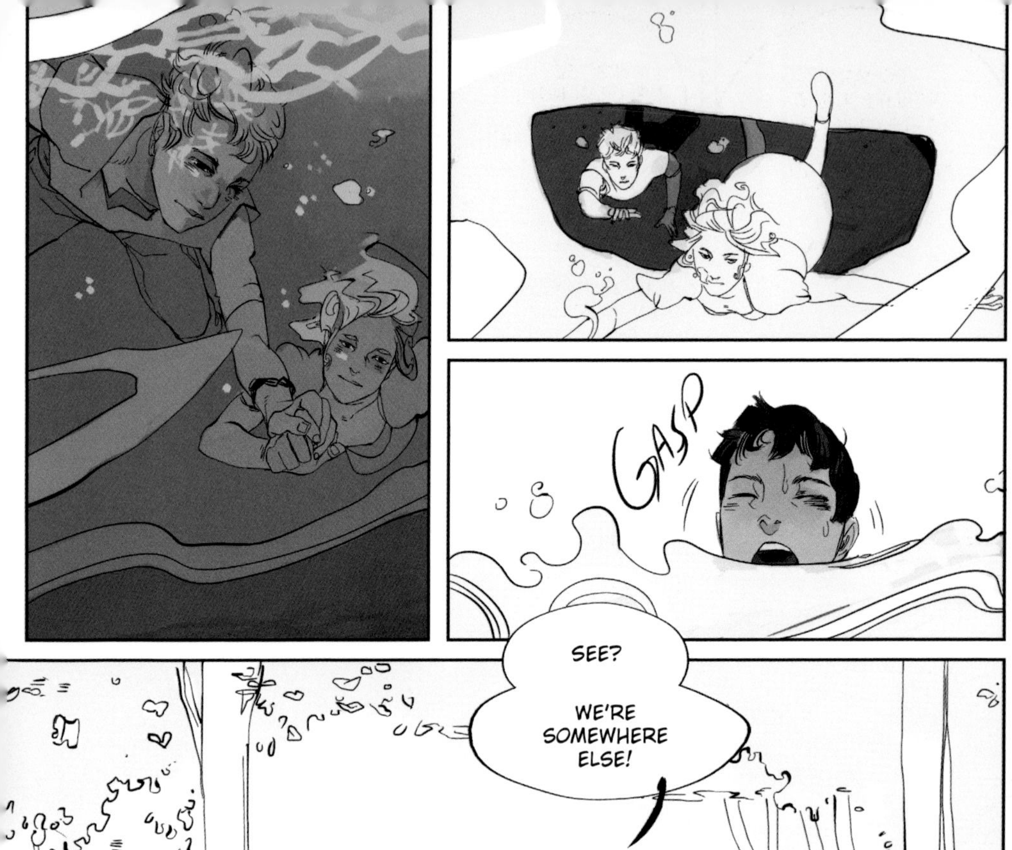
GASP
SEE?
WE'RE SOMEWHERE ELSE!

AND JUST LIKE THAT, WE'D ENTERED A LOOP—ABANDONED A MILD MORNING IN 1940 FOR A HOT AFTERNOON IN SOME OTHER, OLDER YEAR, THOUGH IT WAS DIFFICULT TO TELL JUST HOW MUCH OLDER, HERE IN THE FOREST, AWAY FROM THE EASILY DATABLE CUES OF CIVILIZATION.

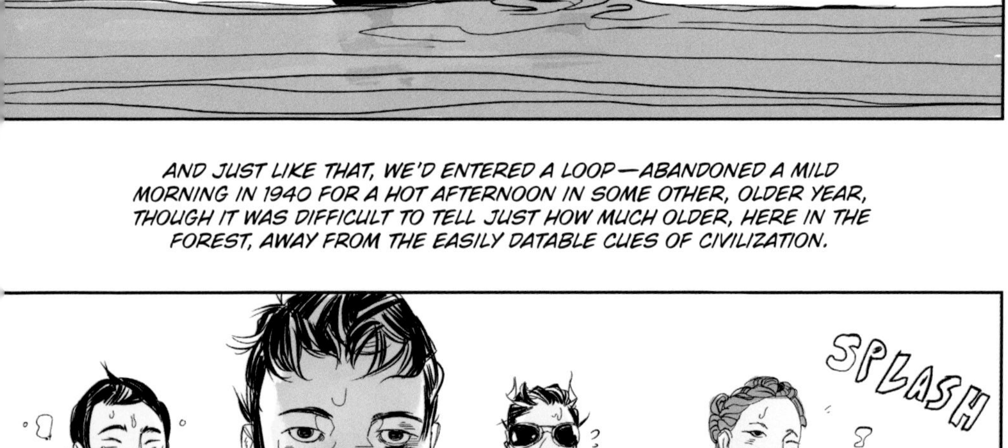
SPLASH

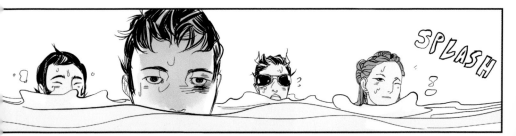

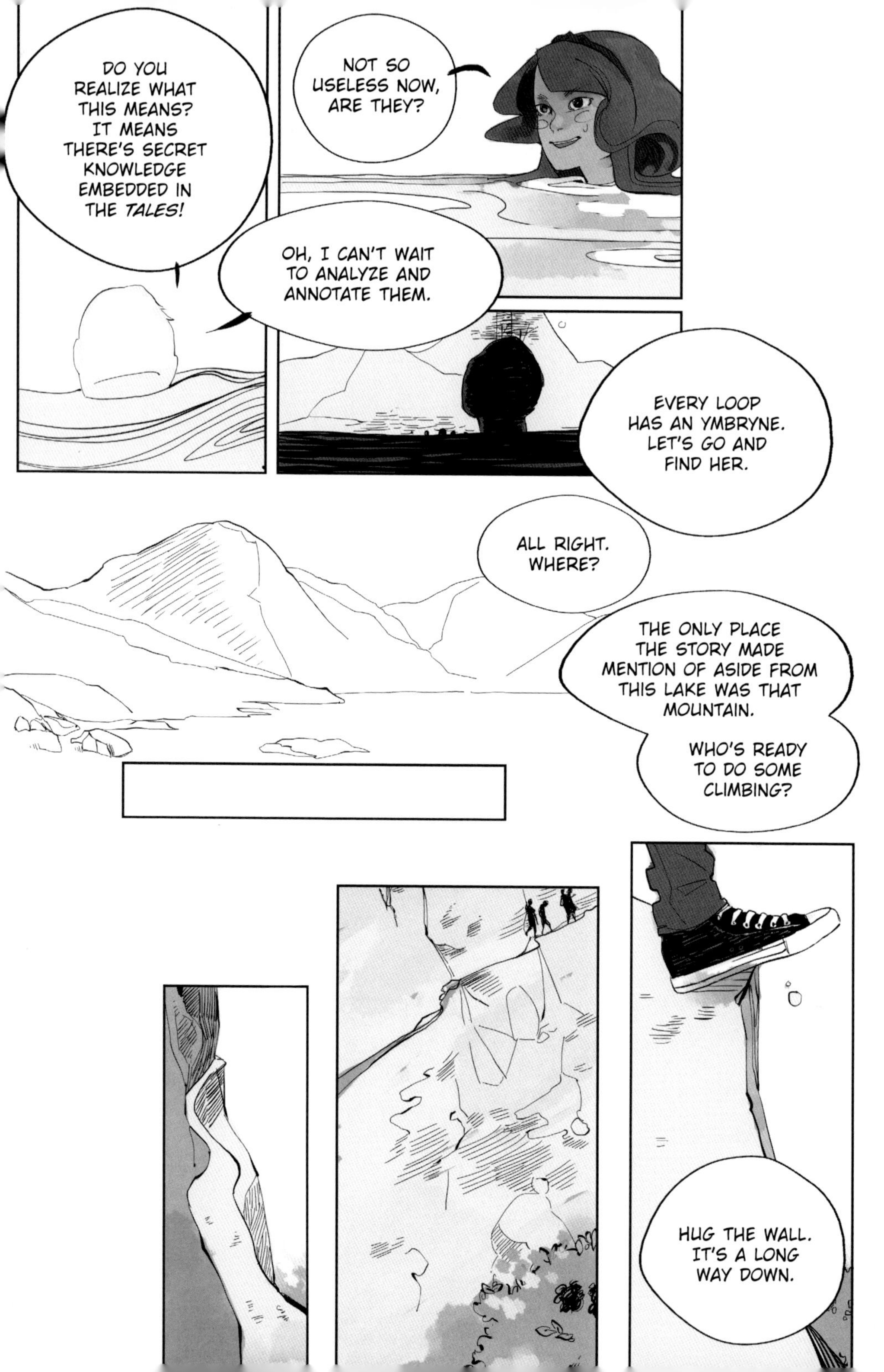
DO YOU REALIZE WHAT THIS MEANS? IT MEANS THERE'S SECRET KNOWLEDGE EMBEDDED IN THE *TALES*!
NOT SO USELESS NOW, ARE THEY?
OH, I CAN'T WAIT TO ANALYZE AND ANNOTATE THEM.
EVERY LOOP HAS AN YMBRYNE. LET'S GO AND FIND HER.
ALL RIGHT. WHERE?
THE ONLY PLACE THE STORY MADE MENTION OF ASIDE FROM THIS LAKE WAS THAT MOUNTAIN.
WHO'S READY TO DO SOME CLIMBING?
HUG THE WALL. IT'S A LONG WAY DOWN.

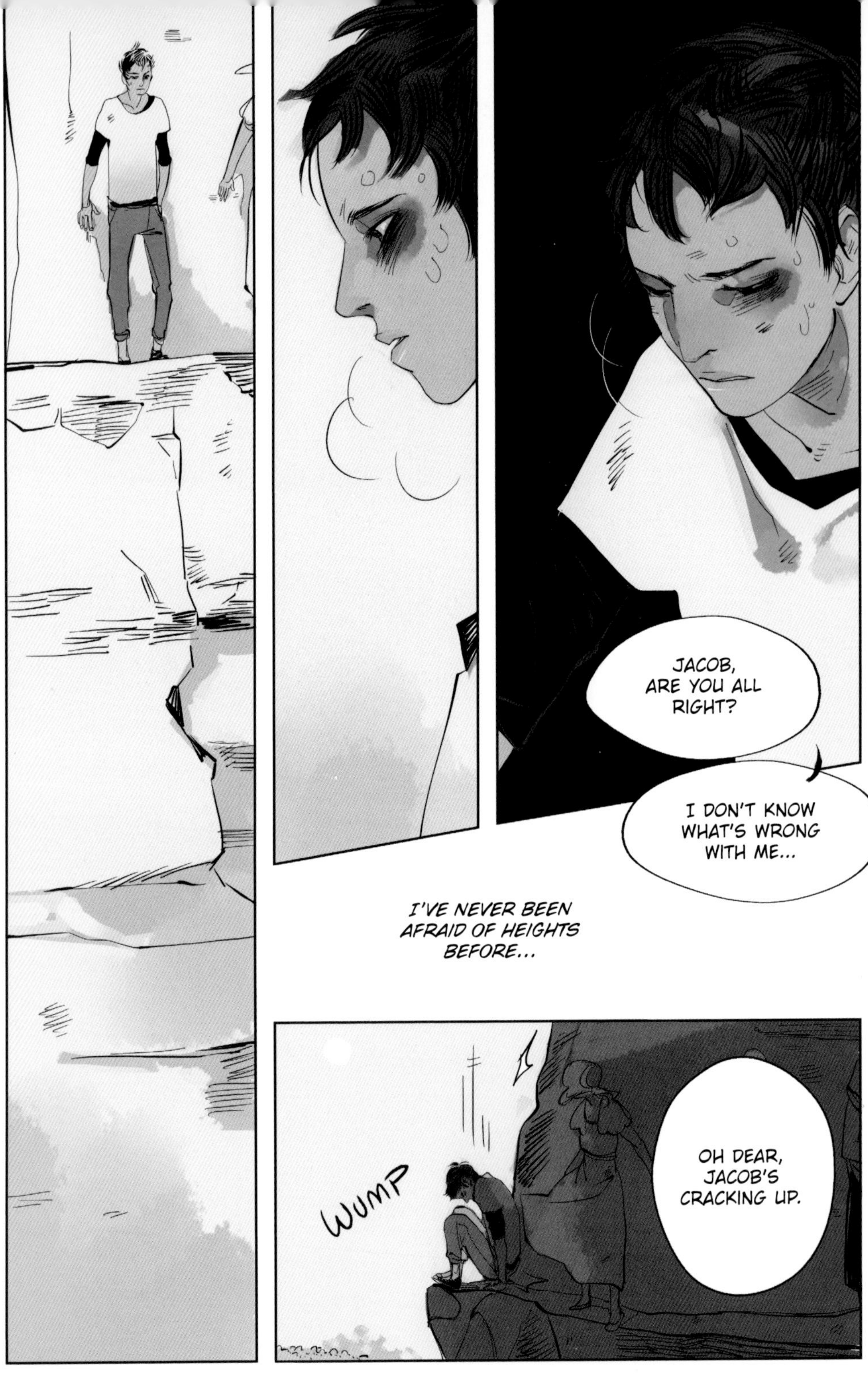
JACOB, ARE YOU ALL RIGHT?
I DON'T KNOW WHAT'S WRONG WITH ME...
I'VE NEVER BEEN AFRAID OF HEIGHTS BEFORE...
WUMP
OH DEAR, JACOB'S CRACKING UP.

WAIT. WHAT IF IT'S NOT A FEAR OF HEIGHTS...

WHAT IF IT'S...

NO...

WE'RE INSIDE A LOOP.

...A HOLLOW.

THEY...CAN'T COME HERE.

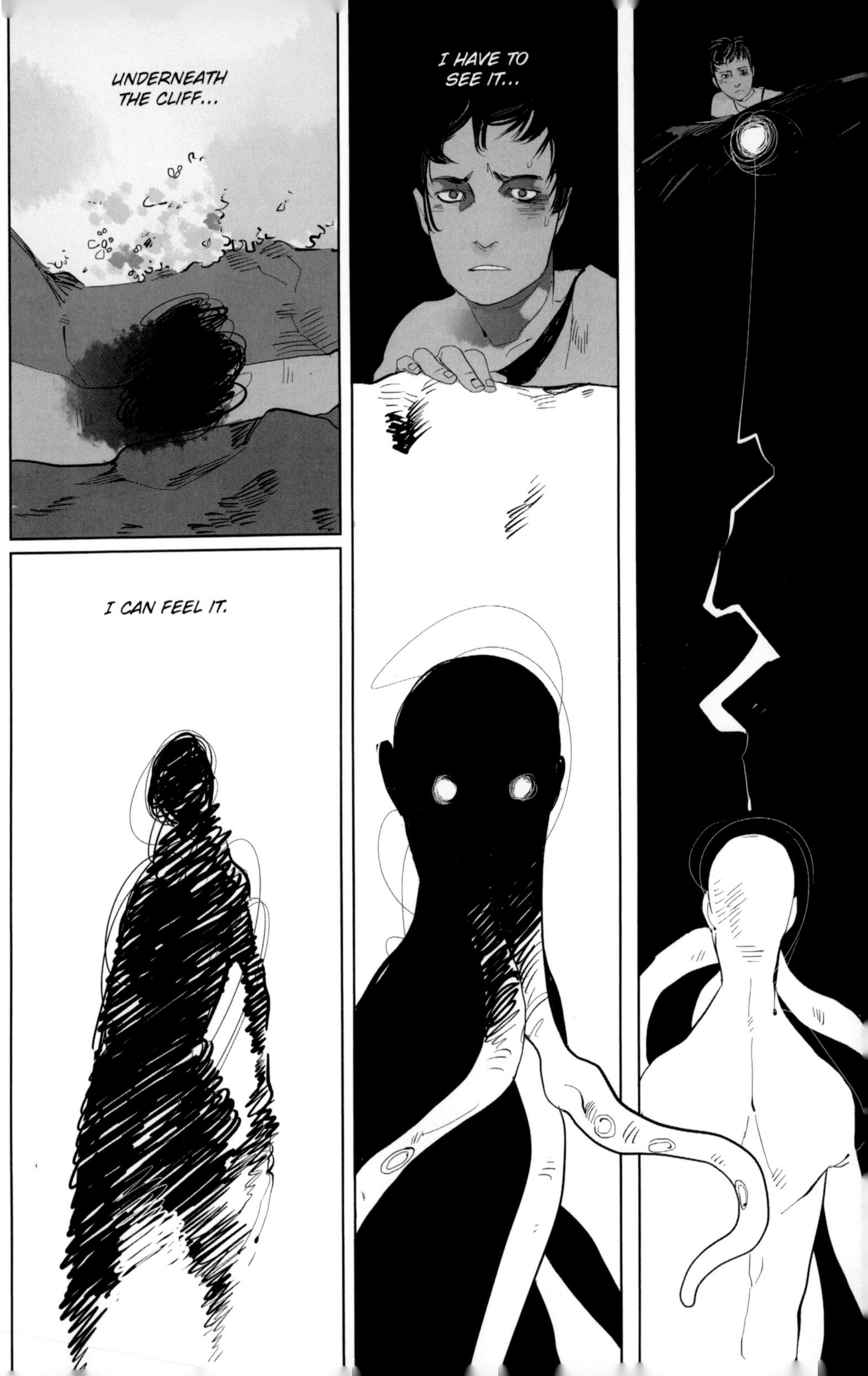
UNDERNEATH THE CLIFF...
I CAN FEEL IT.
I HAVE TO SEE IT...

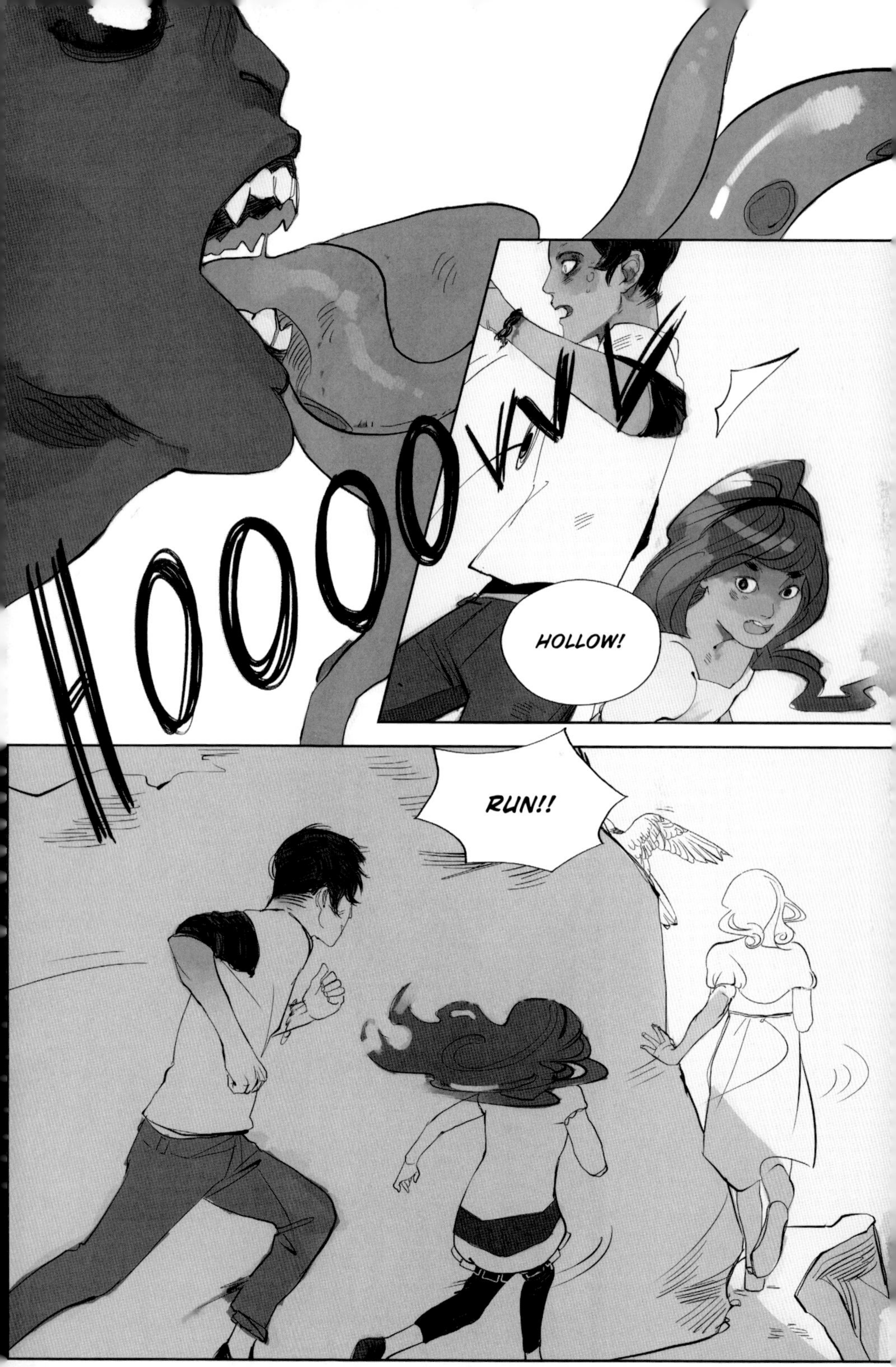
HOOOOOWW
HOLLOW!
RUN!!

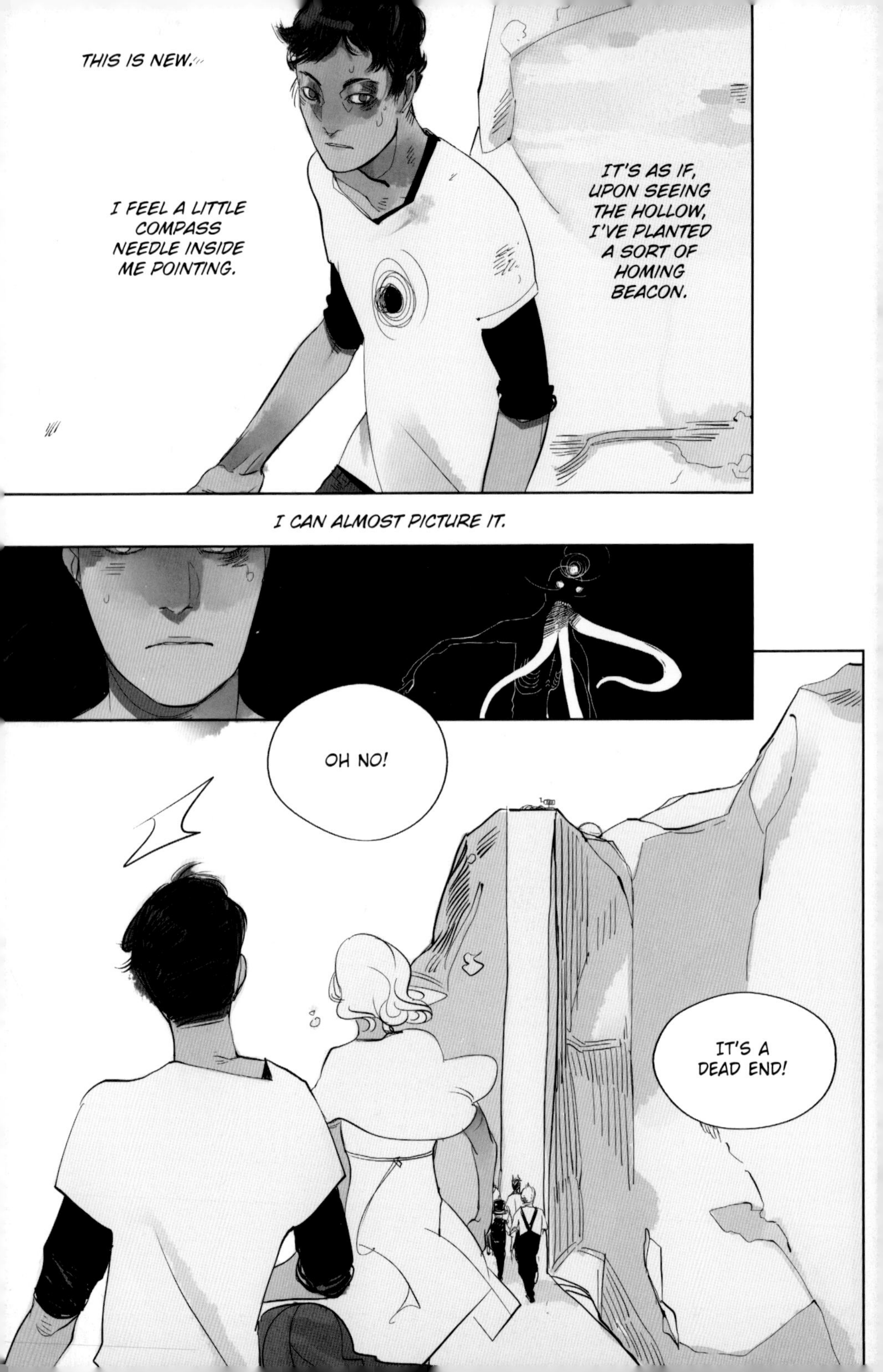
THIS IS NEW.
I FEEL A LITTLE COMPASS NEEDLE INSIDE ME POINTING.
IT'S AS IF, UPON SEEING THE HOLLOW, I'VE PLANTED A SORT OF HOMING BEACON.
I CAN ALMOST PICTURE IT.
OH NO!
IT'S A DEAD END!

CHAPTER TWO

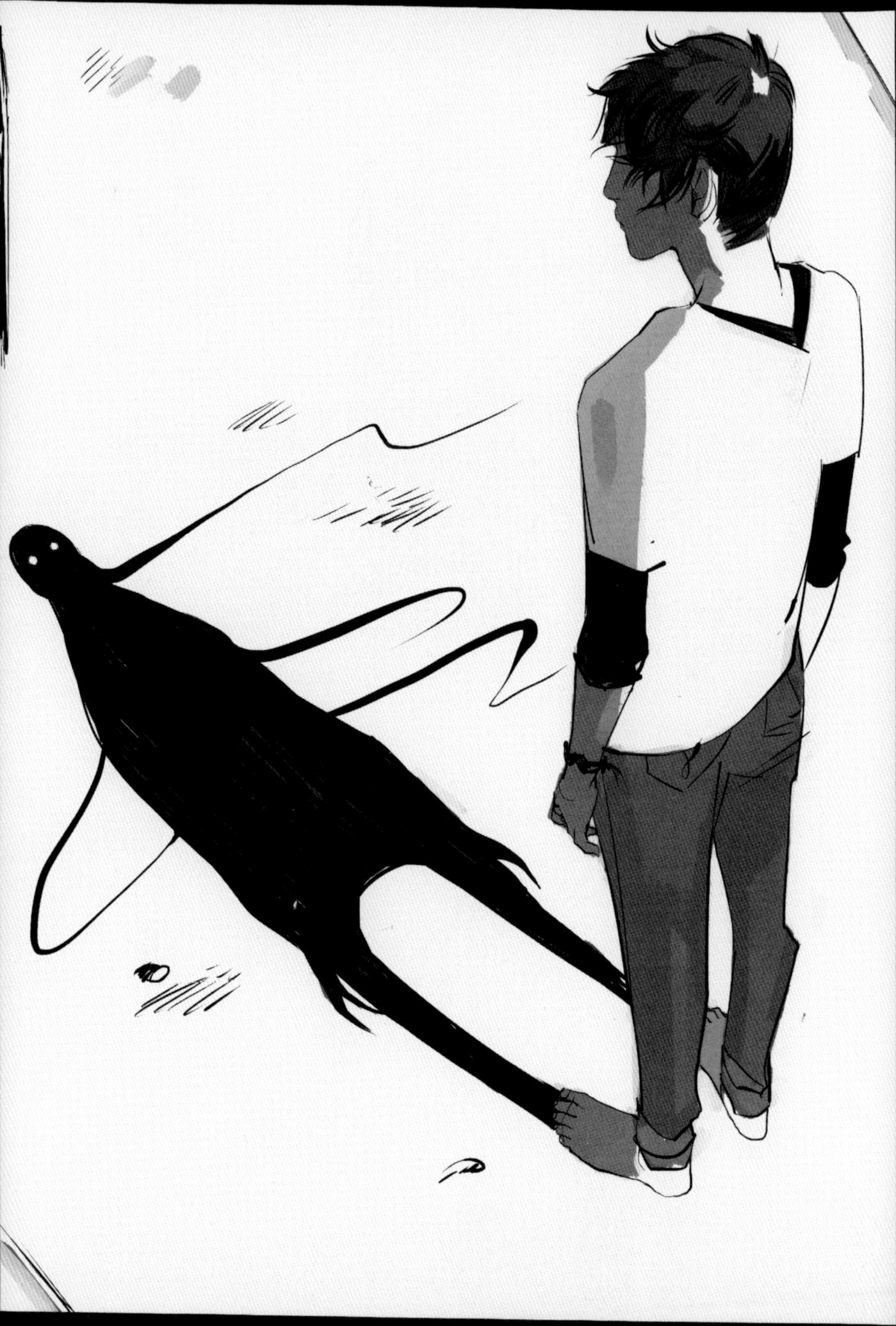

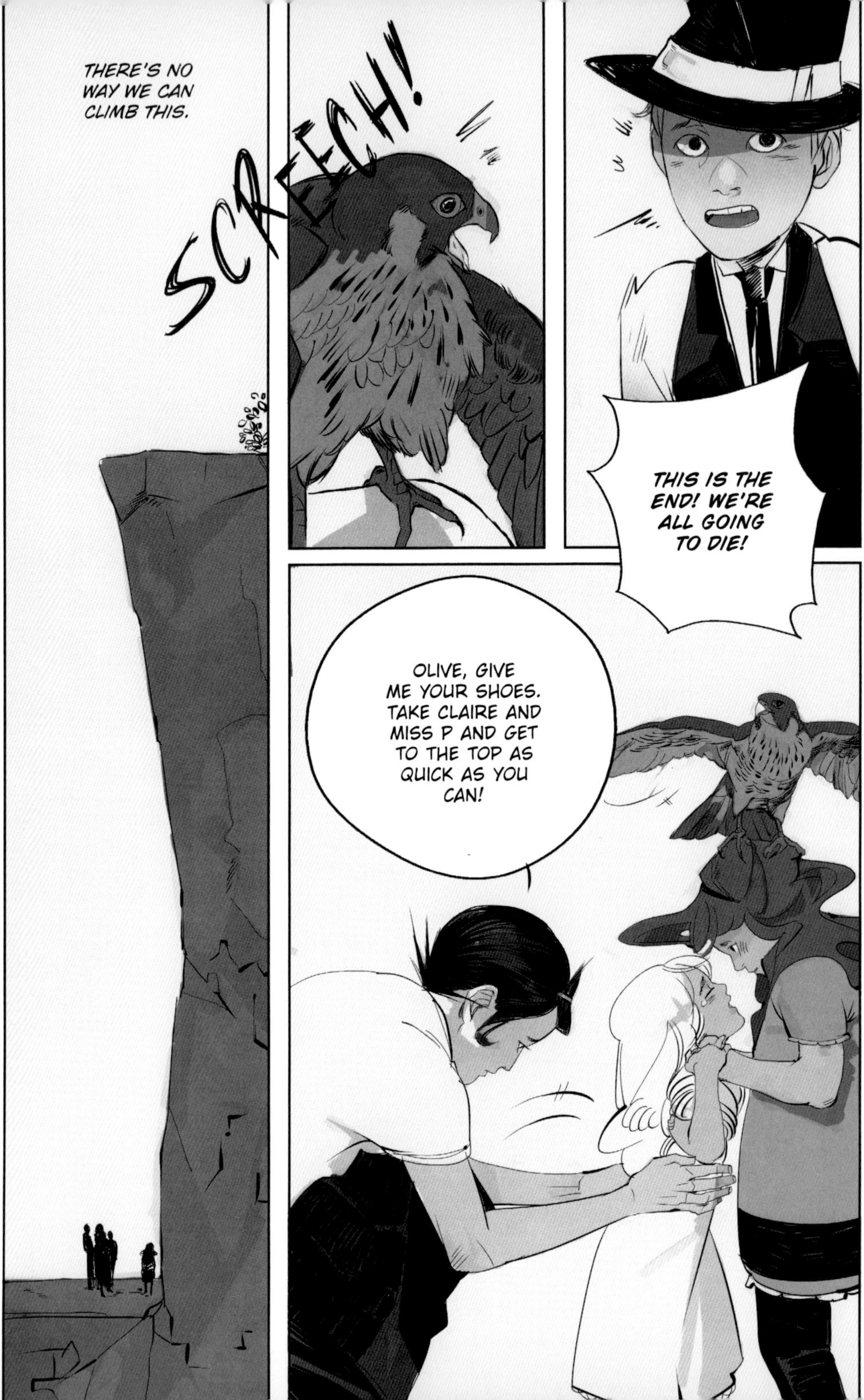
THERE'S NO WAY WE CAN CLIMB THIS.
SCREECH!
THIS IS THE END! WE'RE ALL GOING TO DIE!
OLIVE, GIVE ME YOUR SHOES. TAKE CLAIRE AND MISS P AND GET TO THE TOP AS QUICK AS YOU CAN!

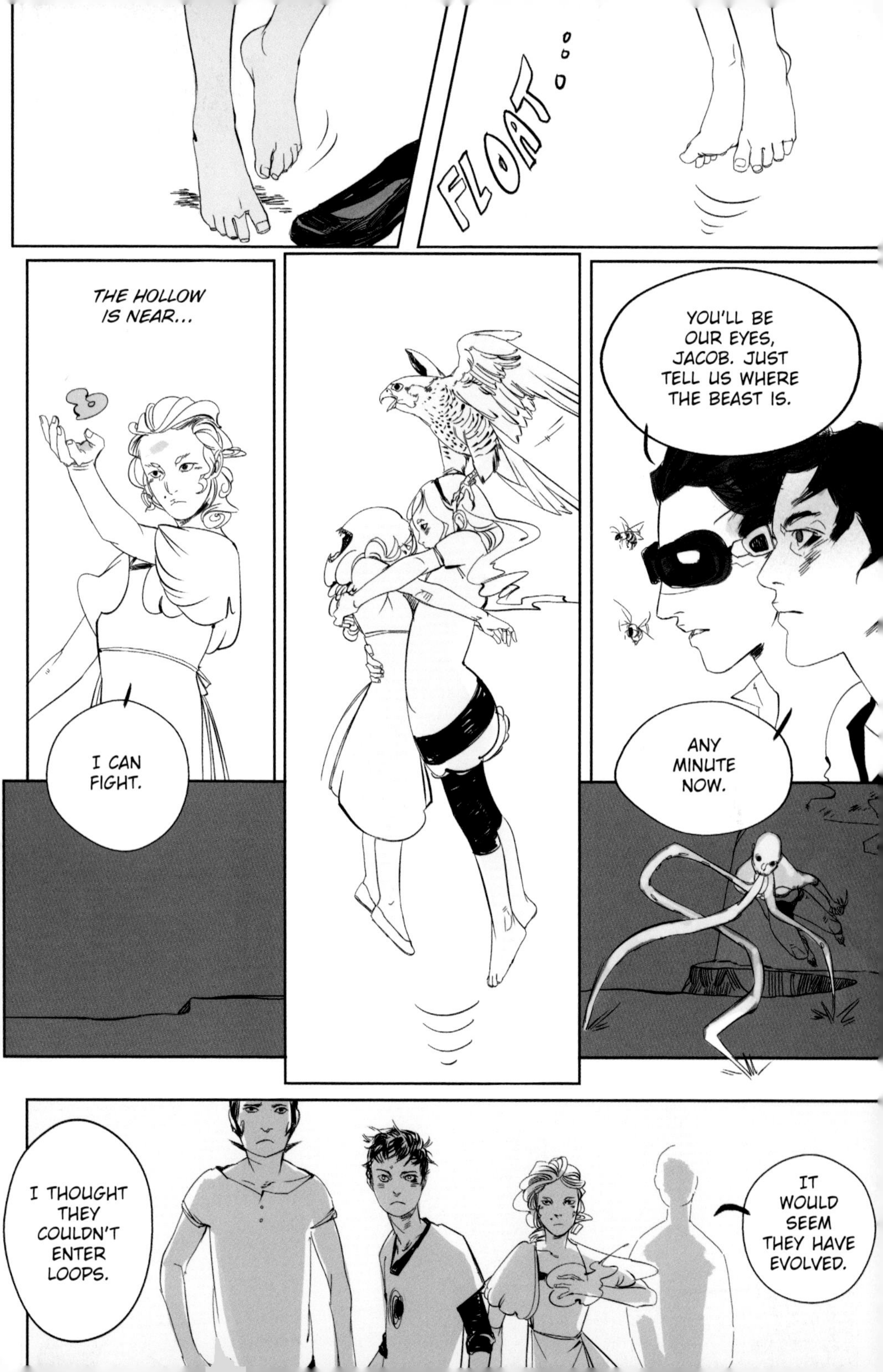
FLOAT...
THE HOLLOW IS NEAR...
I CAN FIGHT.
YOU'LL BE OUR EYES, JACOB. JUST TELL US WHERE THE BEAST IS.
ANY MINUTE NOW.
I THOUGHT THEY COULDN'T ENTER LOOPS.
IT WOULD SEEM THEY HAVE EVOLVED.

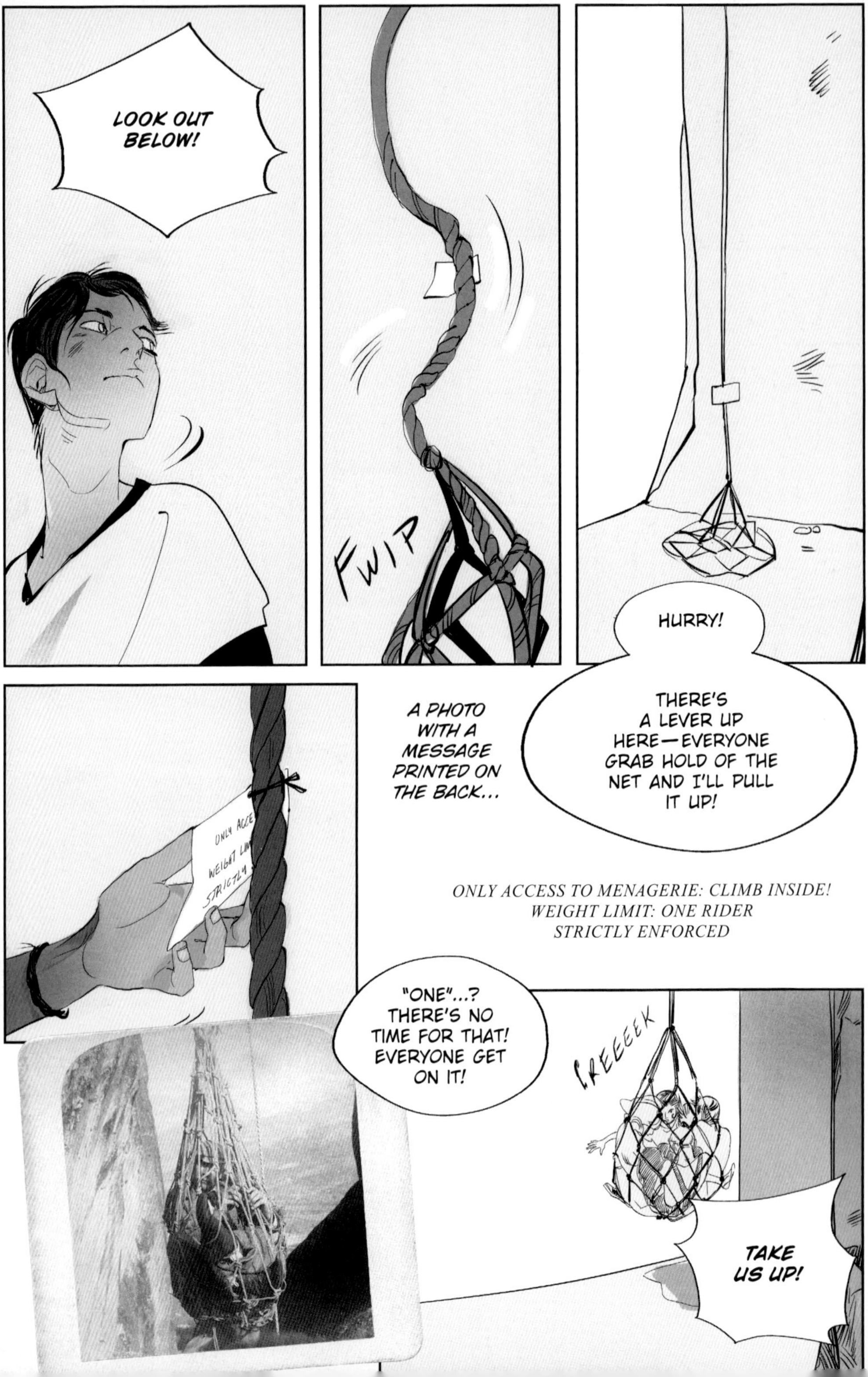
LOOK OUT BELOW!
FWIP
HURRY!
THERE'S A LEVER UP HERE—EVERYONE GRAB HOLD OF THE NET AND I'LL PULL IT UP!
A PHOTO WITH A MESSAGE PRINTED ON THE BACK...
ONLY ACCESS TO MENAGERIE: CLIMB INSIDE!
WEIGHT LIMIT: ONE RIDER
STRICTLY ENFORCED
"ONE"...? THERE'S NO TIME FOR THAT! EVERYONE GET ON IT!
CREEEEK
TAKE US UP!

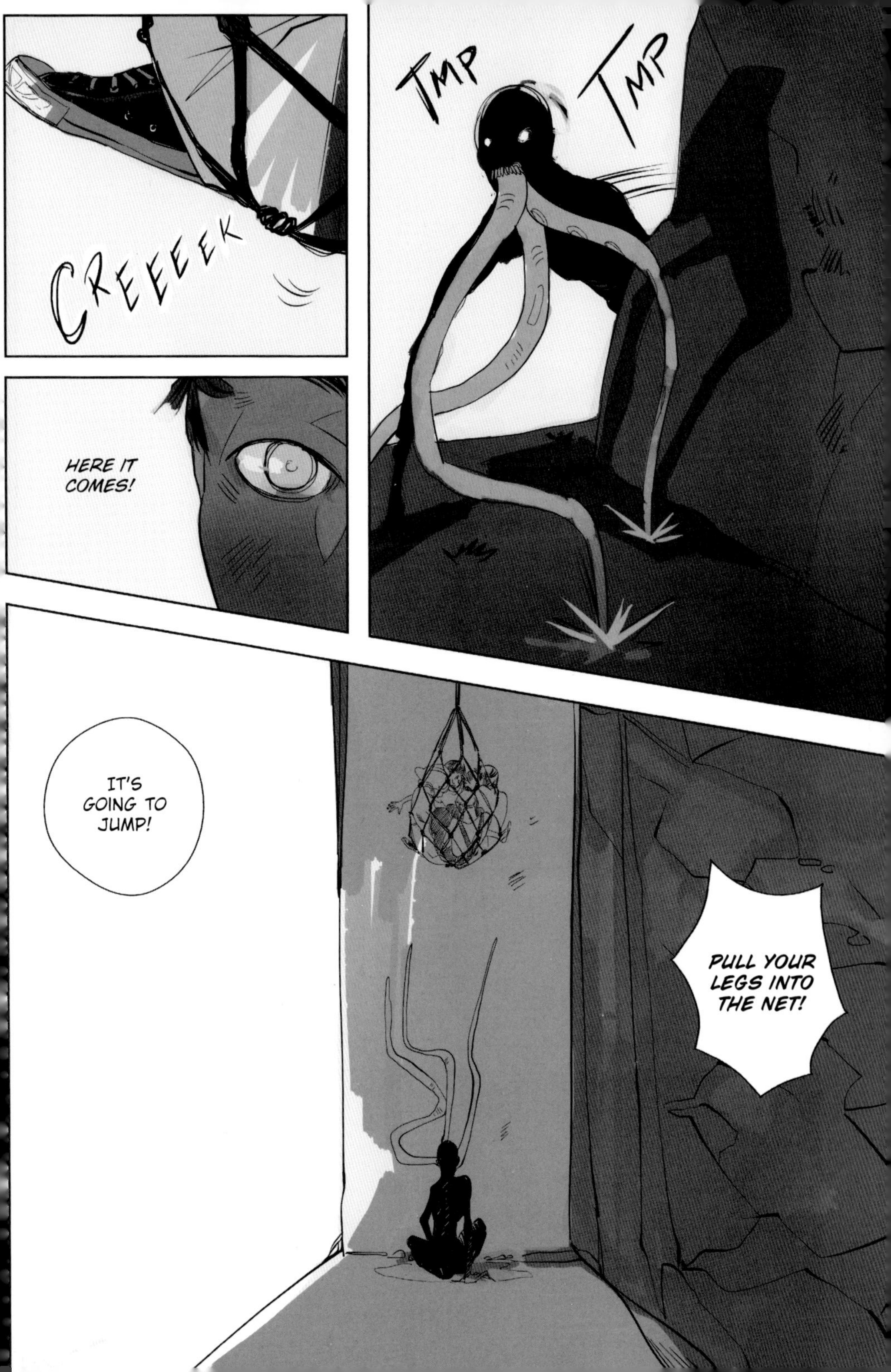
CREEEEK
HERE IT COMES!
TMP
TMP
IT'S GOING TO JUMP!
PULL YOUR LEGS INTO THE NET!

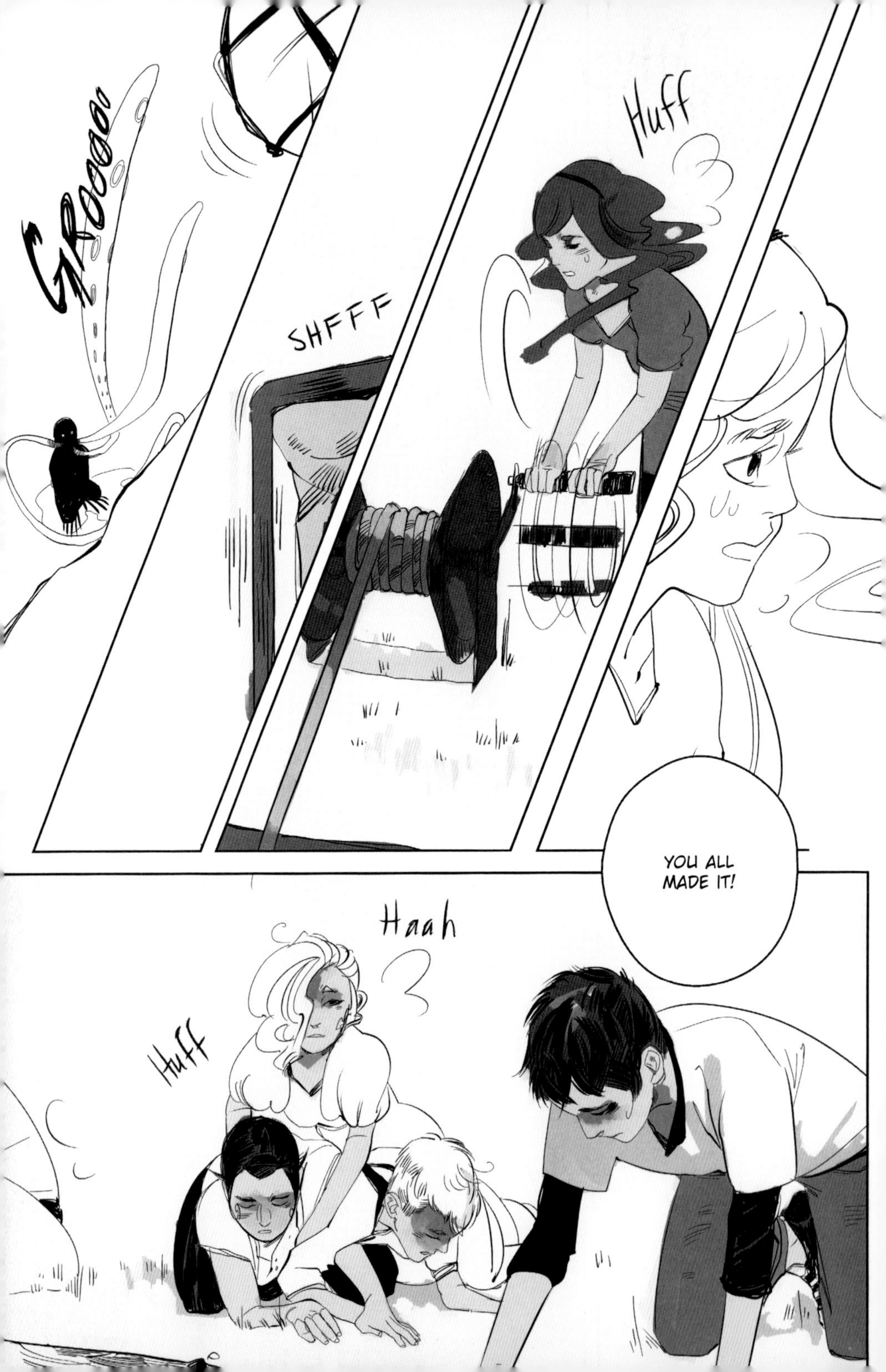
GROOOOOO
SHFFF
Huff
YOU ALL MADE IT!
Haah
Huff

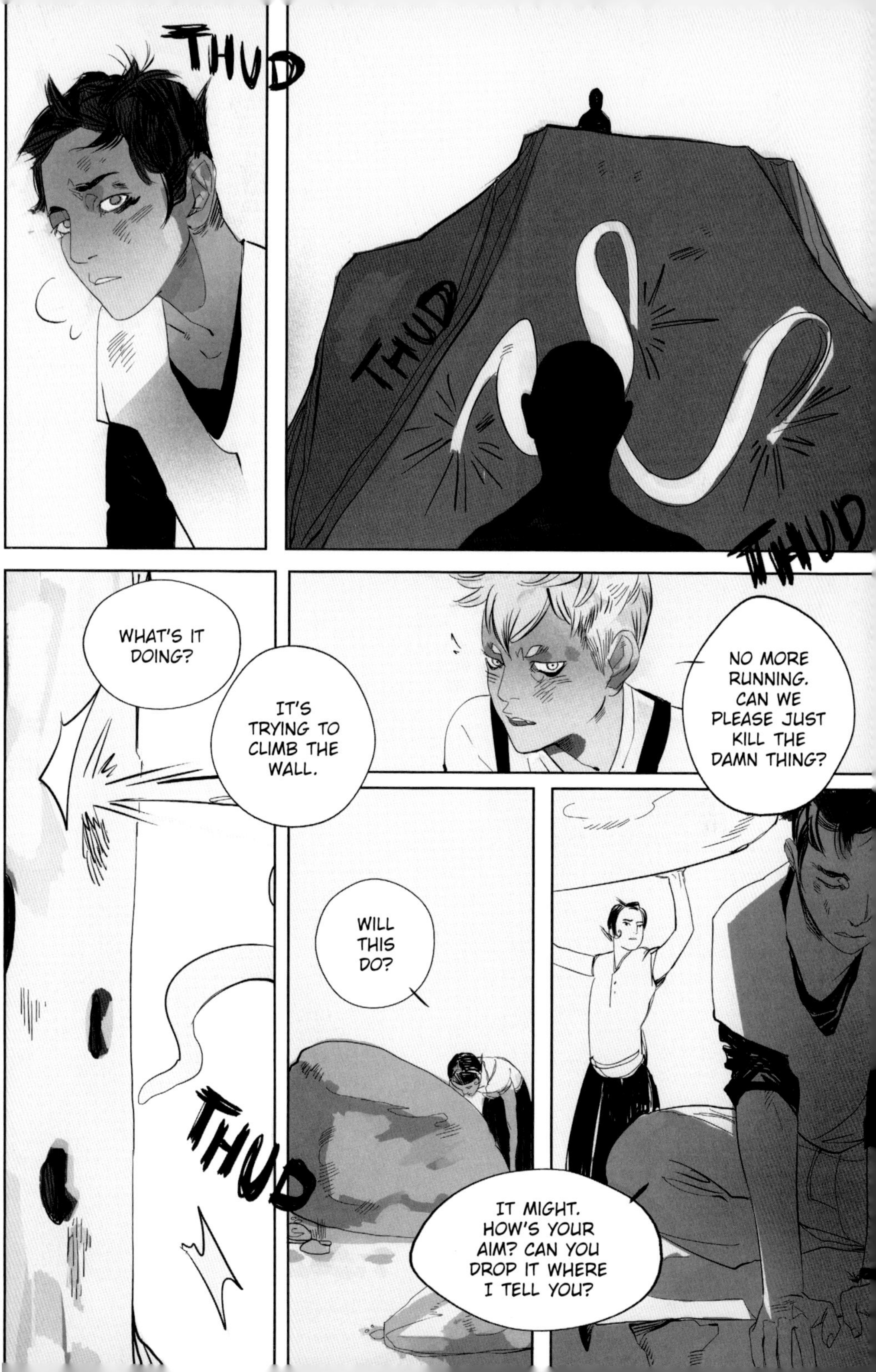
THUD
THUD
THUD
WHAT'S IT DOING?
IT'S TRYING TO CLIMB THE WALL.
THUD
NO MORE RUNNING. CAN WE PLEASE JUST KILL THE DAMN THING?
WILL THIS DO?
IT MIGHT. HOW'S YOUR AIM? CAN YOU DROP IT WHERE I TELL YOU?

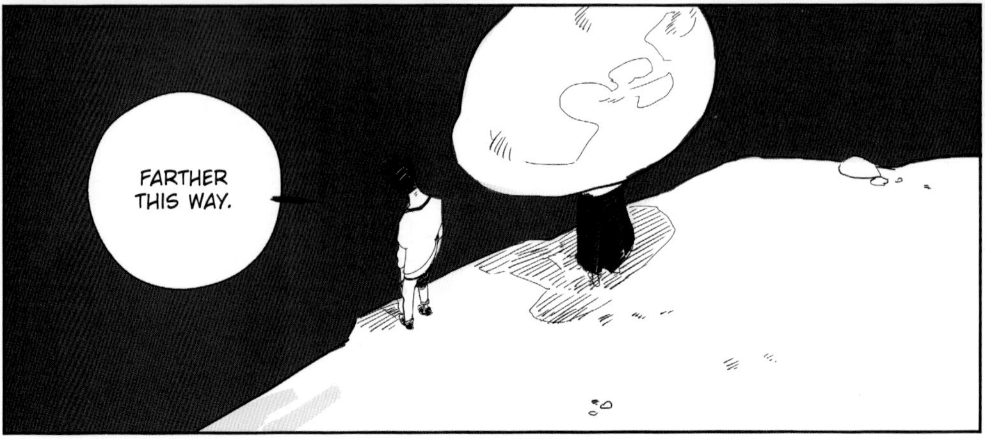
FARTHER THIS WAY.

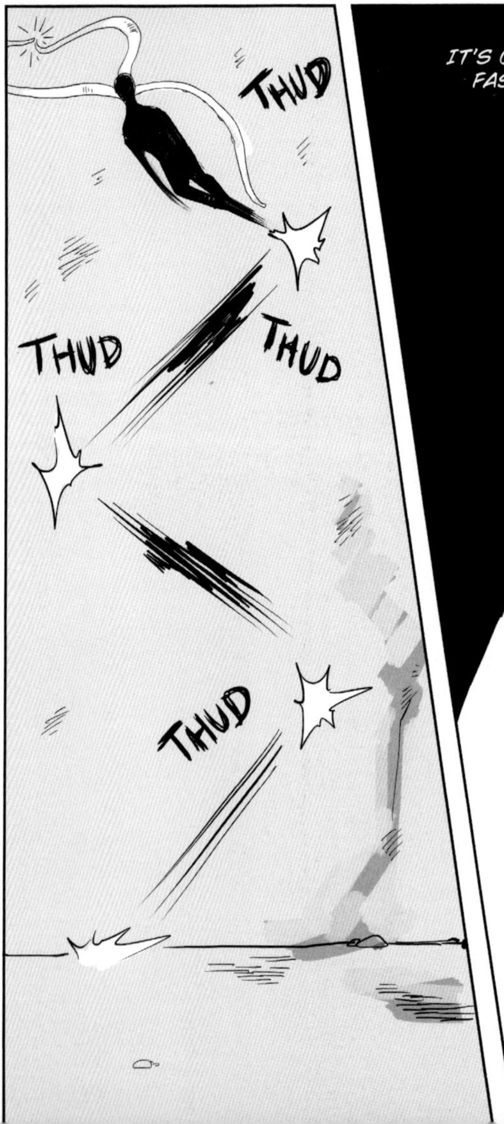
THUD
THUD
THUD
THUD

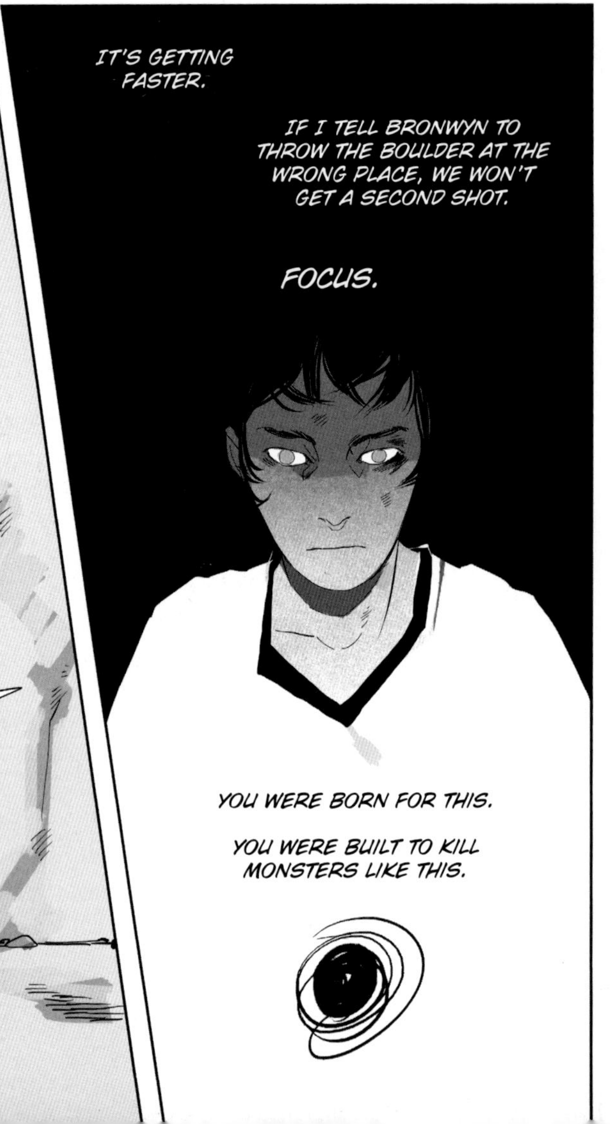
IT'S GETTING FASTER.
IF I TELL BRONWYN TO THROW THE BOULDER AT THE WRONG PLACE, WE WON'T GET A SECOND SHOT.
FOCUS.
YOU WERE BORN FOR THIS.
YOU WERE BUILT TO KILL MONSTERS LIKE THIS.

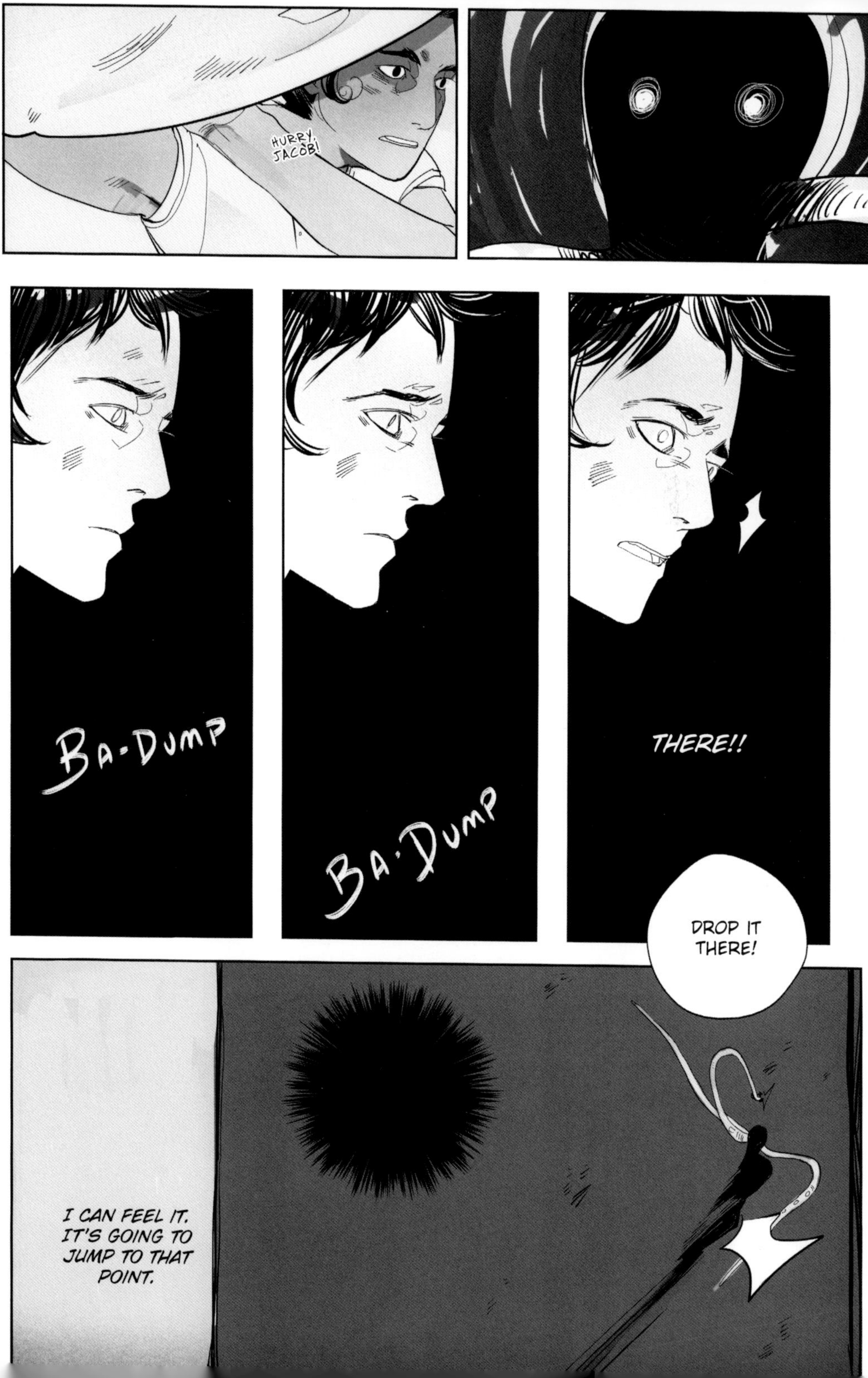
HURRY, JACOB!
BA-DUMP
BA-DUMP
THERE!!
DROP IT THERE!
I CAN FEEL IT. IT'S GOING TO JUMP TO THAT POINT.

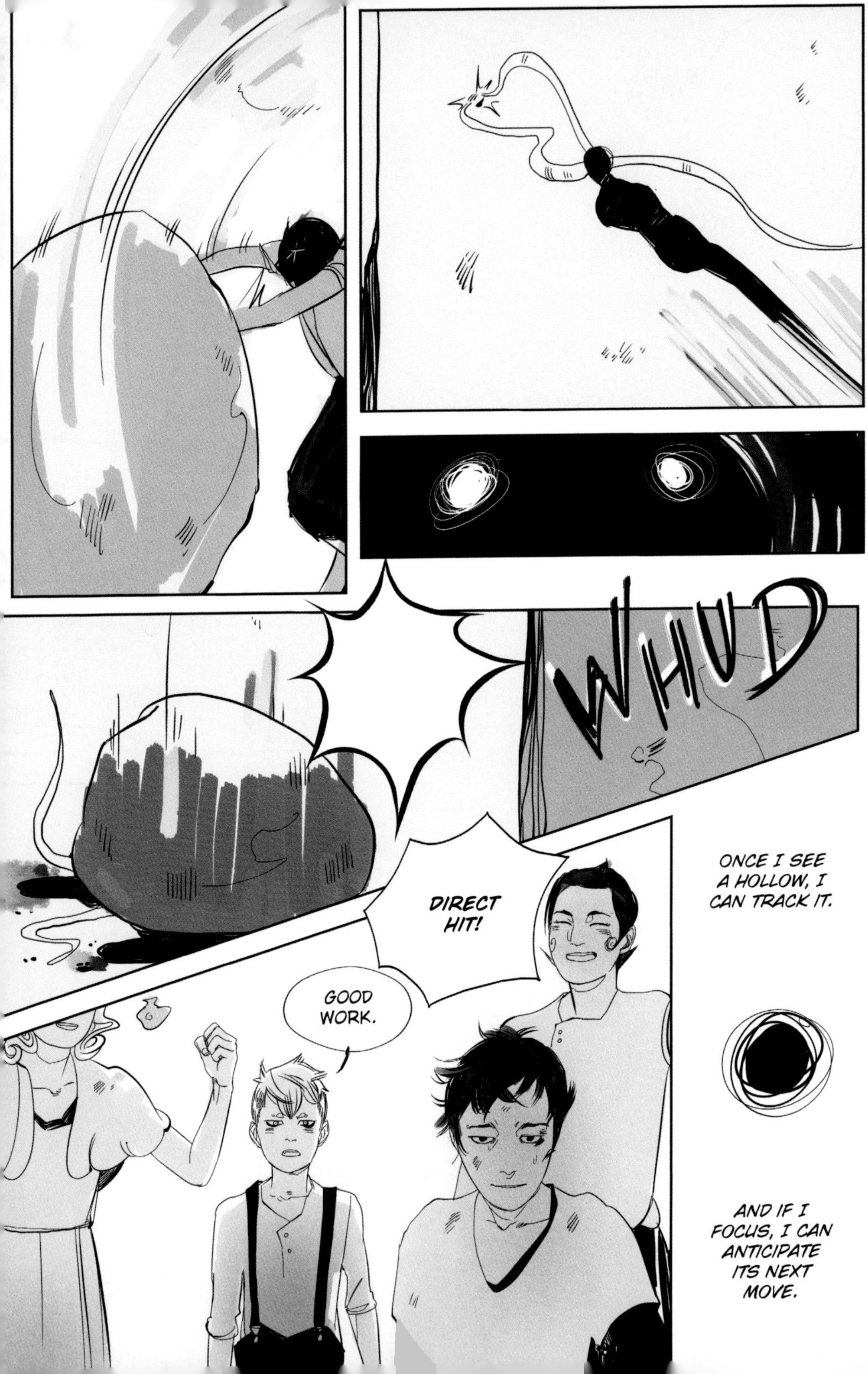
WHUD
DIRECT HIT!
GOOD WORK.
ONCE I SEE A HOLLOW, I CAN TRACK IT.
AND IF I FOCUS, I CAN ANTICIPATE ITS NEXT MOVE.

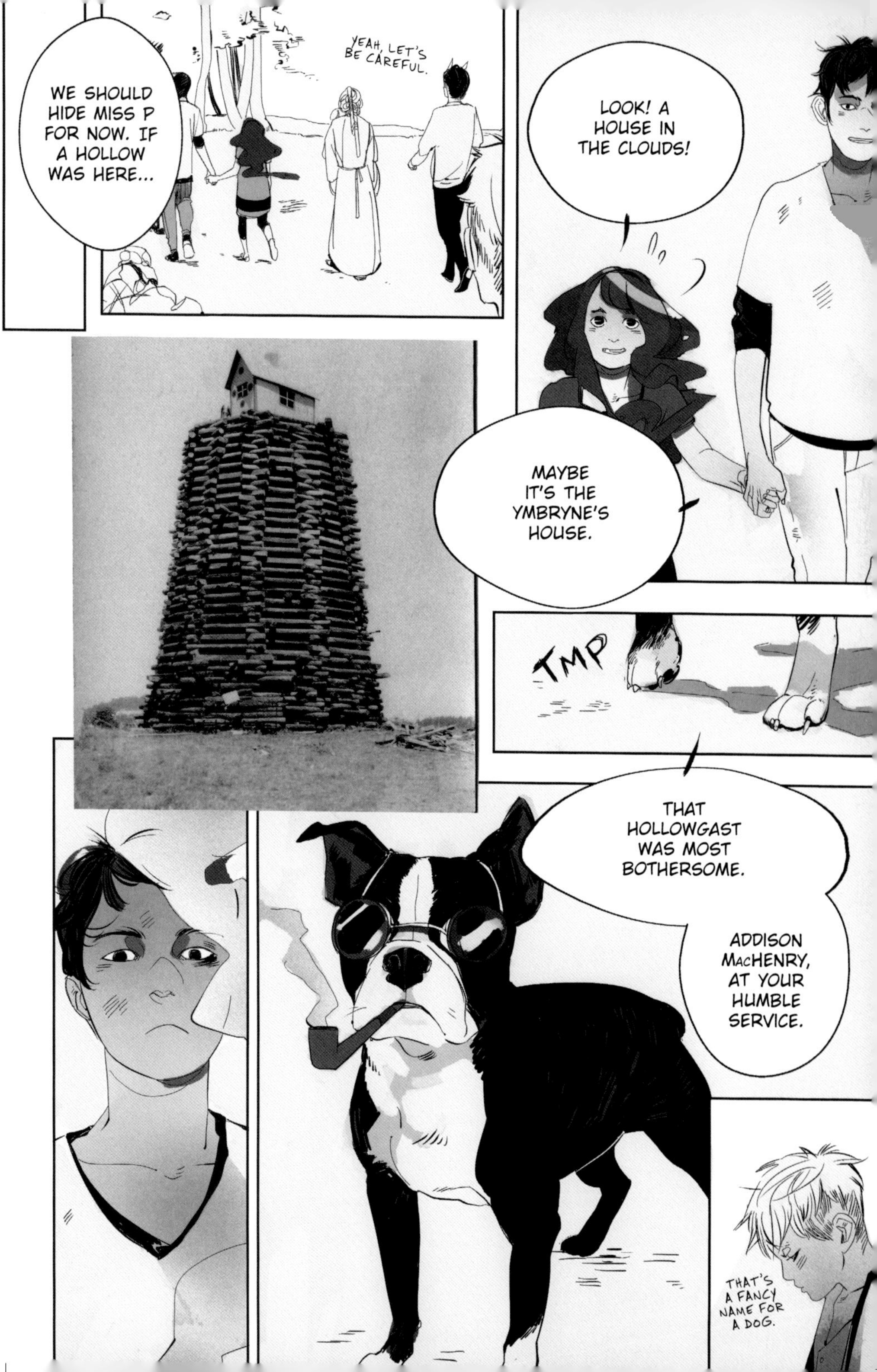
WE SHOULD HIDE MISS P FOR NOW. IF A HOLLOW WAS HERE...
YEAH, LET'S BE CAREFUL.
LOOK! A HOUSE IN THE CLOUDS!
MAYBE IT'S THE YMBRYNE'S HOUSE.
TMP
THAT HOLLOWGAST WAS MOST BOTHERSOME.
ADDISON MacHENRY, AT YOUR HUMBLE SERVICE.
THAT'S A FANCY NAME FOR A DOG.

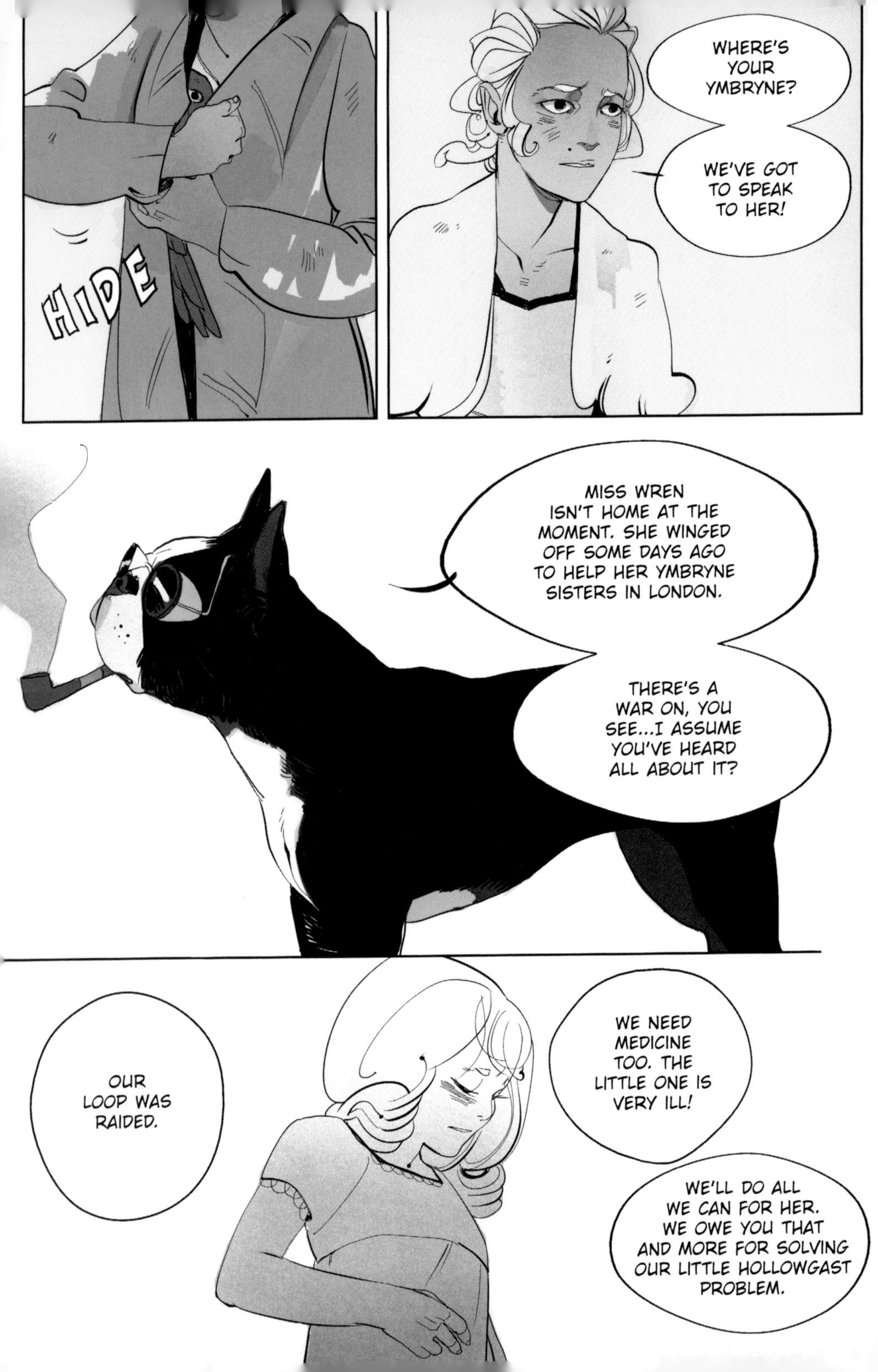
HIDE
WHERE'S YOUR YMBRYNE?
WE'VE GOT TO SPEAK TO HER!
MISS WREN ISN'T HOME AT THE MOMENT. SHE WINGED OFF SOME DAYS AGO TO HELP HER YMBRYNE SISTERS IN LONDON.
THERE'S A WAR ON, YOU SEE...I ASSUME YOU'VE HEARD ALL ABOUT IT?
OUR LOOP WAS RAIDED.
WE NEED MEDICINE TOO. THE LITTLE ONE IS VERY ILL!
WE'LL DO ALL WE CAN FOR HER. WE OWE YOU THAT AND MORE FOR SOLVING OUR LITTLE HOLLOWGAST PROBLEM.

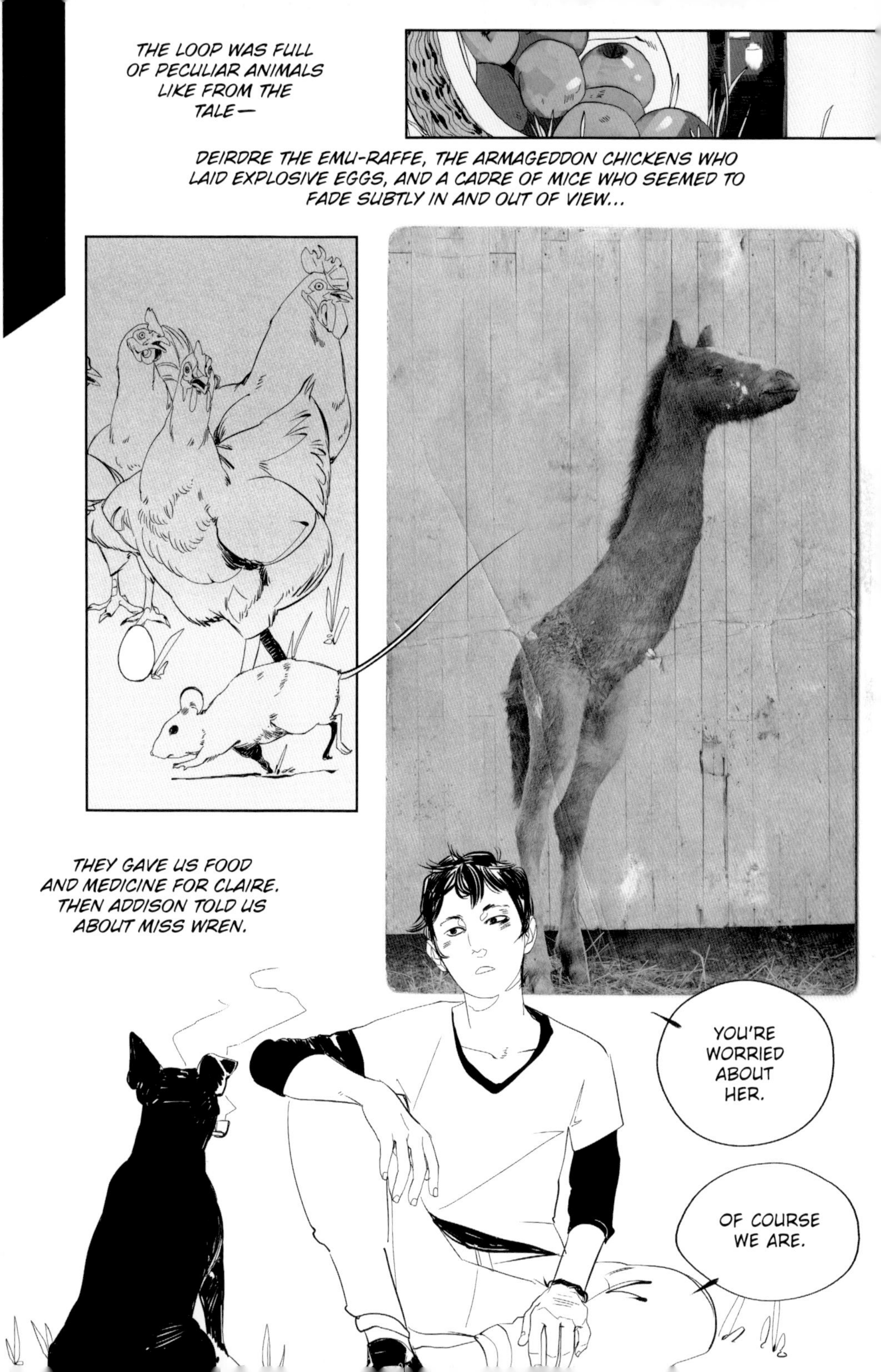
THE LOOP WAS FULL OF PECULIAR ANIMALS LIKE FROM THE TALE—
DEIRDRE THE EMU-RAFFE, THE ARMAGEDDON CHICKENS WHO LAID EXPLOSIVE EGGS, AND A CADRE OF MICE WHO SEEMED TO FADE SUBTLY IN AND OUT OF VIEW...
THEY GAVE US FOOD AND MEDICINE FOR CLAIRE. THEN ADDISON TOLD US ABOUT MISS WREN.
YOU'RE WORRIED ABOUT HER.
OF COURSE WE ARE.

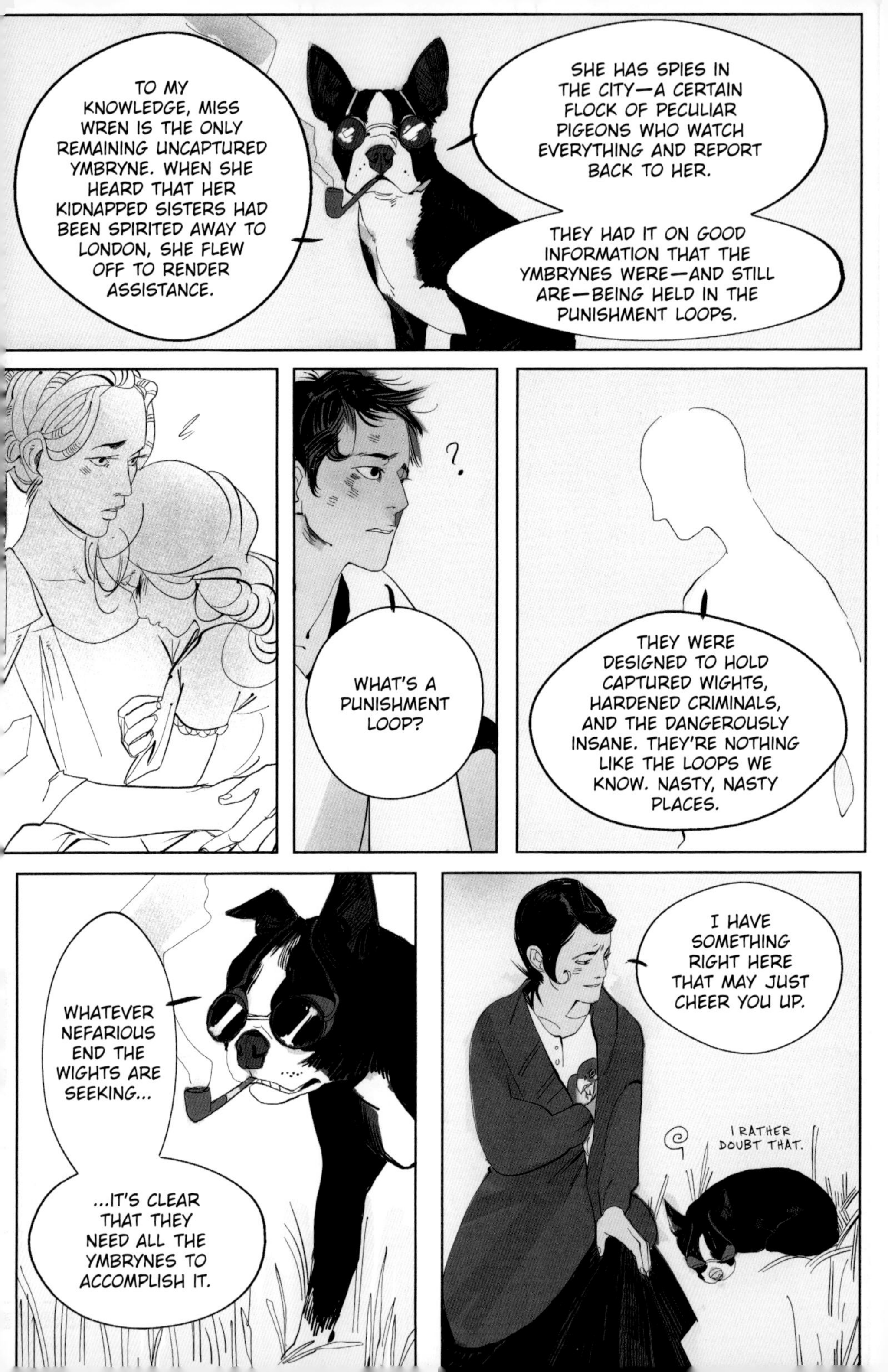
TO MY KNOWLEDGE, MISS WREN IS THE ONLY REMAINING UNCAPTURED YMBRYNE. WHEN SHE HEARD THAT HER KIDNAPPED SISTERS HAD BEEN SPIRITED AWAY TO LONDON, SHE FLEW OFF TO RENDER ASSISTANCE.
SHE HAS SPIES IN THE CITY—A CERTAIN FLOCK OF PECULIAR PIGEONS WHO WATCH EVERYTHING AND REPORT BACK TO HER.
THEY HAD IT ON GOOD INFORMATION THAT THE YMBRYNES WERE—AND STILL ARE—BEING HELD IN THE PUNISHMENT LOOPS.
?
WHAT'S A PUNISHMENT LOOP?
THEY WERE DESIGNED TO HOLD CAPTURED WIGHTS, HARDENED CRIMINALS, AND THE DANGEROUSLY INSANE. THEY'RE NOTHING LIKE THE LOOPS WE KNOW. NASTY, NASTY PLACES.
WHATEVER NEFARIOUS END THE WIGHTS ARE SEEKING...
...IT'S CLEAR THAT THEY NEED ALL THE YMBRYNES TO ACCOMPLISH IT.
I HAVE SOMETHING RIGHT HERE THAT MAY JUST CHEER YOU UP.
I RATHER DOUBT THAT.

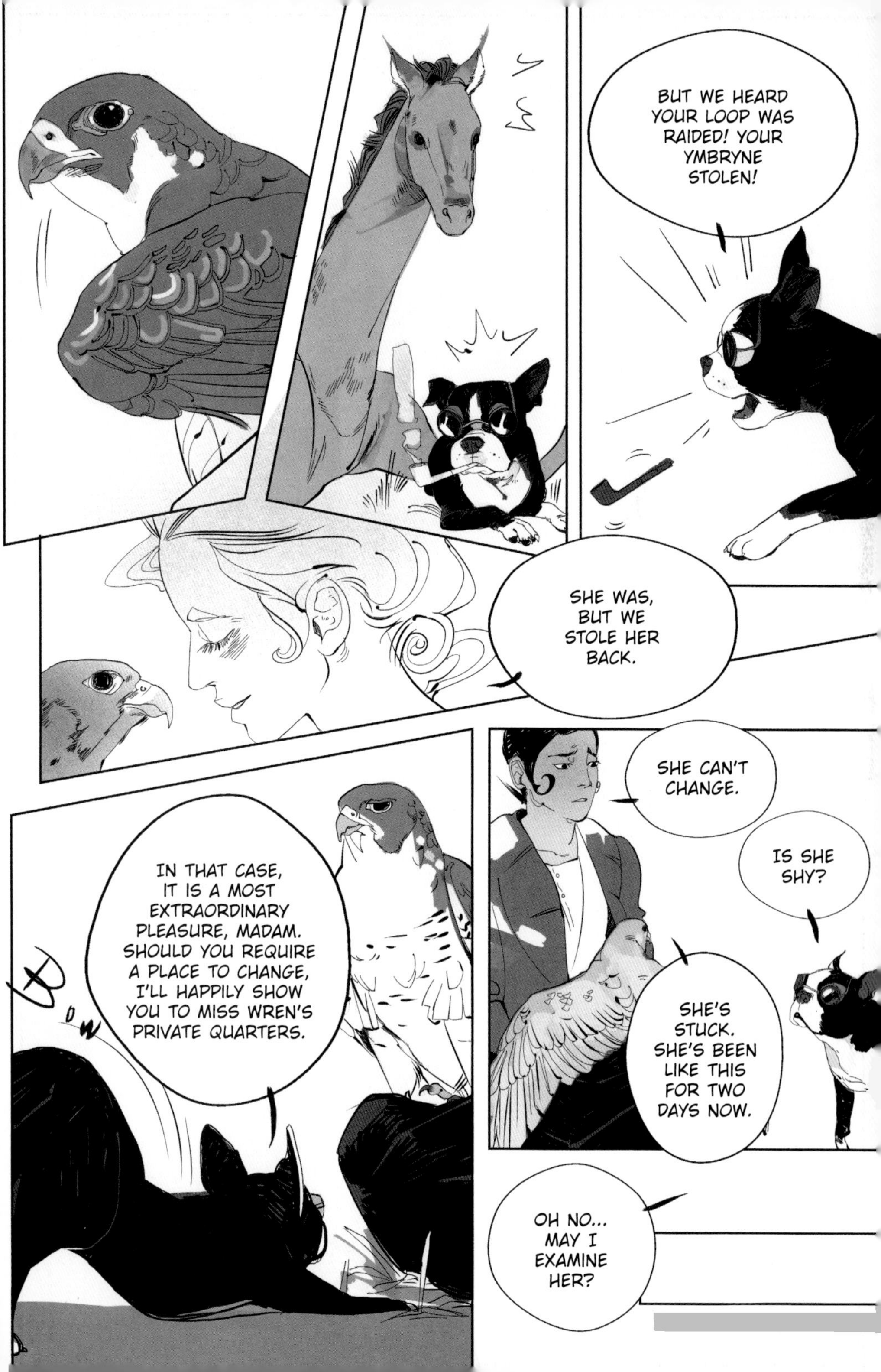
BUT WE HEARD YOUR LOOP WAS RAIDED! YOUR YMBRYNE STOLEN!
SHE WAS, BUT WE STOLE HER BACK.
IN THAT CASE, IT IS A MOST EXTRAORDINARY PLEASURE, MADAM. SHOULD YOU REQUIRE A PLACE TO CHANGE, I'LL HAPPILY SHOW YOU TO MISS WREN'S PRIVATE QUARTERS.
BOW
SHE CAN'T CHANGE.
IS SHE SHY?
SHE'S STUCK. SHE'S BEEN LIKE THIS FOR TWO DAYS NOW.
OH NO... MAY I EXAMINE HER?

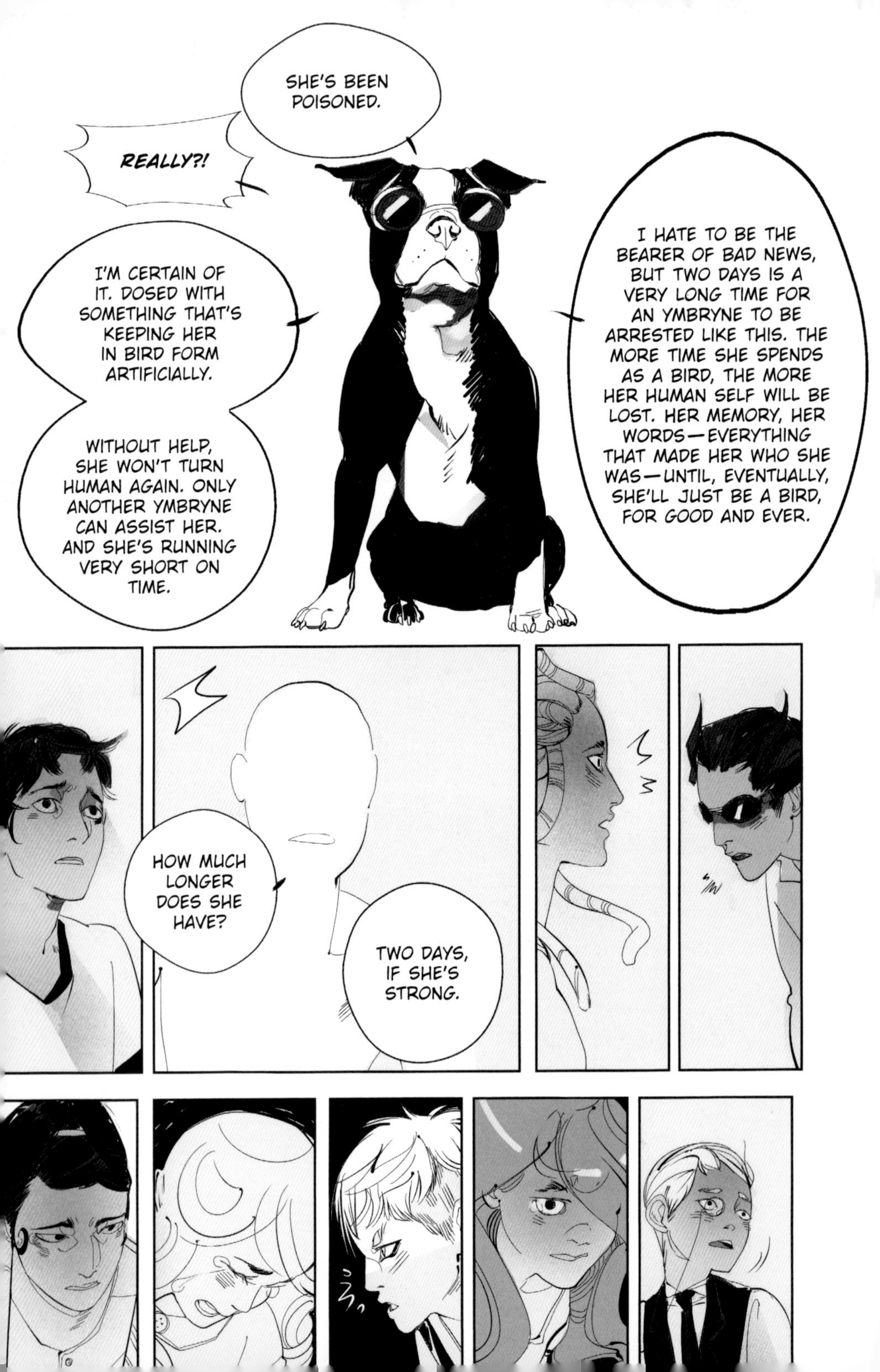
SHE'S BEEN POISONED.
REALLY?!
I'M CERTAIN OF IT. DOSED WITH SOMETHING THAT'S KEEPING HER IN BIRD FORM ARTIFICIALLY.
WITHOUT HELP, SHE WON'T TURN HUMAN AGAIN. ONLY ANOTHER YMBRYNE CAN ASSIST HER. AND SHE'S RUNNING VERY SHORT ON TIME.
I HATE TO BE THE BEARER OF BAD NEWS, BUT TWO DAYS IS A VERY LONG TIME FOR AN YMBRYNE TO BE ARRESTED LIKE THIS. THE MORE TIME SHE SPENDS AS A BIRD, THE MORE HER HUMAN SELF WILL BE LOST. HER MEMORY, HER WORDS—EVERYTHING THAT MADE HER WHO SHE WAS—UNTIL, EVENTUALLY, SHE'LL JUST BE A BIRD, FOR GOOD AND EVER.
HOW MUCH LONGER DOES SHE HAVE?
TWO DAYS, IF SHE'S STRONG.

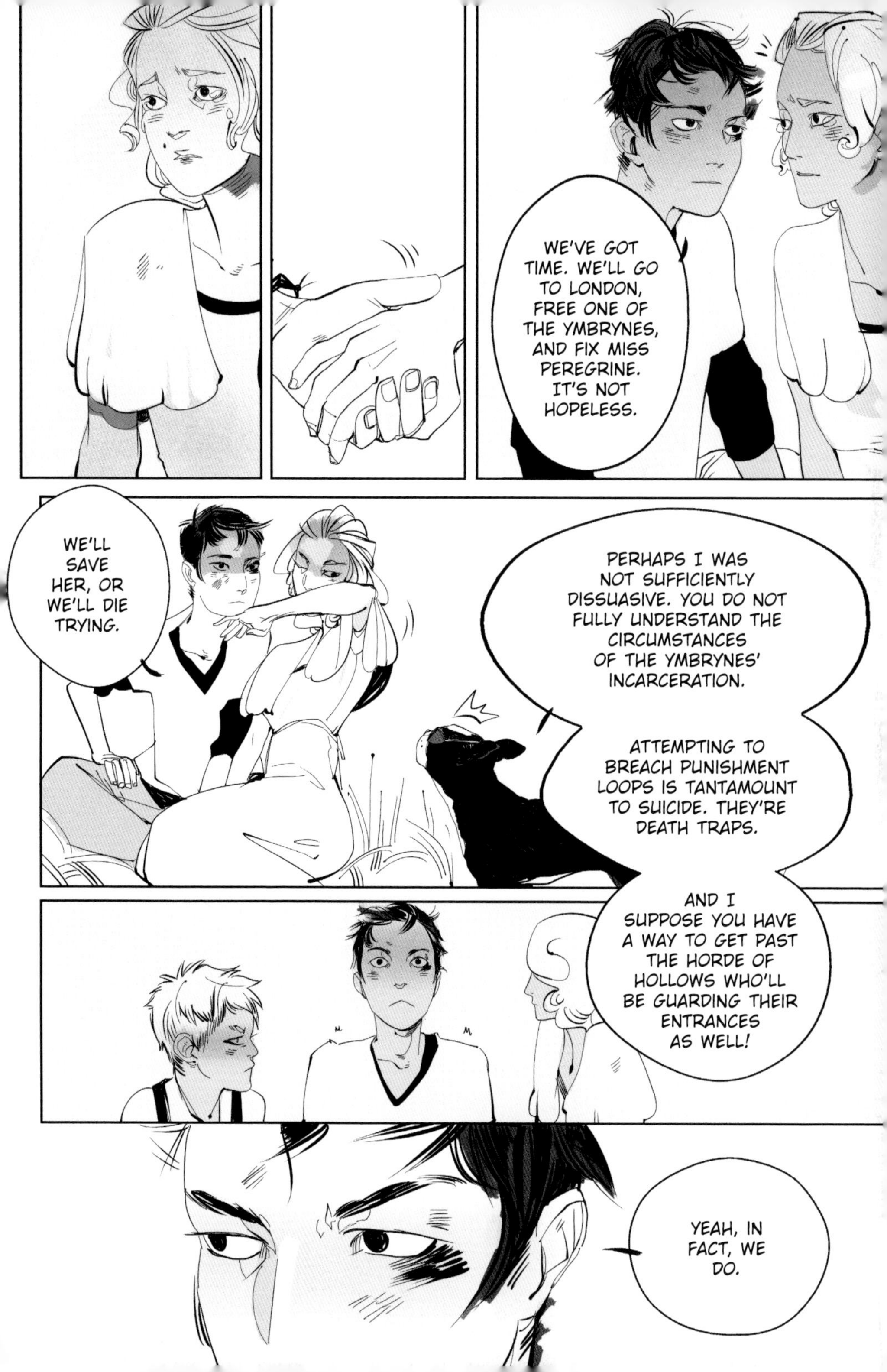
WE'VE GOT TIME. WE'LL GO TO LONDON, FREE ONE OF THE YMBRYNES, AND FIX MISS PEREGRINE. IT'S NOT HOPELESS.
WE'LL SAVE HER, OR WE'LL DIE TRYING.
PERHAPS I WAS NOT SUFFICIENTLY DISSUASIVE. YOU DO NOT FULLY UNDERSTAND THE CIRCUMSTANCES OF THE YMBRYNES' INCARCERATION.
ATTEMPTING TO BREACH PUNISHMENT LOOPS IS TANTAMOUNT TO SUICIDE. THEY'RE DEATH TRAPS.
AND I SUPPOSE YOU HAVE A WAY TO GET PAST THE HORDE OF HOLLOWS WHO'LL BE GUARDING THEIR ENTRANCES AS WELL!
YEAH, IN FACT, WE DO.

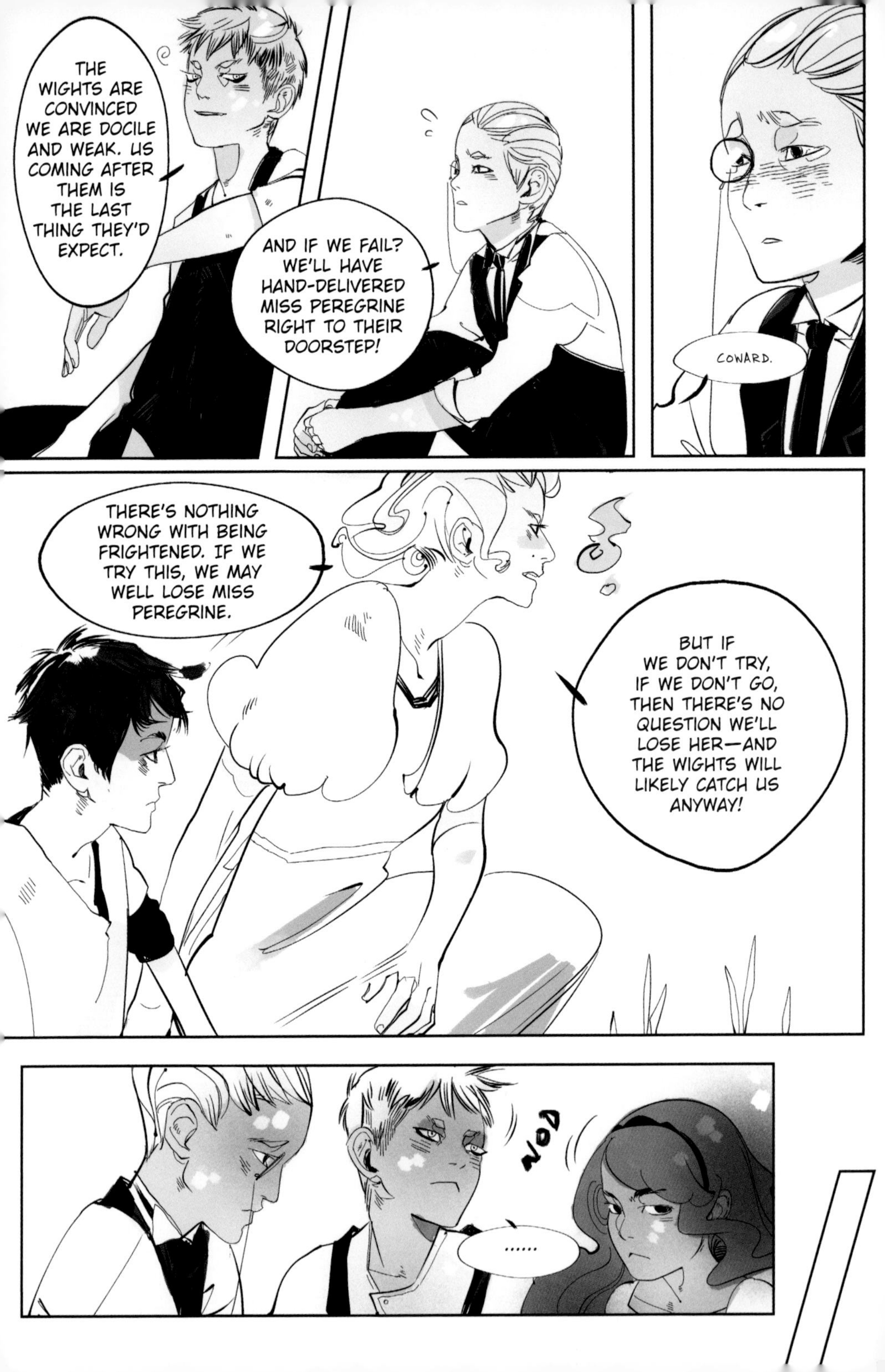
THE WIGHTS ARE CONVINCED WE ARE DOCILE AND WEAK. US COMING AFTER THEM IS THE LAST THING THEY'D EXPECT.
AND IF WE FAIL? WE'LL HAVE HAND-DELIVERED MISS PEREGRINE RIGHT TO THEIR DOORSTEP!
COWARD.
THERE'S NOTHING WRONG WITH BEING FRIGHTENED. IF WE TRY THIS, WE MAY WELL LOSE MISS PEREGRINE.
BUT IF WE DON'T TRY, IF WE DON'T GO, THEN THERE'S NO QUESTION WE'LL LOSE HER—AND THE WIGHTS WILL LIKELY CATCH US ANYWAY!
NOD
......

WE LEFT THE LOOP, BACK INTO SEPTEMBER 1940, TO TAKE THE TRAIN TO LONDON—THEIR LOOP ONLY HAS HORSES AND CARRIAGES.

FIONA STAYED BEHIND TO TAKE CARE OF CLAIRE, WHO WAS TOO SICK TO COME WITH US.

ADDISON GAVE US ALL EXPLODING EGGS AND SWEATERS MADE OF WOOL FROM PECULIAR SHEEP.

ONCE HE GAVE US DIRECTIONS, WE WERE ON OUR WAY.

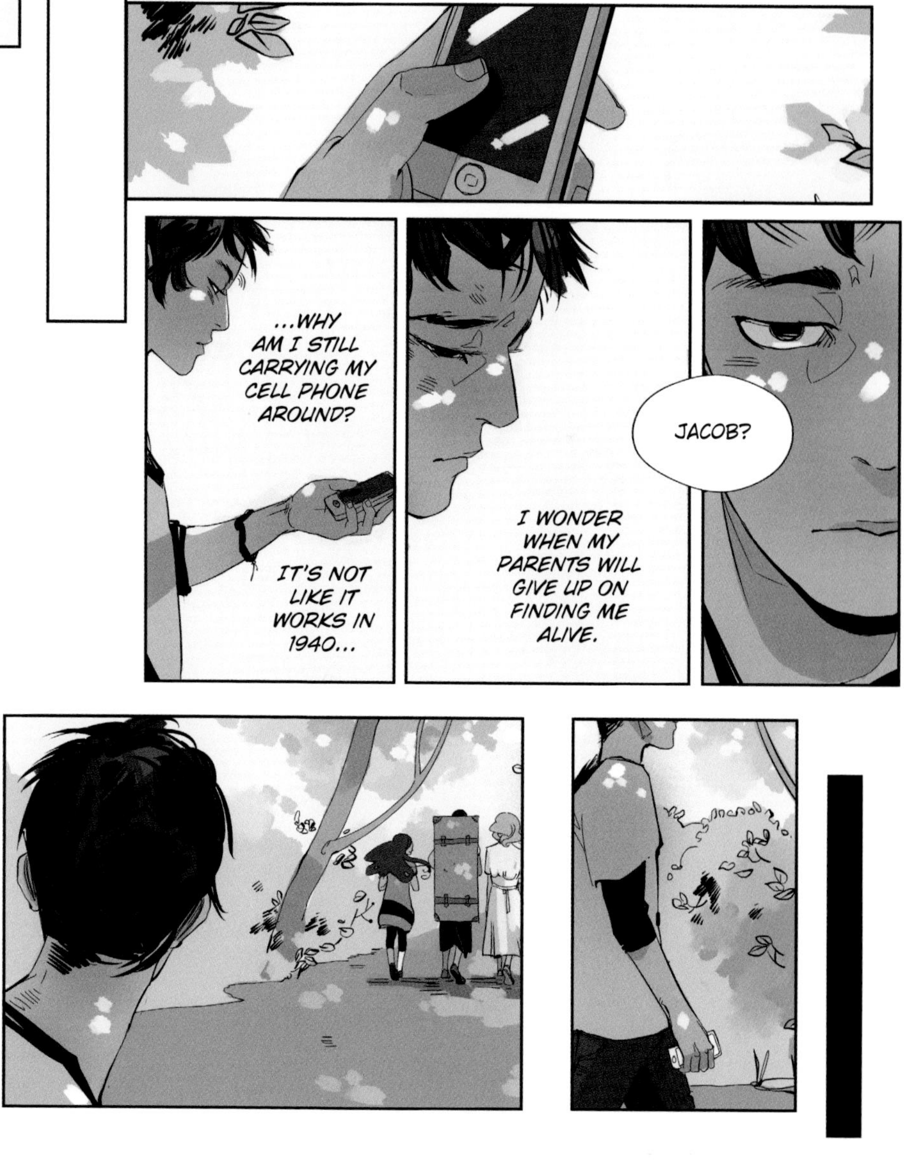
...WHY AM I STILL CARRYING MY CELL PHONE AROUND?
IT'S NOT LIKE IT WORKS IN 1940...
I WONDER WHEN MY PARENTS WILL GIVE UP ON FINDING ME ALIVE.
JACOB?

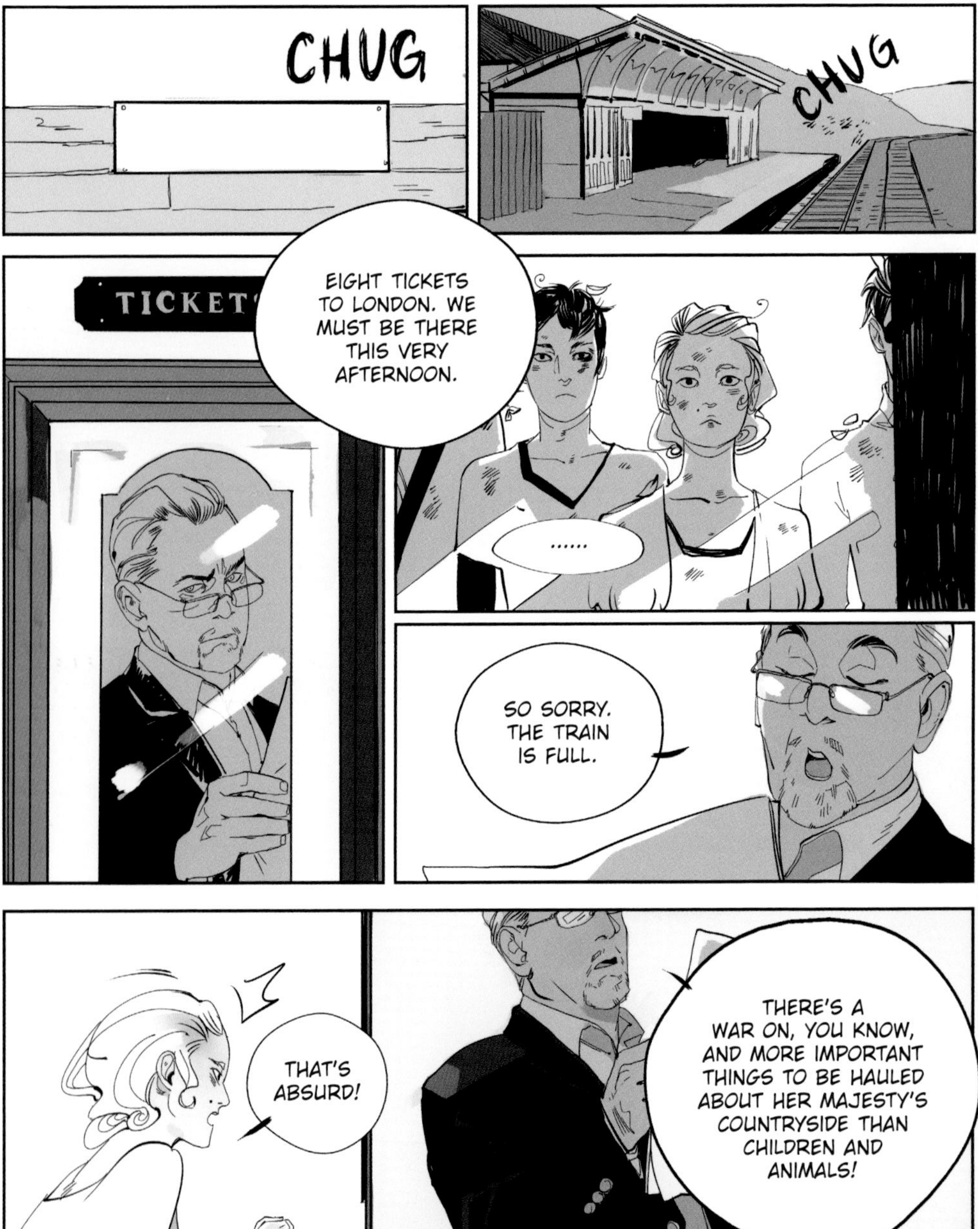
CHUG
CHUG
TICKET
EIGHT TICKETS TO LONDON. WE MUST BE THERE THIS VERY AFTERNOON.
......
SO SORRY. THE TRAIN IS FULL.
THAT'S ABSURD!
THERE'S A WAR ON, YOU KNOW, AND MORE IMPORTANT THINGS TO BE HAULED ABOUT HER MAJESTY'S COUNTRYSIDE THAN CHILDREN AND ANIMALS!

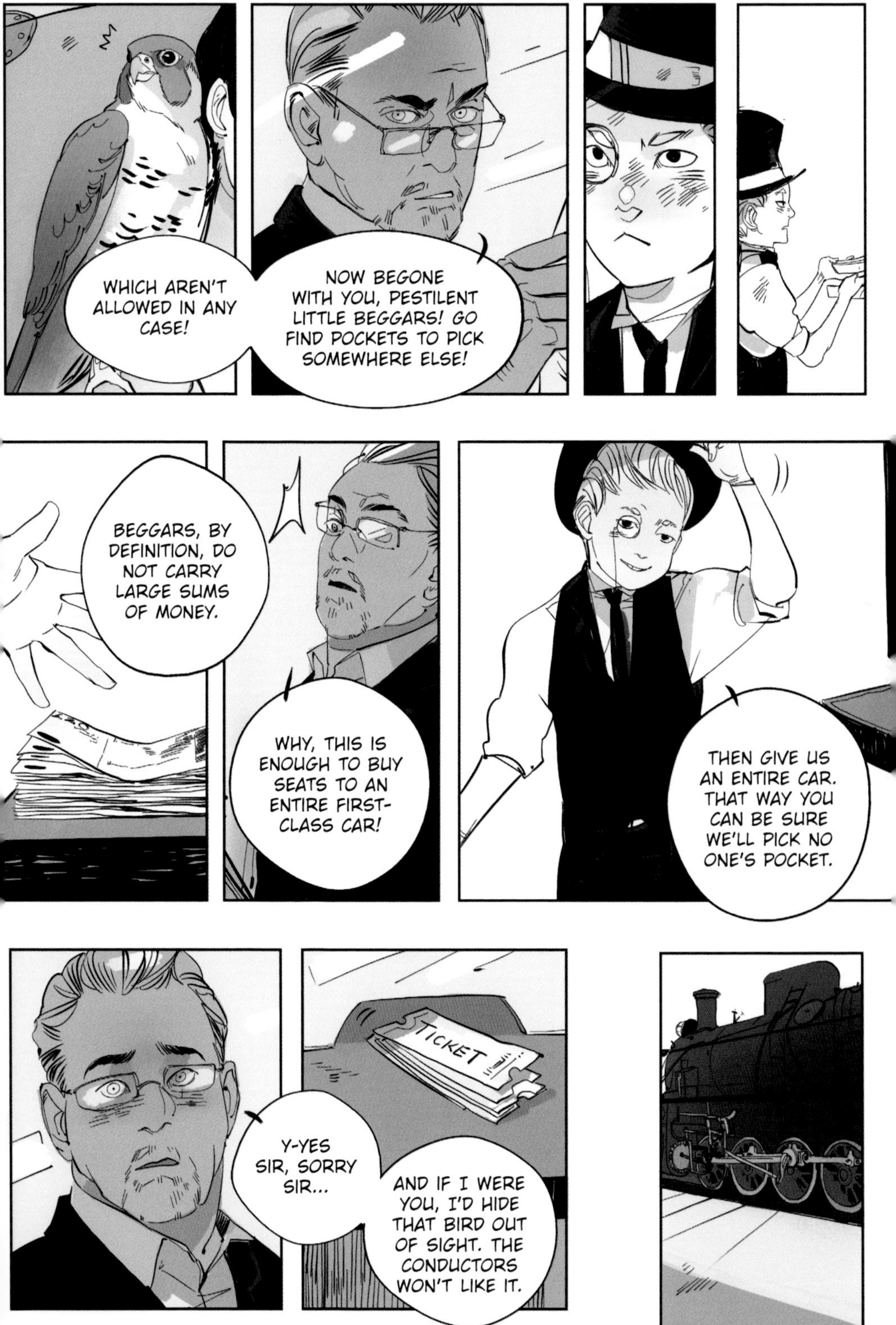
WHICH AREN'T ALLOWED IN ANY CASE!
NOW BEGONE WITH YOU, PESTILENT LITTLE BEGGARS! GO FIND POCKETS TO PICK SOMEWHERE ELSE!
BEGGARS, BY DEFINITION, DO NOT CARRY LARGE SUMS OF MONEY.
WHY, THIS IS ENOUGH TO BUY SEATS TO AN ENTIRE FIRST-CLASS CAR!
THEN GIVE US AN ENTIRE CAR. THAT WAY YOU CAN BE SURE WE'LL PICK NO ONE'S POCKET.
Y-YES SIR, SORRY SIR...
AND IF I WERE YOU, I'D HIDE THAT BIRD OUT OF SIGHT. THE CONDUCTORS WON'T LIKE IT.
TICKET

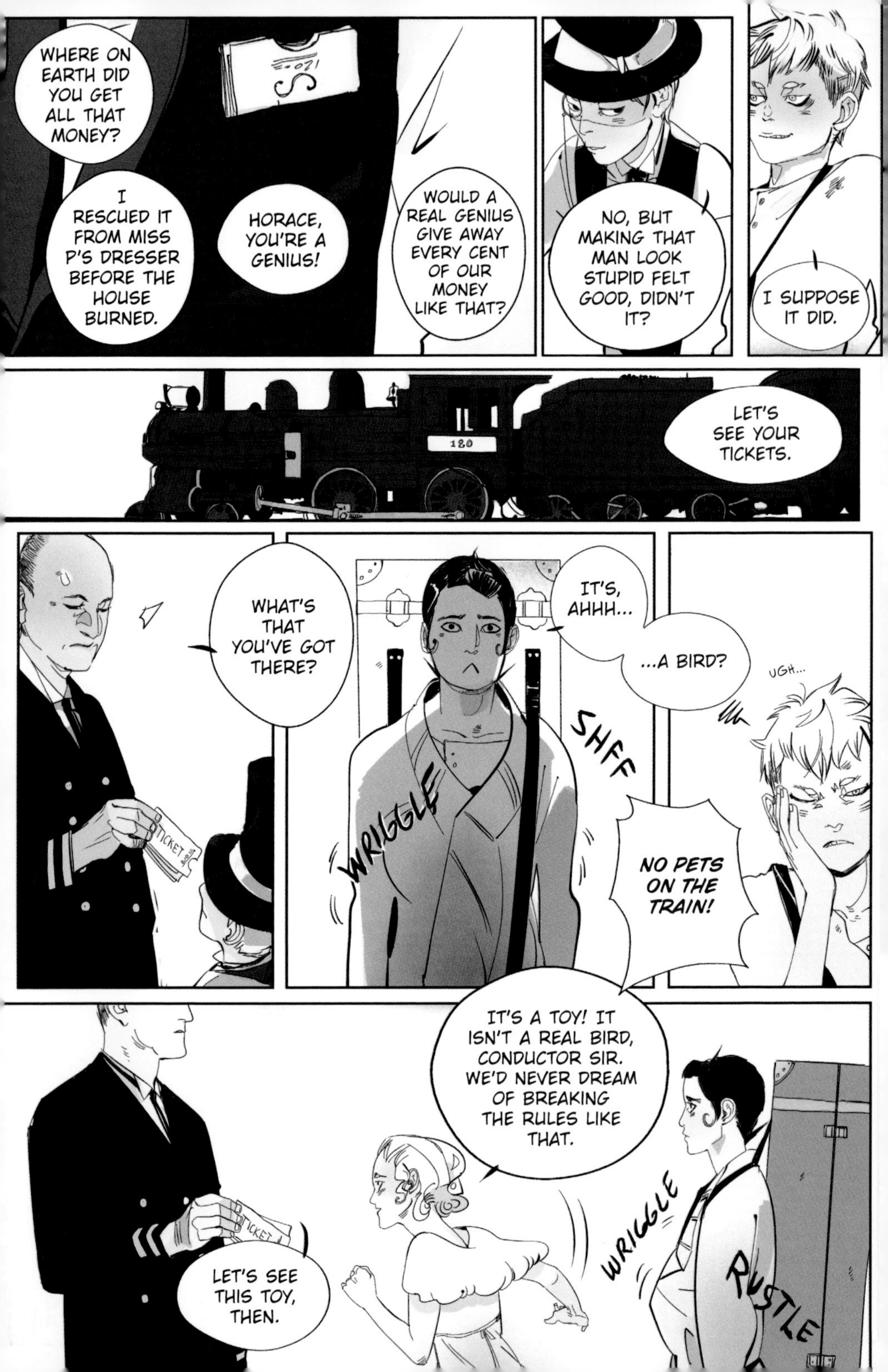
WHERE ON EARTH DID YOU GET ALL THAT MONEY?
I RESCUED IT FROM MISS P'S DRESSER BEFORE THE HOUSE BURNED.
HORACE, YOU'RE A GENIUS!
WOULD A REAL GENIUS GIVE AWAY EVERY CENT OF OUR MONEY LIKE THAT?
NO, BUT MAKING THAT MAN LOOK STUPID FELT GOOD, DIDN'T IT?
I SUPPOSE IT DID.
120
LET'S SEE YOUR TICKETS.
TICKET
WHAT'S THAT YOU'VE GOT THERE?
IT'S, AHHH...
...A BIRD?
SHFF
WRIGGLE
UGH...
NO PETS ON THE TRAIN!
IT'S A TOY! IT ISN'T A REAL BIRD, CONDUCTOR SIR. WE'D NEVER DREAM OF BREAKING THE RULES LIKE THAT.
TICKET
LET'S SEE THIS TOY, THEN.
WRIGGLE
RUSTLE

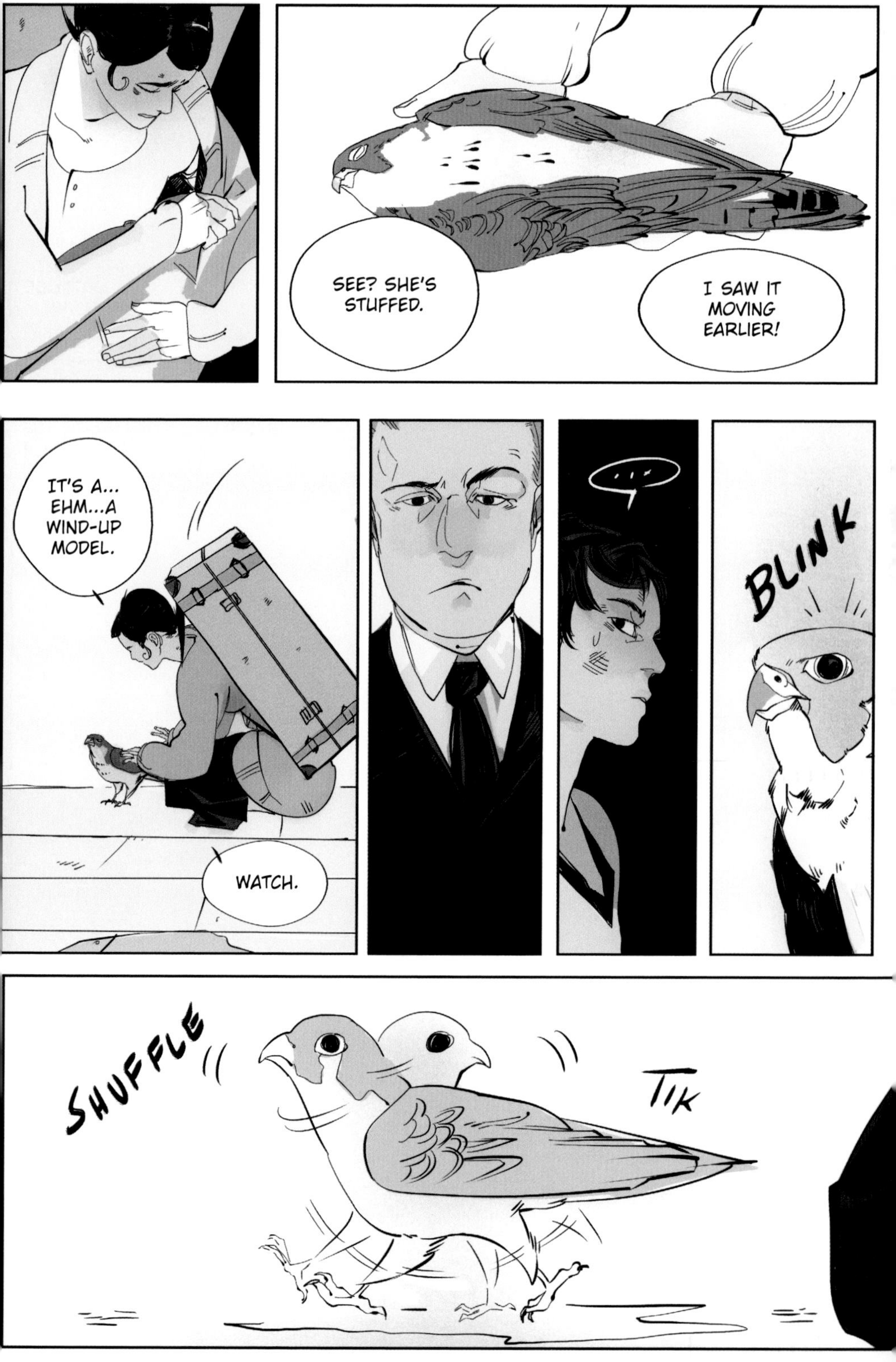
SEE? SHE'S STUFFED.
I SAW IT MOVING EARLIER!
IT'S A... EHM...A WIND-UP MODEL.
WATCH.
BLINK
SHUFFLE
TIK

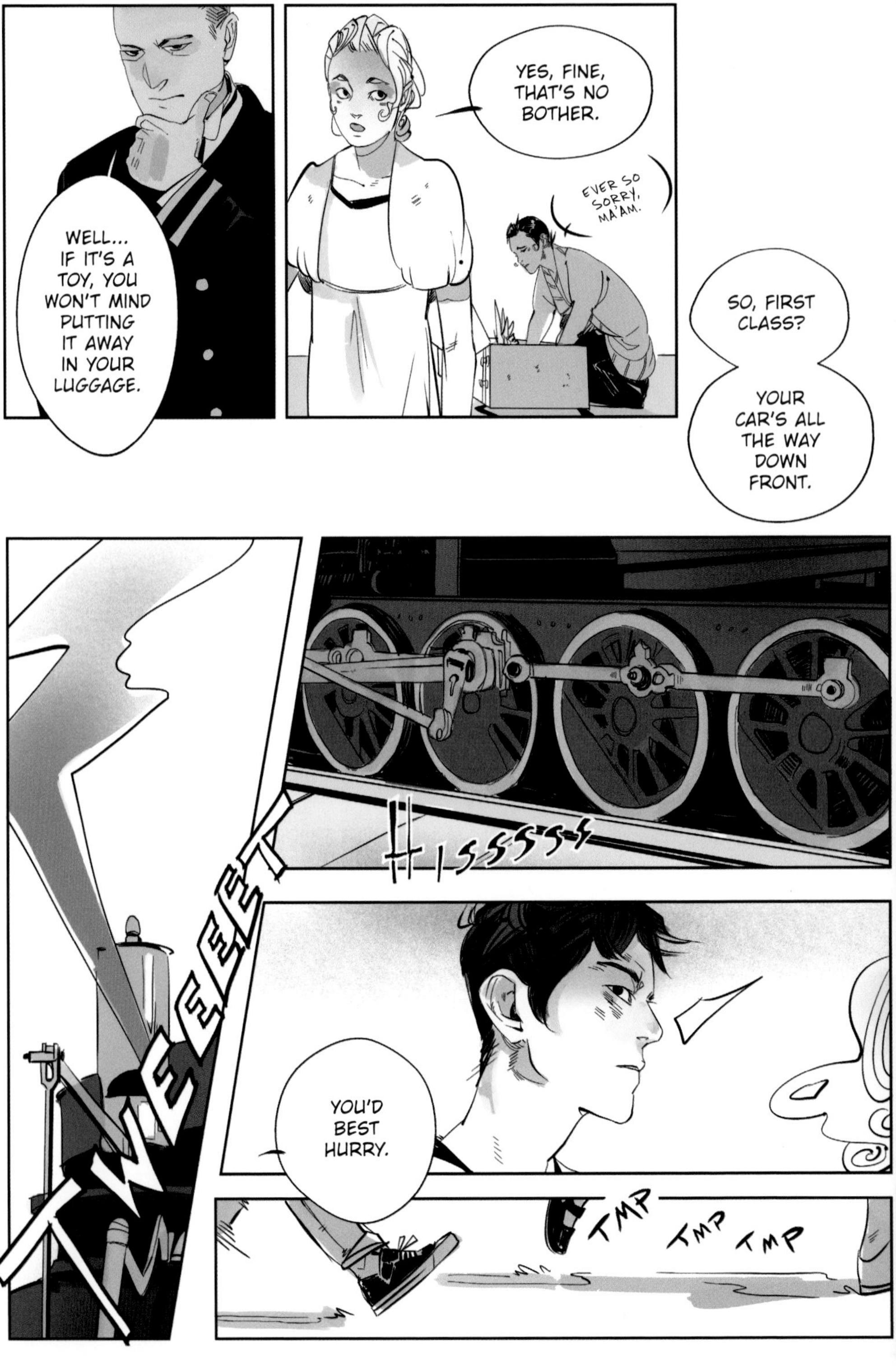
WELL... IF IT'S A TOY, YOU WON'T MIND PUTTING IT AWAY IN YOUR LUGGAGE.
YES, FINE, THAT'S NO BOTHER.
EVER SO SORRY, MA'AM.
SO, FIRST CLASS?
YOUR CAR'S ALL THE WAY DOWN FRONT.
TWEEET
HISSSSS
YOU'D BEST HURRY.
TMP
TMP
TMP

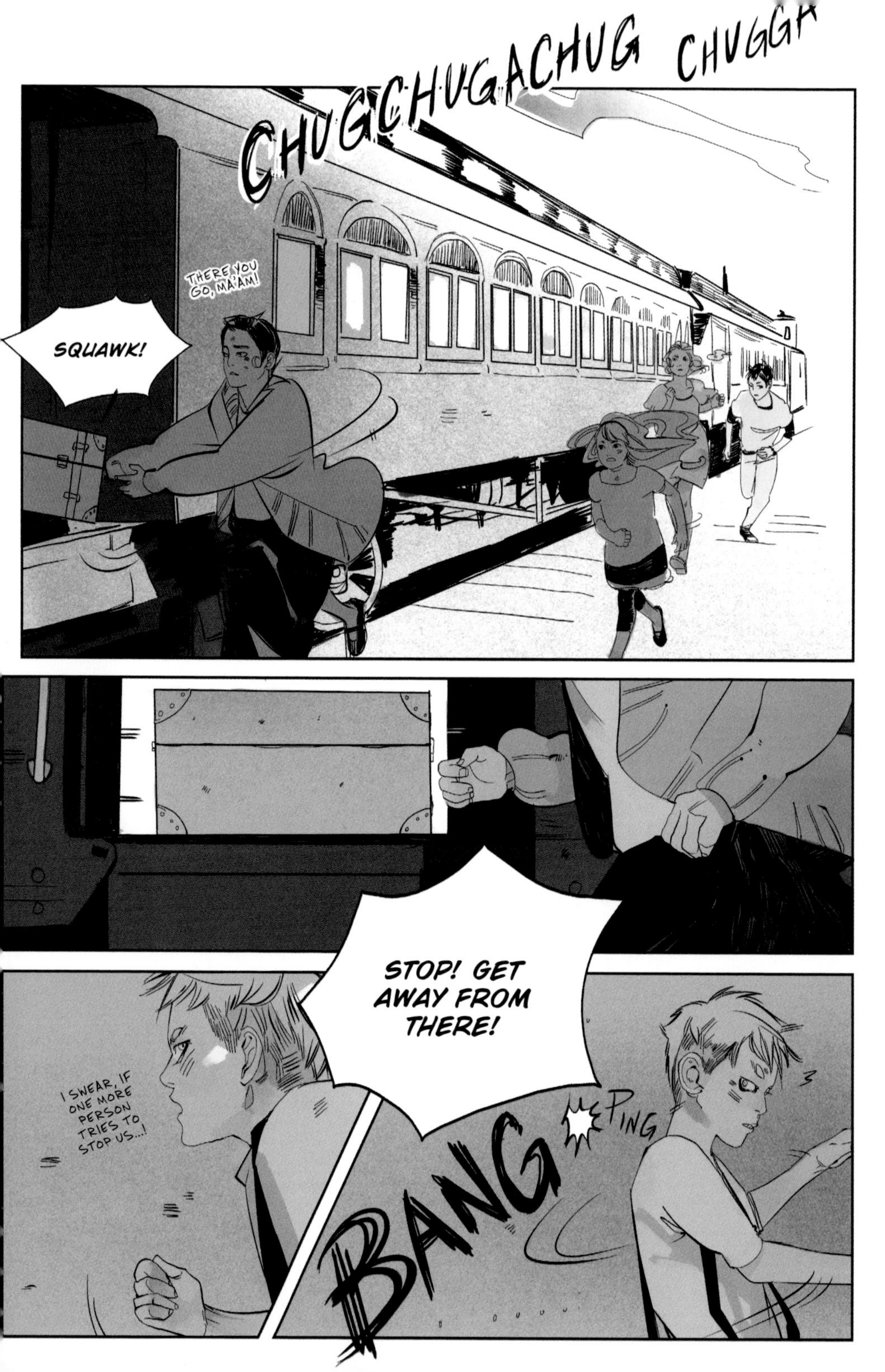
CHUGCHUGACHUG CHUGGA
THERE YOU GO, MA'AM!
SQUAWK!
STOP! GET AWAY FROM THERE!
I SWEAR, IF ONE MORE PERSON TRIES TO STOP US...!
BANG
PING

I SAID STOP!

GET AWAY FROM THE TRAIN!

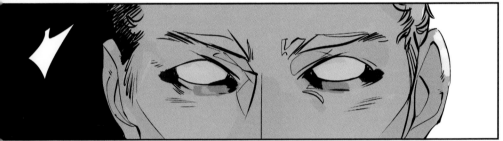

WE WERE SO CLOSE.

AND MISS P IS STUCK IN A TRUNK IN THAT TRAIN!!

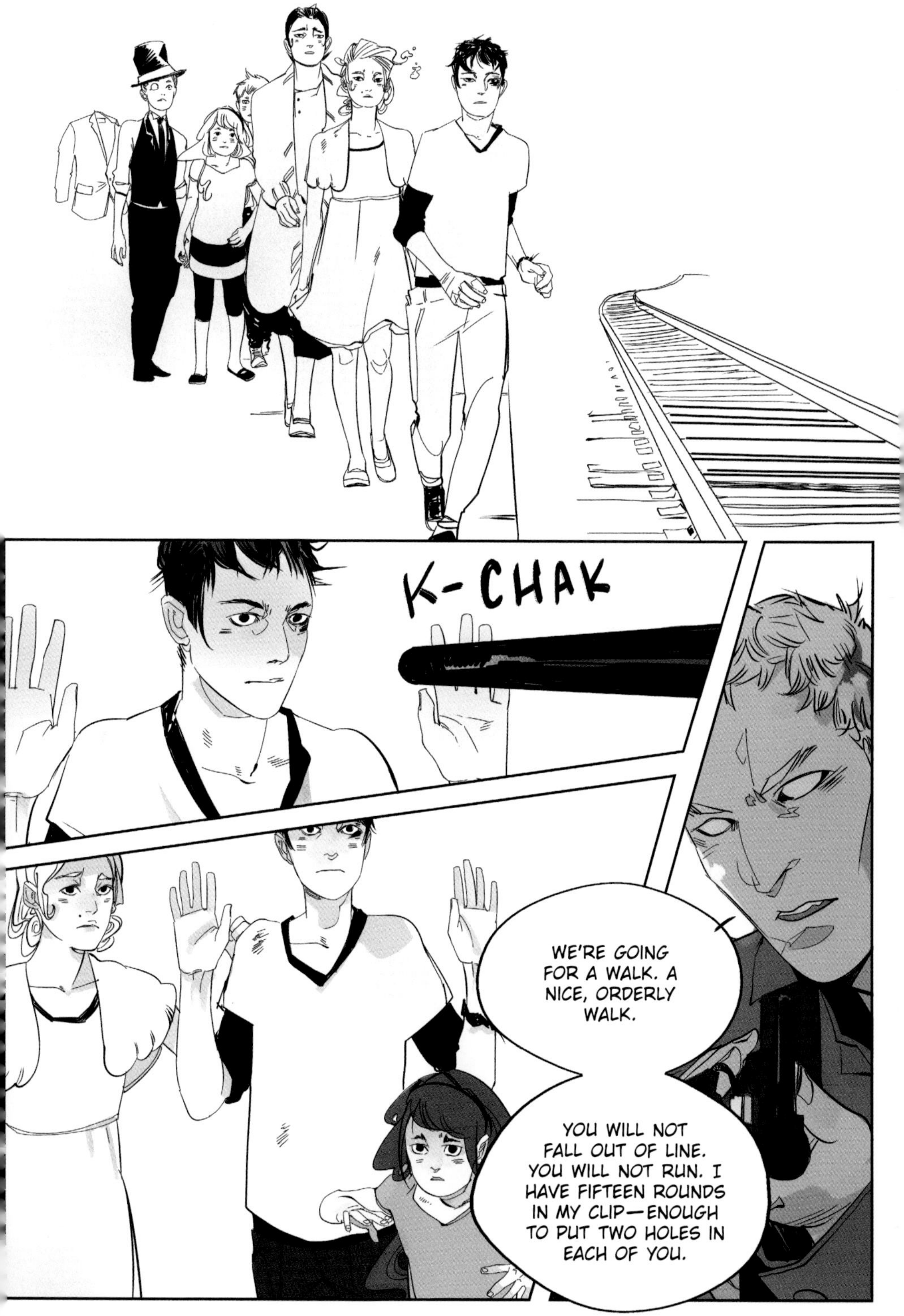
K-CHAK
WE'RE GOING FOR A WALK. A NICE, ORDERLY WALK.
YOU WILL NOT FALL OUT OF LINE. YOU WILL NOT RUN. I HAVE FIFTEEN ROUNDS IN MY CLIP—ENOUGH TO PUT TWO HOLES IN EACH OF YOU.

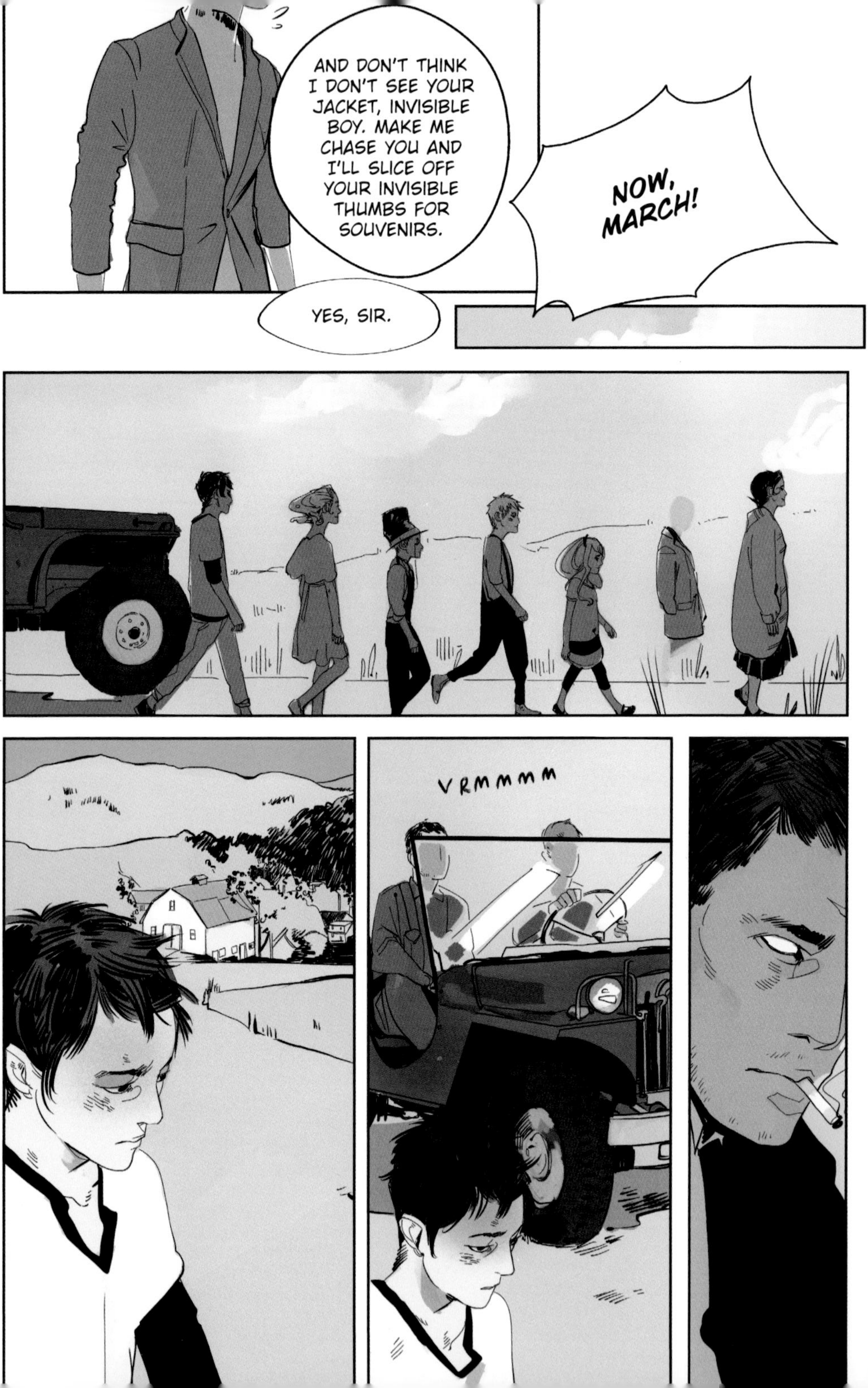
AND DON'T THINK I DON'T SEE YOUR JACKET, INVISIBLE BOY. MAKE ME CHASE YOU AND I'LL SLICE OFF YOUR INVISIBLE THUMBS FOR SOUVENIRS.
NOW, MARCH!
YES, SIR.
VRMMMM

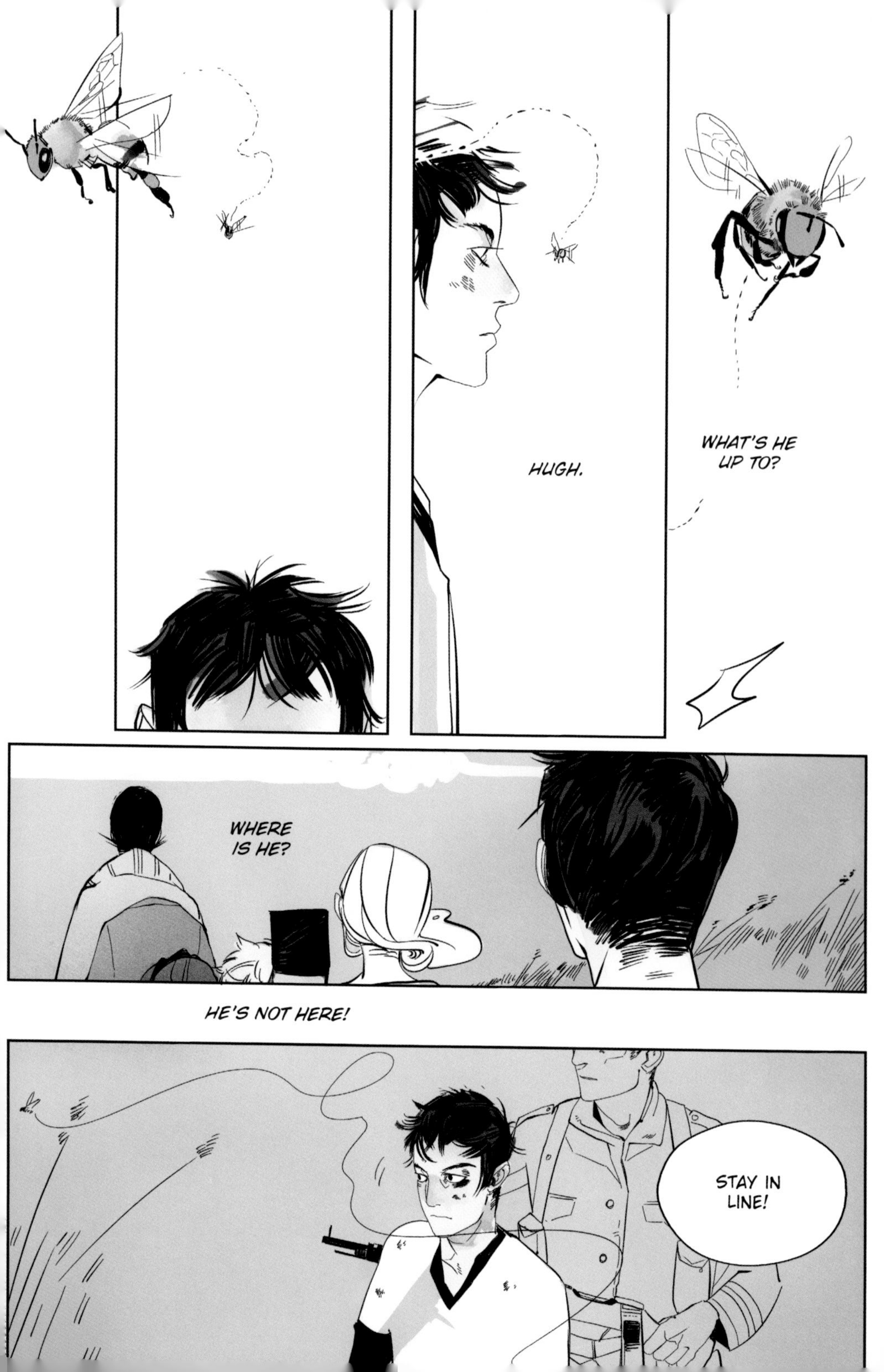
HUGH.
WHAT'S HE UP TO?
WHERE IS HE?
HE'S NOT HERE!
STAY IN LINE!

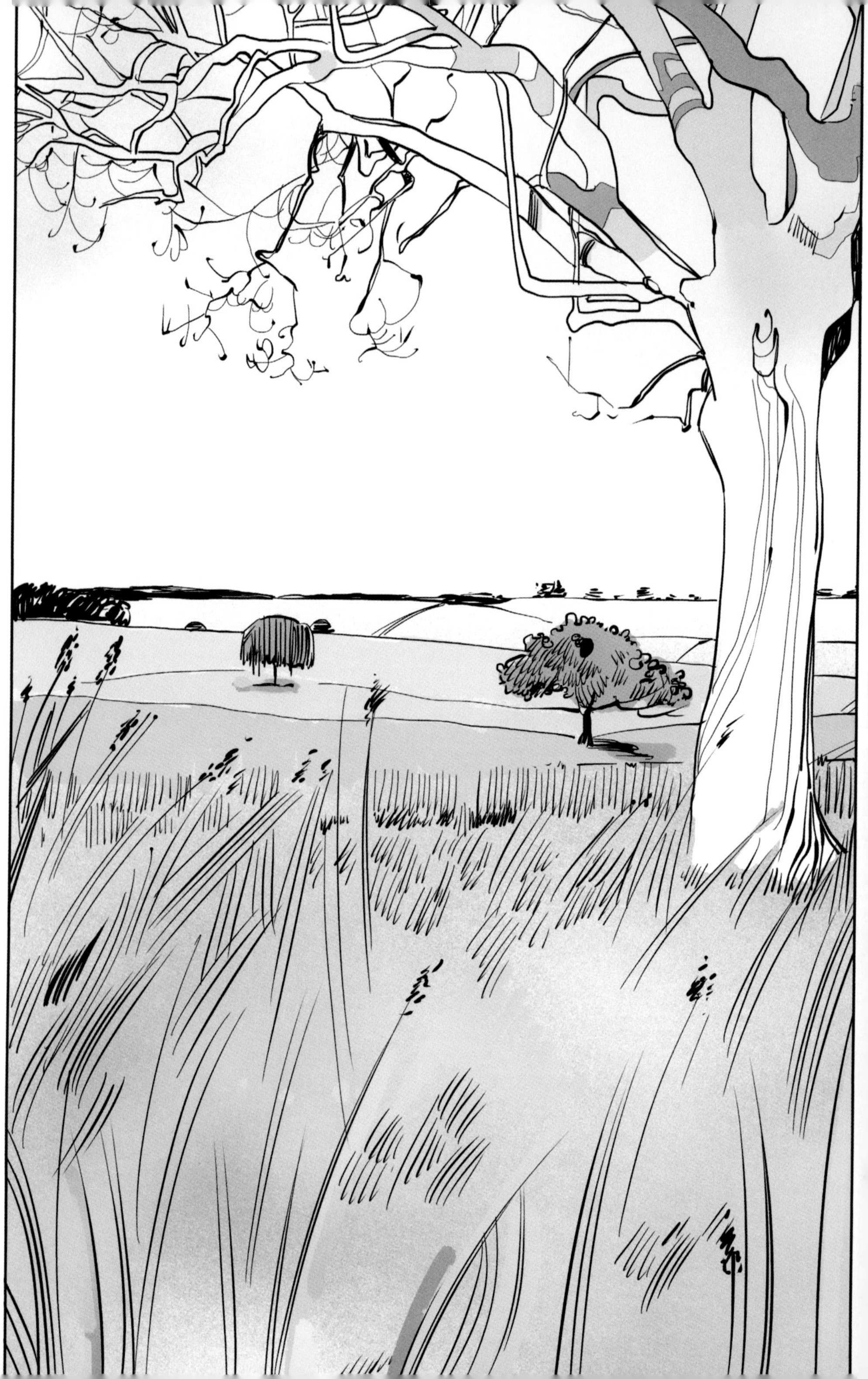

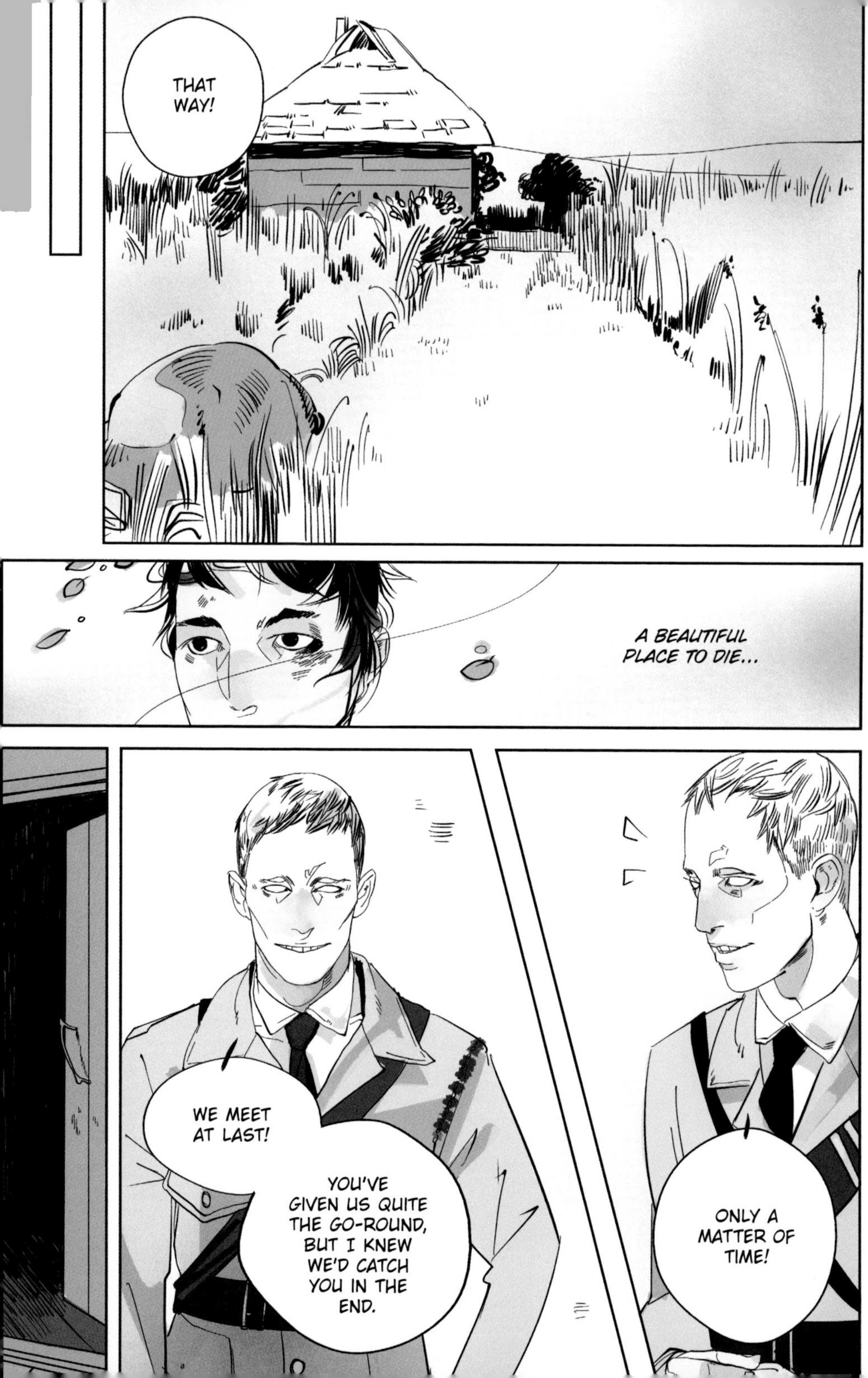
THAT WAY!
A BEAUTIFUL PLACE TO DIE...
WE MEET AT LAST!
YOU'VE GIVEN US QUITE THE GO-ROUND, BUT I KNEW WE'D CATCH YOU IN THE END.
ONLY A MATTER OF TIME!

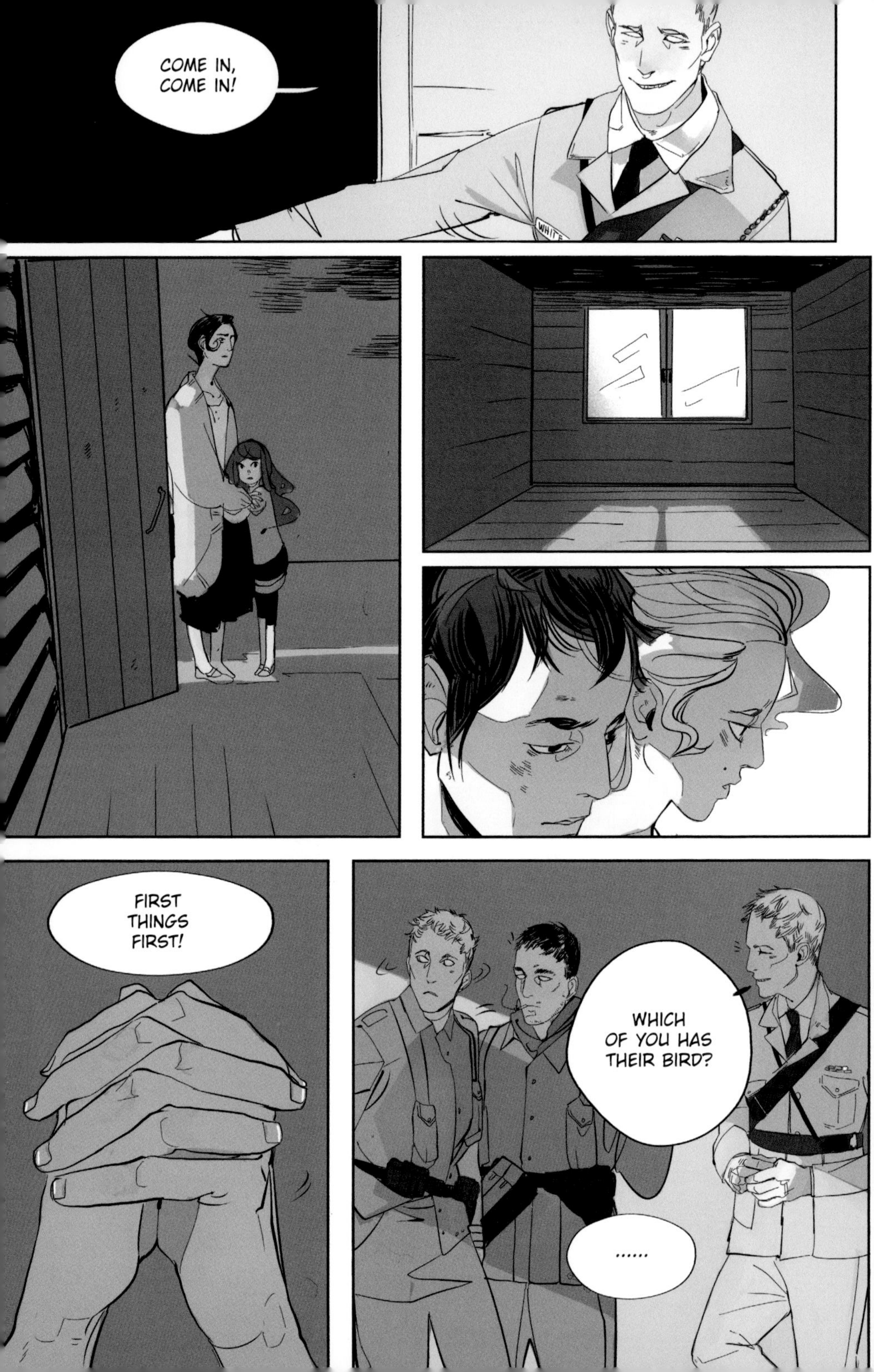
COME IN, COME IN!
WHITE
FIRST THINGS FIRST!
WHICH OF YOU HAS THEIR BIRD?
......

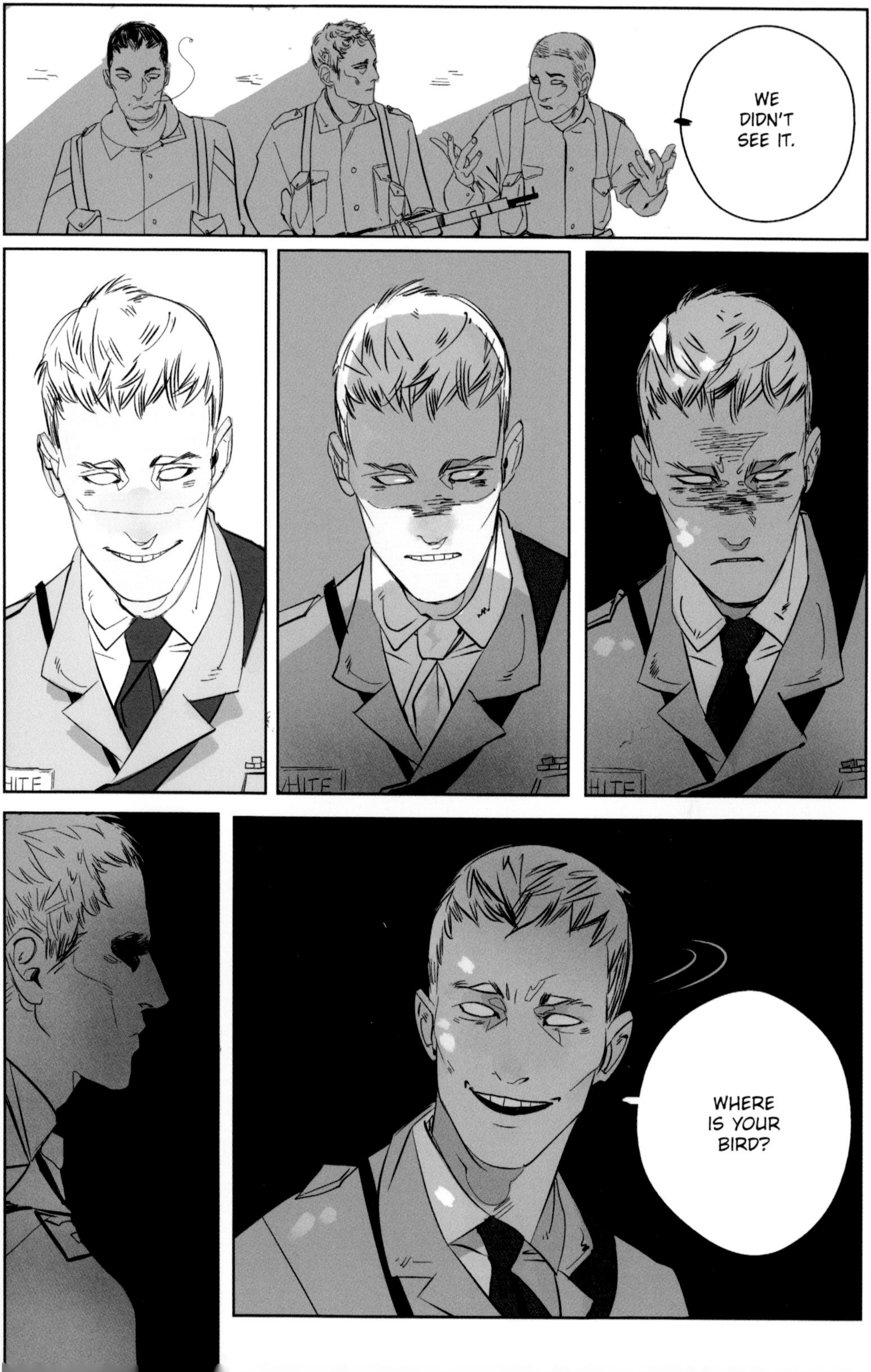
WE DIDN'T SEE IT.
WHERE IS YOUR BIRD?

CHAPTER THREE

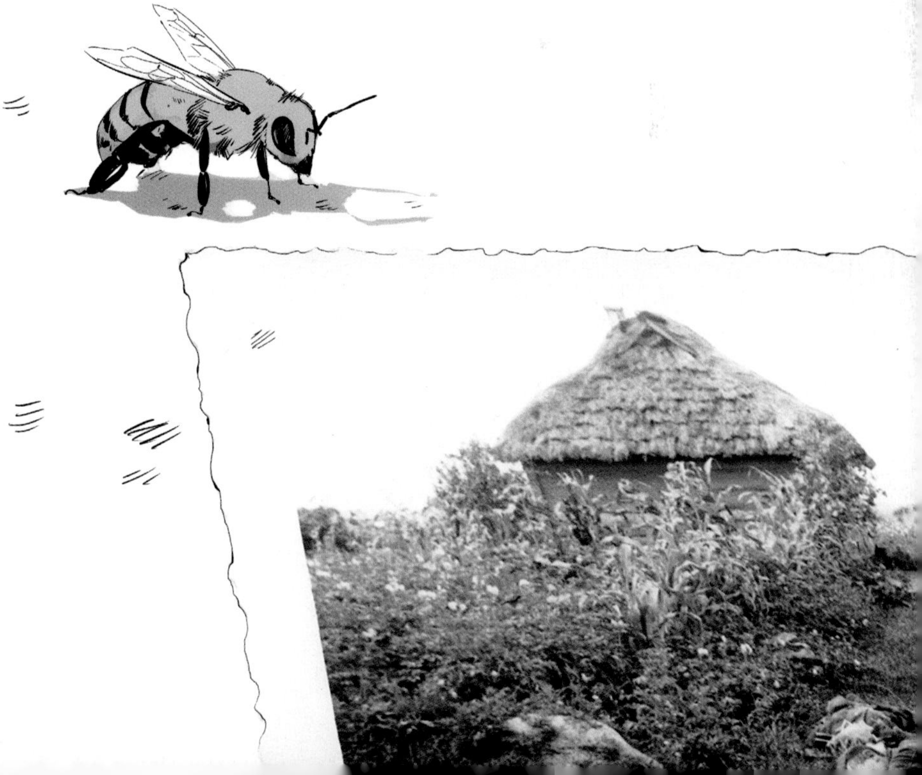

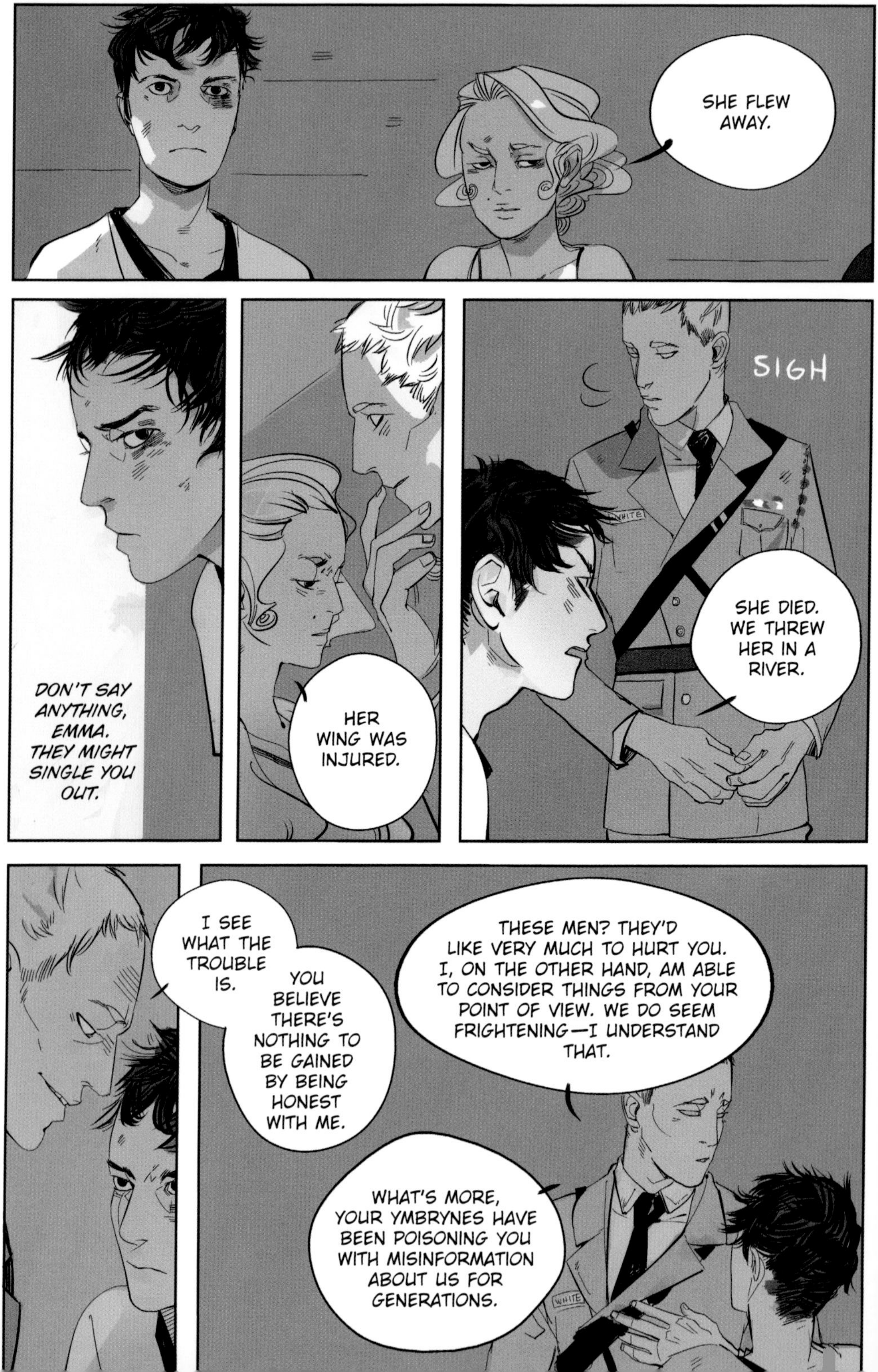
SHE FLEW AWAY.
DON'T SAY ANYTHING, EMMA. THEY MIGHT SINGLE YOU OUT.
HER WING WAS INJURED.
SIGH
WHITE
SHE DIED. WE THREW HER IN A RIVER.
I SEE WHAT THE TROUBLE IS.
YOU BELIEVE THERE'S NOTHING TO BE GAINED BY BEING HONEST WITH ME.
THESE MEN? THEY'D LIKE VERY MUCH TO HURT YOU. I, ON THE OTHER HAND, AM ABLE TO CONSIDER THINGS FROM YOUR POINT OF VIEW. WE DO SEEM FRIGHTENING—I UNDERSTAND THAT.
WHAT'S MORE, YOUR YMBRYNES HAVE BEEN POISONING YOU WITH MISINFORMATION ABOUT US FOR GENERATIONS.
WHITE

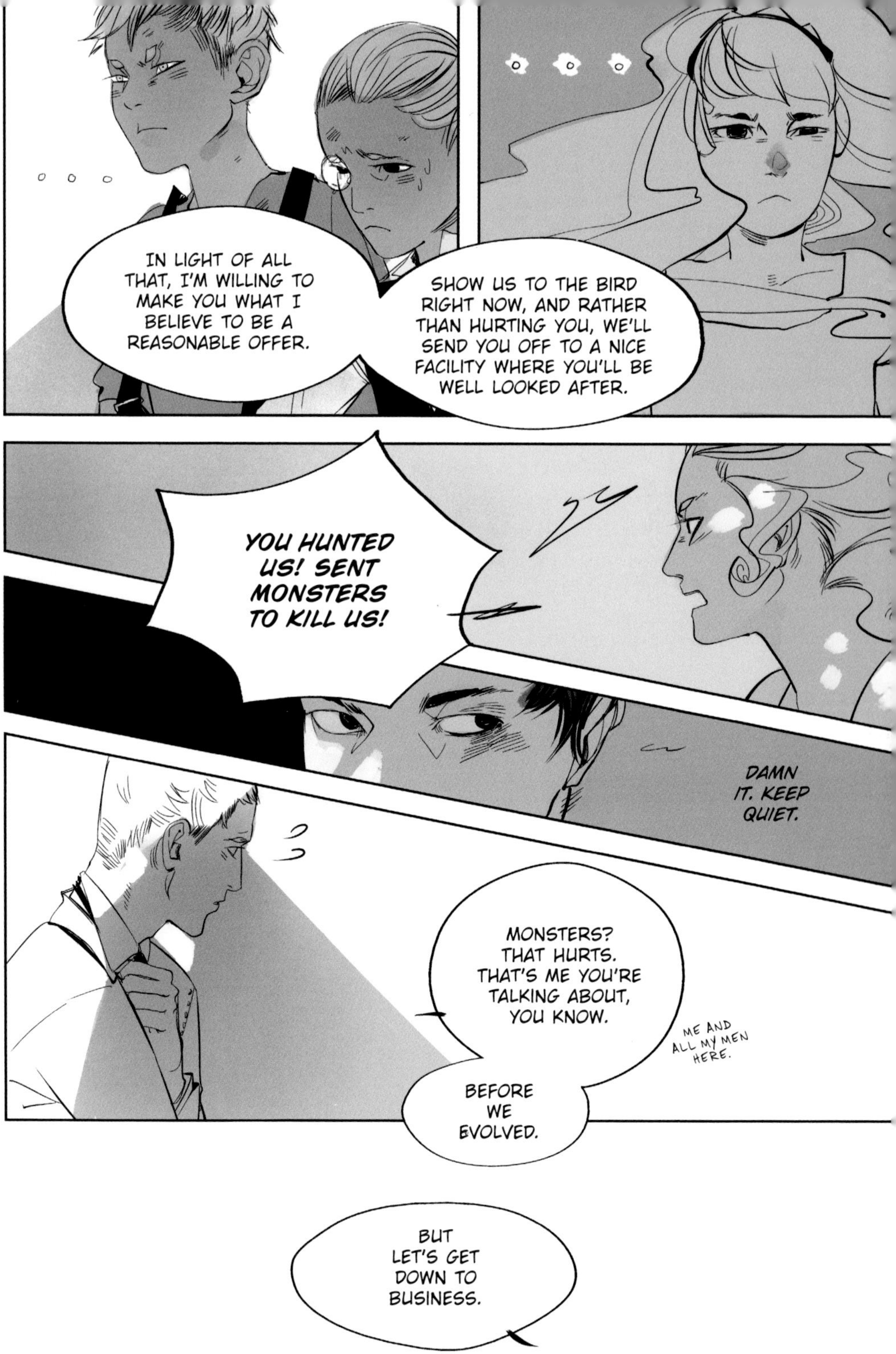

IN LIGHT OF ALL THAT, I'M WILLING TO MAKE YOU WHAT I BELIEVE TO BE A REASONABLE OFFER.
SHOW US TO THE BIRD RIGHT NOW, AND RATHER THAN HURTING YOU, WE'LL SEND YOU OFF TO A NICE FACILITY WHERE YOU'LL BE WELL LOOKED AFTER.
YOU HUNTED US! SENT MONSTERS TO KILL US!
DAMN IT. KEEP QUIET.
MONSTERS? THAT HURTS. THAT'S ME YOU'RE TALKING ABOUT, YOU KNOW.
ME AND ALL MY MEN HERE.
BEFORE WE EVOLVED.
BUT LET'S GET DOWN TO BUSINESS.

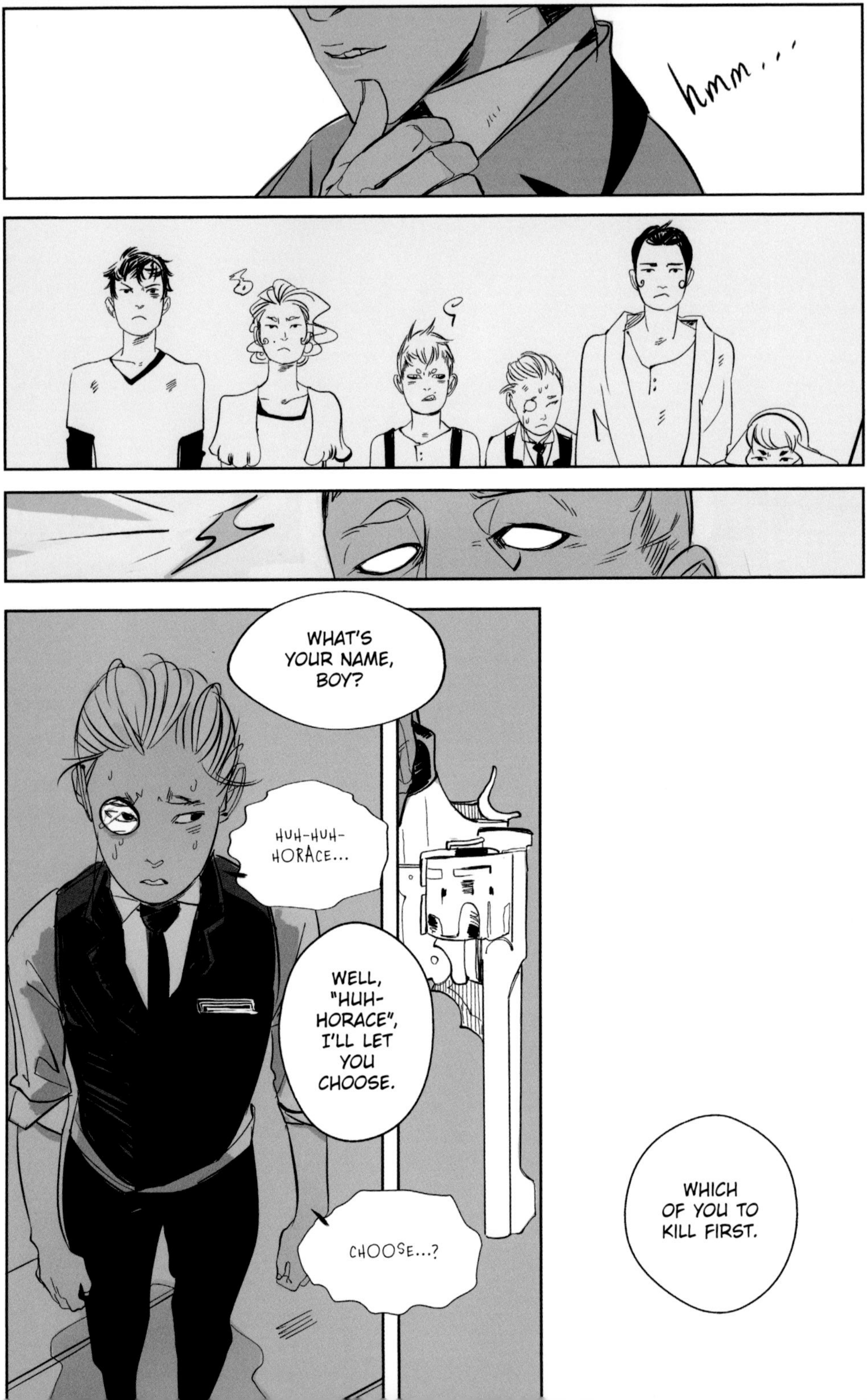
hmm...
WHAT'S YOUR NAME, BOY?
HUH-HUH-HORACE...
WELL, "HUH-HORACE", I'LL LET YOU CHOOSE.
CHOOSE...?
WHICH OF YOU TO KILL FIRST.

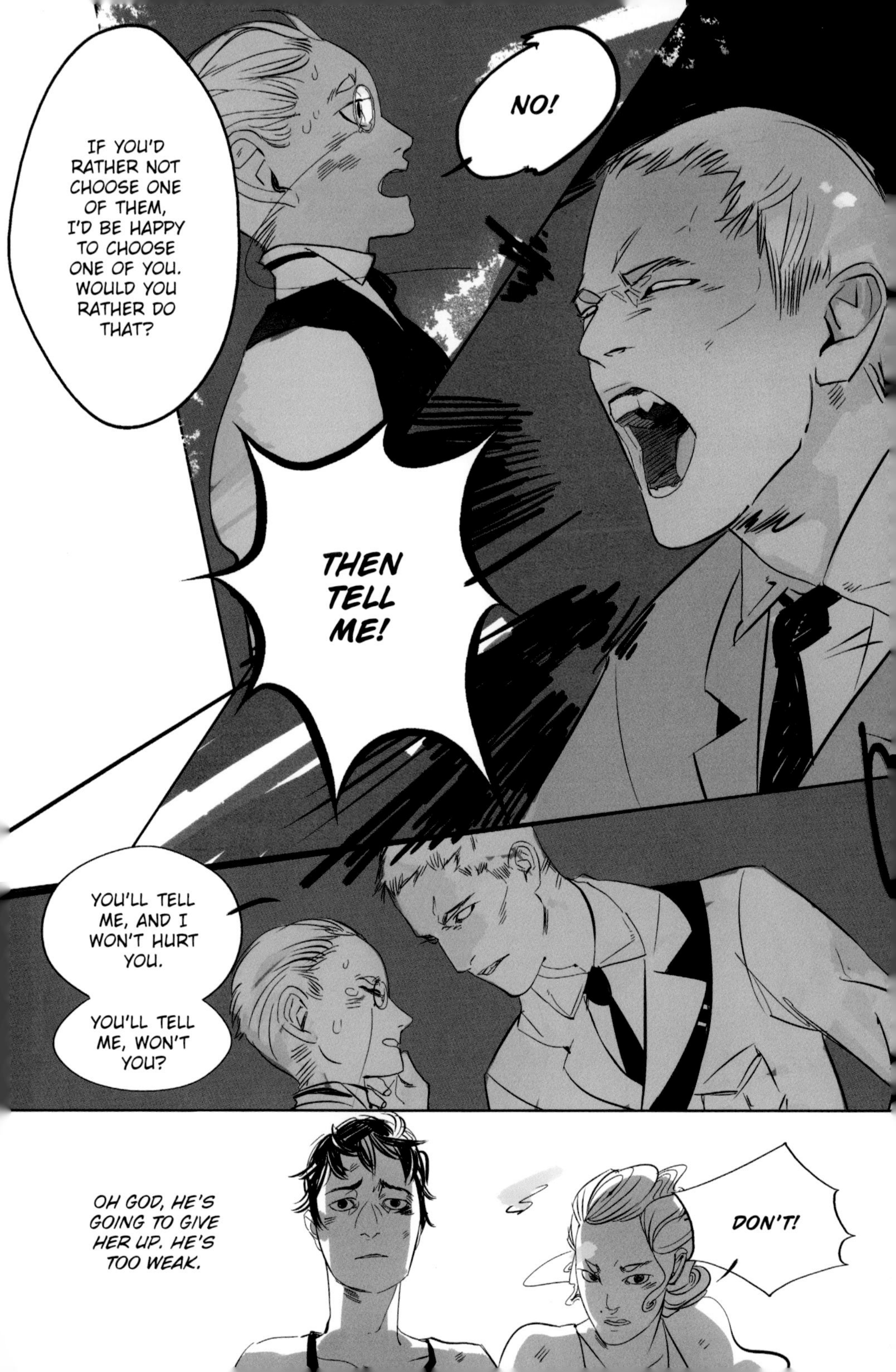
IF YOU'D RATHER NOT CHOOSE ONE OF THEM, I'D BE HAPPY TO CHOOSE ONE OF YOU. WOULD YOU RATHER DO THAT?
NO!
THEN TELL ME!
YOU'LL TELL ME, AND I WON'T HURT YOU.
YOU'LL TELL ME, WON'T YOU?
OH GOD, HE'S GOING TO GIVE HER UP. HE'S TOO WEAK.
DON'T!

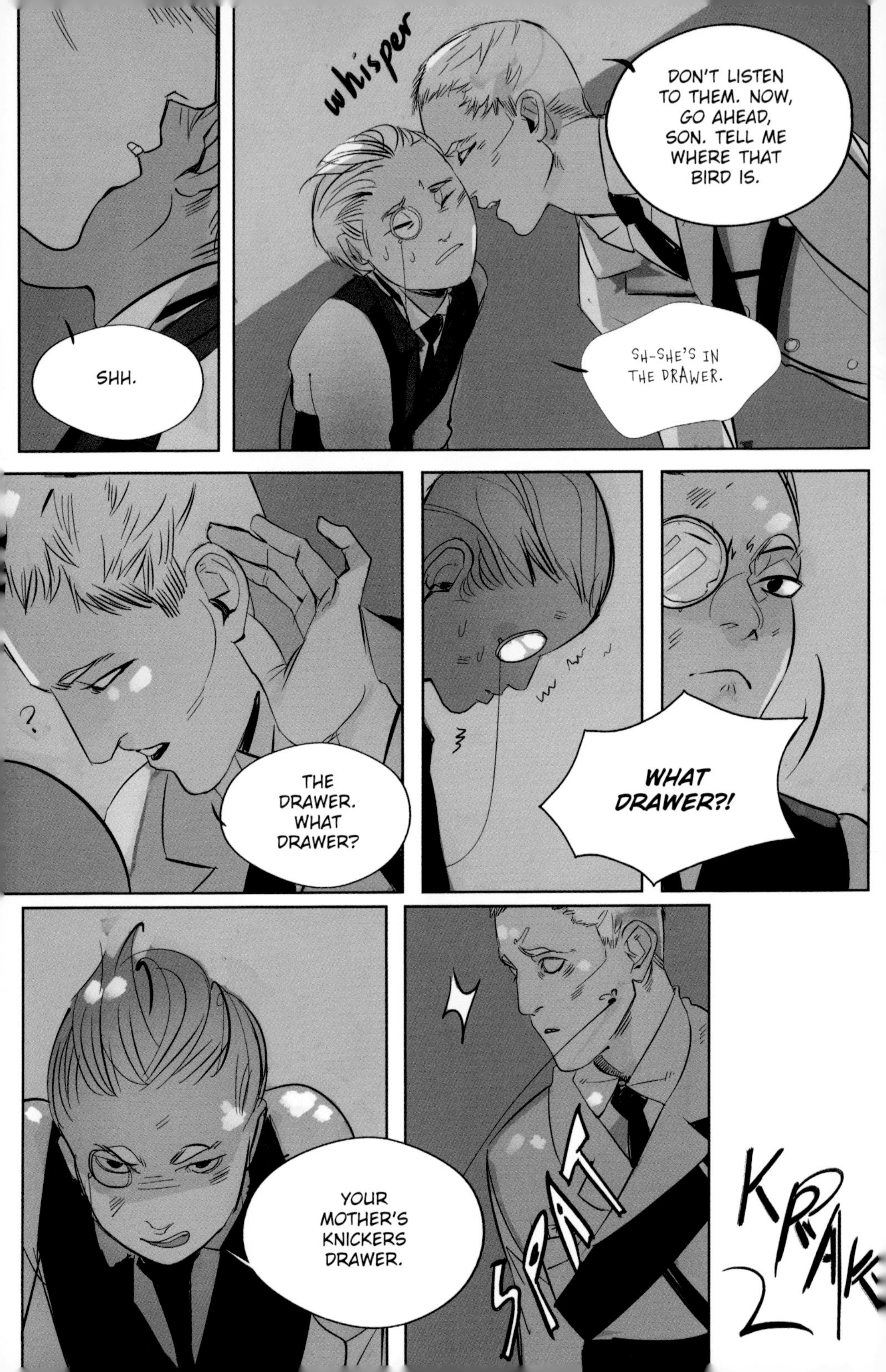
SHH.
whisper
DON'T LISTEN TO THEM. NOW, GO AHEAD, SON. TELL ME WHERE THAT BIRD IS.
SH-SHE'S IN THE DRAWER.
THE DRAWER. WHAT DRAWER?
WHAT DRAWER?!
YOUR MOTHER'S KNICKERS DRAWER.
SPAT
KRAKE

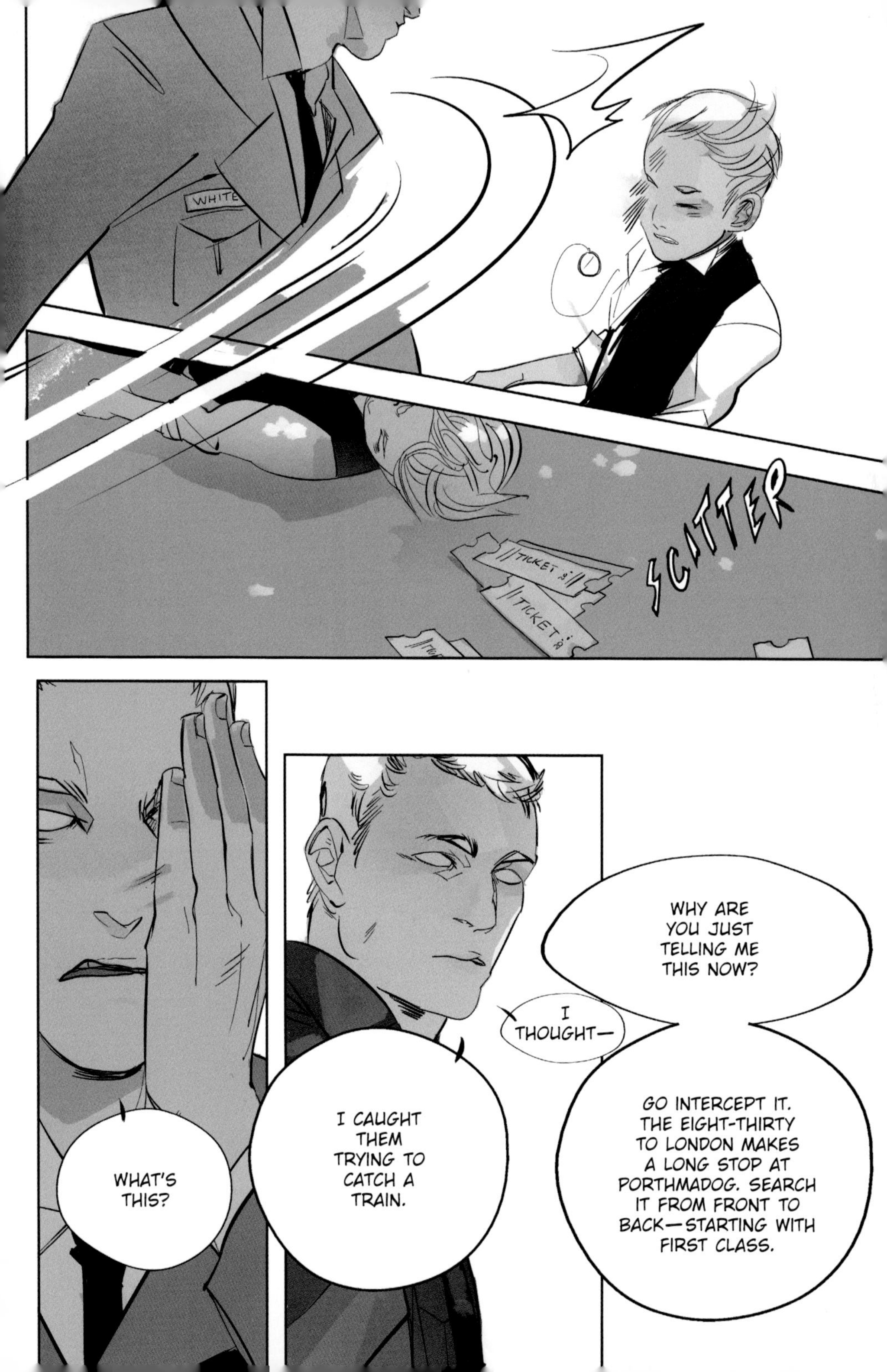
WHITE
TICKET
TICKET
SCATTER
WHAT'S THIS?
I CAUGHT THEM TRYING TO CATCH A TRAIN.
WHY ARE YOU JUST TELLING ME THIS NOW?
I THOUGHT—
GO INTERCEPT IT. THE EIGHT-THIRTY TO LONDON MAKES A LONG STOP AT PORTHMADOG. SEARCH IT FROM FRONT TO BACK—STARTING WITH FIRST CLASS.

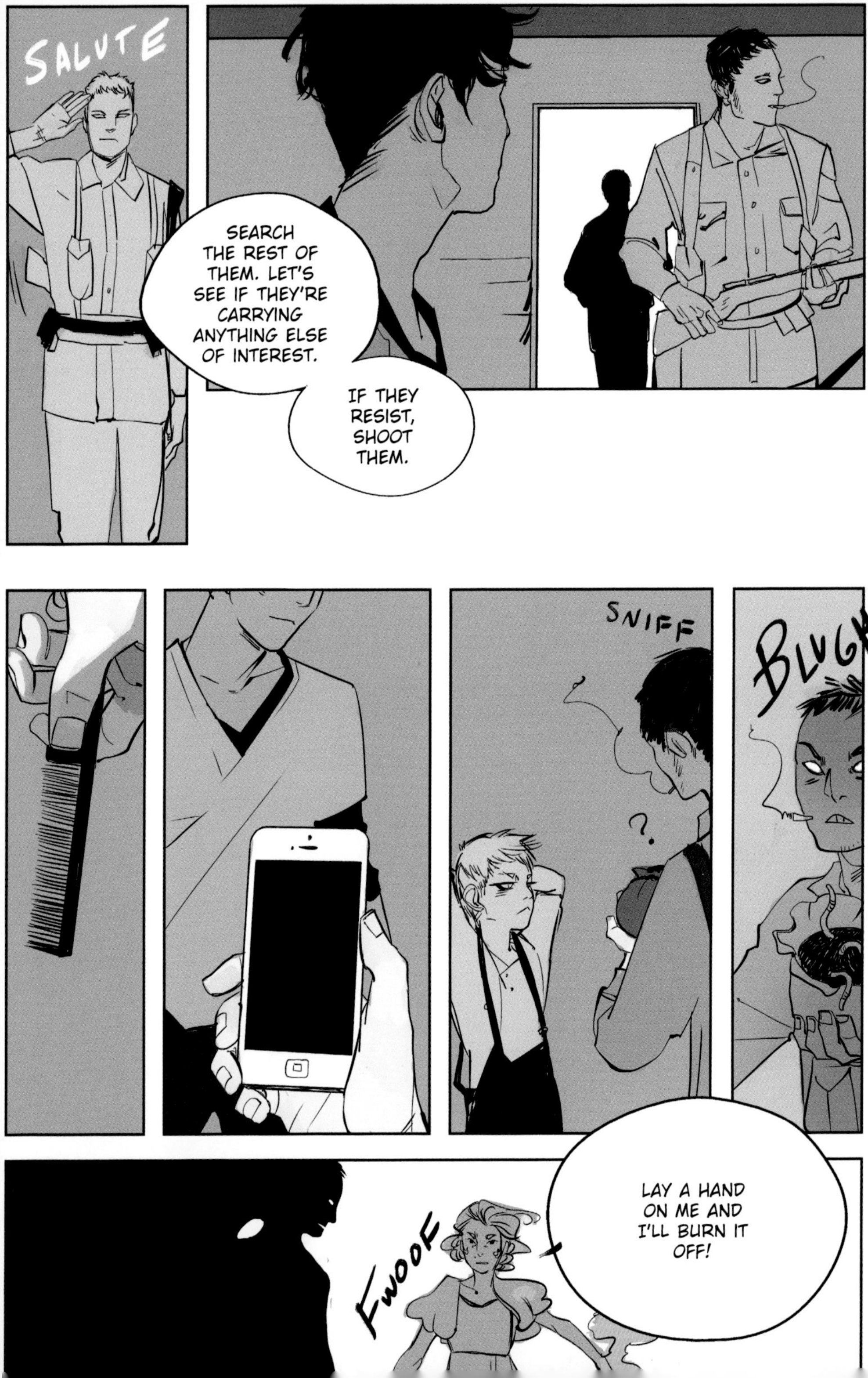
SALUTE
SEARCH THE REST OF THEM. LET'S SEE IF THEY'RE CARRYING ANYTHING ELSE OF INTEREST.
IF THEY RESIST, SHOOT THEM.
SNIFF
?
BLUGH
FWOOF
LAY A HAND ON ME AND I'LL BURN IT OFF!

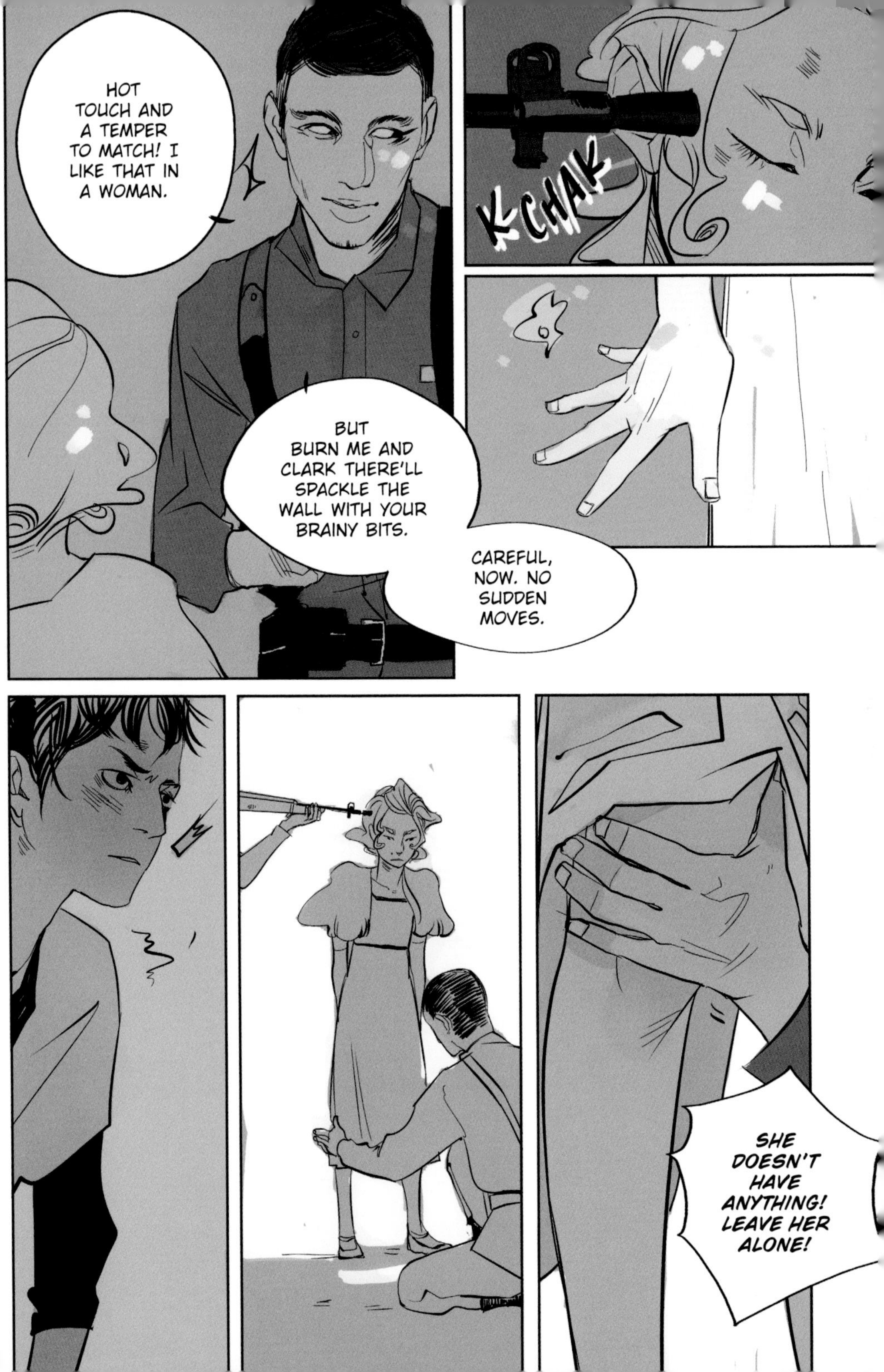
HOT TOUCH AND A TEMPER TO MATCH! I LIKE THAT IN A WOMAN.
K-CHAK
BUT BURN ME AND CLARK THERE'LL SPACKLE THE WALL WITH YOUR BRAINY BITS.
CAREFUL, NOW. NO SUDDEN MOVES.
SHE DOESN'T HAVE ANYTHING! LEAVE HER ALONE!

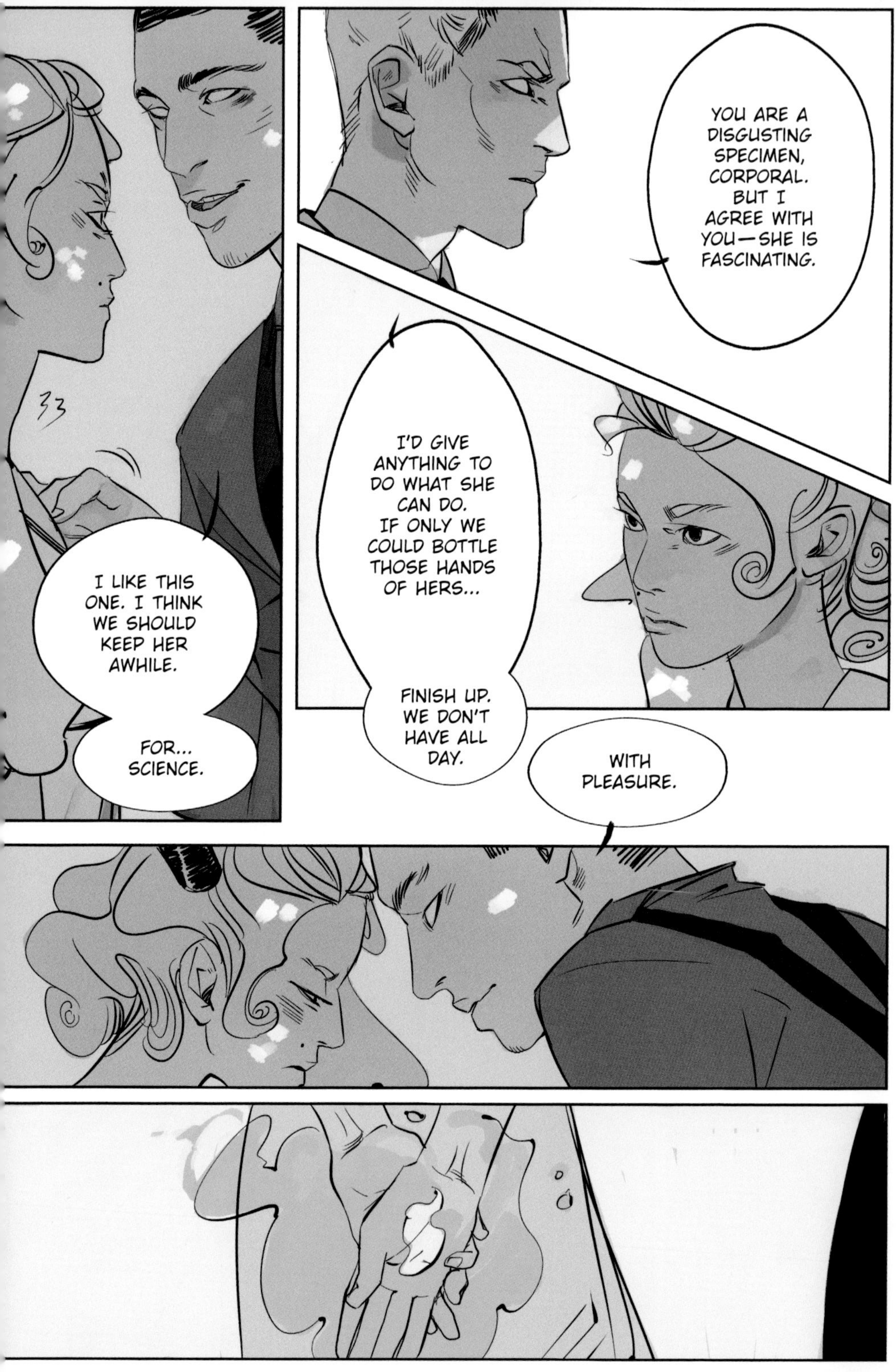
I LIKE THIS ONE. I THINK WE SHOULD KEEP HER AWHILE.
FOR... SCIENCE.
YOU ARE A DISGUSTING SPECIMEN, CORPORAL. BUT I AGREE WITH YOU—SHE IS FASCINATING.
I'D GIVE ANYTHING TO DO WHAT SHE CAN DO. IF ONLY WE COULD BOTTLE THOSE HANDS OF HERS...
FINISH UP. WE DON'T HAVE ALL DAY.
WITH PLEASURE.

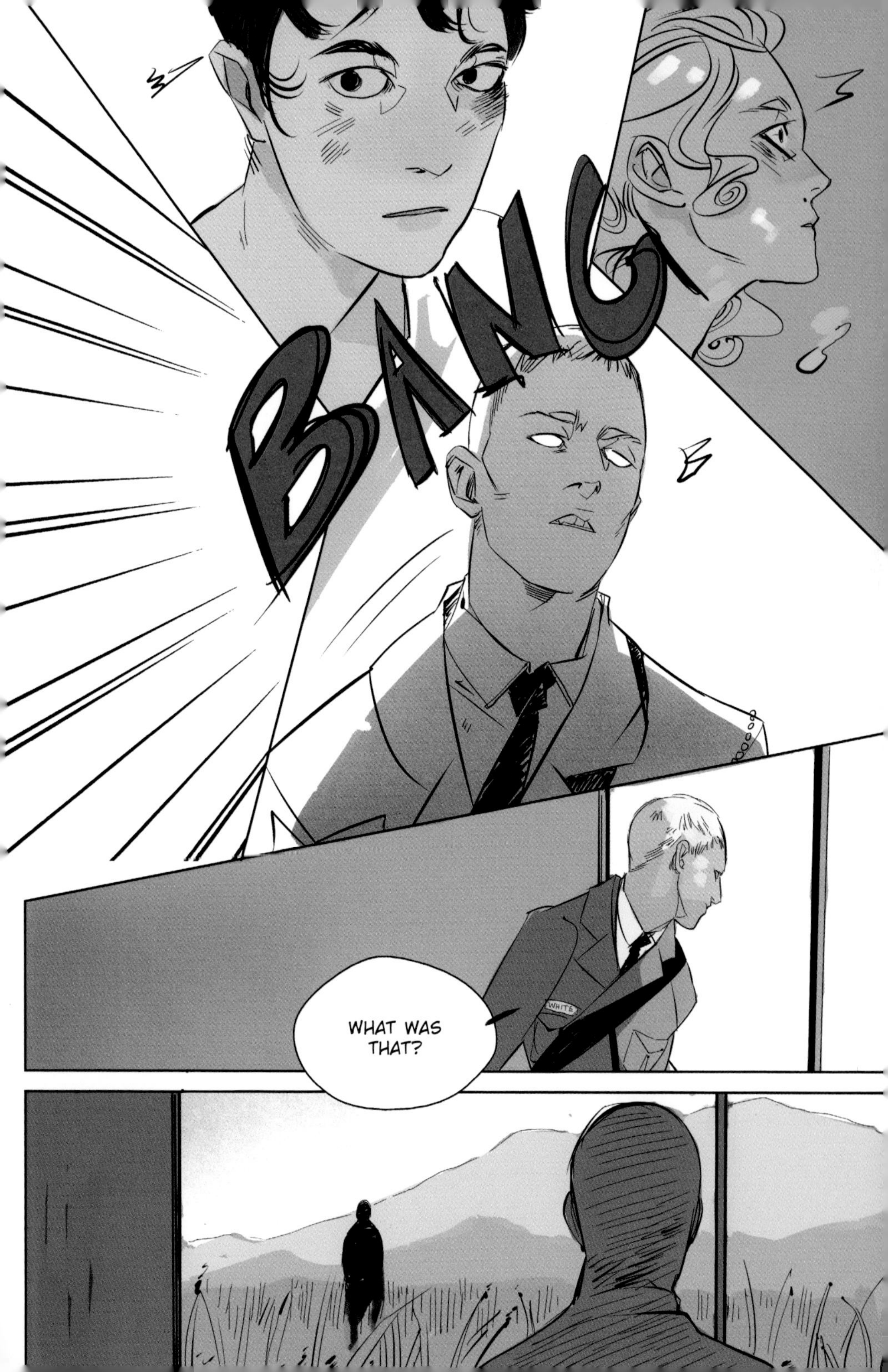
BANG
WHITE
WHAT WAS THAT?

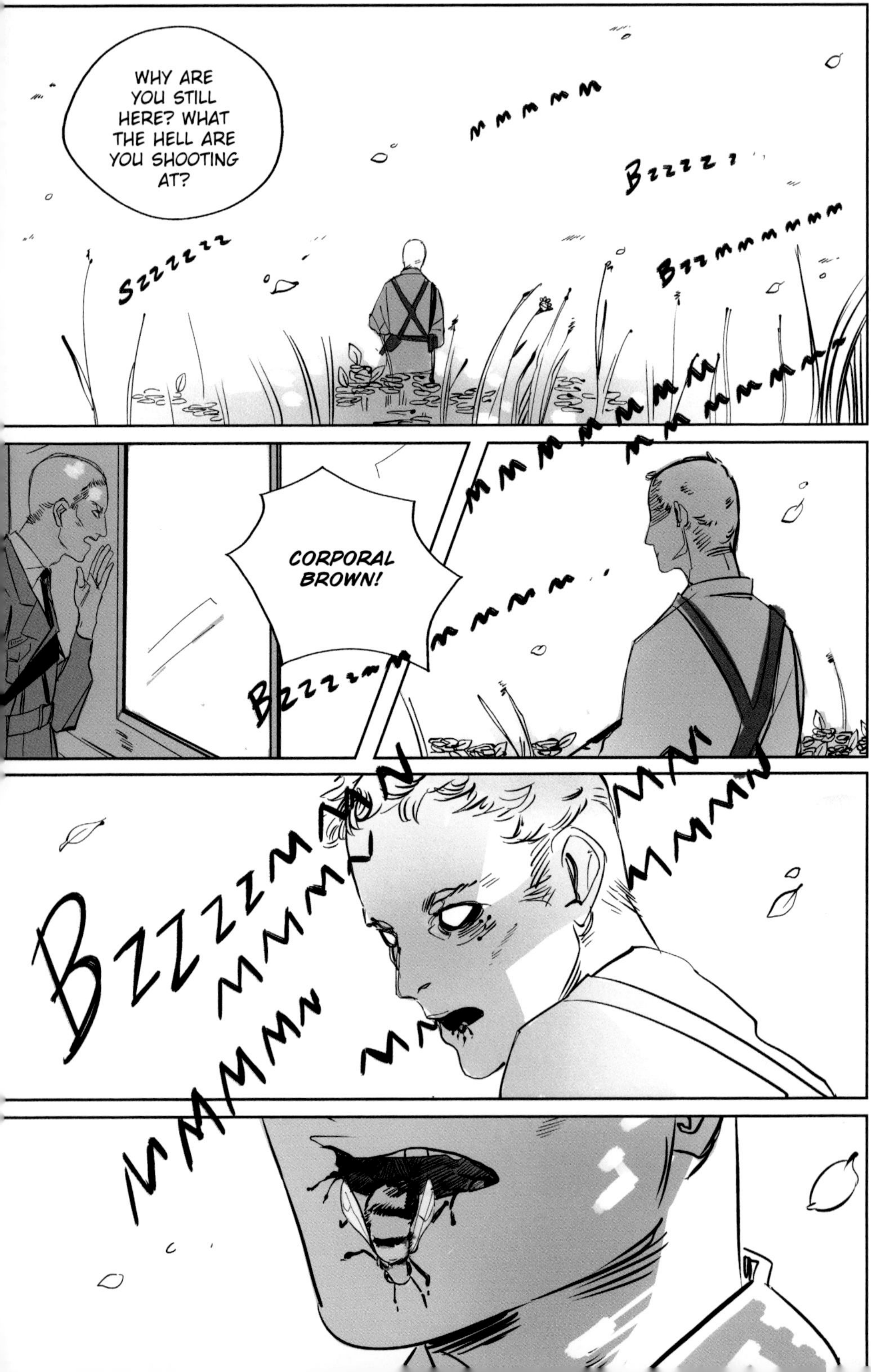
WHY ARE YOU STILL HERE? WHAT THE HELL ARE YOU SHOOTING AT?
mmmmm
Bzzzz
Szzzzzz
Bzzmmmmmm
CORPORAL BROWN!
Bzzzzmmmmmmmm
BZZZMMMMMMMN
MMMMMMMMM

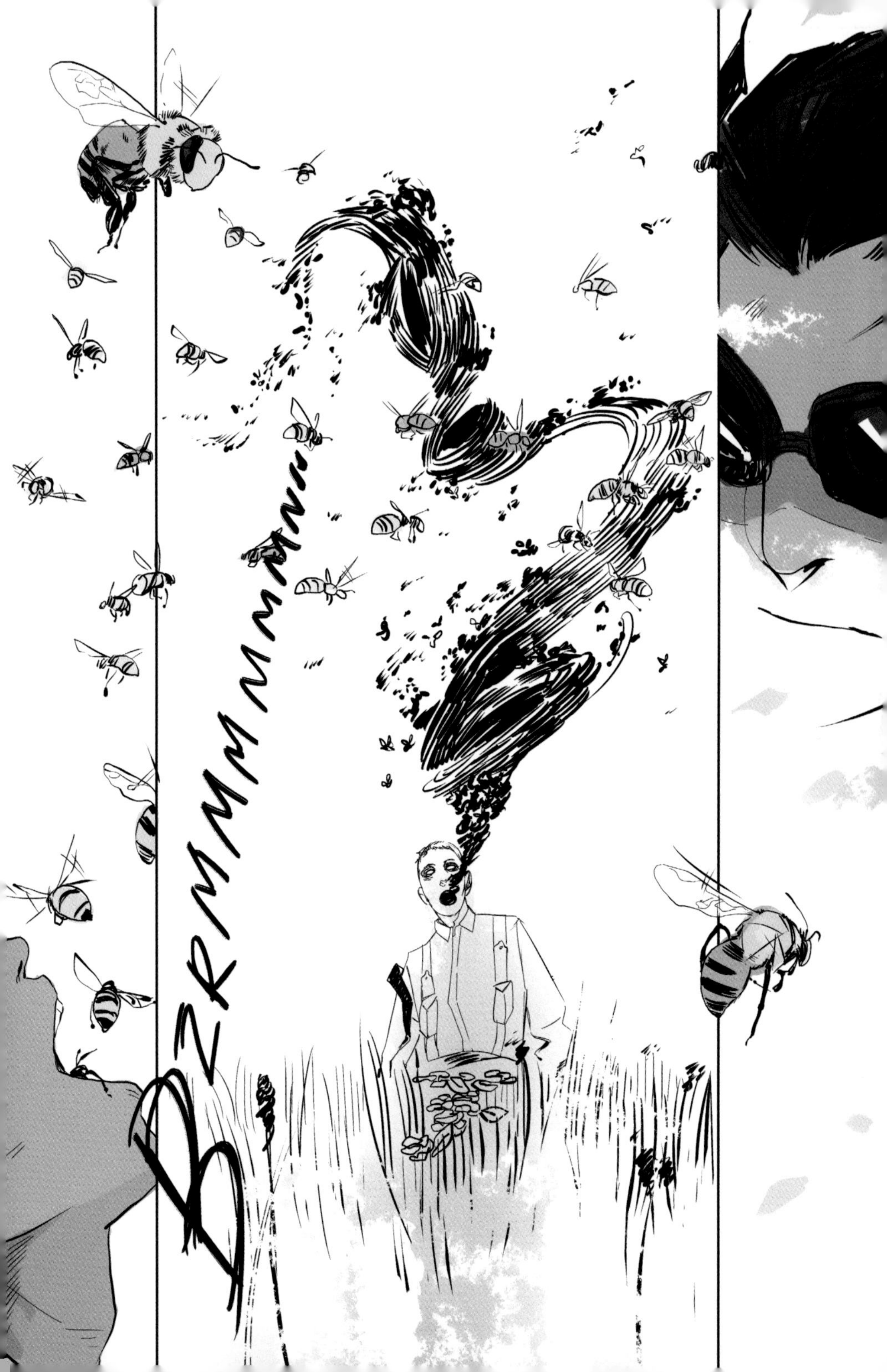
BZRMMMMMMNN

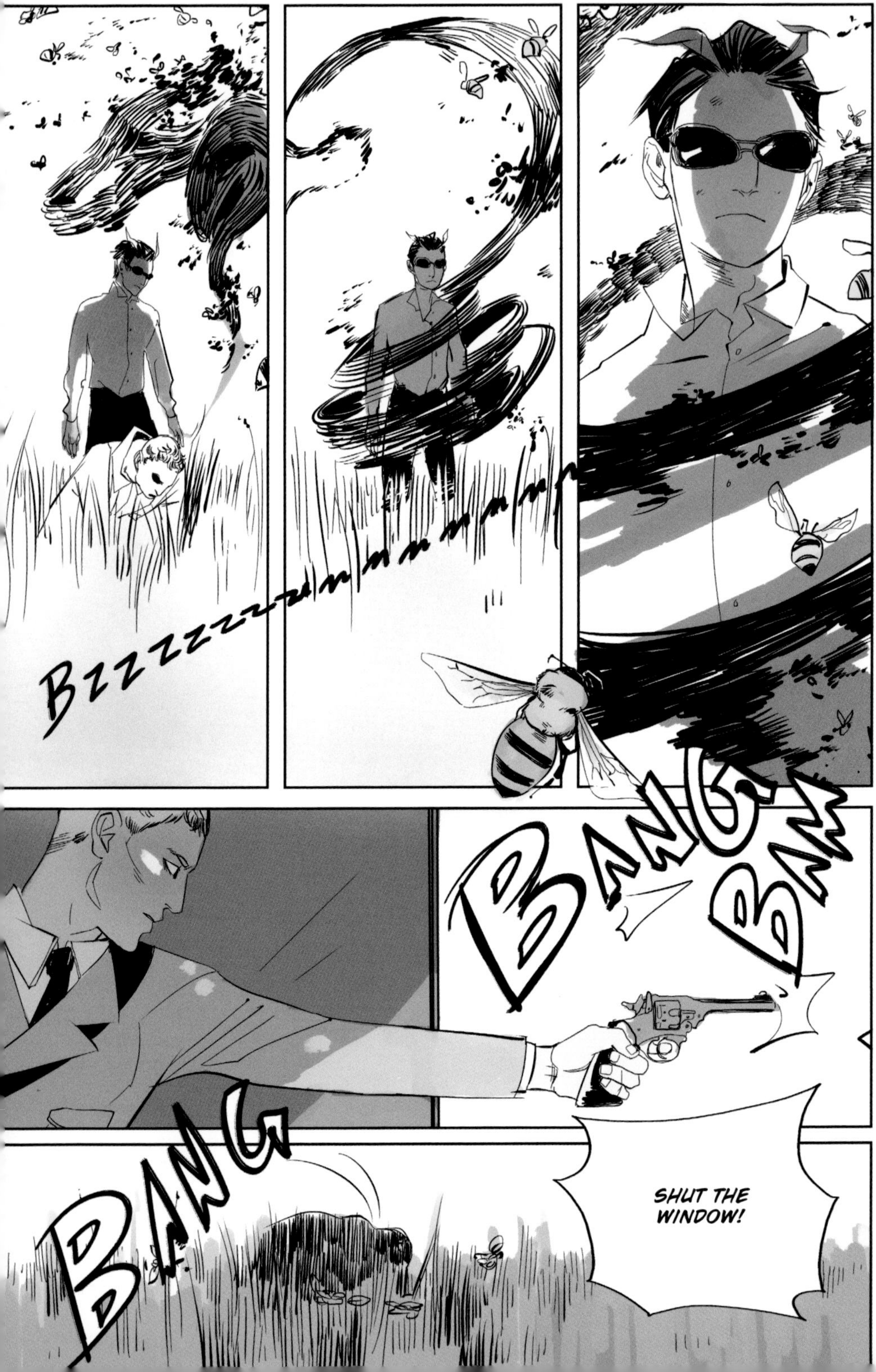
Bzzzzzzzzunnnnnnnnnp
BANG
BAM
BANG
SHUT THE WINDOW!

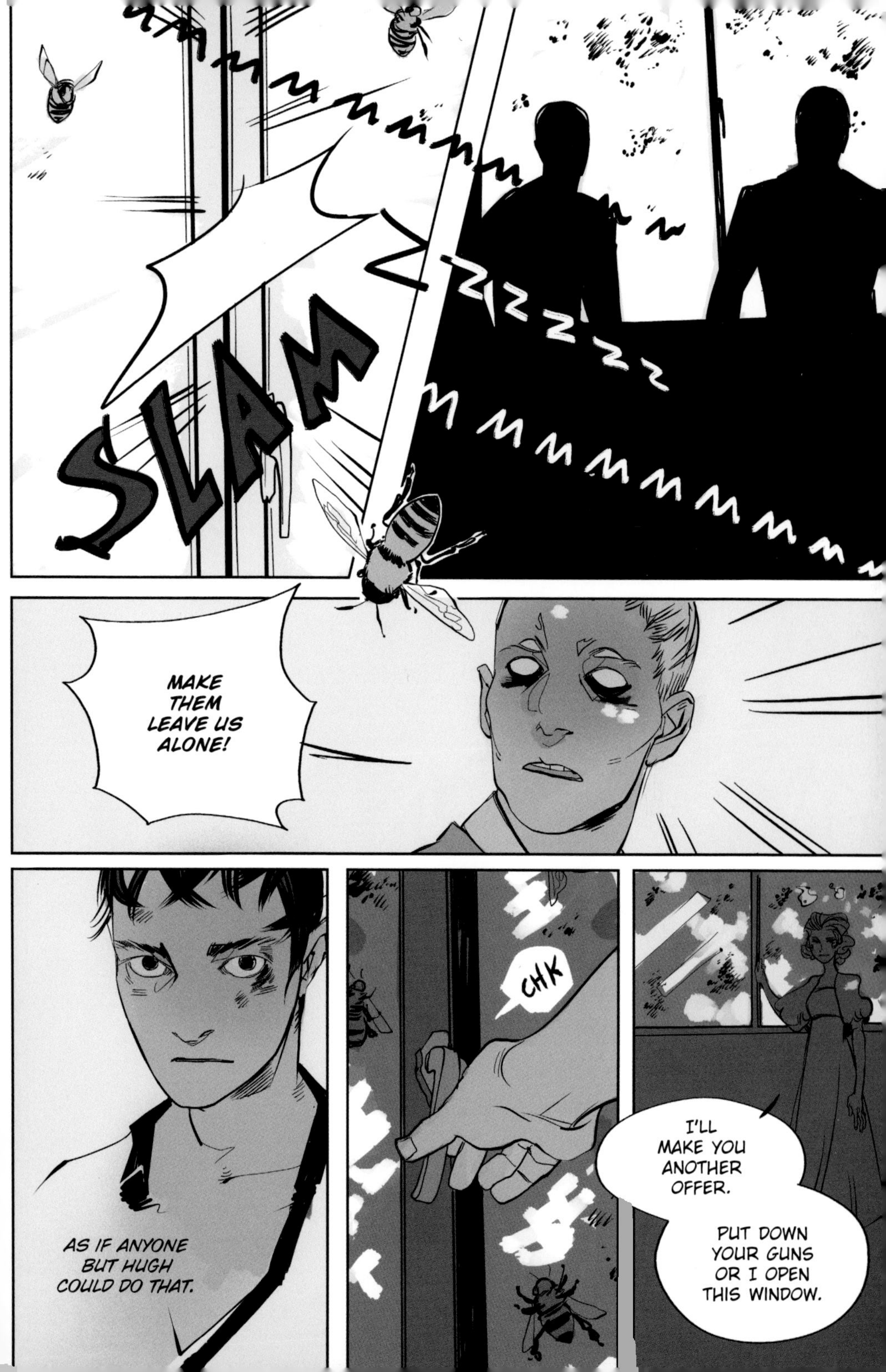
SLAM
ZZZZZZZ
MAKE THEM LEAVE US ALONE!
AS IF ANYONE BUT HUGH COULD DO THAT.
CHK
I'LL MAKE YOU ANOTHER OFFER.
PUT DOWN YOUR GUNS OR I OPEN THIS WINDOW.

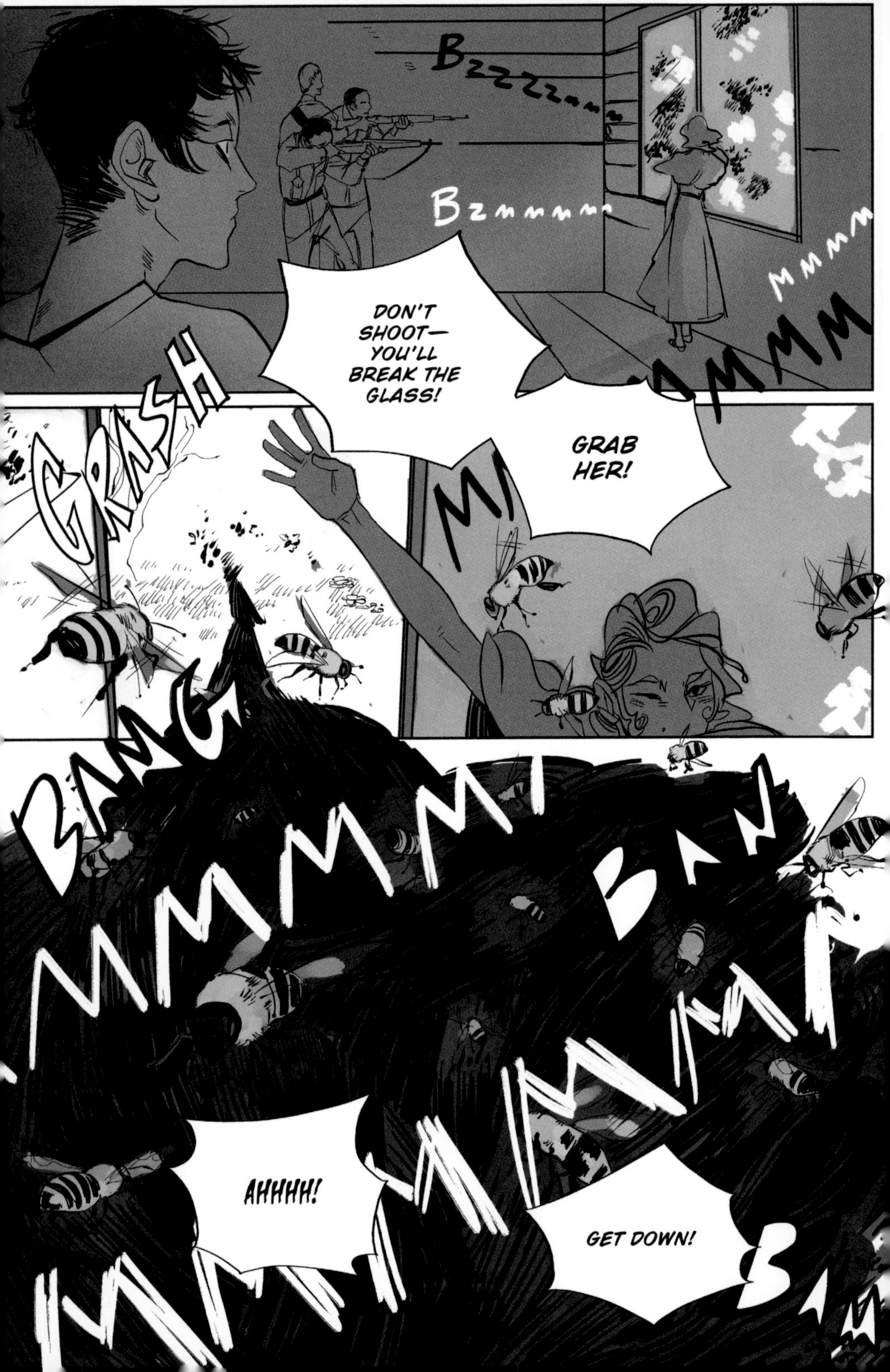
Bzzzzz
Bzmmmm
MMMM
MMMM
DON'T SHOOT—YOU'LL BREAK THE GLASS!
CRASH
GRAB HER!
BANG
MMMMM
BAM
AHHHH!
GET DOWN!

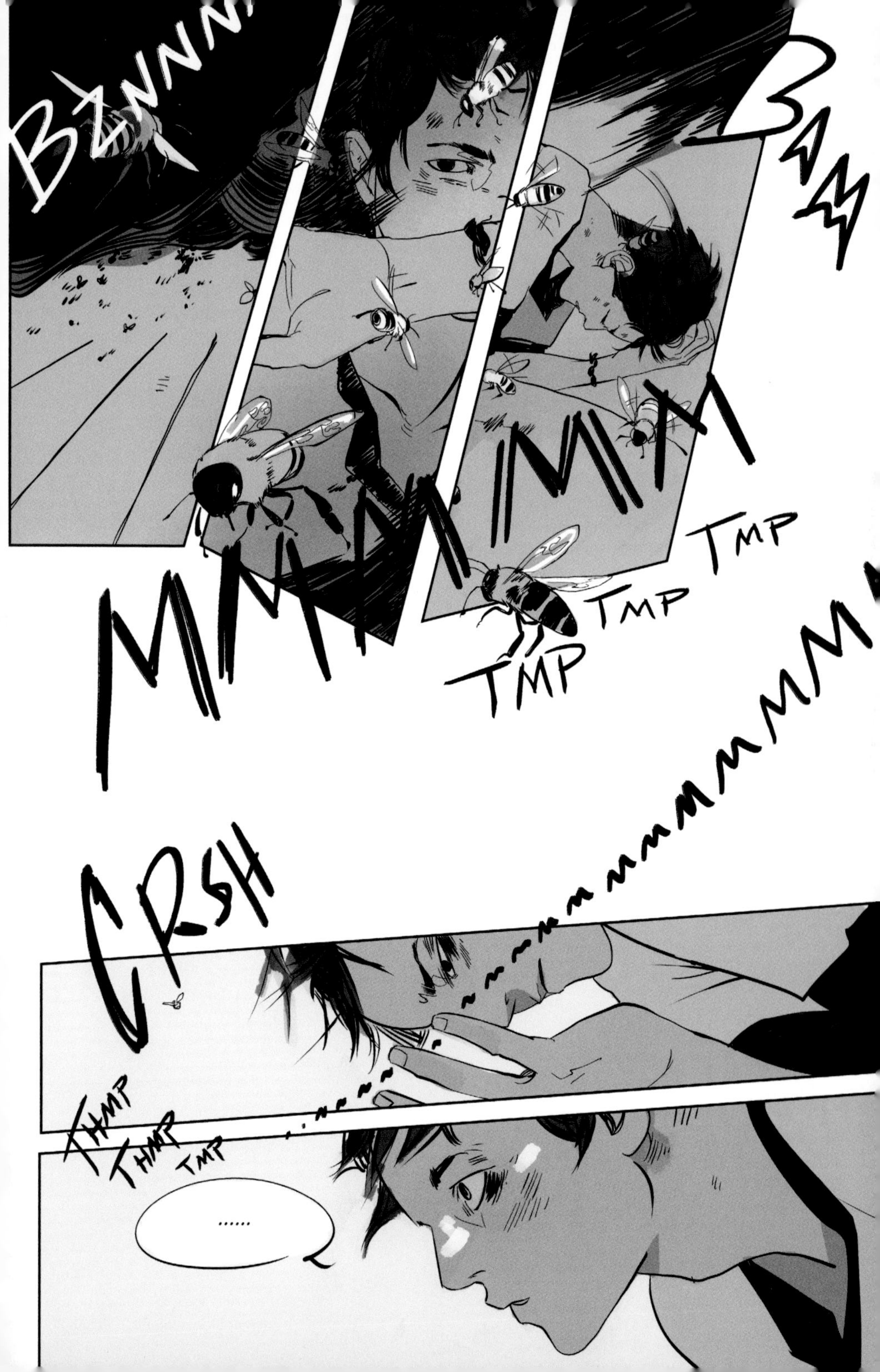
BZNNN
BAM
MMMM
TMP TMP TMP TMP
MMMMMMMMMMmmmmmm
CRSH
THMP THMP TMP
......

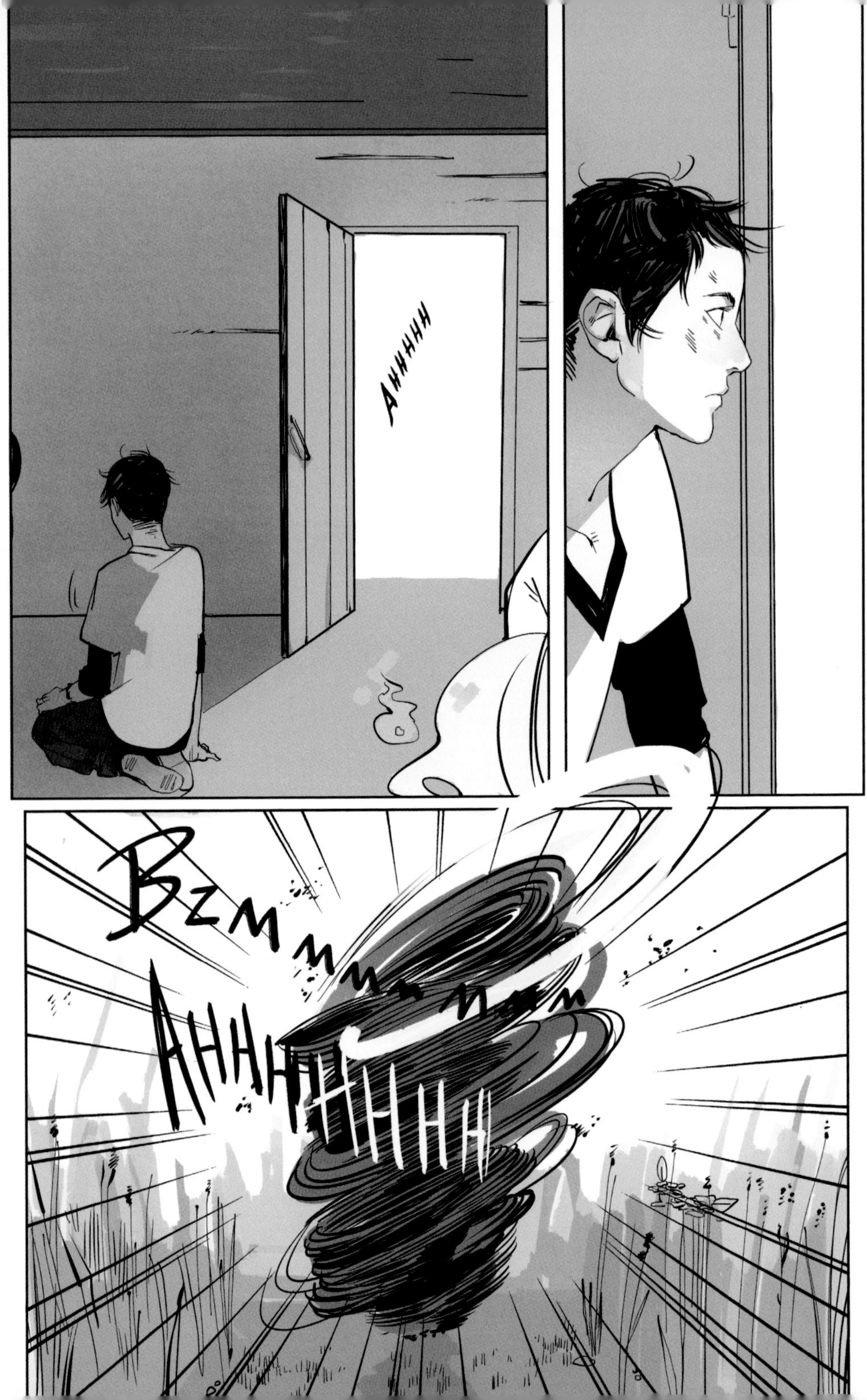
AHHHHH
BZMMMMMMM
AHHHHHHHHHH

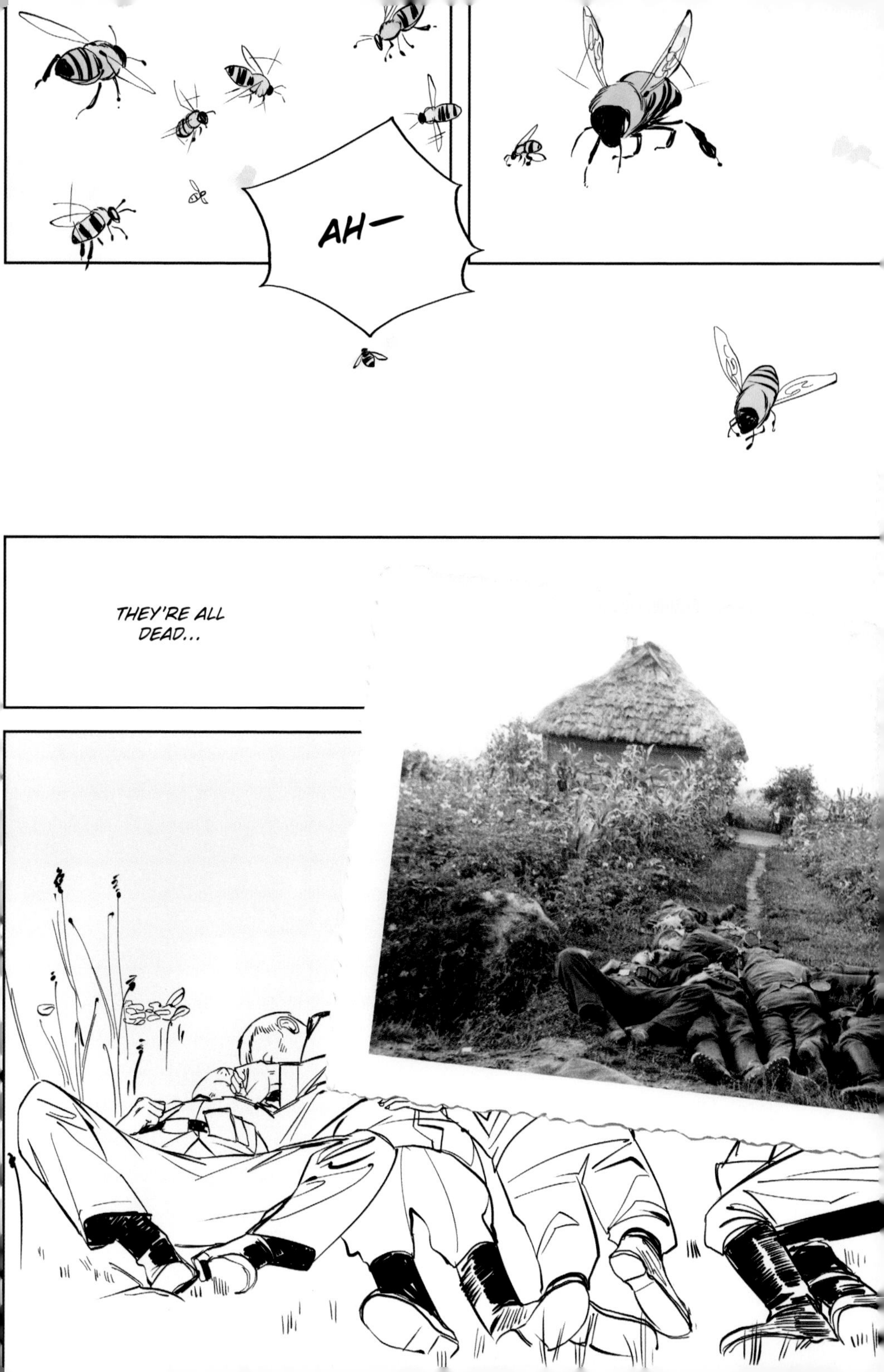
AH—
THEY'RE ALL DEAD...

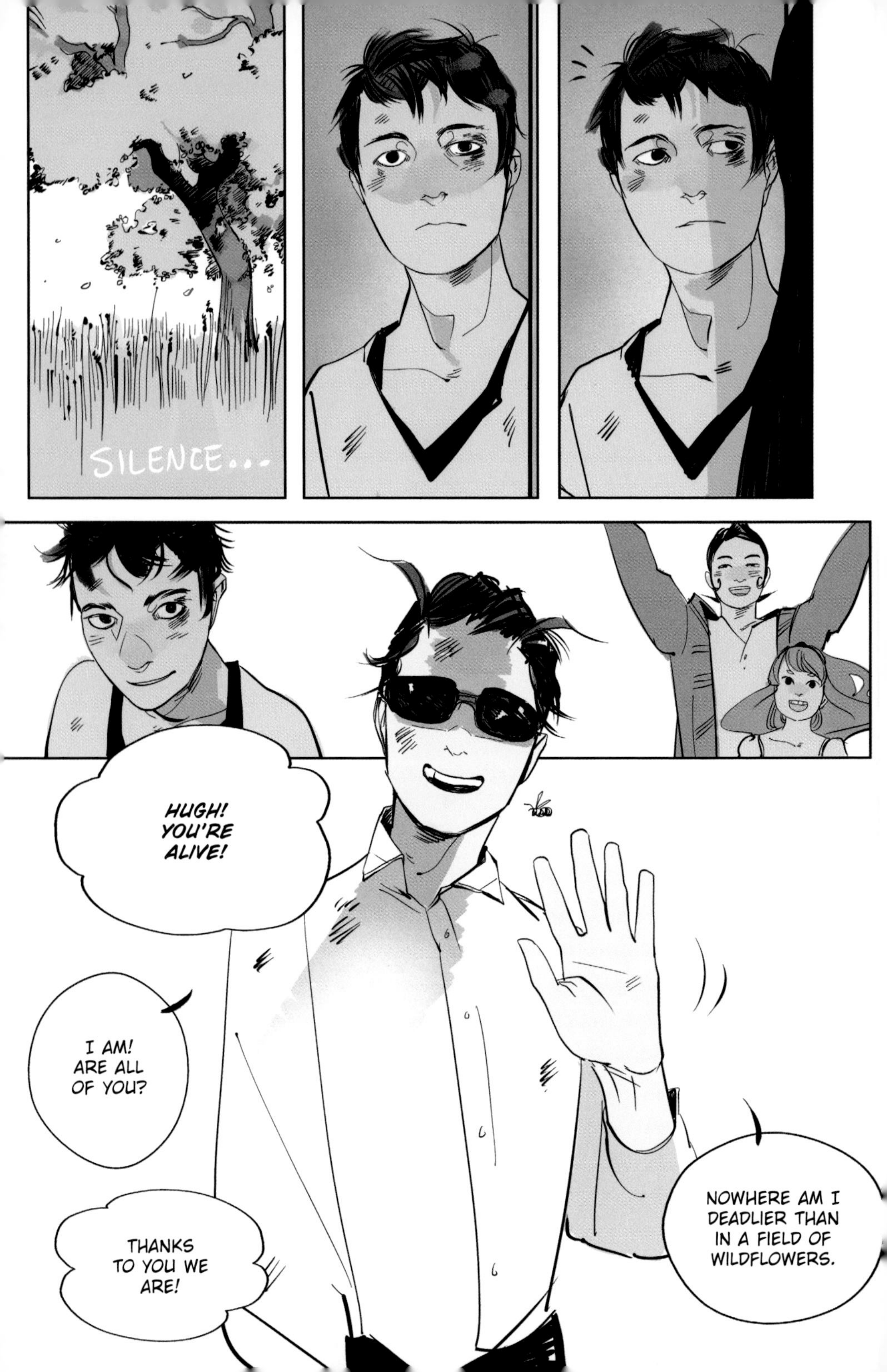
SILENCE...
HUGH! YOU'RE ALIVE!
I AM! ARE ALL OF YOU?
THANKS TO YOU WE ARE!
NOWHERE AM I DEADLIER THAN IN A FIELD OF WILDFLOWERS.

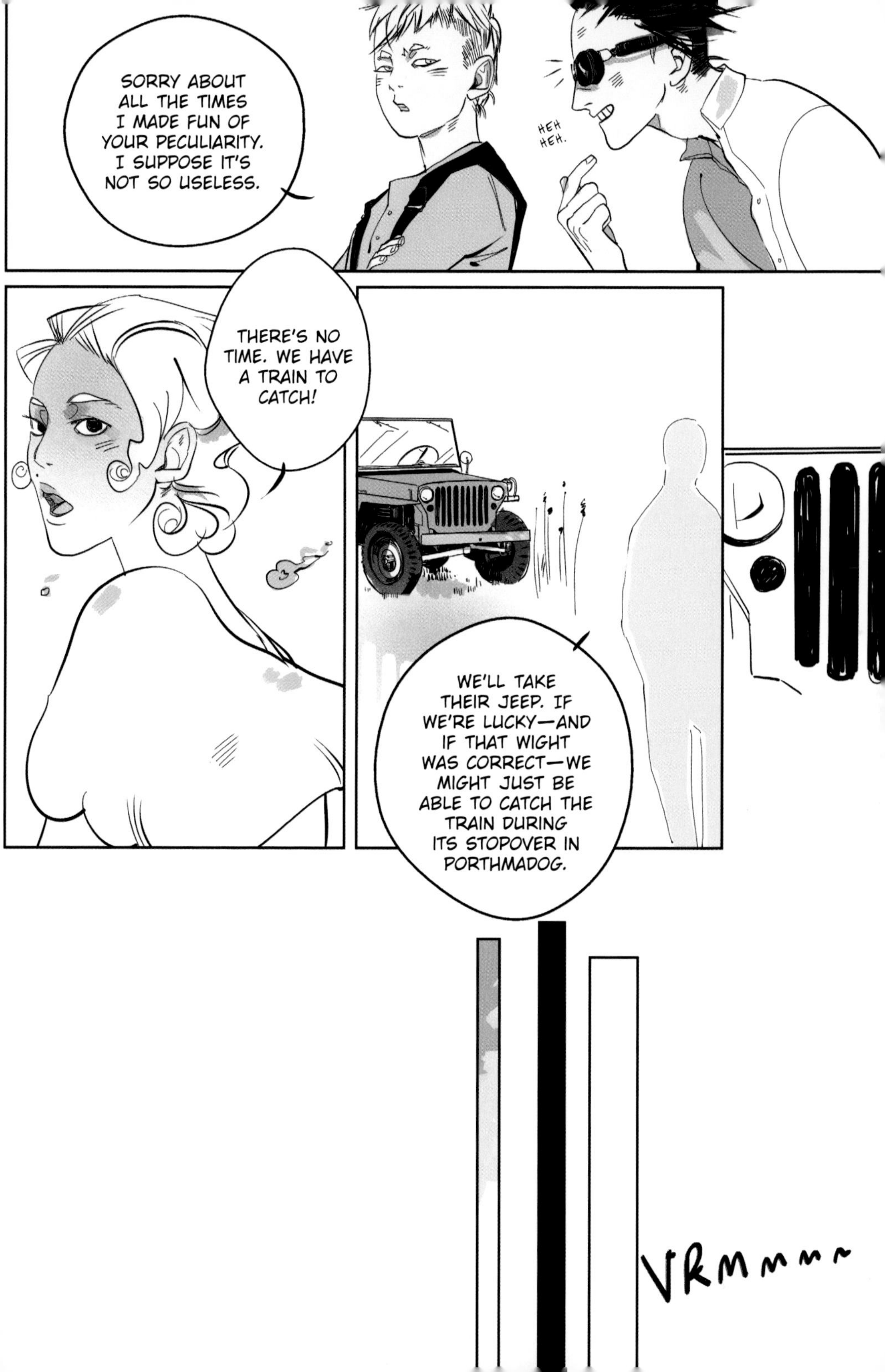
SORRY ABOUT ALL THE TIMES I MADE FUN OF YOUR PECULIARITY. I SUPPOSE IT'S NOT SO USELESS.
HEH HEH.
THERE'S NO TIME. WE HAVE A TRAIN TO CATCH!
WE'LL TAKE THEIR JEEP. IF WE'RE LUCKY—AND IF THAT WIGHT WAS CORRECT—WE MIGHT JUST BE ABLE TO CATCH THE TRAIN DURING ITS STOPOVER IN PORTHMADOG.
VRMMMM

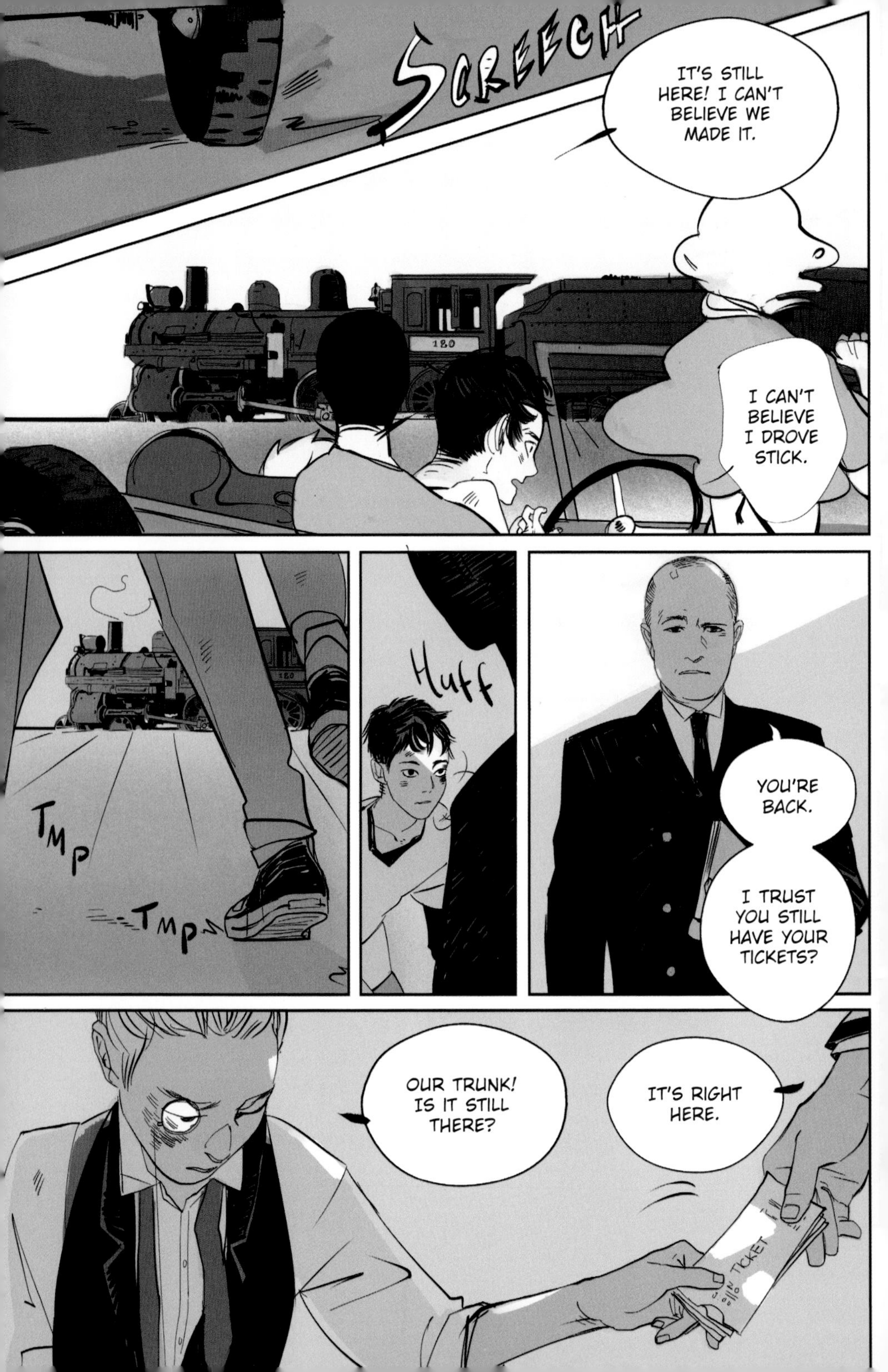
SCREECH
IT'S STILL HERE! I CAN'T BELIEVE WE MADE IT.
120
I CAN'T BELIEVE I DROVE STICK.
120
TMP
TMP
HUFF
YOU'RE BACK.
I TRUST YOU STILL HAVE YOUR TICKETS?
OUR TRUNK! IS IT STILL THERE?
IT'S RIGHT HERE.
TICKET

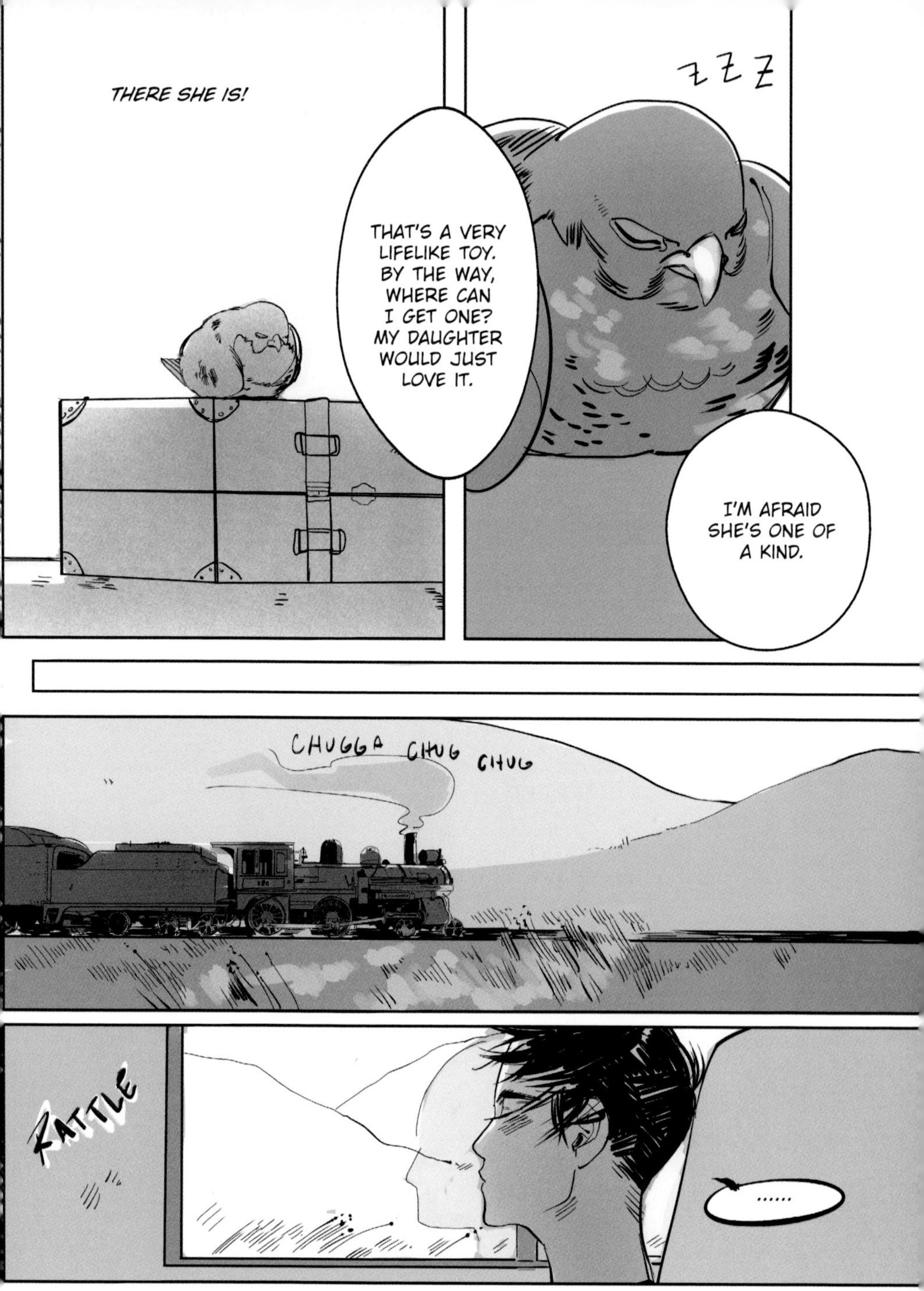
THERE SHE IS!
ZZZ
THAT'S A VERY LIFELIKE TOY. BY THE WAY, WHERE CAN I GET ONE? MY DAUGHTER WOULD JUST LOVE IT.
I'M AFRAID SHE'S ONE OF A KIND.
CHUGGA CHUG CHUG
RATTLE
......

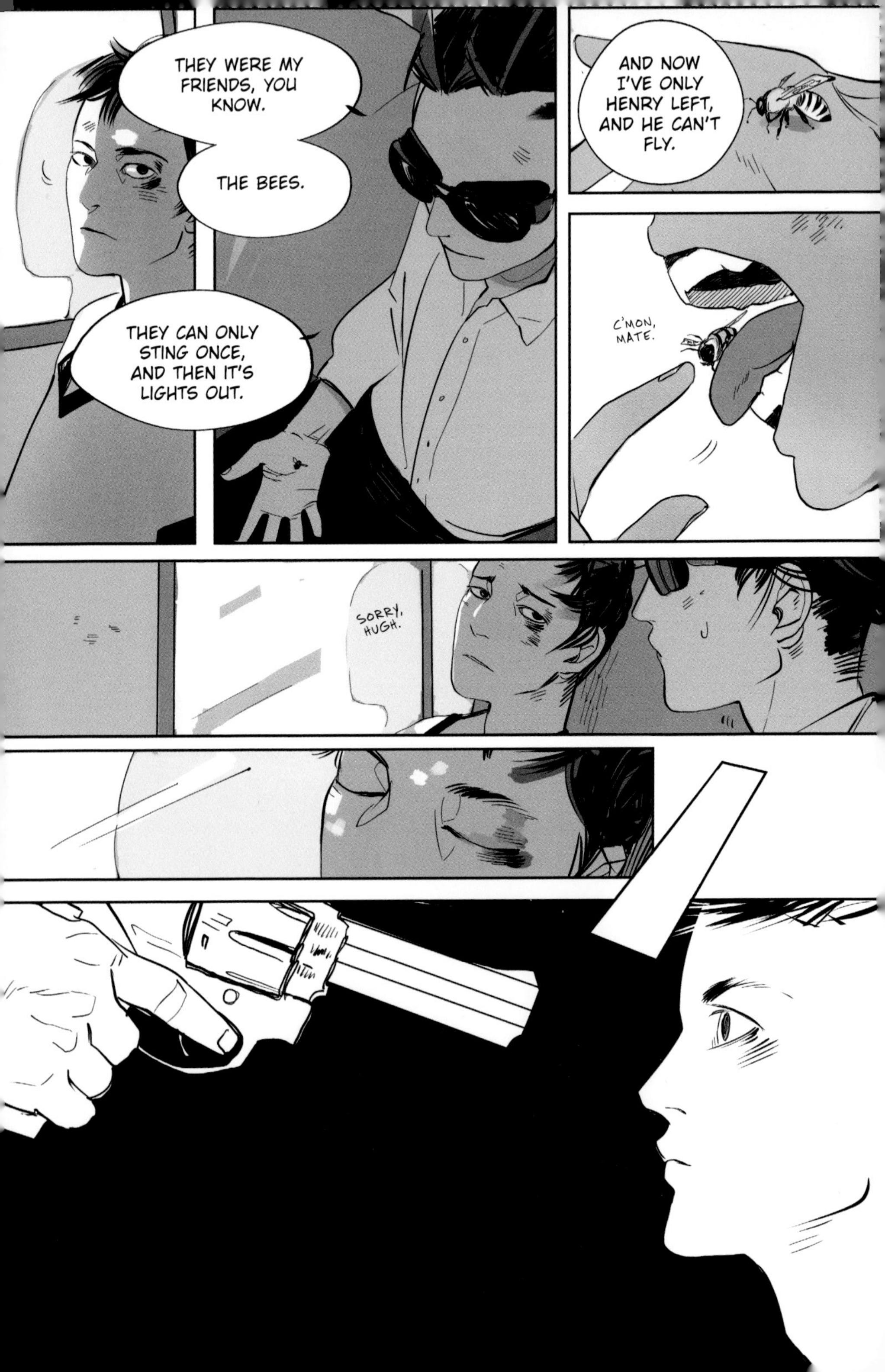
THEY WERE MY FRIENDS, YOU KNOW.
THE BEES.
THEY CAN ONLY STING ONCE, AND THEN IT'S LIGHTS OUT.
AND NOW I'VE ONLY HENRY LEFT, AND HE CAN'T FLY.
C'MON, MATE.
SORRY, HUGH.

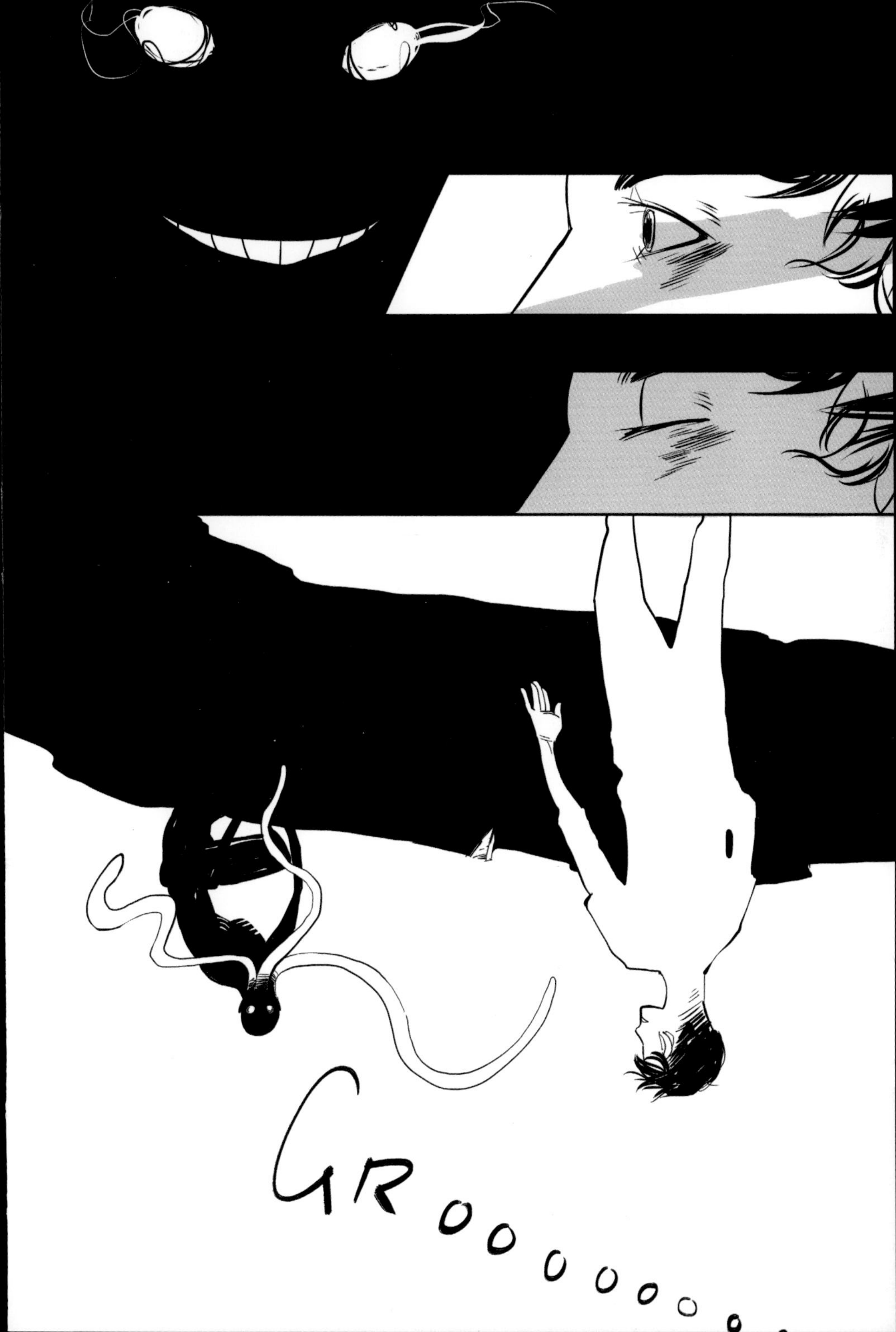
GROOOOOOO

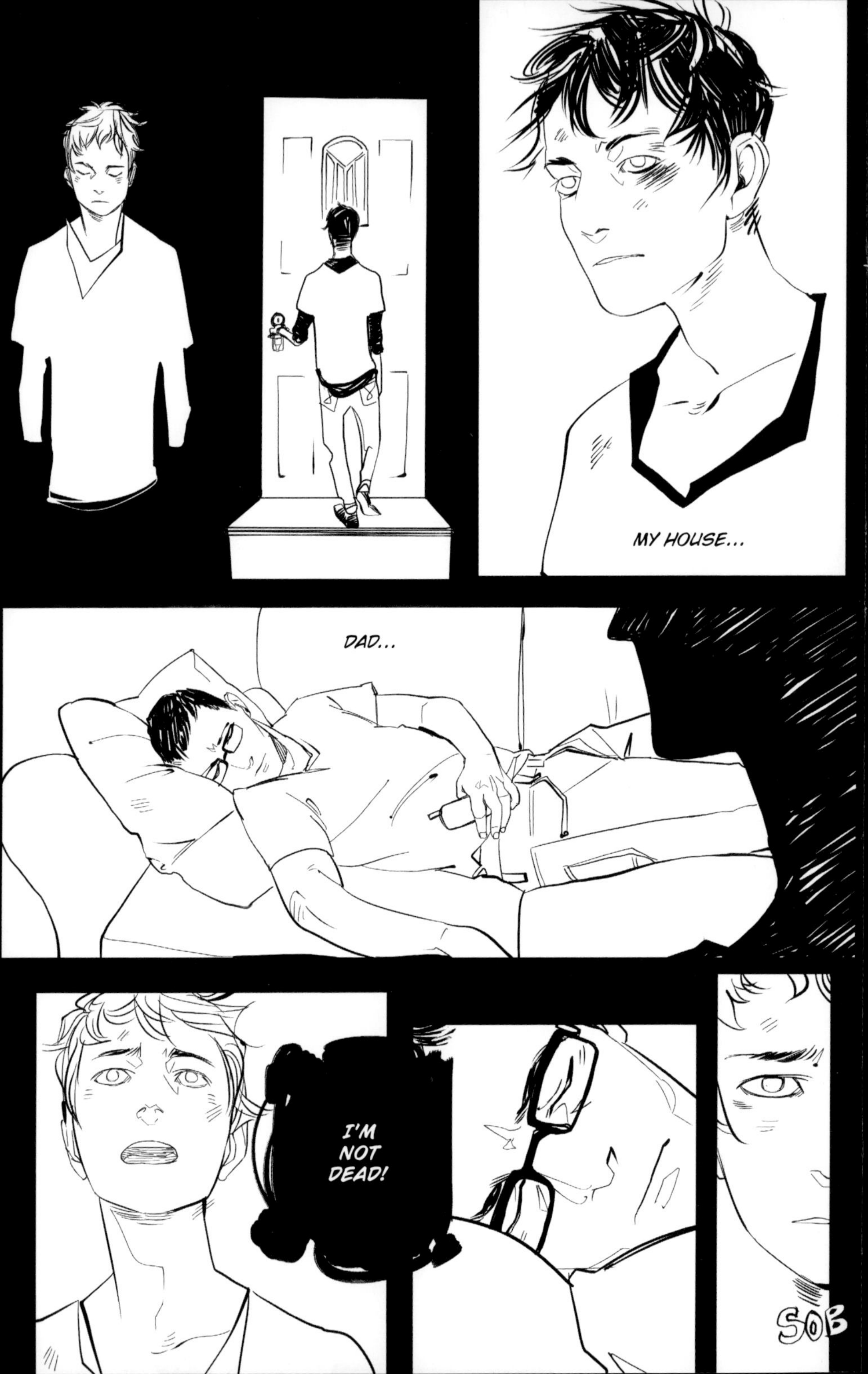
MY HOUSE...
DAD...
I'M NOT DEAD!
SOB

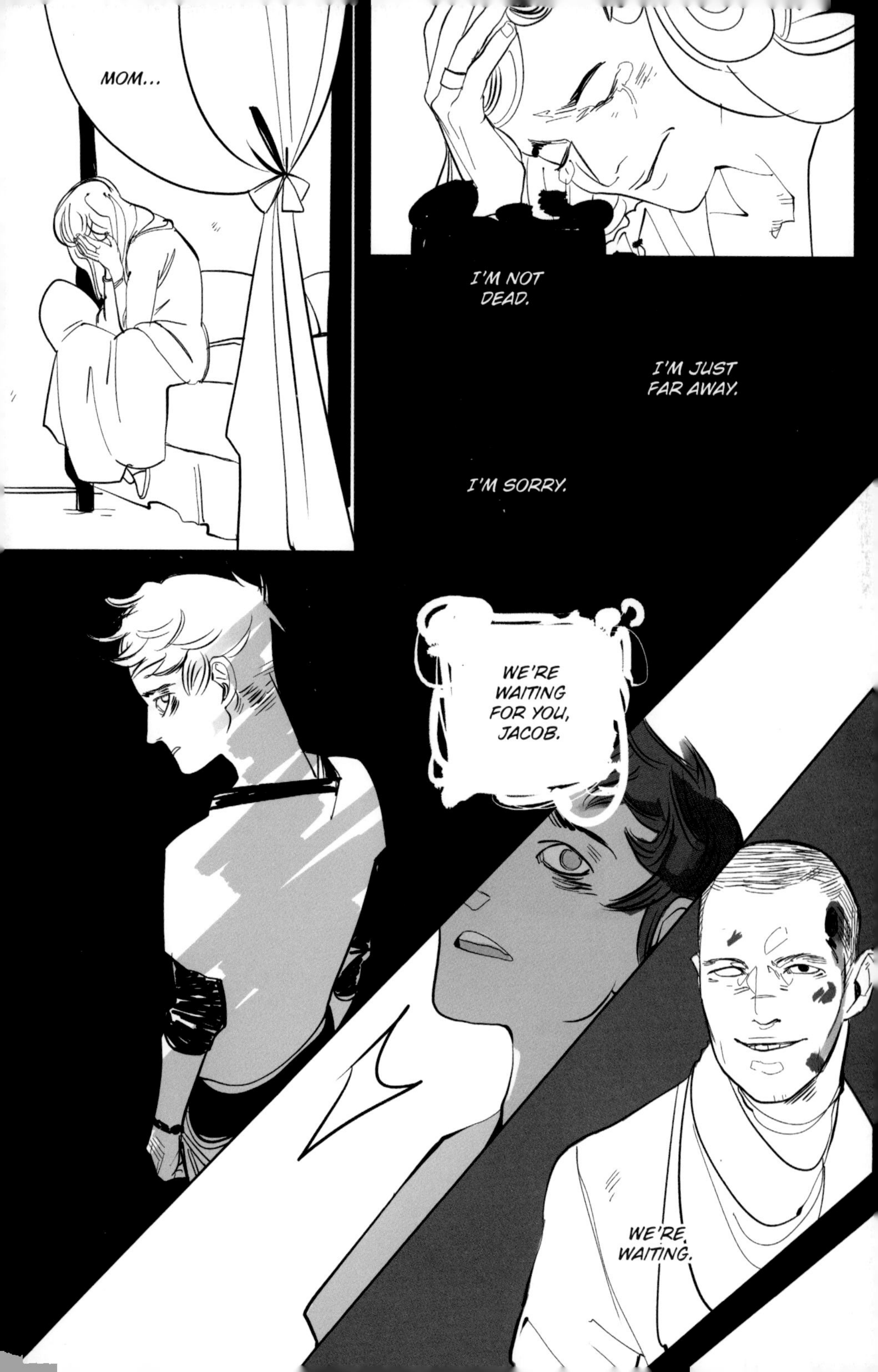
MOM...
I'M NOT DEAD.
I'M JUST FAR AWAY.
I'M SORRY.
WE'RE WAITING FOR YOU, JACOB.
WE'RE WAITING.

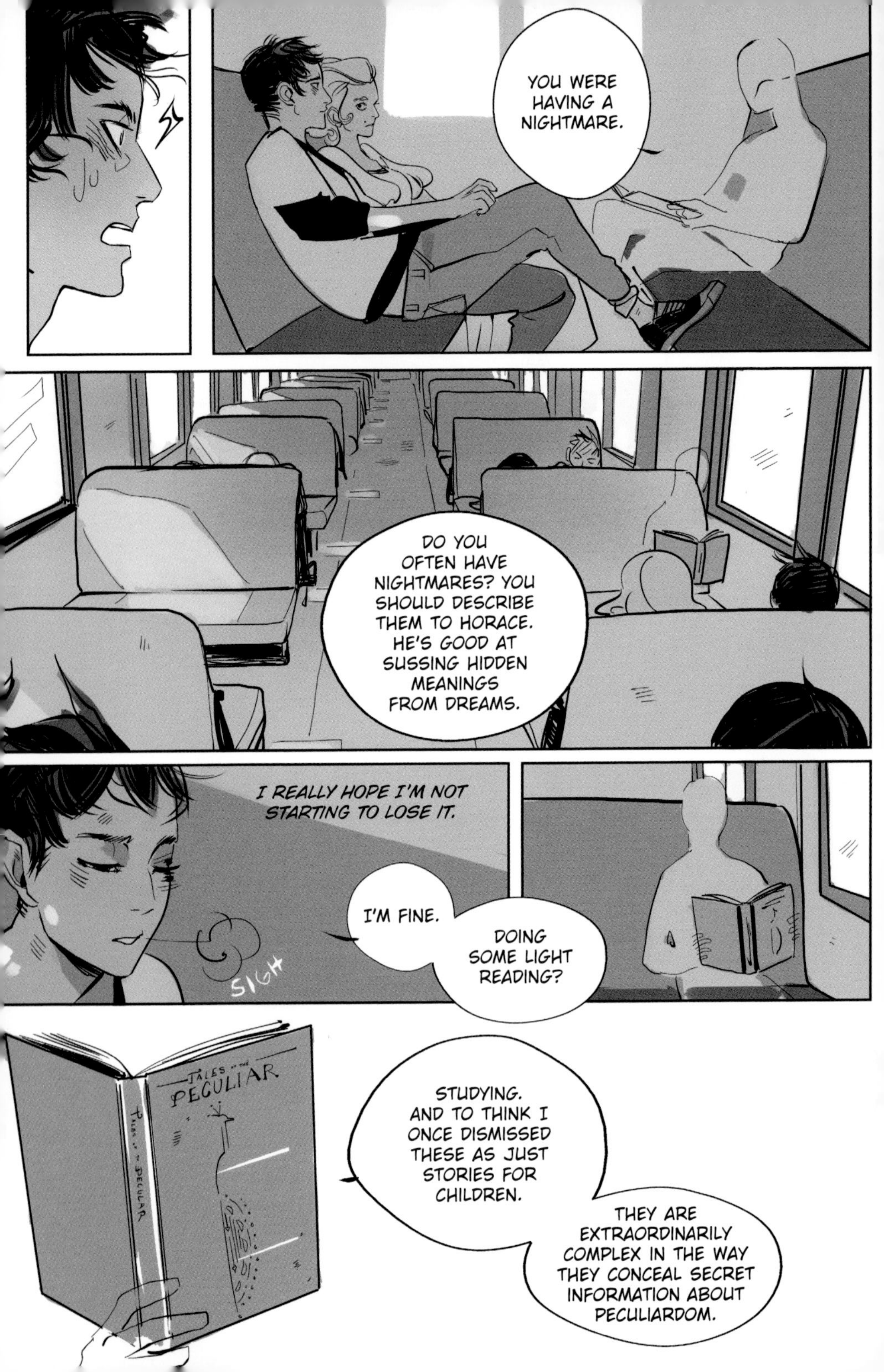

YOU WERE HAVING A NIGHTMARE.
DO YOU OFTEN HAVE NIGHTMARES? YOU SHOULD DESCRIBE THEM TO HORACE. HE'S GOOD AT SUSSING HIDDEN MEANINGS FROM DREAMS.
I REALLY HOPE I'M NOT STARTING TO LOSE IT.
SIGH
I'M FINE.
DOING SOME LIGHT READING?
TALES OF THE PECULIAR
STUDYING. AND TO THINK I ONCE DISMISSED THESE AS JUST STORIES FOR CHILDREN.
THEY ARE EXTRAORDINARILY COMPLEX IN THE WAY THEY CONCEAL SECRET INFORMATION ABOUT PECULIARDOM.

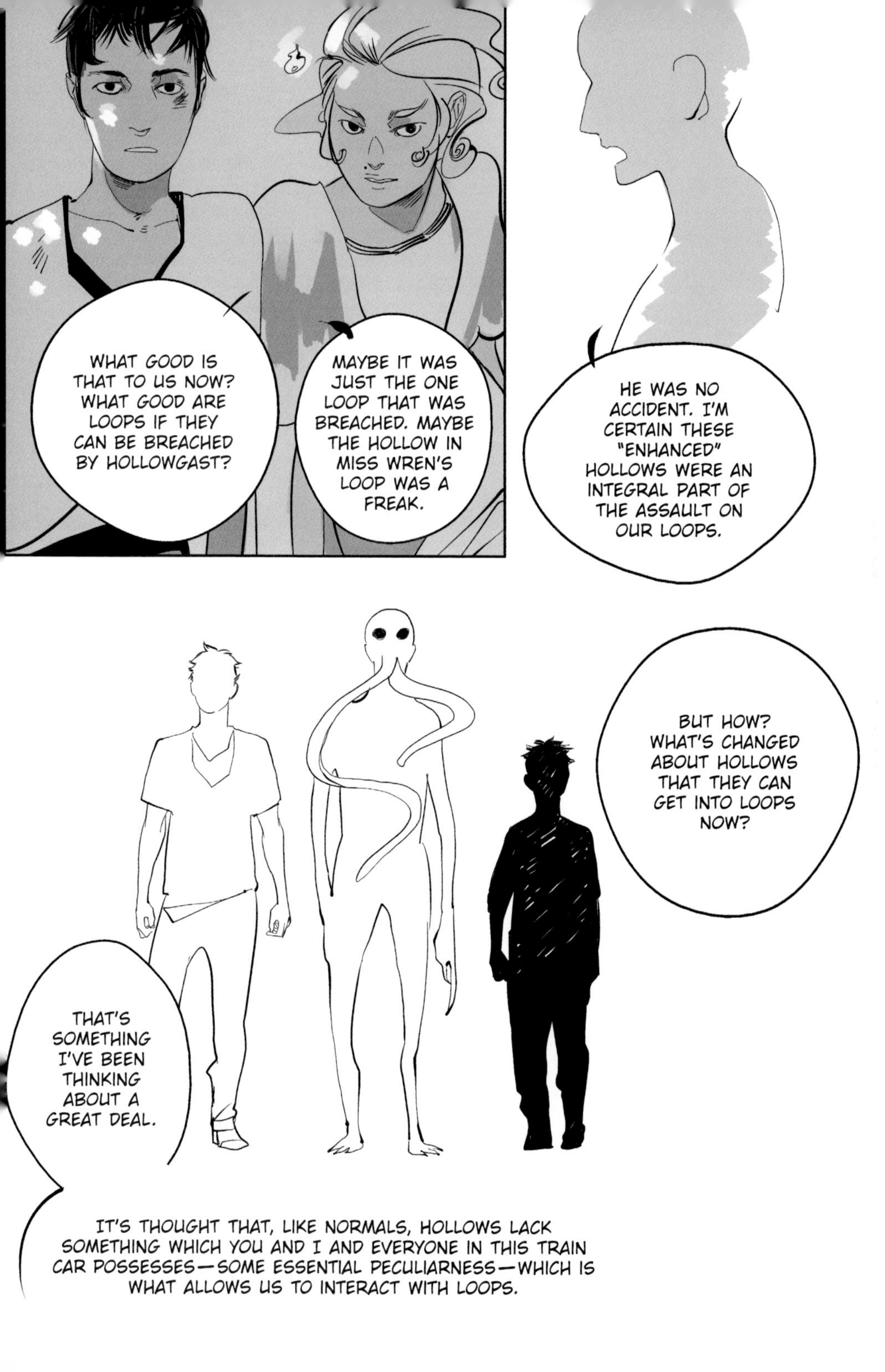
WHAT GOOD IS THAT TO US NOW? WHAT GOOD ARE LOOPS IF THEY CAN BE BREACHED BY HOLLOWGAST?
MAYBE IT WAS JUST THE ONE LOOP THAT WAS BREACHED. MAYBE THE HOLLOW IN MISS WREN'S LOOP WAS A FREAK.
HE WAS NO ACCIDENT. I'M CERTAIN THESE "ENHANCED" HOLLOWS WERE AN INTEGRAL PART OF THE ASSAULT ON OUR LOOPS.
BUT HOW? WHAT'S CHANGED ABOUT HOLLOWS THAT THEY CAN GET INTO LOOPS NOW?
THAT'S SOMETHING I'VE BEEN THINKING ABOUT A GREAT DEAL.
IT'S THOUGHT THAT, LIKE NORMALS, HOLLOWS LACK SOMETHING WHICH YOU AND I AND EVERYONE IN THIS TRAIN CAR POSSESSES—SOME ESSENTIAL PECULIARNESS—WHICH IS WHAT ALLOWS US TO INTERACT WITH LOOPS.

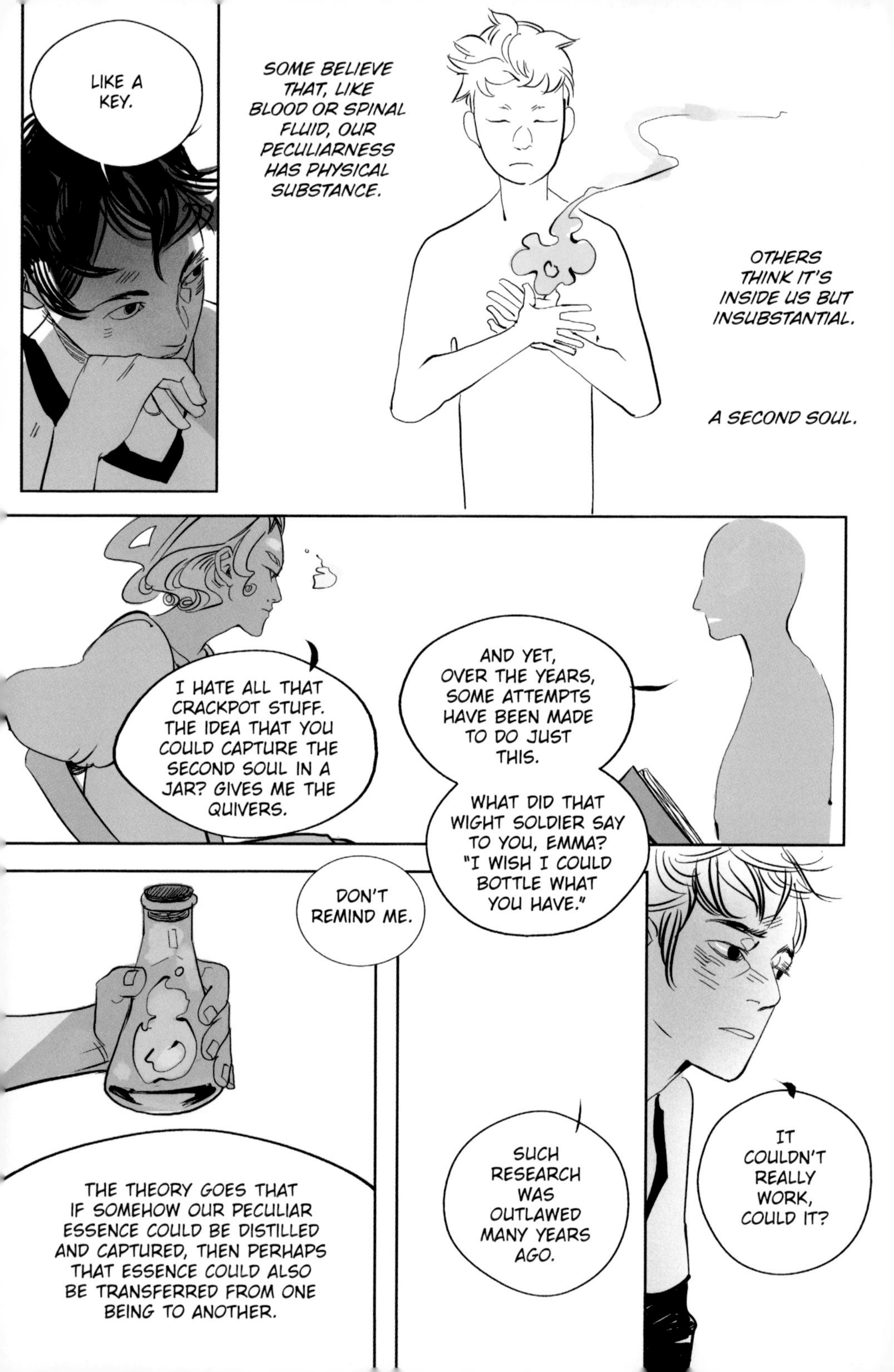
LIKE A KEY.
SOME BELIEVE THAT, LIKE BLOOD OR SPINAL FLUID, OUR PECULIARNESS HAS PHYSICAL SUBSTANCE.
OTHERS THINK IT'S INSIDE US BUT INSUBSTANTIAL.
A SECOND SOUL.
I HATE ALL THAT CRACKPOT STUFF. THE IDEA THAT YOU COULD CAPTURE THE SECOND SOUL IN A JAR? GIVES ME THE QUIVERS.
AND YET, OVER THE YEARS, SOME ATTEMPTS HAVE BEEN MADE TO DO JUST THIS.
WHAT DID THAT WIGHT SOLDIER SAY TO YOU, EMMA? "I WISH I COULD BOTTLE WHAT YOU HAVE."
DON'T REMIND ME.
THE THEORY GOES THAT IF SOMEHOW OUR PECULIAR ESSENCE COULD BE DISTILLED AND CAPTURED, THEN PERHAPS THAT ESSENCE COULD ALSO BE TRANSFERRED FROM ONE BEING TO ANOTHER.
SUCH RESEARCH WAS OUTLAWED MANY YEARS AGO.
IT COULDN'T REALLY WORK, COULD IT?

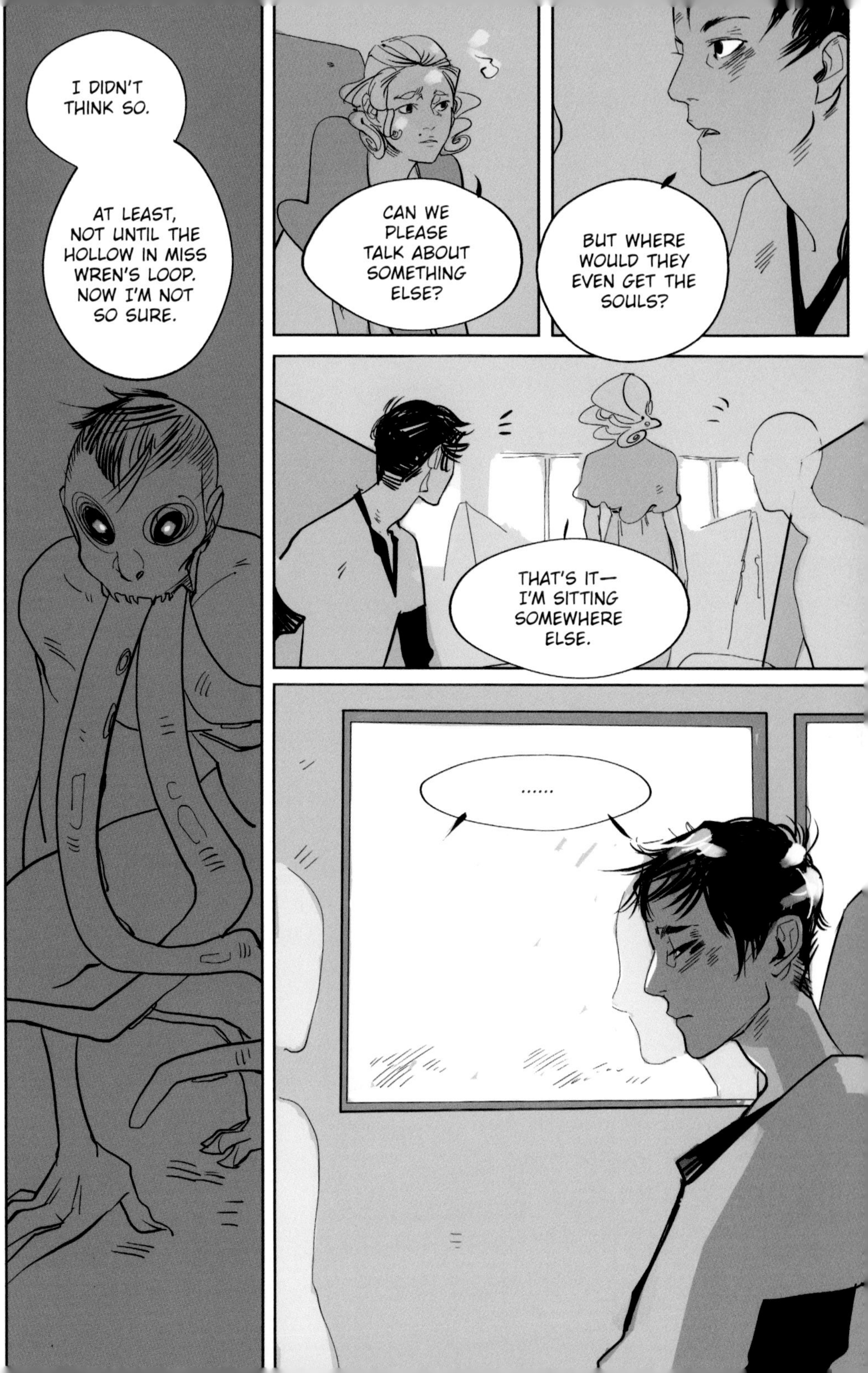
I DIDN'T THINK SO.
AT LEAST, NOT UNTIL THE HOLLOW IN MISS WREN'S LOOP. NOW I'M NOT SO SURE.
CAN WE PLEASE TALK ABOUT SOMETHING ELSE?
BUT WHERE WOULD THEY EVEN GET THE SOULS?
THAT'S IT— I'M SITTING SOMEWHERE ELSE.
......

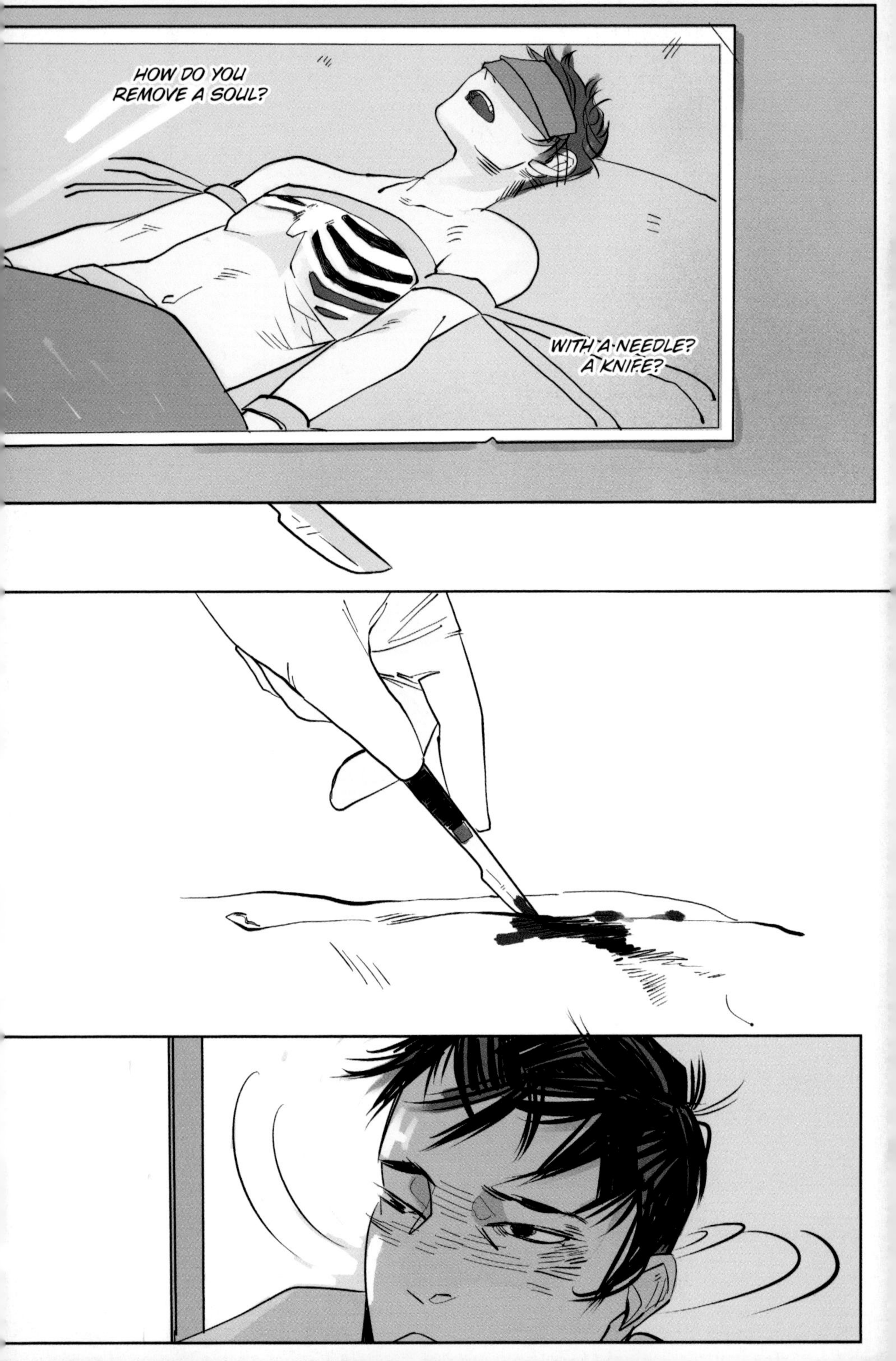
HOW DO YOU
REMOVE A SOUL?
WITH A NEEDLE?
A KNIFE?

CHAPTER FOUR

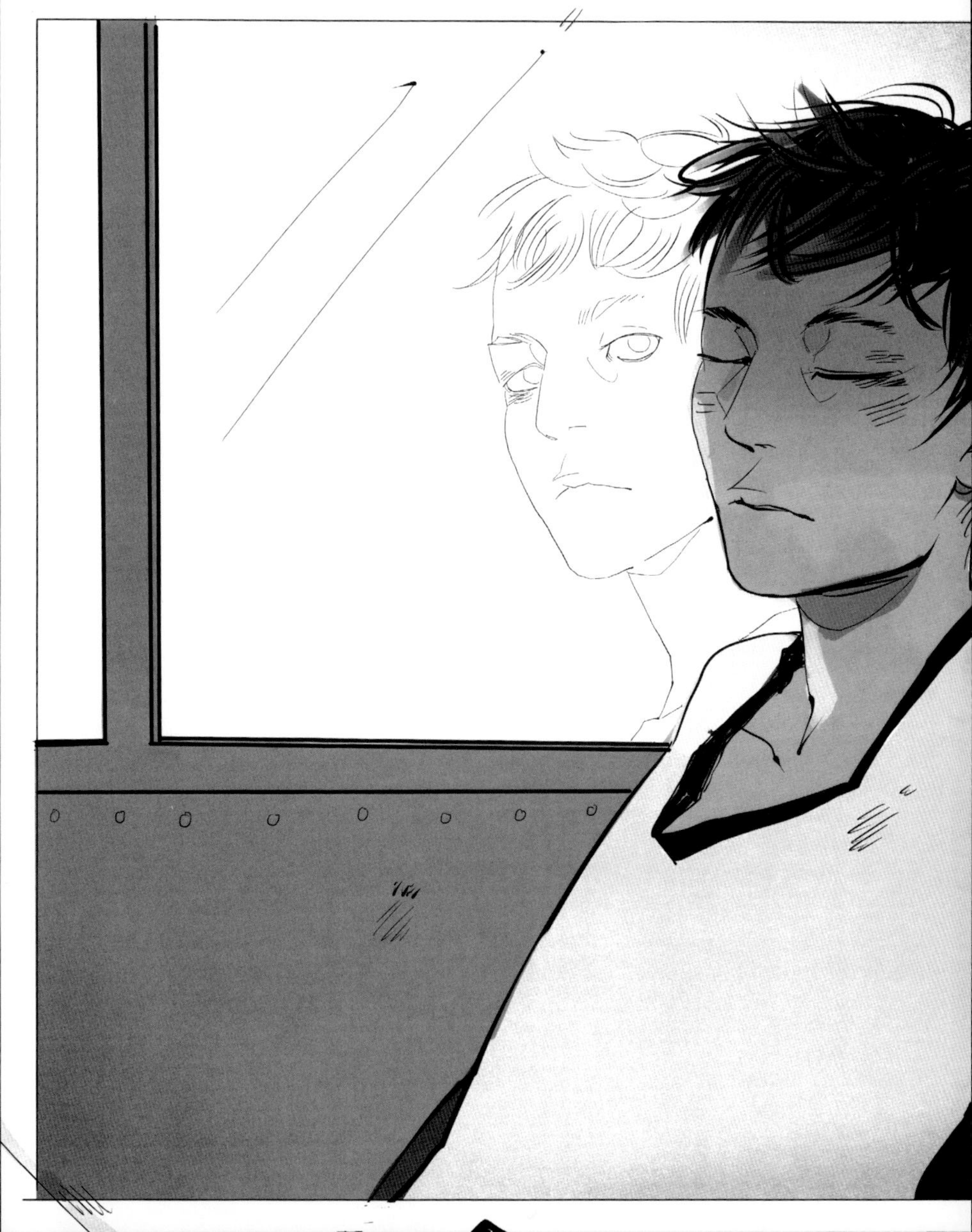

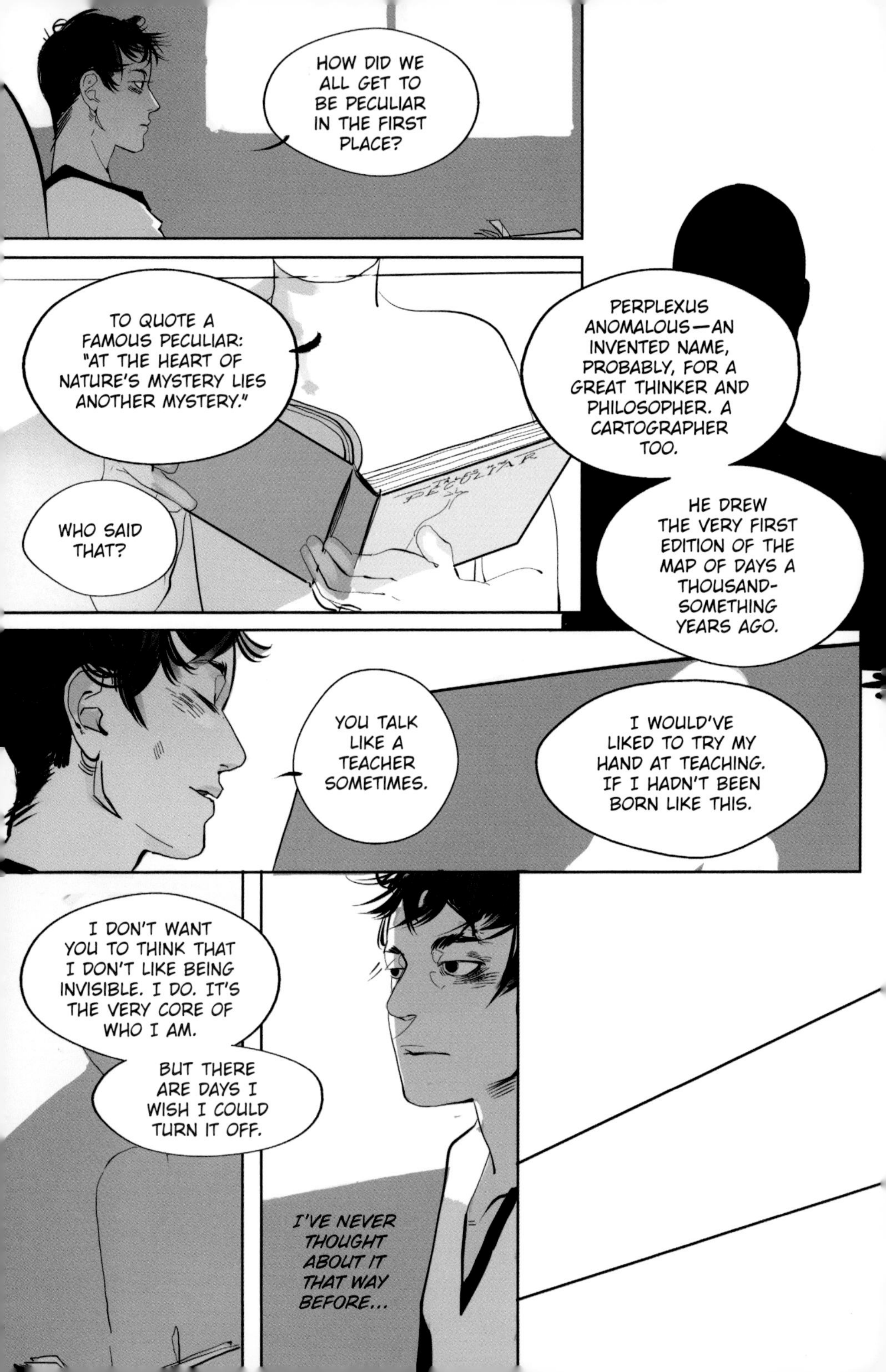
HOW DID WE ALL GET TO BE PECULIAR IN THE FIRST PLACE?
TO QUOTE A FAMOUS PECULIAR: "AT THE HEART OF NATURE'S MYSTERY LIES ANOTHER MYSTERY."
WHO SAID THAT?
PERPLEXUS ANOMALOUS—AN INVENTED NAME, PROBABLY, FOR A GREAT THINKER AND PHILOSOPHER. A CARTOGRAPHER TOO.
HE DREW THE VERY FIRST EDITION OF THE MAP OF DAYS A THOUSAND-SOMETHING YEARS AGO.
YOU TALK LIKE A TEACHER SOMETIMES.
I WOULD'VE LIKED TO TRY MY HAND AT TEACHING. IF I HADN'T BEEN BORN LIKE THIS.
I DON'T WANT YOU TO THINK THAT I DON'T LIKE BEING INVISIBLE. I DO. IT'S THE VERY CORE OF WHO I AM.
BUT THERE ARE DAYS I WISH I COULD TURN IT OFF.
I'VE NEVER THOUGHT ABOUT IT THAT WAY BEFORE...

TO PASS TIME, THE CHILDREN TOLD THEIR STORIES.

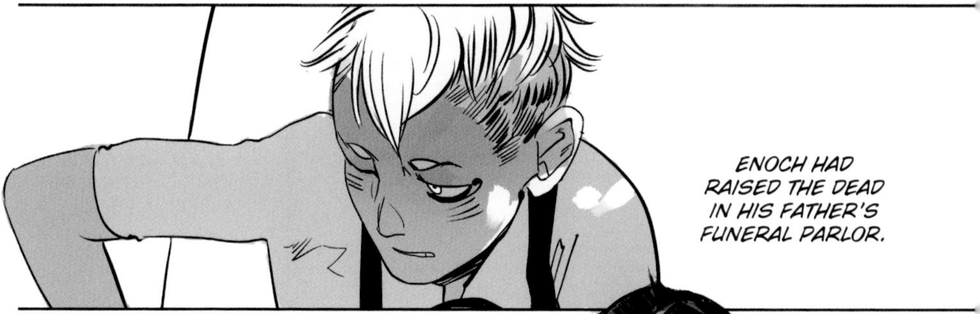
ENOCH HAD RAISED THE DEAD IN HIS FATHER'S FUNERAL PARLOR.

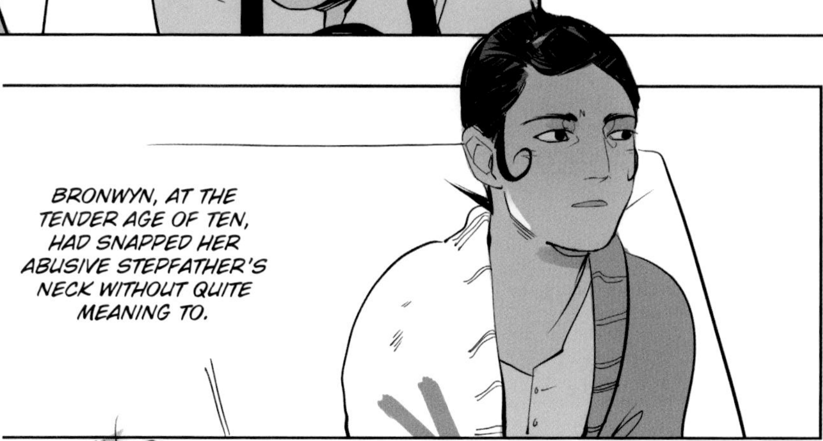
BRONWYN, AT THE TENDER AGE OF TEN, HAD SNAPPED HER ABUSIVE STEPFATHER'S NECK WITHOUT QUITE MEANING TO.

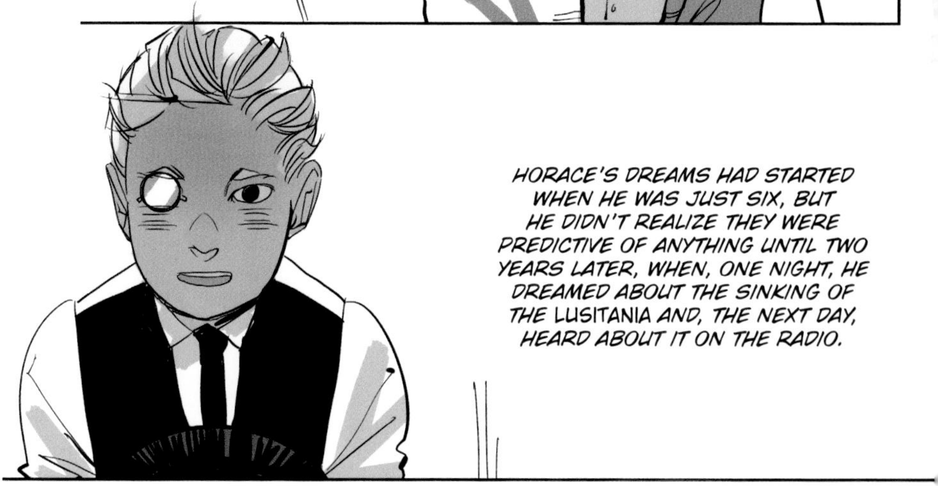
HORACE'S DREAMS HAD STARTED WHEN HE WAS JUST SIX, BUT HE DIDN'T REALIZE THEY WERE PREDICTIVE OF ANYTHING UNTIL TWO YEARS LATER, WHEN, ONE NIGHT, HE DREAMED ABOUT THE SINKING OF THE LUSITANIA AND, THE NEXT DAY, HEARD ABOUT IT ON THE RADIO.

HUGH, FROM A YOUNG AGE, HAD LOVED HONEY MORE THAN ANY OTHER FOOD, AND AT FIVE HE'D STARTED EATING HONEYCOMB ALONG WITH IT—SO RAVENOUSLY THAT THE FIRST TIME HE ACCIDENTALLY SWALLOWED A BEE, HE DIDN'T NOTICE UNTIL HE FELT IT BUZZING AROUND IN HIS STOMACH.

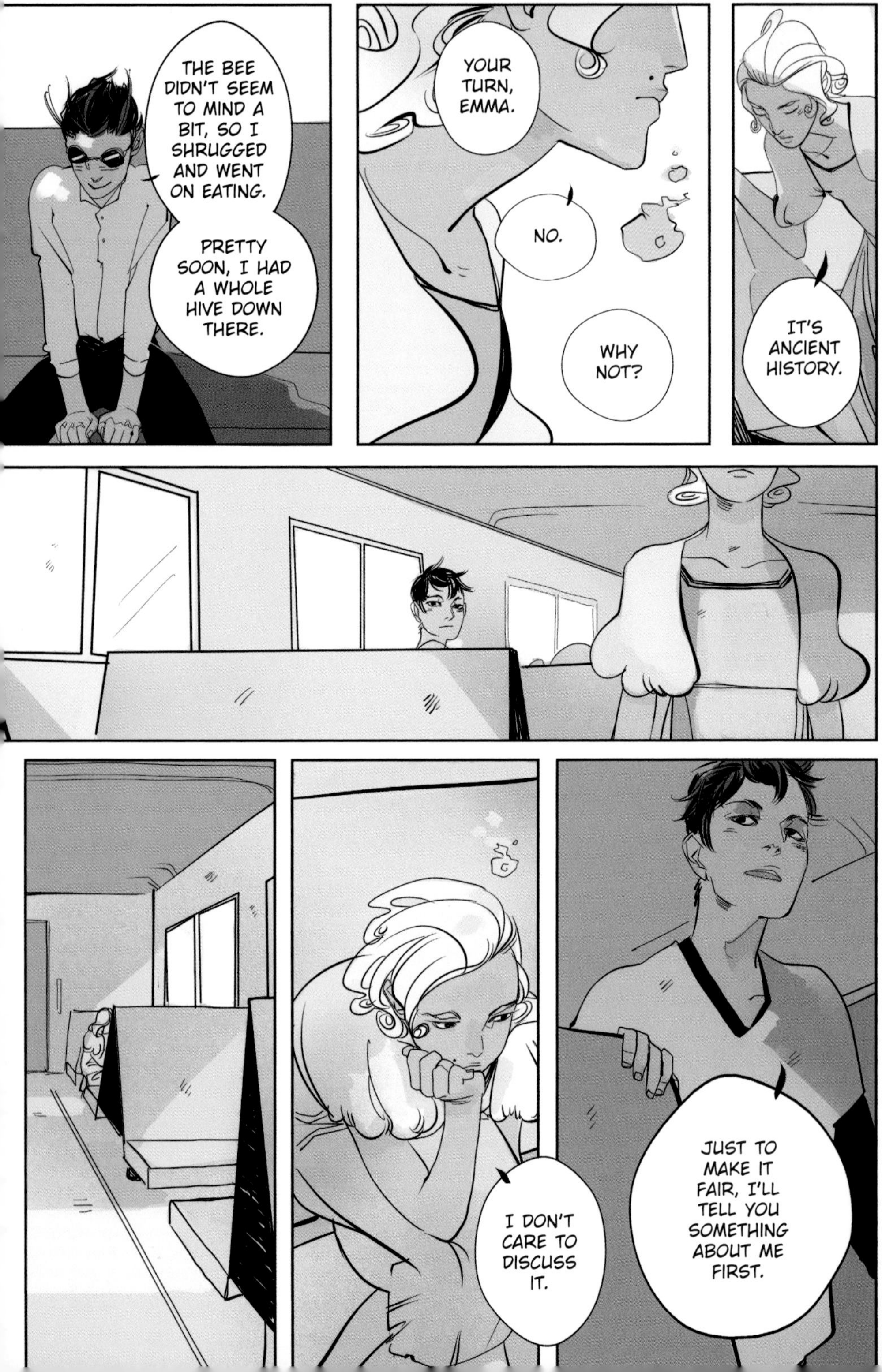
THE BEE DIDN'T SEEM TO MIND A BIT, SO I SHRUGGED AND WENT ON EATING.
PRETTY SOON, I HAD A WHOLE HIVE DOWN THERE.
YOUR TURN, EMMA.
NO.
WHY NOT?
IT'S ANCIENT HISTORY.
I DON'T CARE TO DISCUSS IT.
JUST TO MAKE IT FAIR, I'LL TELL YOU SOMETHING ABOUT ME FIRST.

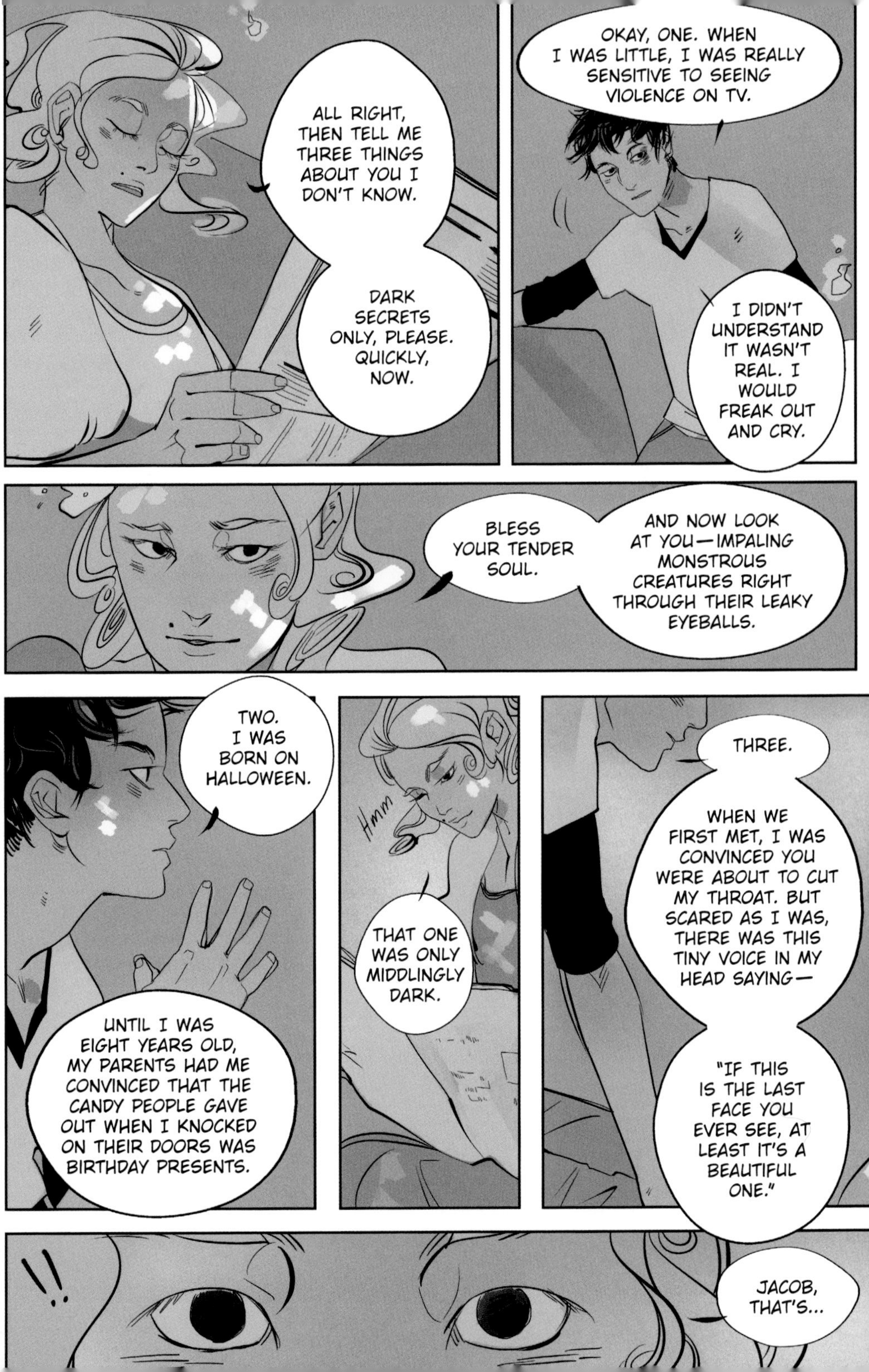
ALL RIGHT, THEN TELL ME THREE THINGS ABOUT YOU I DON'T KNOW.
DARK SECRETS ONLY, PLEASE. QUICKLY, NOW.
OKAY, ONE. WHEN I WAS LITTLE, I WAS REALLY SENSITIVE TO SEEING VIOLENCE ON TV.
I DIDN'T UNDERSTAND IT WASN'T REAL. I WOULD FREAK OUT AND CRY.
BLESS YOUR TENDER SOUL.
AND NOW LOOK AT YOU—IMPALING MONSTROUS CREATURES RIGHT THROUGH THEIR LEAKY EYEBALLS.
TWO. I WAS BORN ON HALLOWEEN.
UNTIL I WAS EIGHT YEARS OLD, MY PARENTS HAD ME CONVINCED THAT THE CANDY PEOPLE GAVE OUT WHEN I KNOCKED ON THEIR DOORS WAS BIRTHDAY PRESENTS.
Hmm
THAT ONE WAS ONLY MIDDLINGLY DARK.
THREE.
WHEN WE FIRST MET, I WAS CONVINCED YOU WERE ABOUT TO CUT MY THROAT. BUT SCARED AS I WAS, THERE WAS THIS TINY VOICE IN MY HEAD SAYING—
"IF THIS IS THE LAST FACE YOU EVER SEE, AT LEAST IT'S A BEAUTIFUL ONE."
!!
JACOB, THAT'S...

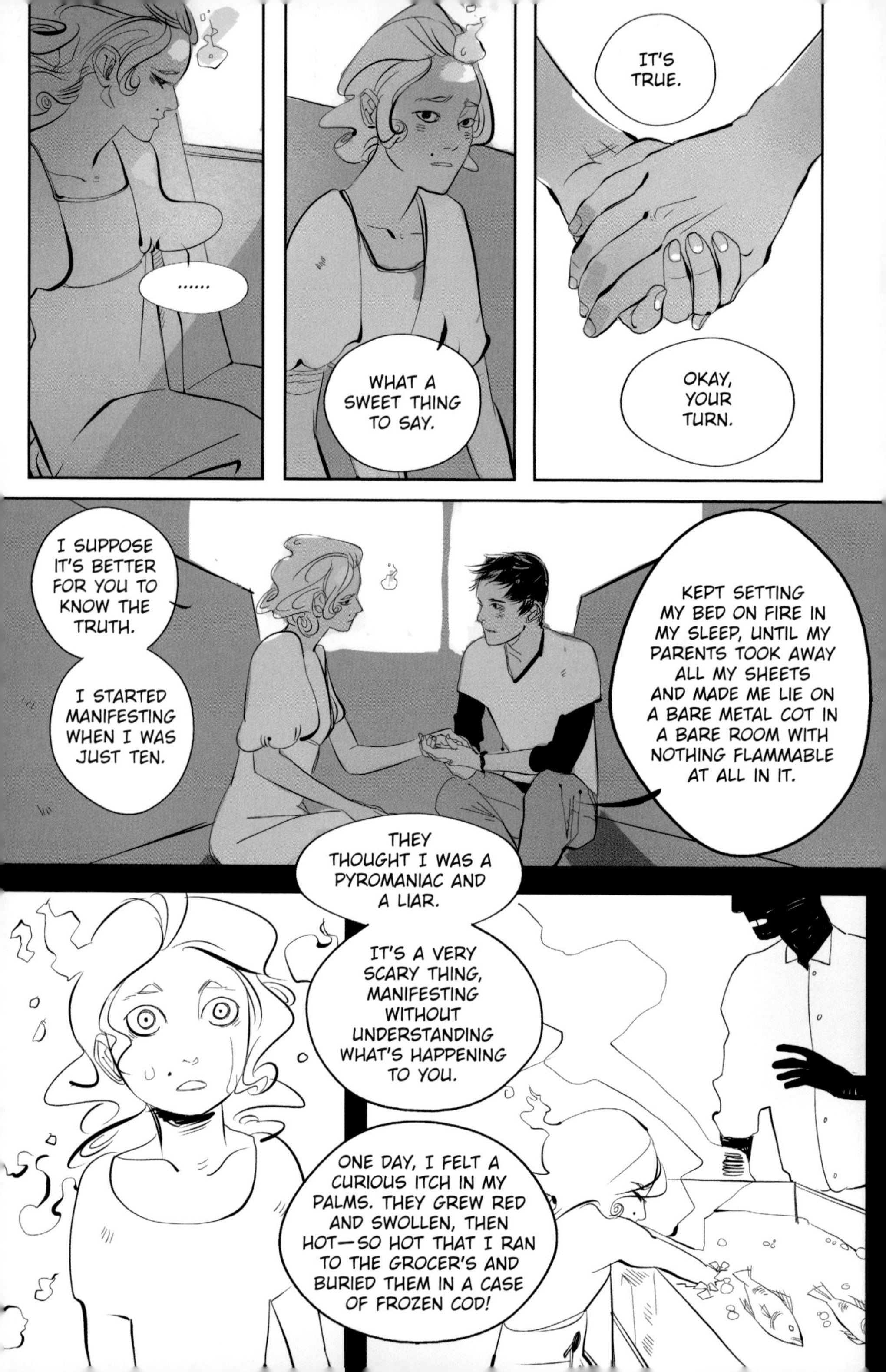
......
WHAT A SWEET THING TO SAY.
IT'S TRUE.
OKAY, YOUR TURN.
I SUPPOSE IT'S BETTER FOR YOU TO KNOW THE TRUTH.
I STARTED MANIFESTING WHEN I WAS JUST TEN.
KEPT SETTING MY BED ON FIRE IN MY SLEEP, UNTIL MY PARENTS TOOK AWAY ALL MY SHEETS AND MADE ME LIE ON A BARE METAL COT IN A BARE ROOM WITH NOTHING FLAMMABLE AT ALL IN IT.
THEY THOUGHT I WAS A PYROMANIAC AND A LIAR.
IT'S A VERY SCARY THING, MANIFESTING WITHOUT UNDERSTANDING WHAT'S HAPPENING TO YOU.
ONE DAY, I FELT A CURIOUS ITCH IN MY PALMS. THEY GREW RED AND SWOLLEN, THEN HOT—SO HOT THAT I RAN TO THE GROCER'S AND BURIED THEM IN A CASE OF FROZEN COD!

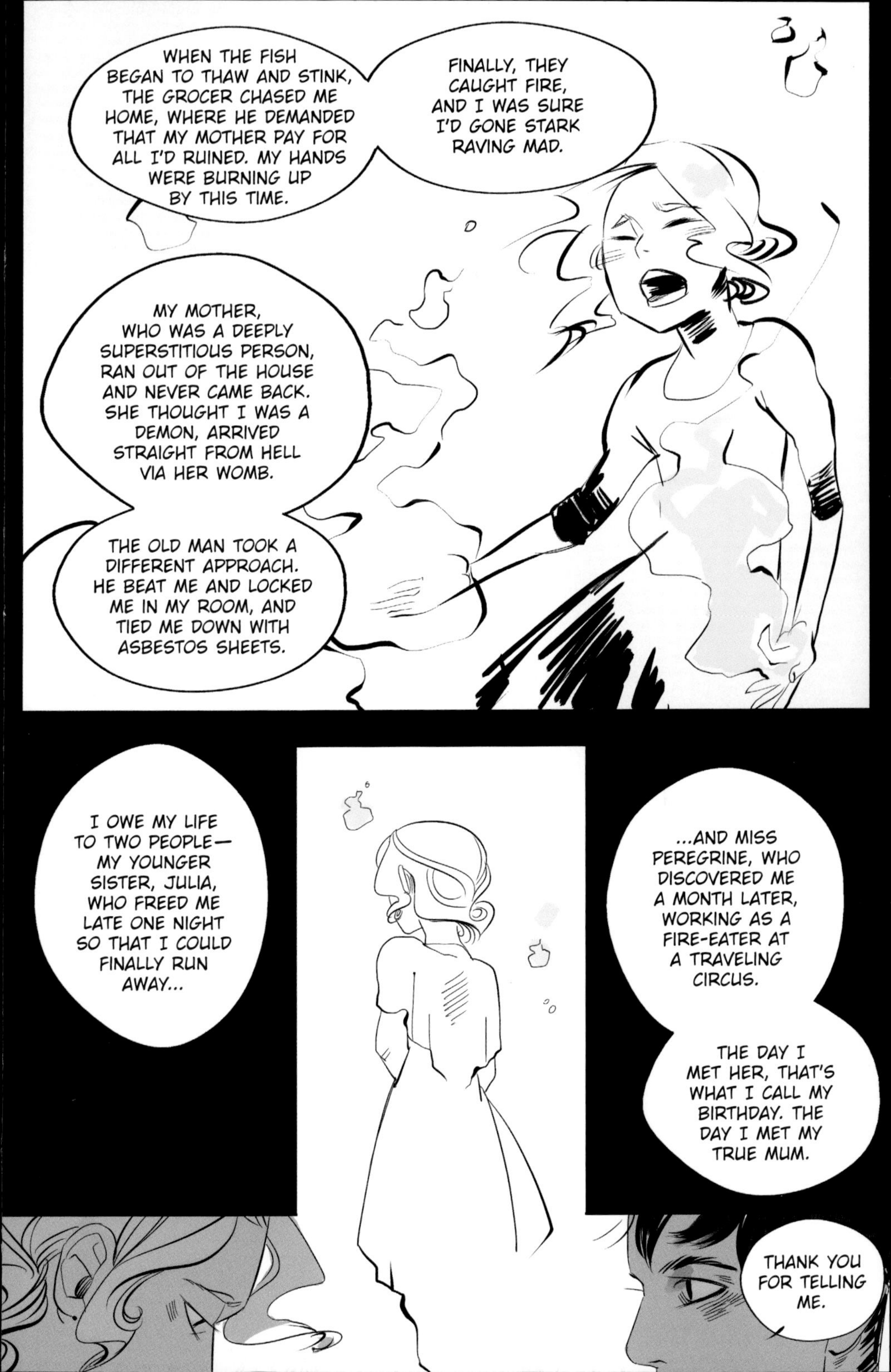
WHEN THE FISH BEGAN TO THAW AND STINK, THE GROCER CHASED ME HOME, WHERE HE DEMANDED THAT MY MOTHER PAY FOR ALL I'D RUINED. MY HANDS WERE BURNING UP BY THIS TIME.
FINALLY, THEY CAUGHT FIRE, AND I WAS SURE I'D GONE STARK RAVING MAD.
MY MOTHER, WHO WAS A DEEPLY SUPERSTITIOUS PERSON, RAN OUT OF THE HOUSE AND NEVER CAME BACK. SHE THOUGHT I WAS A DEMON, ARRIVED STRAIGHT FROM HELL VIA HER WOMB.
THE OLD MAN TOOK A DIFFERENT APPROACH. HE BEAT ME AND LOCKED ME IN MY ROOM, AND TIED ME DOWN WITH ASBESTOS SHEETS.
I OWE MY LIFE TO TWO PEOPLE— MY YOUNGER SISTER, JULIA, WHO FREED ME LATE ONE NIGHT SO THAT I COULD FINALLY RUN AWAY...
...AND MISS PEREGRINE, WHO DISCOVERED ME A MONTH LATER, WORKING AS A FIRE-EATER AT A TRAVELING CIRCUS.
THE DAY I MET HER, THAT'S WHAT I CALL MY BIRTHDAY. THE DAY I MET MY TRUE MUM.
THANK YOU FOR TELLING ME.

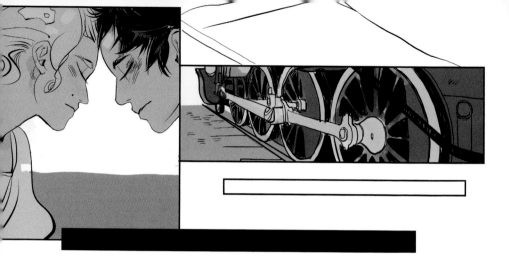

LONDON.

IT LOOKS LIKE THEY'RE EVACUATING ALL THE KIDS.

WHAT ABOUT HOLLOWS?

I DON'T SENSE ANY.

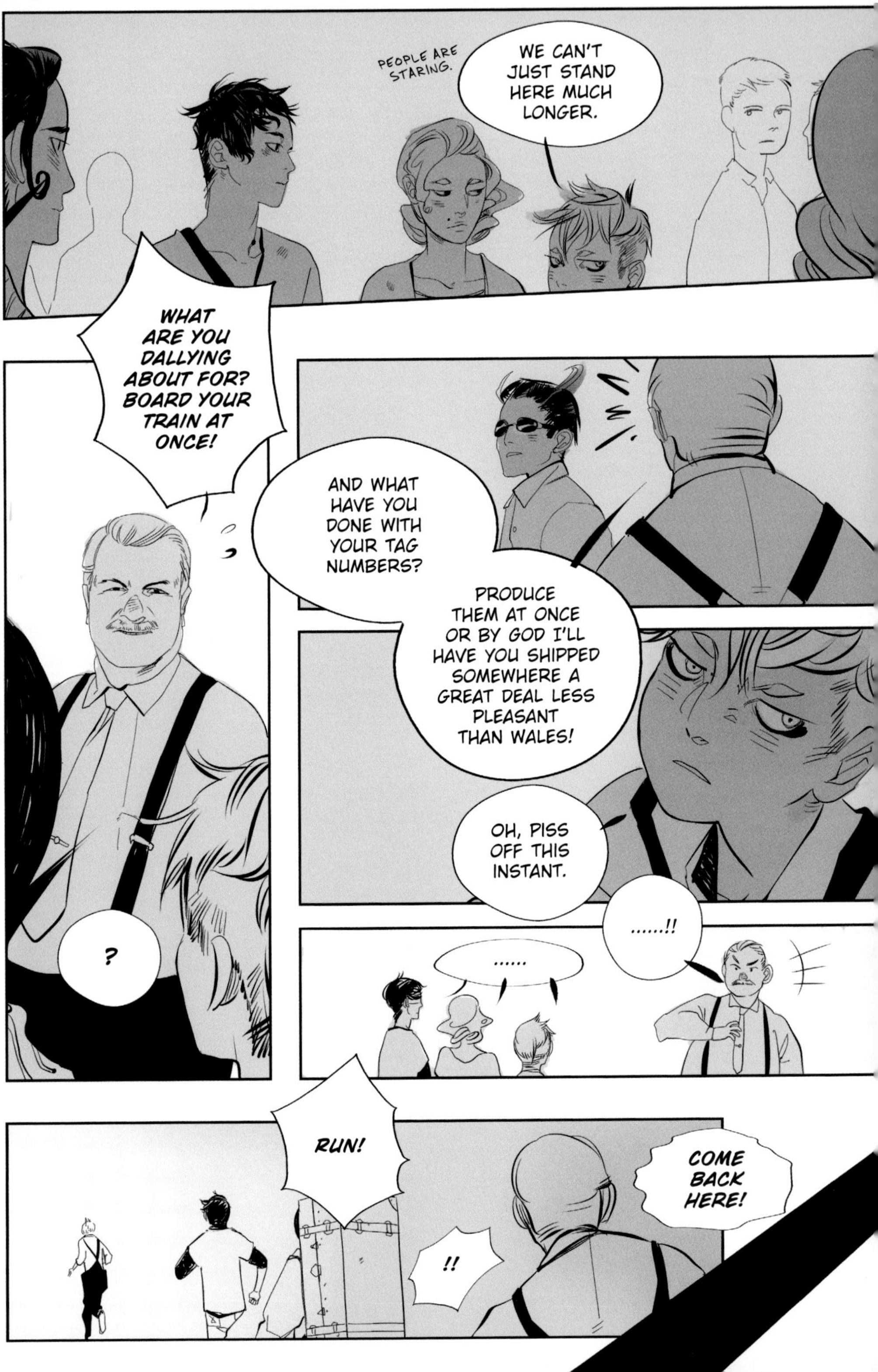
PEOPLE ARE STARING.
WE CAN'T JUST STAND HERE MUCH LONGER.
WHAT ARE YOU DALLYING ABOUT FOR? BOARD YOUR TRAIN AT ONCE!
?
AND WHAT HAVE YOU DONE WITH YOUR TAG NUMBERS?
PRODUCE THEM AT ONCE OR BY GOD I'LL HAVE YOU SHIPPED SOMEWHERE A GREAT DEAL LESS PLEASANT THAN WALES!
OH, PISS OFF THIS INSTANT.
......!!
......
RUN!
!!
COME BACK HERE!

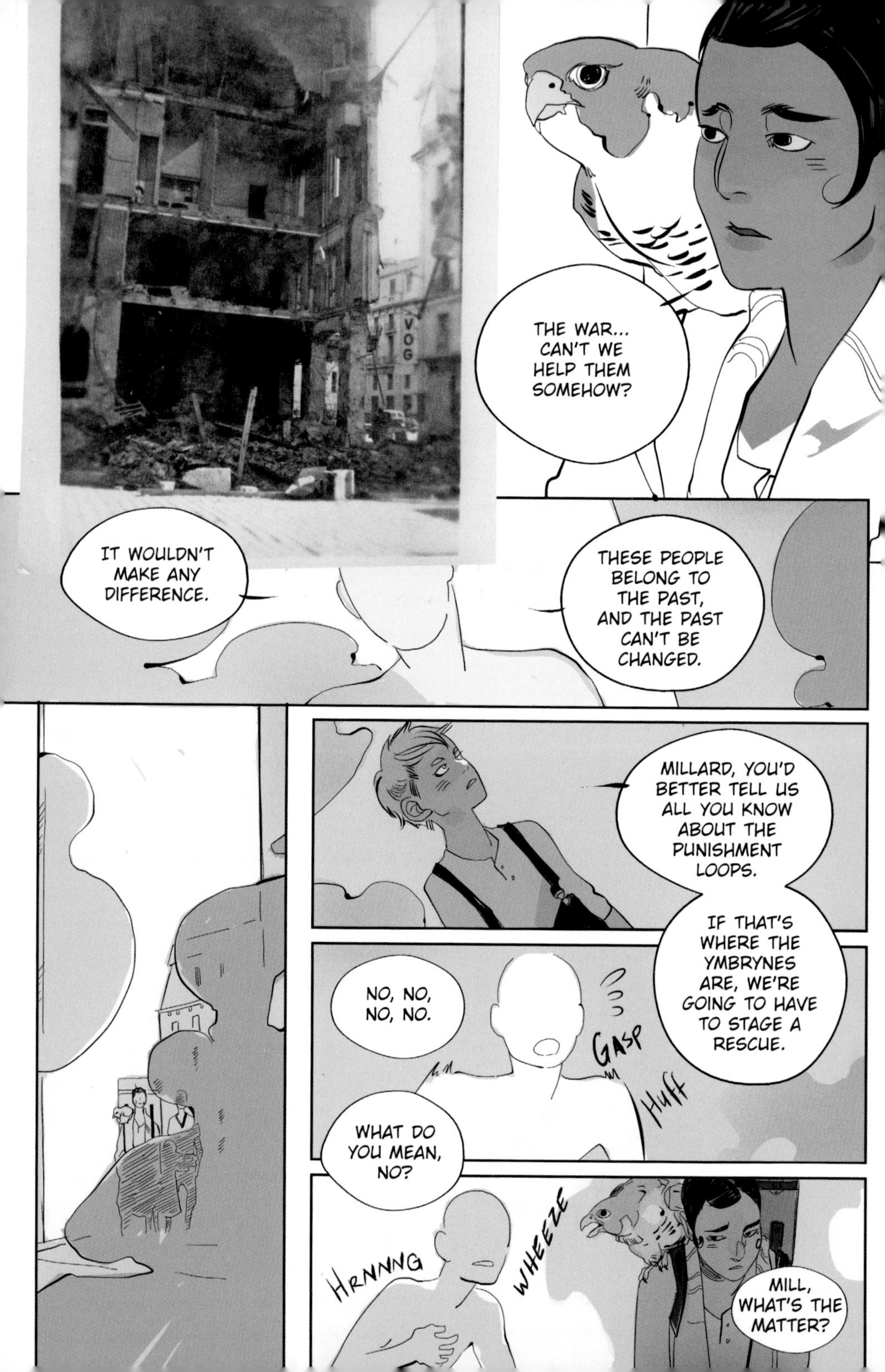
THE WAR... CAN'T WE HELP THEM SOMEHOW?
IT WOULDN'T MAKE ANY DIFFERENCE.
THESE PEOPLE BELONG TO THE PAST, AND THE PAST CAN'T BE CHANGED.
MILLARD, YOU'D BETTER TELL US ALL YOU KNOW ABOUT THE PUNISHMENT LOOPS.
IF THAT'S WHERE THE YMBRYNES ARE, WE'RE GOING TO HAVE TO STAGE A RESCUE.
NO, NO, NO, NO.
GASP
HUFF
WHAT DO YOU MEAN, NO?
HRNNNG
WHEEZE
MILL, WHAT'S THE MATTER?

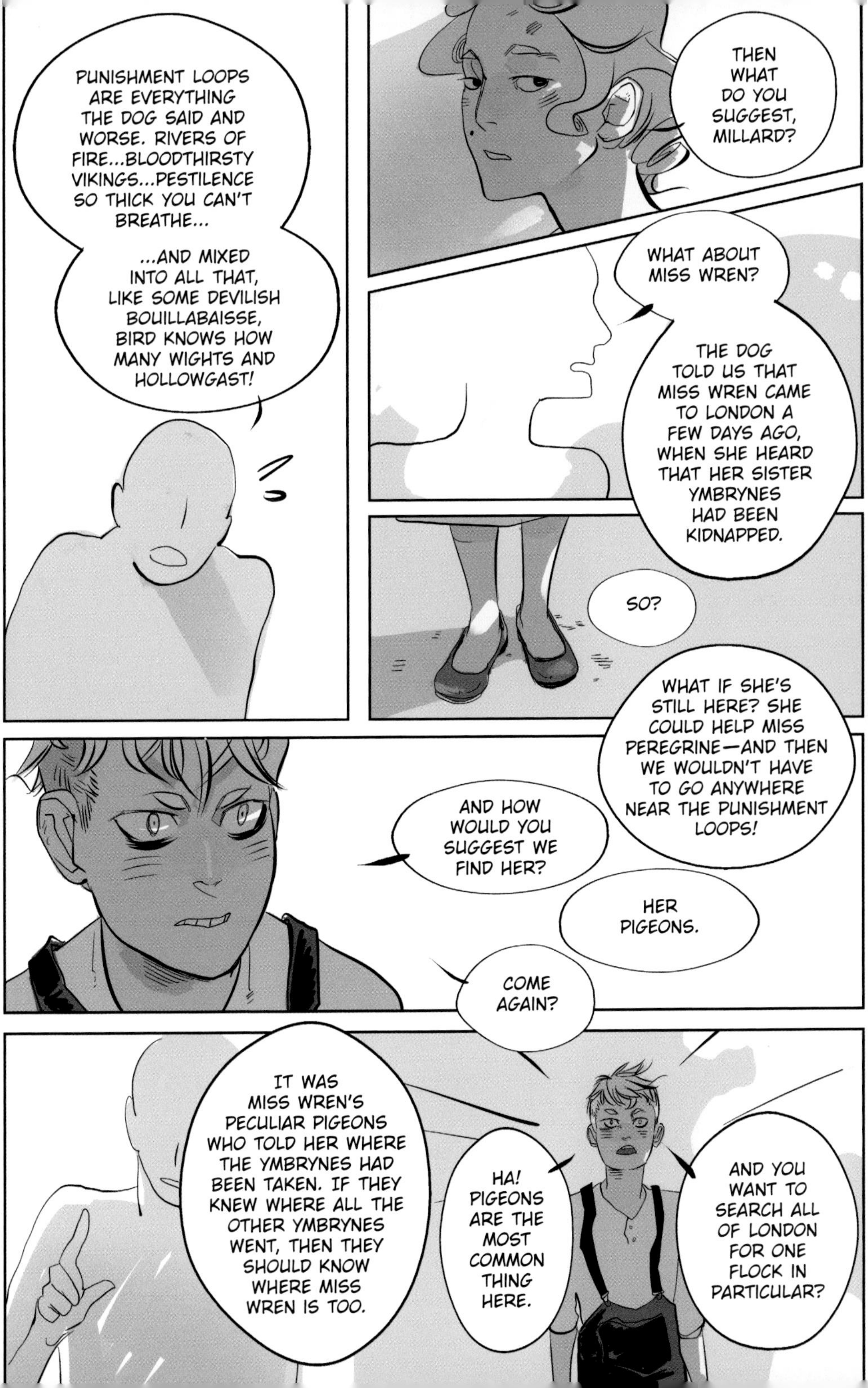
PUNISHMENT LOOPS ARE EVERYTHING THE DOG SAID AND WORSE. RIVERS OF FIRE...BLOODTHIRSTY VIKINGS...PESTILENCE SO THICK YOU CAN'T BREATHE...
...AND MIXED INTO ALL THAT, LIKE SOME DEVILISH BOUILLABAISSE, BIRD KNOWS HOW MANY WIGHTS AND HOLLOWGAST!
THEN WHAT DO YOU SUGGEST, MILLARD?
WHAT ABOUT MISS WREN?
THE DOG TOLD US THAT MISS WREN CAME TO LONDON A FEW DAYS AGO, WHEN SHE HEARD THAT HER SISTER YMBRYNES HAD BEEN KIDNAPPED.
SO?
WHAT IF SHE'S STILL HERE? SHE COULD HELP MISS PEREGRINE—AND THEN WE WOULDN'T HAVE TO GO ANYWHERE NEAR THE PUNISHMENT LOOPS!
AND HOW WOULD YOU SUGGEST WE FIND HER?
HER PIGEONS.
COME AGAIN?
IT WAS MISS WREN'S PECULIAR PIGEONS WHO TOLD HER WHERE THE YMBRYNES HAD BEEN TAKEN. IF THEY KNEW WHERE ALL THE OTHER YMBRYNES WENT, THEN THEY SHOULD KNOW WHERE MISS WREN IS TOO.
HA! PIGEONS ARE THE MOST COMMON THING HERE.
AND YOU WANT TO SEARCH ALL OF LONDON FOR ONE FLOCK IN PARTICULAR?

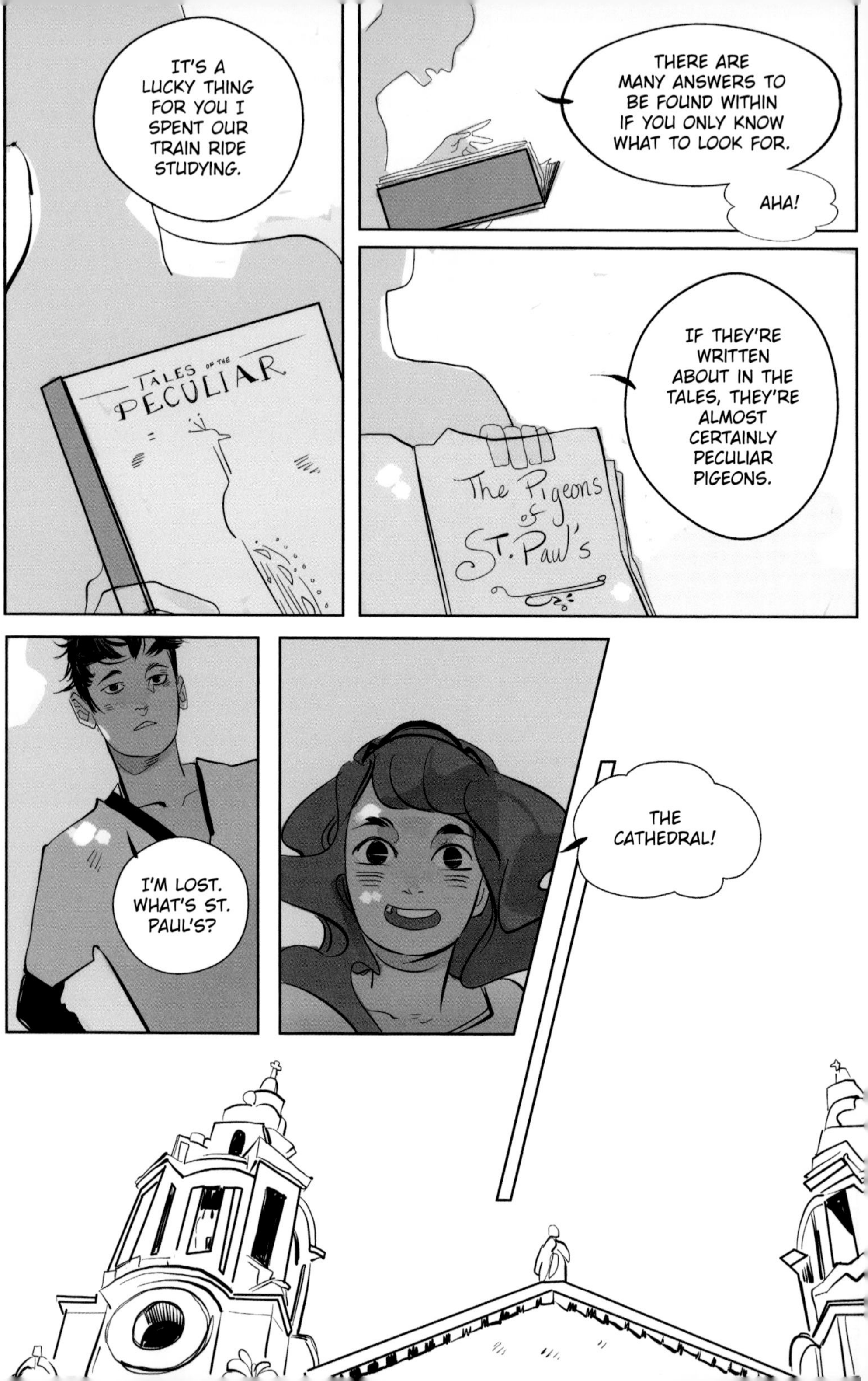
IT'S A LUCKY THING FOR YOU I SPENT OUR TRAIN RIDE STUDYING.
TALES OF THE PECULIAR
THERE ARE MANY ANSWERS TO BE FOUND WITHIN IF YOU ONLY KNOW WHAT TO LOOK FOR.
AHA!
IF THEY'RE WRITTEN ABOUT IN THE TALES, THEY'RE ALMOST CERTAINLY PECULIAR PIGEONS.
The Pigeons of St. Paul's
I'M LOST. WHAT'S ST. PAUL'S?
THE CATHEDRAL!

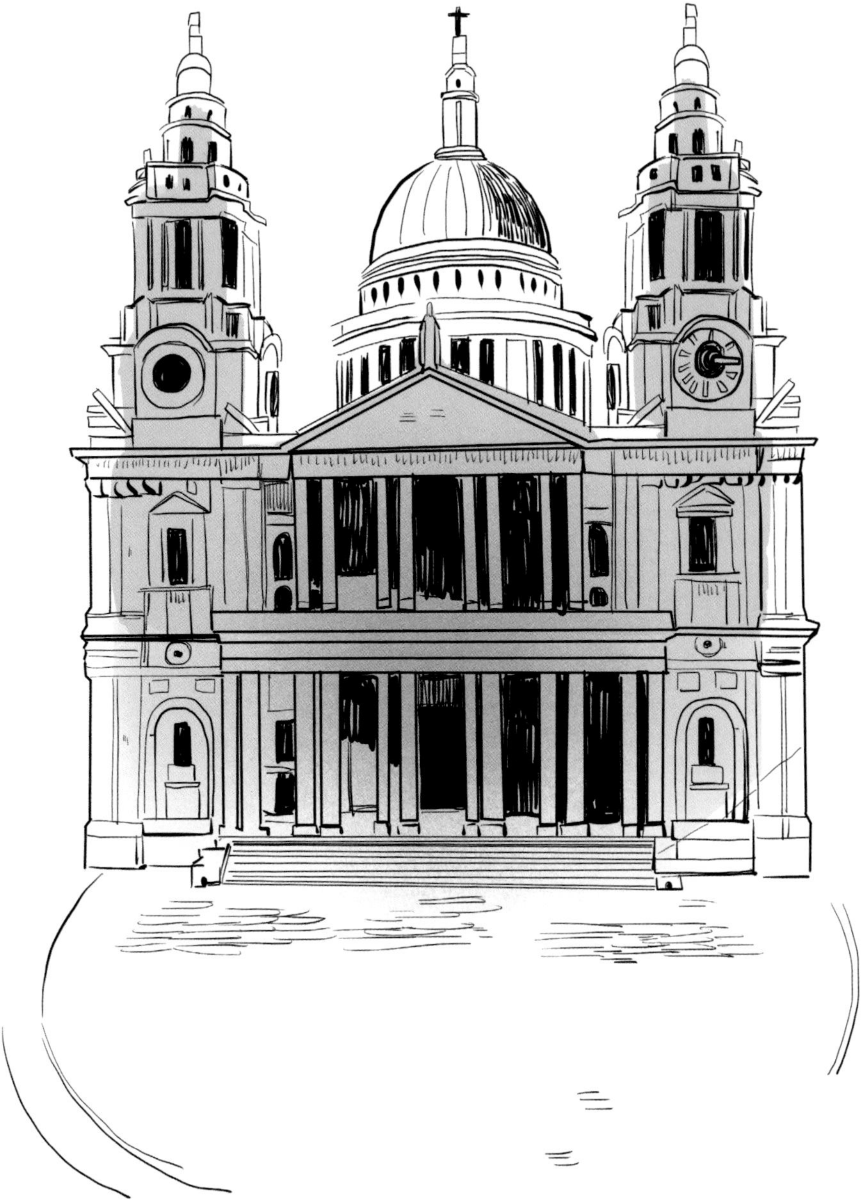

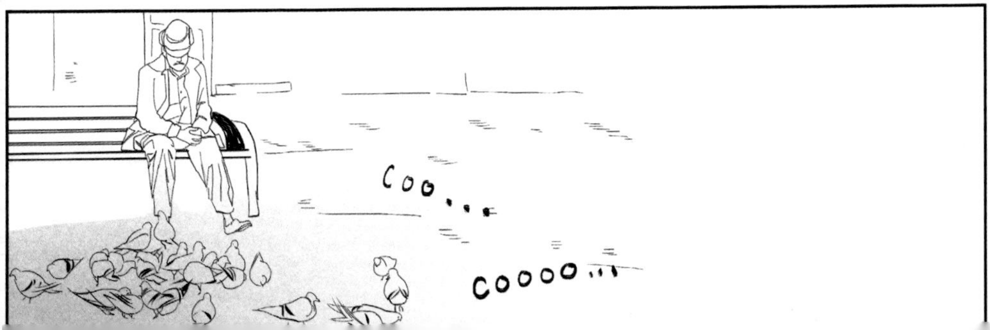
COO...
COOOO...

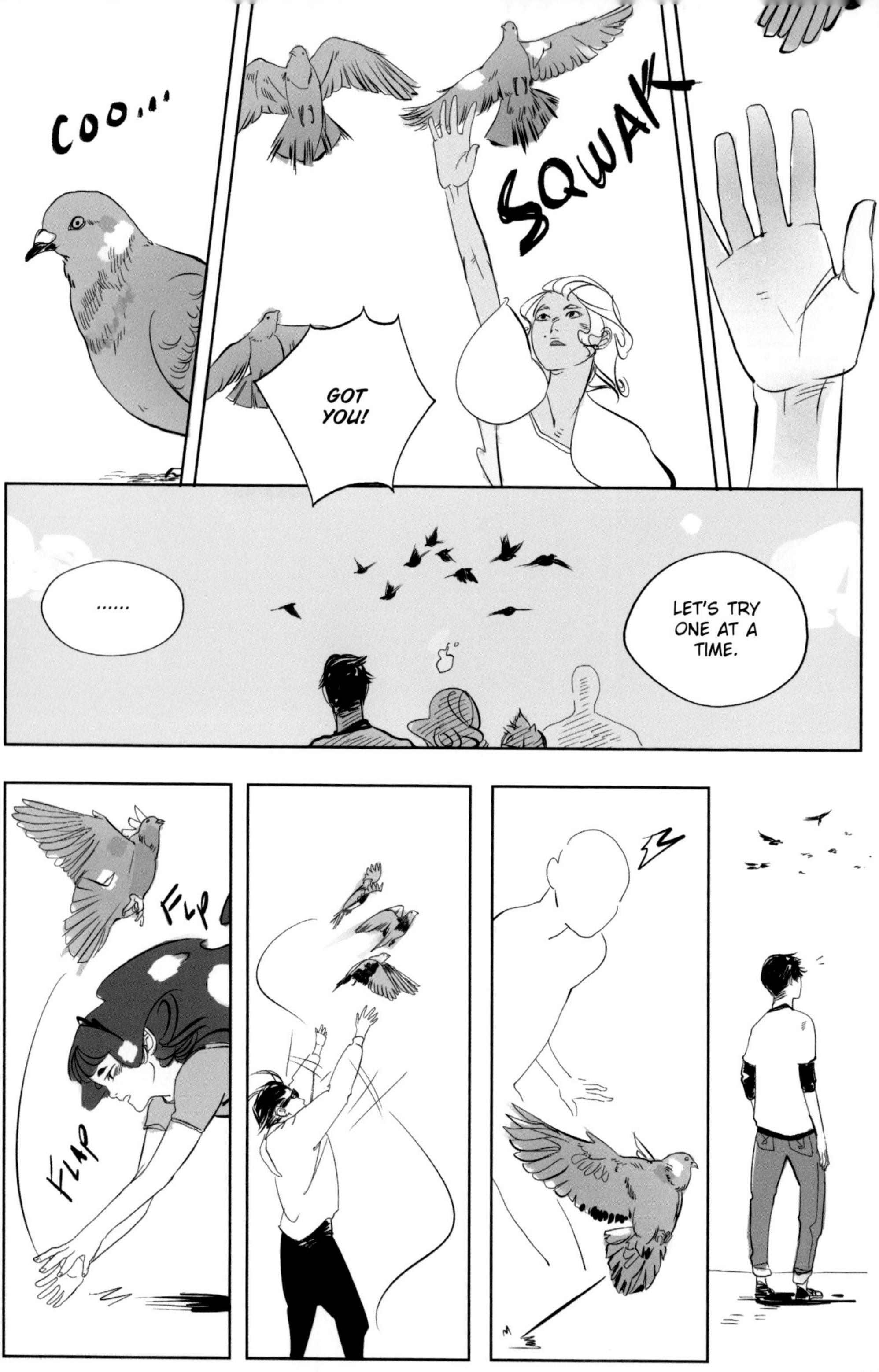
COO...
SQWAK
GOT YOU!
......
LET'S TRY ONE AT A TIME.
FLP
FLAP

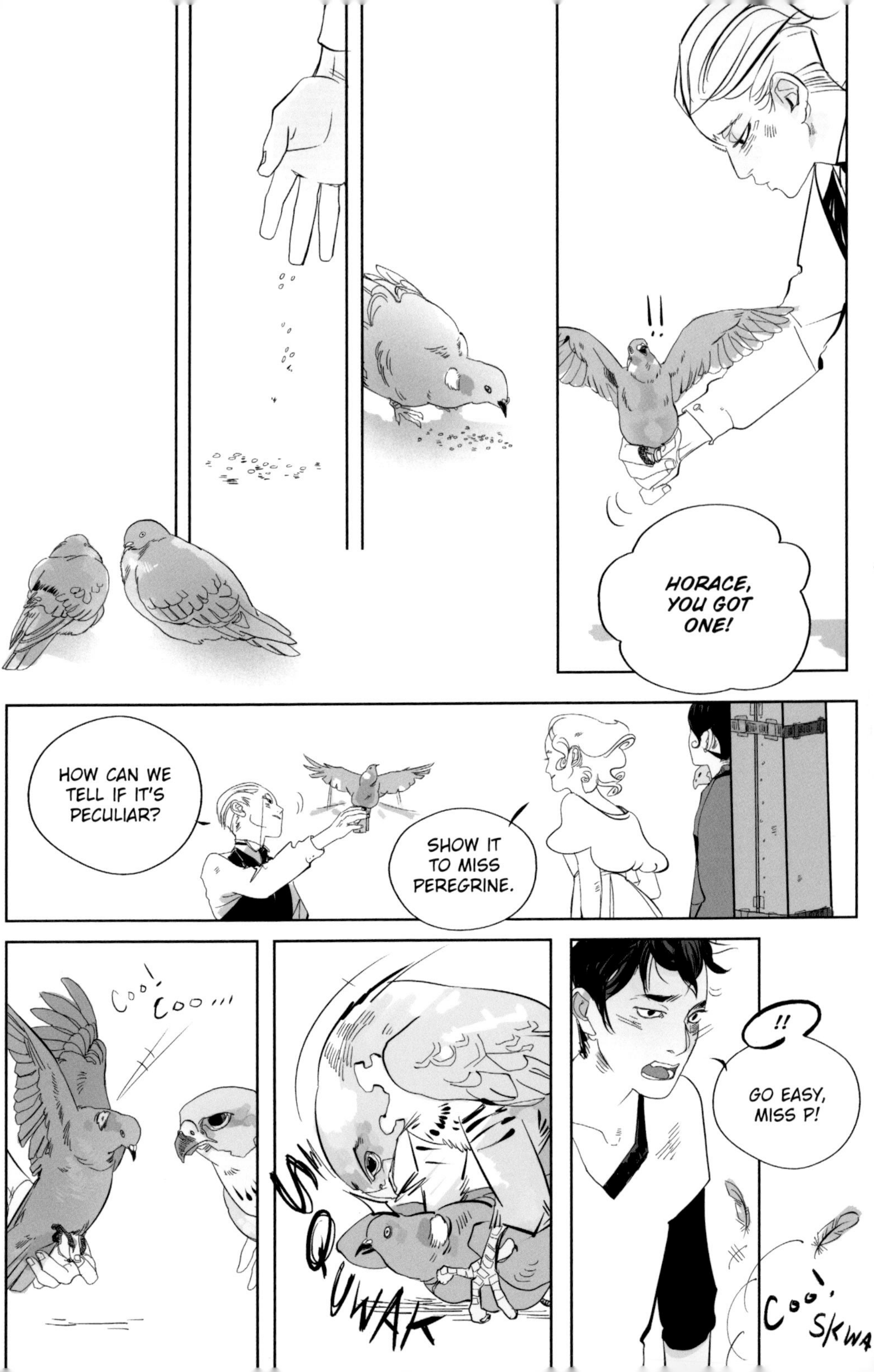
!!
HORACE, YOU GOT ONE!
HOW CAN WE TELL IF IT'S PECULIAR?
SHOW IT TO MISS PEREGRINE.
COO! COO...
SQUWAK
!!
GO EASY, MISS P!
COO, SKWA

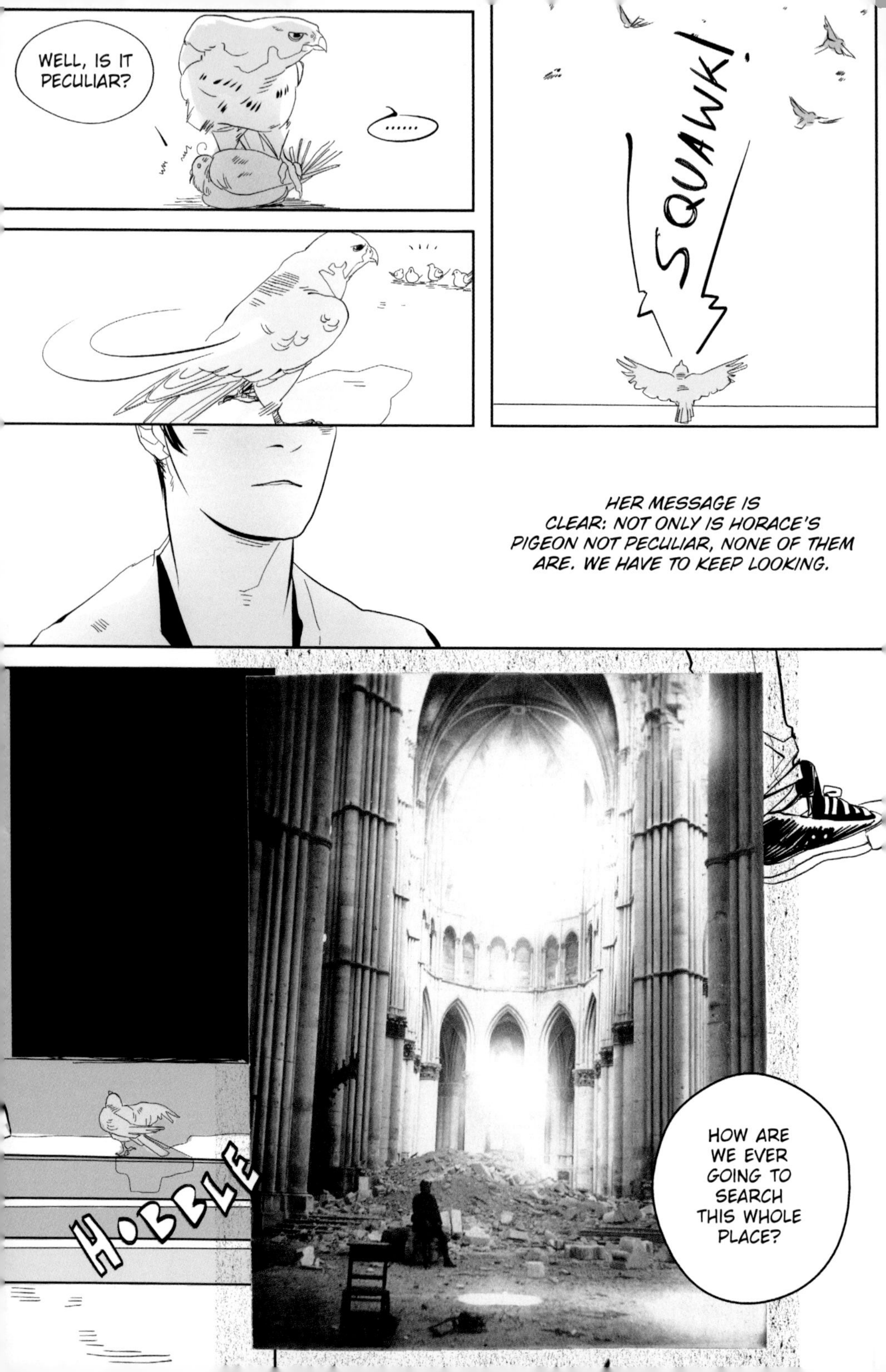
WELL, IS IT PECULIAR?
......
SQUAWK!
HER MESSAGE IS CLEAR: NOT ONLY IS HORACE'S PIGEON NOT PECULIAR, NONE OF THEM ARE. WE HAVE TO KEEP LOOKING.
HOBBLE
HOW ARE WE EVER GOING TO SEARCH THIS WHOLE PLACE?

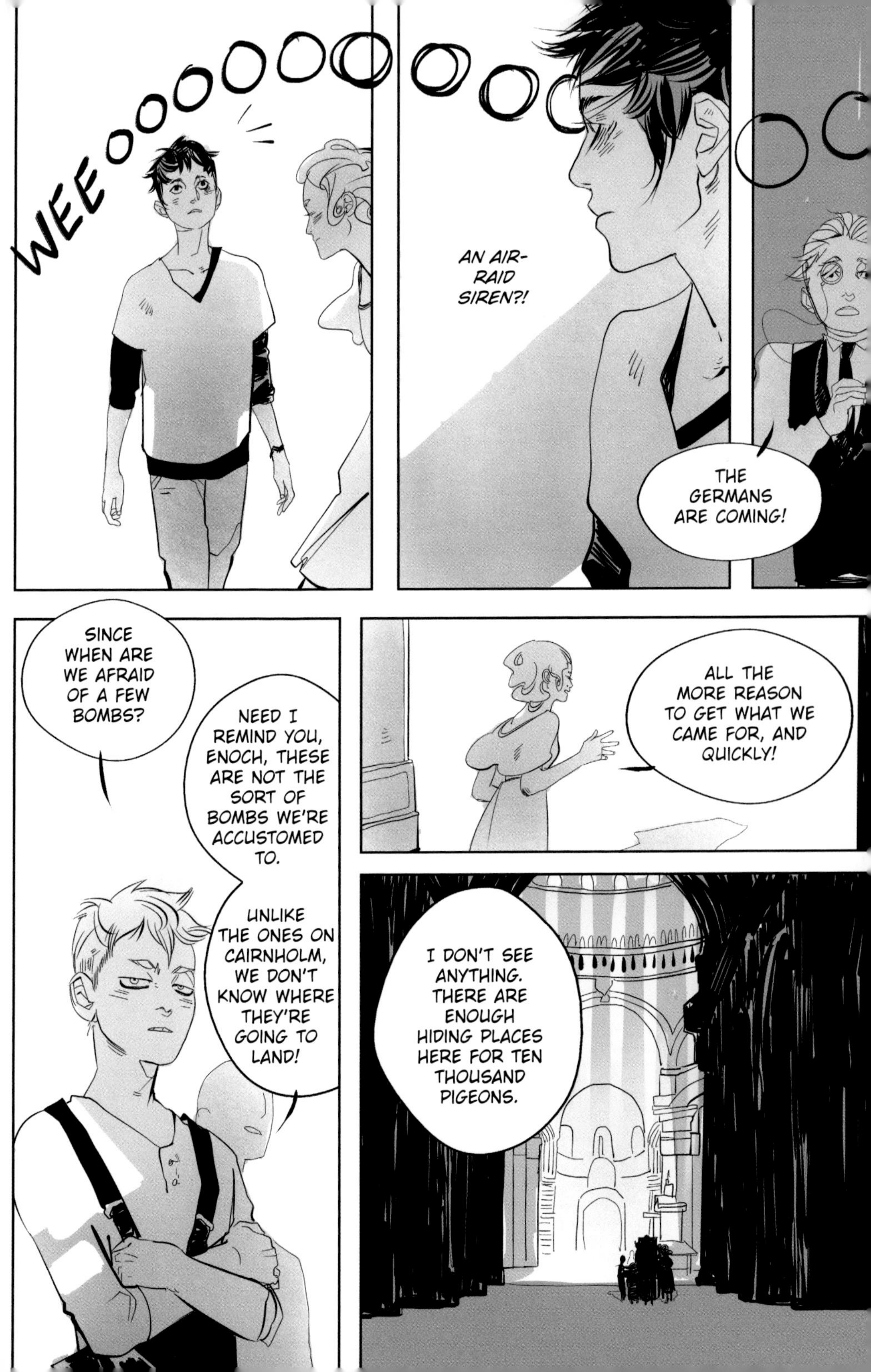
WEEOOOOOOOOOOOOO
AN AIR-RAID SIREN?!
THE GERMANS ARE COMING!
SINCE WHEN ARE WE AFRAID OF A FEW BOMBS?
NEED I REMIND YOU, ENOCH, THESE ARE NOT THE SORT OF BOMBS WE'RE ACCUSTOMED TO.
UNLIKE THE ONES ON CAIRNHOLM, WE DON'T KNOW WHERE THEY'RE GOING TO LAND!
ALL THE MORE REASON TO GET WHAT WE CAME FOR, AND QUICKLY!
I DON'T SEE ANYTHING. THERE ARE ENOUGH HIDING PLACES HERE FOR TEN THOUSAND PIGEONS.

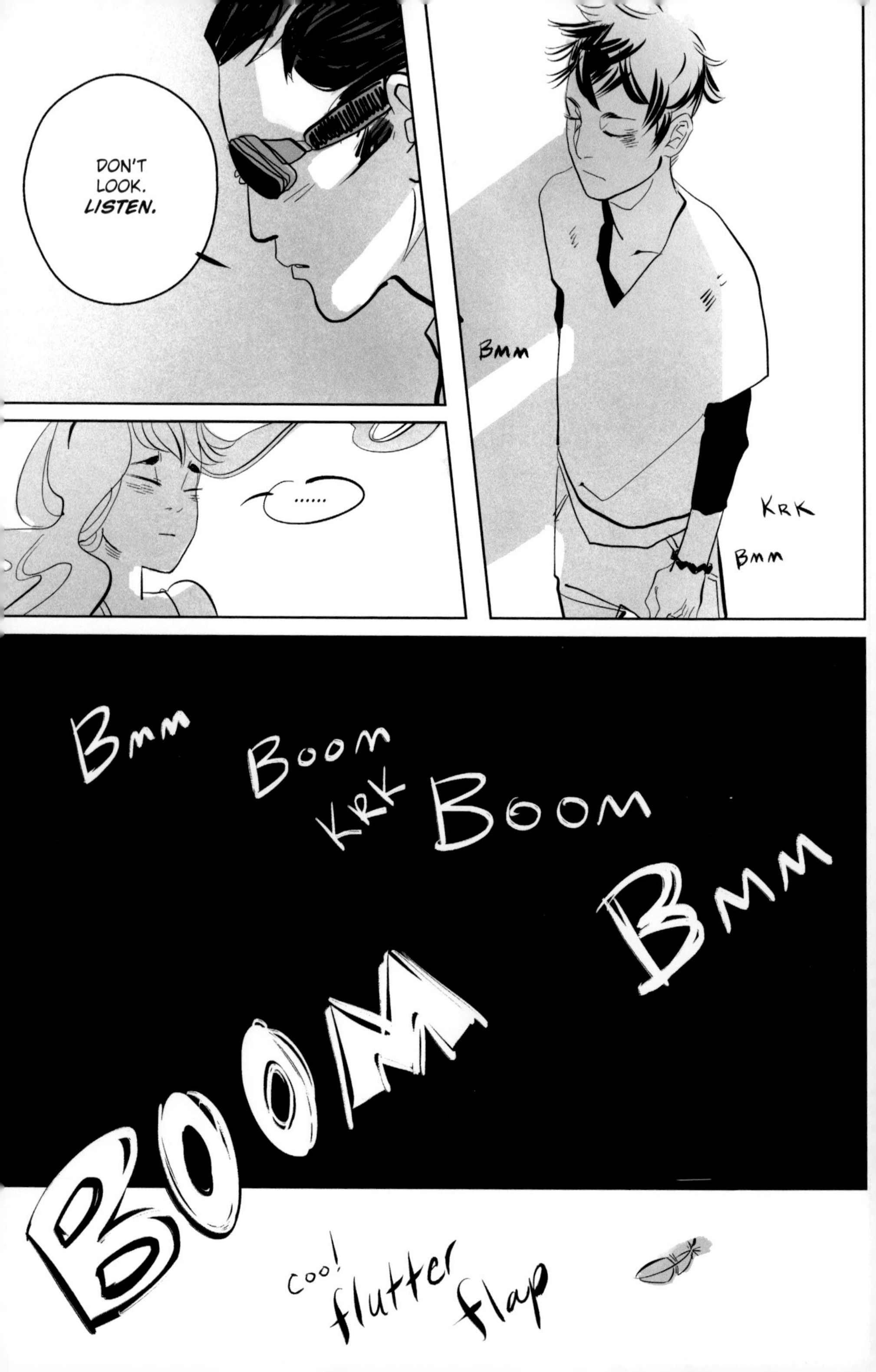
DON'T LOOK. LISTEN.
......
Bmm
Krk
Bmm
Bmm
Boom
Krk
Boom
Bmm
BOOM
coo!
flutter
flap

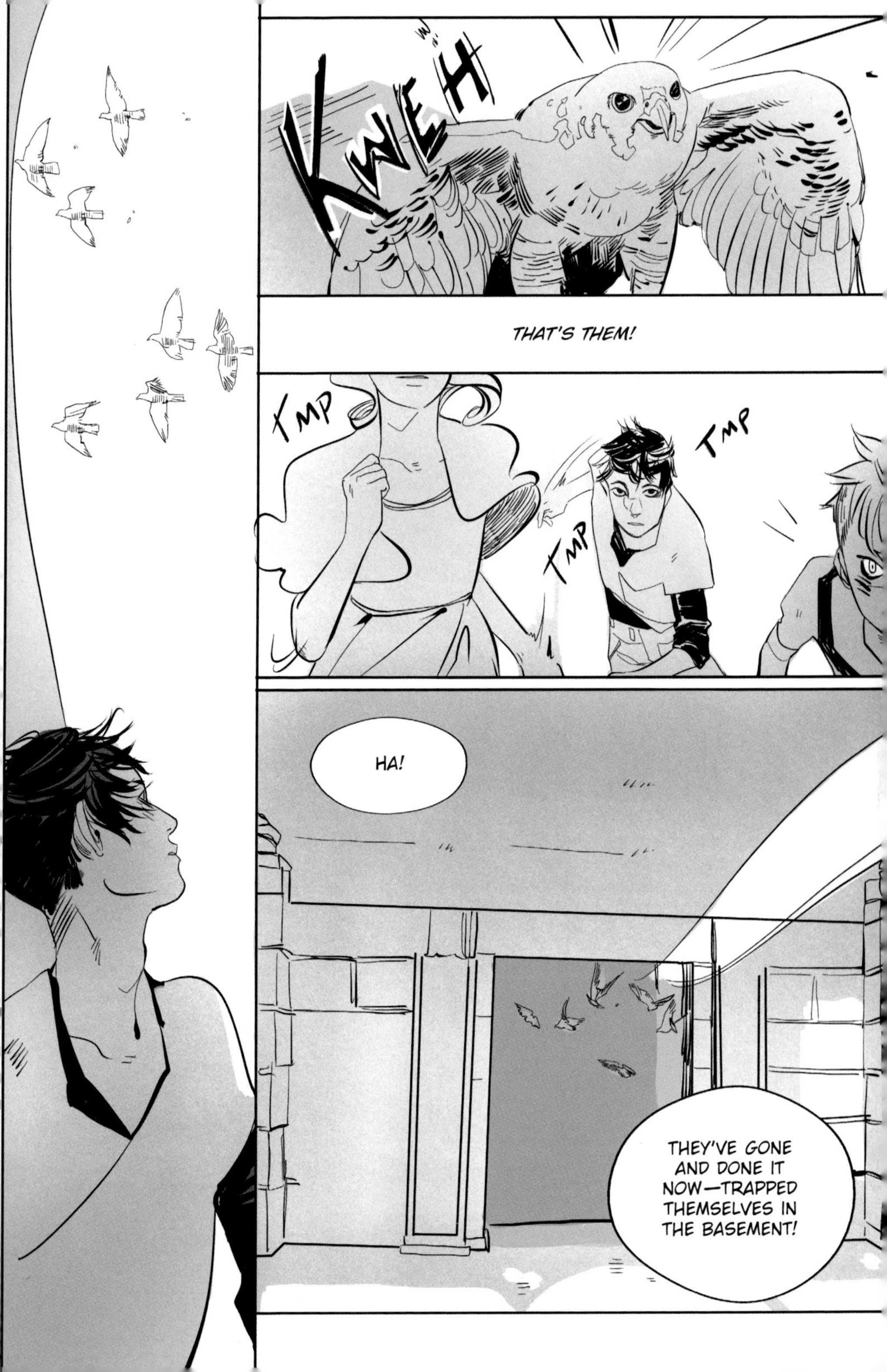
KWEH
THAT'S THEM!
TMP
TMP
TMP
HA!
THEY'VE GONE AND DONE IT NOW—TRAPPED THEMSELVES IN THE BASEMENT!

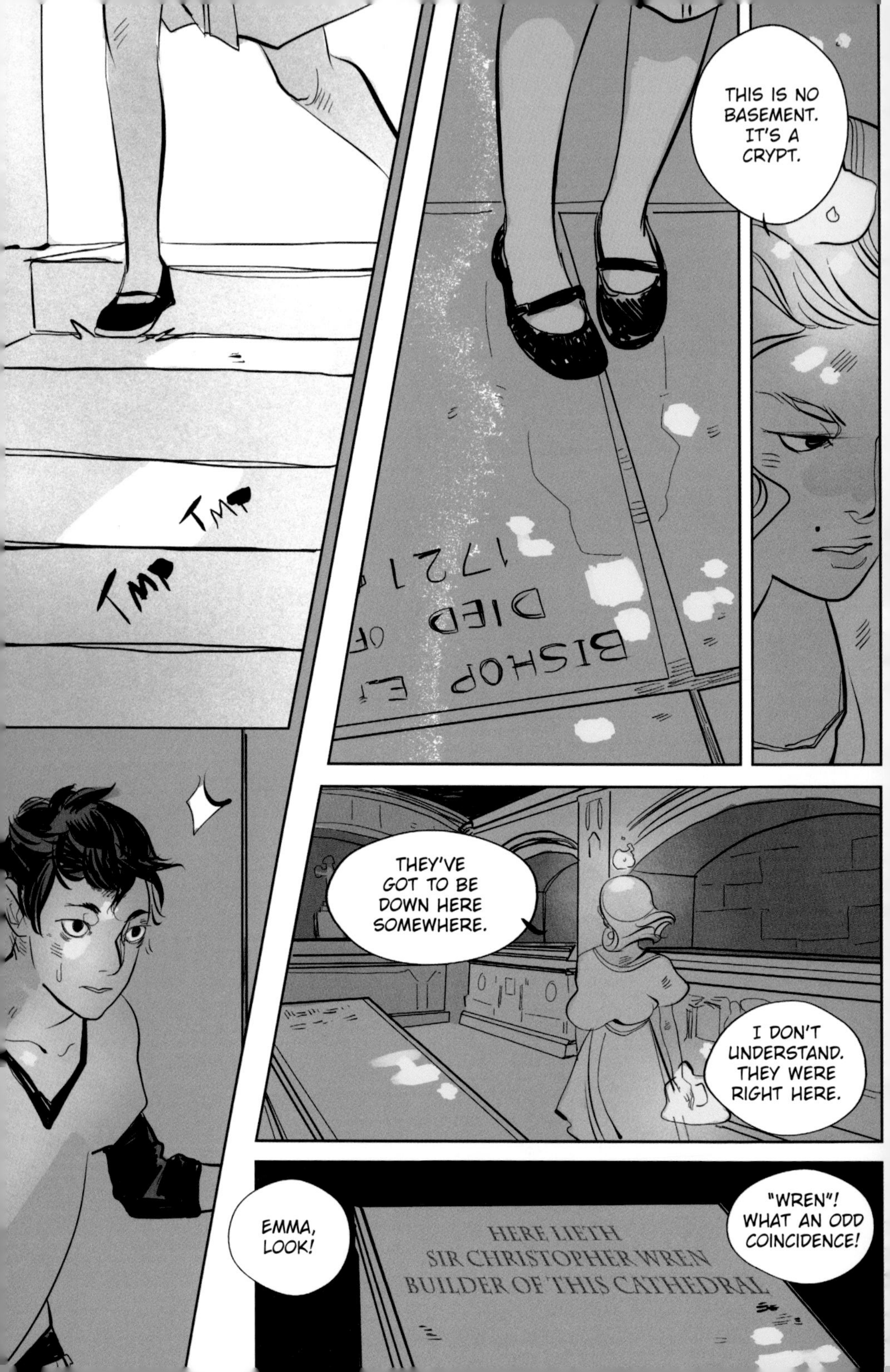
TMP
TMP
BISHOP
DIED
1721
THIS IS NO BASEMENT. IT'S A CRYPT.
THEY'VE GOT TO BE DOWN HERE SOMEWHERE.
I DON'T UNDERSTAND. THEY WERE RIGHT HERE.
EMMA, LOOK!
HERE LIETH
SIR CHRISTOPHER WREN
BUILDER OF THIS CATHEDRAL
"WREN"! WHAT AN ODD COINCIDENCE!

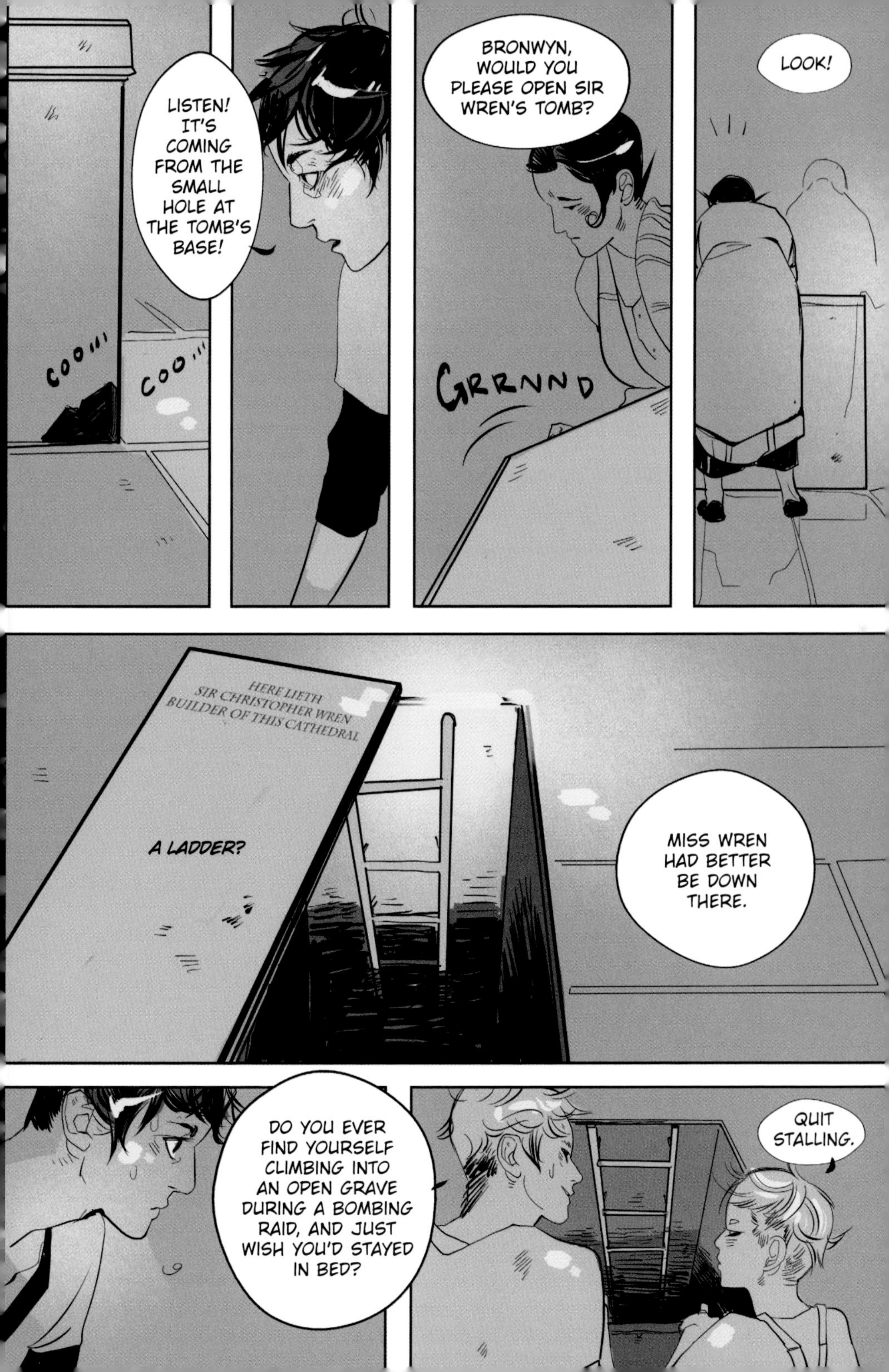
LISTEN! IT'S COMING FROM THE SMALL HOLE AT THE TOMB'S BASE!
COO
COO
BRONWYN, WOULD YOU PLEASE OPEN SIR WREN'S TOMB?
GRRNND
LOOK!
HERE LIETH SIR CHRISTOPHER WREN BUILDER OF THIS CATHEDRAL
A LADDER?
MISS WREN HAD BETTER BE DOWN THERE.
DO YOU EVER FIND YOURSELF CLIMBING INTO AN OPEN GRAVE DURING A BOMBING RAID, AND JUST WISH YOU'D STAYED IN BED?
QUIT STALLING.

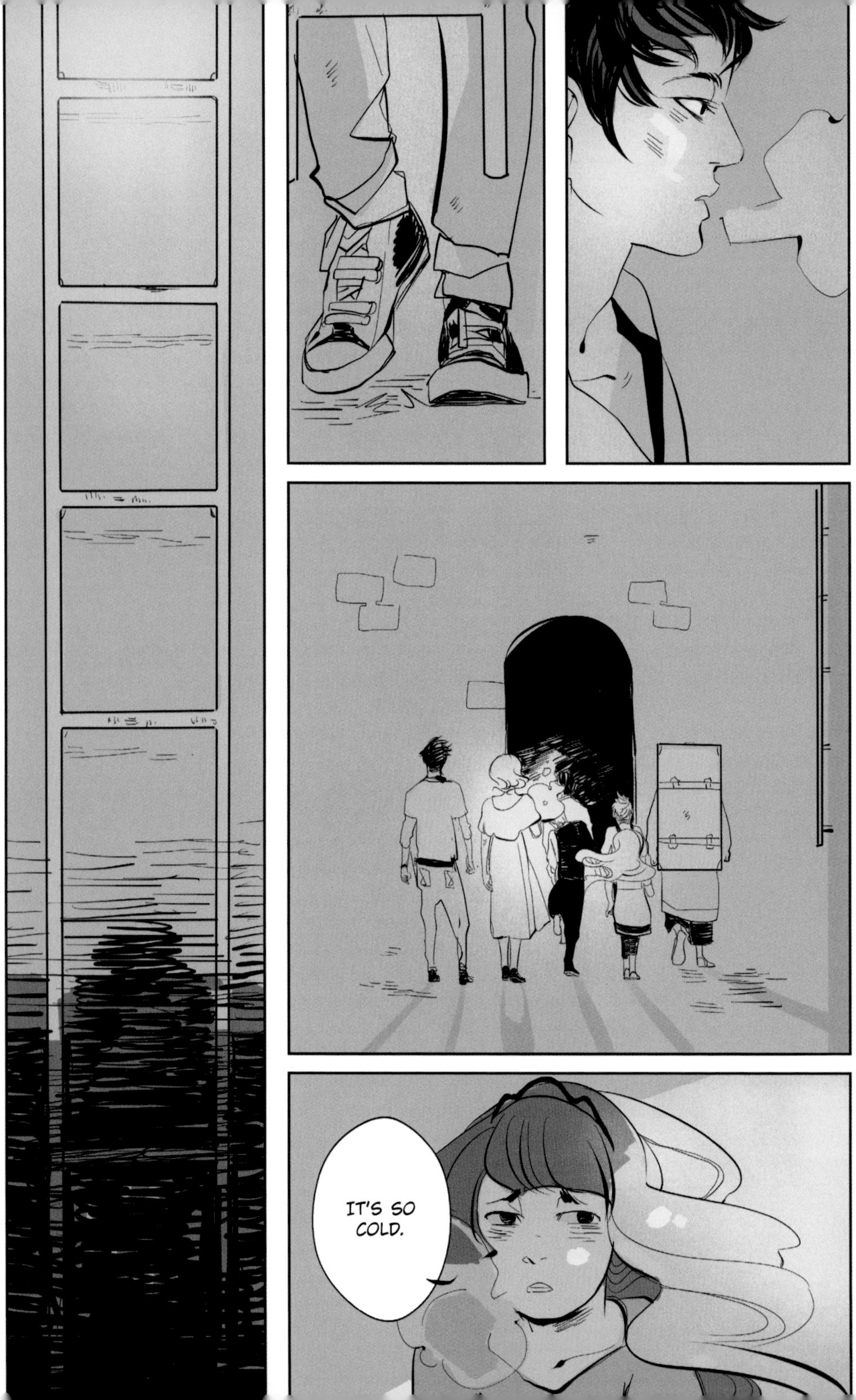
IT'S SO COLD.

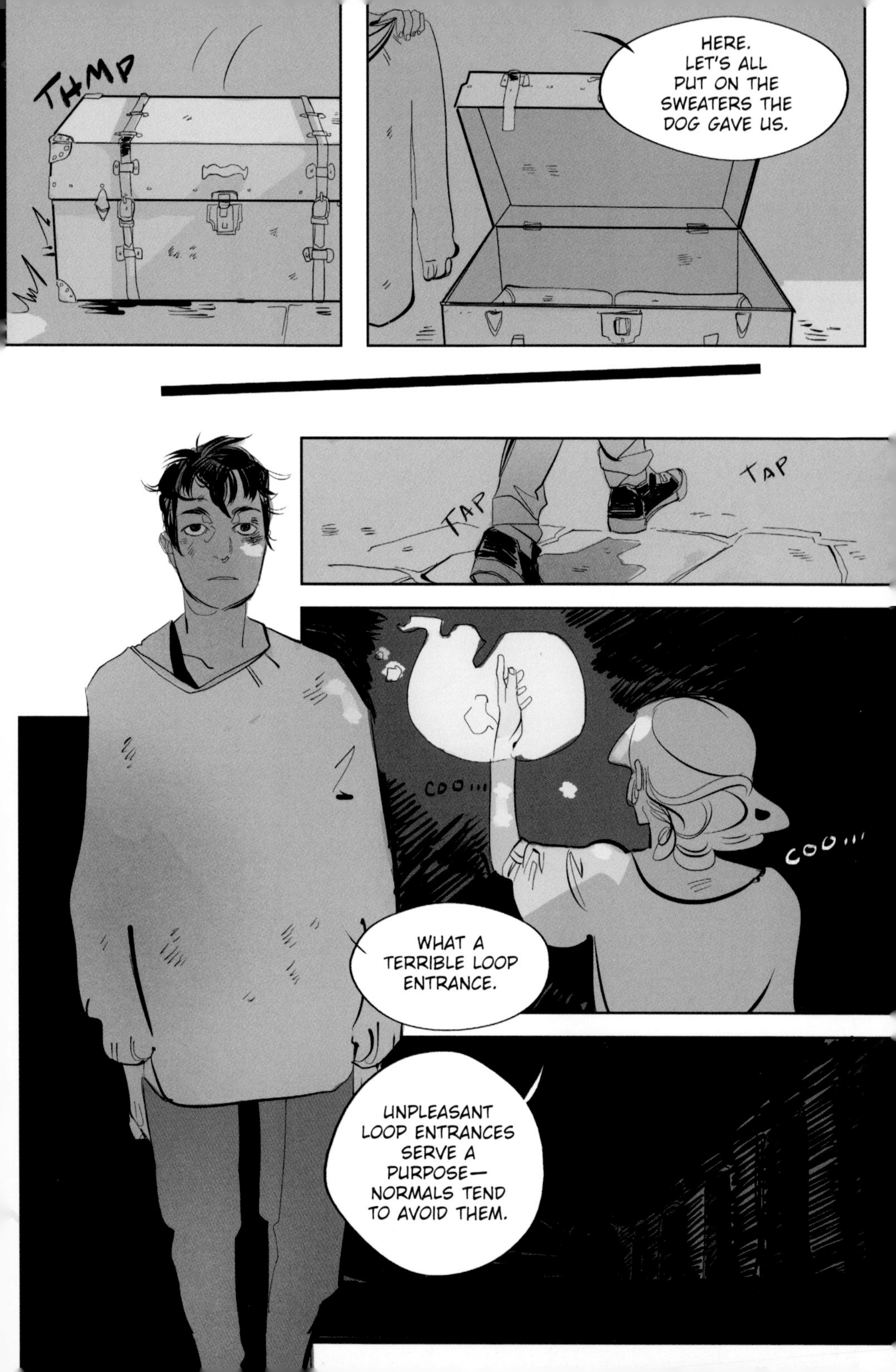
THMP
HERE. LET'S ALL PUT ON THE SWEATERS THE DOG GAVE US.
TAP
TAP
COO!!!
COO!!!
WHAT A TERRIBLE LOOP ENTRANCE.
UNPLEASANT LOOP ENTRANCES SERVE A PURPOSE— NORMALS TEND TO AVOID THEM.

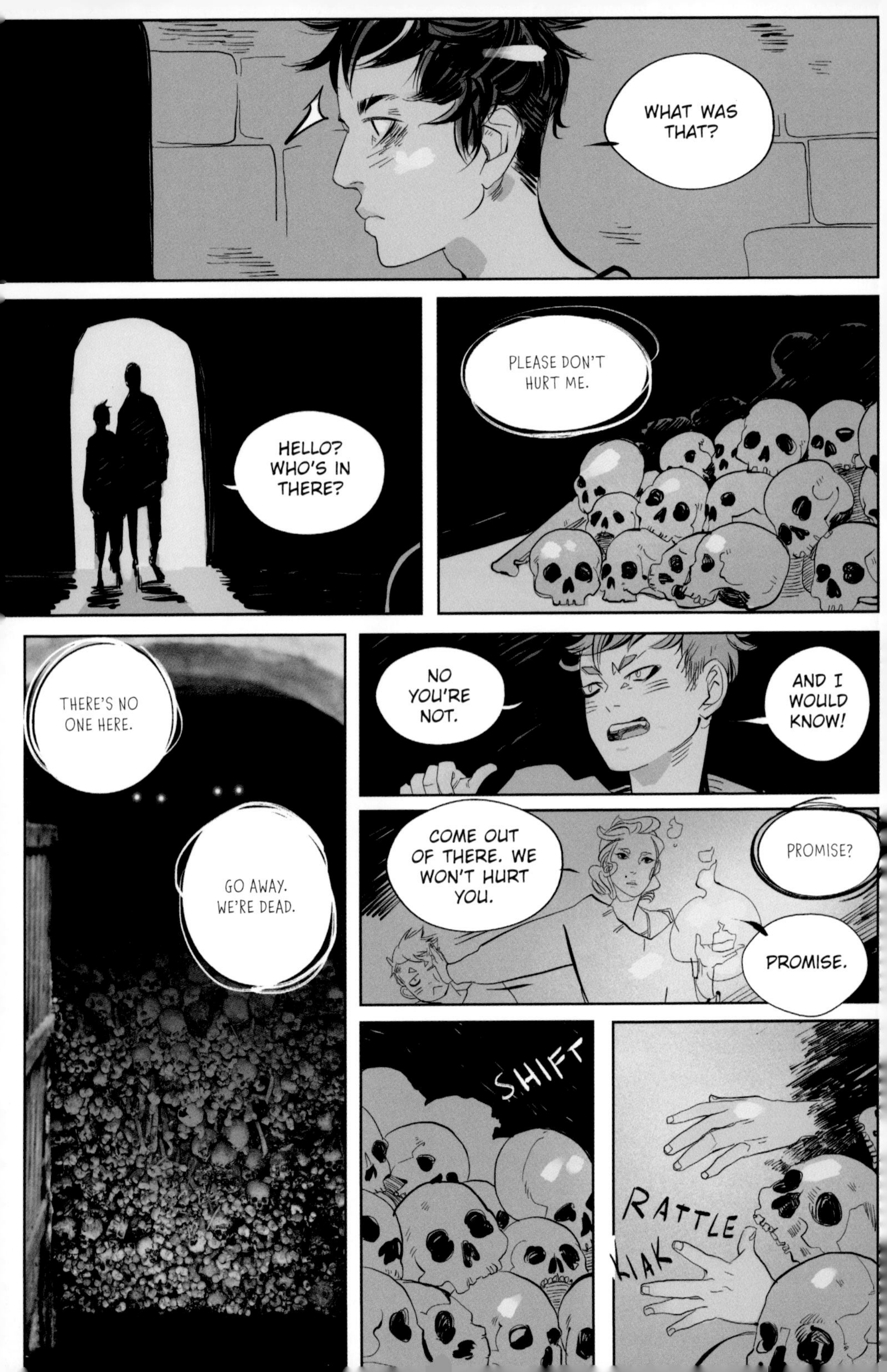
WHAT WAS THAT?
HELLO? WHO'S IN THERE?
PLEASE DON'T HURT ME.
THERE'S NO ONE HERE.
GO AWAY. WE'RE DEAD.
NO YOU'RE NOT.
AND I WOULD KNOW!
COME OUT OF THERE. WE WON'T HURT YOU.
PROMISE?
PROMISE.
SHIFT
RATTLE
KLAK

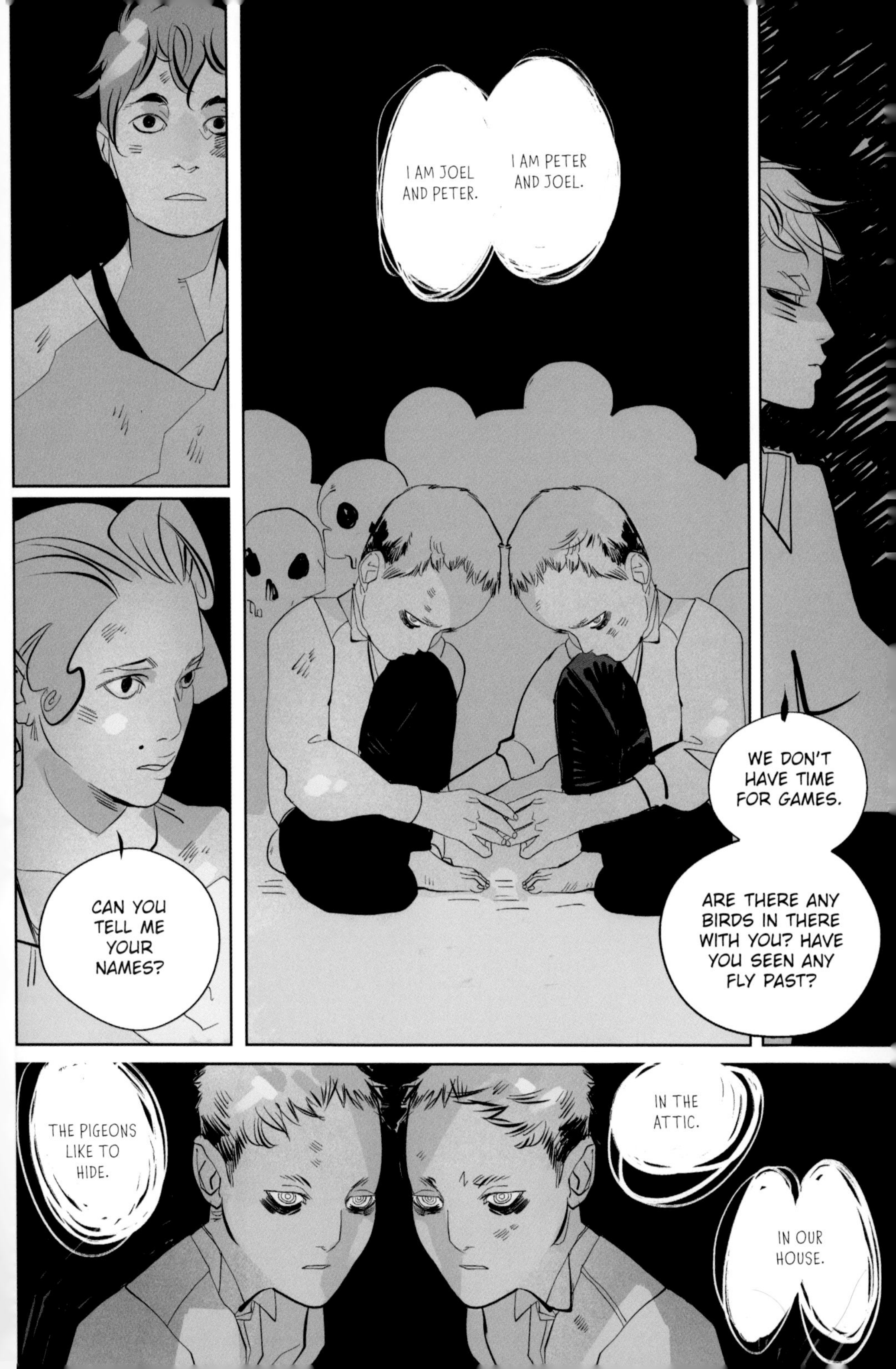
CAN YOU TELL ME YOUR NAMES?
I AM JOEL AND PETER.
I AM PETER AND JOEL.
WE DON'T HAVE TIME FOR GAMES.
ARE THERE ANY BIRDS IN THERE WITH YOU? HAVE YOU SEEN ANY FLY PAST?
THE PIGEONS LIKE TO HIDE.
IN THE ATTIC.
IN OUR HOUSE.

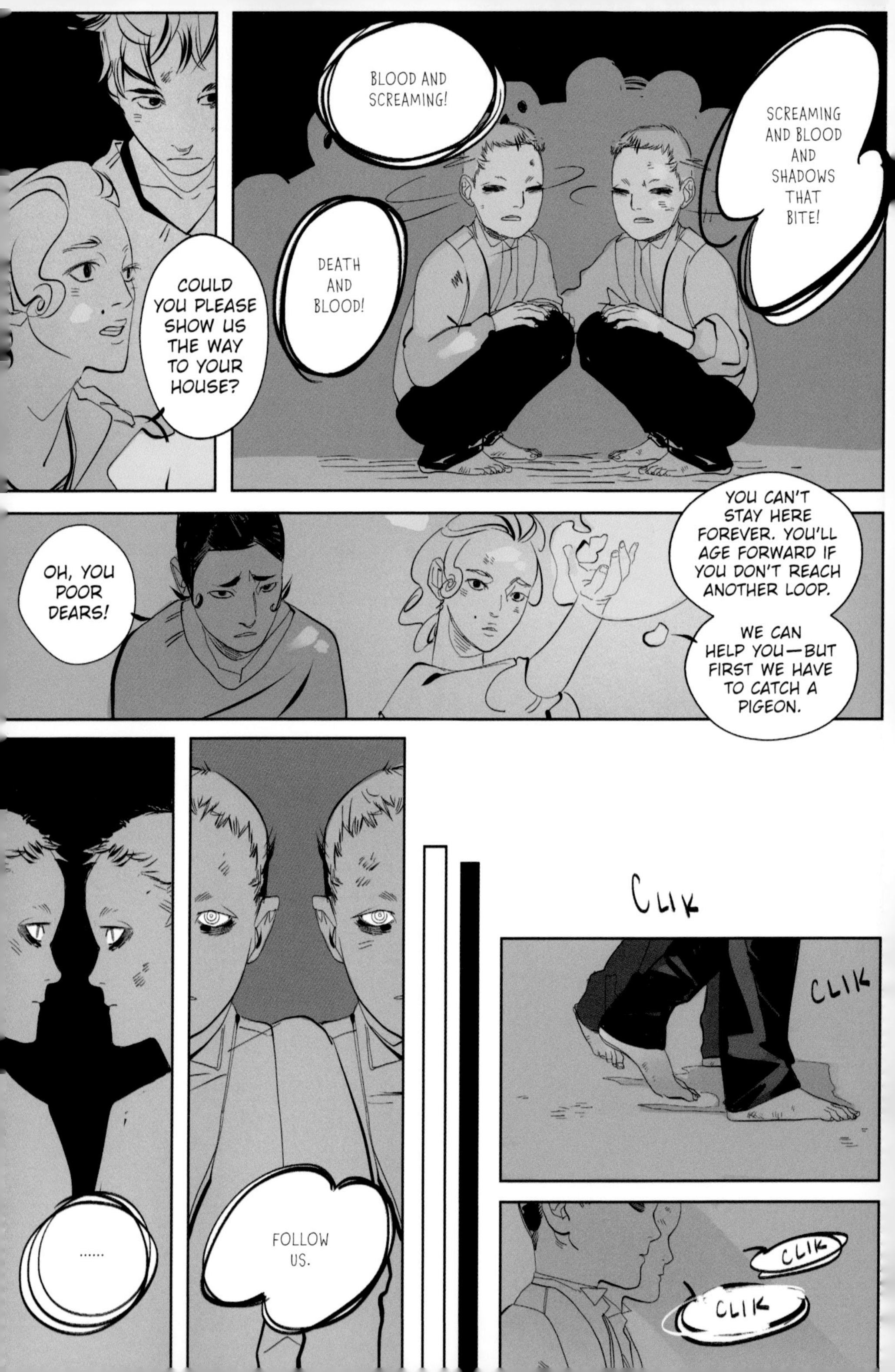
COULD YOU PLEASE SHOW US THE WAY TO YOUR HOUSE?
BLOOD AND SCREAMING!
DEATH AND BLOOD!
SCREAMING AND BLOOD AND SHADOWS THAT BITE!
OH, YOU POOR DEARS!
YOU CAN'T STAY HERE FOREVER. YOU'LL AGE FORWARD IF YOU DON'T REACH ANOTHER LOOP.
WE CAN HELP YOU—BUT FIRST WE HAVE TO CATCH A PIGEON.
......
FOLLOW US.
CLIK
CLIK
CLIK
CLIK

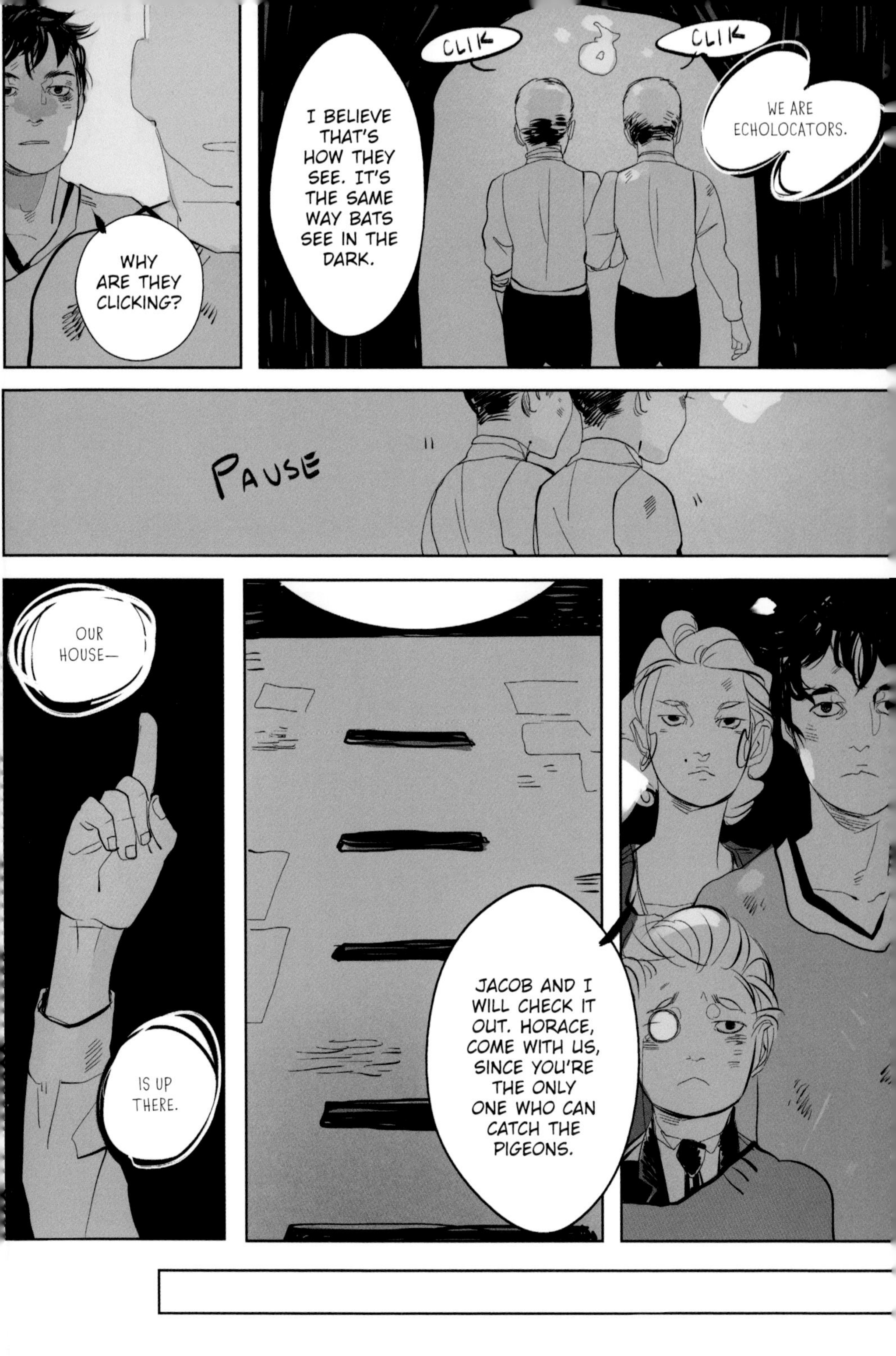
WHY ARE THEY CLICKING?
CLIK
I BELIEVE THAT'S HOW THEY SEE. IT'S THE SAME WAY BATS SEE IN THE DARK.
CLIK
WE ARE ECHOLOCATORS.
PAUSE
OUR HOUSE—
IS UP THERE.
JACOB AND I WILL CHECK IT OUT. HORACE, COME WITH US, SINCE YOU'RE THE ONLY ONE WHO CAN CATCH THE PIGEONS.

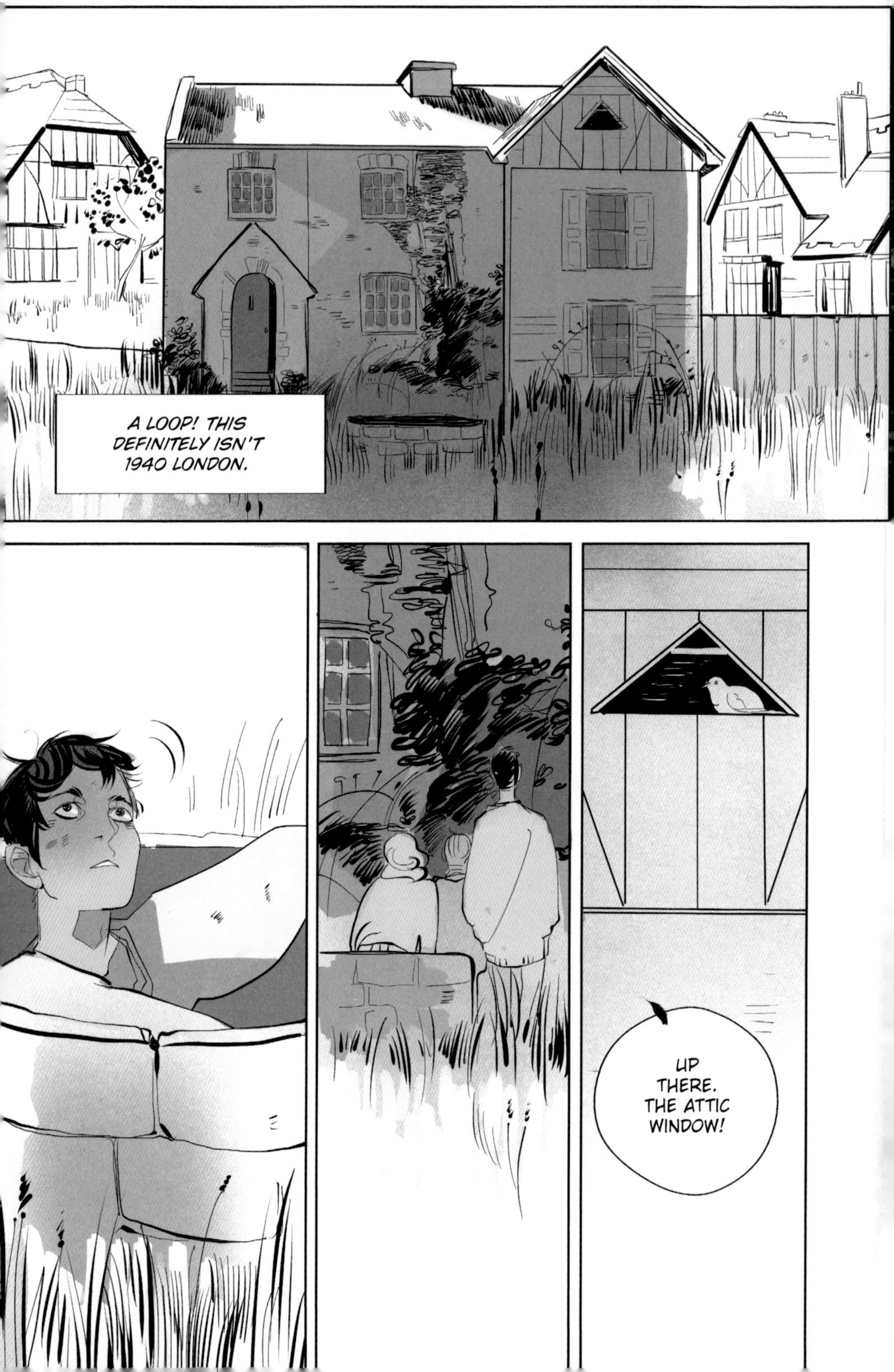
A LOOP! THIS DEFINITELY ISN'T 1940 LONDON.
UP THERE. THE ATTIC WINDOW!

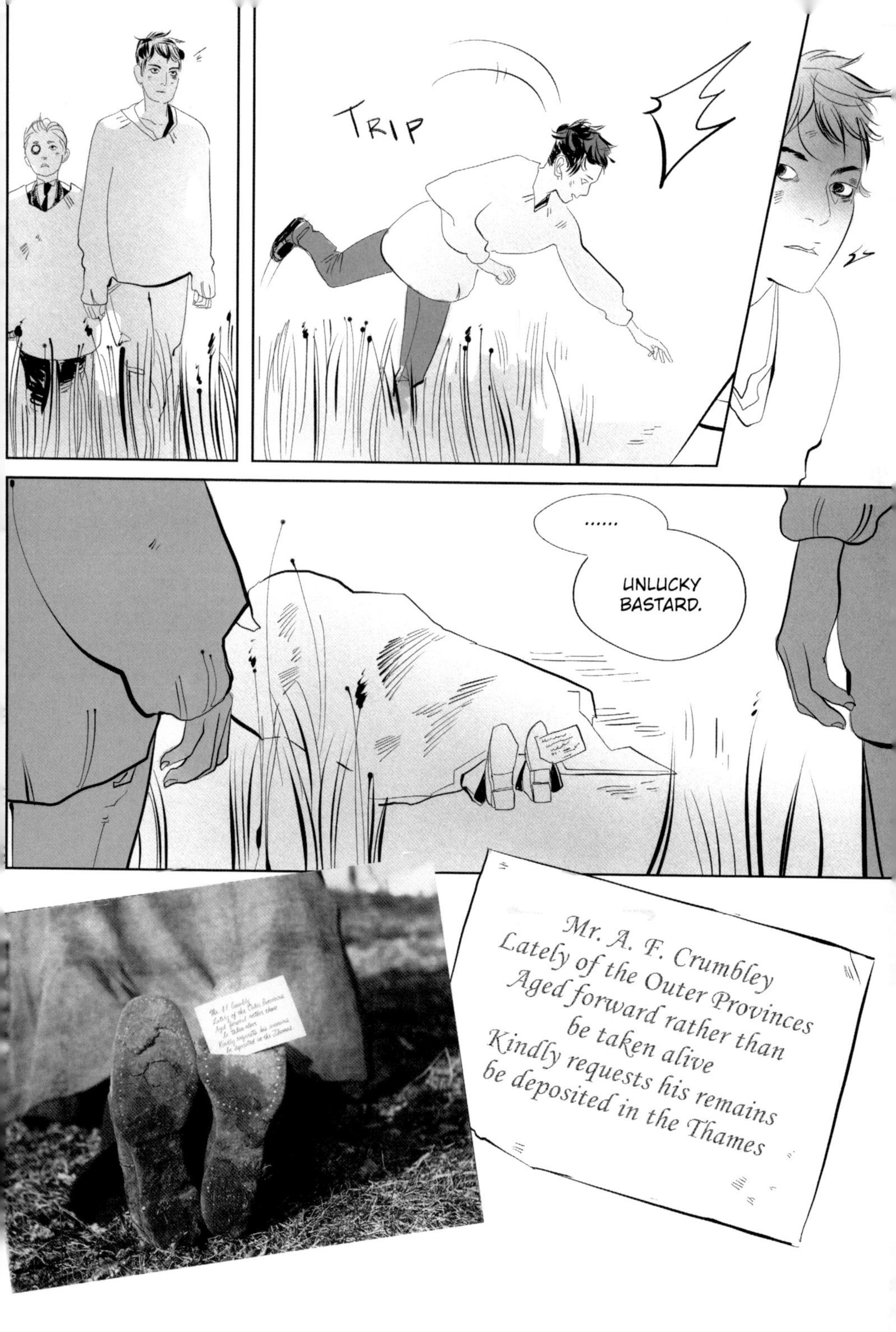
TRIP
......
UNLUCKY BASTARD.
Mr. A. F. Crumbley
Lately of the Outer Provinces
Aged forward rather than
be taken alive
Kindly requests his remains
be deposited in the Thames

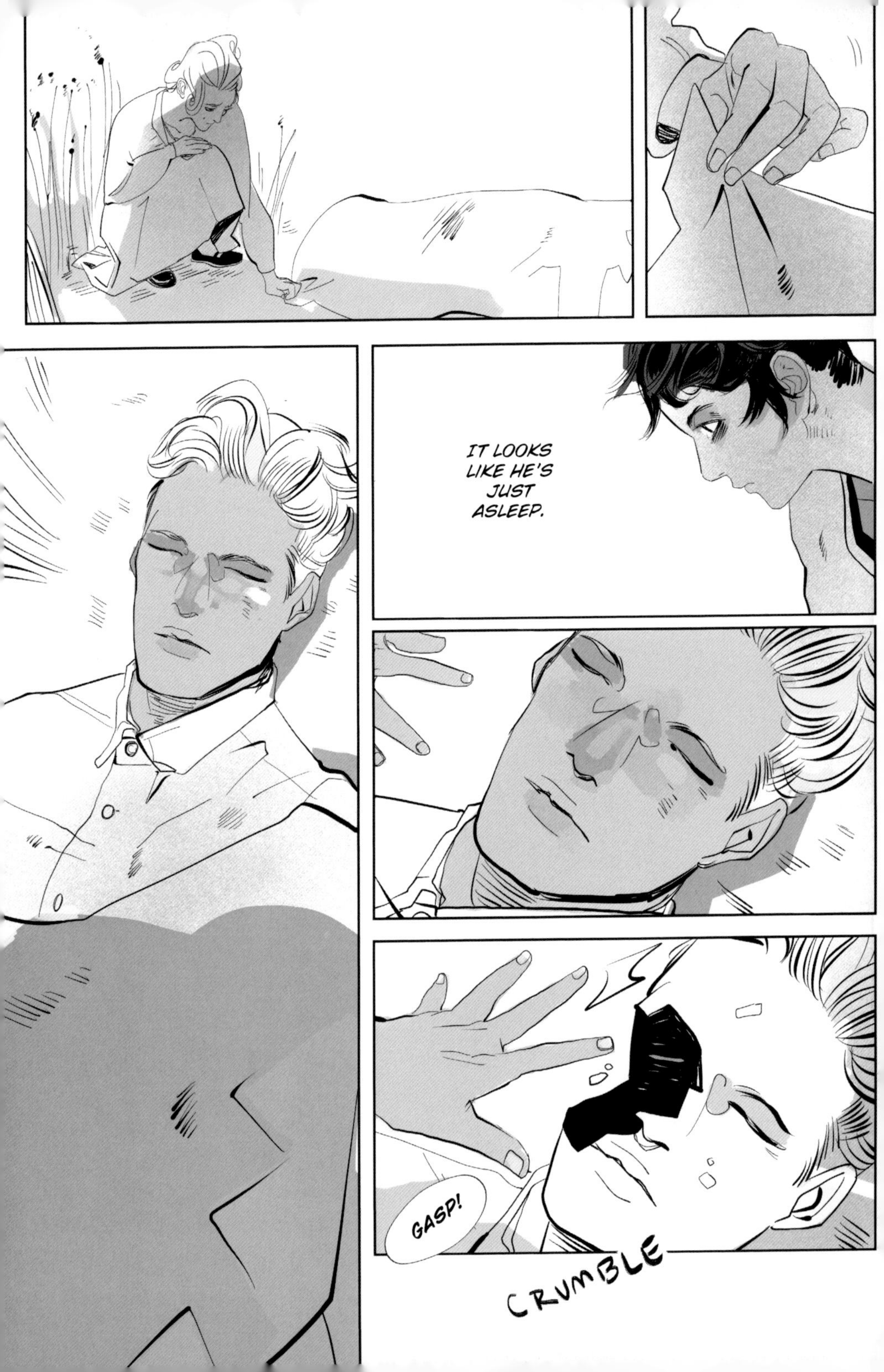
IT LOOKS LIKE HE'S JUST ASLEEP.
GASP!
CRUMBLE

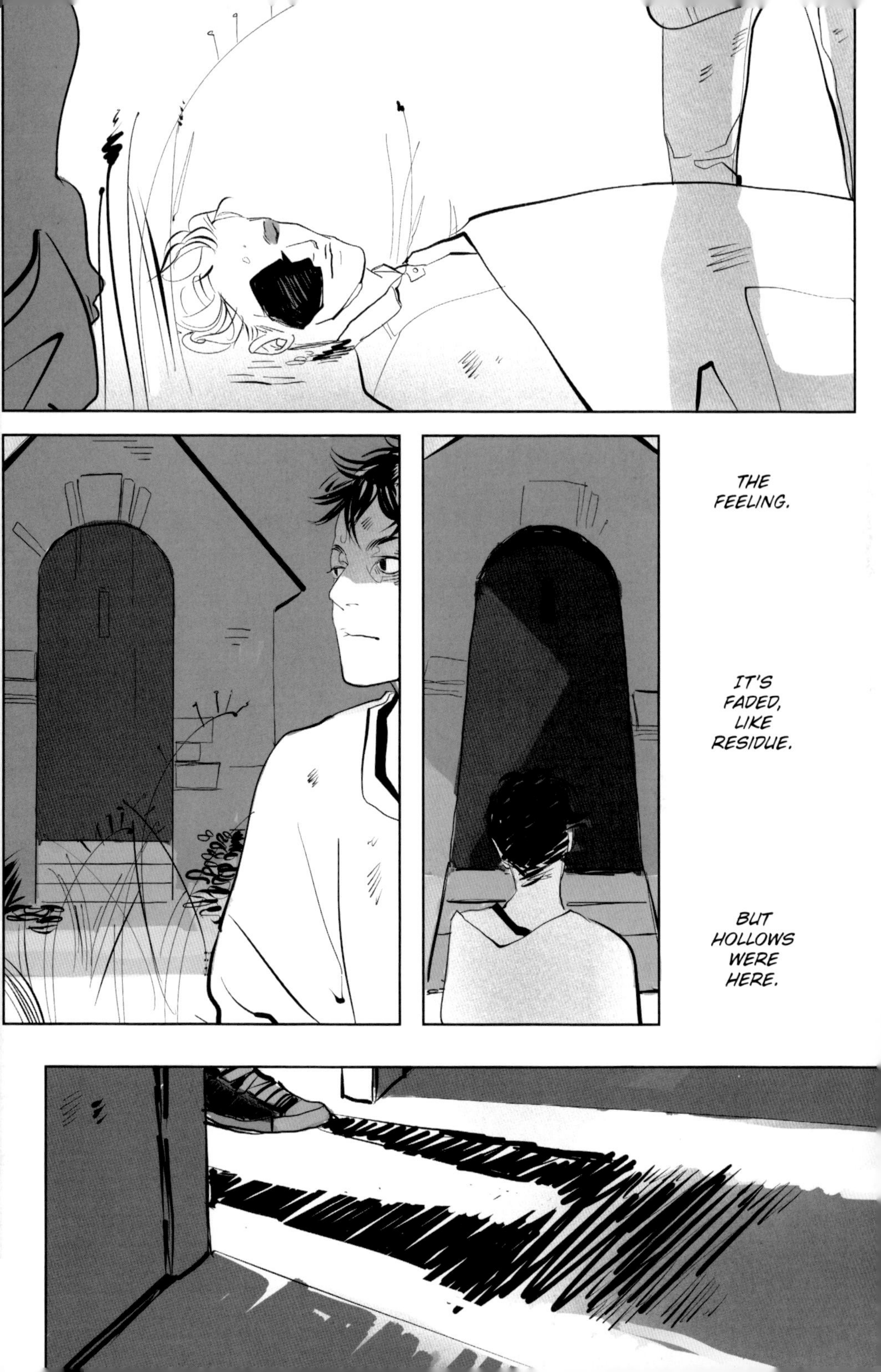
THE FEELING.
IT'S FADED, LIKE RESIDUE.
BUT HOLLOWS WERE HERE.

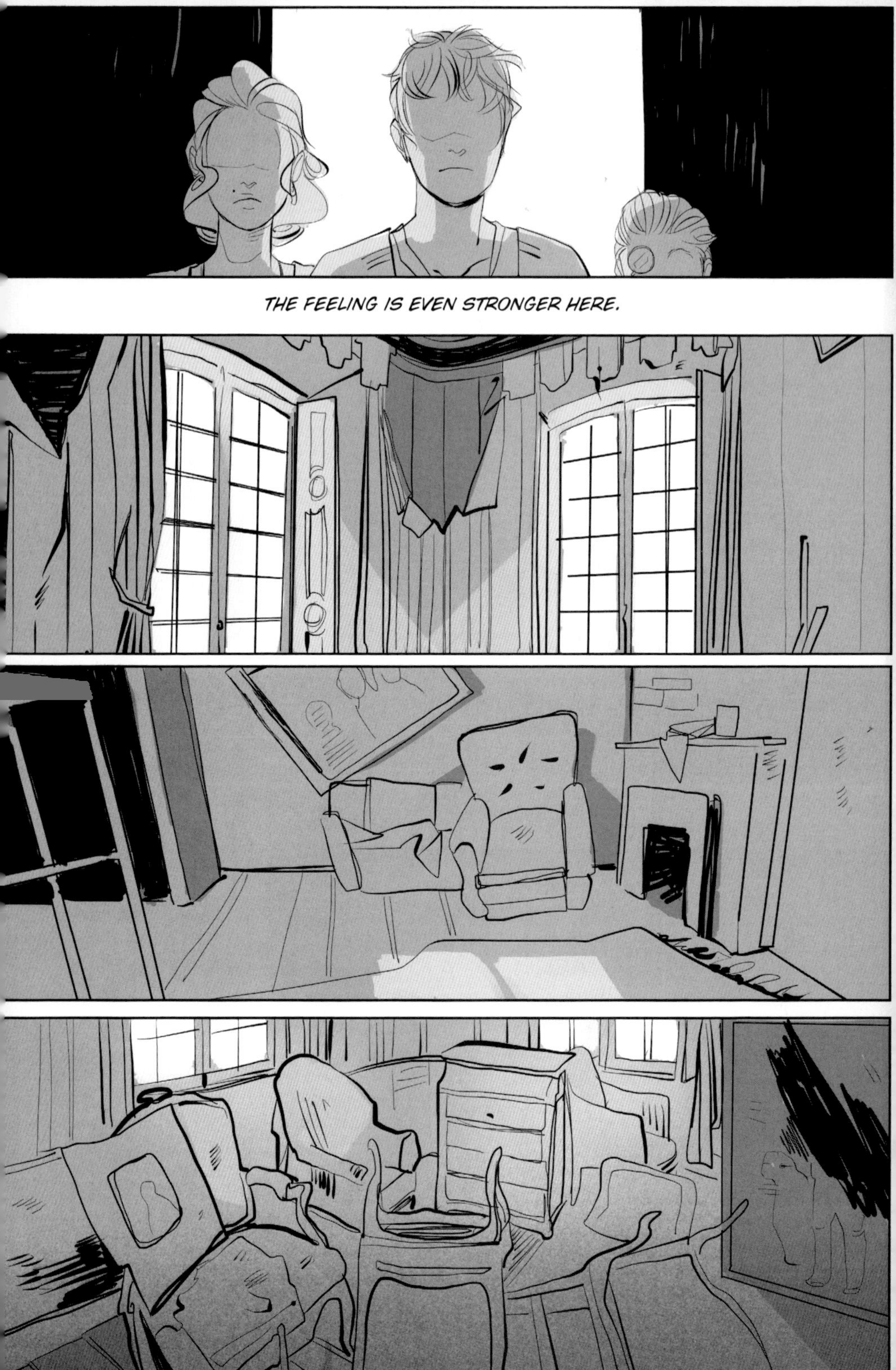
THE FEELING IS EVEN STRONGER HERE.

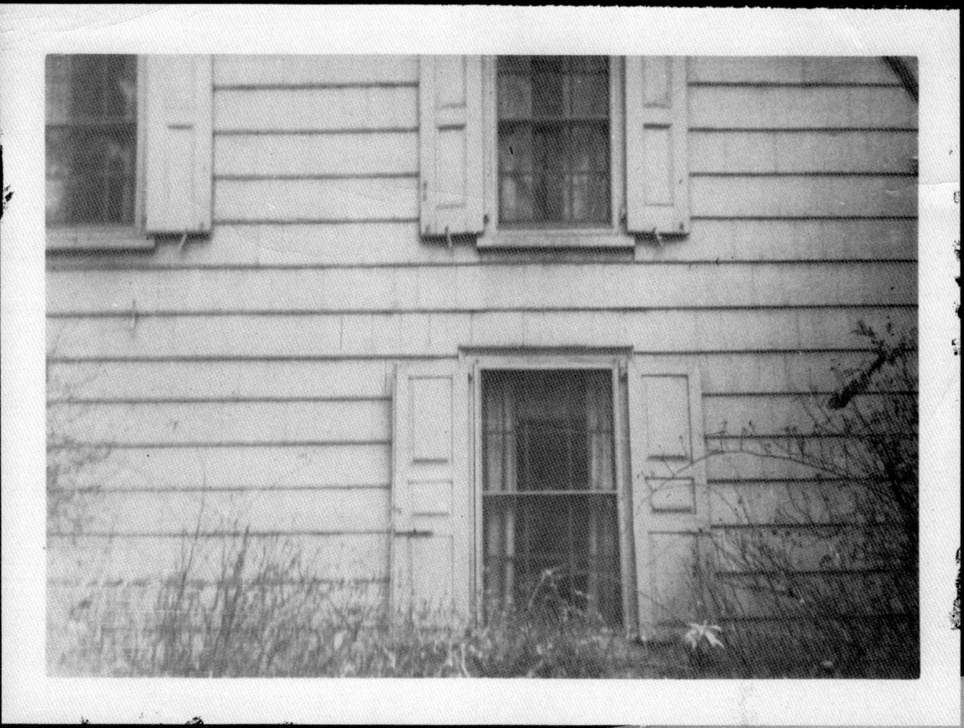

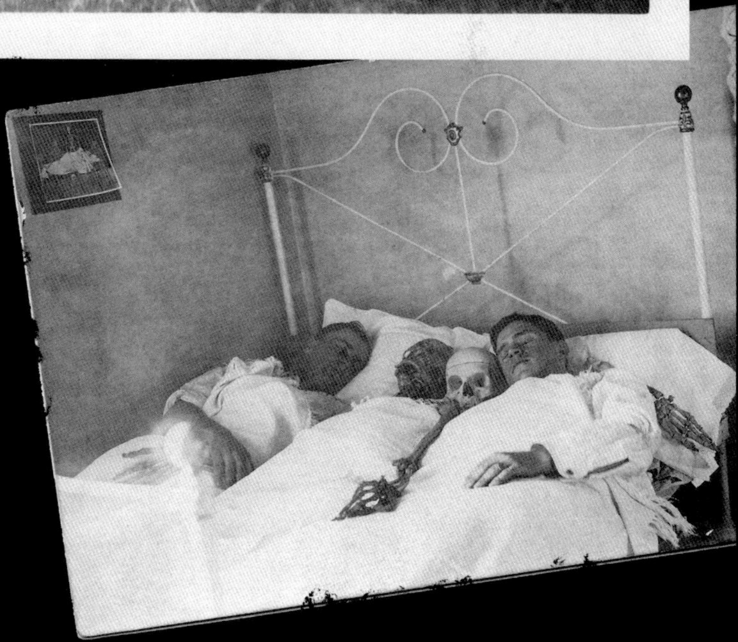

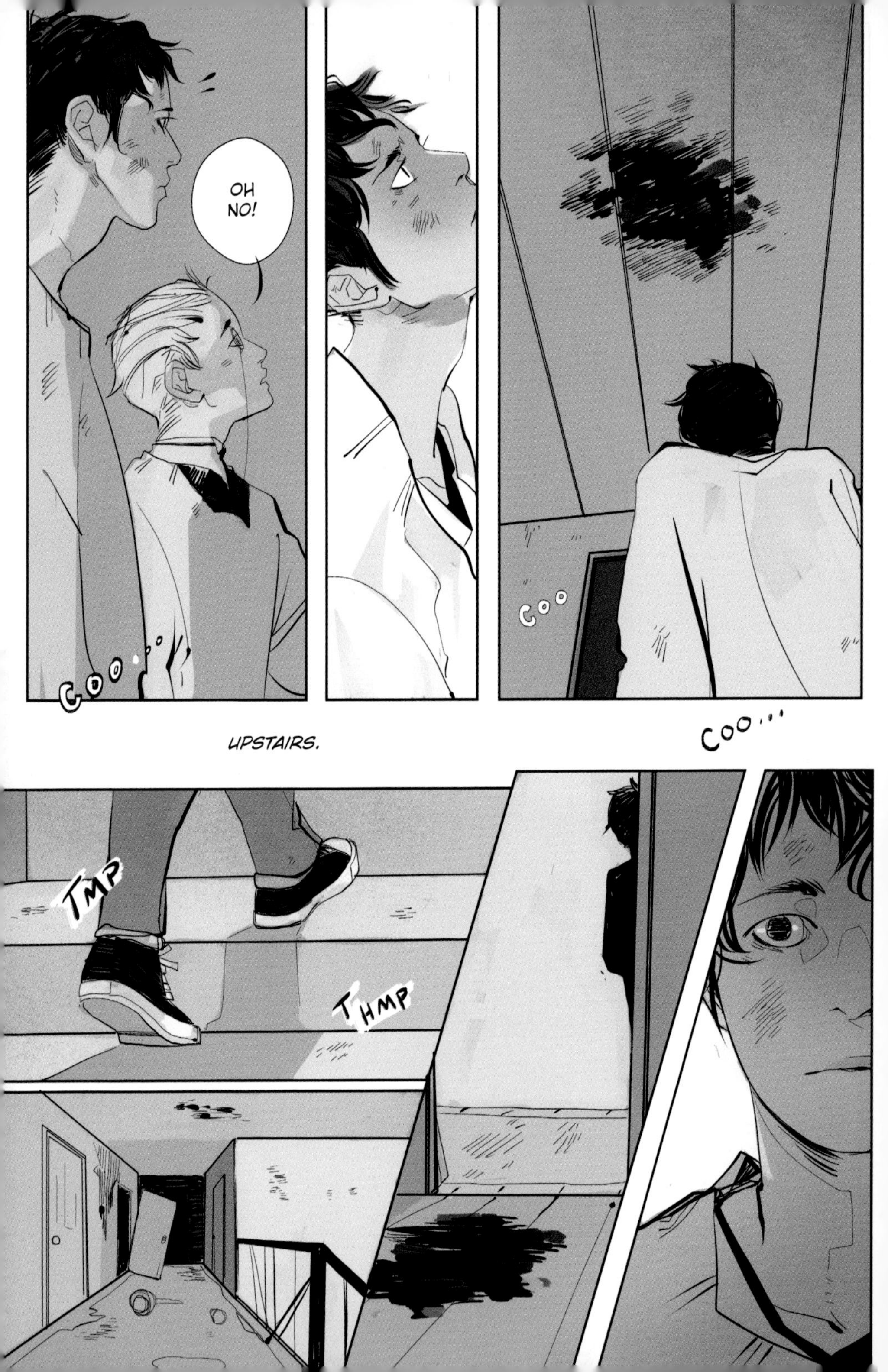
OH NO!
COO...
COO
UPSTAIRS.
COO...
TMP
THMP

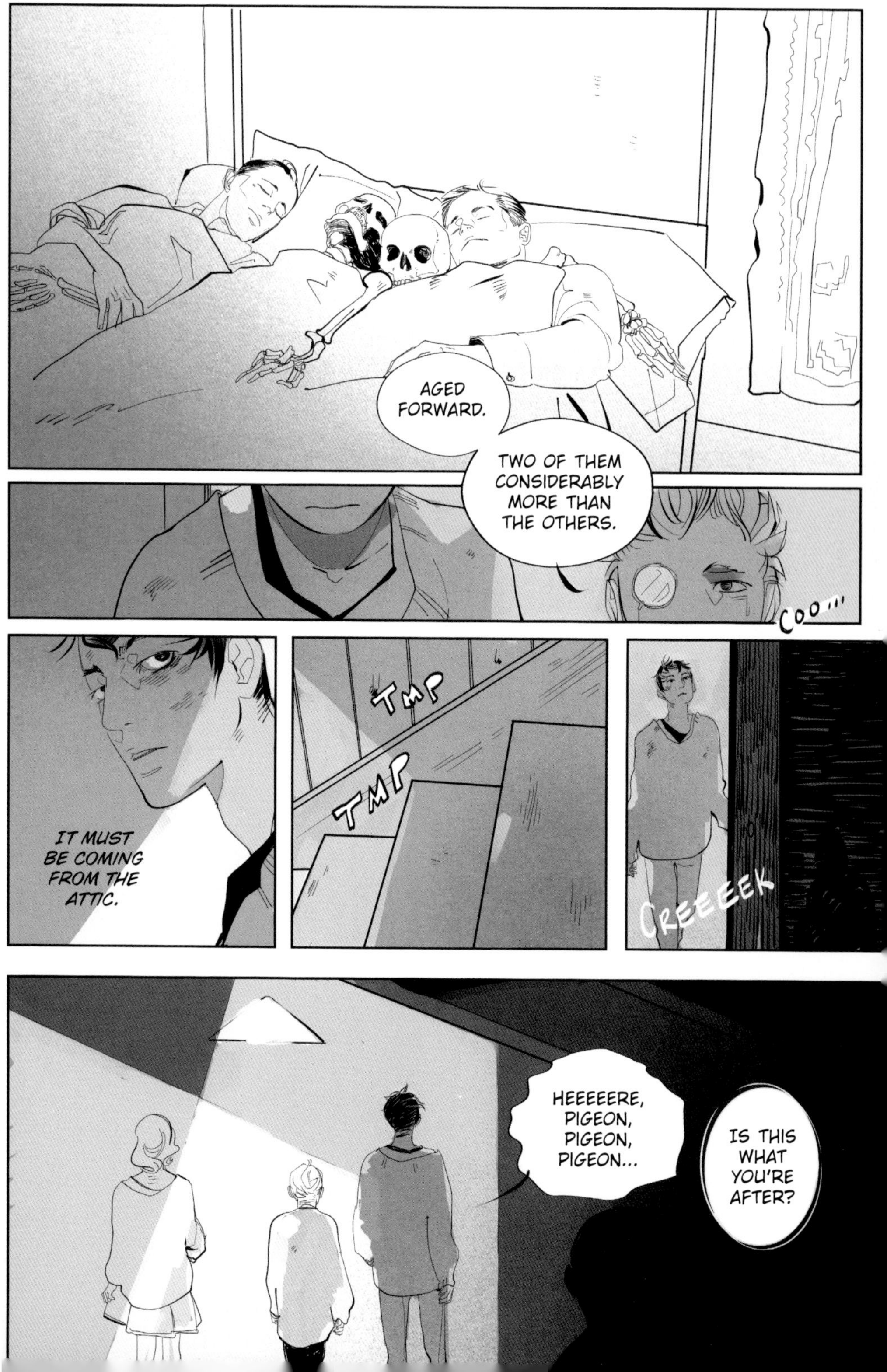
AGED FORWARD.
TWO OF THEM CONSIDERABLY MORE THAN THE OTHERS.
COO...
IT MUST BE COMING FROM THE ATTIC.
TMP
TMP
CREEEEK
HEEEEERE, PIGEON, PIGEON, PIGEON...
IS THIS WHAT YOU'RE AFTER?

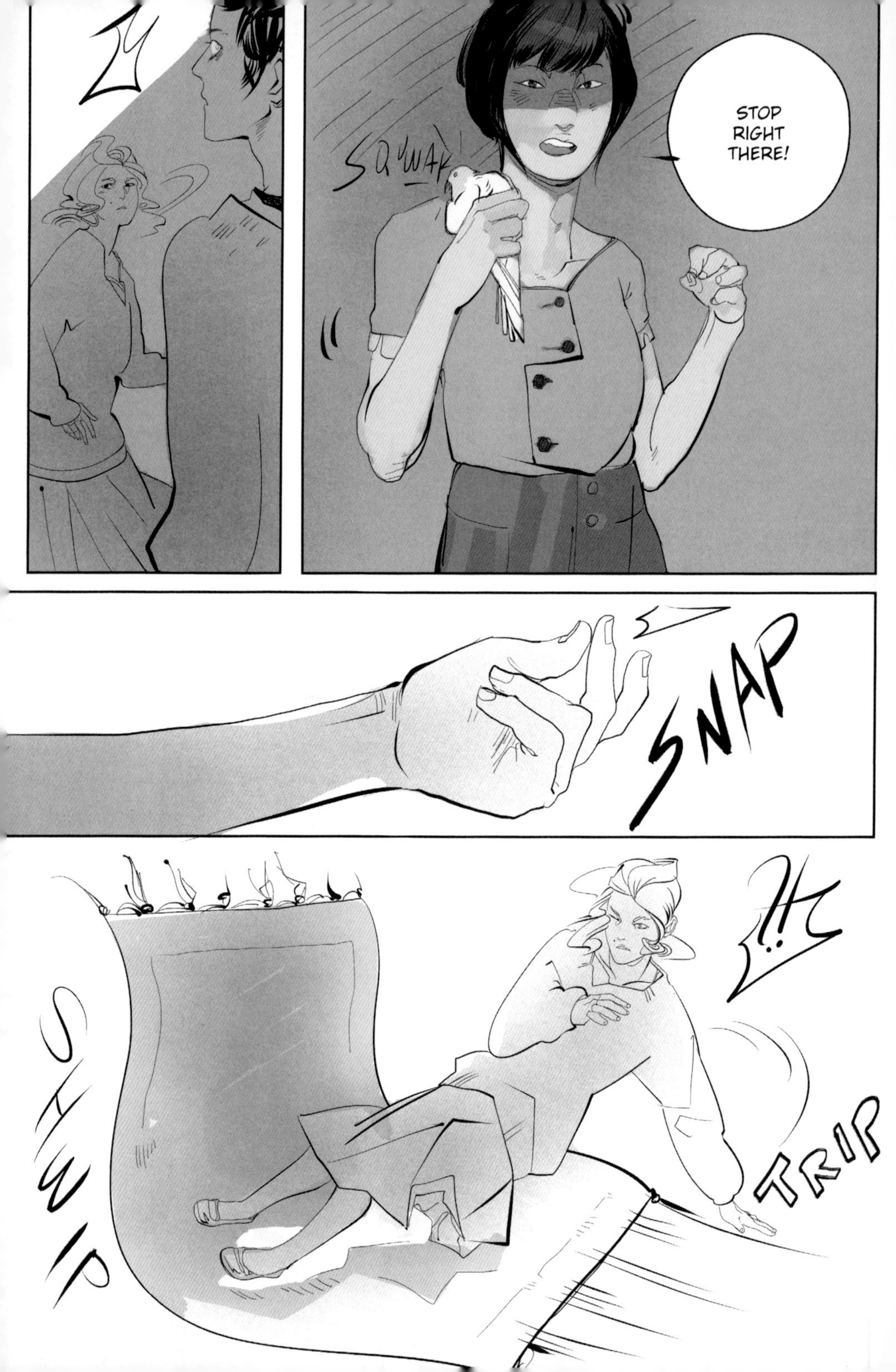
SQUWAK
STOP RIGHT THERE!
SNAP
!?!
SHWIP
TRIP

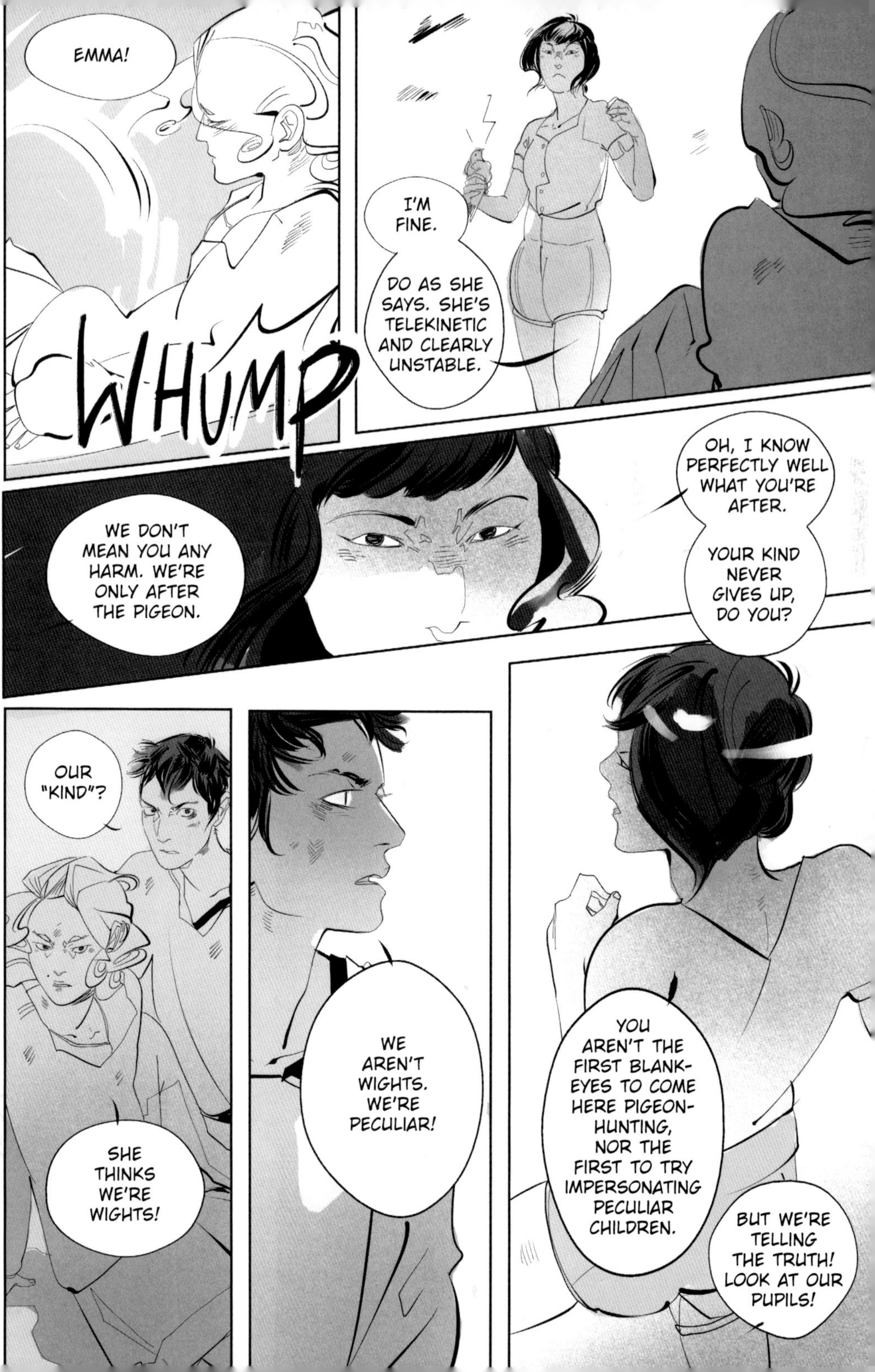
EMMA!
WHUMP
I'M FINE.
DO AS SHE SAYS. SHE'S TELEKINETIC AND CLEARLY UNSTABLE.
WE DON'T MEAN YOU ANY HARM. WE'RE ONLY AFTER THE PIGEON.
OH, I KNOW PERFECTLY WELL WHAT YOU'RE AFTER.
YOUR KIND NEVER GIVES UP, DO YOU?
OUR "KIND"?
SHE THINKS WE'RE WIGHTS!
WE AREN'T WIGHTS. WE'RE PECULIAR!
YOU AREN'T THE FIRST BLANK-EYES TO COME HERE PIGEON-HUNTING, NOR THE FIRST TO TRY IMPERSONATING PECULIAR CHILDREN.
BUT WE'RE TELLING THE TRUTH! LOOK AT OUR PUPILS!

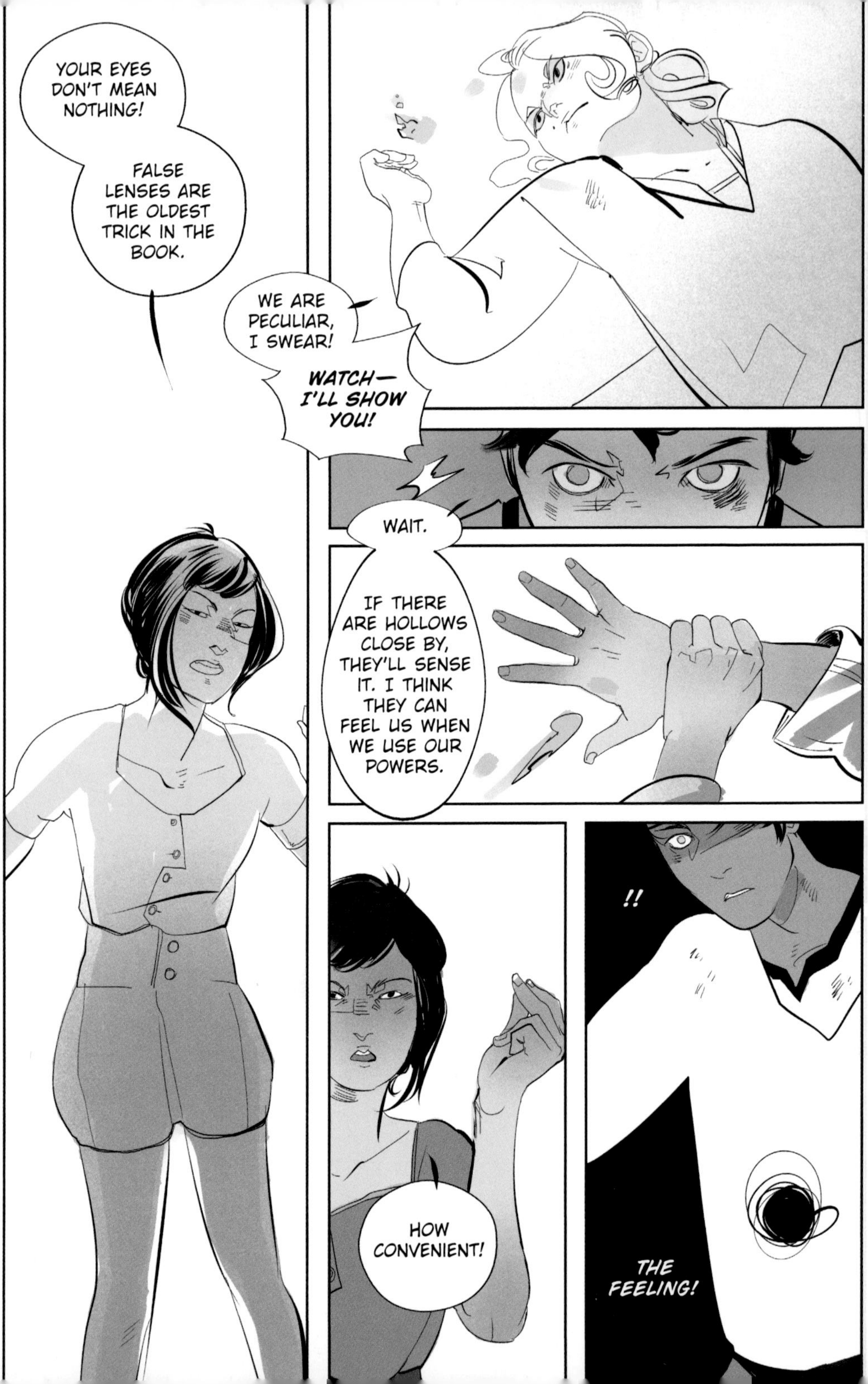
YOUR EYES DON'T MEAN NOTHING!
FALSE LENSES ARE THE OLDEST TRICK IN THE BOOK.
WE ARE PECULIAR, I SWEAR!
WATCH— I'LL SHOW YOU!
WAIT.
IF THERE ARE HOLLOWS CLOSE BY, THEY'LL SENSE IT. I THINK THEY CAN FEEL US WHEN WE USE OUR POWERS.
HOW CONVENIENT!
!!
THE FEELING!

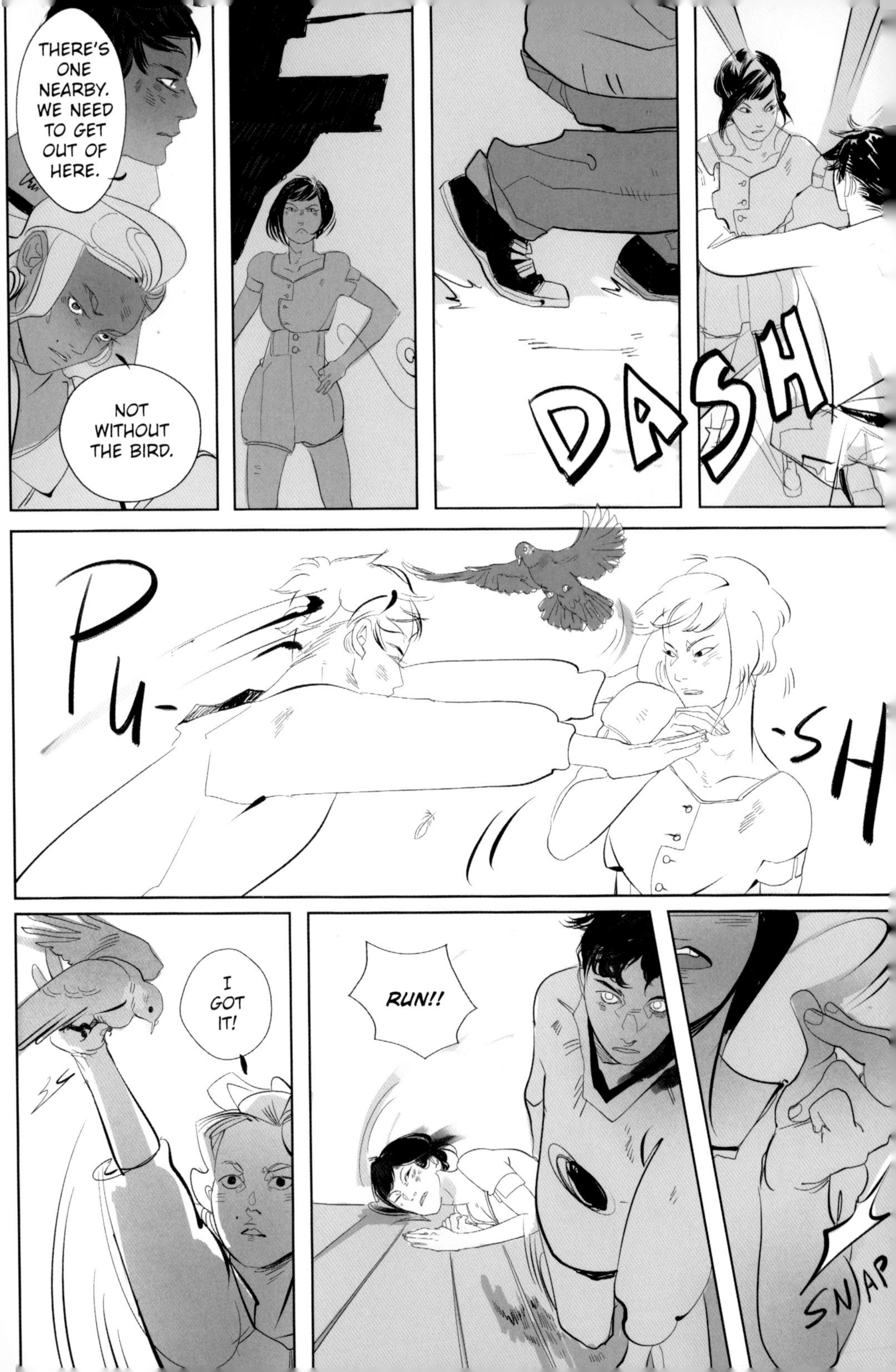
THERE'S ONE NEARBY. WE NEED TO GET OUT OF HERE.
NOT WITHOUT THE BIRD.
DASH
PU-
-SH
I GOT IT!
RUN!!
SNAP

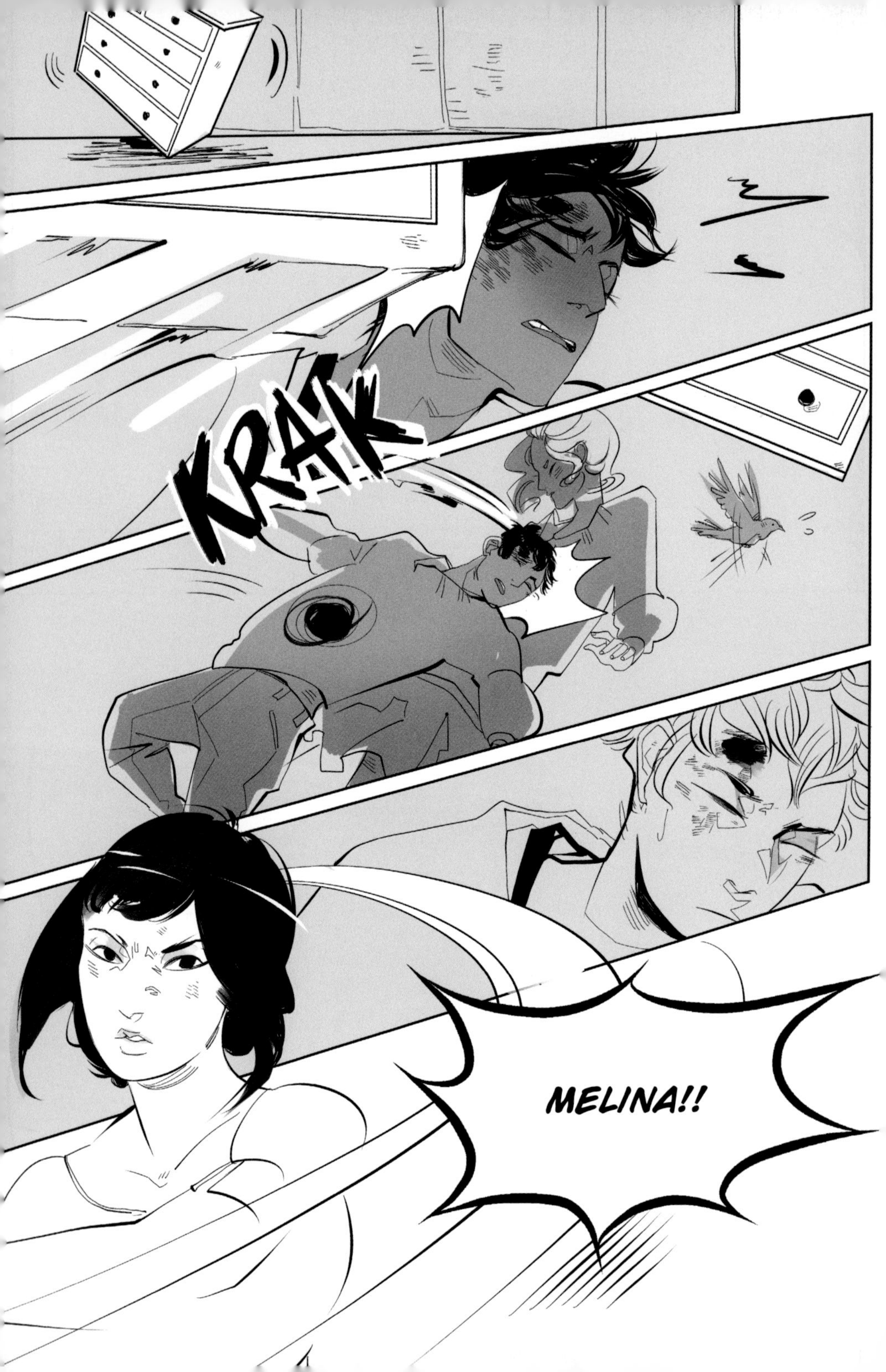
KRAK
MELINA!!

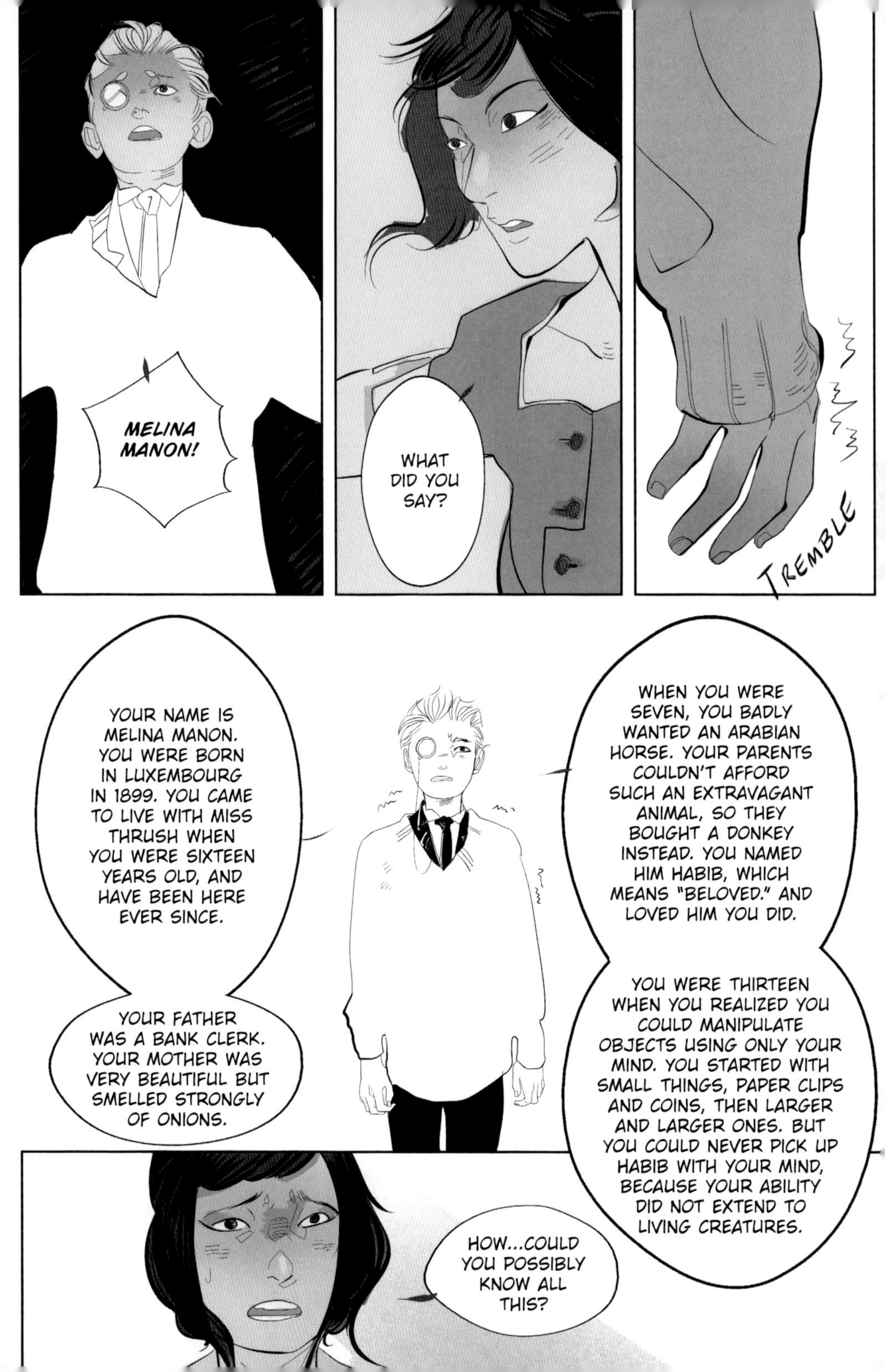
MELINA MANON!
WHAT DID YOU SAY?
TREMBLE
YOUR NAME IS MELINA MANON. YOU WERE BORN IN LUXEMBOURG IN 1899. YOU CAME TO LIVE WITH MISS THRUSH WHEN YOU WERE SIXTEEN YEARS OLD, AND HAVE BEEN HERE EVER SINCE.
YOUR FATHER WAS A BANK CLERK. YOUR MOTHER WAS VERY BEAUTIFUL BUT SMELLED STRONGLY OF ONIONS.
WHEN YOU WERE SEVEN, YOU BADLY WANTED AN ARABIAN HORSE. YOUR PARENTS COULDN'T AFFORD SUCH AN EXTRAVAGANT ANIMAL, SO THEY BOUGHT A DONKEY INSTEAD. YOU NAMED HIM HABIB, WHICH MEANS "BELOVED." AND LOVED HIM YOU DID.
YOU WERE THIRTEEN WHEN YOU REALIZED YOU COULD MANIPULATE OBJECTS USING ONLY YOUR MIND. YOU STARTED WITH SMALL THINGS, PAPER CLIPS AND COINS, THEN LARGER AND LARGER ONES. BUT YOU COULD NEVER PICK UP HABIB WITH YOUR MIND, BECAUSE YOUR ABILITY DID NOT EXTEND TO LIVING CREATURES.
HOW...COULD YOU POSSIBLY KNOW ALL THIS?

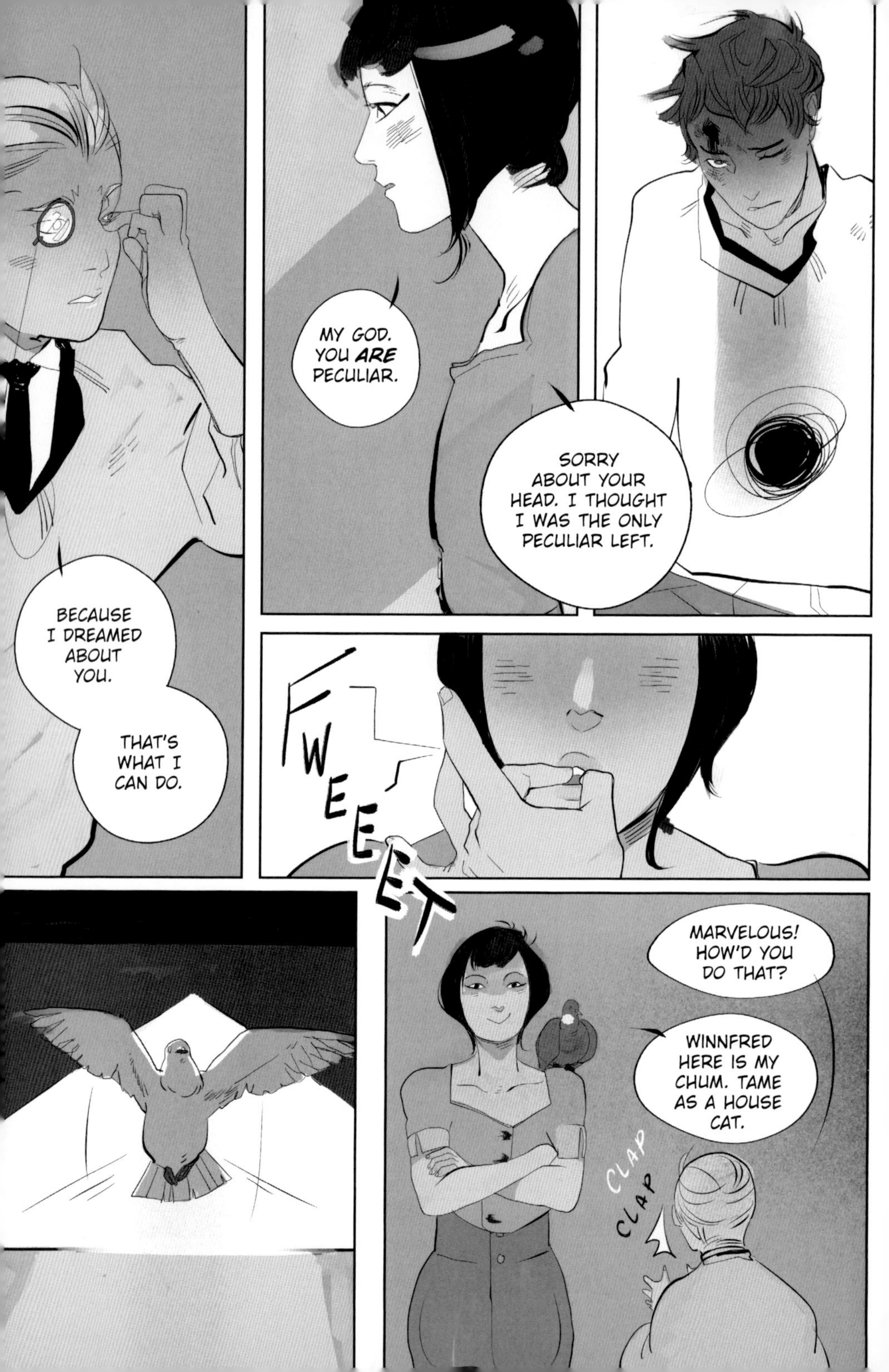
MY GOD. YOU ARE PECULIAR.
SORRY ABOUT YOUR HEAD. I THOUGHT I WAS THE ONLY PECULIAR LEFT.
BECAUSE I DREAMED ABOUT YOU.
THAT'S WHAT I CAN DO.
FWEEET
MARVELOUS! HOW'D YOU DO THAT?
WINNFRED HERE IS MY CHUM. TAME AS A HOUSE CAT.
CLAP CLAP

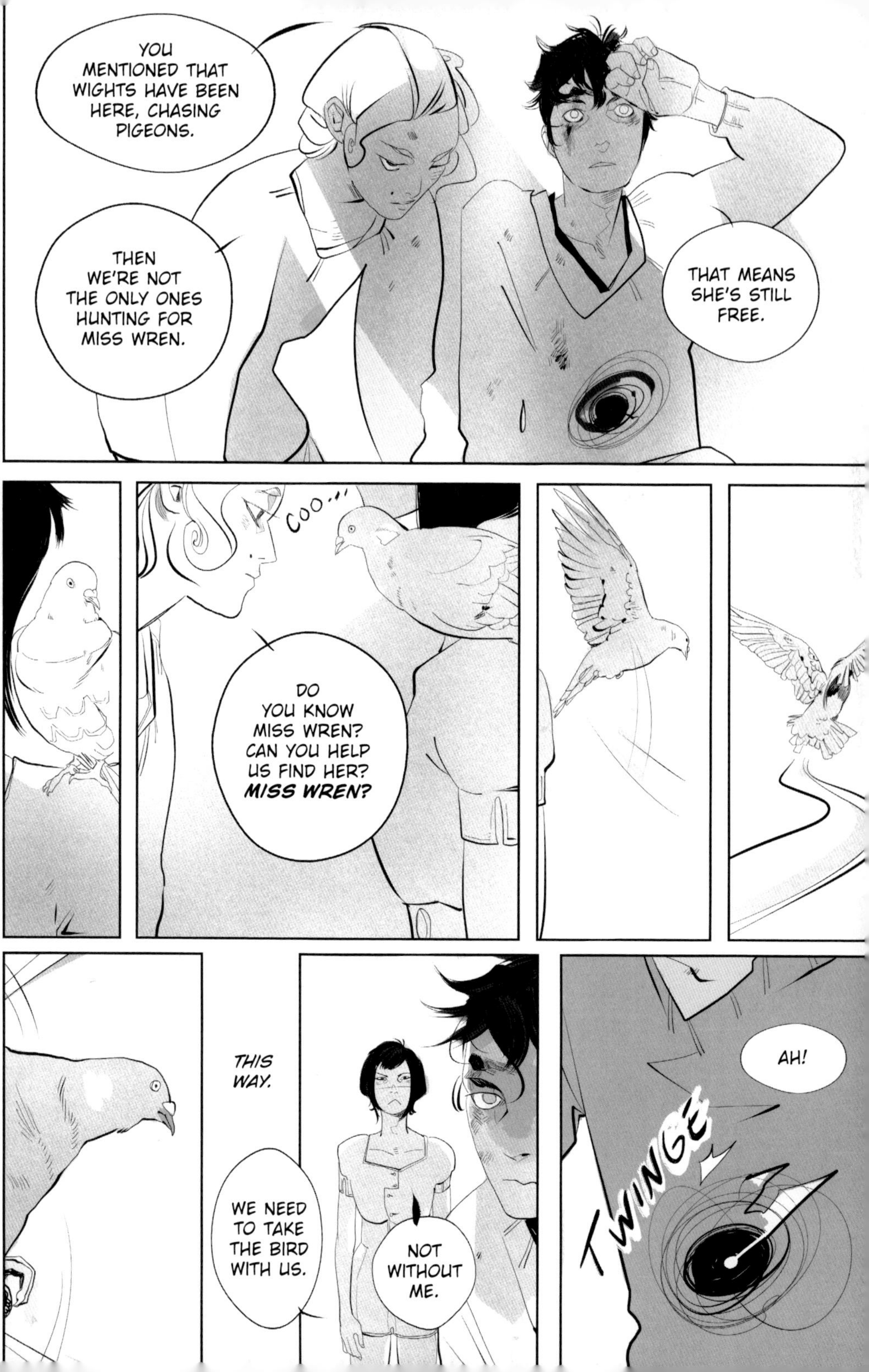
YOU MENTIONED THAT WIGHTS HAVE BEEN HERE, CHASING PIGEONS.
THEN WE'RE NOT THE ONLY ONES HUNTING FOR MISS WREN.
THAT MEANS SHE'S STILL FREE.
COO...!
DO YOU KNOW MISS WREN? CAN YOU HELP US FIND HER? MISS WREN?
THIS WAY.
WE NEED TO TAKE THE BIRD WITH US.
NOT WITHOUT ME.
AH!
TWINGE

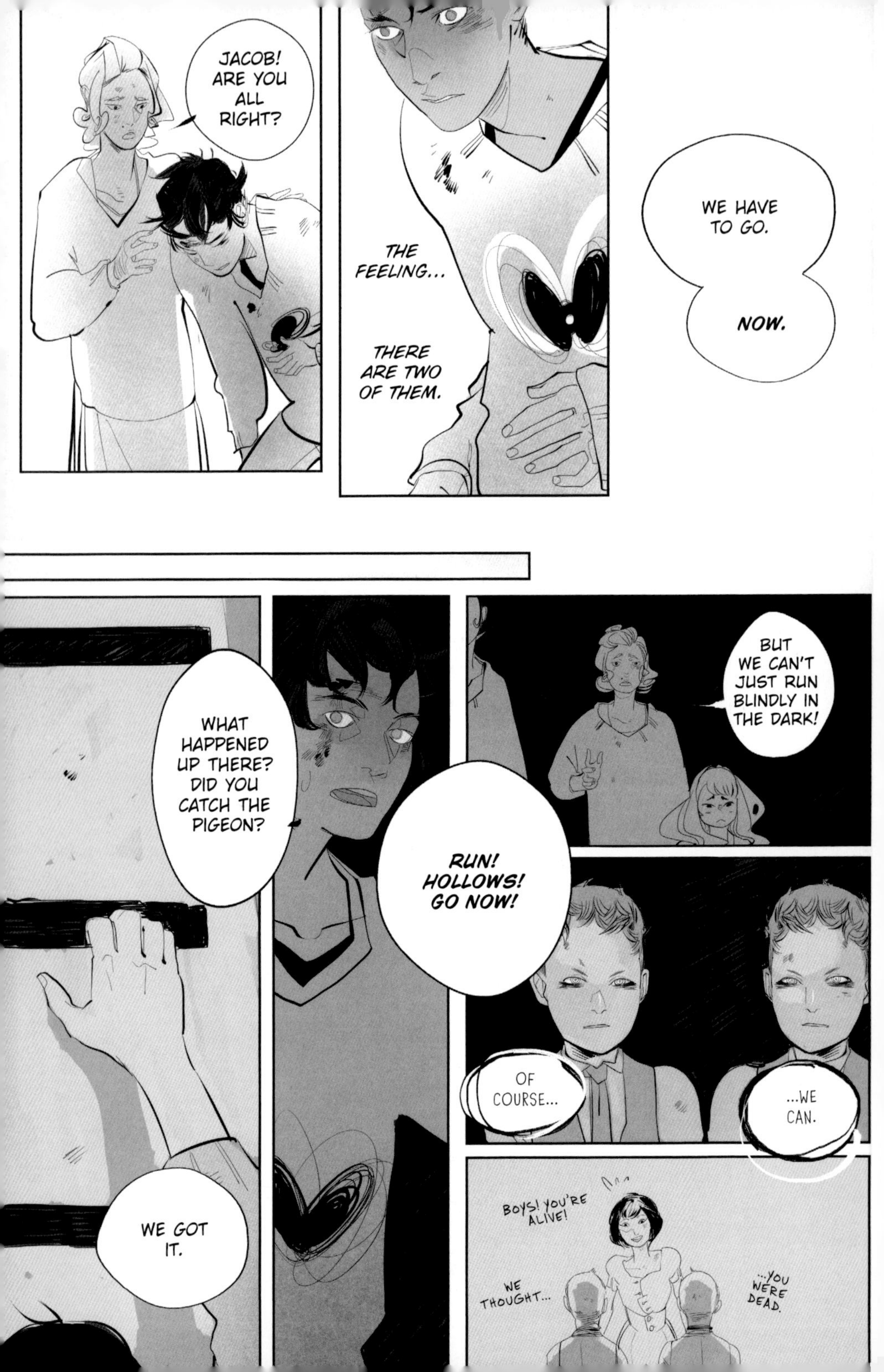
JACOB! ARE YOU ALL RIGHT?
THE FEELING...
THERE ARE TWO OF THEM.
WE HAVE TO GO.
NOW.
WHAT HAPPENED UP THERE? DID YOU CATCH THE PIGEON?
WE GOT IT.
RUN! HOLLOWS! GO NOW!
BUT WE CAN'T JUST RUN BLINDLY IN THE DARK!
OF COURSE...
...WE CAN.
BOYS! YOU'RE ALIVE!
WE THOUGHT...
...YOU WERE DEAD.

EVERYONE LINK HANDS! LET THE BOYS LEAD THE WAY!

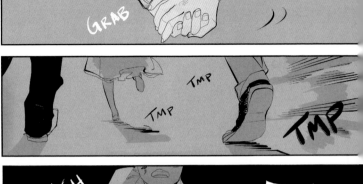

GRAB

TMP TMP TMP TMP

CRASH SMASH

THEY'RE IN THE TUNNELS!

STOP! EVERYONE STOP!

STUMBLE

ONE OF US WILL HAVE TO PASS THROUGH THE LOOP EXIT BEFORE THE ECHOLOCATORS, OR THEY WILL CROSS INTO THE PRESENT AND WE INTO 1940. WE'LL BE SEPARATED.

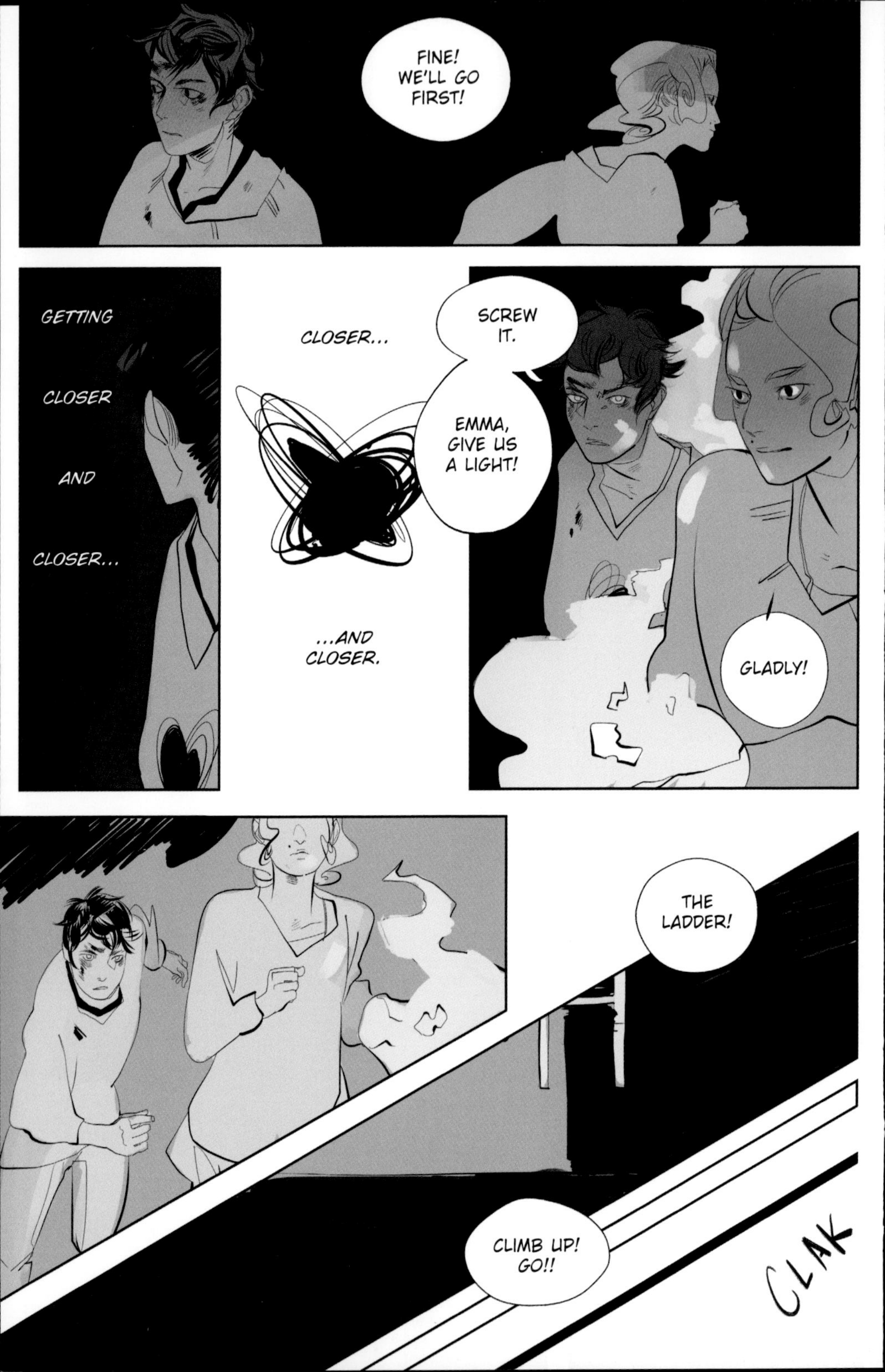
FINE! WE'LL GO FIRST!
GETTING
CLOSER
AND
CLOSER...
CLOSER...
...AND CLOSER.
SCREW IT.
EMMA, GIVE US A LIGHT!
GLADLY!
THE LADDER!
CLIMB UP! GO!!
CLAK

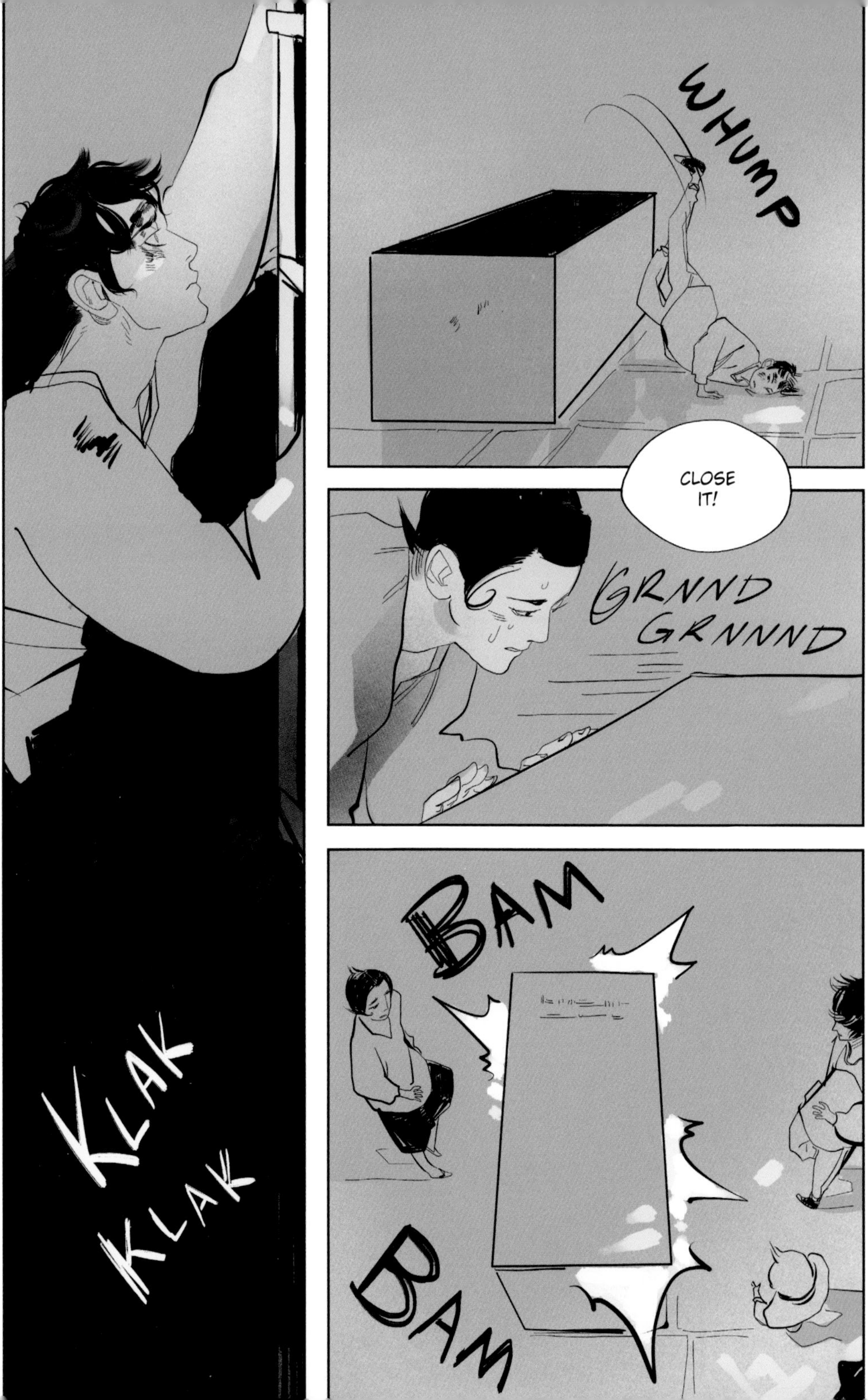
KLAK
KLAK
WHUMP
CLOSE IT!
GRNND
GRNNND
BAM
BAM

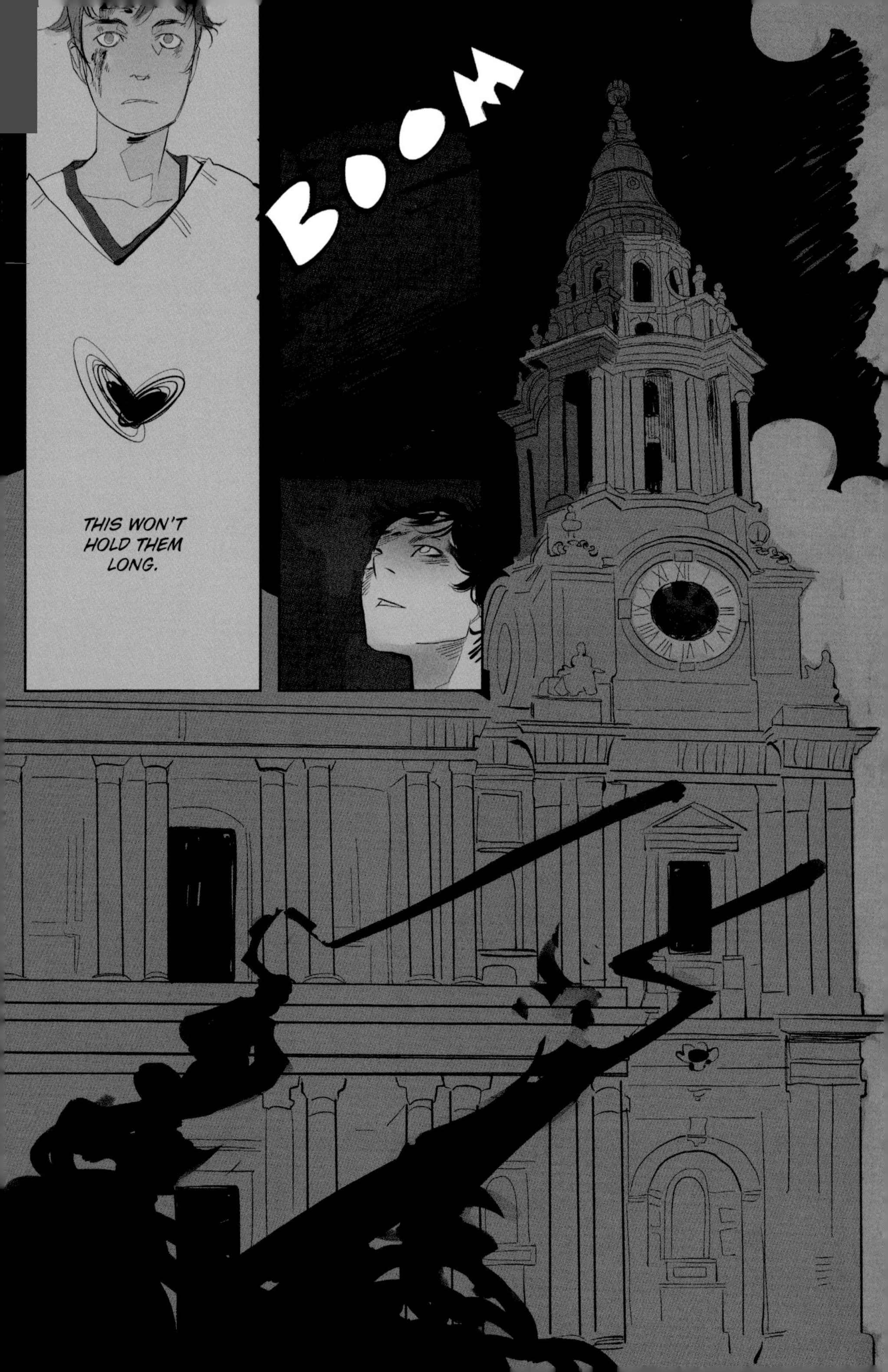
THIS WON'T HOLD THEM LONG.
BOOM

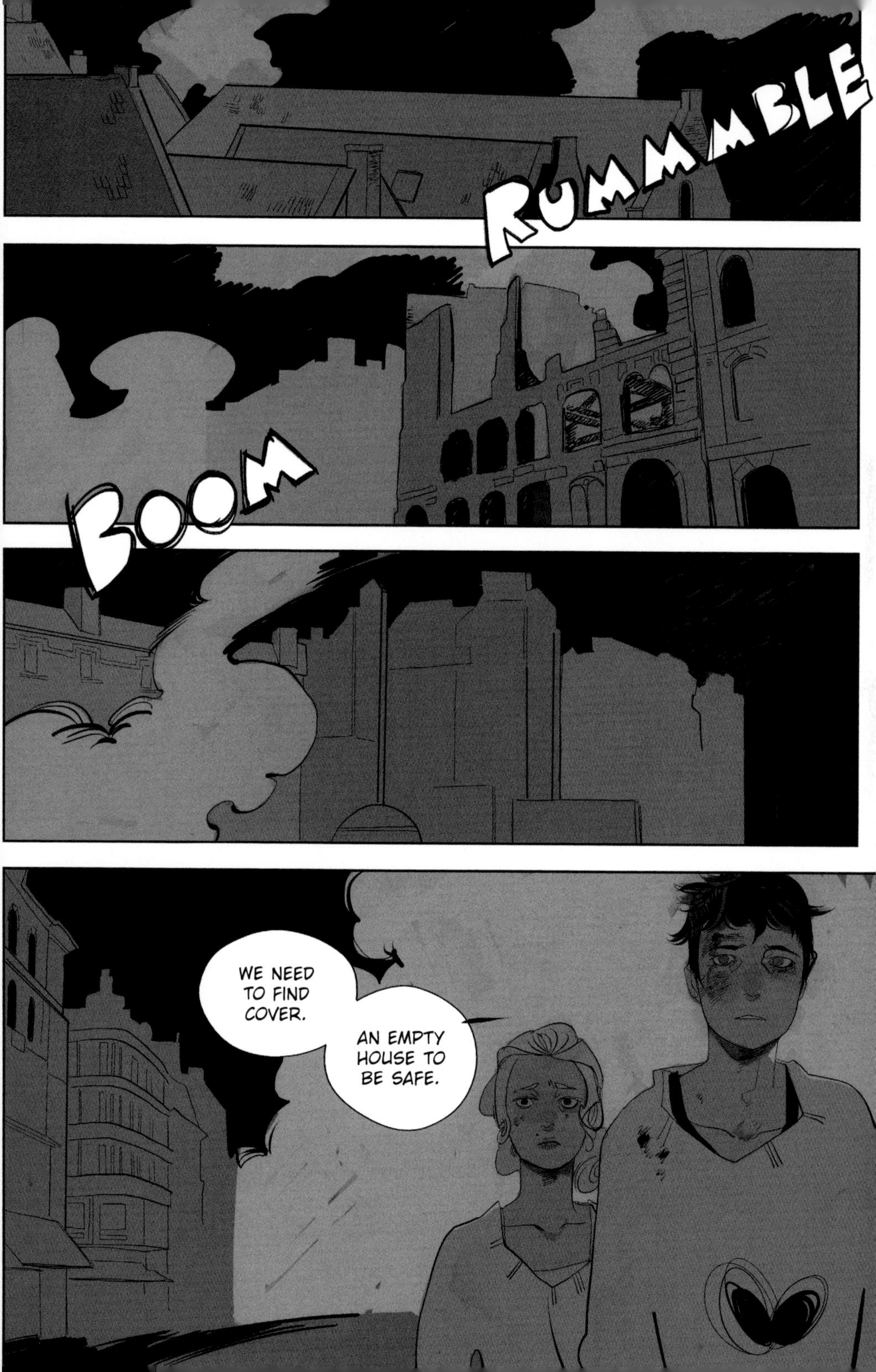
RUMMMBLE
BOOM
WE NEED TO FIND COVER.
AN EMPTY HOUSE TO BE SAFE.

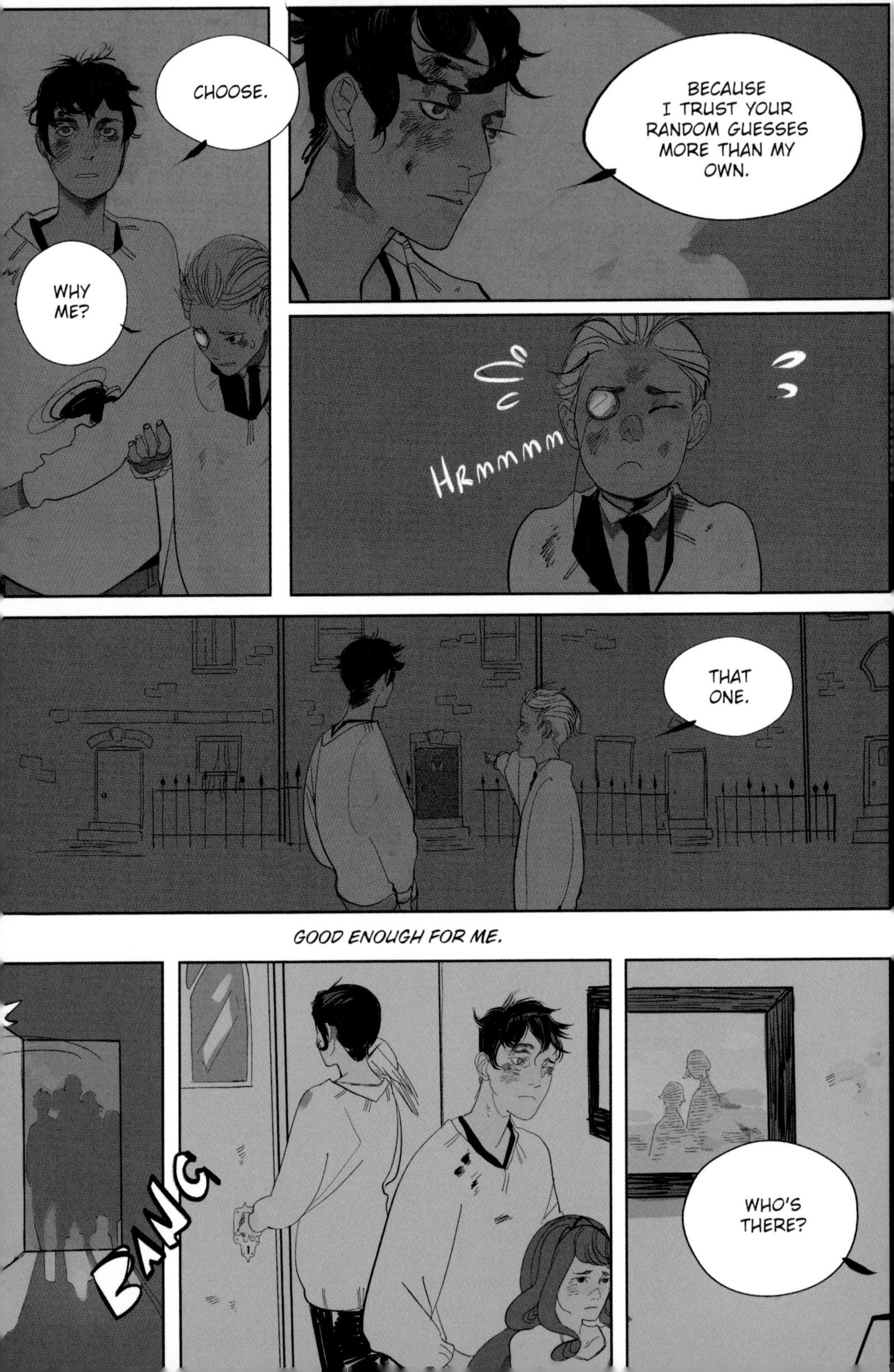
CHOOSE.
WHY ME?
BECAUSE I TRUST YOUR RANDOM GUESSES MORE THAN MY OWN.
HRmmmm
THAT ONE.
GOOD ENOUGH FOR ME.
BANG
WHO'S THERE?

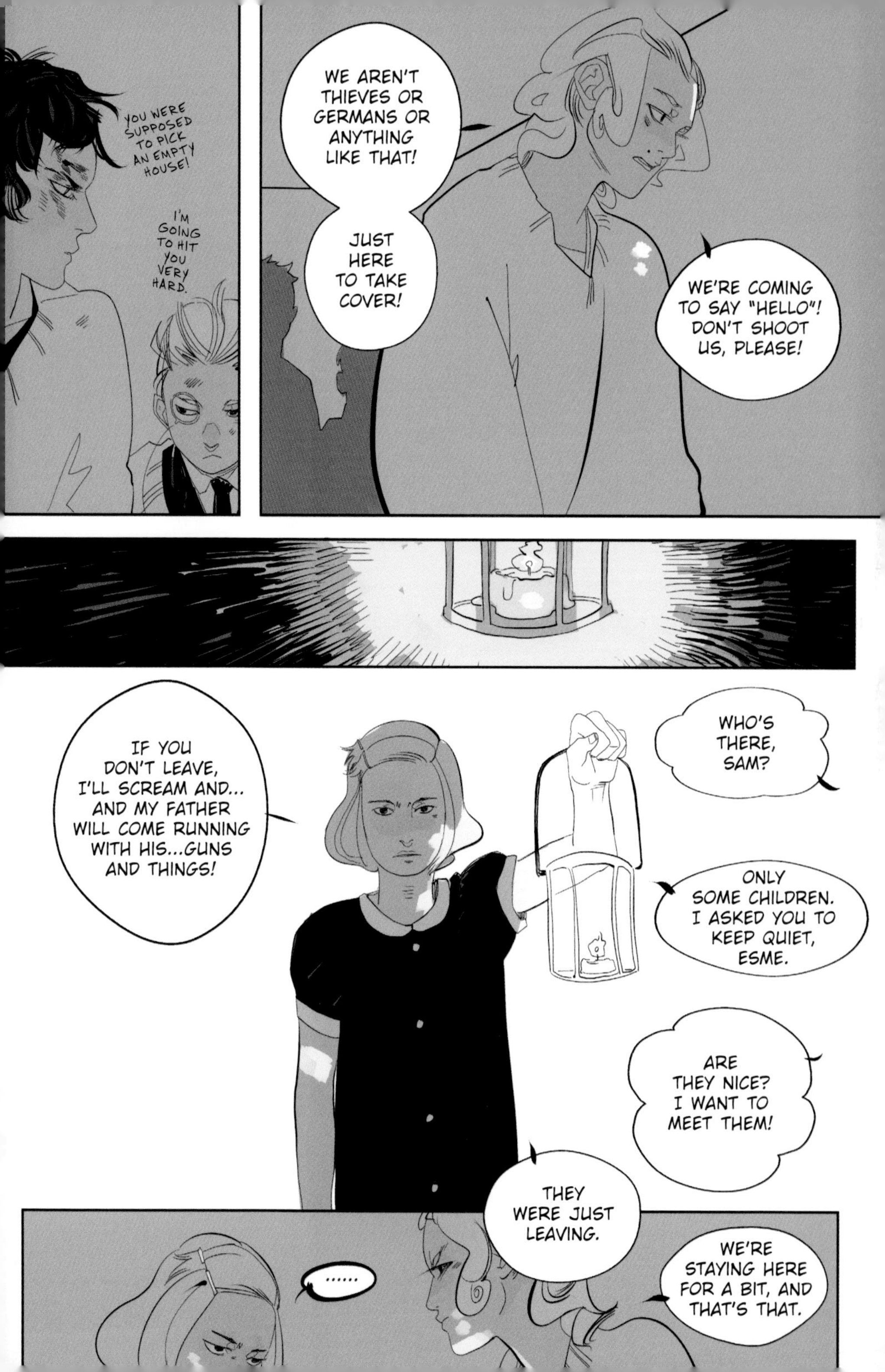
YOU WERE SUPPOSED TO PICK AN EMPTY HOUSE!
I'M GOING TO HIT YOU VERY HARD.
WE AREN'T THIEVES OR GERMANS OR ANYTHING LIKE THAT!
JUST HERE TO TAKE COVER!
WE'RE COMING TO SAY "HELLO"! DON'T SHOOT US, PLEASE!
IF YOU DON'T LEAVE, I'LL SCREAM AND... AND MY FATHER WILL COME RUNNING WITH HIS...GUNS AND THINGS!
WHO'S THERE, SAM?
ONLY SOME CHILDREN. I ASKED YOU TO KEEP QUIET, ESME.
ARE THEY NICE? I WANT TO MEET THEM!
THEY WERE JUST LEAVING.
......
WE'RE STAYING HERE FOR A BIT, AND THAT'S THAT.

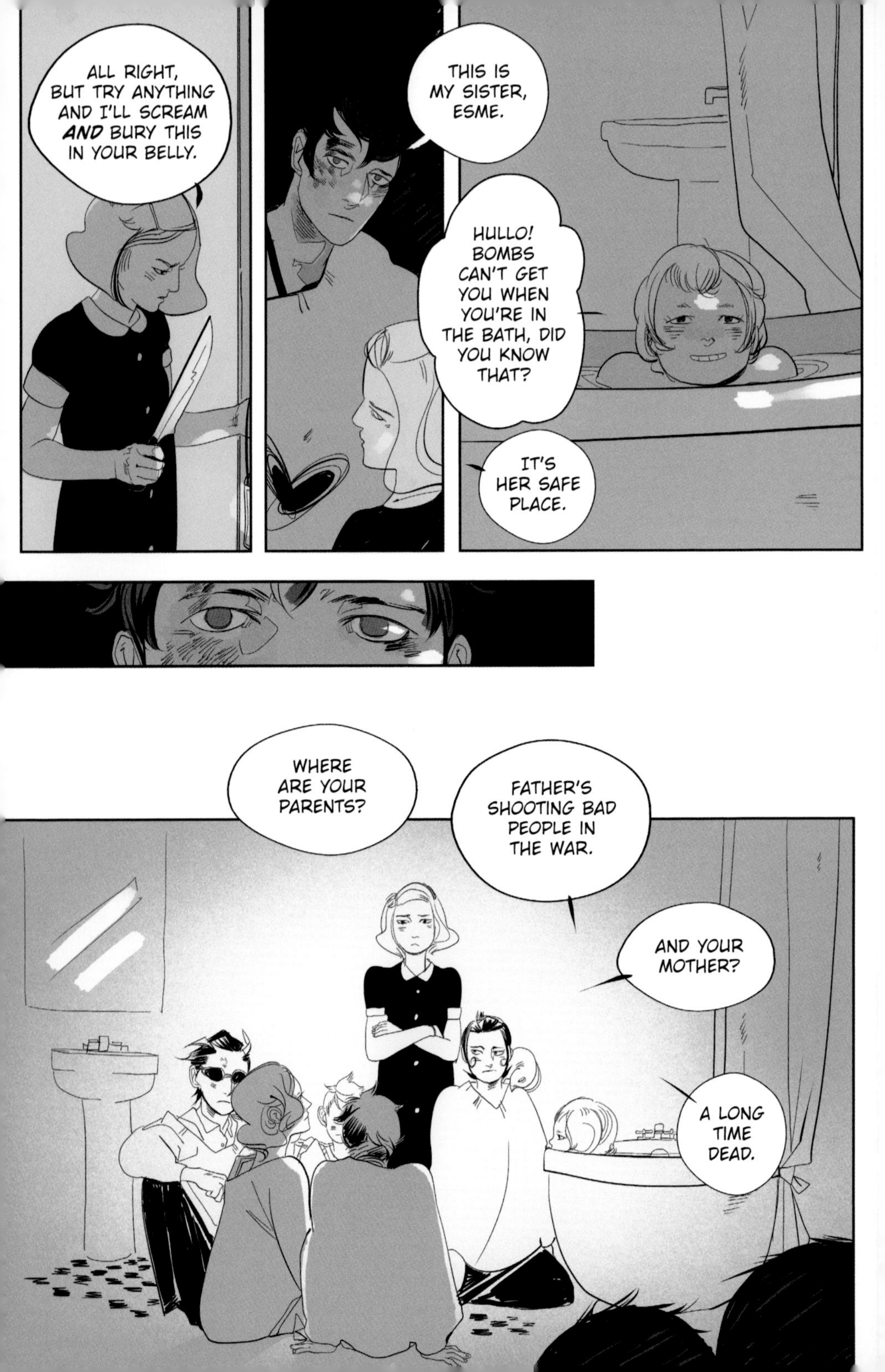
ALL RIGHT, BUT TRY ANYTHING AND I'LL SCREAM **AND** BURY THIS IN YOUR BELLY.
THIS IS MY SISTER, ESME.
HULLO! BOMBS CAN'T GET YOU WHEN YOU'RE IN THE BATH, DID YOU KNOW THAT?
IT'S HER SAFE PLACE.
WHERE ARE YOUR PARENTS?
FATHER'S SHOOTING BAD PEOPLE IN THE WAR.
AND YOUR MOTHER?
A LONG TIME DEAD.

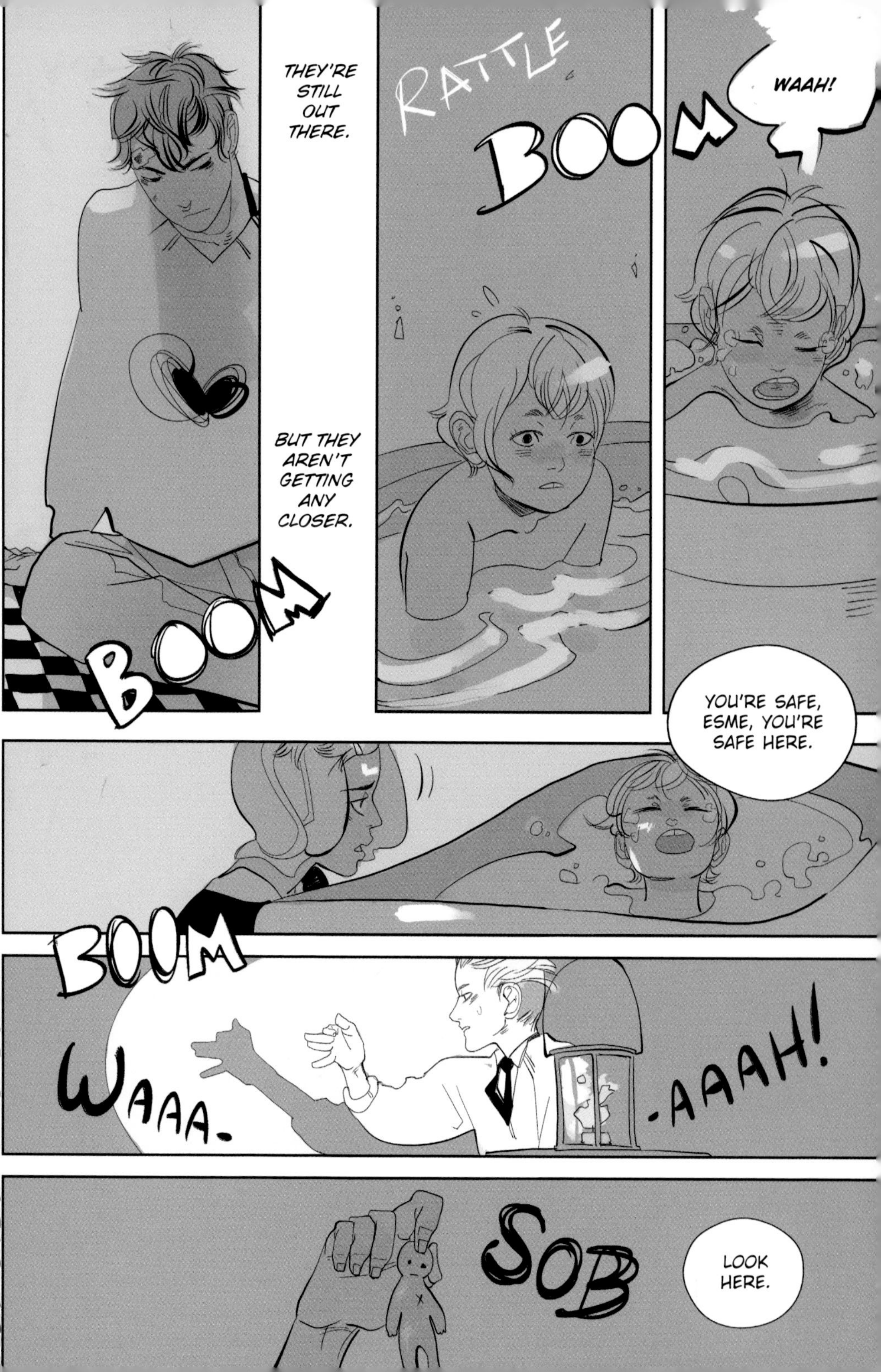
THEY'RE STILL OUT THERE.
BUT THEY AREN'T GETTING ANY CLOSER.
BOOM
RATTLE
BOOM
WAAH!
YOU'RE SAFE, ESME, YOU'RE SAFE HERE.
BOOM
WAAA-
-AAAH!
SOB
LOOK HERE.

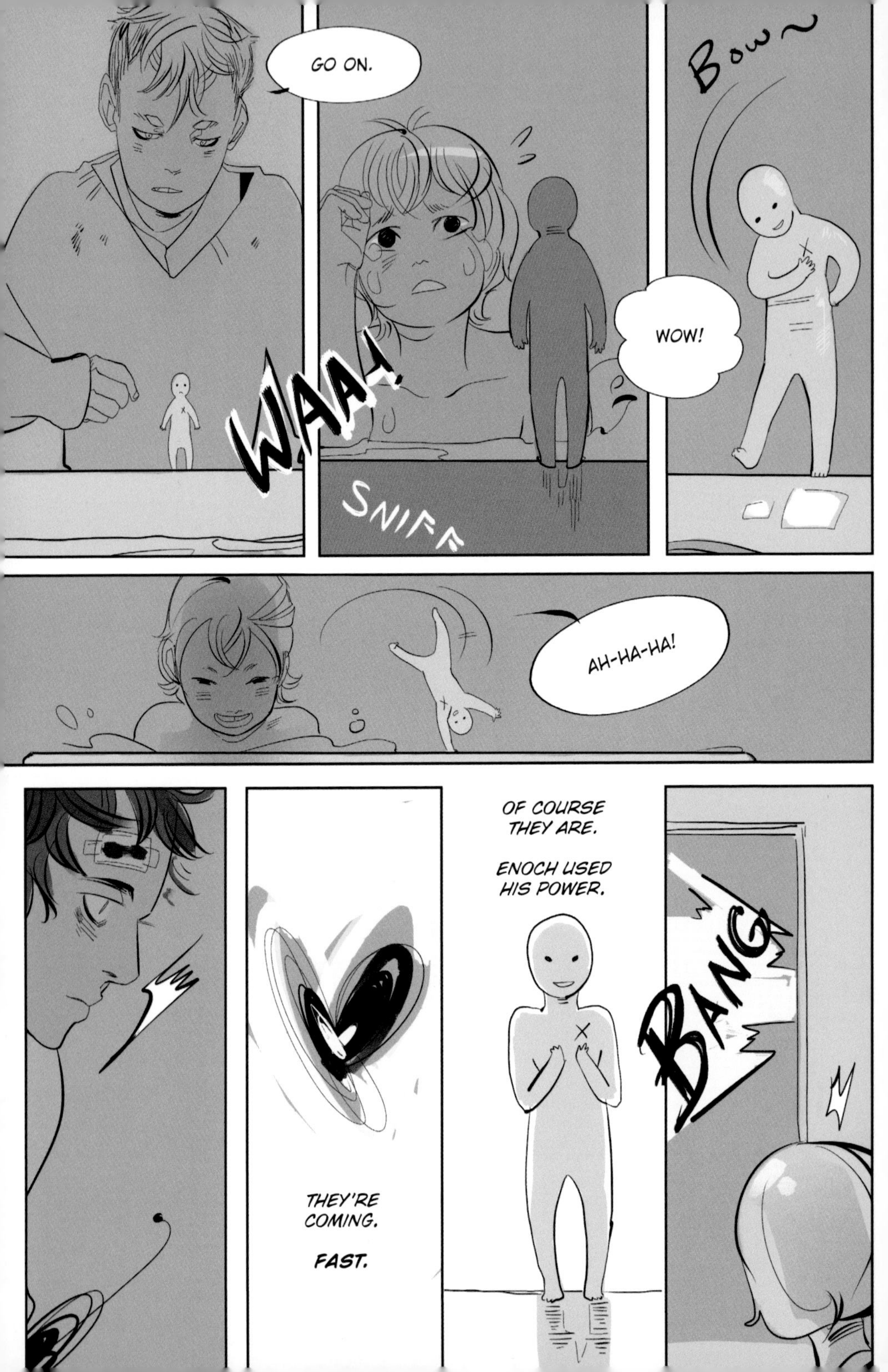
GO ON.
WAAA!
SNIFF
BOW~
WOW!
AH-HA-HA!
THEY'RE COMING.
FAST.
OF COURSE THEY ARE.
ENOCH USED HIS POWER.
BANG

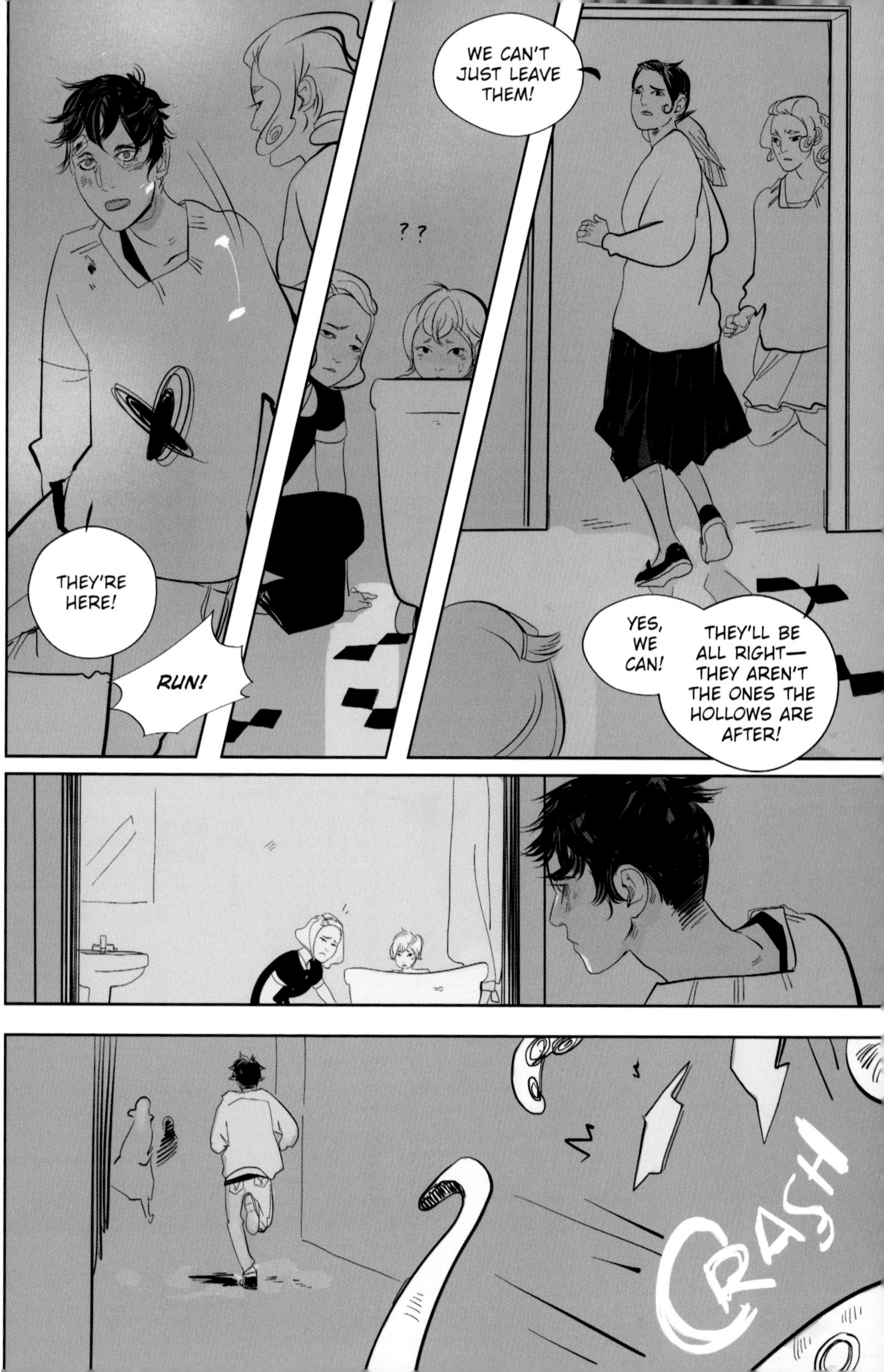
THEY'RE HERE!
RUN!
? ?
WE CAN'T JUST LEAVE THEM!
YES, WE CAN!
THEY'LL BE ALL RIGHT— THEY AREN'T THE ONES THE HOLLOWS ARE AFTER!
CRASH

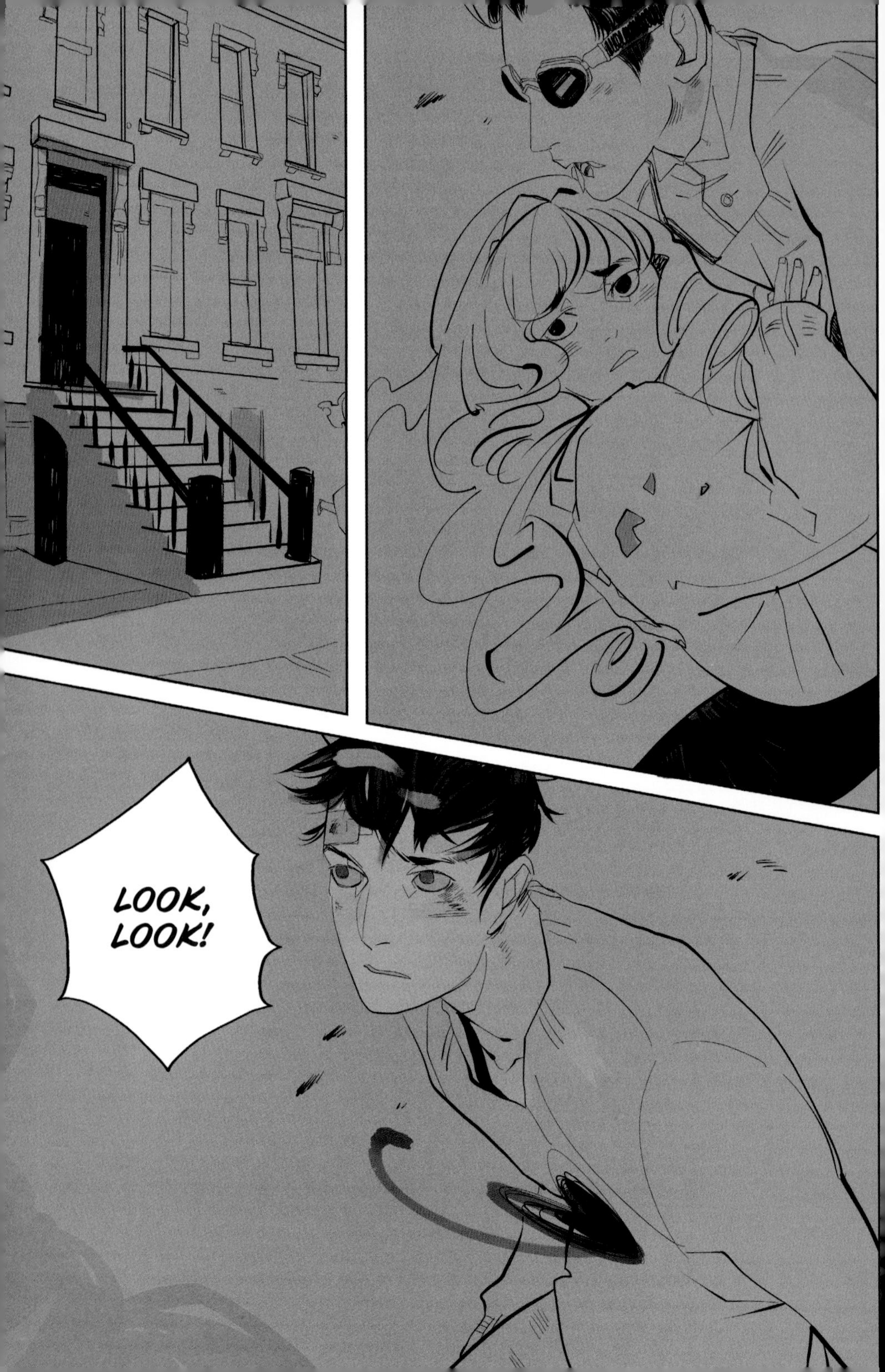
LOOK, LOOK!

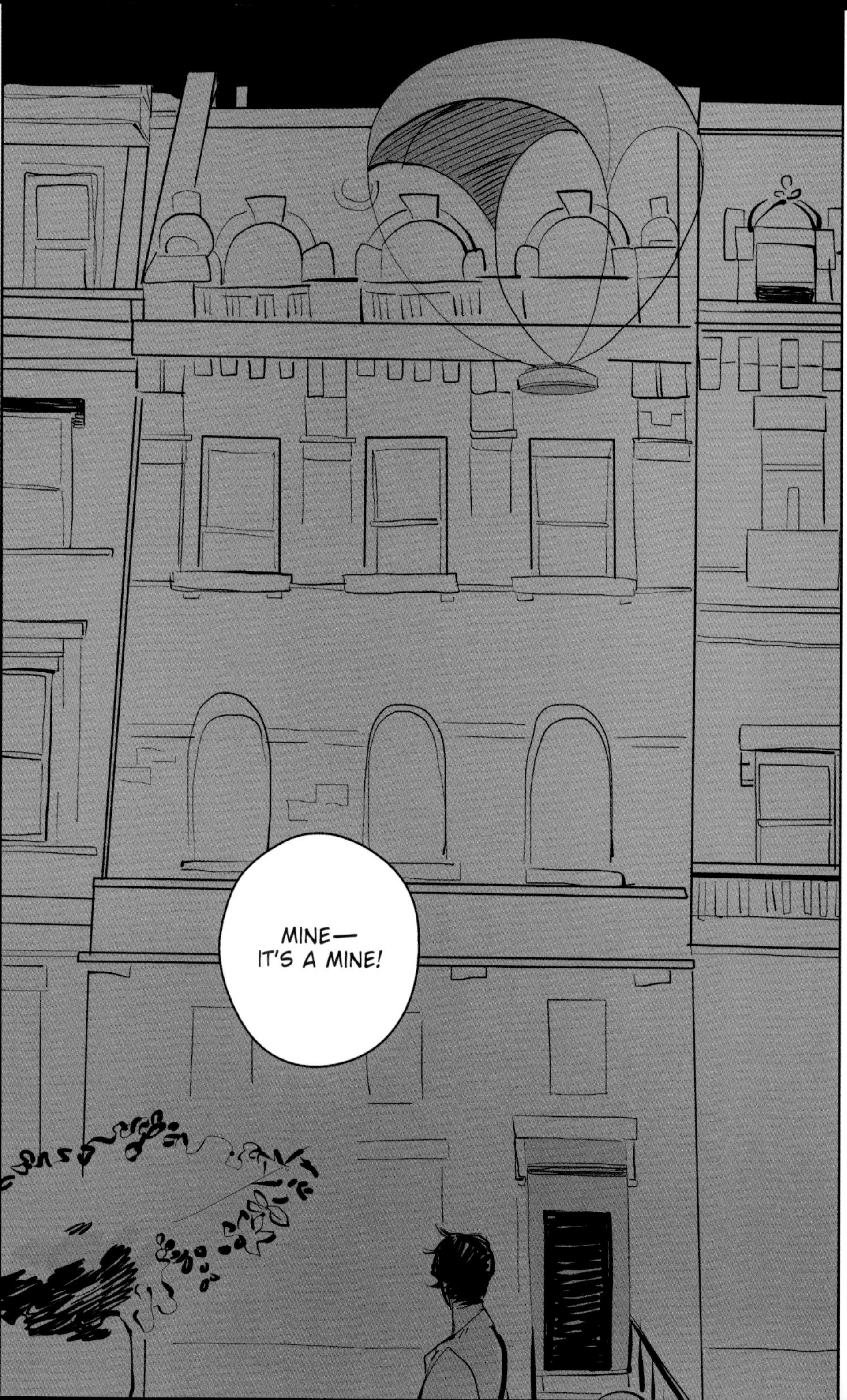
MINE—
IT'S A MINE!

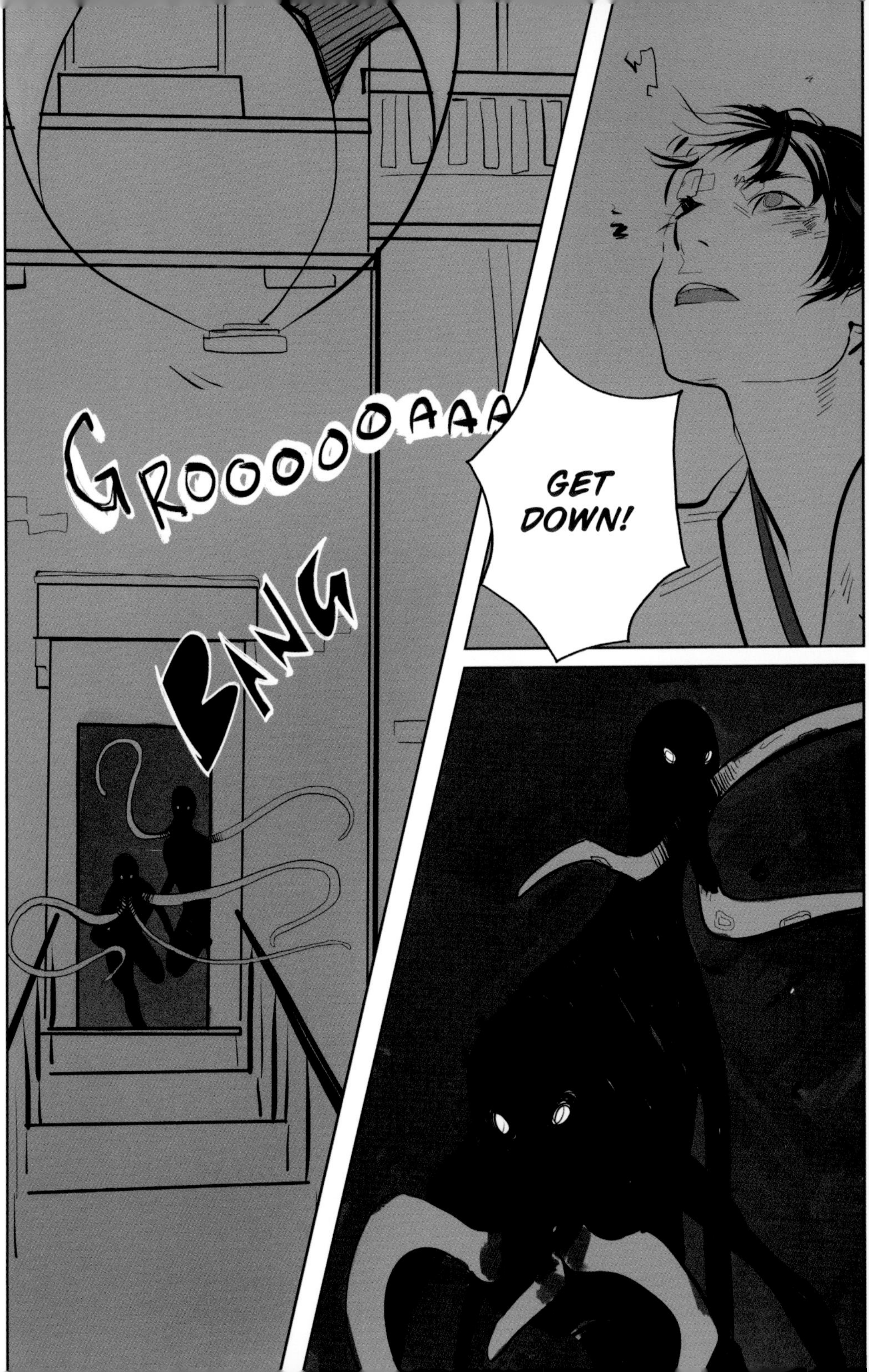
GROOOOOAAA
BANG
GET DOWN!

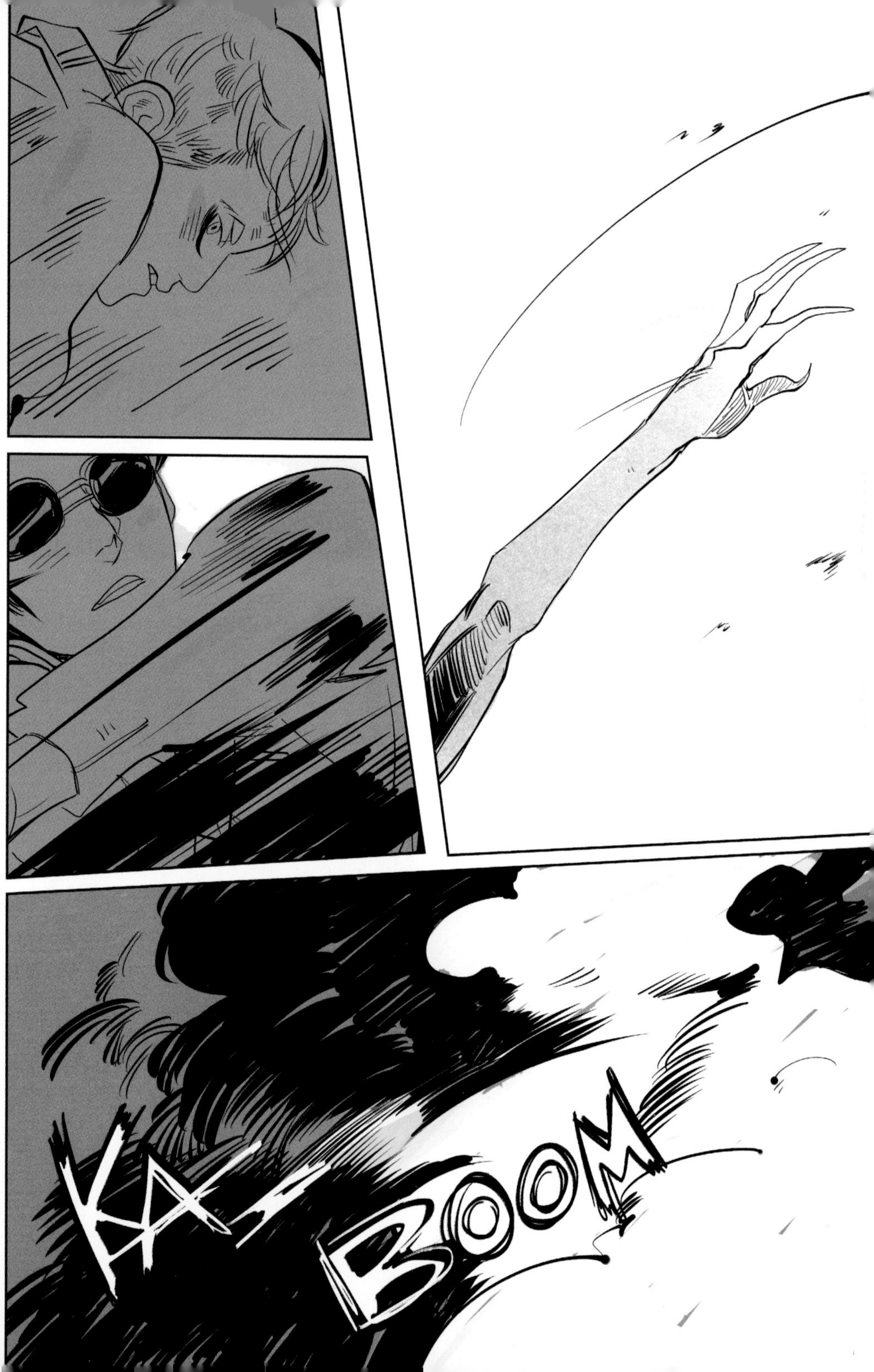
KA-
BOOM

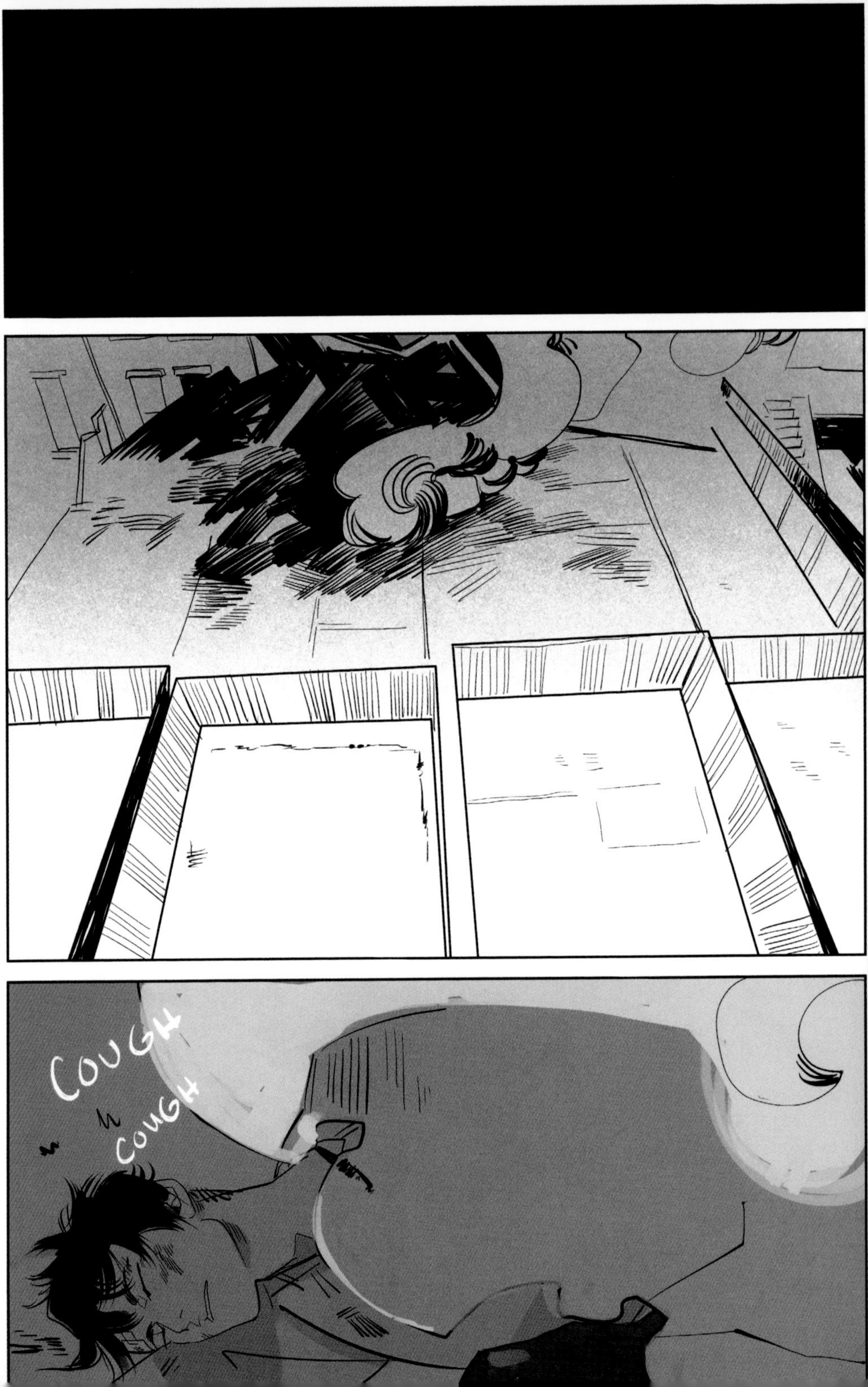
COUGH
COUGH

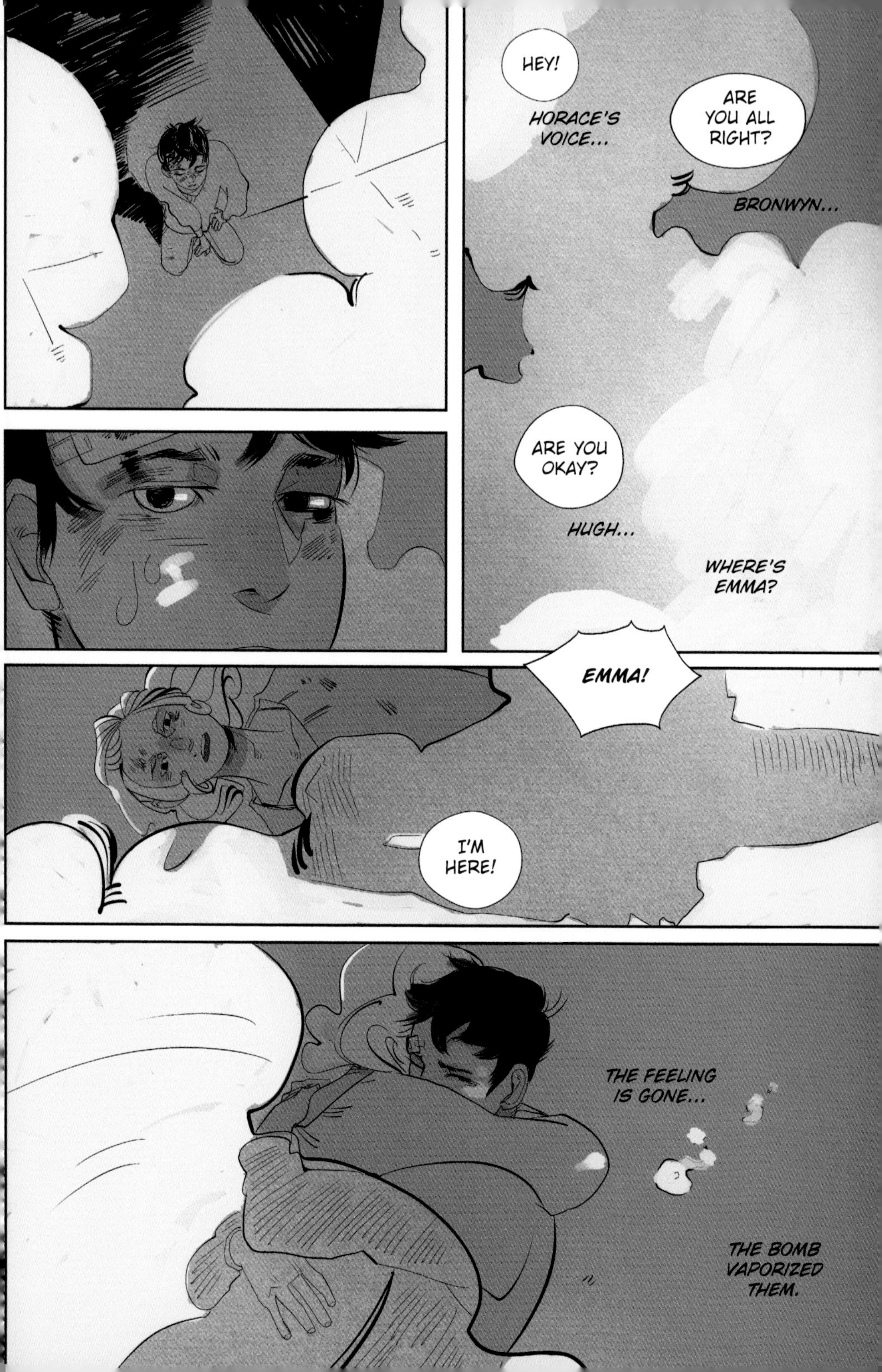
HEY!
HORACE'S VOICE...
ARE YOU ALL RIGHT?
BRONWYN...
ARE YOU OKAY?
HUGH...
WHERE'S EMMA?
EMMA!
I'M HERE!
THE FEELING IS GONE...
THE BOMB VAPORIZED THEM.

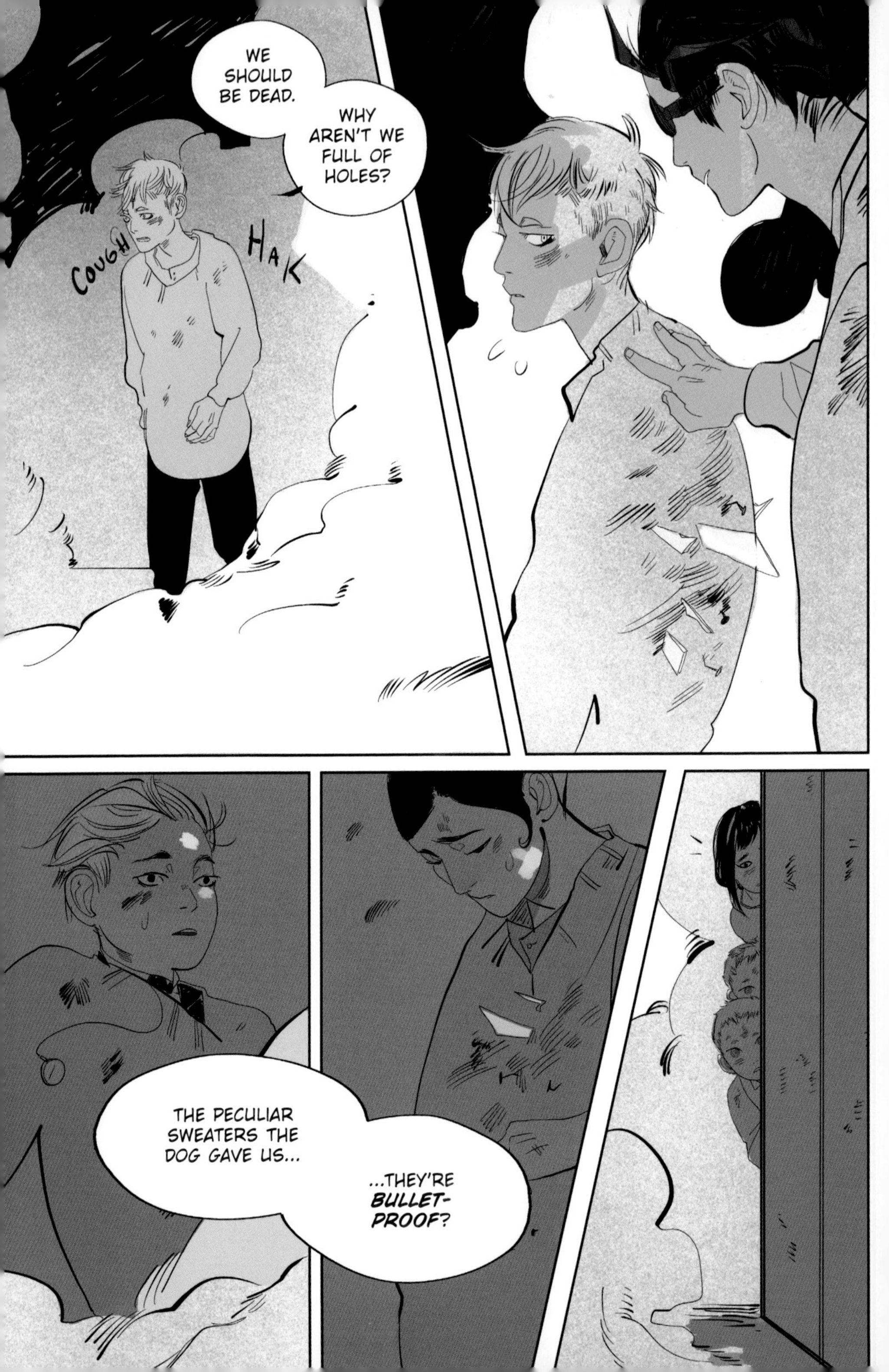
WE SHOULD BE DEAD.
WHY AREN'T WE FULL OF HOLES?
COUGH
HAK
THE PECULIAR SWEATERS THE DOG GAVE US...
...THEY'RE *BULLET-PROOF*?

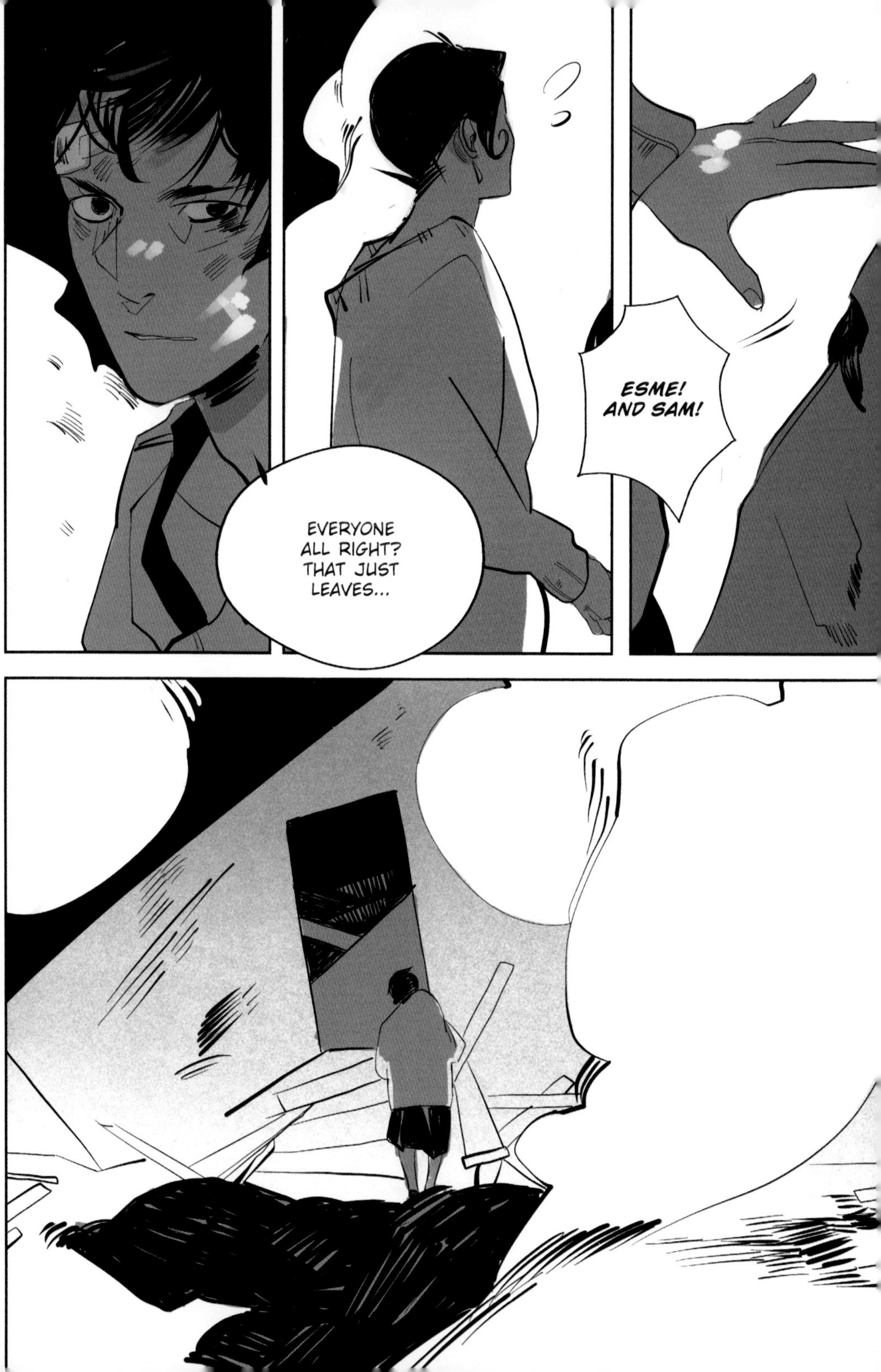
EVERYONE ALL RIGHT? THAT JUST LEAVES...
ESME! AND SAM!

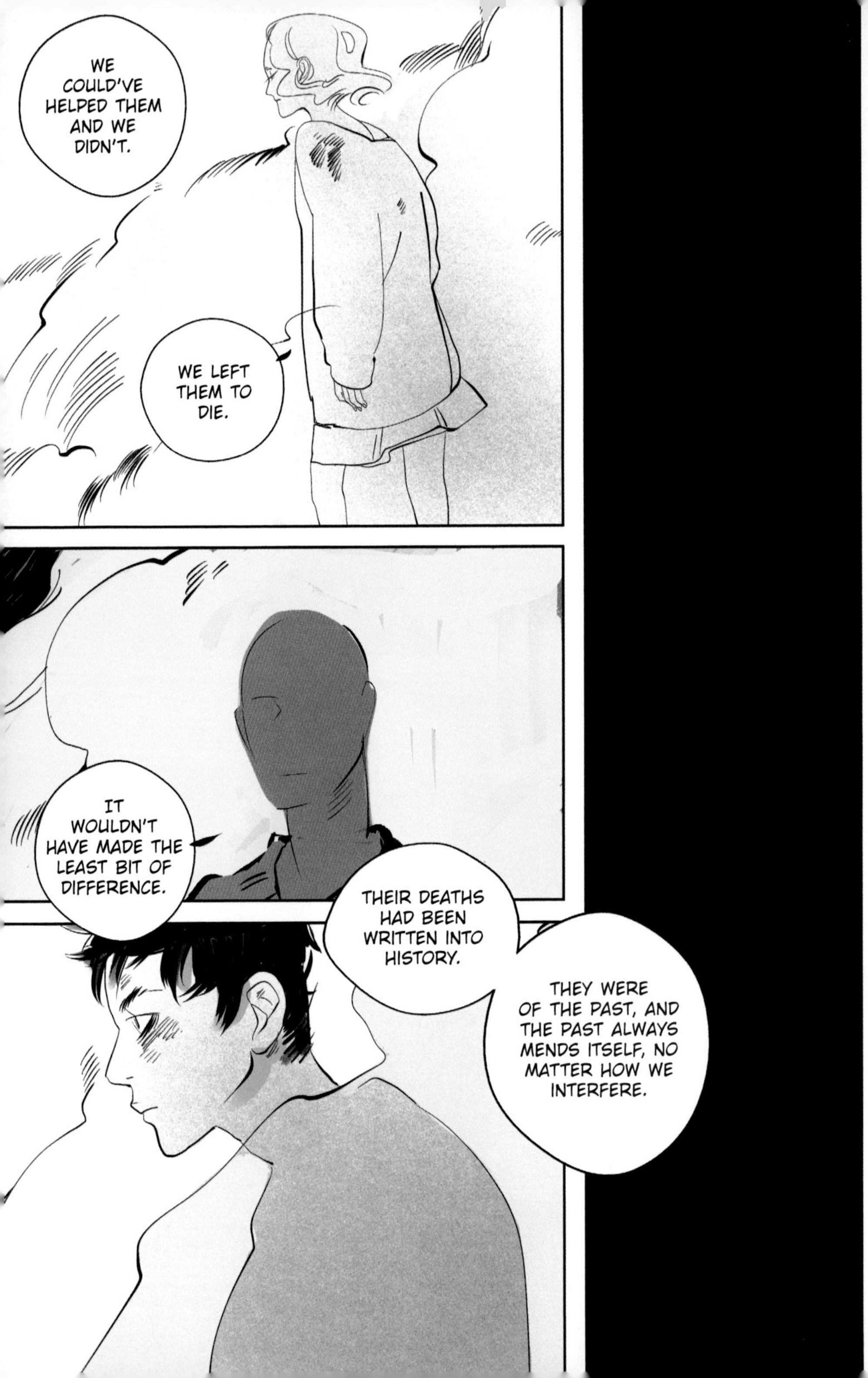
WE COULD'VE HELPED THEM AND WE DIDN'T.
WE LEFT THEM TO DIE.
IT WOULDN'T HAVE MADE THE LEAST BIT OF DIFFERENCE.
THEIR DEATHS HAD BEEN WRITTEN INTO HISTORY.
THEY WERE OF THE PAST, AND THE PAST ALWAYS MENDS ITSELF, NO MATTER HOW WE INTERFERE.

CHAPTER SIX

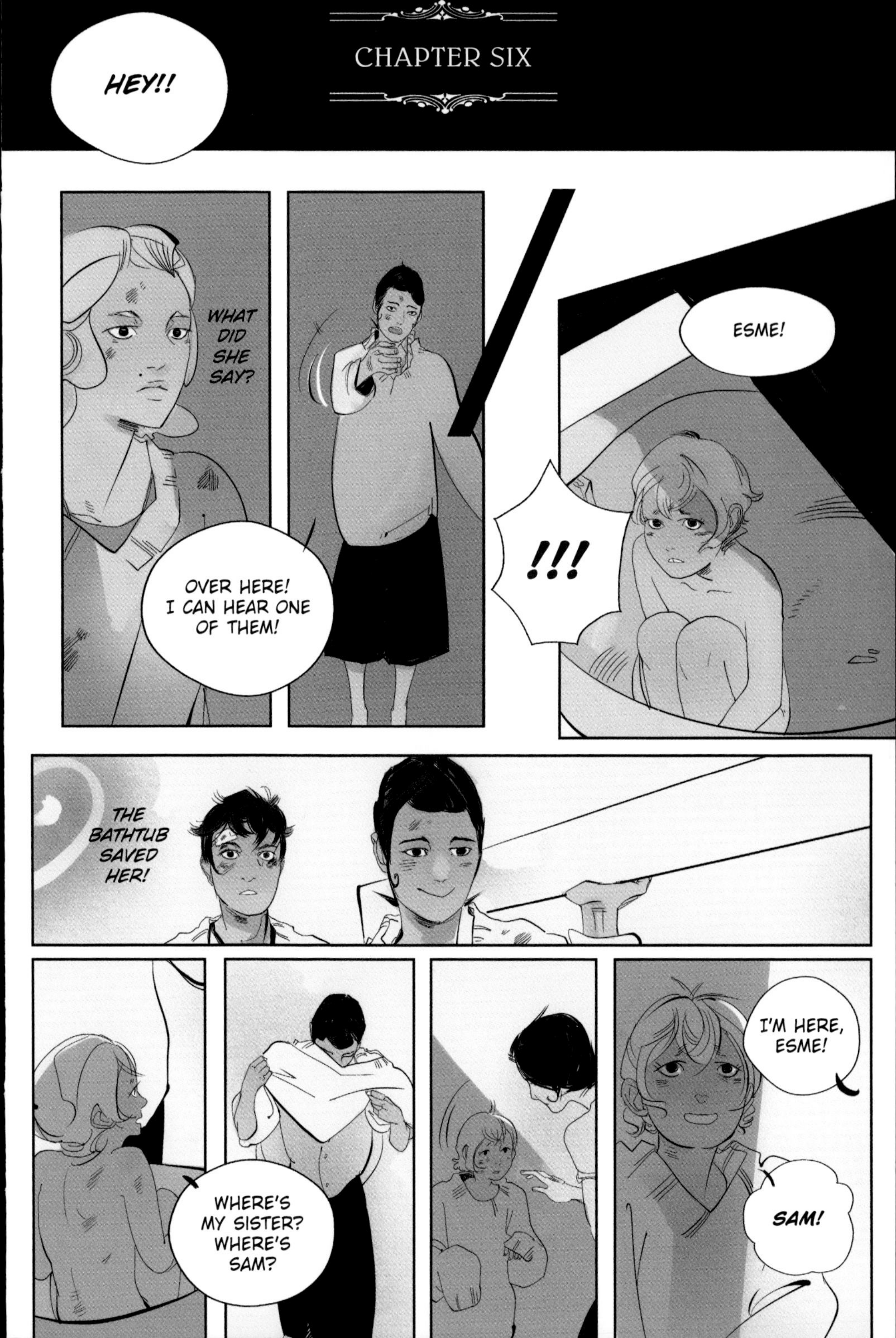
HEY!!
WHAT DID SHE SAY?
OVER HERE! I CAN HEAR ONE OF THEM!
ESME!
!!!
THE BATHTUB SAVED HER!
WHERE'S MY SISTER? WHERE'S SAM?
I'M HERE, ESME!
SAM!

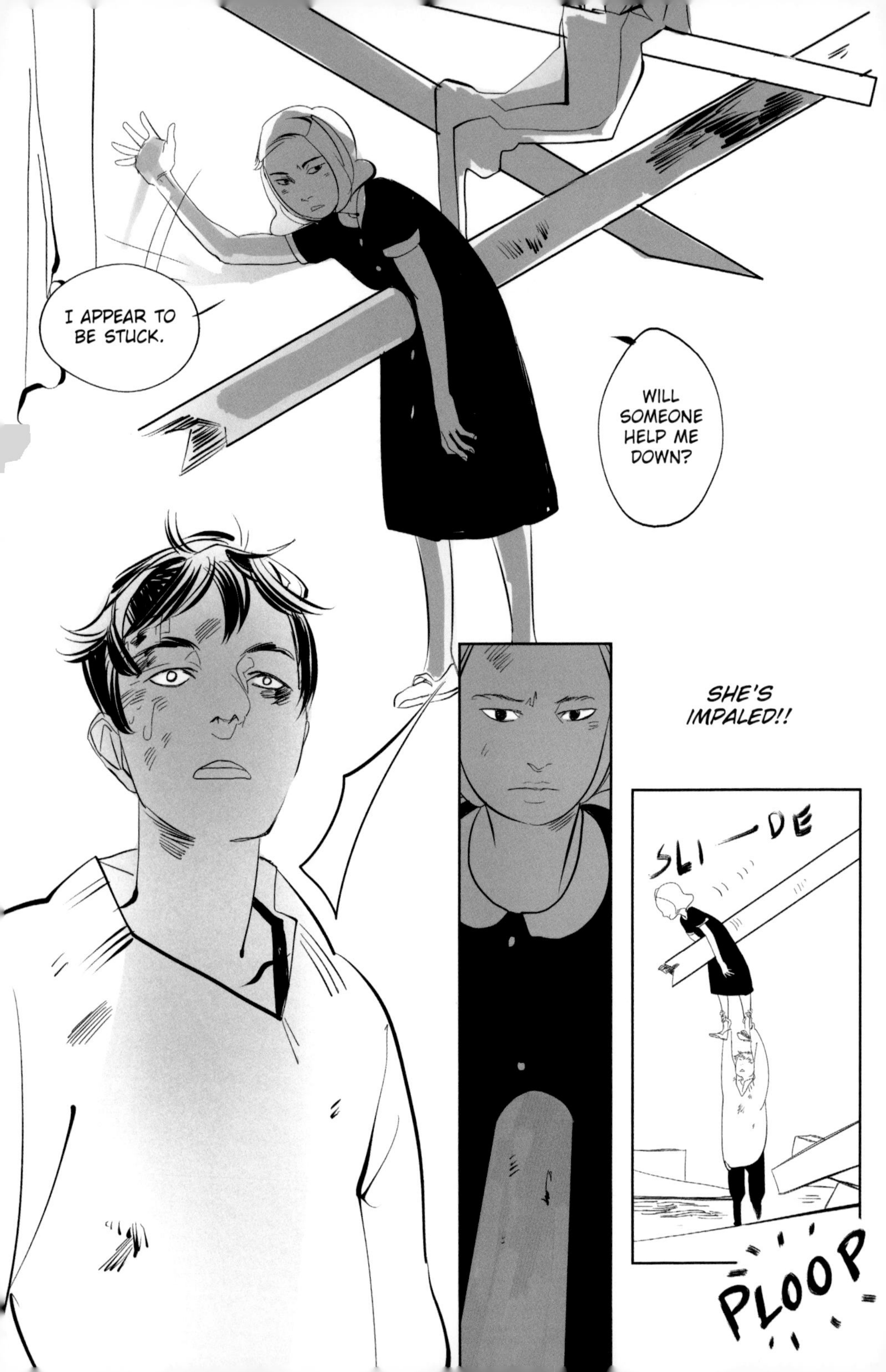
I APPEAR TO BE STUCK.
WILL SOMEONE HELP ME DOWN?
SHE'S IMPALED!!
SLI—DE
PLOOP

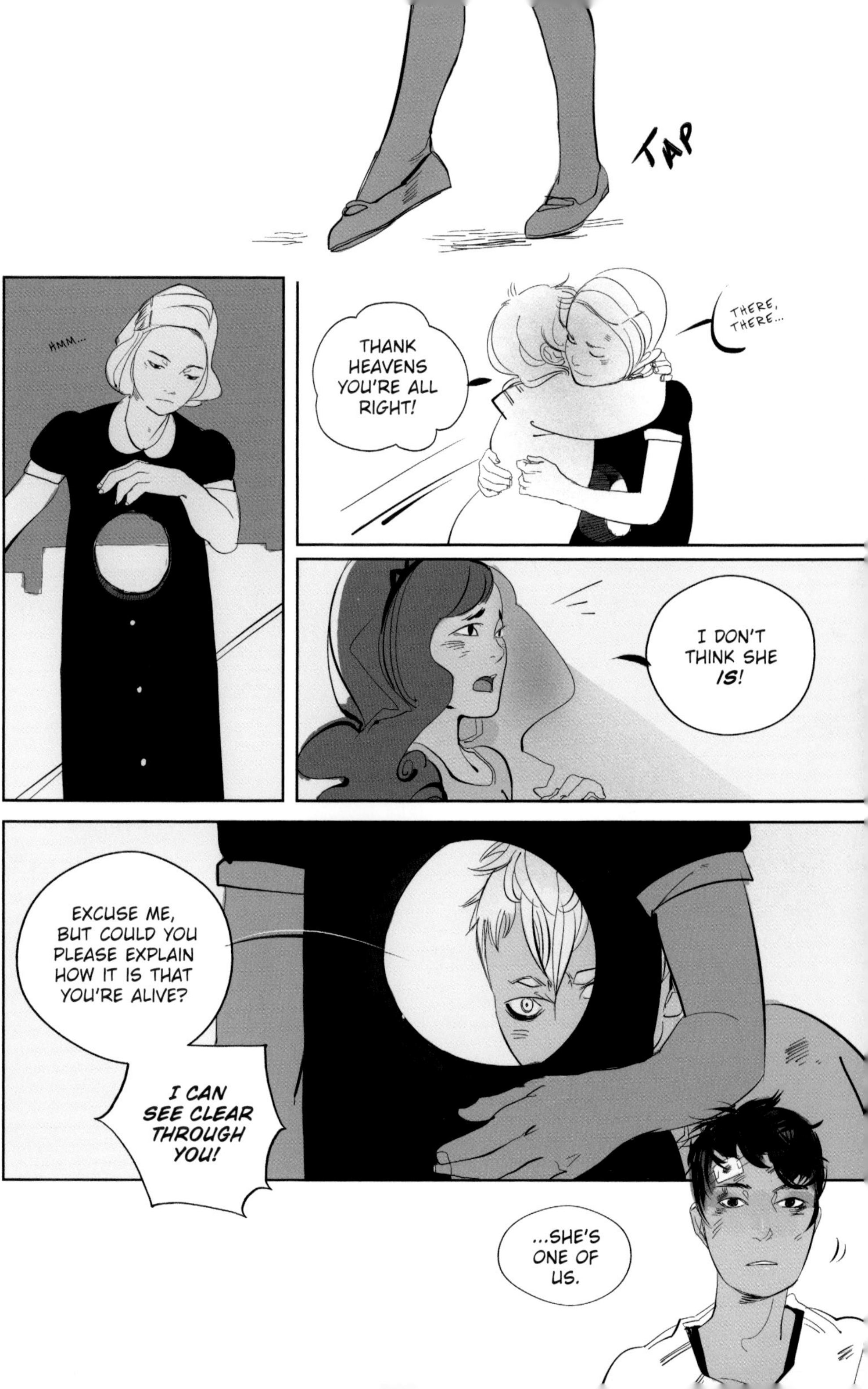
TAP
HMM...
THANK HEAVENS YOU'RE ALL RIGHT!
THERE, THERE...
I DON'T THINK SHE IS!
EXCUSE ME, BUT COULD YOU PLEASE EXPLAIN HOW IT IS THAT YOU'RE ALIVE?
I CAN SEE CLEAR THROUGH YOU!
...SHE'S ONE OF US.

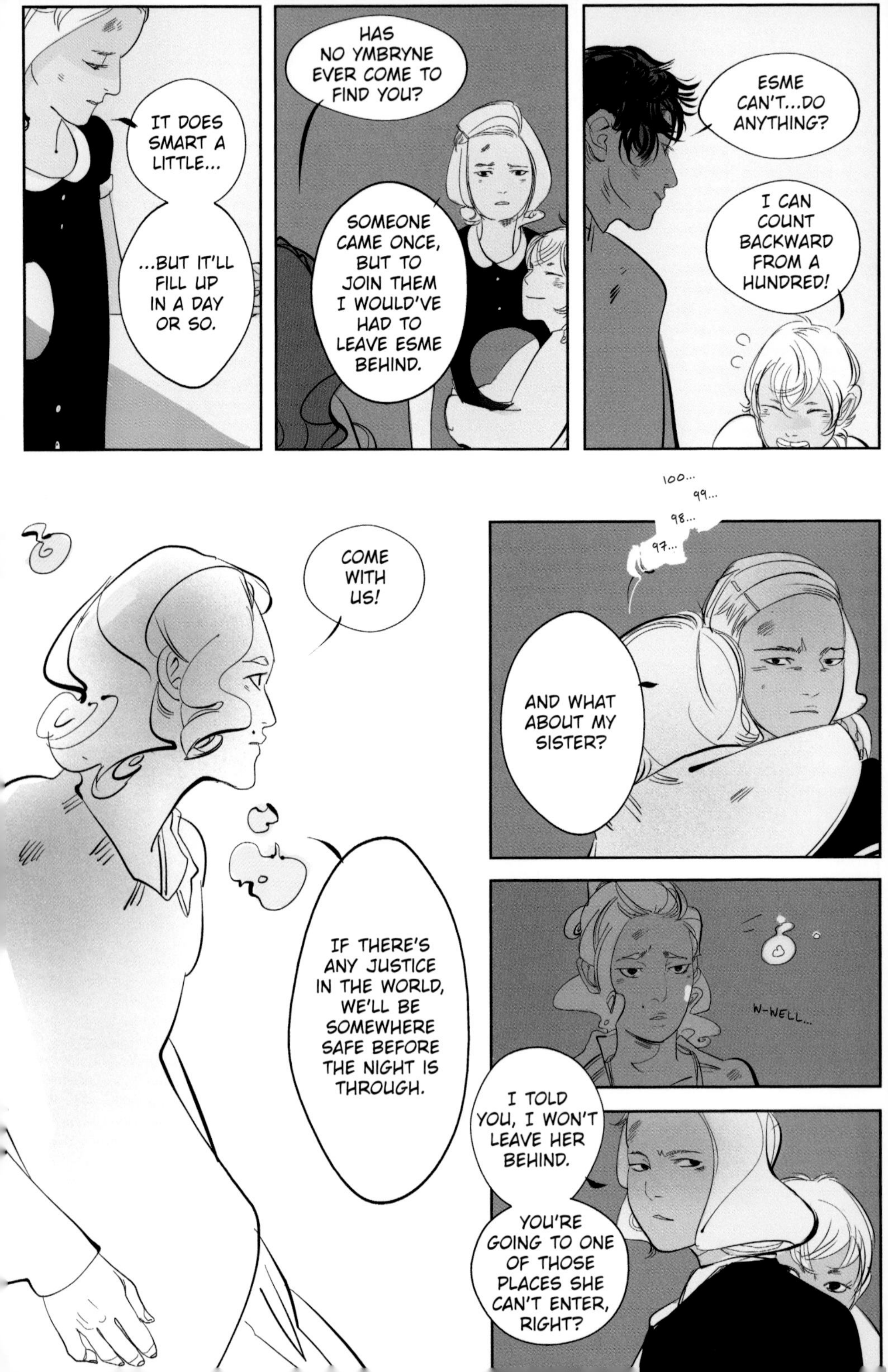
IT DOES SMART A LITTLE...
...BUT IT'LL FILL UP IN A DAY OR SO.
HAS NO YMBRYNE EVER COME TO FIND YOU?
SOMEONE CAME ONCE, BUT TO JOIN THEM I WOULD'VE HAD TO LEAVE ESME BEHIND.
ESME CAN'T...DO ANYTHING?
I CAN COUNT BACKWARD FROM A HUNDRED!
COME WITH US!
IF THERE'S ANY JUSTICE IN THE WORLD, WE'LL BE SOMEWHERE SAFE BEFORE THE NIGHT IS THROUGH.
100...
99...
98...
97...
AND WHAT ABOUT MY SISTER?
W-WELL...
I TOLD YOU, I WON'T LEAVE HER BEHIND.
YOU'RE GOING TO ONE OF THOSE PLACES SHE CAN'T ENTER, RIGHT?

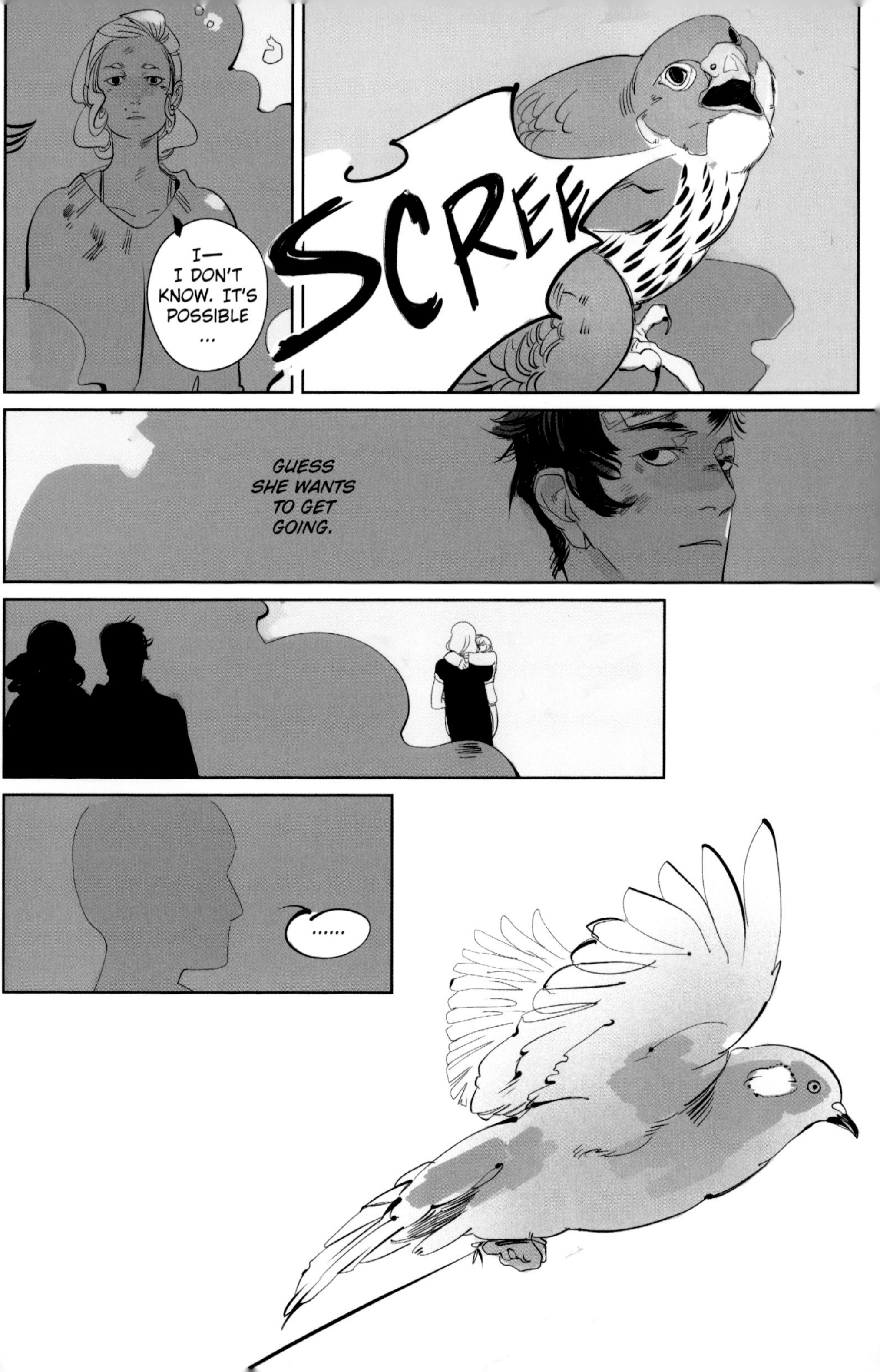
I— I DON'T KNOW. IT'S POSSIBLE ...
SCREE
GUESS SHE WANTS TO GET GOING.
......

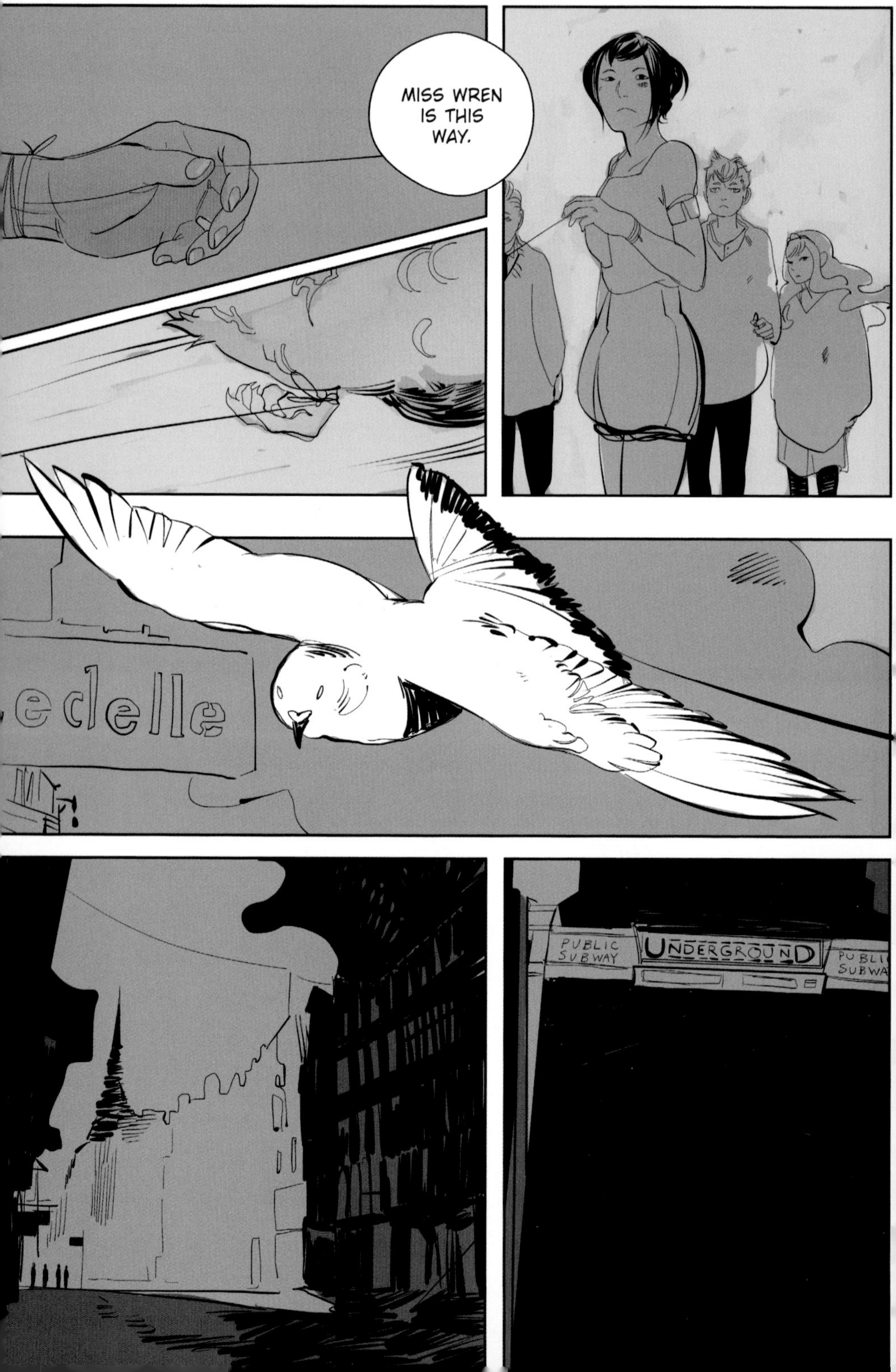
MISS WREN IS THIS WAY.
edelle
PUBLIC SUBWAY
UNDERGROUND
PUBLIC SUBWAY

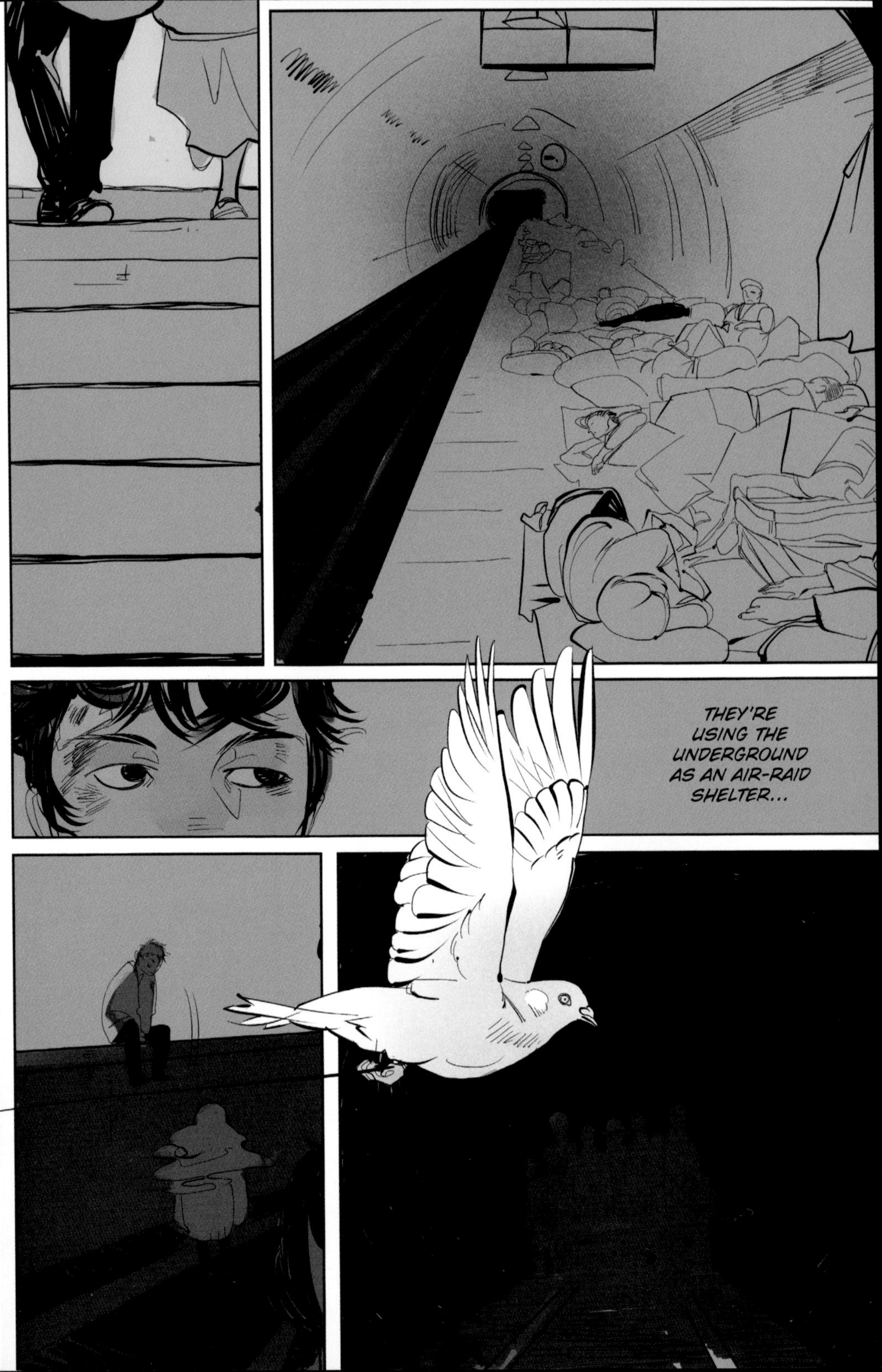
THEY'RE USING THE UNDERGROUND AS AN AIR-RAID SHELTER...

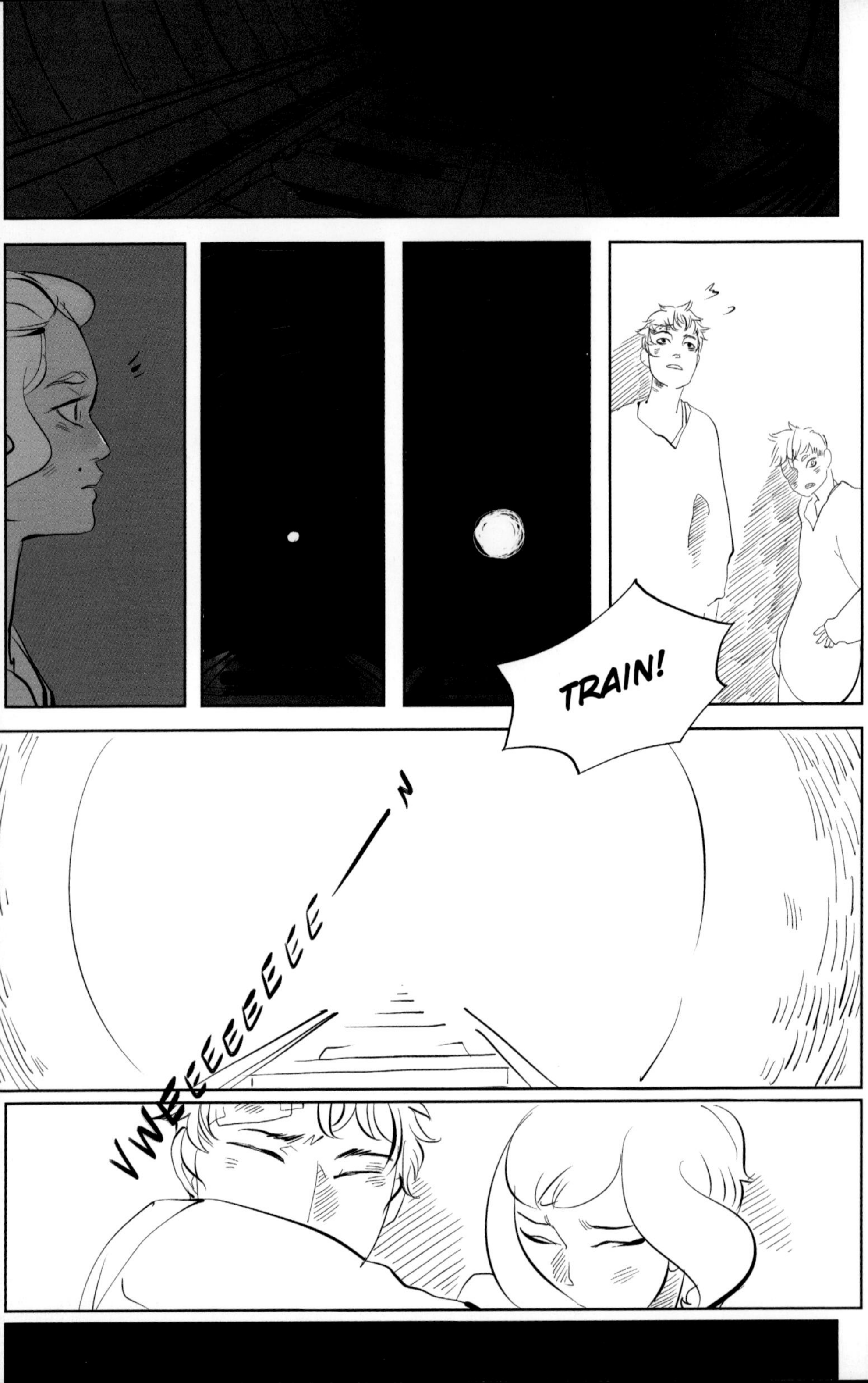
TRAIN!
VWEEEEEEEEE——N

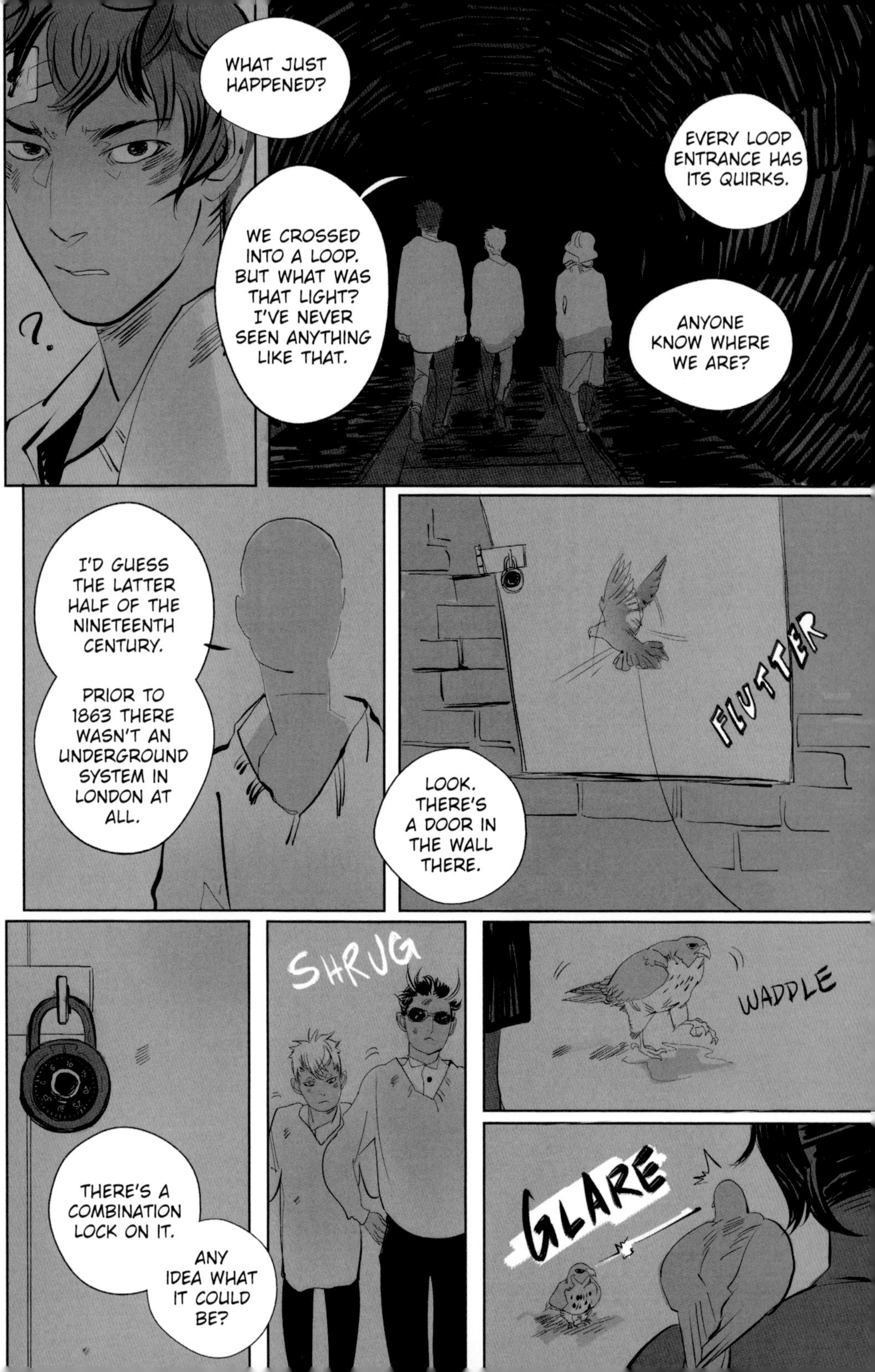
WHAT JUST HAPPENED?
WE CROSSED INTO A LOOP. BUT WHAT WAS THAT LIGHT? I'VE NEVER SEEN ANYTHING LIKE THAT.
EVERY LOOP ENTRANCE HAS ITS QUIRKS.
ANYONE KNOW WHERE WE ARE?
I'D GUESS THE LATTER HALF OF THE NINETEENTH CENTURY.
PRIOR TO 1863 THERE WASN'T AN UNDERGROUND SYSTEM IN LONDON AT ALL.
FLUTTER
LOOK. THERE'S A DOOR IN THE WALL THERE.
THERE'S A COMBINATION LOCK ON IT.
ANY IDEA WHAT IT COULD BE?
SHRUG
WADDLE
GLARE

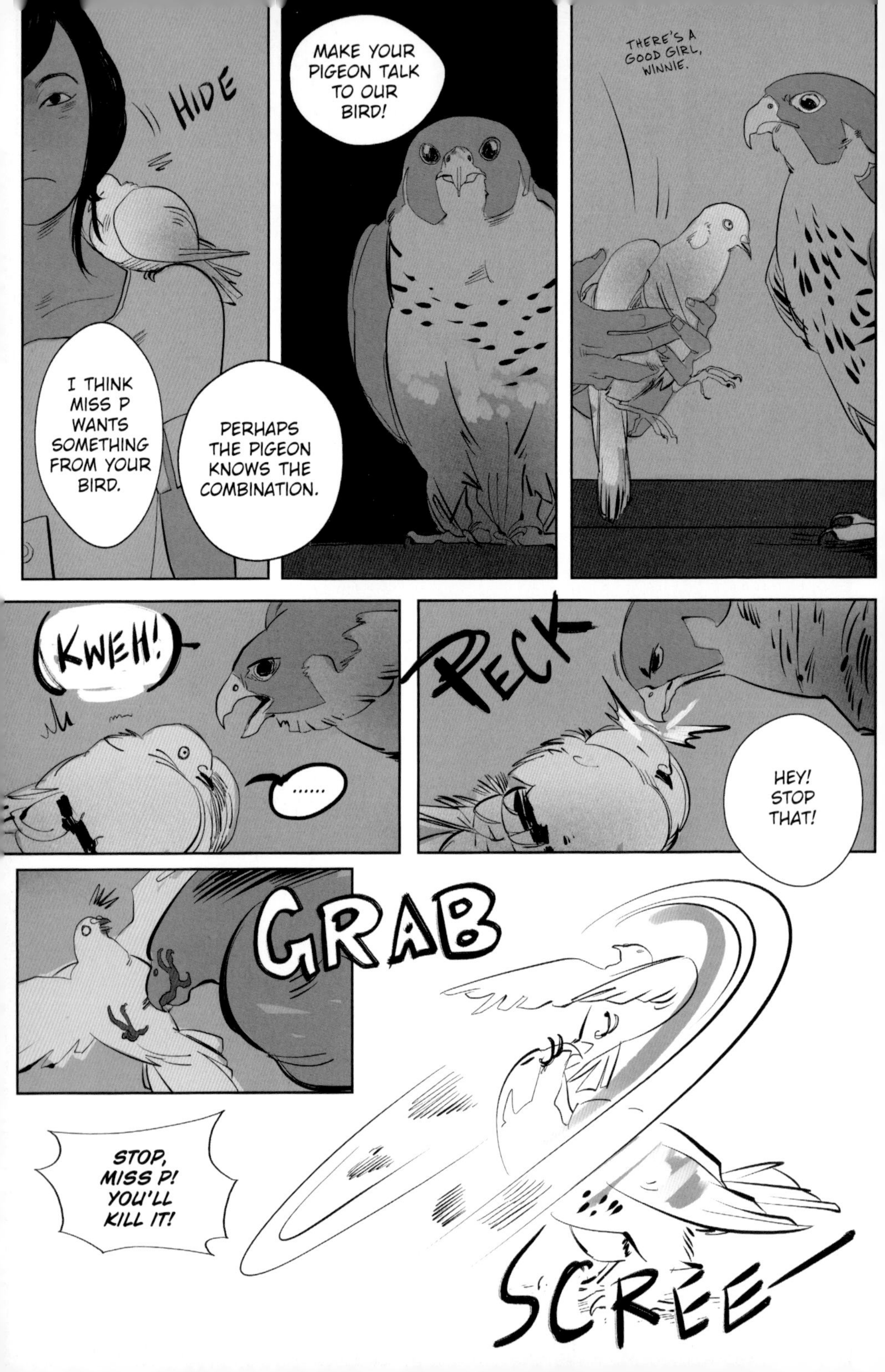
HIDE
I THINK MISS P WANTS SOMETHING FROM YOUR BIRD.
PERHAPS THE PIGEON KNOWS THE COMBINATION.
MAKE YOUR PIGEON TALK TO OUR BIRD!
THERE'S A GOOD GIRL, WINNIE.
KWEH!
......
PECK
HEY! STOP THAT!
GRAB
STOP, MISS P! YOU'LL KILL IT!
SCREE

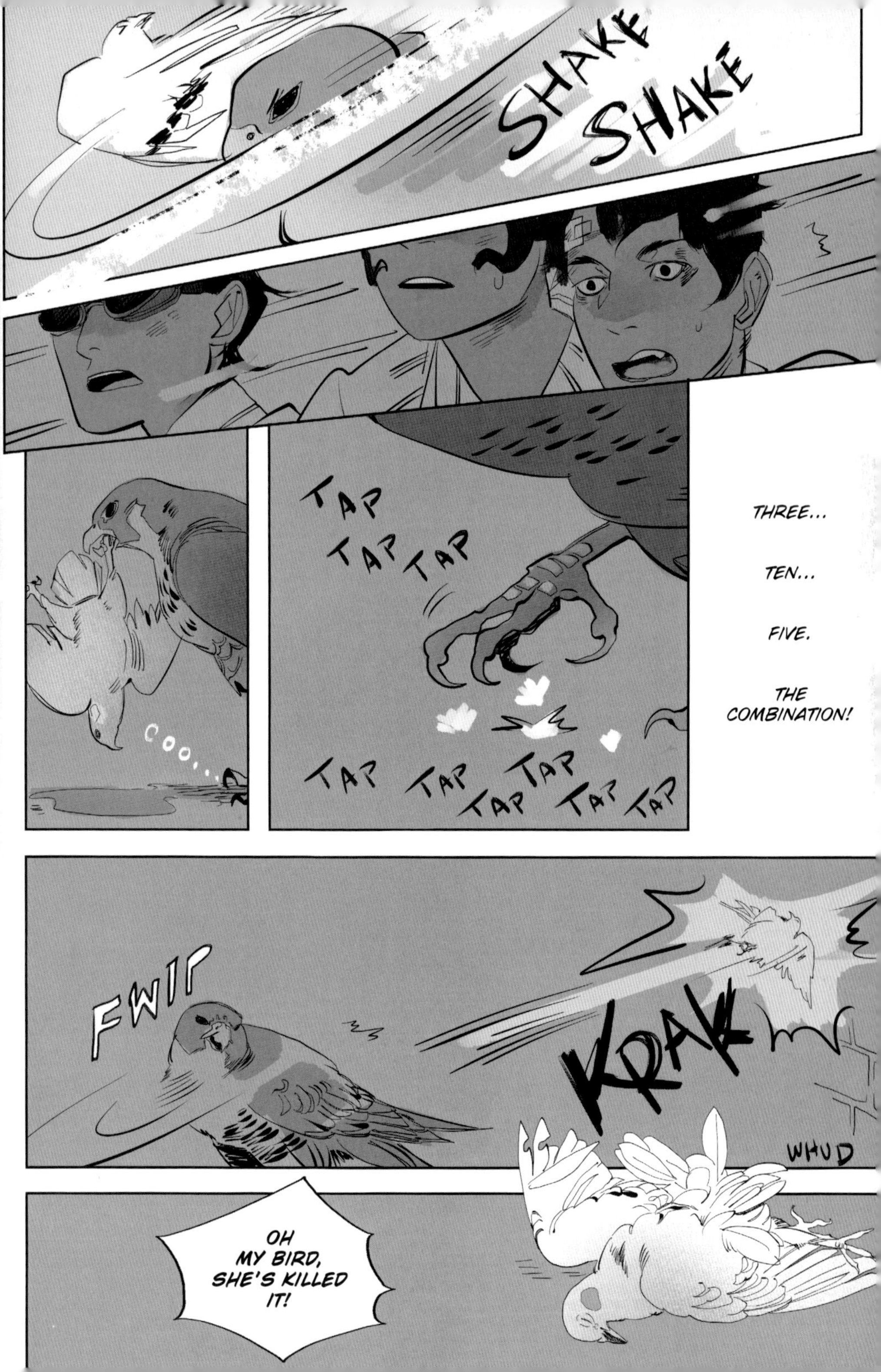
SHAKE SHAKE
COO...
TAP TAP TAP
TAP TAP TAP TAP TAP TAP
THREE...
TEN...
FIVE.
THE COMBINATION!
FWIP
KRAK
WHUD
OH MY BIRD, SHE'S KILLED IT!

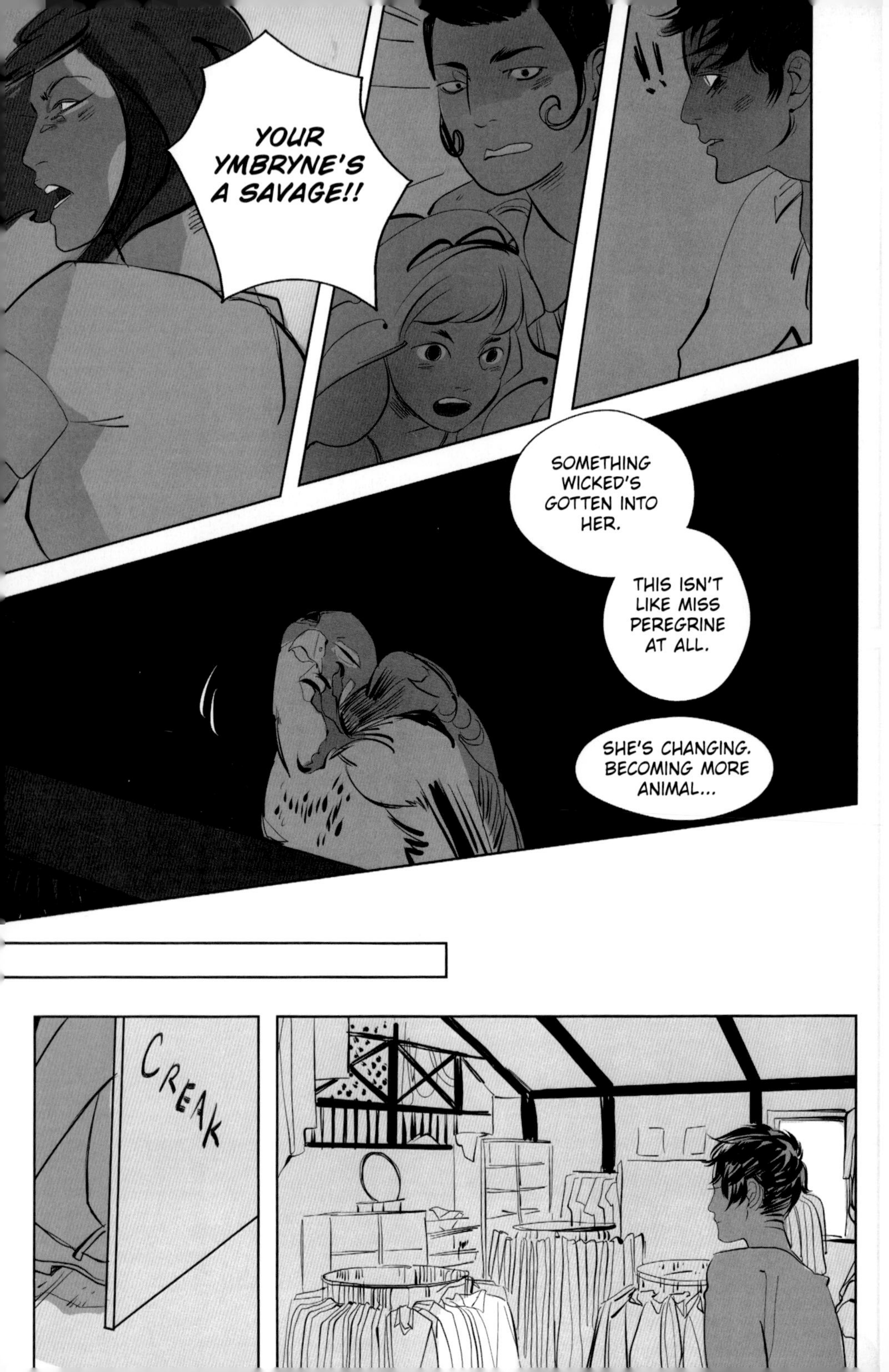
YOUR YMBRYNE'S A SAVAGE!!
!!
SOMETHING WICKED'S GOTTEN INTO HER.
THIS ISN'T LIKE MISS PEREGRINE AT ALL.
SHE'S CHANGING. BECOMING MORE ANIMAL...
CREAK

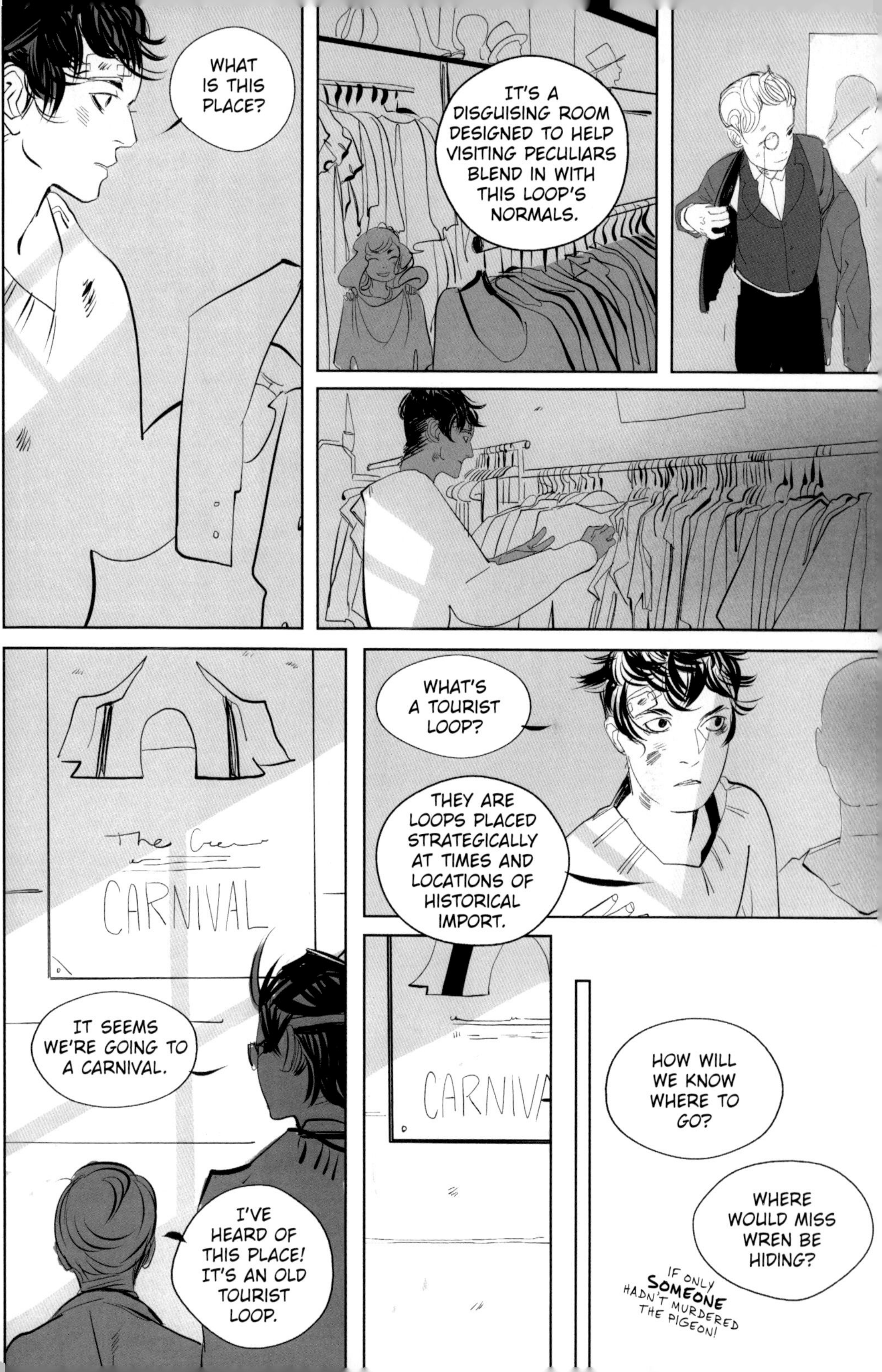
WHAT IS THIS PLACE?
IT'S A DISGUISING ROOM DESIGNED TO HELP VISITING PECULIARS BLEND IN WITH THIS LOOP'S NORMALS.
CARNIVAL
IT SEEMS WE'RE GOING TO A CARNIVAL.
I'VE HEARD OF THIS PLACE! IT'S AN OLD TOURIST LOOP.
WHAT'S A TOURIST LOOP?
THEY ARE LOOPS PLACED STRATEGICALLY AT TIMES AND LOCATIONS OF HISTORICAL IMPORT.
CARNIVA
HOW WILL WE KNOW WHERE TO GO?
WHERE WOULD MISS WREN BE HIDING?
IF ONLY SOMEONE HADN'T MURDERED THE PIGEON!

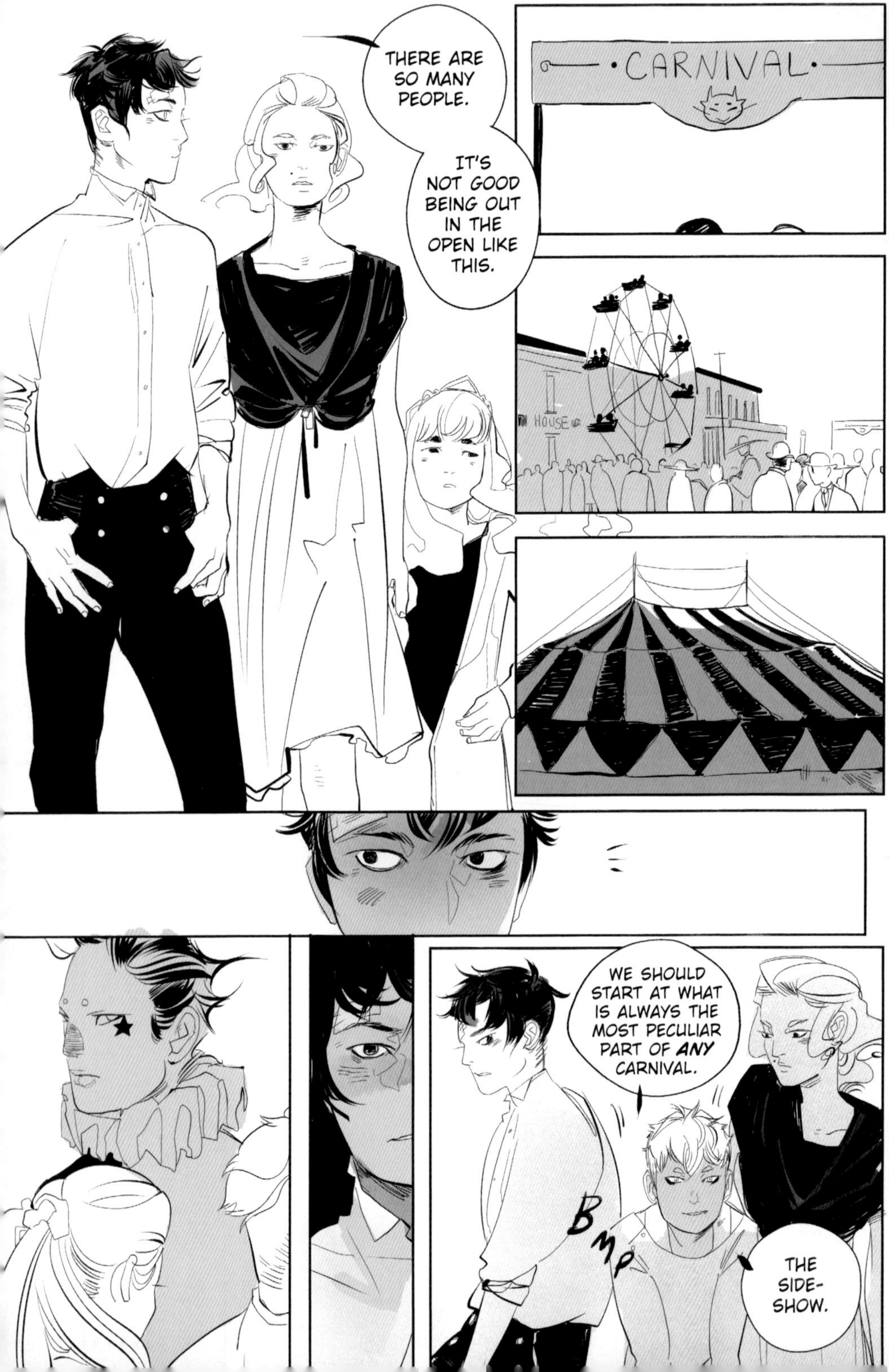
THERE ARE SO MANY PEOPLE.
IT'S NOT GOOD BEING OUT IN THE OPEN LIKE THIS.
CARNIVAL
HOUSE
WE SHOULD START AT WHAT IS ALWAYS THE MOST PECULIAR PART OF *ANY* CARNIVAL.
BMP
THE SIDE-SHOW.

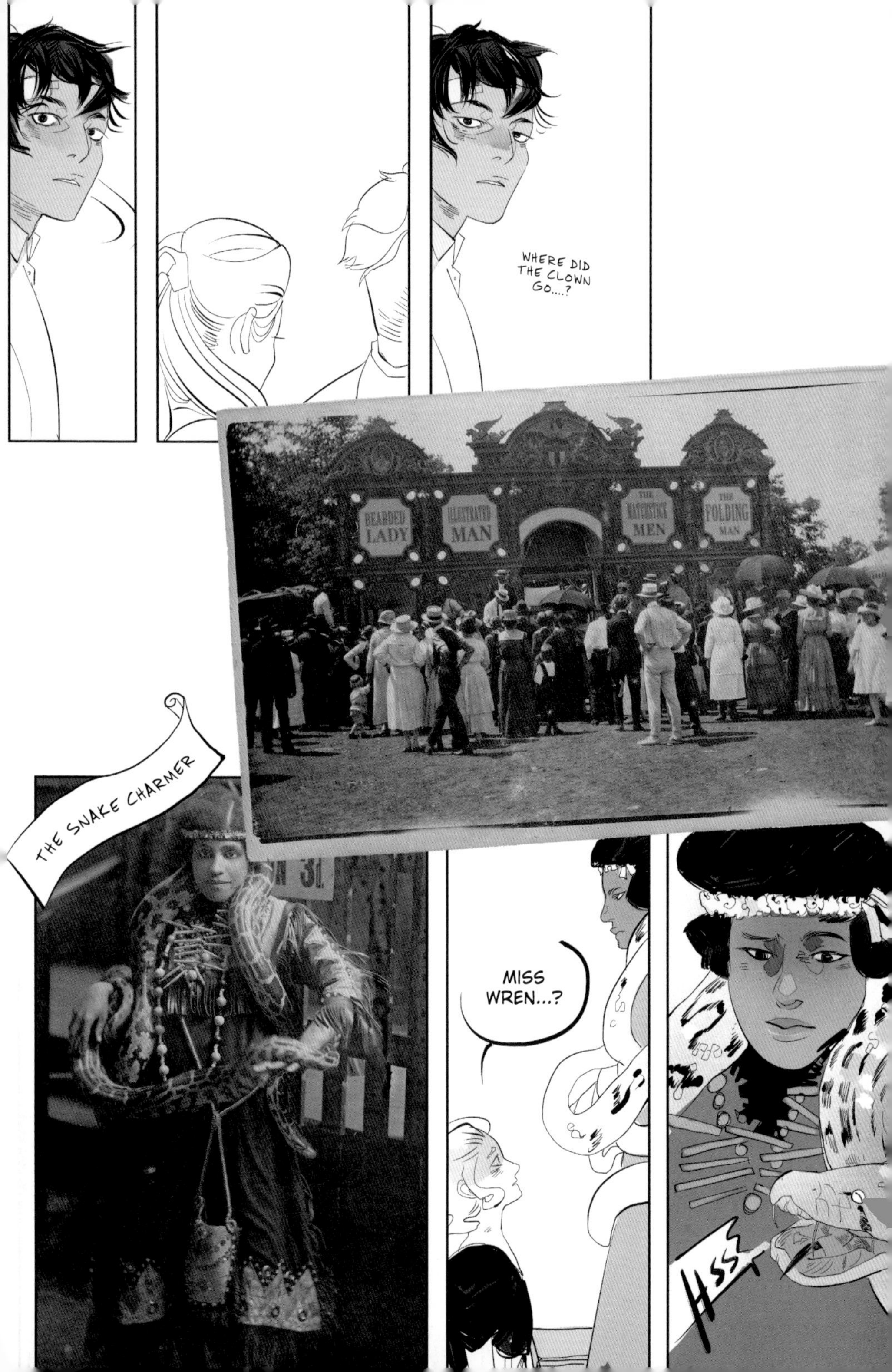
WHERE DID THE CLOWN GO....?
BEARDED LADY
ILLUSTRATED MAN
THE MATCHSTICK MEN
THE FOLDING MAN
THE SNAKE CHARMER
MISS WREN...?
HSSS

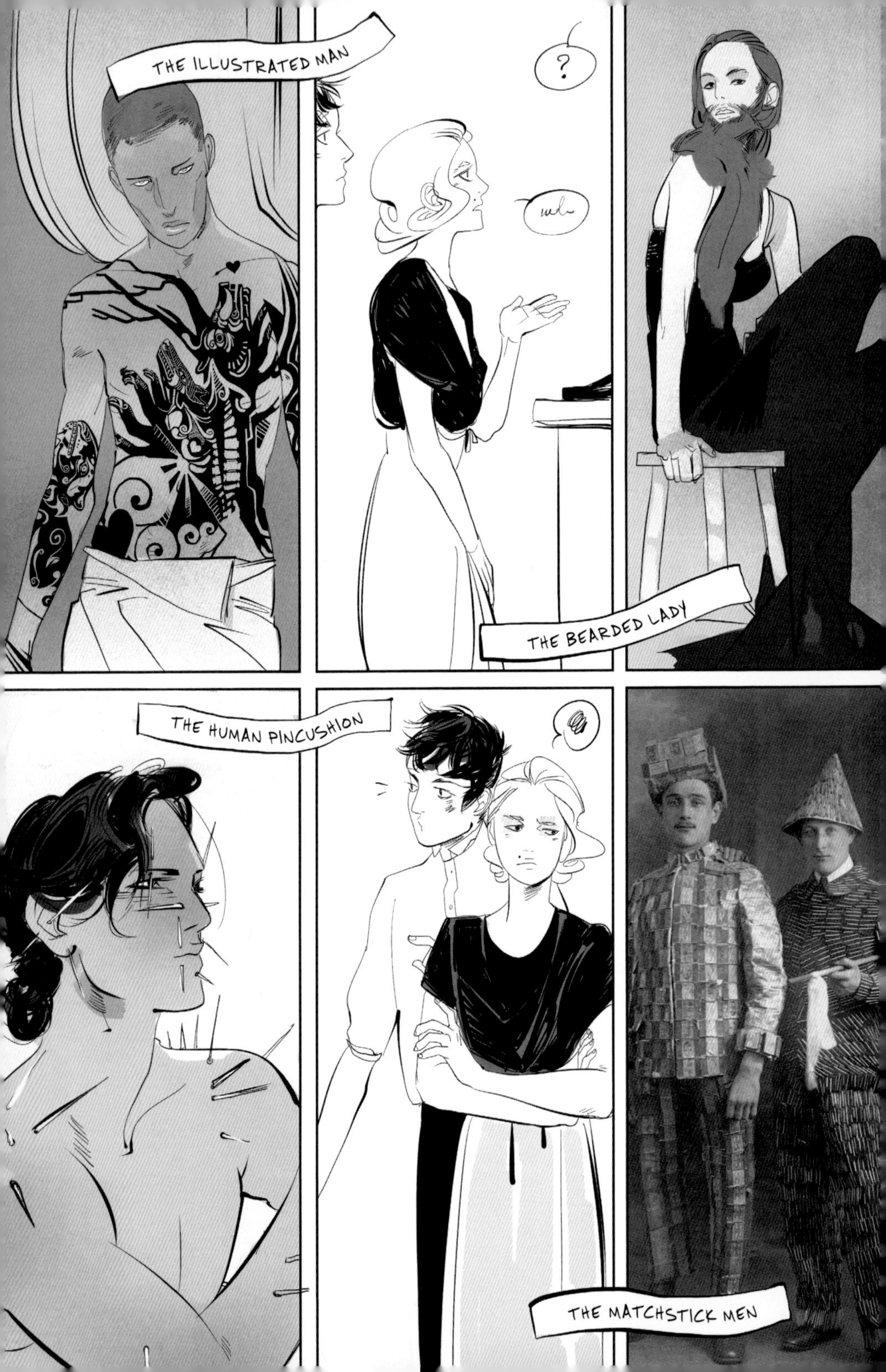
THE ILLUSTRATED MAN
?
THE BEARDED LADY
THE HUMAN PINCUSHION
THE MATCHSTICK MEN

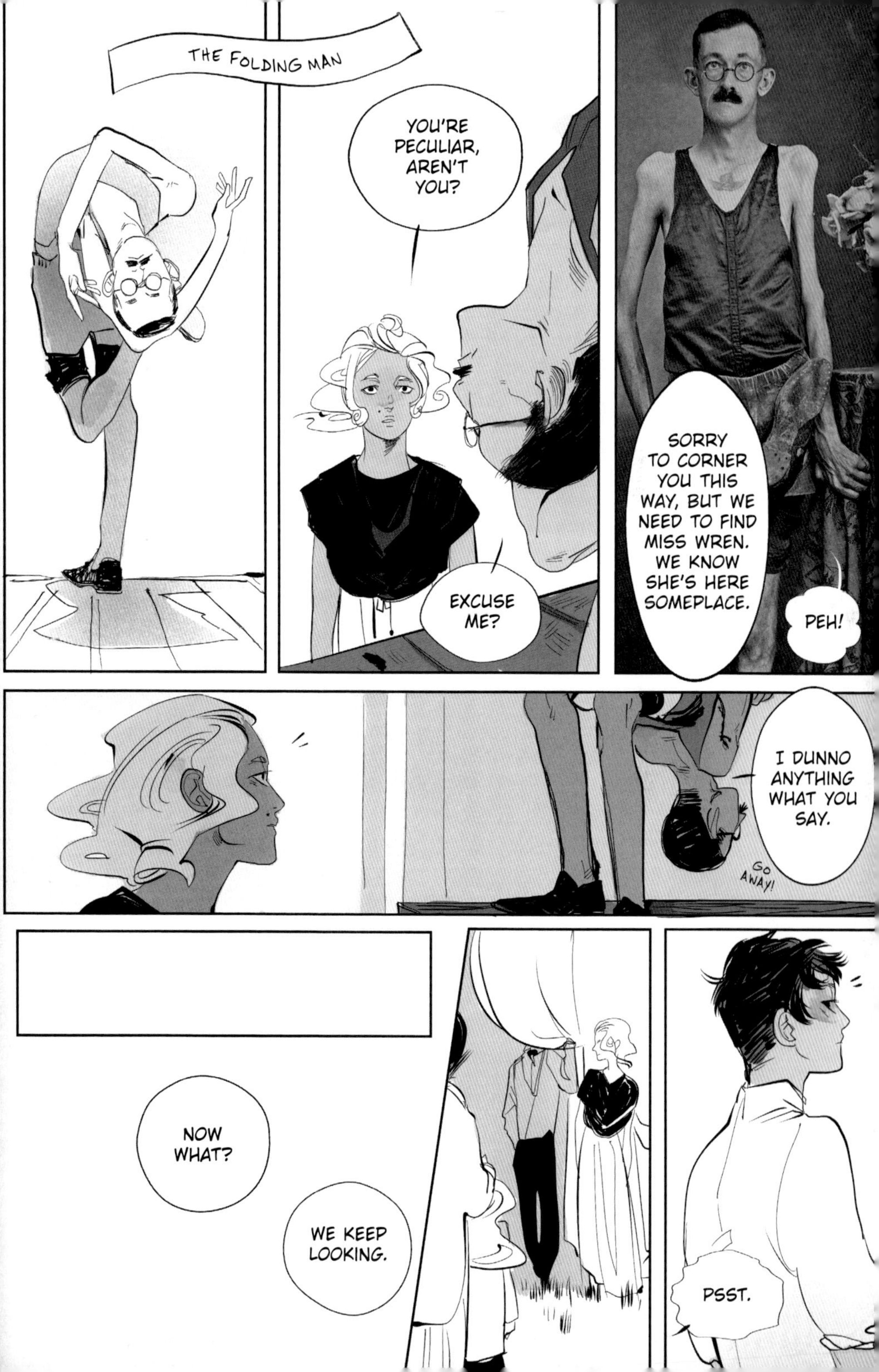
THE FOLDING MAN
YOU'RE PECULIAR, AREN'T YOU?
EXCUSE ME?
SORRY TO CORNER YOU THIS WAY, BUT WE NEED TO FIND MISS WREN. WE KNOW SHE'S HERE SOMEPLACE.
PEH!
I DUNNO ANYTHING WHAT YOU SAY.
GO AWAY!
NOW WHAT?
WE KEEP LOOKING.
PSST.

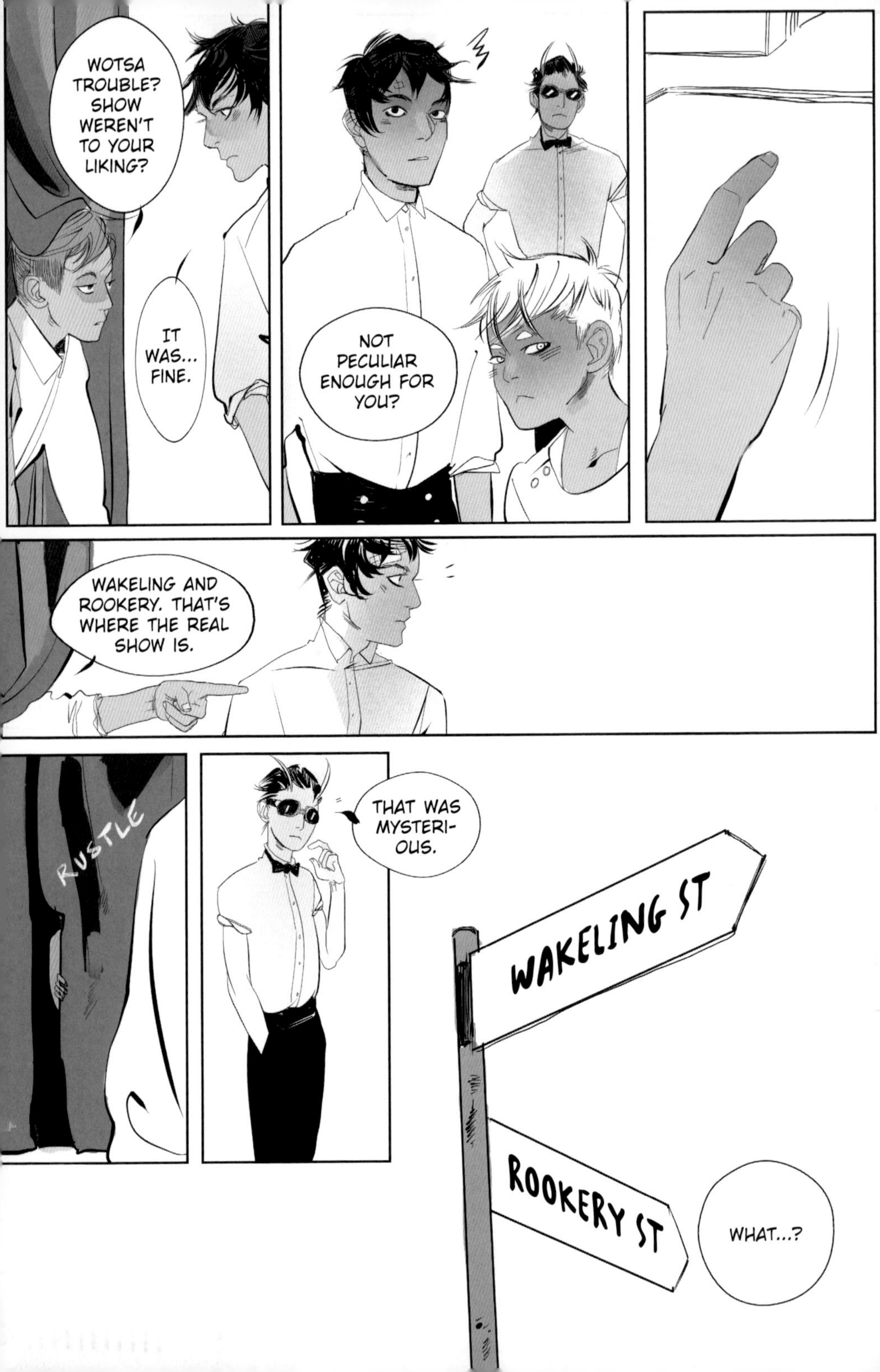
WOTSA TROUBLE? SHOW WEREN'T TO YOUR LIKING?
IT WAS... FINE.
NOT PECULIAR ENOUGH FOR YOU?
WAKELING AND ROOKERY. THAT'S WHERE THE REAL SHOW IS.
RUSTLE
THAT WAS MYSTERI-OUS.
WAKELING ST
ROOKERY ST
WHAT...?

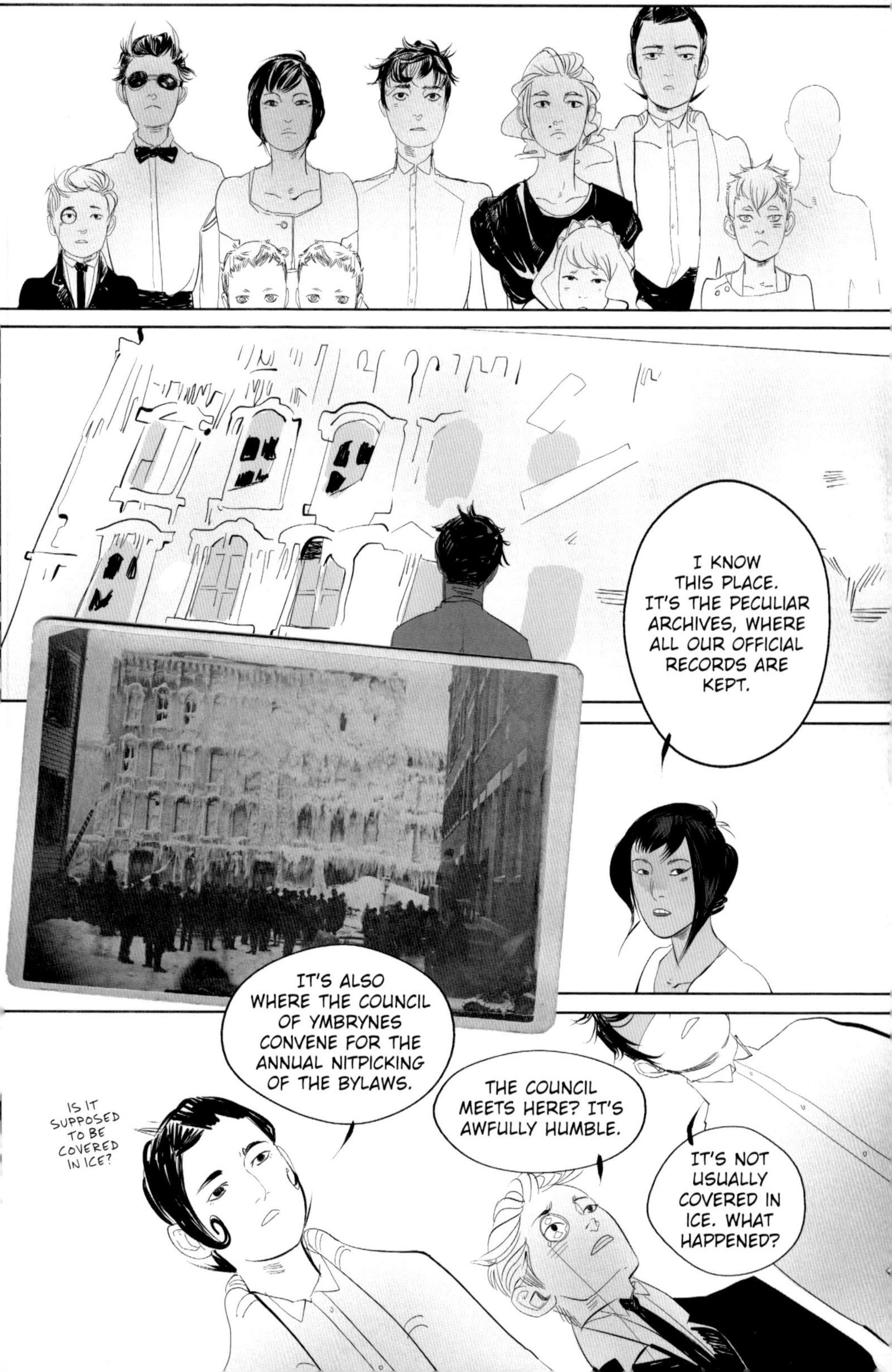
I KNOW THIS PLACE. IT'S THE PECULIAR ARCHIVES, WHERE ALL OUR OFFICIAL RECORDS ARE KEPT.
IT'S ALSO WHERE THE COUNCIL OF YMBRYNES CONVENE FOR THE ANNUAL NITPICKING OF THE BYLAWS.
IS IT SUPPOSED TO BE COVERED IN ICE?
THE COUNCIL MEETS HERE? IT'S AWFULLY HUMBLE.
IT'S NOT USUALLY COVERED IN ICE. WHAT HAPPENED?

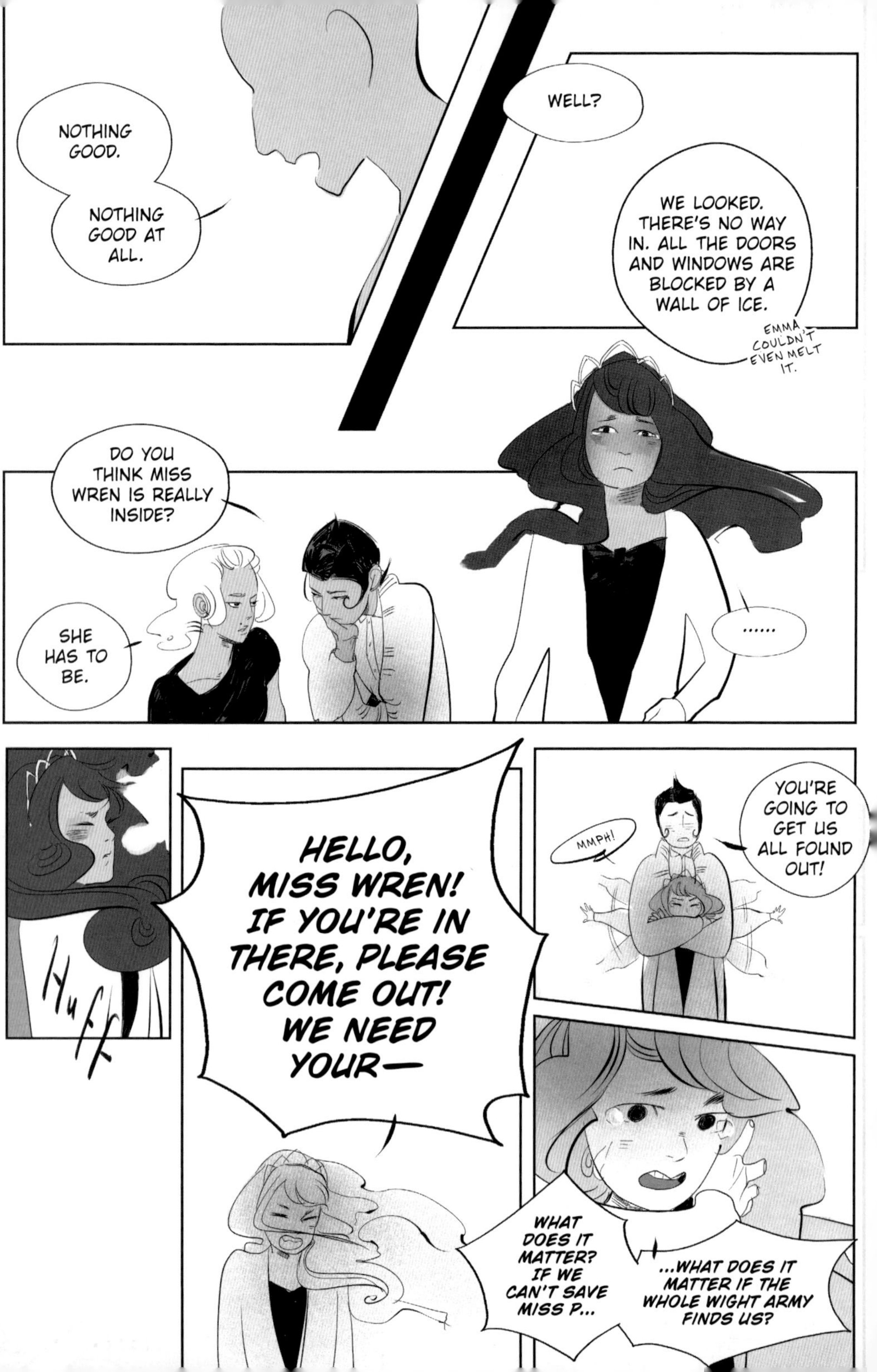
NOTHING GOOD.
NOTHING GOOD AT ALL.
WELL?
WE LOOKED. THERE'S NO WAY IN. ALL THE DOORS AND WINDOWS ARE BLOCKED BY A WALL OF ICE.
EMMA COULDN'T EVEN MELT IT.
DO YOU THINK MISS WREN IS REALLY INSIDE?
SHE HAS TO BE.
......
HUFF
HELLO, MISS WREN! IF YOU'RE IN THERE, PLEASE COME OUT! WE NEED YOUR—
MMPH!
YOU'RE GOING TO GET US ALL FOUND OUT!
WHAT DOES IT MATTER? IF WE CAN'T SAVE MISS P...
...WHAT DOES IT MATTER IF THE WHOLE WIGHT ARMY FINDS US?

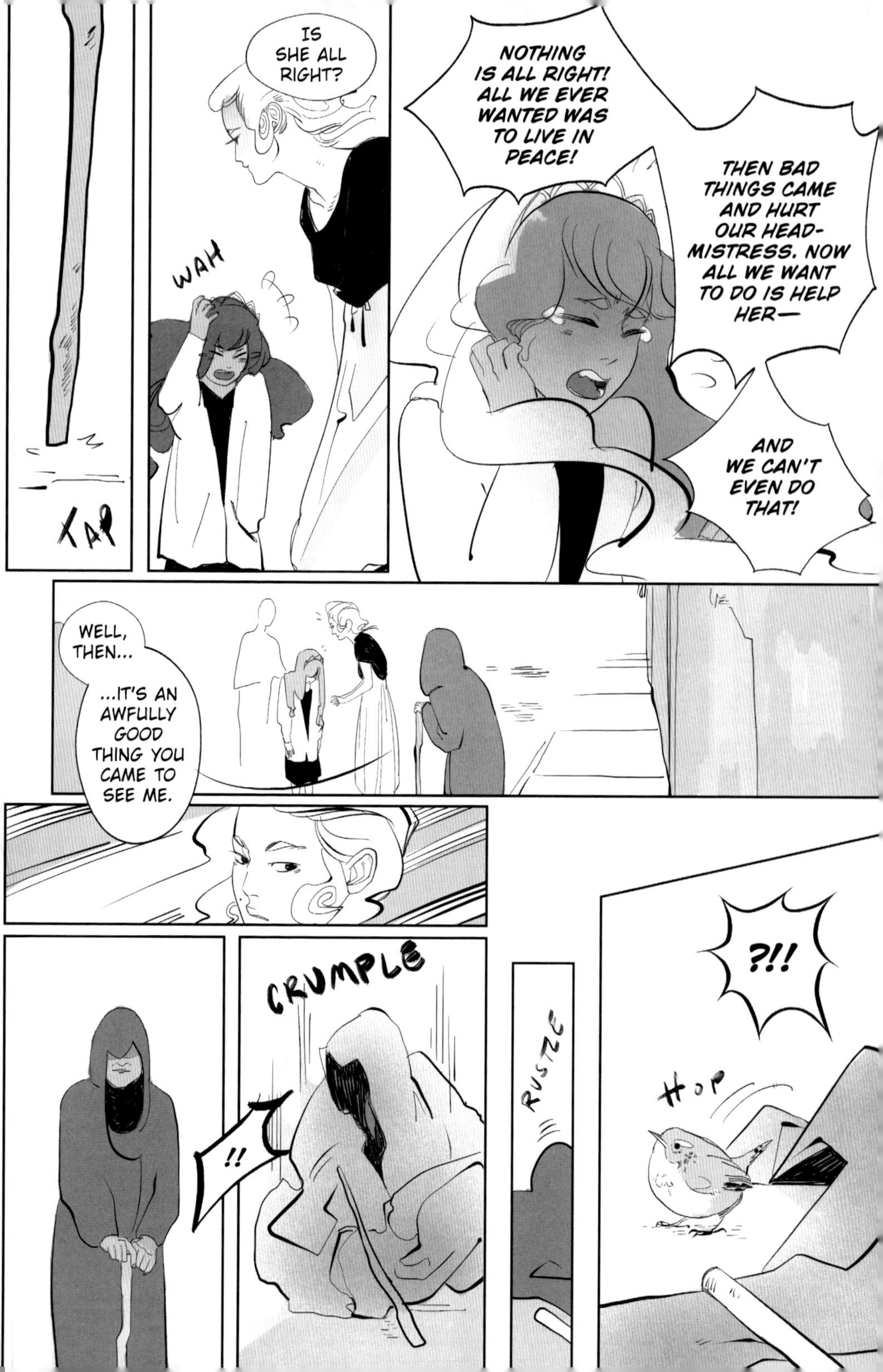
TAP
IS SHE ALL RIGHT?
WAH
NOTHING IS ALL RIGHT! ALL WE EVER WANTED WAS TO LIVE IN PEACE!
THEN BAD THINGS CAME AND HURT OUR HEAD-MISTRESS. NOW ALL WE WANT TO DO IS HELP HER—
AND WE CAN'T EVEN DO THAT!
WELL, THEN...
...IT'S AN AWFULLY GOOD THING YOU CAME TO SEE ME.
CRUMPLE
!!
RUSTLE
?!!
HOP

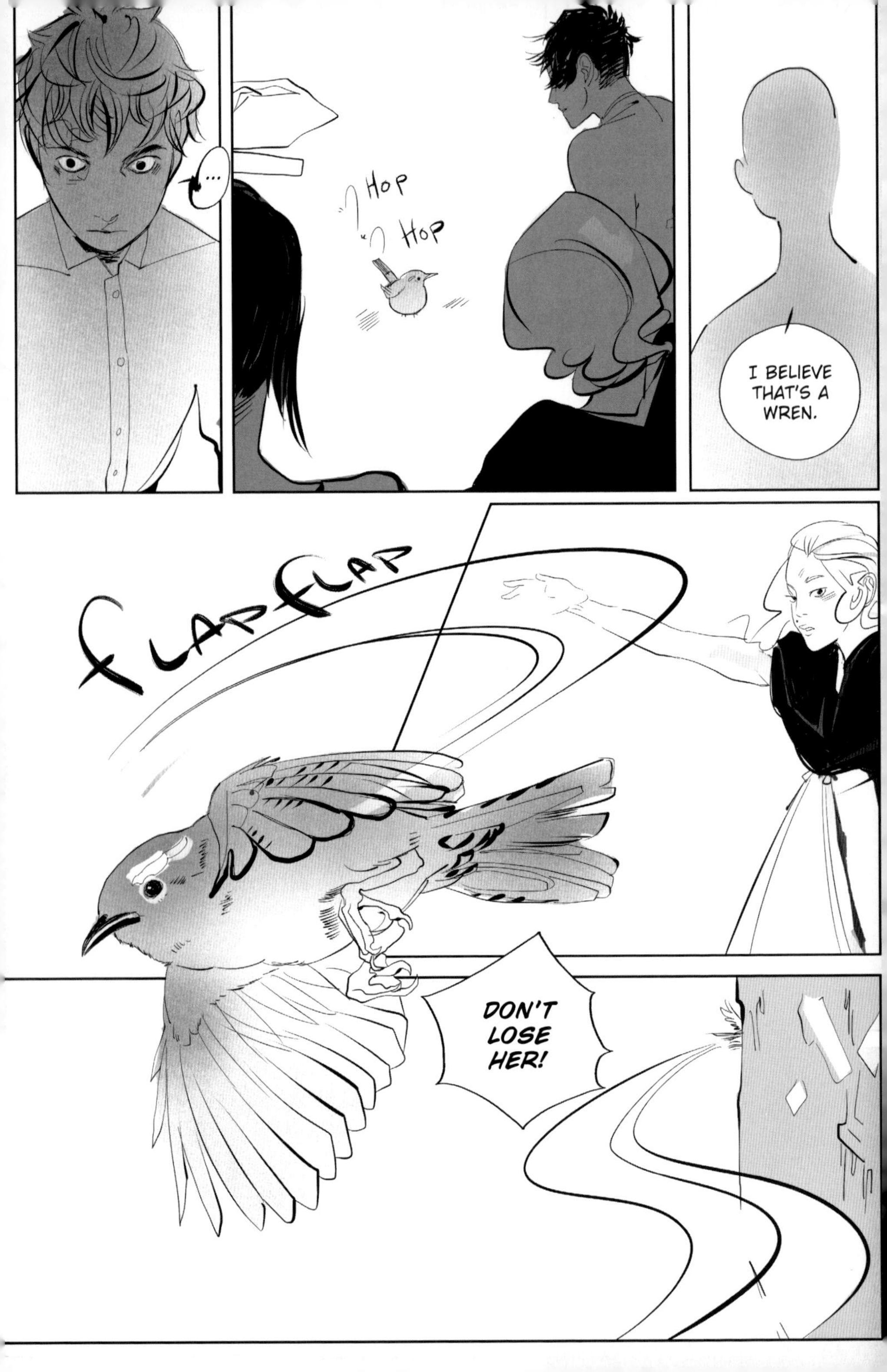
...
HOP
HOP
I BELIEVE THAT'S A WREN.
FLAP FLAP
DON'T LOSE HER!

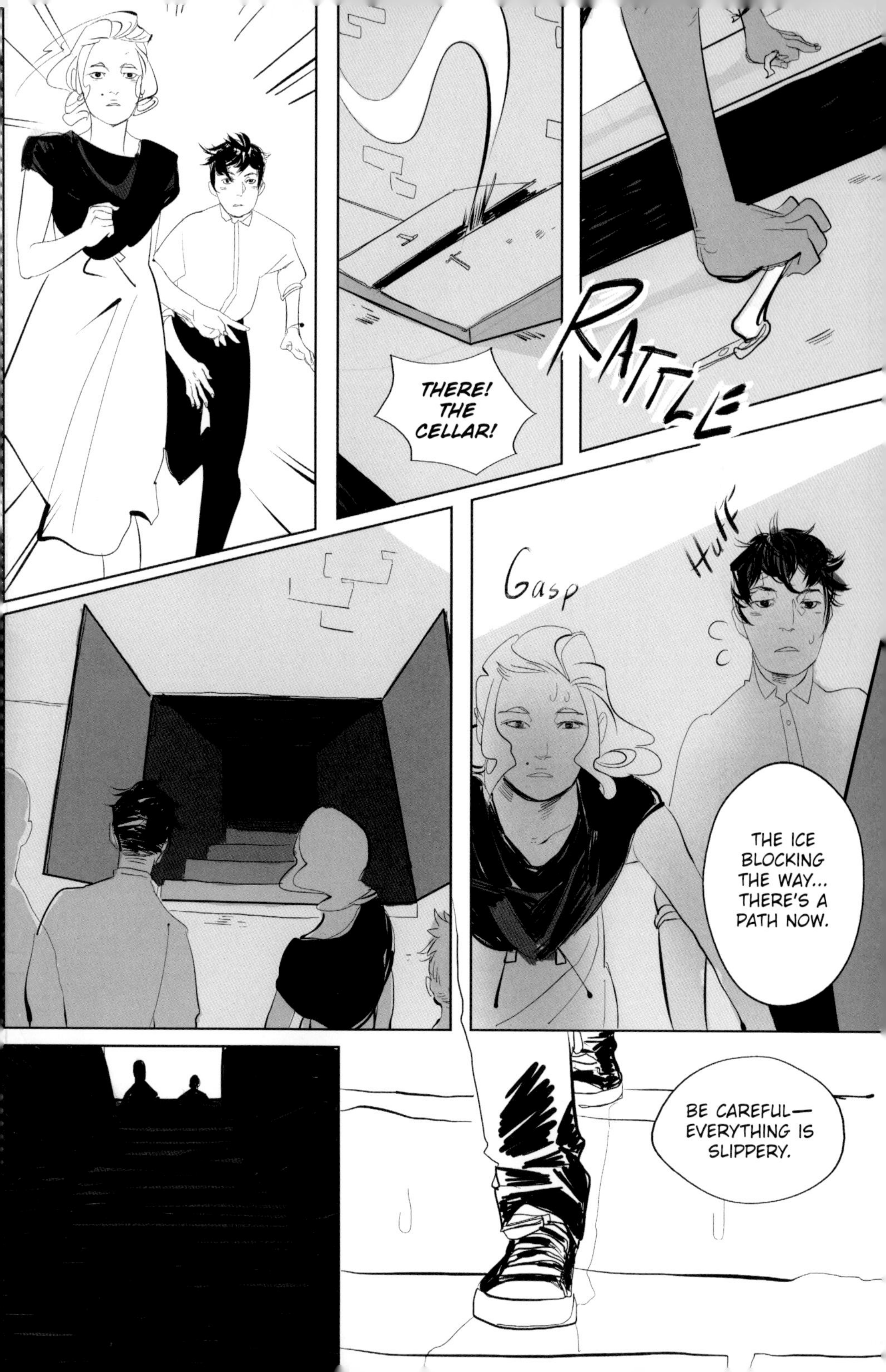
THERE! THE CELLAR!
RATTLE
Gasp
Huff
THE ICE BLOCKING THE WAY... THERE'S A PATH NOW.
BE CAREFUL— EVERYTHING IS SLIPPERY.

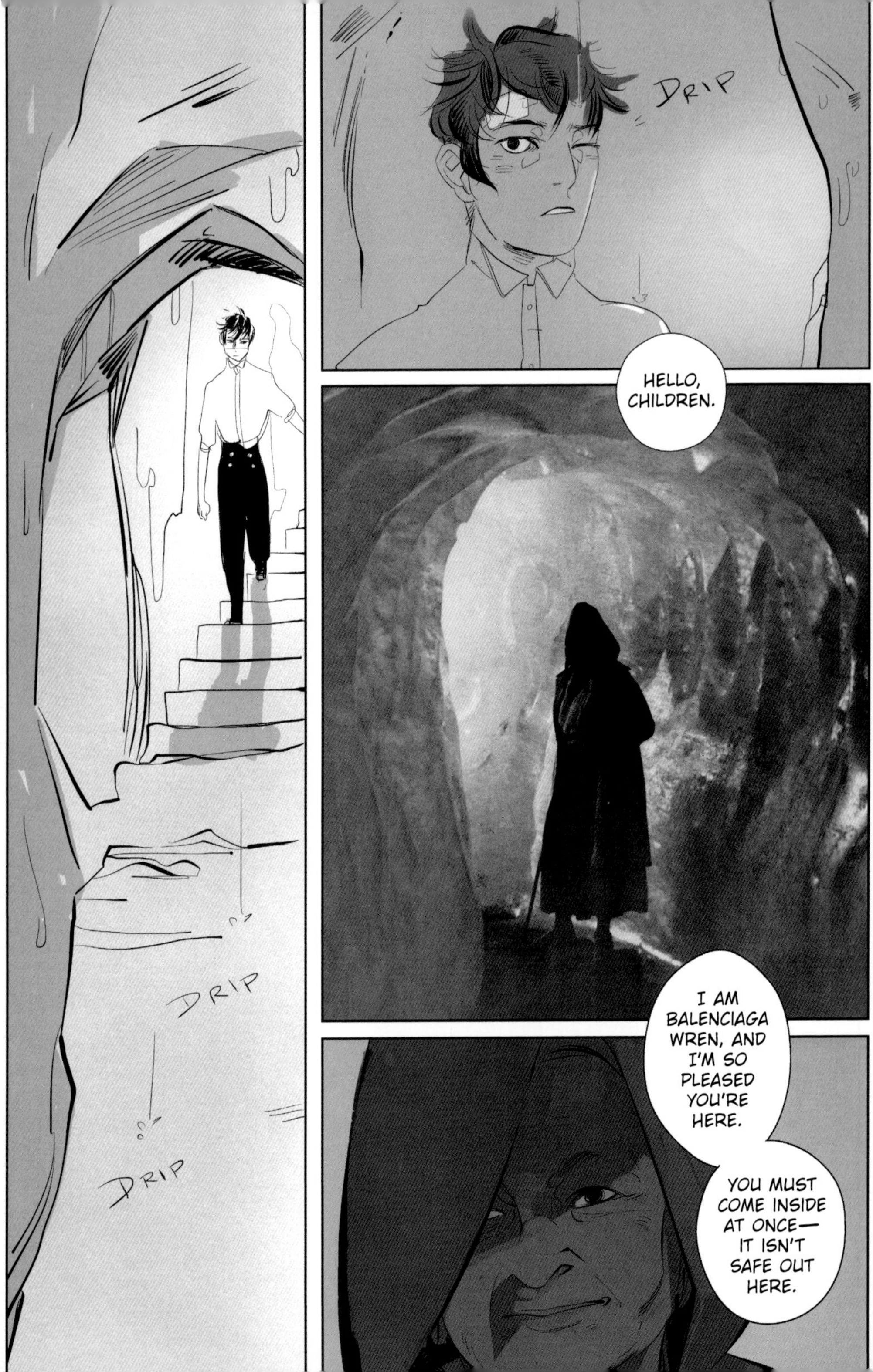
DRIP
DRIP
DRIP
HELLO, CHILDREN.
I AM BALENCIAGA WREN, AND I'M SO PLEASED YOU'RE HERE.
YOU MUST COME INSIDE AT ONCE— IT ISN'T SAFE OUT HERE.

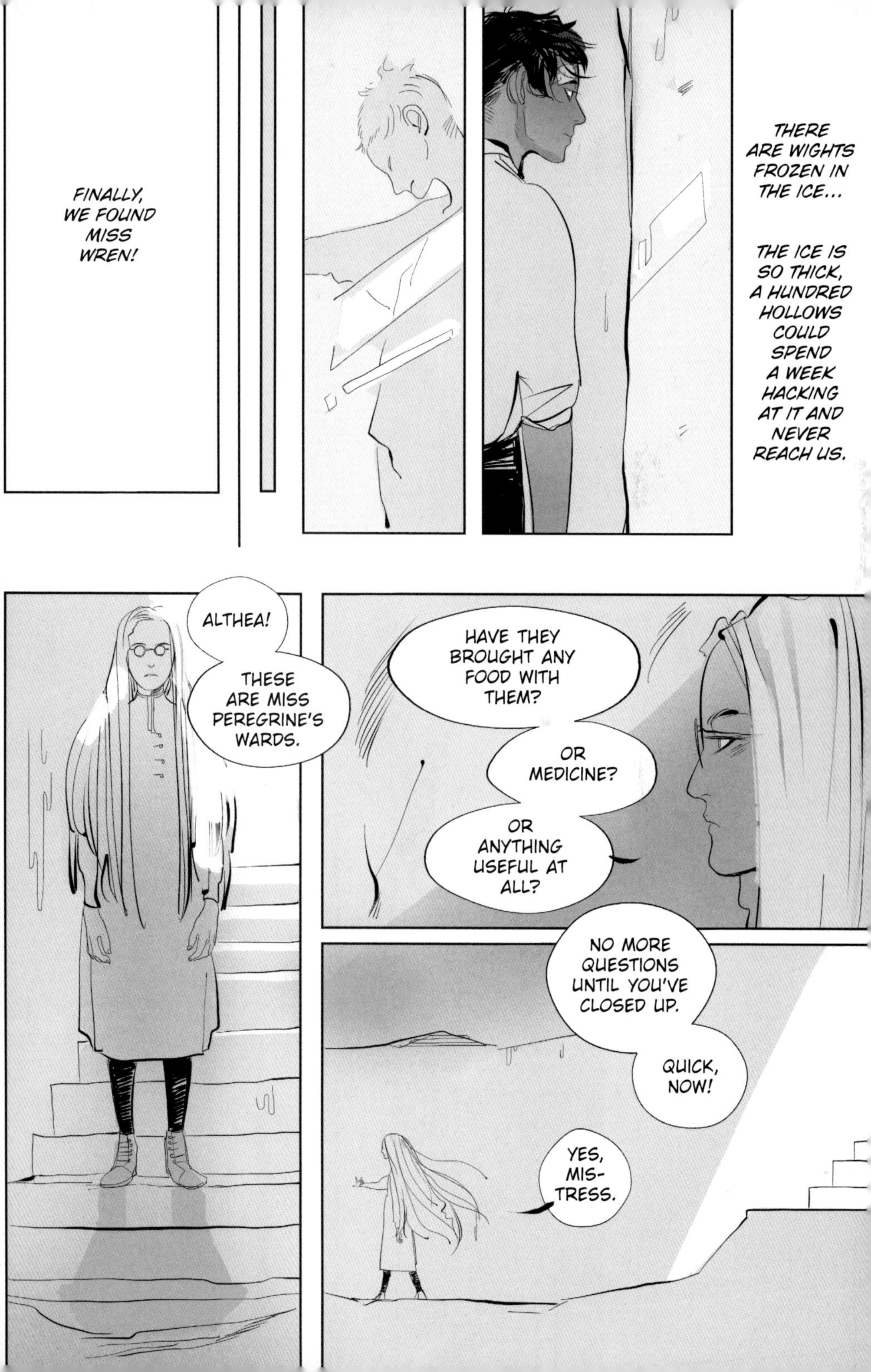
FINALLY, WE FOUND MISS WREN!
THERE ARE WIGHTS FROZEN IN THE ICE...
THE ICE IS SO THICK, A HUNDRED HOLLOWS COULD SPEND A WEEK HACKING AT IT AND NEVER REACH US.
ALTHEA!
THESE ARE MISS PEREGRINE'S WARDS.
HAVE THEY BROUGHT ANY FOOD WITH THEM?
OR MEDICINE?
OR ANYTHING USEFUL AT ALL?
NO MORE QUESTIONS UNTIL YOU'VE CLOSED UP.
QUICK, NOW!
YES, MIS-TRESS.

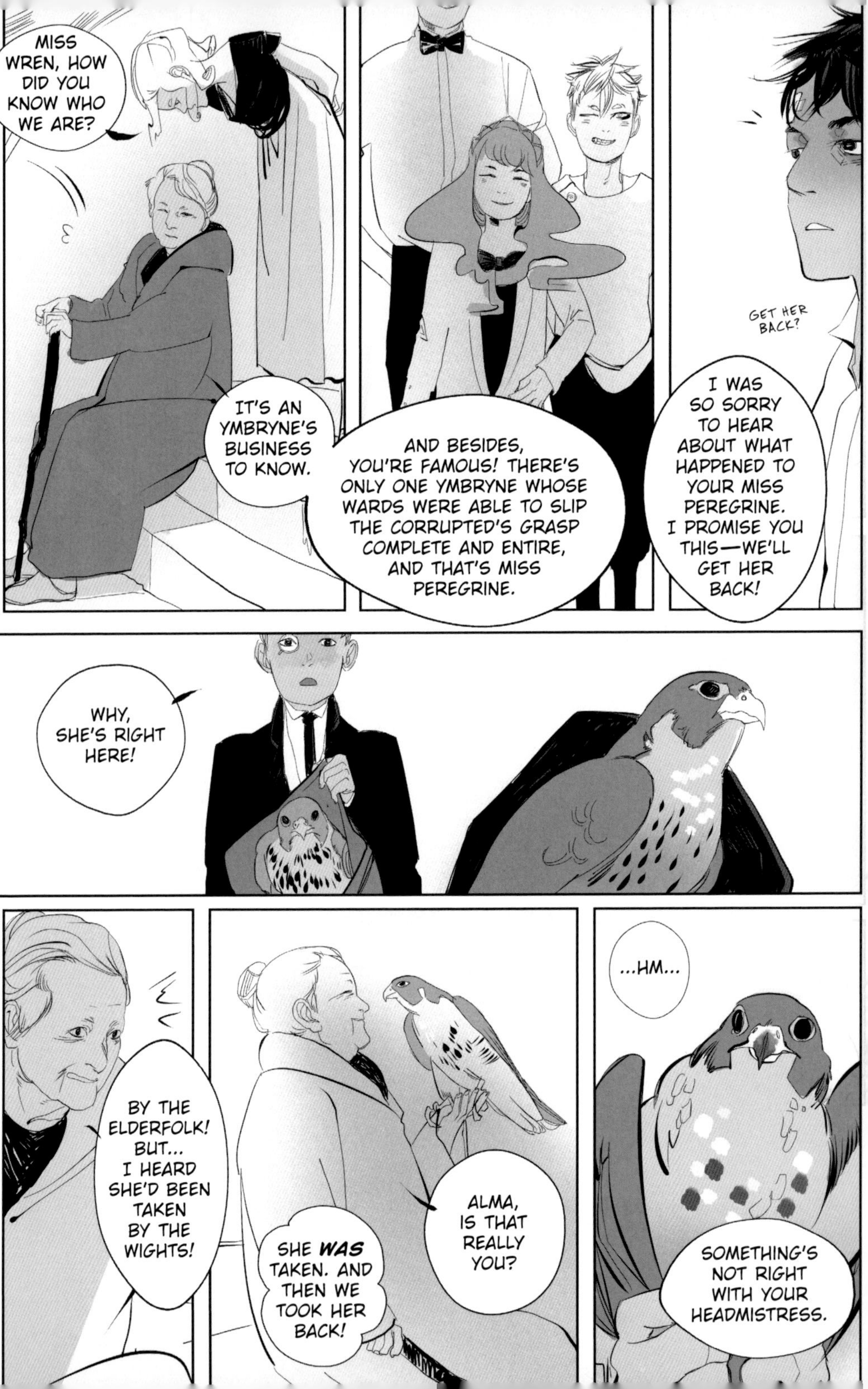
MISS WREN, HOW DID YOU KNOW WHO WE ARE?
IT'S AN YMBRYNE'S BUSINESS TO KNOW.
AND BESIDES, YOU'RE FAMOUS! THERE'S ONLY ONE YMBRYNE WHOSE WARDS WERE ABLE TO SLIP THE CORRUPTED'S GRASP COMPLETE AND ENTIRE, AND THAT'S MISS PEREGRINE.
GET HER BACK?
I WAS SO SORRY TO HEAR ABOUT WHAT HAPPENED TO YOUR MISS PEREGRINE. I PROMISE YOU THIS—WE'LL GET HER BACK!
WHY, SHE'S RIGHT HERE!
BY THE ELDERFOLK! BUT... I HEARD SHE'D BEEN TAKEN BY THE WIGHTS!
SHE **WAS** TAKEN. AND THEN WE TOOK HER BACK!
ALMA, IS THAT REALLY YOU?
...HM...
SOMETHING'S NOT RIGHT WITH YOUR HEADMISTRESS.

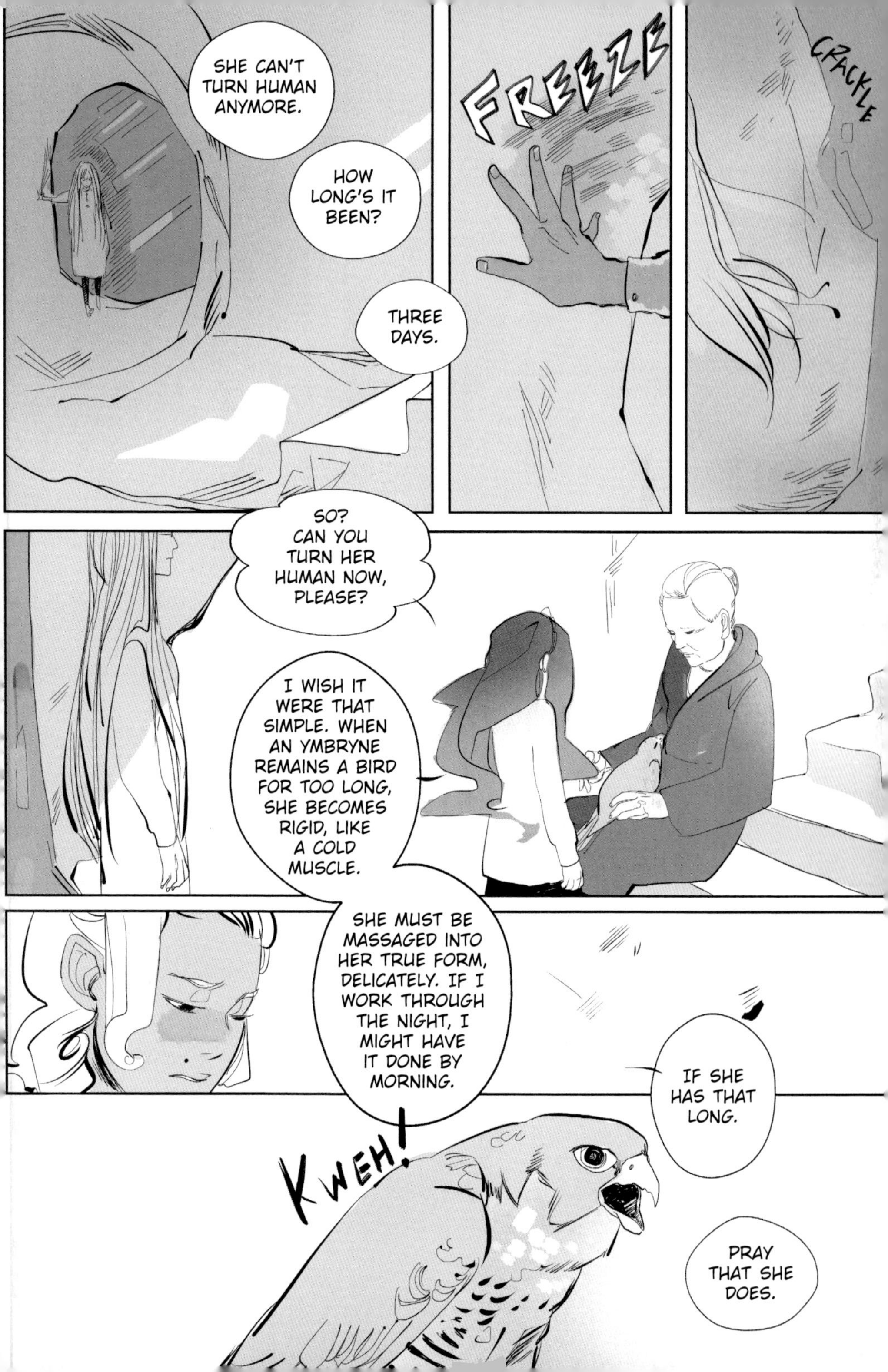
SHE CAN'T TURN HUMAN ANYMORE.
HOW LONG'S IT BEEN?
THREE DAYS.
FREEZE
CRACKLE
SO? CAN YOU TURN HER HUMAN NOW, PLEASE?
I WISH IT WERE THAT SIMPLE. WHEN AN YMBRYNE REMAINS A BIRD FOR TOO LONG, SHE BECOMES RIGID, LIKE A COLD MUSCLE.
SHE MUST BE MASSAGED INTO HER TRUE FORM, DELICATELY. IF I WORK THROUGH THE NIGHT, I MIGHT HAVE IT DONE BY MORNING.
IF SHE HAS THAT LONG.
KWEH!
PRAY THAT SHE DOES.

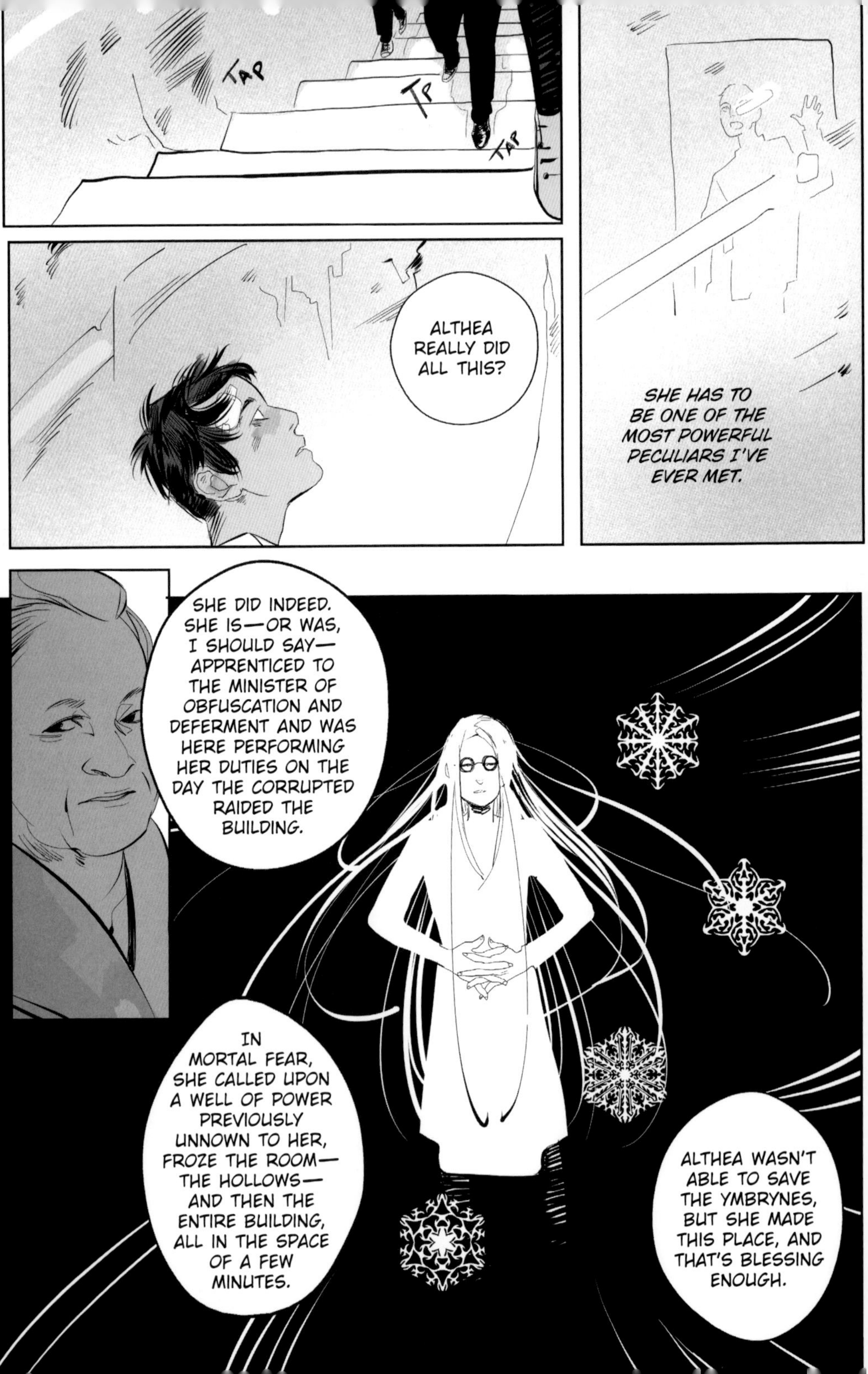
TAP
TP
TAP
ALTHEA REALLY DID ALL THIS?
SHE HAS TO BE ONE OF THE MOST POWERFUL PECULIARS I'VE EVER MET.
SHE DID INDEED. SHE IS—OR WAS, I SHOULD SAY—APPRENTICED TO THE MINISTER OF OBFUSCATION AND DEFERMENT AND WAS HERE PERFORMING HER DUTIES ON THE DAY THE CORRUPTED RAIDED THE BUILDING.
IN MORTAL FEAR, SHE CALLED UPON A WELL OF POWER PREVIOUSLY UNNOWN TO HER, FROZE THE ROOM—THE HOLLOWS—AND THEN THE ENTIRE BUILDING, ALL IN THE SPACE OF A FEW MINUTES.
ALTHEA WASN'T ABLE TO SAVE THE YMBRYNES, BUT SHE MADE THIS PLACE, AND THAT'S BLESSING ENOUGH.

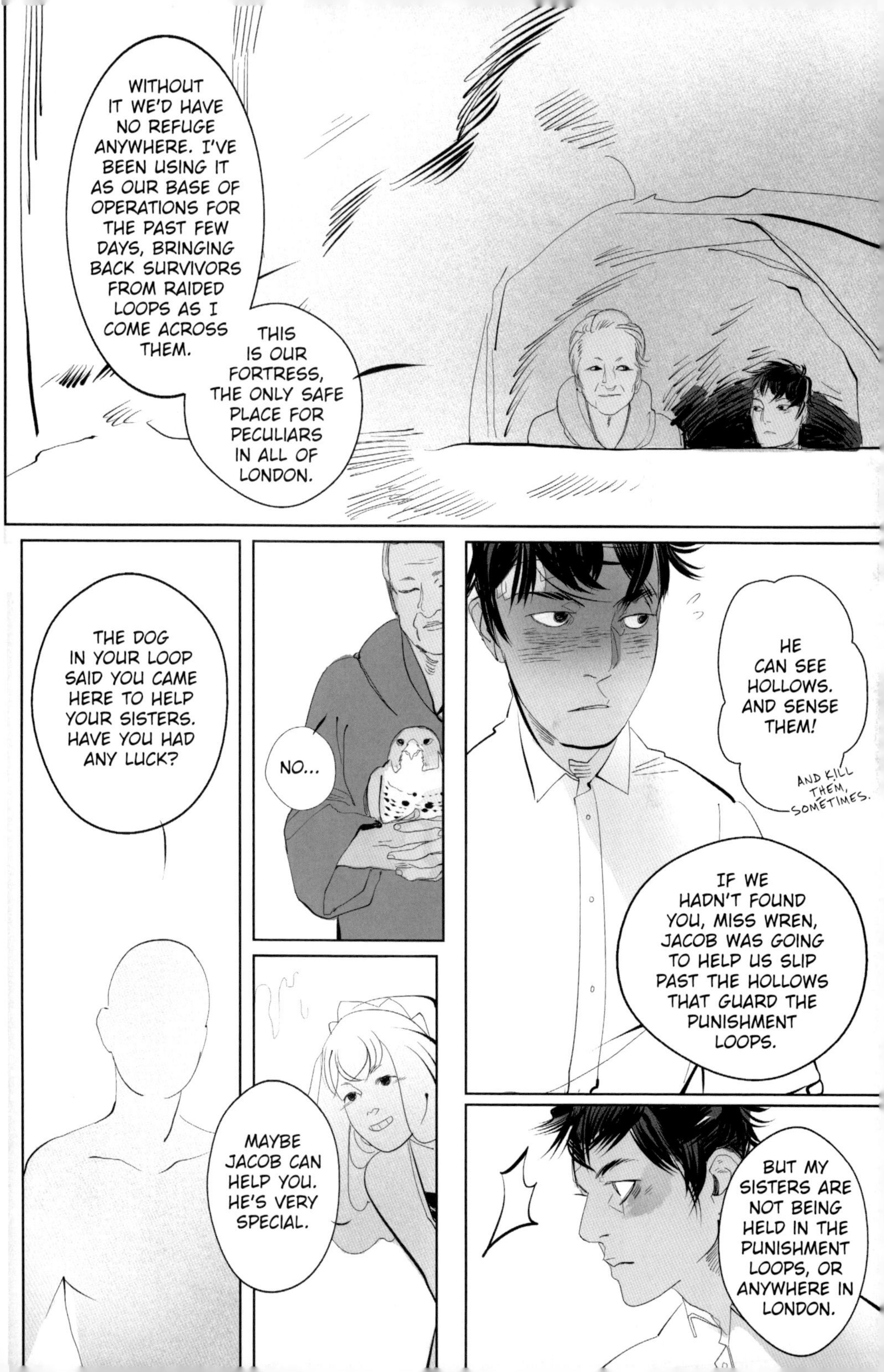
WITHOUT IT WE'D HAVE NO REFUGE ANYWHERE. I'VE BEEN USING IT AS OUR BASE OF OPERATIONS FOR THE PAST FEW DAYS, BRINGING BACK SURVIVORS FROM RAIDED LOOPS AS I COME ACROSS THEM.
THIS IS OUR FORTRESS, THE ONLY SAFE PLACE FOR PECULIARS IN ALL OF LONDON.
THE DOG IN YOUR LOOP SAID YOU CAME HERE TO HELP YOUR SISTERS. HAVE YOU HAD ANY LUCK?
NO...
MAYBE JACOB CAN HELP YOU. HE'S VERY SPECIAL.
HE CAN SEE HOLLOWS. AND SENSE THEM!
AND KILL THEM, SOMETIMES.
IF WE HADN'T FOUND YOU, MISS WREN, JACOB WAS GOING TO HELP US SLIP PAST THE HOLLOWS THAT GUARD THE PUNISHMENT LOOPS.
BUT MY SISTERS ARE NOT BEING HELD IN THE PUNISHMENT LOOPS, OR ANYWHERE IN LONDON.

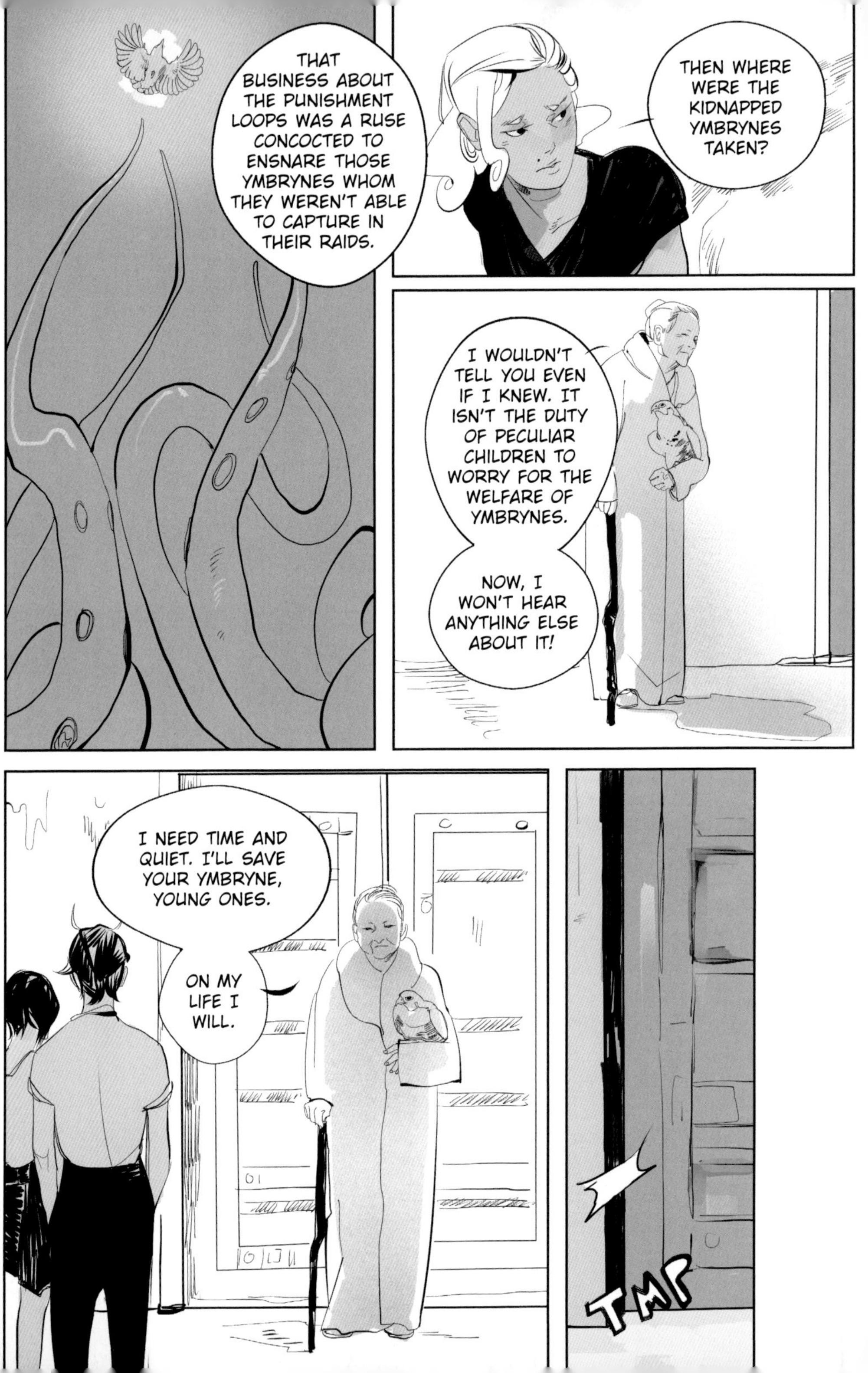
THAT BUSINESS ABOUT THE PUNISHMENT LOOPS WAS A RUSE CONCOCTED TO ENSNARE THOSE YMBRYNES WHOM THEY WEREN'T ABLE TO CAPTURE IN THEIR RAIDS.
THEN WHERE WERE THE KIDNAPPED YMBRYNES TAKEN?
I WOULDN'T TELL YOU EVEN IF I KNEW. IT ISN'T THE DUTY OF PECULIAR CHILDREN TO WORRY FOR THE WELFARE OF YMBRYNES.
NOW, I WON'T HEAR ANYTHING ELSE ABOUT IT!
I NEED TIME AND QUIET. I'LL SAVE YOUR YMBRYNE, YOUNG ONES.
ON MY LIFE I WILL.
TMP

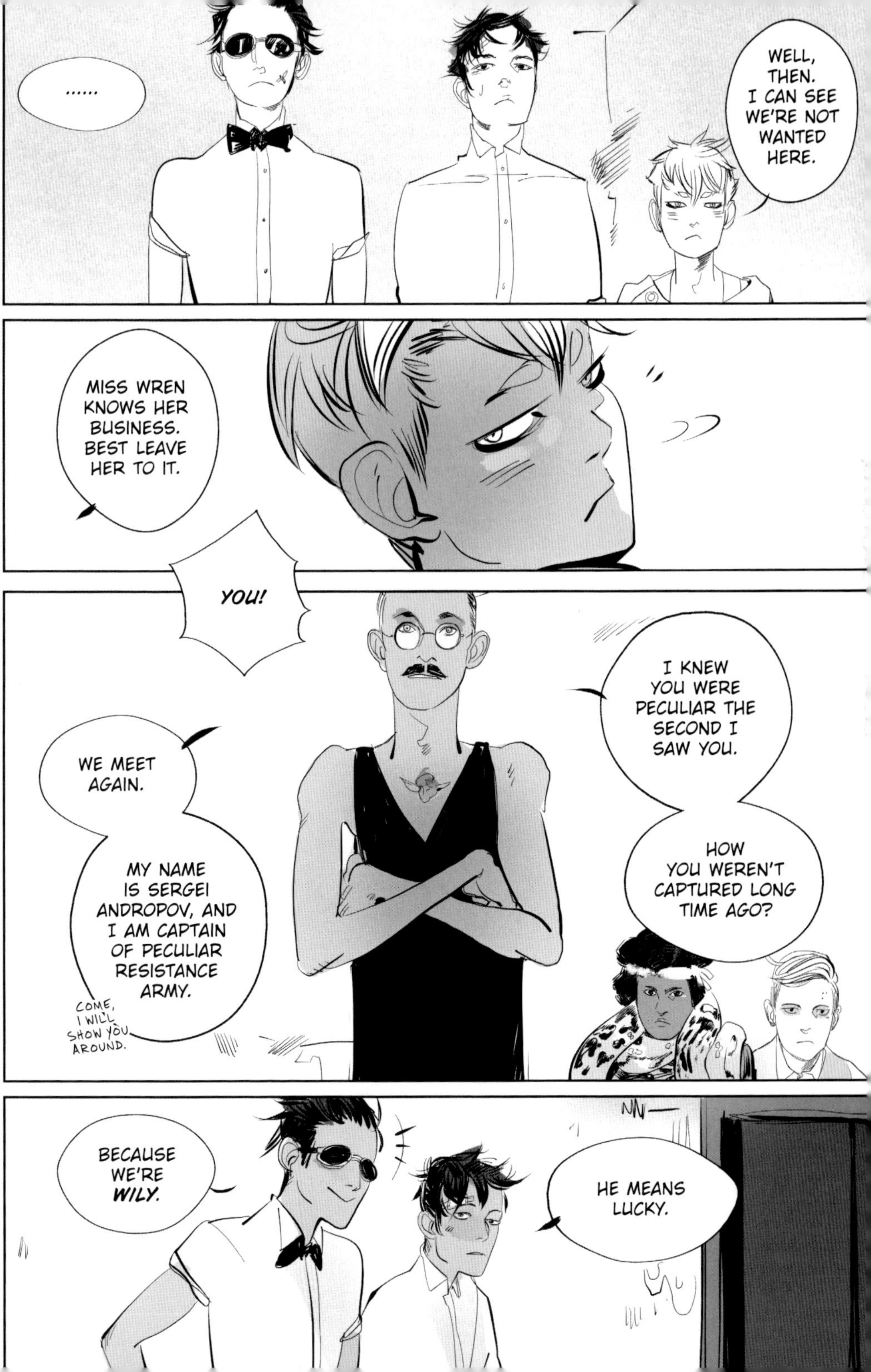
......
WELL, THEN. I CAN SEE WE'RE NOT WANTED HERE.
MISS WREN KNOWS HER BUSINESS. BEST LEAVE HER TO IT.
YOU!
WE MEET AGAIN.
MY NAME IS SERGEI ANDROPOV, AND I AM CAPTAIN OF PECULIAR RESISTANCE ARMY.
COME, I WILL SHOW YOU AROUND.
I KNEW YOU WERE PECULIAR THE SECOND I SAW YOU.
HOW YOU WEREN'T CAPTURED LONG TIME AGO?
BECAUSE WE'RE *WILY*.
HE MEANS LUCKY.

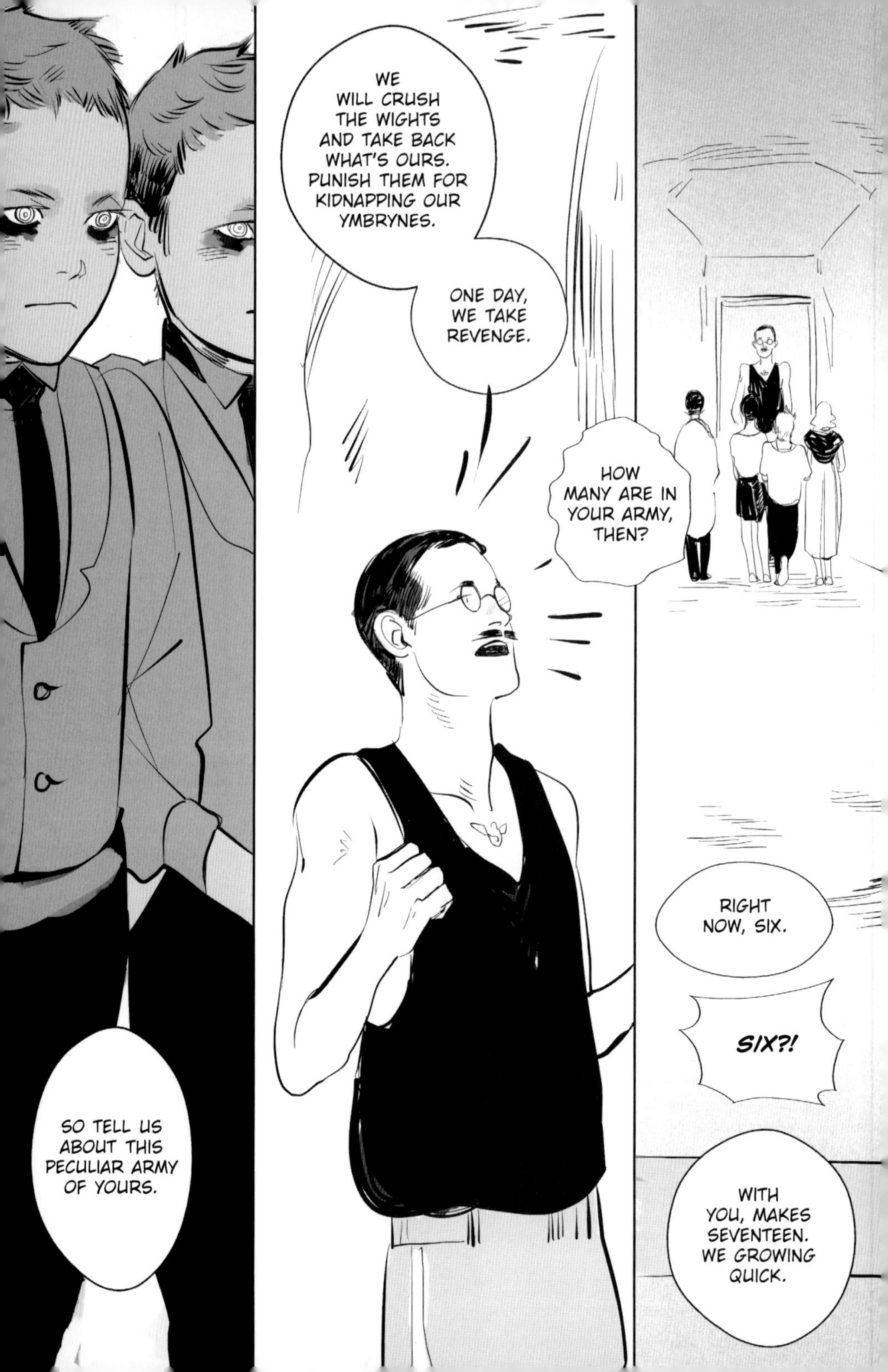
SO TELL US ABOUT THIS PECULIAR ARMY OF YOURS.
WE WILL CRUSH THE WIGHTS AND TAKE BACK WHAT'S OURS. PUNISH THEM FOR KIDNAPPING OUR YMBRYNES.
ONE DAY, WE TAKE REVENGE.
HOW MANY ARE IN YOUR ARMY, THEN?
RIGHT NOW, SIX.
SIX?!
WITH YOU, MAKES SEVENTEEN. WE GROWING QUICK.

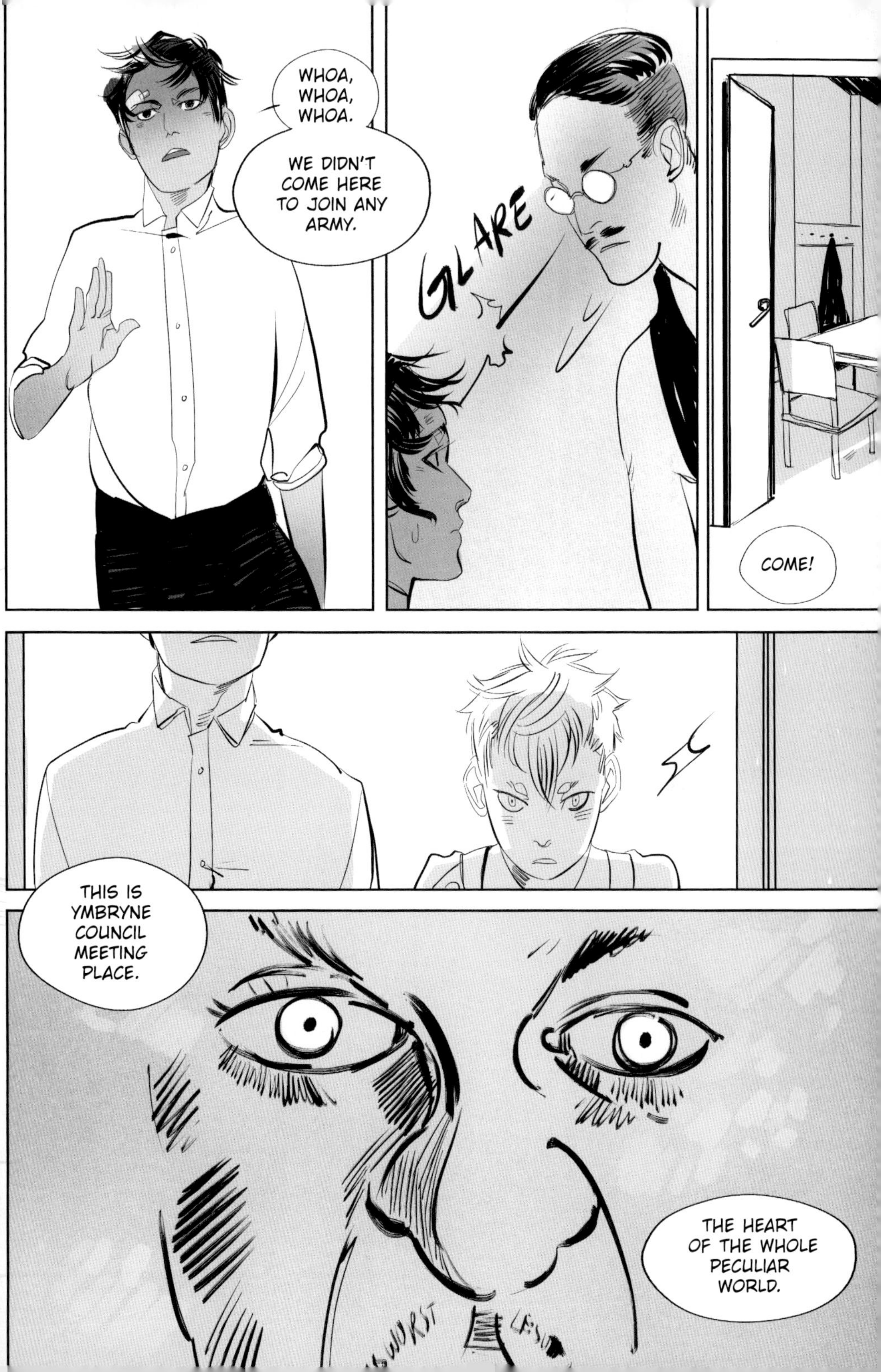
WHOA, WHOA, WHOA.
WE DIDN'T COME HERE TO JOIN ANY ARMY.
GLARE
COME!
THIS IS YMBRYNE COUNCIL MEETING PLACE.
THE HEART OF THE WHOLE PECULIAR WORLD.

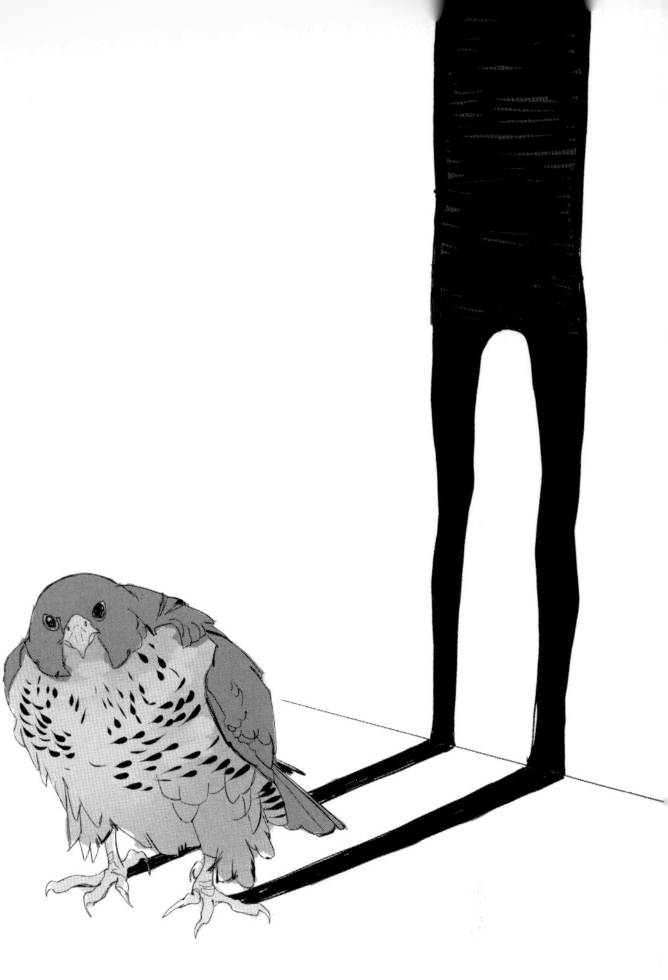

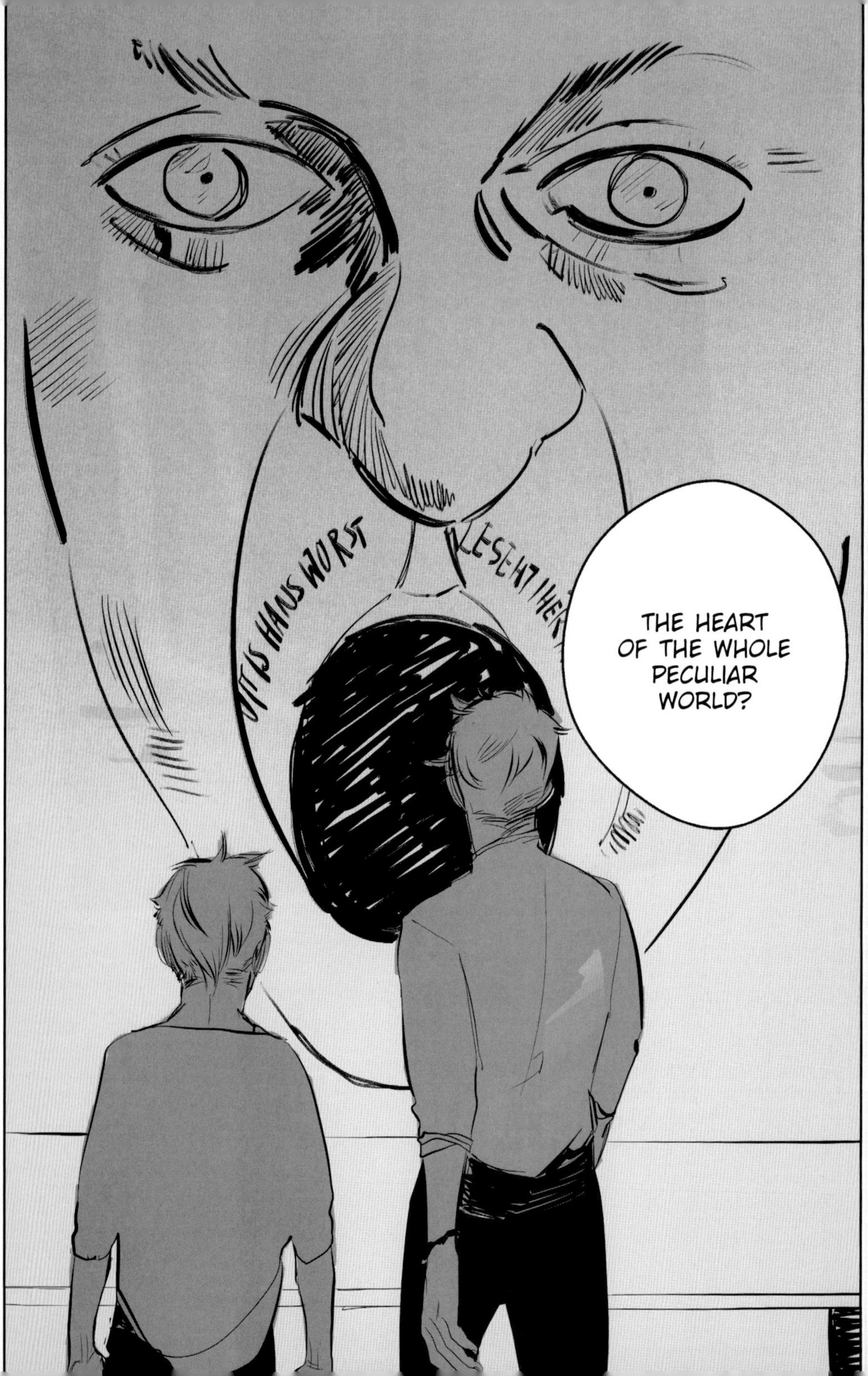
THE HEART OF THE WHOLE PECULIAR WORLD?

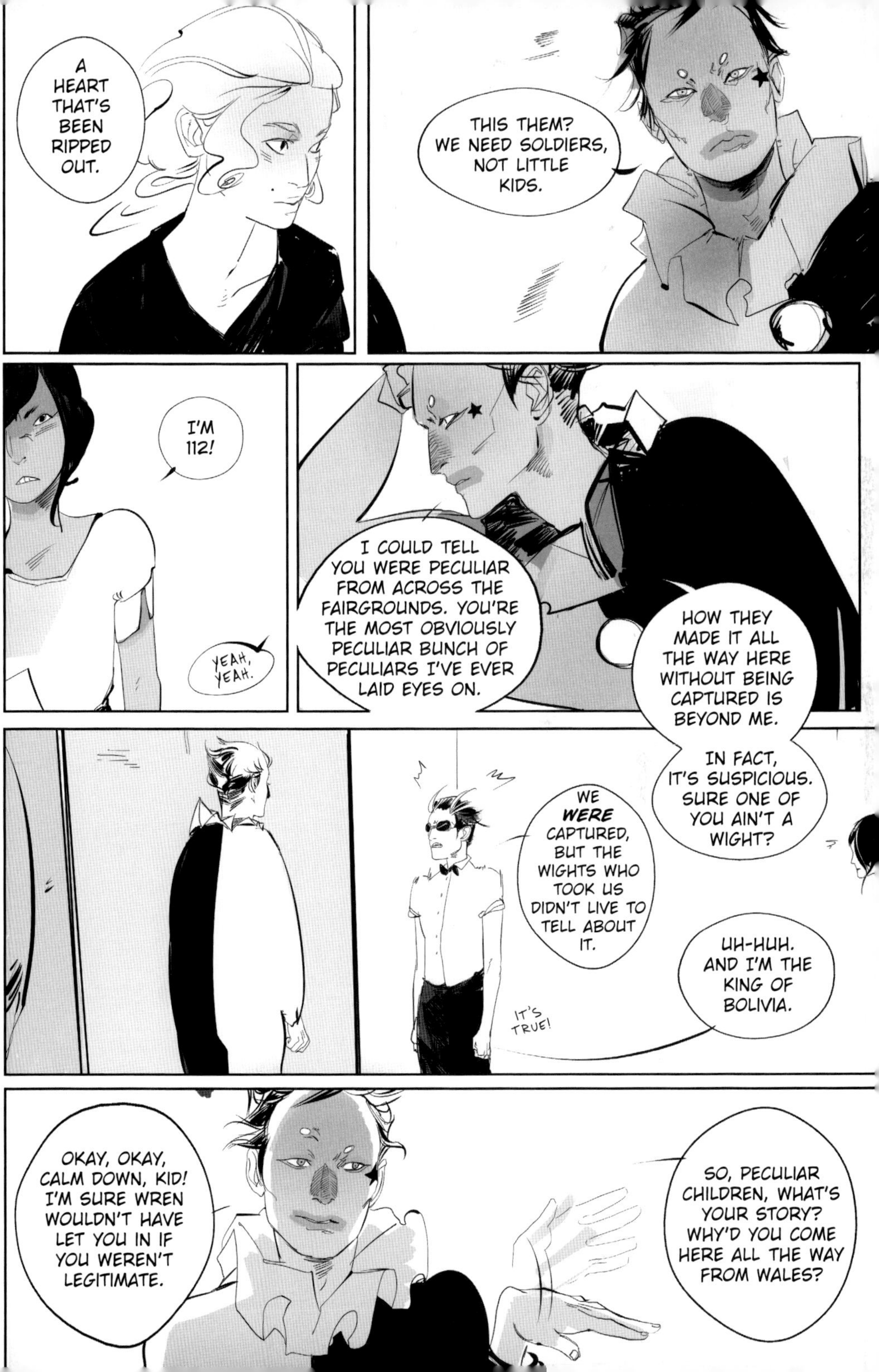
A HEART THAT'S BEEN RIPPED OUT.
THIS THEM? WE NEED SOLDIERS, NOT LITTLE KIDS.
I'M 112!
YEAH, YEAH.
I COULD TELL YOU WERE PECULIAR FROM ACROSS THE FAIRGROUNDS. YOU'RE THE MOST OBVIOUSLY PECULIAR BUNCH OF PECULIARS I'VE EVER LAID EYES ON.
HOW THEY MADE IT ALL THE WAY HERE WITHOUT BEING CAPTURED IS BEYOND ME.
IN FACT, IT'S SUSPICIOUS. SURE ONE OF YOU AIN'T A WIGHT?
WE *WERE* CAPTURED, BUT THE WIGHTS WHO TOOK US DIDN'T LIVE TO TELL ABOUT IT.
UH-HUH. AND I'M THE KING OF BOLIVIA.
IT'S TRUE!
OKAY, OKAY, CALM DOWN, KID! I'M SURE WREN WOULDN'T HAVE LET YOU IN IF YOU WEREN'T LEGITIMATE.
SO, PECULIAR CHILDREN, WHAT'S YOUR STORY? WHY'D YOU COME HERE ALL THE WAY FROM WALES?

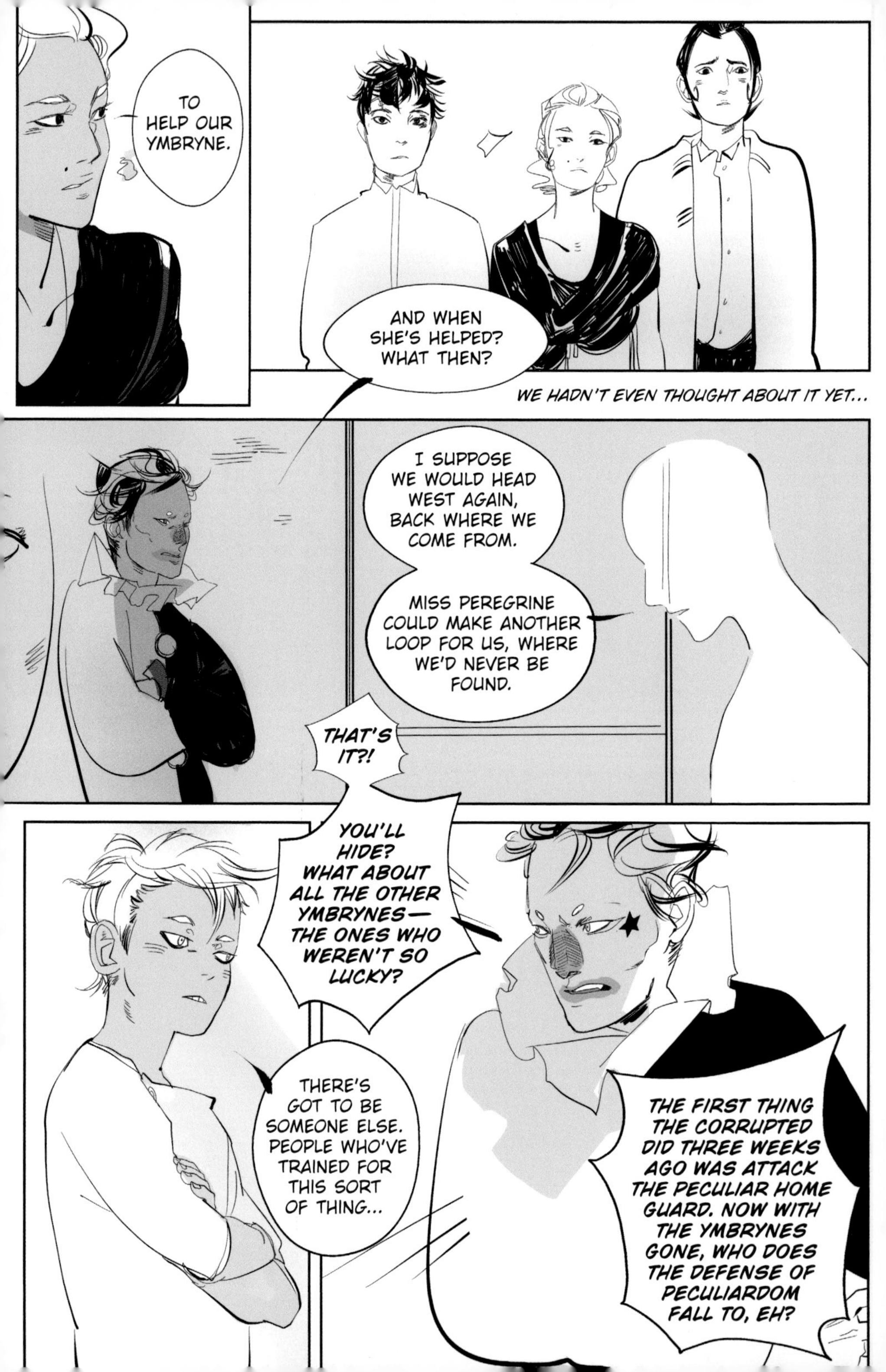
TO HELP OUR YMBRYNE.
AND WHEN SHE'S HELPED? WHAT THEN?
WE HADN'T EVEN THOUGHT ABOUT IT YET...
I SUPPOSE WE WOULD HEAD WEST AGAIN, BACK WHERE WE COME FROM.
MISS PEREGRINE COULD MAKE ANOTHER LOOP FOR US, WHERE WE'D NEVER BE FOUND.
THAT'S IT?!
YOU'LL HIDE? WHAT ABOUT ALL THE OTHER YMBRYNES— THE ONES WHO WEREN'T SO LUCKY?
THERE'S GOT TO BE SOMEONE ELSE. PEOPLE WHO'VE TRAINED FOR THIS SORT OF THING...
THE FIRST THING THE CORRUPTED DID THREE WEEKS AGO WAS ATTACK THE PECULIAR HOME GUARD. NOW WITH THE YMBRYNES GONE, WHO DOES THE DEFENSE OF PECULIARDOM FALL TO, EH?

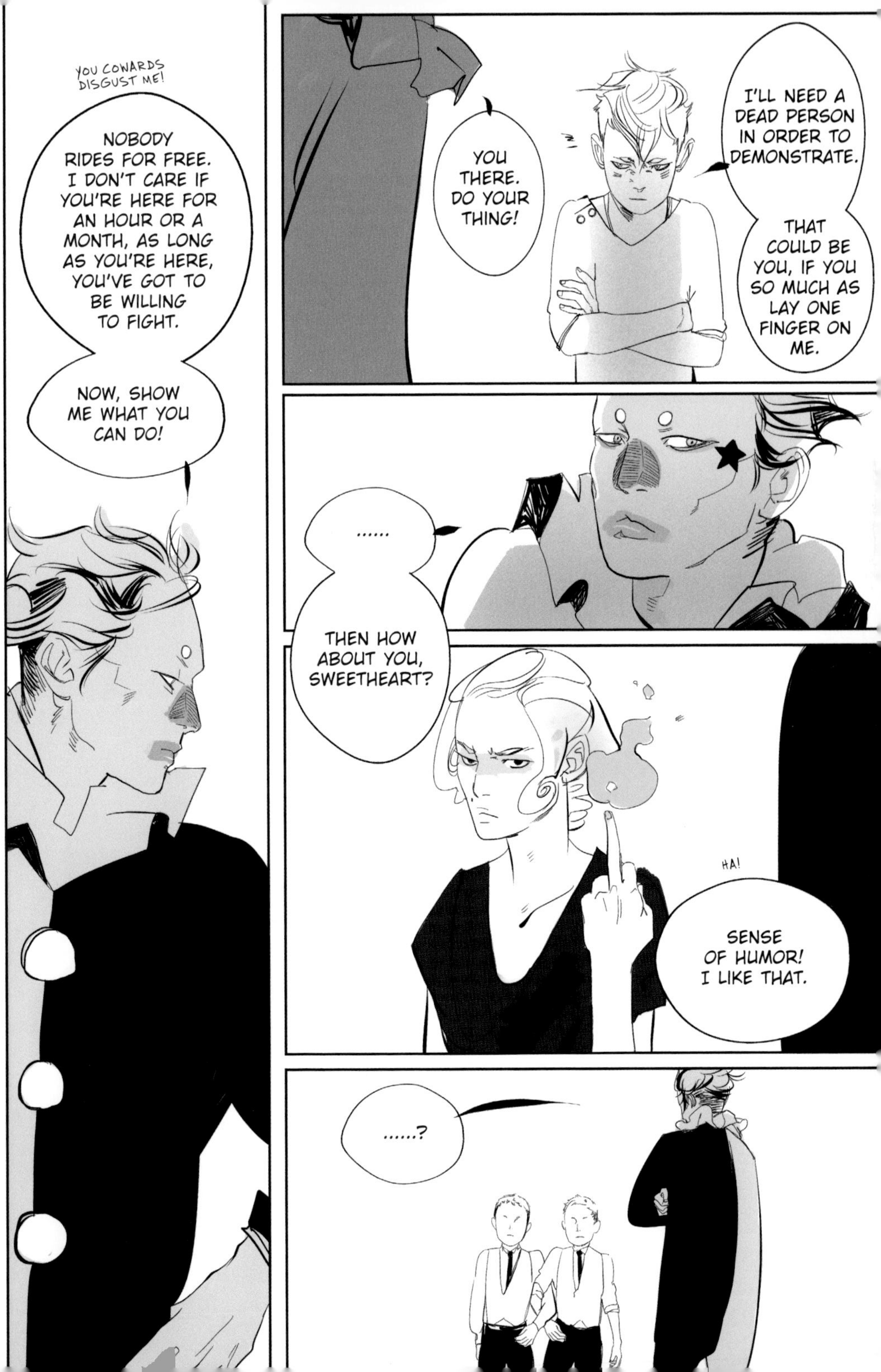
YOU COWARDS DISGUST ME!
NOBODY RIDES FOR FREE. I DON'T CARE IF YOU'RE HERE FOR AN HOUR OR A MONTH, AS LONG AS YOU'RE HERE, YOU'VE GOT TO BE WILLING TO FIGHT.
NOW, SHOW ME WHAT YOU CAN DO!
YOU THERE. DO YOUR THING!
I'LL NEED A DEAD PERSON IN ORDER TO DEMONSTRATE.
THAT COULD BE YOU, IF YOU SO MUCH AS LAY ONE FINGER ON ME.
......
THEN HOW ABOUT YOU, SWEETHEART?
HA!
SENSE OF HUMOR! I LIKE THAT.
......?

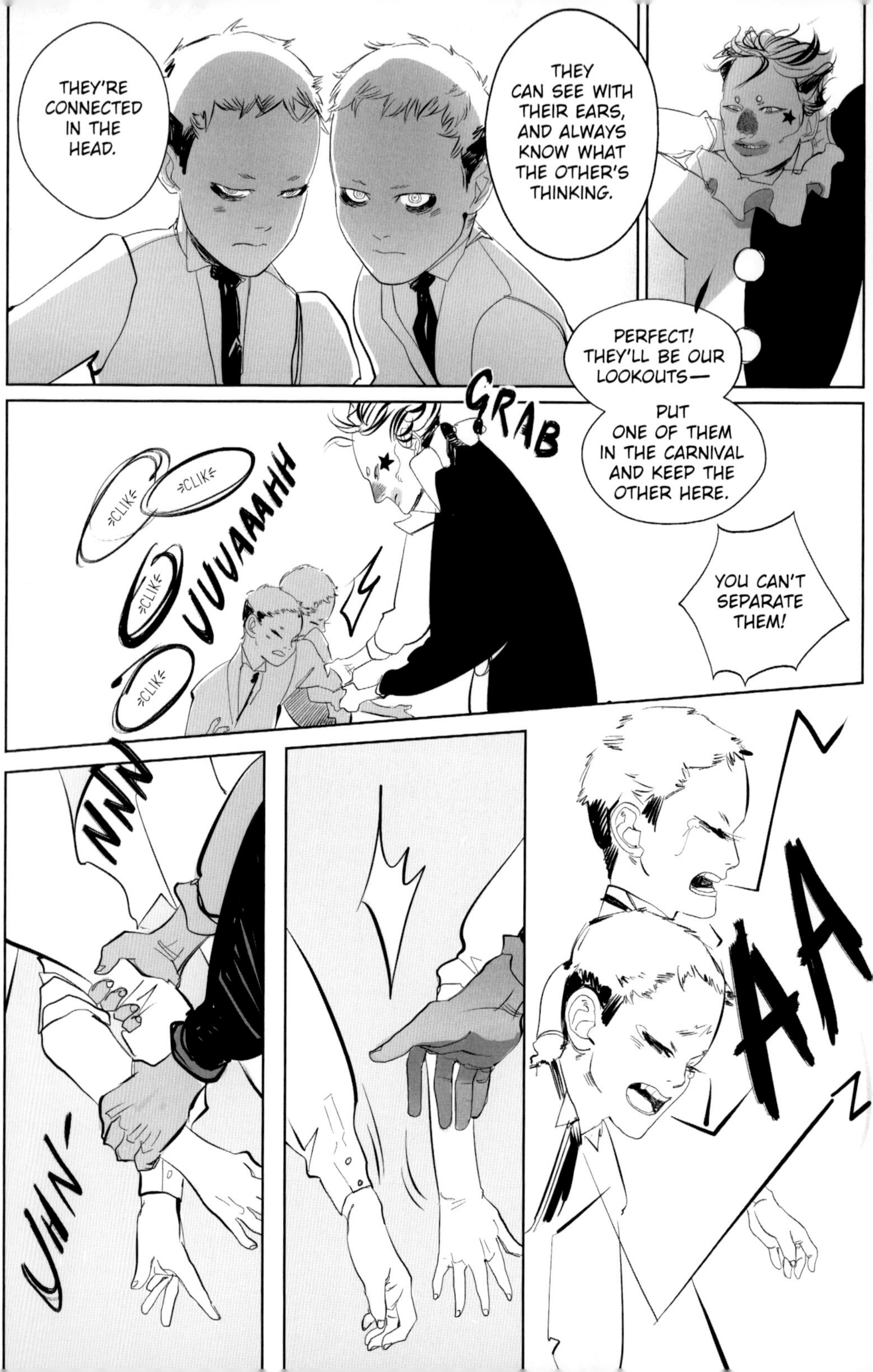
THEY'RE CONNECTED IN THE HEAD.
THEY CAN SEE WITH THEIR EARS, AND ALWAYS KNOW WHAT THE OTHER'S THINKING.
PERFECT! THEY'LL BE OUR LOOKOUTS—
PUT ONE OF THEM IN THE CARNIVAL AND KEEP THE OTHER HERE.
CLIK
CLIK
CLIK
CLIK
UUUAAAHH
GRAB
YOU CAN'T SEPARATE THEM!
NNN
UHN-
AA

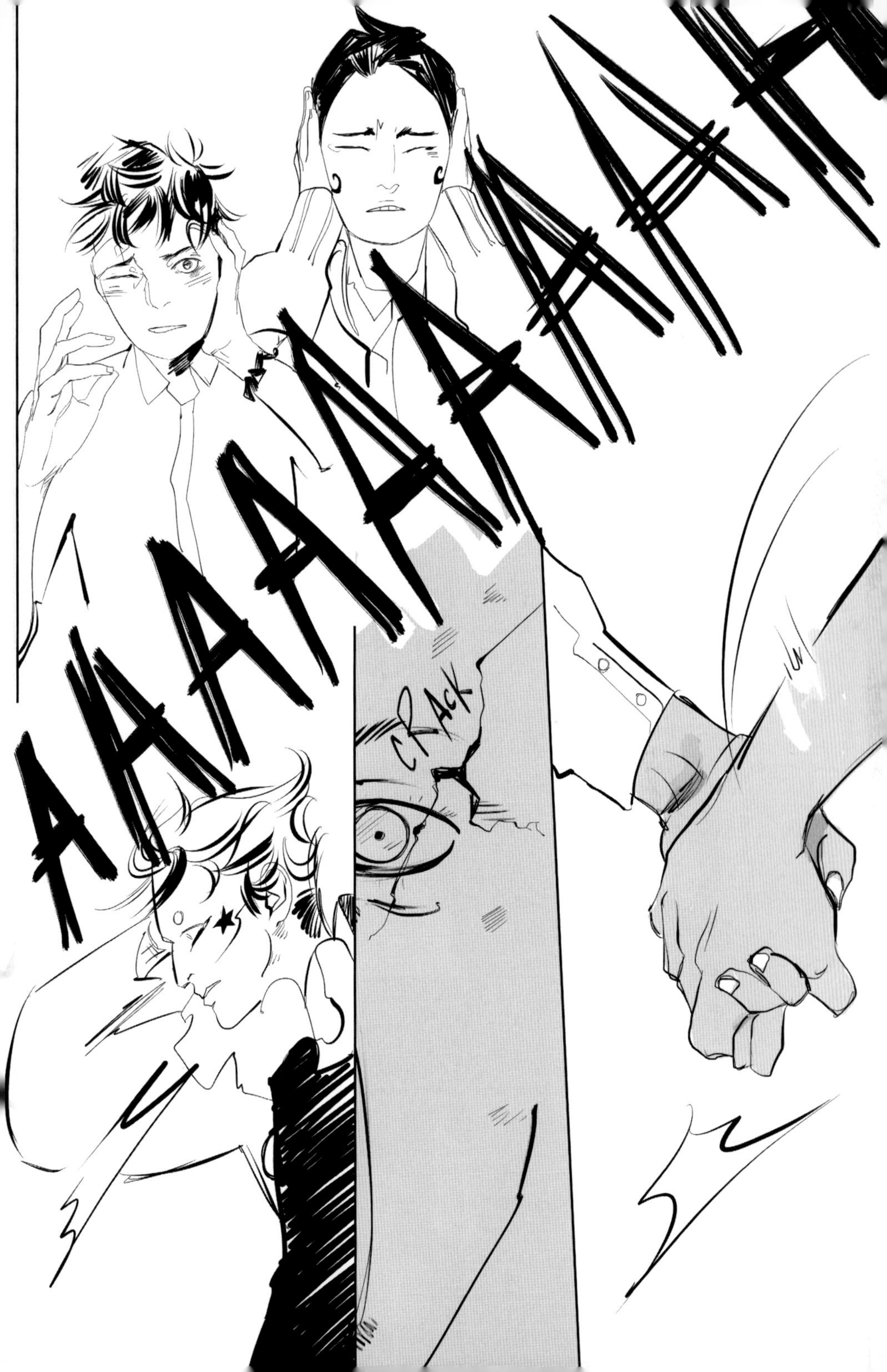
AAAAAAAAAH
CRACK

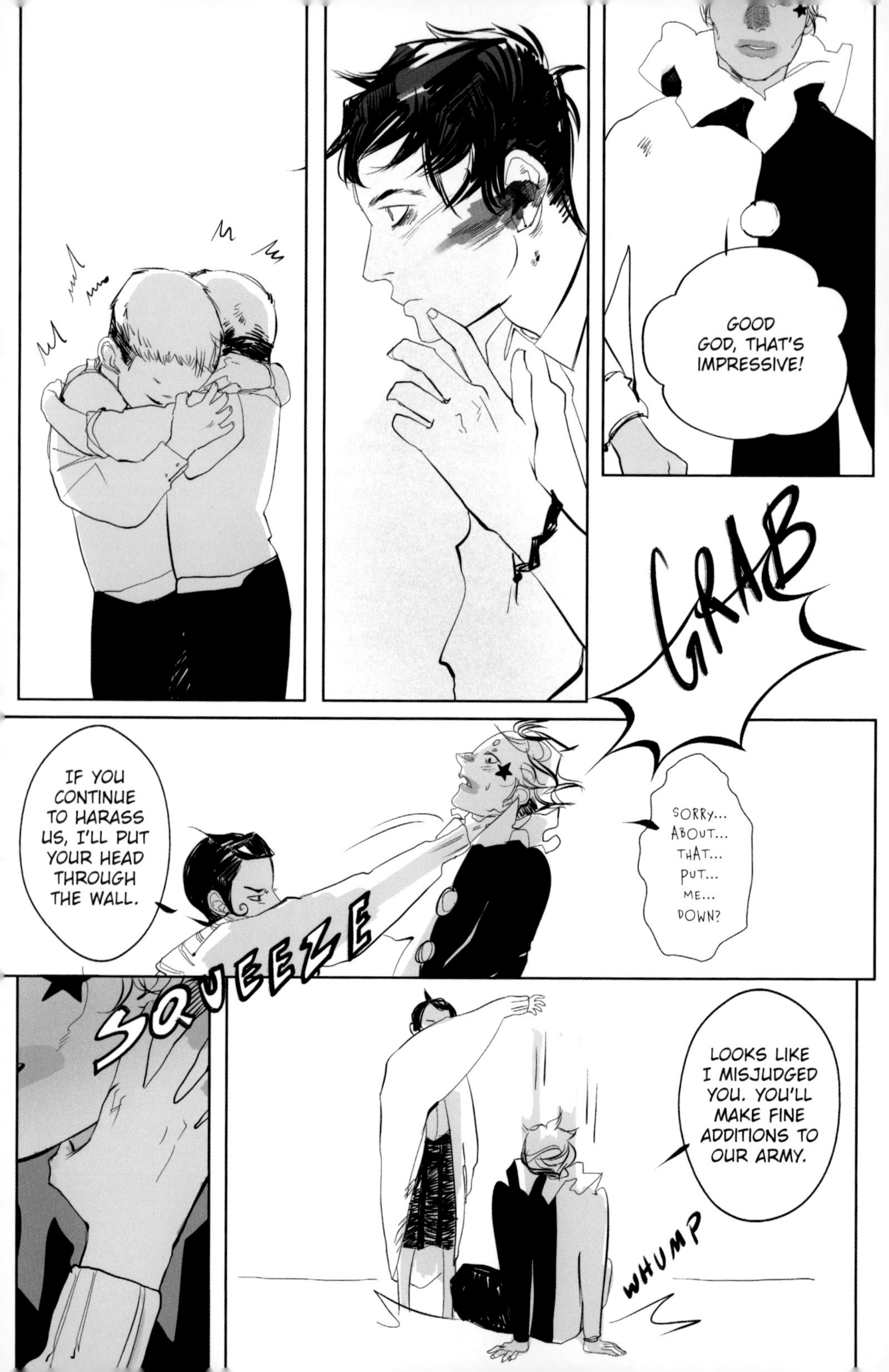
GOOD GOD, THAT'S IMPRESSIVE!
GRAB
IF YOU CONTINUE TO HARASS US, I'LL PUT YOUR HEAD THROUGH THE WALL.
SQUEEZE
SORRY... ABOUT... THAT... PUT... ME... DOWN?
LOOKS LIKE I MISJUDGED YOU. YOU'LL MAKE FINE ADDITIONS TO OUR ARMY.
WHUMP

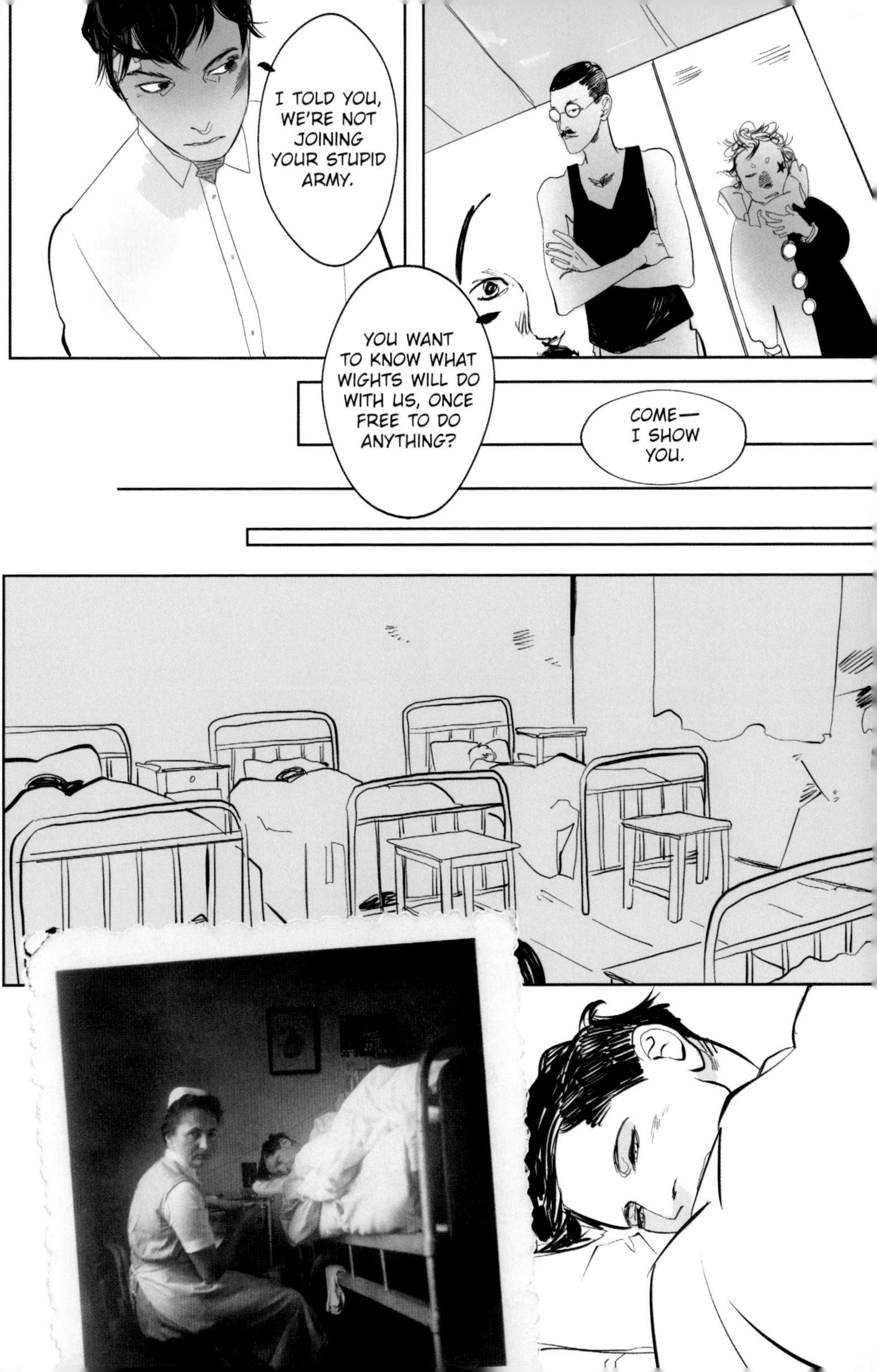
I TOLD YOU, WE'RE NOT JOINING YOUR STUPID ARMY.
YOU WANT TO KNOW WHAT WIGHTS WILL DO WITH US, ONCE FREE TO DO ANYTHING?
COME— I SHOW YOU.

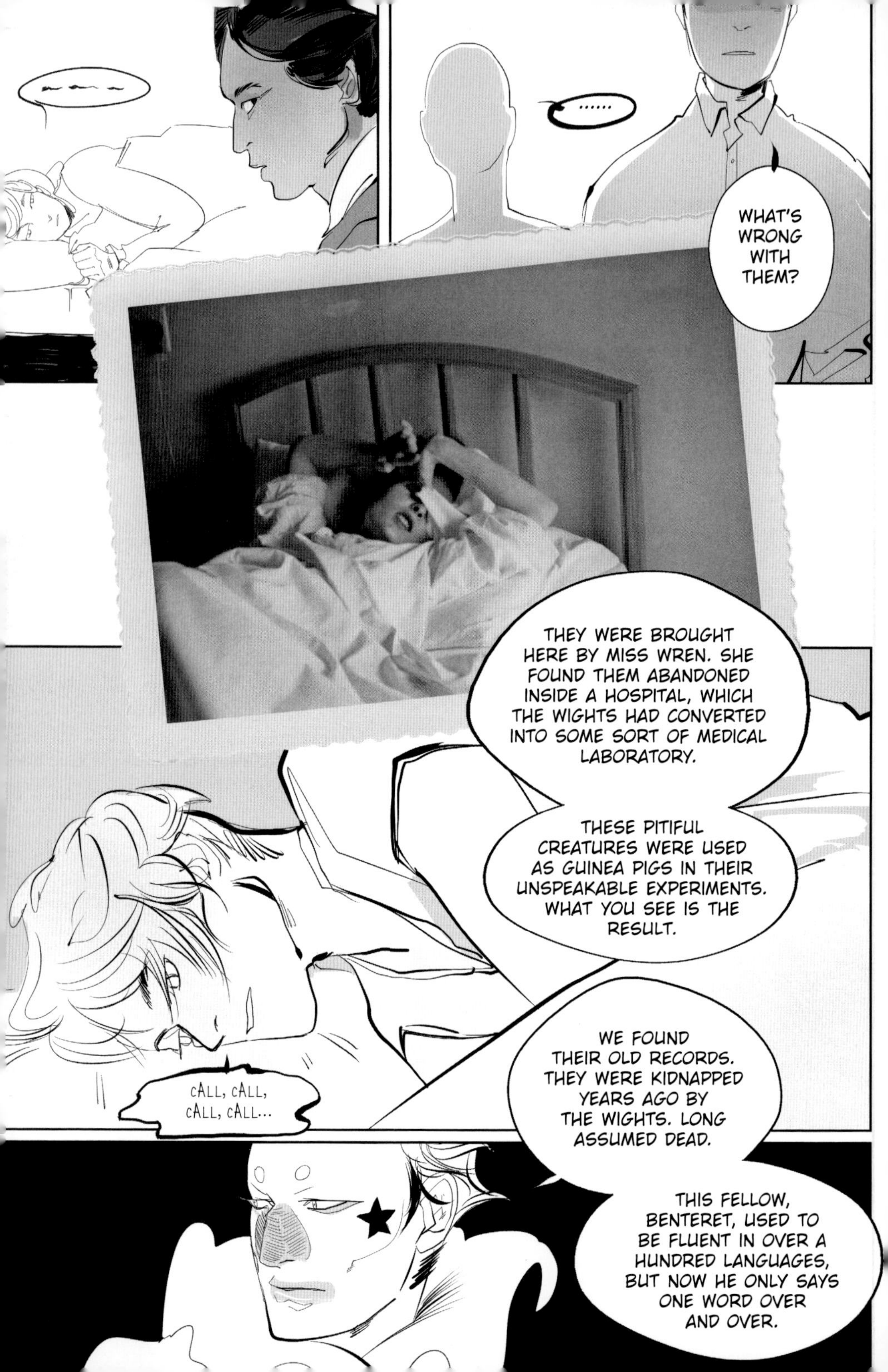

......
WHAT'S WRONG WITH THEM?
THEY WERE BROUGHT HERE BY MISS WREN. SHE FOUND THEM ABANDONED INSIDE A HOSPITAL, WHICH THE WIGHTS HAD CONVERTED INTO SOME SORT OF MEDICAL LABORATORY.
THESE PITIFUL CREATURES WERE USED AS GUINEA PIGS IN THEIR UNSPEAKABLE EXPERIMENTS. WHAT YOU SEE IS THE RESULT.
cALL, cALL, cALL, cALL...
WE FOUND THEIR OLD RECORDS. THEY WERE KIDNAPPED YEARS AGO BY THE WIGHTS. LONG ASSUMED DEAD.
THIS FELLOW, BENTERET, USED TO BE FLUENT IN OVER A HUNDRED LANGUAGES, BUT NOW HE ONLY SAYS ONE WORD OVER AND OVER.

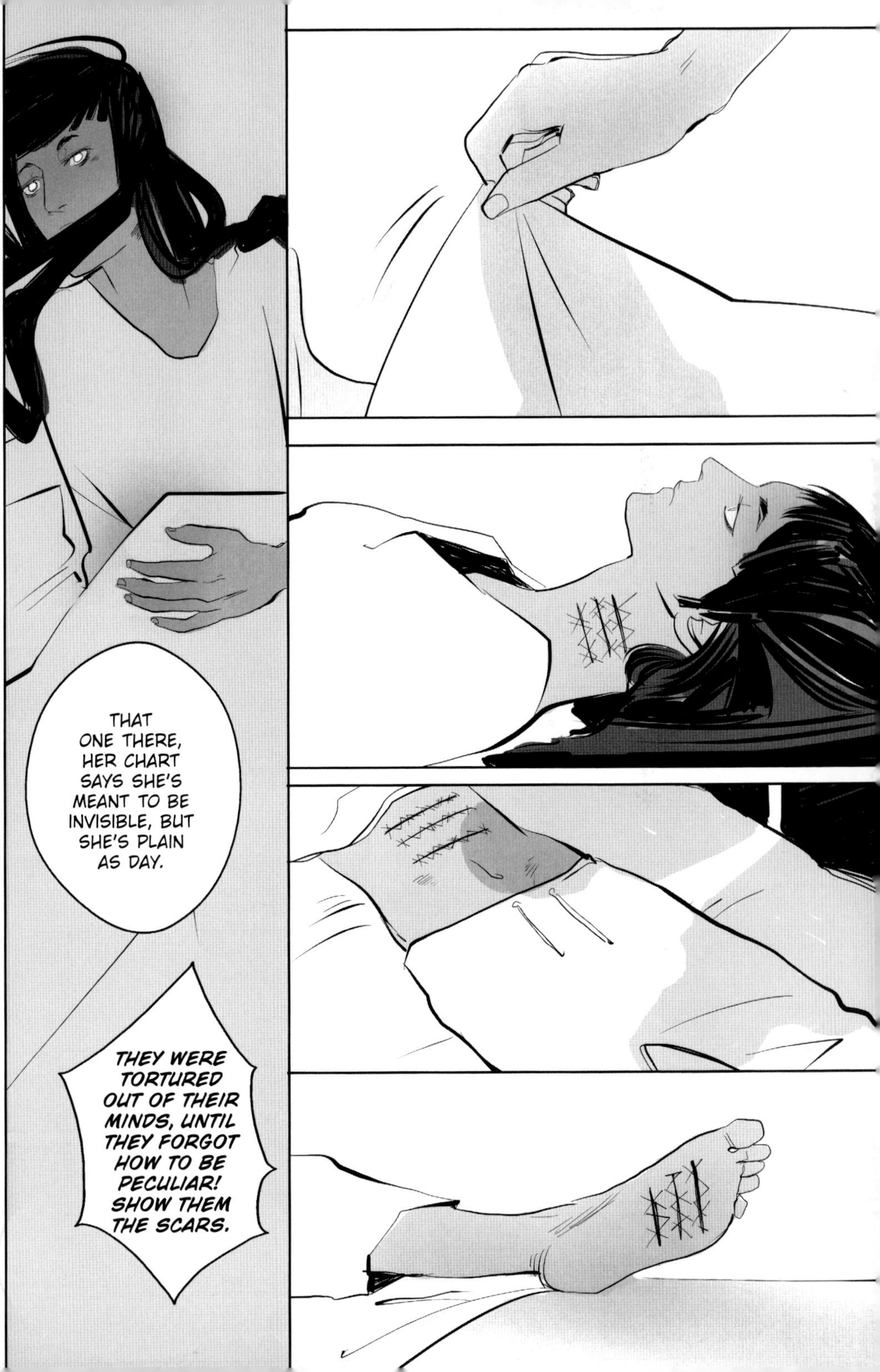
THAT ONE THERE, HER CHART SAYS SHE'S MEANT TO BE INVISIBLE, BUT SHE'S PLAIN AS DAY.
THEY WERE TORTURED OUT OF THEIR MINDS, UNTIL THEY FORGOT HOW TO BE PECULIAR! SHOW THEM THE SCARS.

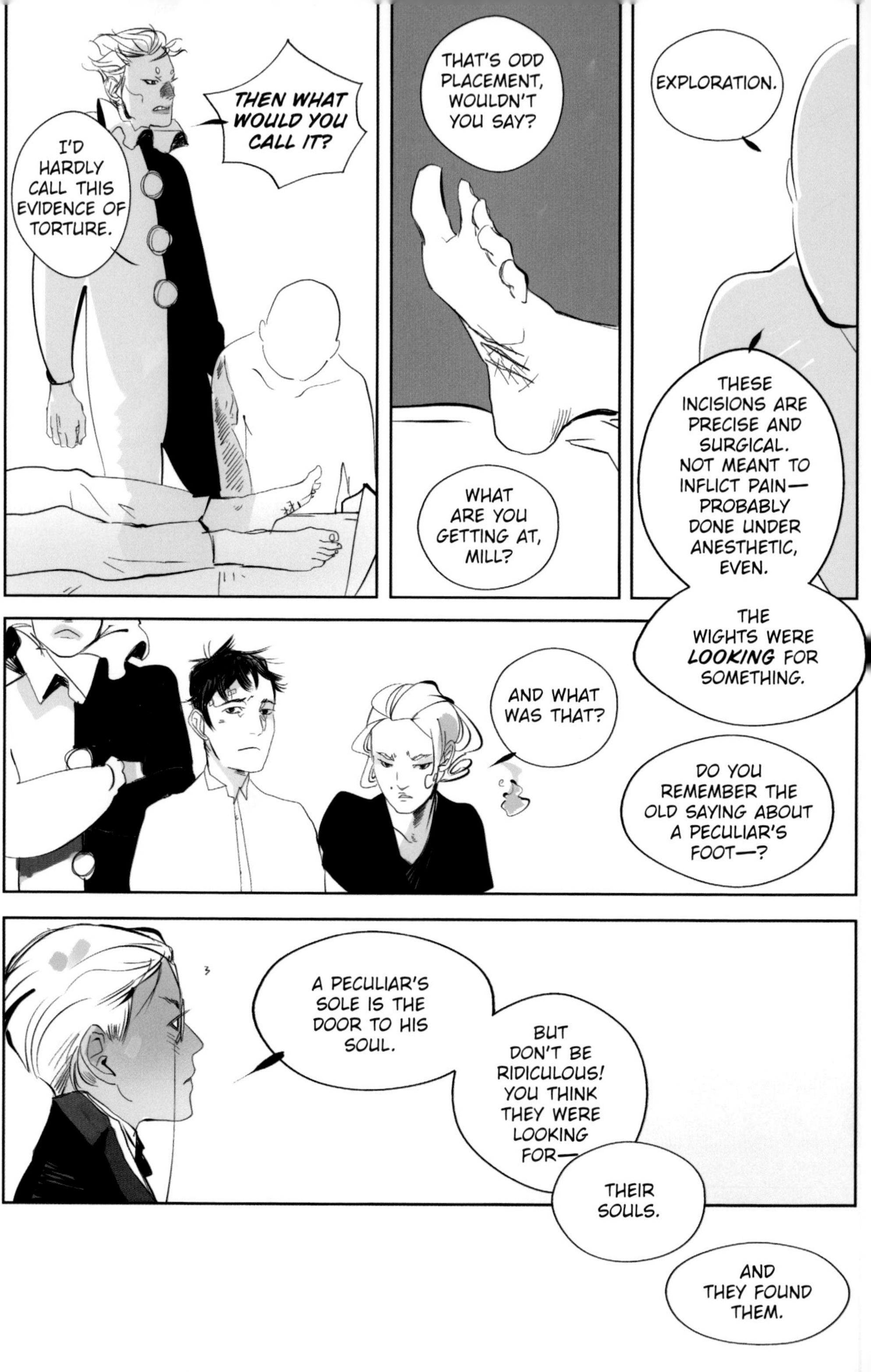
I'D HARDLY CALL THIS EVIDENCE OF TORTURE.
THEN WHAT WOULD YOU CALL IT?
THAT'S ODD PLACEMENT, WOULDN'T YOU SAY?
WHAT ARE YOU GETTING AT, MILL?
EXPLORATION.
THESE INCISIONS ARE PRECISE AND SURGICAL. NOT MEANT TO INFLICT PAIN—PROBABLY DONE UNDER ANESTHETIC, EVEN.
THE WIGHTS WERE LOOKING FOR SOMETHING.
AND WHAT WAS THAT?
DO YOU REMEMBER THE OLD SAYING ABOUT A PECULIAR'S FOOT—?
A PECULIAR'S SOLE IS THE DOOR TO HIS SOUL.
BUT DON'T BE RIDICULOUS! YOU THINK THEY WERE LOOKING FOR—
THEIR SOULS.
AND THEY FOUND THEM.

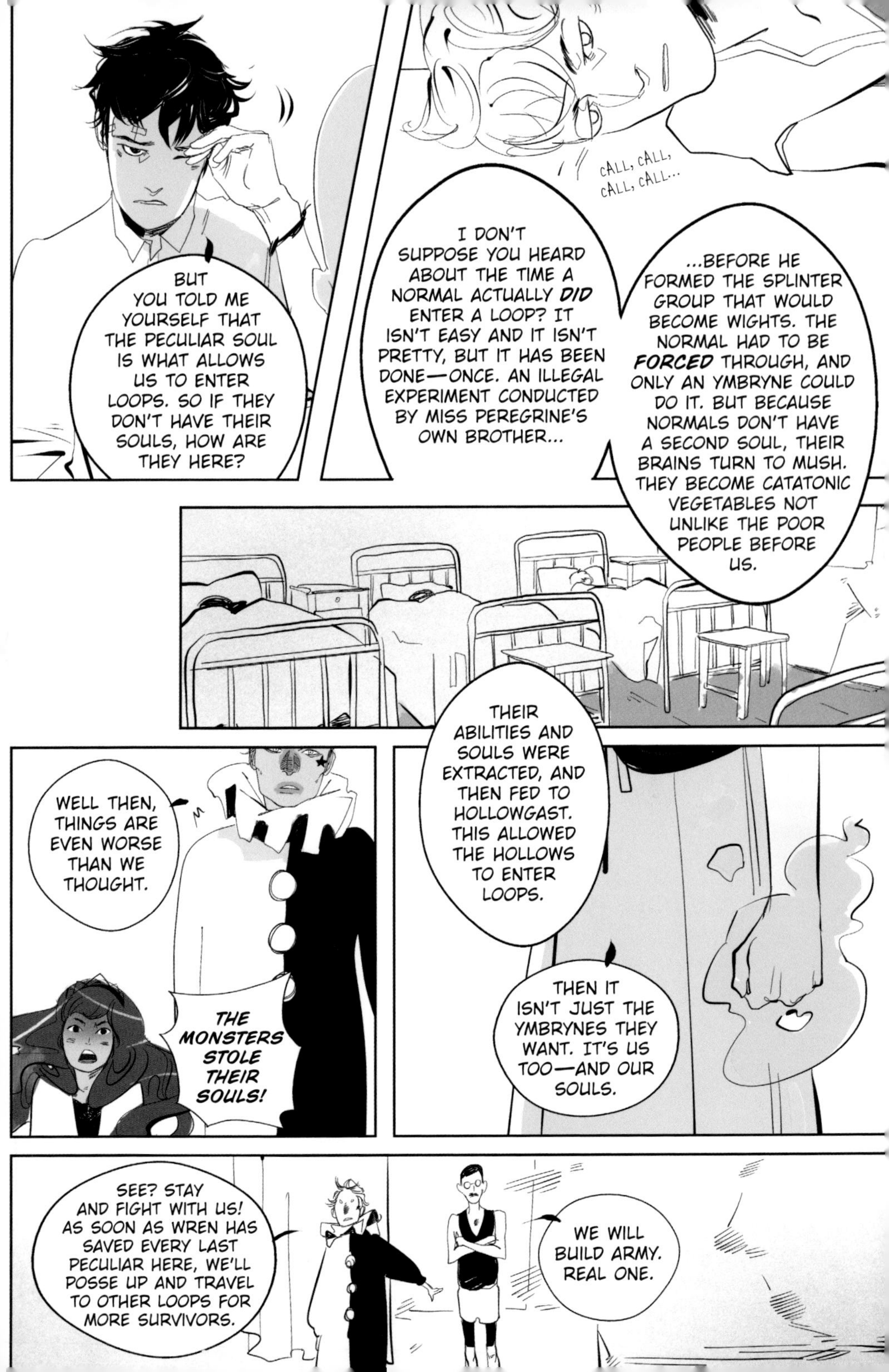
BUT YOU TOLD ME YOURSELF THAT THE PECULIAR SOUL IS WHAT ALLOWS US TO ENTER LOOPS. SO IF THEY DON'T HAVE THEIR SOULS, HOW ARE THEY HERE?
CALL, CALL, CALL, CALL...
I DON'T SUPPOSE YOU HEARD ABOUT THE TIME A NORMAL ACTUALLY *DID* ENTER A LOOP? IT ISN'T EASY AND IT ISN'T PRETTY, BUT IT HAS BEEN DONE—ONCE. AN ILLEGAL EXPERIMENT CONDUCTED BY MISS PEREGRINE'S OWN BROTHER...
...BEFORE HE FORMED THE SPLINTER GROUP THAT WOULD BECOME WIGHTS. THE NORMAL HAD TO BE ***FORCED*** THROUGH, AND ONLY AN YMBRYNE COULD DO IT. BUT BECAUSE NORMALS DON'T HAVE A SECOND SOUL, THEIR BRAINS TURN TO MUSH. THEY BECOME CATATONIC VEGETABLES NOT UNLIKE THE POOR PEOPLE BEFORE US.
THEIR ABILITIES AND SOULS WERE EXTRACTED, AND THEN FED TO HOLLOWGAST. THIS ALLOWED THE HOLLOWS TO ENTER LOOPS.
WELL THEN, THINGS ARE EVEN WORSE THAN WE THOUGHT.
THE MONSTERS STOLE THEIR SOULS!
THEN IT ISN'T JUST THE YMBRYNES THEY WANT. IT'S US TOO—AND OUR SOULS.
SEE? STAY AND FIGHT WITH US! AS SOON AS WREN HAS SAVED EVERY LAST PECULIAR HERE, WE'LL POSSE UP AND TRAVEL TO OTHER LOOPS FOR MORE SURVIVORS.
WE WILL BUILD ARMY. REAL ONE.

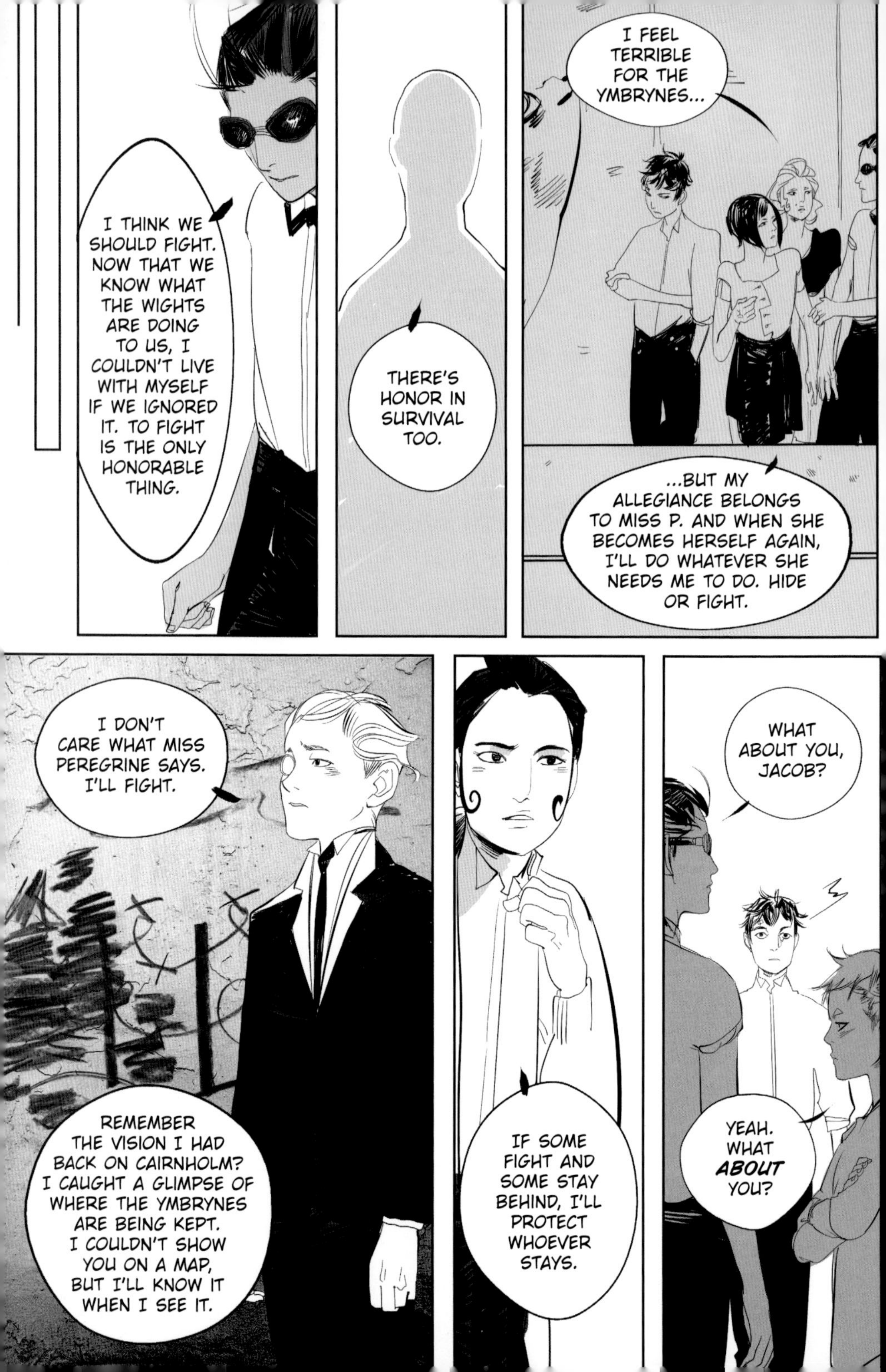
I THINK WE SHOULD FIGHT. NOW THAT WE KNOW WHAT THE WIGHTS ARE DOING TO US, I COULDN'T LIVE WITH MYSELF IF WE IGNORED IT. TO FIGHT IS THE ONLY HONORABLE THING.
THERE'S HONOR IN SURVIVAL TOO.
I FEEL TERRIBLE FOR THE YMBRYNES...
...BUT MY ALLEGIANCE BELONGS TO MISS P. AND WHEN SHE BECOMES HERSELF AGAIN, I'LL DO WHATEVER SHE NEEDS ME TO DO. HIDE OR FIGHT.
I DON'T CARE WHAT MISS PEREGRINE SAYS. I'LL FIGHT.
REMEMBER THE VISION I HAD BACK ON CAIRNHOLM? I CAUGHT A GLIMPSE OF WHERE THE YMBRYNES ARE BEING KEPT. I COULDN'T SHOW YOU ON A MAP, BUT I'LL KNOW IT WHEN I SEE IT.
IF SOME FIGHT AND SOME STAY BEHIND, I'LL PROTECT WHOEVER STAYS.
WHAT ABOUT YOU, JACOB?
YEAH. WHAT ABOUT YOU?

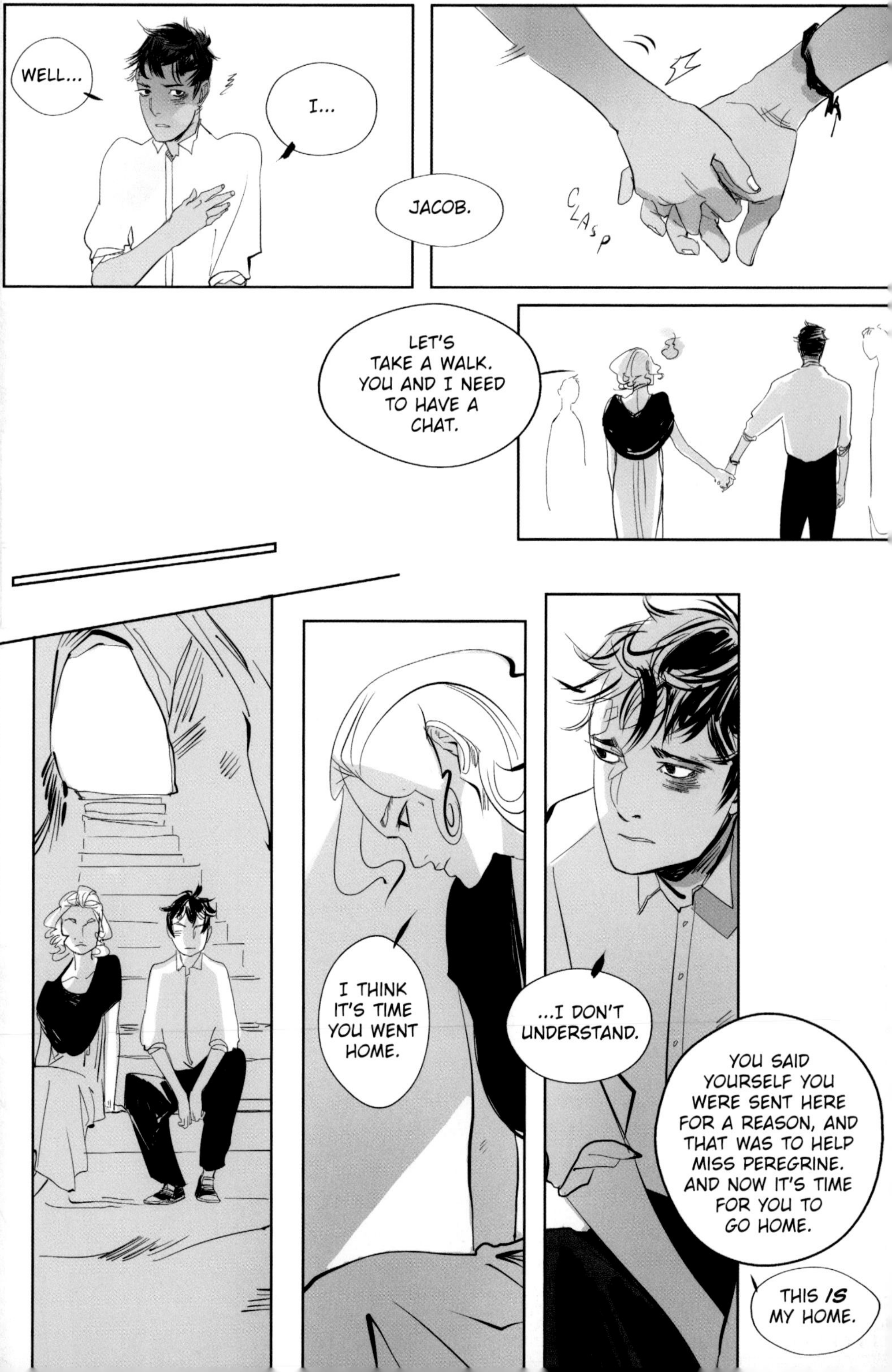
WELL...
I...
JACOB.
CLASP
LET'S TAKE A WALK. YOU AND I NEED TO HAVE A CHAT.
I THINK IT'S TIME YOU WENT HOME.
...I DON'T UNDERSTAND.
YOU SAID YOURSELF YOU WERE SENT HERE FOR A REASON, AND THAT WAS TO HELP MISS PEREGRINE. AND NOW IT'S TIME FOR YOU TO GO HOME.
THIS *IS* MY HOME.

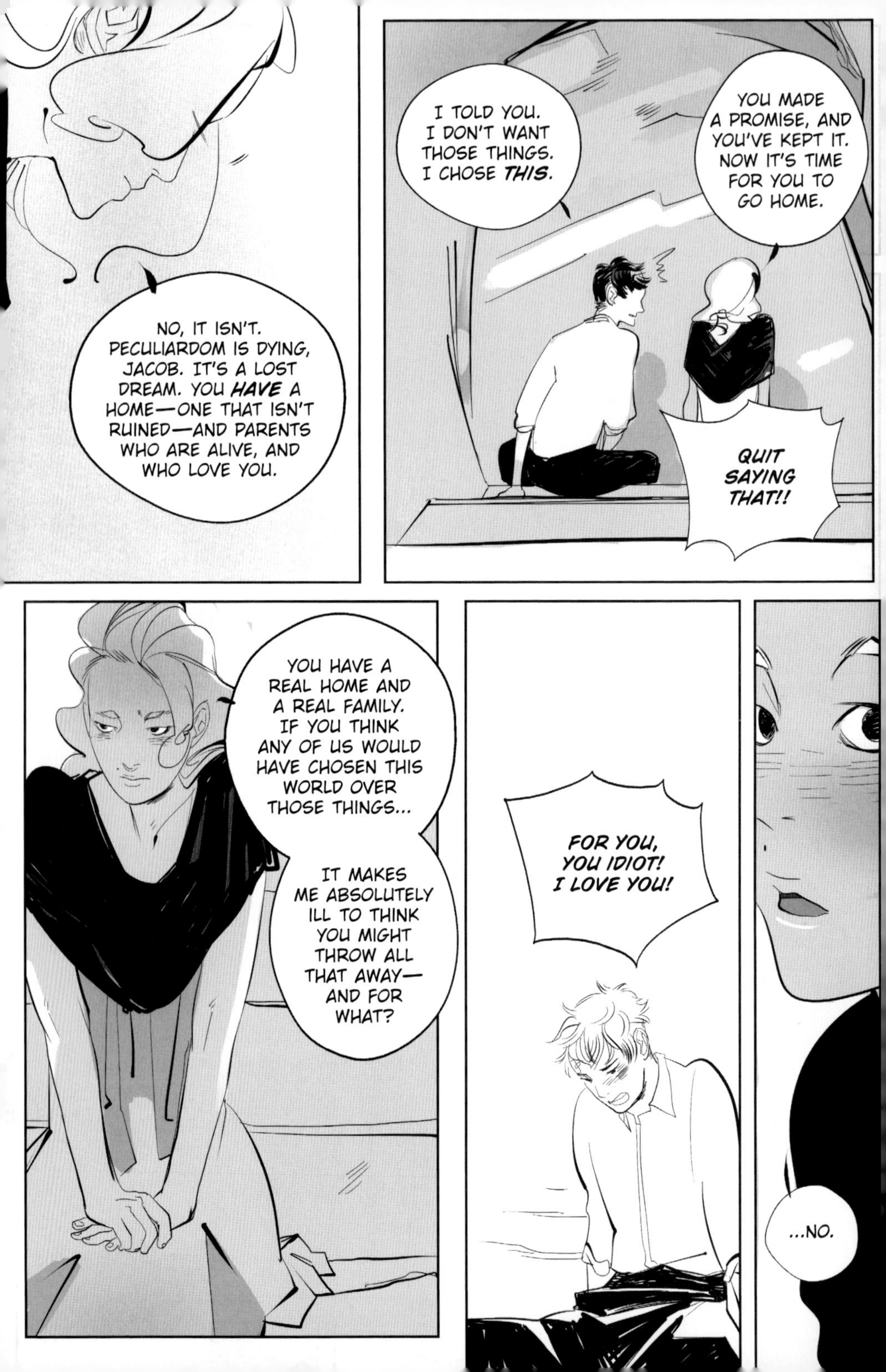
NO, IT ISN'T. PECULIARDOM IS DYING, JACOB. IT'S A LOST DREAM. YOU **HAVE** A HOME—ONE THAT ISN'T RUINED—AND PARENTS WHO ARE ALIVE, AND WHO LOVE YOU.
I TOLD YOU. I DON'T WANT THOSE THINGS. I CHOSE **THIS**.
YOU MADE A PROMISE, AND YOU'VE KEPT IT. NOW IT'S TIME FOR YOU TO GO HOME.
QUIT SAYING THAT!!
YOU HAVE A REAL HOME AND A REAL FAMILY. IF YOU THINK ANY OF US WOULD HAVE CHOSEN THIS WORLD OVER THOSE THINGS...
IT MAKES ME ABSOLUTELY ILL TO THINK YOU MIGHT THROW ALL THAT AWAY—AND FOR WHAT?
FOR YOU, YOU IDIOT! I LOVE YOU!
...NO.

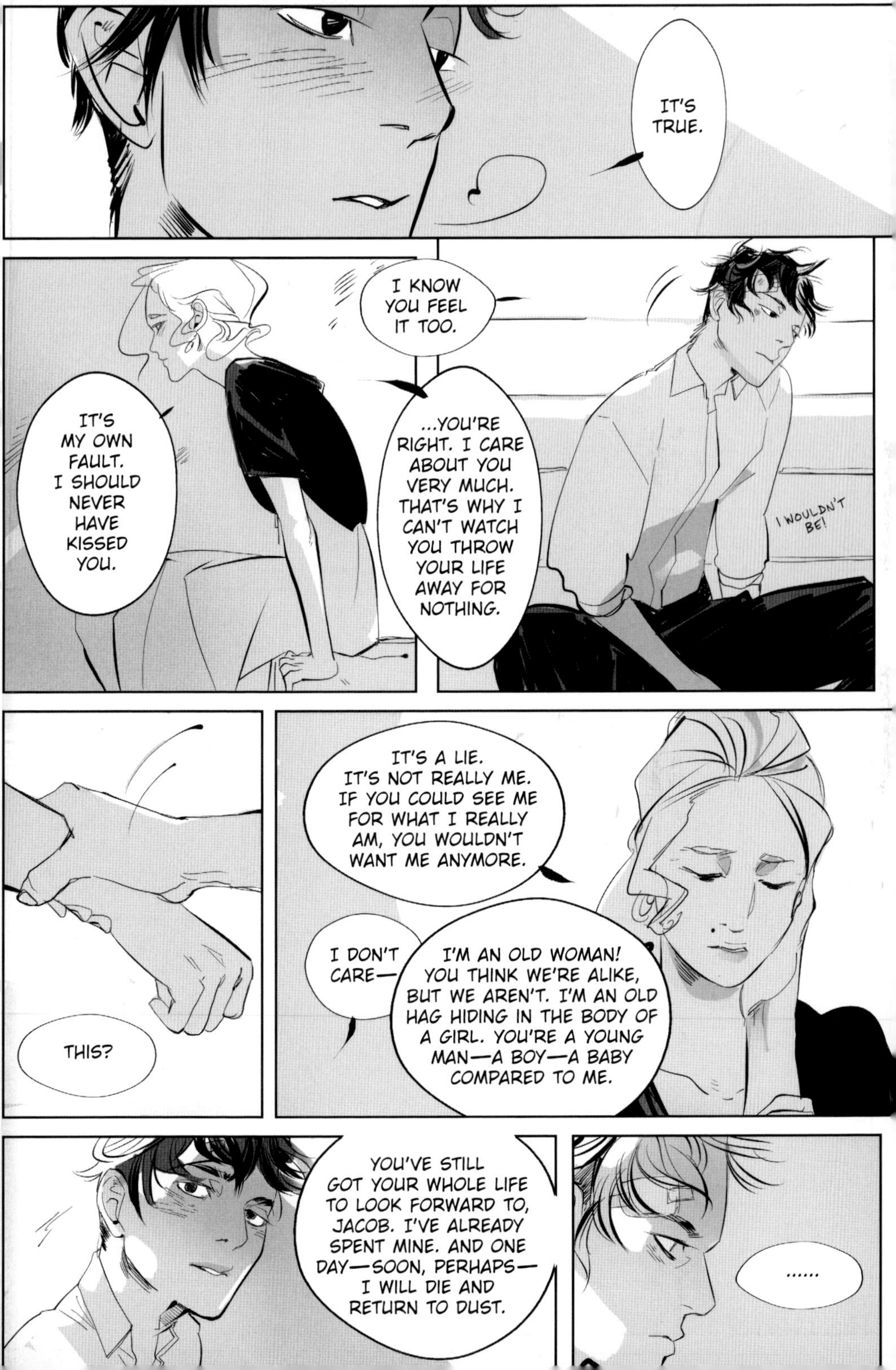
IT'S TRUE.
I KNOW YOU FEEL IT TOO.
IT'S MY OWN FAULT. I SHOULD NEVER HAVE KISSED YOU.
...YOU'RE RIGHT. I CARE ABOUT YOU VERY MUCH. THAT'S WHY I CAN'T WATCH YOU THROW YOUR LIFE AWAY FOR NOTHING.
I WOULDN'T BE!
THIS?
IT'S A LIE. IT'S NOT REALLY ME. IF YOU COULD SEE ME FOR WHAT I REALLY AM, YOU WOULDN'T WANT ME ANYMORE.
I DON'T CARE—
I'M AN OLD WOMAN! YOU THINK WE'RE ALIKE, BUT WE AREN'T. I'M AN OLD HAG HIDING IN THE BODY OF A GIRL. YOU'RE A YOUNG MAN—A BOY—A BABY COMPARED TO ME.
YOU'VE STILL GOT YOUR WHOLE LIFE TO LOOK FORWARD TO, JACOB. I'VE ALREADY SPENT MINE. AND ONE DAY—SOON, PERHAPS—I WILL DIE AND RETURN TO DUST.
......

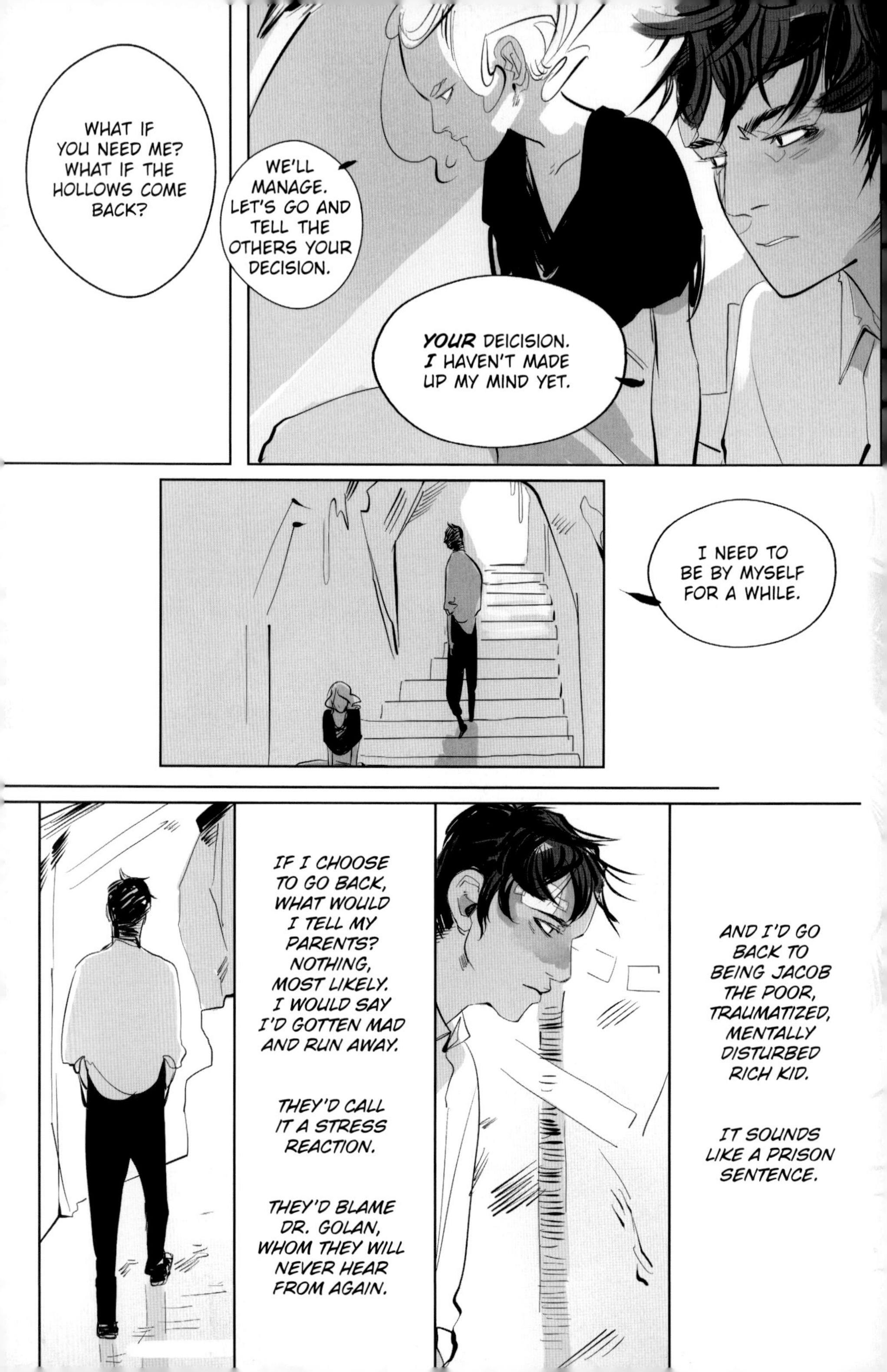
WHAT IF YOU NEED ME? WHAT IF THE HOLLOWS COME BACK?
WE'LL MANAGE. LET'S GO AND TELL THE OTHERS YOUR DECISION.
YOUR DEICISION. I HAVEN'T MADE UP MY MIND YET.
I NEED TO BE BY MYSELF FOR A WHILE.
IF I CHOOSE TO GO BACK, WHAT WOULD I TELL MY PARENTS? NOTHING, MOST LIKELY. I WOULD SAY I'D GOTTEN MAD AND RUN AWAY.
THEY'D CALL IT A STRESS REACTION.
THEY'D BLAME DR. GOLAN, WHOM THEY WILL NEVER HEAR FROM AGAIN.
AND I'D GO BACK TO BEING JACOB THE POOR, TRAUMATIZED, MENTALLY DISTURBED RICH KID.
IT SOUNDS LIKE A PRISON SENTENCE.

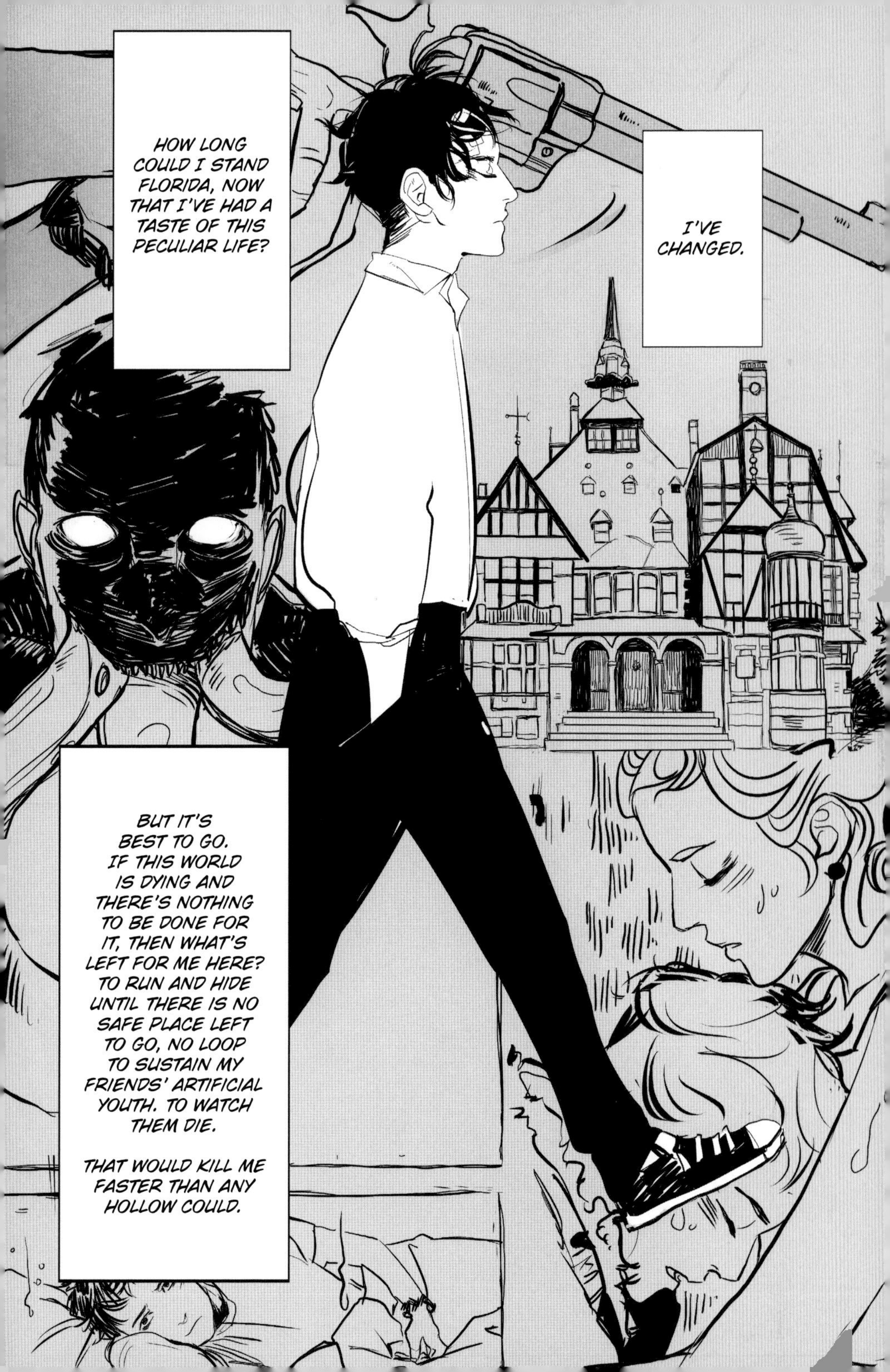
HOW LONG COULD I STAND FLORIDA, NOW THAT I'VE HAD A TASTE OF THIS PECULIAR LIFE?
I'VE CHANGED.
BUT IT'S BEST TO GO. IF THIS WORLD IS DYING AND THERE'S NOTHING TO BE DONE FOR IT, THEN WHAT'S LEFT FOR ME HERE? TO RUN AND HIDE UNTIL THERE IS NO SAFE PLACE LEFT TO GO, NO LOOP TO SUSTAIN MY FRIENDS' ARTIFICIAL YOUTH. TO WATCH THEM DIE.
THAT WOULD KILL ME FASTER THAN ANY HOLLOW COULD.

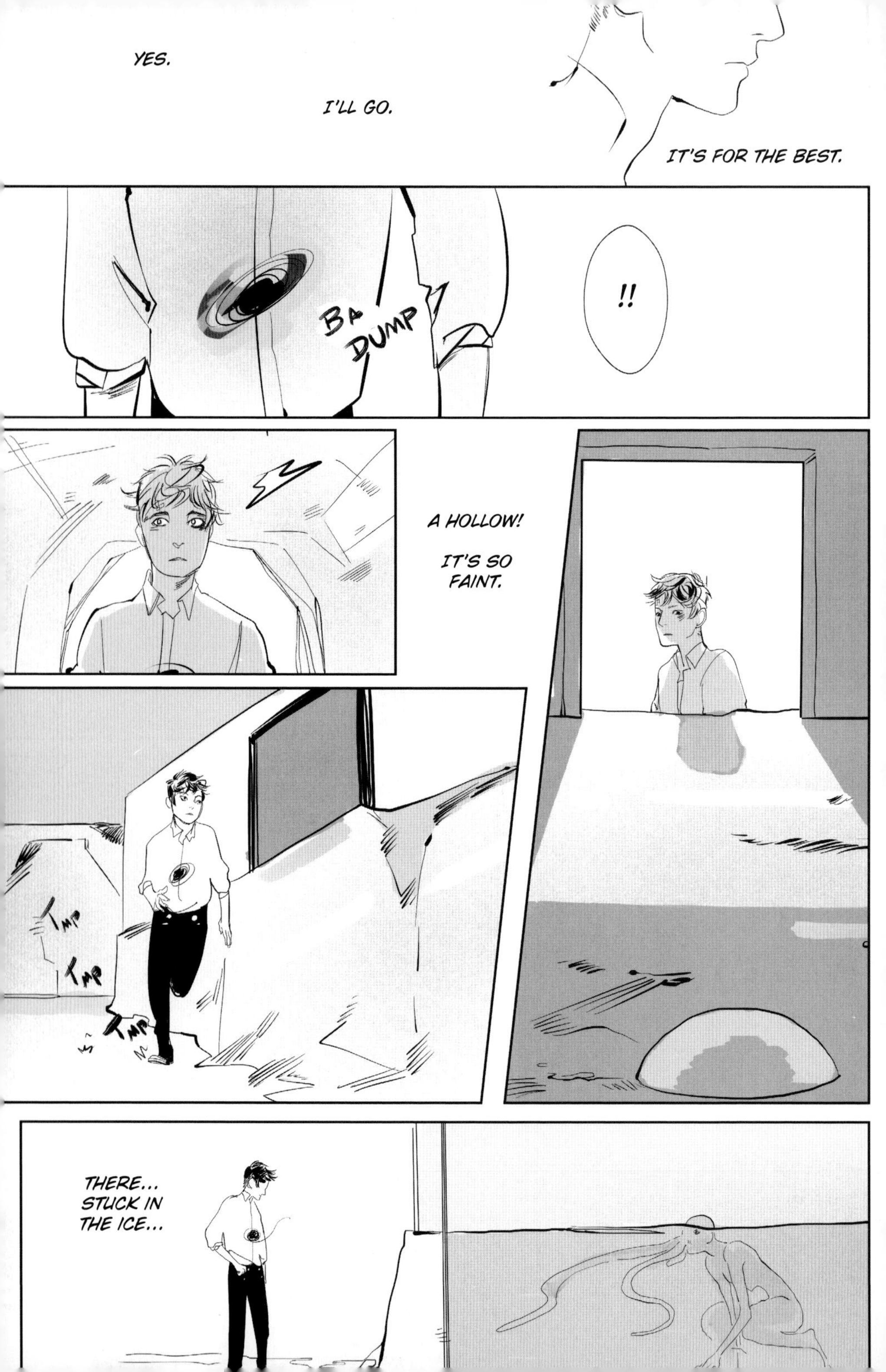
YES.
I'LL GO.
IT'S FOR THE BEST.
BA DUMP
!!
A HOLLOW!
IT'S SO FAINT.
TMP
TMP
TMP
THERE... STUCK IN THE ICE...

IT'S BARELY ALIVE.

VULNERABLE.

THEY MUST NOT KNOW IT'S HERE, OR ANYONE WOULD HAVE KILLED IT...

I SHOULD KILL IT.

BADUMP

BA-DUMP

NO. I DON'T WANT TO HAVE NIGHTMARES ABOUT THIS ONE TOO.

I'M NOT JACOB THE HOLLOW-SLAYER ANYMORE.

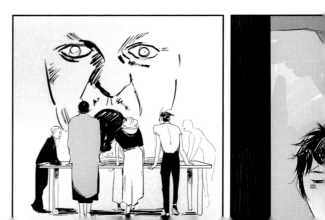

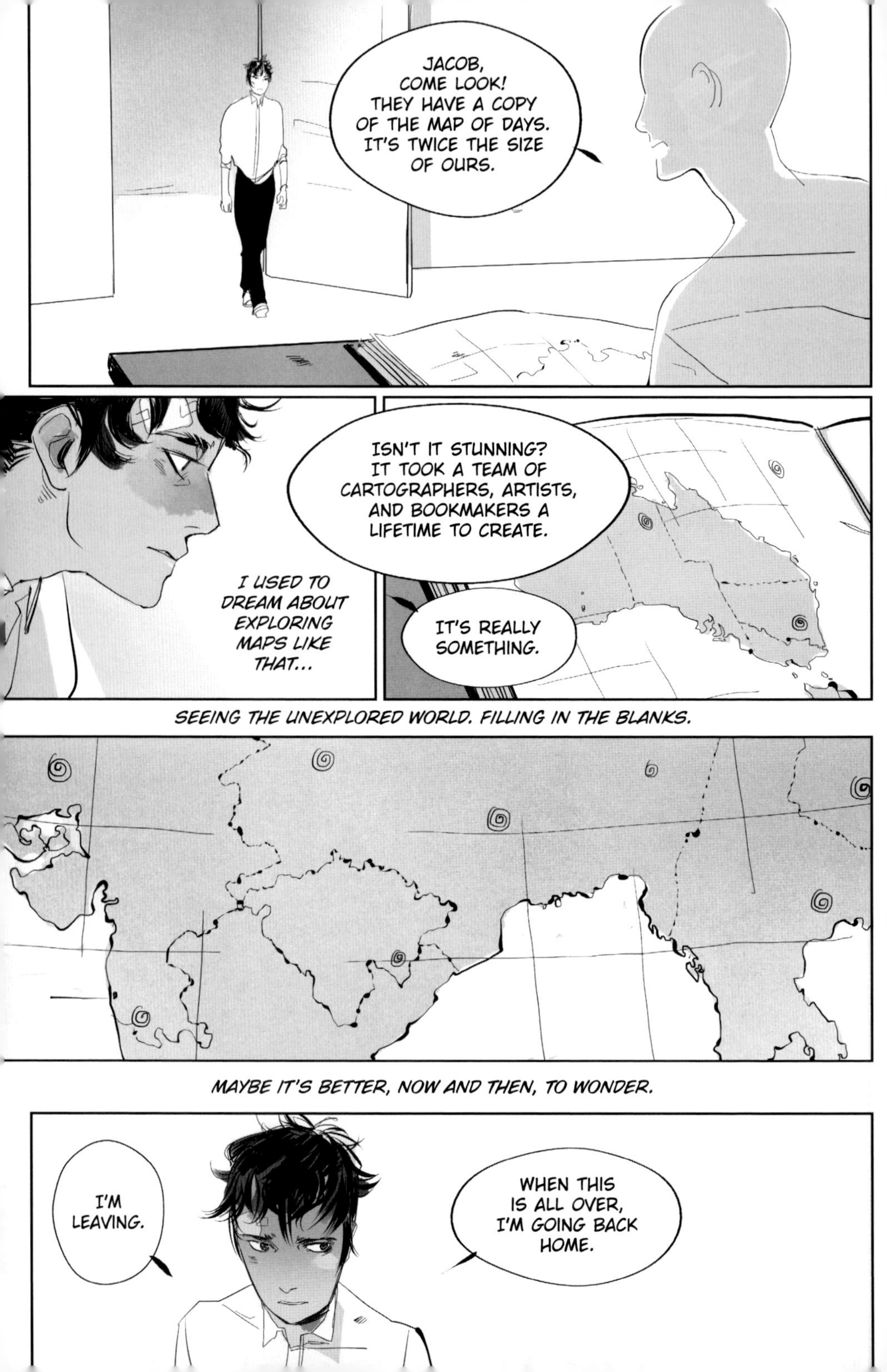
JACOB, COME LOOK! THEY HAVE A COPY OF THE MAP OF DAYS. IT'S TWICE THE SIZE OF OURS.
I USED TO DREAM ABOUT EXPLORING MAPS LIKE THAT...
ISN'T IT STUNNING? IT TOOK A TEAM OF CARTOGRAPHERS, ARTISTS, AND BOOKMAKERS A LIFETIME TO CREATE.
IT'S REALLY SOMETHING.
SEEING THE UNEXPLORED WORLD. FILLING IN THE BLANKS.
MAYBE IT'S BETTER, NOW AND THEN, TO WONDER.
I'M LEAVING.
WHEN THIS IS ALL OVER, I'M GOING BACK HOME.

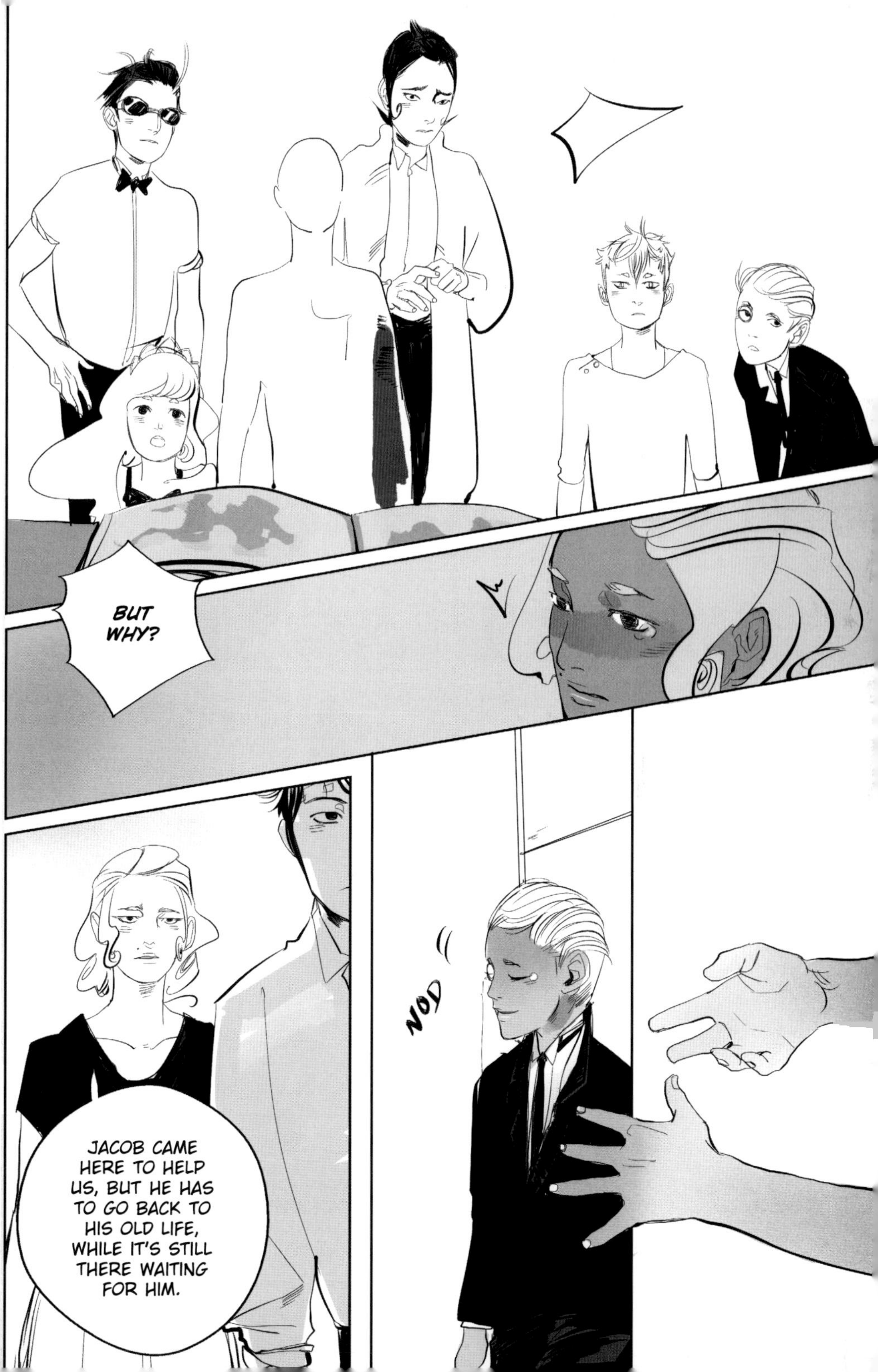
BUT WHY?
JACOB CAME HERE TO HELP US, BUT HE HAS TO GO BACK TO HIS OLD LIFE, WHILE IT'S STILL THERE WAITING FOR HIM.
NOD

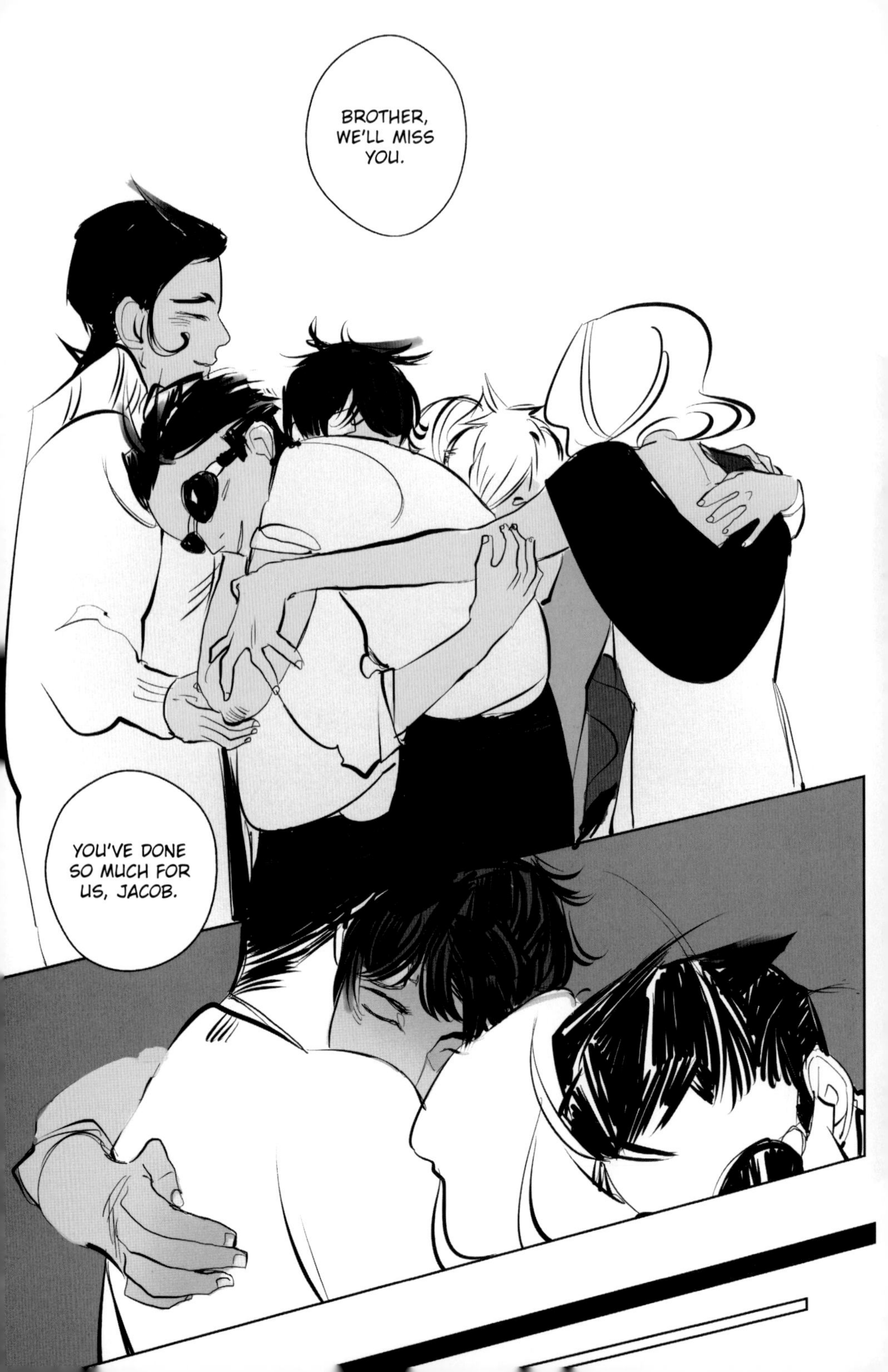
BROTHER, WE'LL MISS YOU.
YOU'VE DONE SO MUCH FOR US, JACOB.

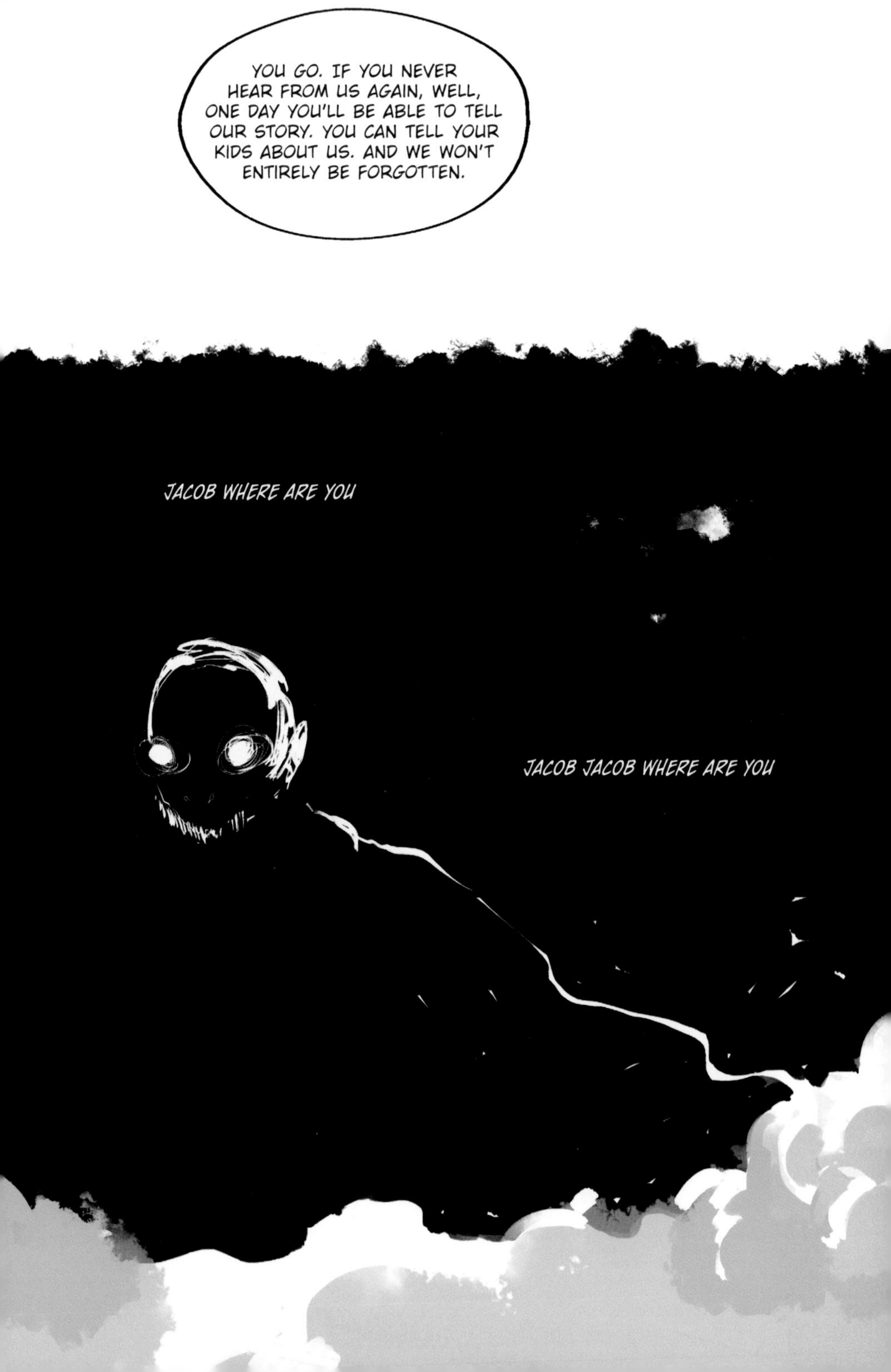
YOU GO. IF YOU NEVER HEAR FROM US AGAIN, WELL, ONE DAY YOU'LL BE ABLE TO TELL OUR STORY. YOU CAN TELL YOUR KIDS ABOUT US. AND WE WON'T ENTIRELY BE FORGOTTEN.
JACOB WHERE ARE YOU
JACOB JACOB WHERE ARE YOU

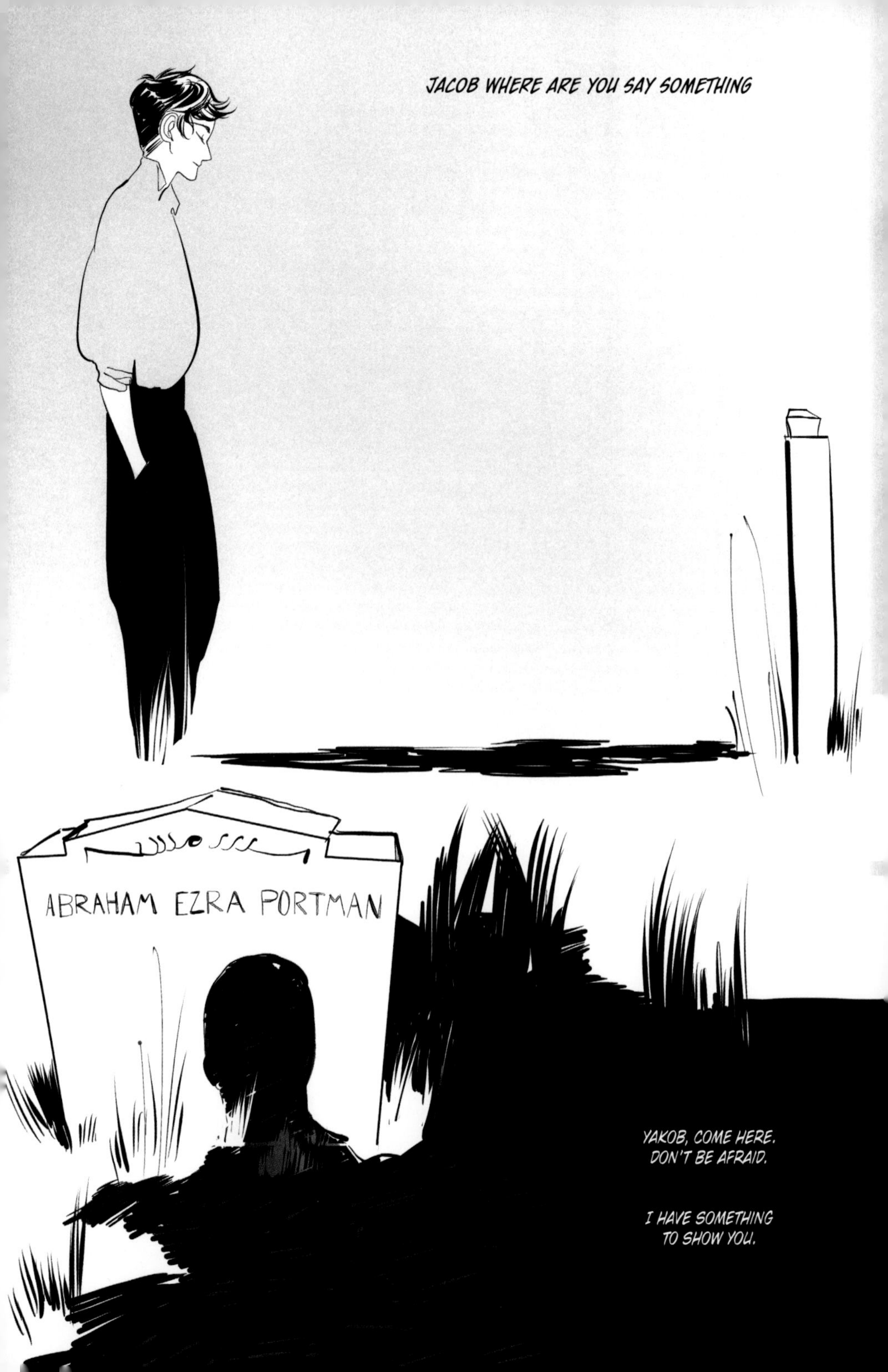
JACOB WHERE ARE YOU SAY SOMETHING
ABRAHAM EZRA PORTMAN
YAKOB, COME HERE. DON'T BE AFRAID.
I HAVE SOMETHING TO SHOW YOU.

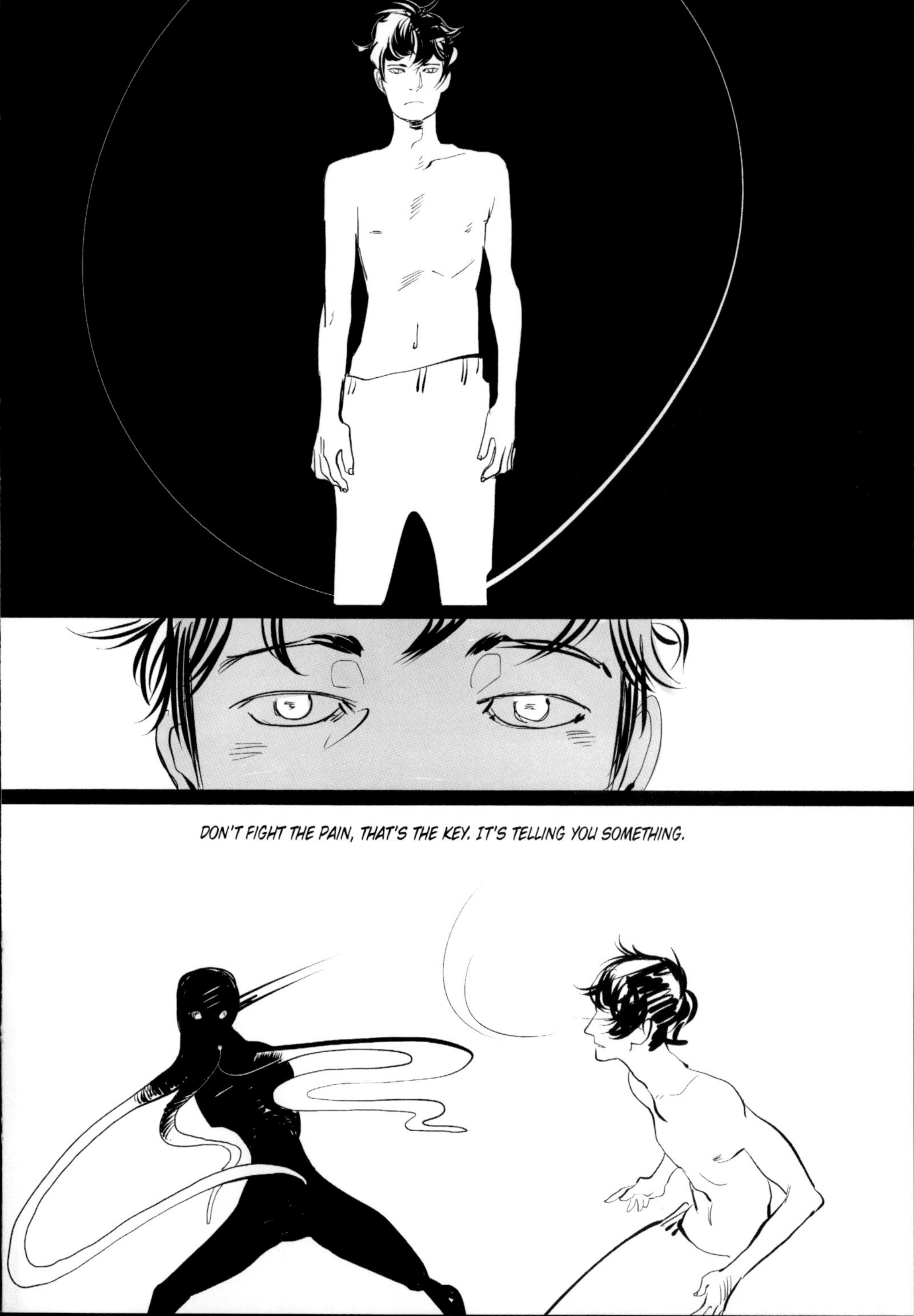
DON'T FIGHT THE PAIN, THAT'S THE KEY. IT'S TELLING YOU SOMETHING.

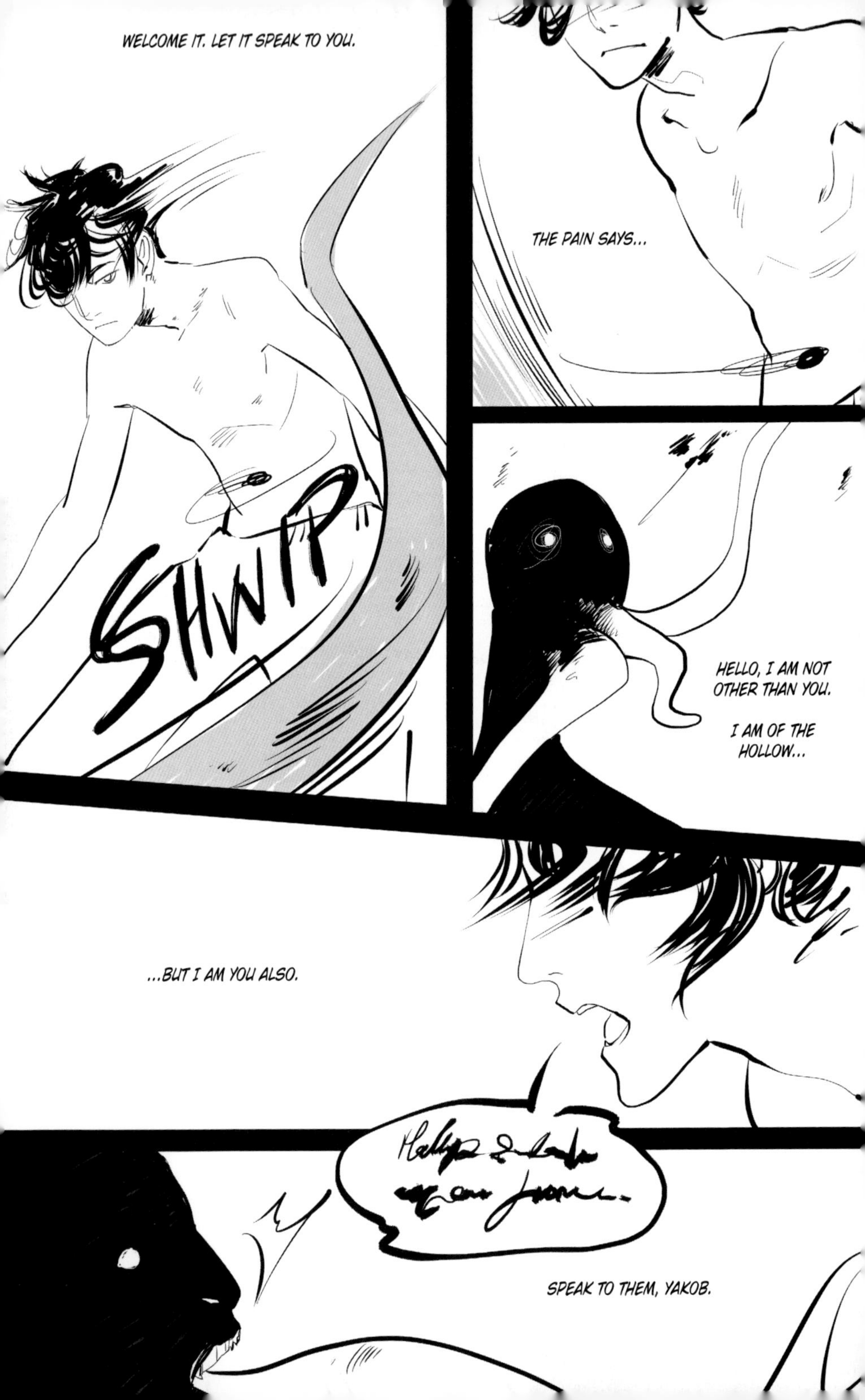
WELCOME IT. LET IT SPEAK TO YOU.
SHWIP
THE PAIN SAYS...
HELLO, I AM NOT OTHER THAN YOU.
I AM OF THE HOLLOW...
...BUT I AM YOU ALSO.
SPEAK TO THEM, YAKOB.

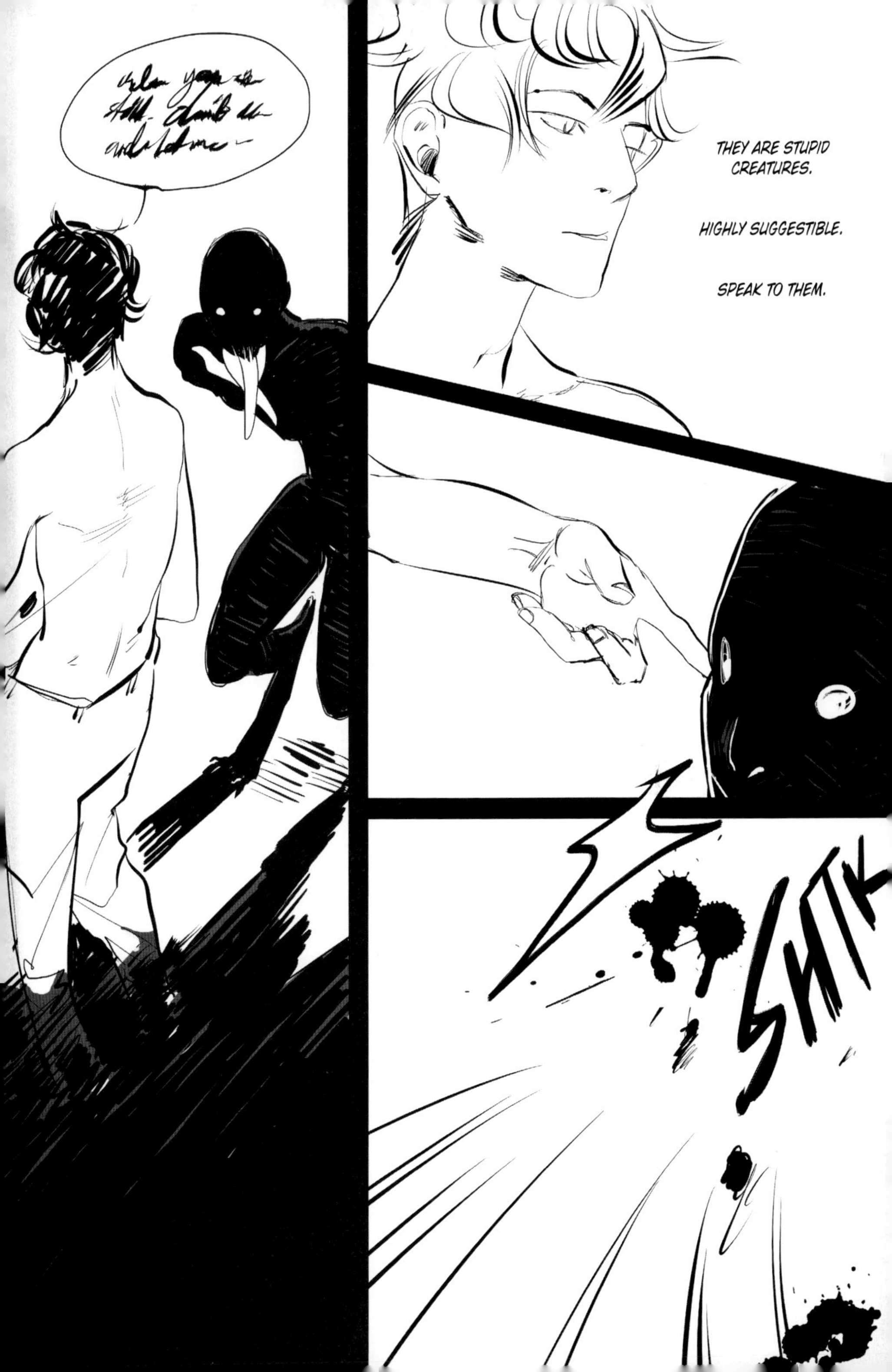
THEY ARE STUPID CREATURES.
HIGHLY SUGGESTIBLE.
SPEAK TO THEM.
SHTK

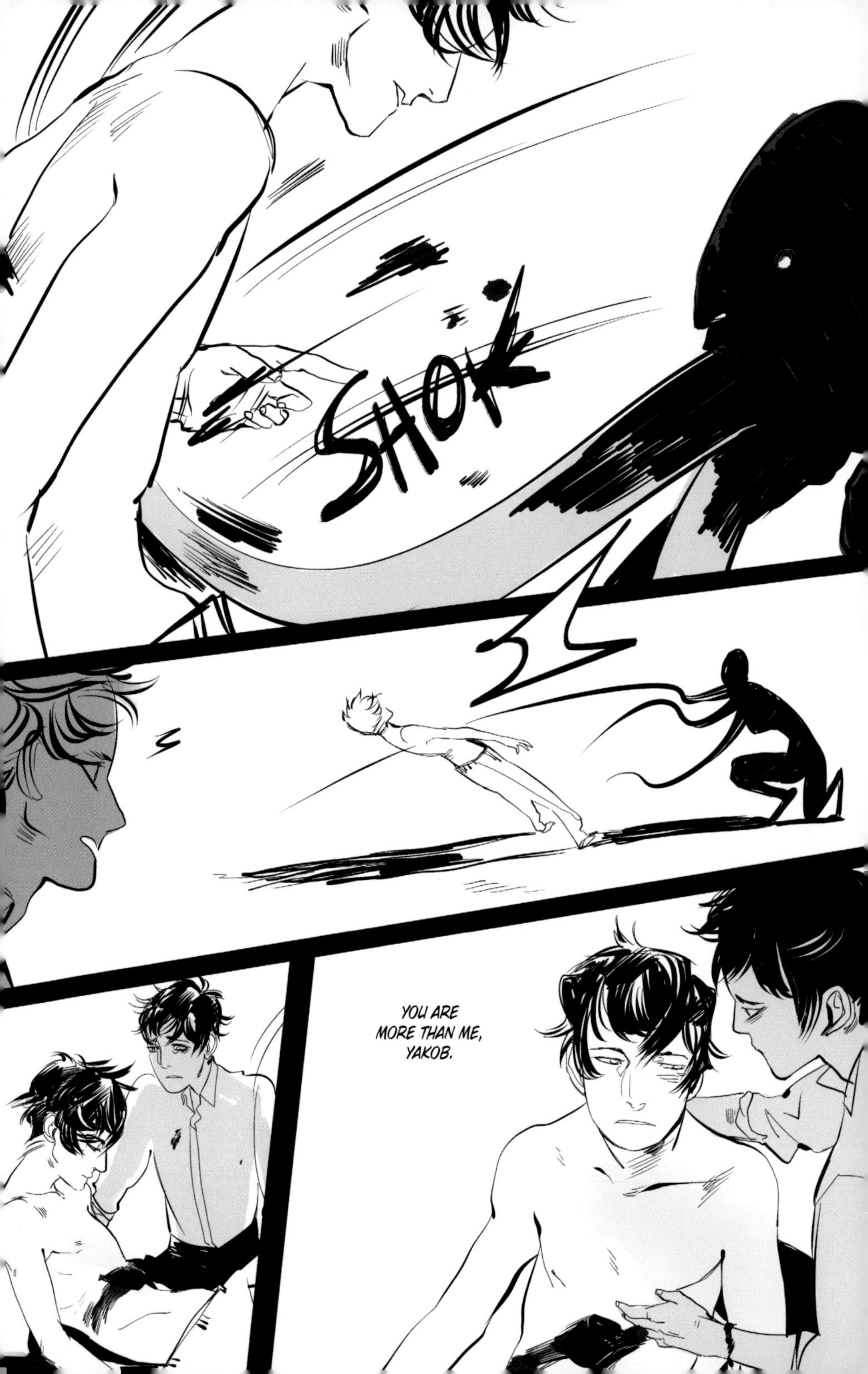
SHOK
YOU ARE MORE THAN ME, YAKOB.

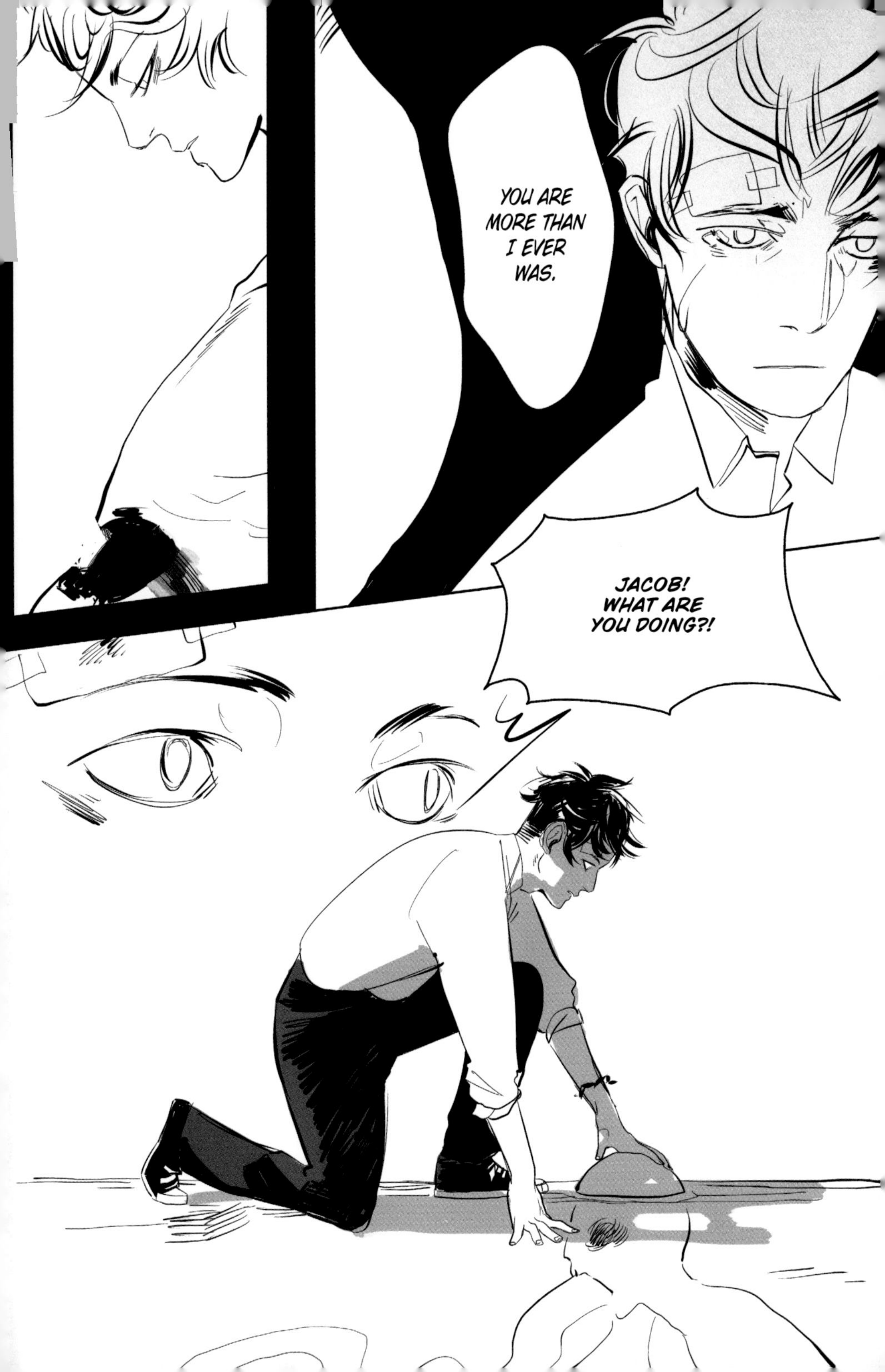
YOU ARE MORE THAN I EVER WAS.
JACOB! WHAT ARE YOU DOING?!

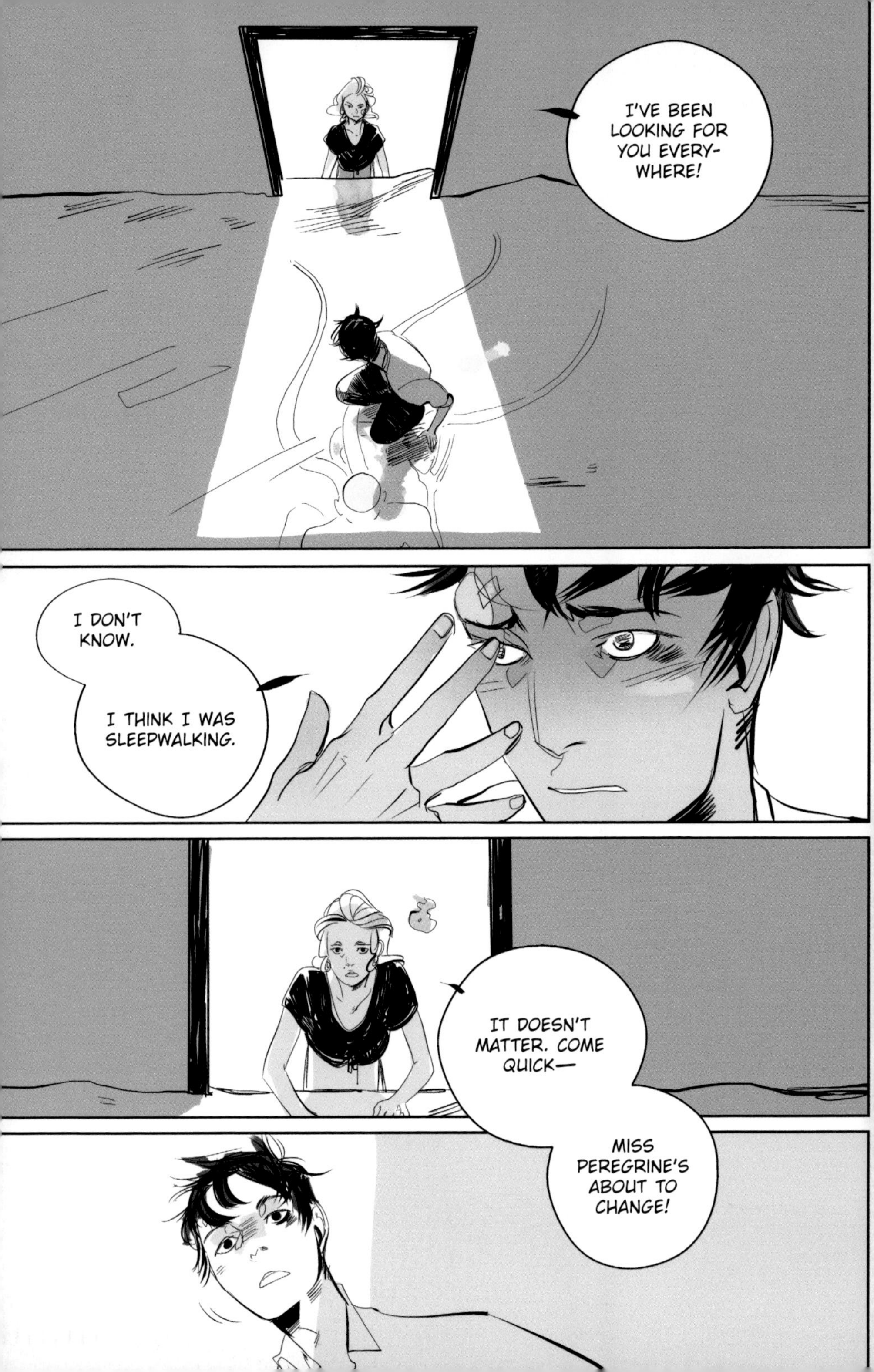
I'VE BEEN LOOKING FOR YOU EVERY-WHERE!
I DON'T KNOW.
I THINK I WAS SLEEPWALKING.
IT DOESN'T MATTER. COME QUICK—
MISS PEREGRINE'S ABOUT TO CHANGE!

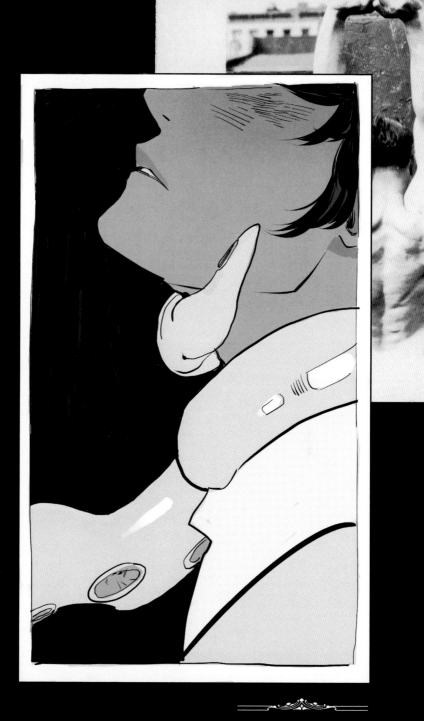

CHAPTER EIGHT

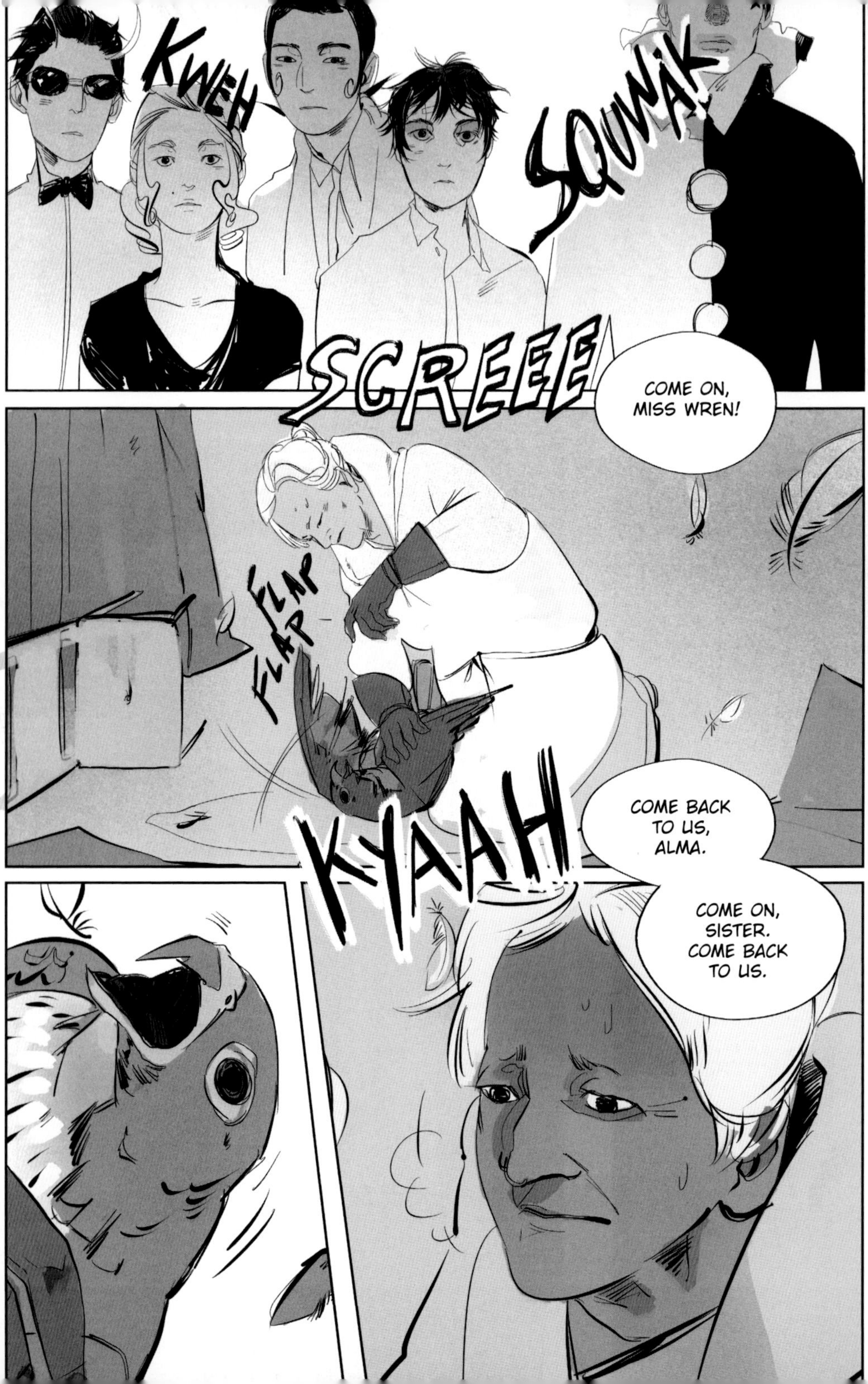
KWEH
SQUWAK
SCREEE
COME ON, MISS WREN!
FLAP FLAP
KYAAH
COME BACK TO US, ALMA.
COME ON, SISTER. COME BACK TO US.

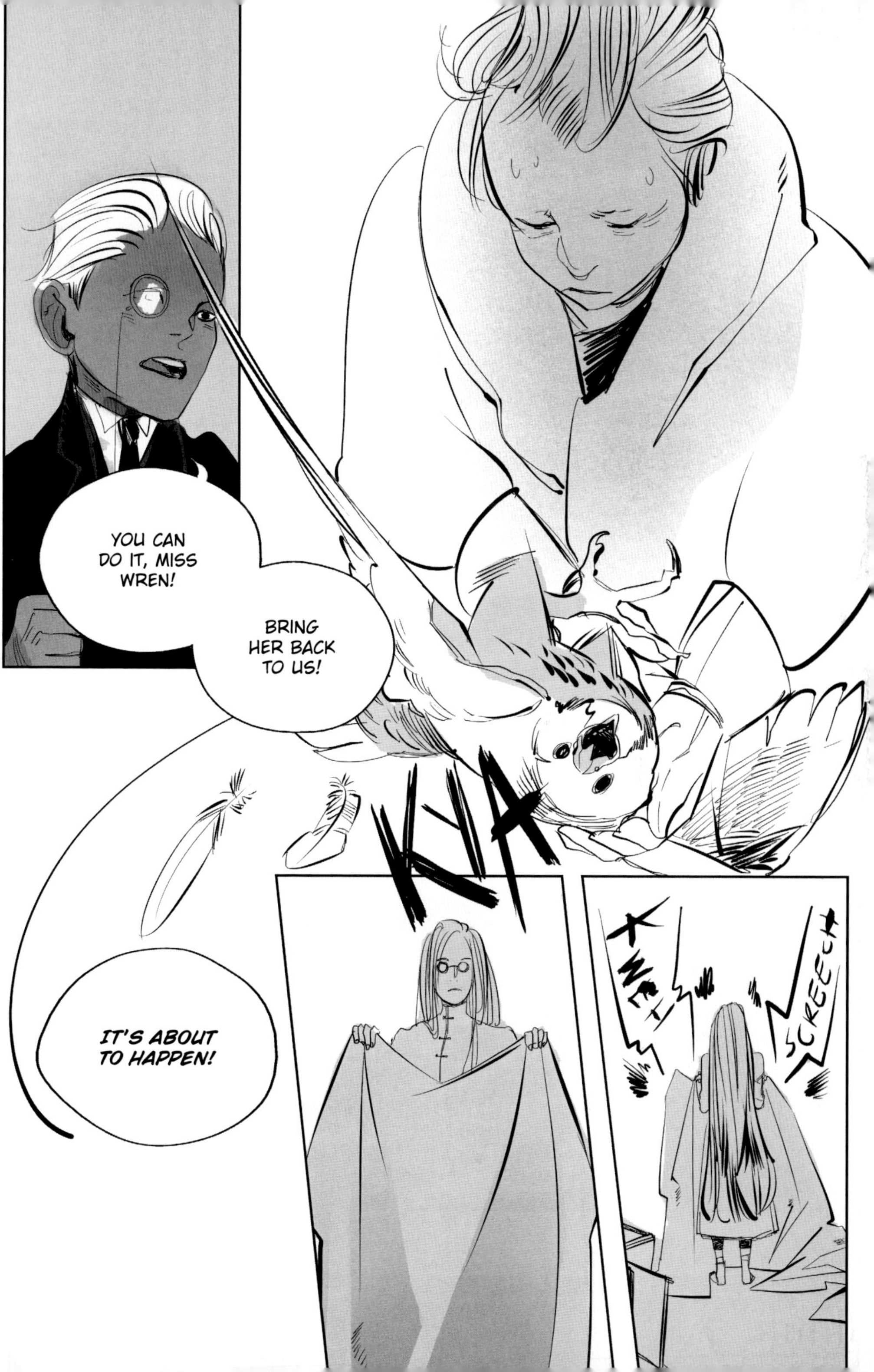
YOU CAN DO IT, MISS WREN!
BRING HER BACK TO US!
KYA
IT'S ABOUT TO HAPPEN!
KWEE!
SCREECH

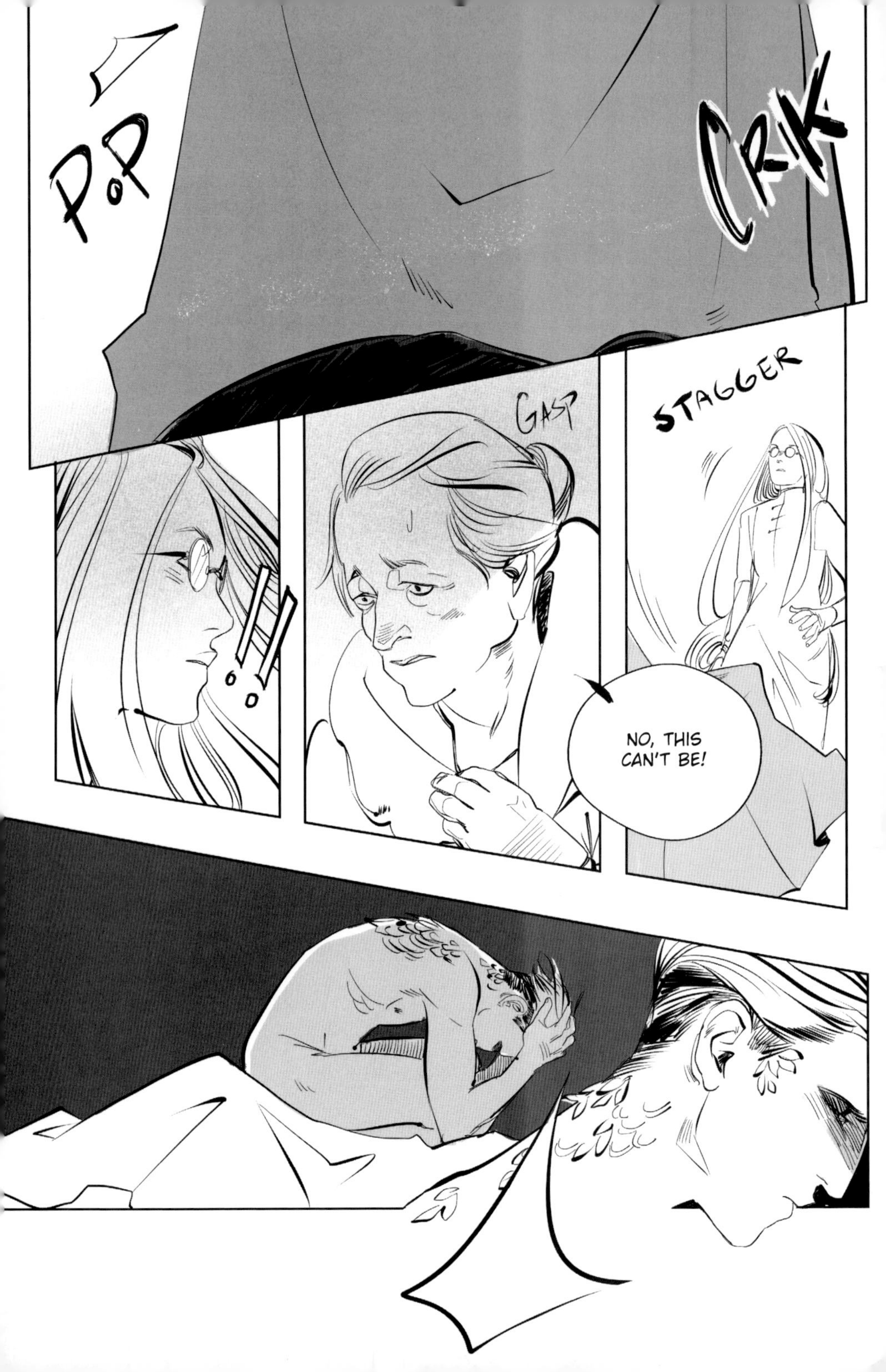
POP
CRK
GASP
STAGGER
NO, THIS CAN'T BE!

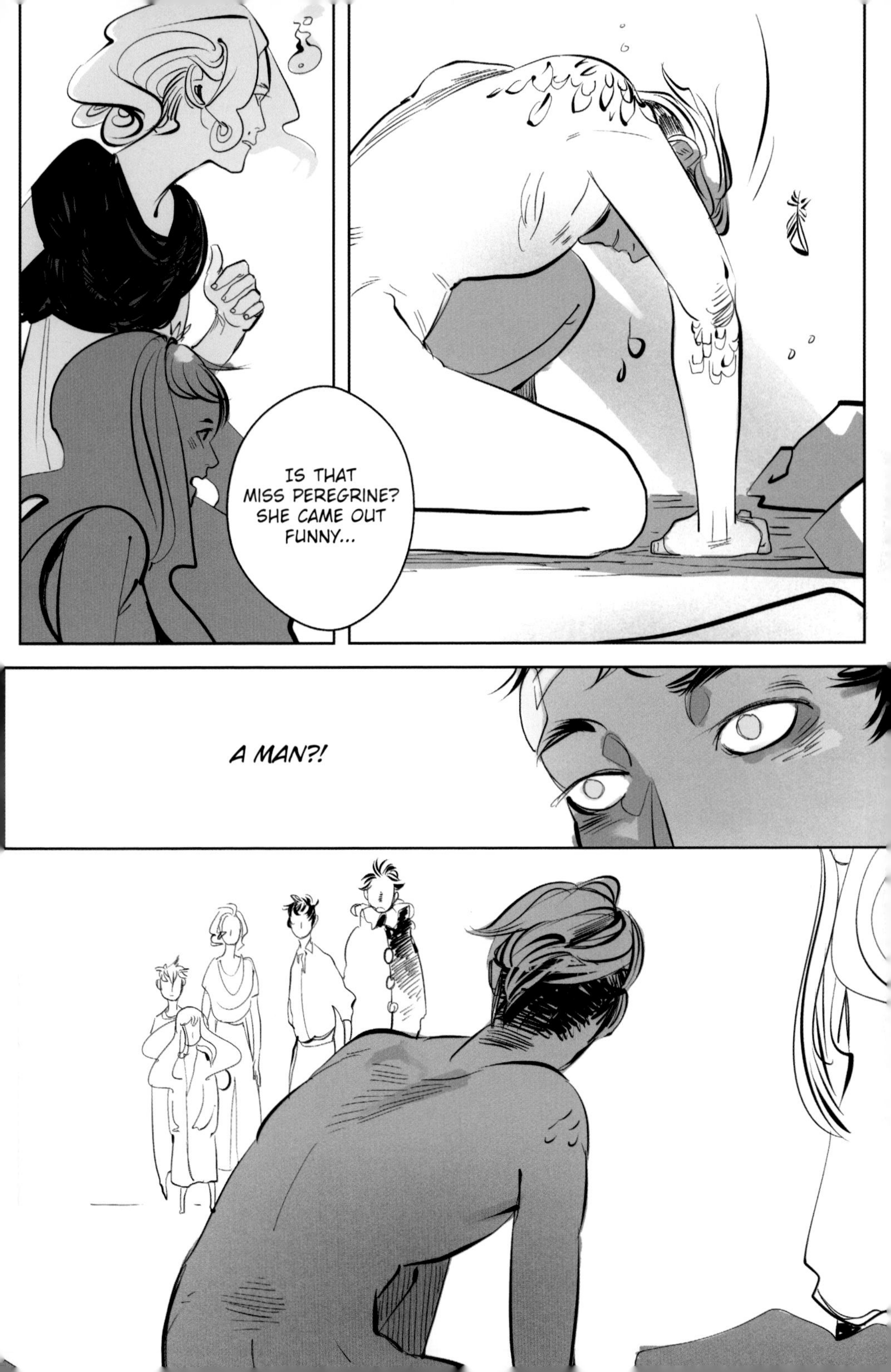
IS THAT MISS PEREGRINE? SHE CAME OUT FUNNY...
A MAN?!

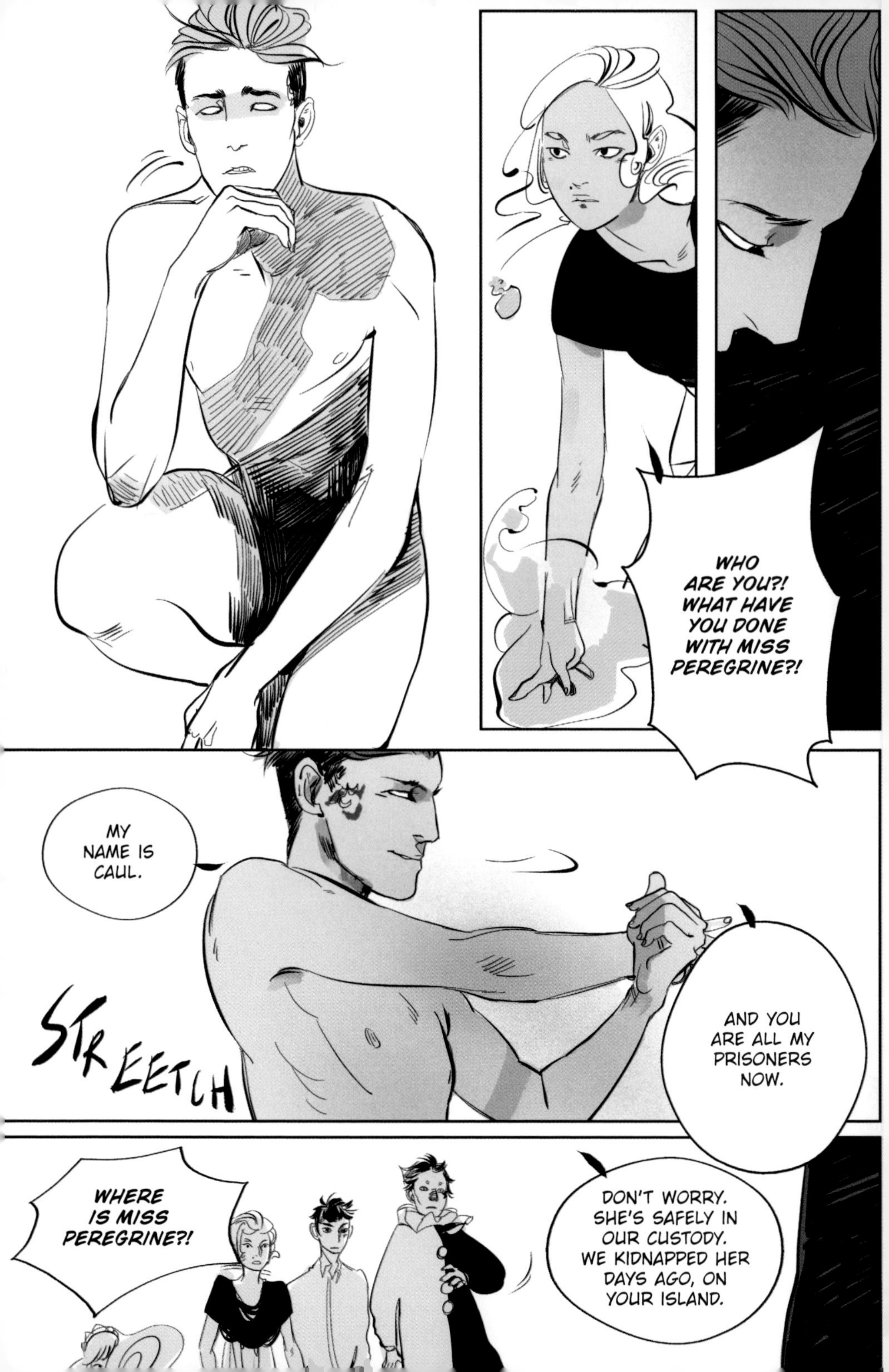
WHO ARE YOU?! WHAT HAVE YOU DONE WITH MISS PEREGRINE?!
MY NAME IS CAUL.
STREETCH
AND YOU ARE ALL MY PRISONERS NOW.
WHERE IS MISS PEREGRINE?!
DON'T WORRY. SHE'S SAFELY IN OUR CUSTODY. WE KIDNAPPED HER DAYS AGO, ON YOUR ISLAND.

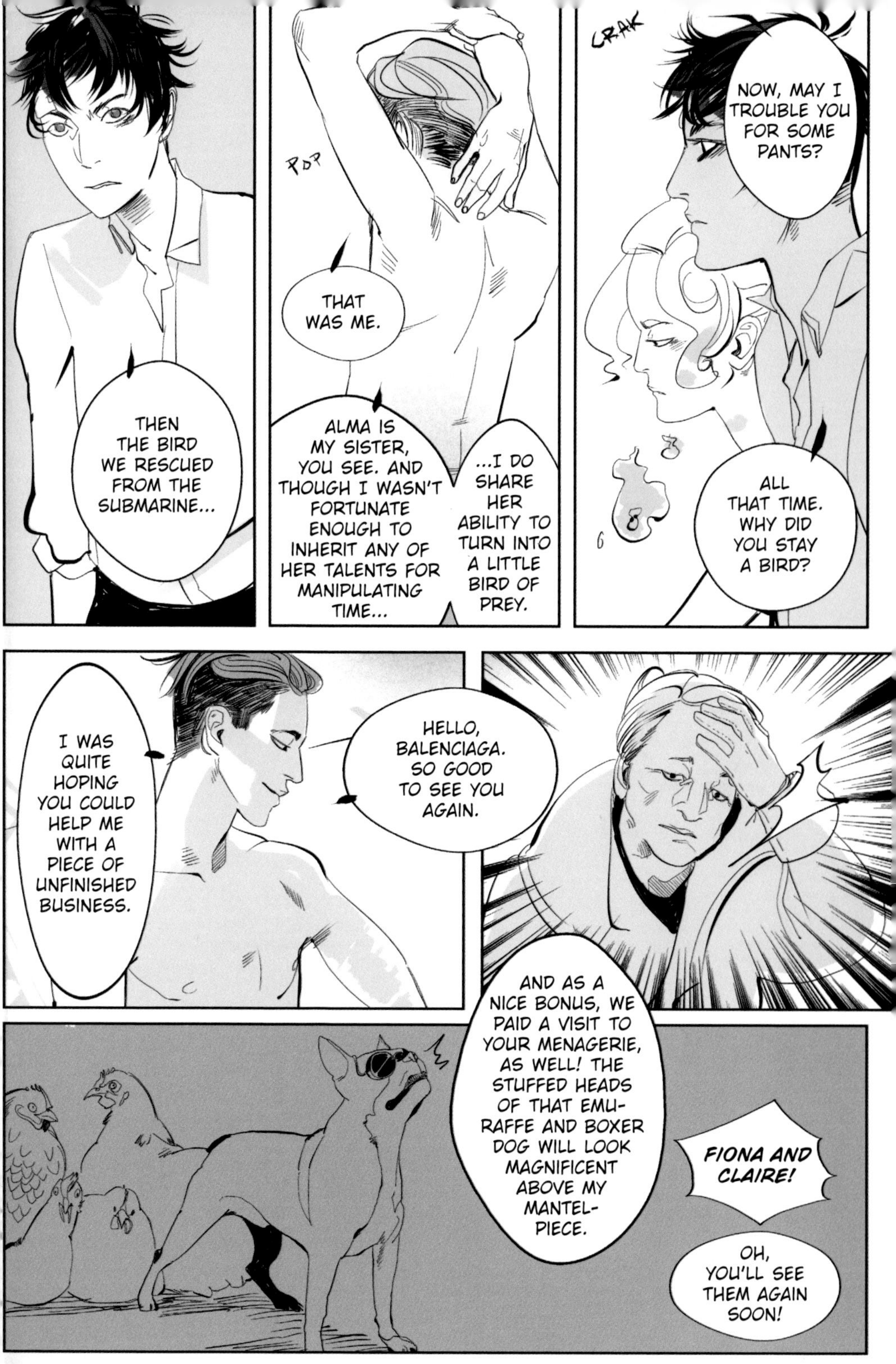
THEN THE BIRD WE RESCUED FROM THE SUBMARINE...
POP
THAT WAS ME.
ALMA IS MY SISTER, YOU SEE. AND THOUGH I WASN'T FORTUNATE ENOUGH TO INHERIT ANY OF HER TALENTS FOR MANIPULATING TIME...
...I DO SHARE HER ABILITY TO TURN INTO A LITTLE BIRD OF PREY.
CRAK
NOW, MAY I TROUBLE YOU FOR SOME PANTS?
ALL THAT TIME. WHY DID YOU STAY A BIRD?
I WAS QUITE HOPING YOU COULD HELP ME WITH A PIECE OF UNFINISHED BUSINESS.
HELLO, BALENCIAGA. SO GOOD TO SEE YOU AGAIN.
AND AS A NICE BONUS, WE PAID A VISIT TO YOUR MENAGERIE, AS WELL! THE STUFFED HEADS OF THAT EMU-RAFFE AND BOXER DOG WILL LOOK MAGNIFICENT ABOVE MY MANTEL-PIECE.
FIONA AND CLAIRE!
OH, YOU'LL SEE THEM AGAIN SOON!

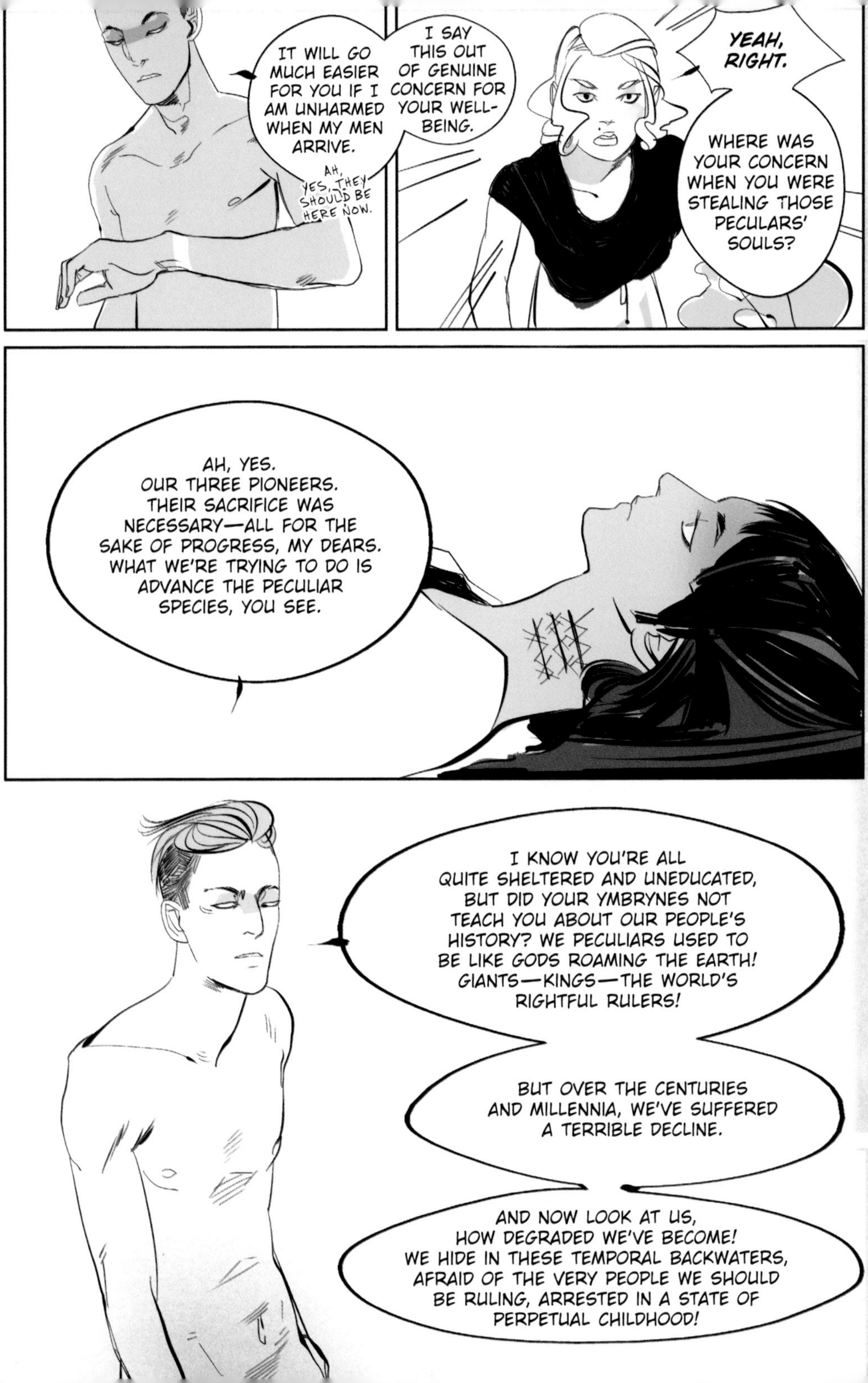

IT WILL GO MUCH EASIER FOR YOU IF I AM UNHARMED WHEN MY MEN ARRIVE.
I SAY THIS OUT OF GENUINE CONCERN FOR YOUR WELL-BEING.
AH, YES, THEY SHOULD BE HERE NOW.
YEAH, RIGHT.
WHERE WAS YOUR CONCERN WHEN YOU WERE STEALING THOSE PECULARS' SOULS?
AH, YES. OUR THREE PIONEERS. THEIR SACRIFICE WAS NECESSARY—ALL FOR THE SAKE OF PROGRESS, MY DEARS. WHAT WE'RE TRYING TO DO IS ADVANCE THE PECULIAR SPECIES, YOU SEE.
I KNOW YOU'RE ALL QUITE SHELTERED AND UNEDUCATED, BUT DID YOUR YMBRYNES NOT TEACH YOU ABOUT OUR PEOPLE'S HISTORY? WE PECULIARS USED TO BE LIKE GODS ROAMING THE EARTH! GIANTS—KINGS—THE WORLD'S RIGHTFUL RULERS!
BUT OVER THE CENTURIES AND MILLENNIA, WE'VE SUFFERED A TERRIBLE DECLINE.
AND NOW LOOK AT US, HOW DEGRADED WE'VE BECOME! WE HIDE IN THESE TEMPORAL BACKWATERS, AFRAID OF THE VERY PEOPLE WE SHOULD BE RULING, ARRESTED IN A STATE OF PERPETUAL CHILDHOOD!

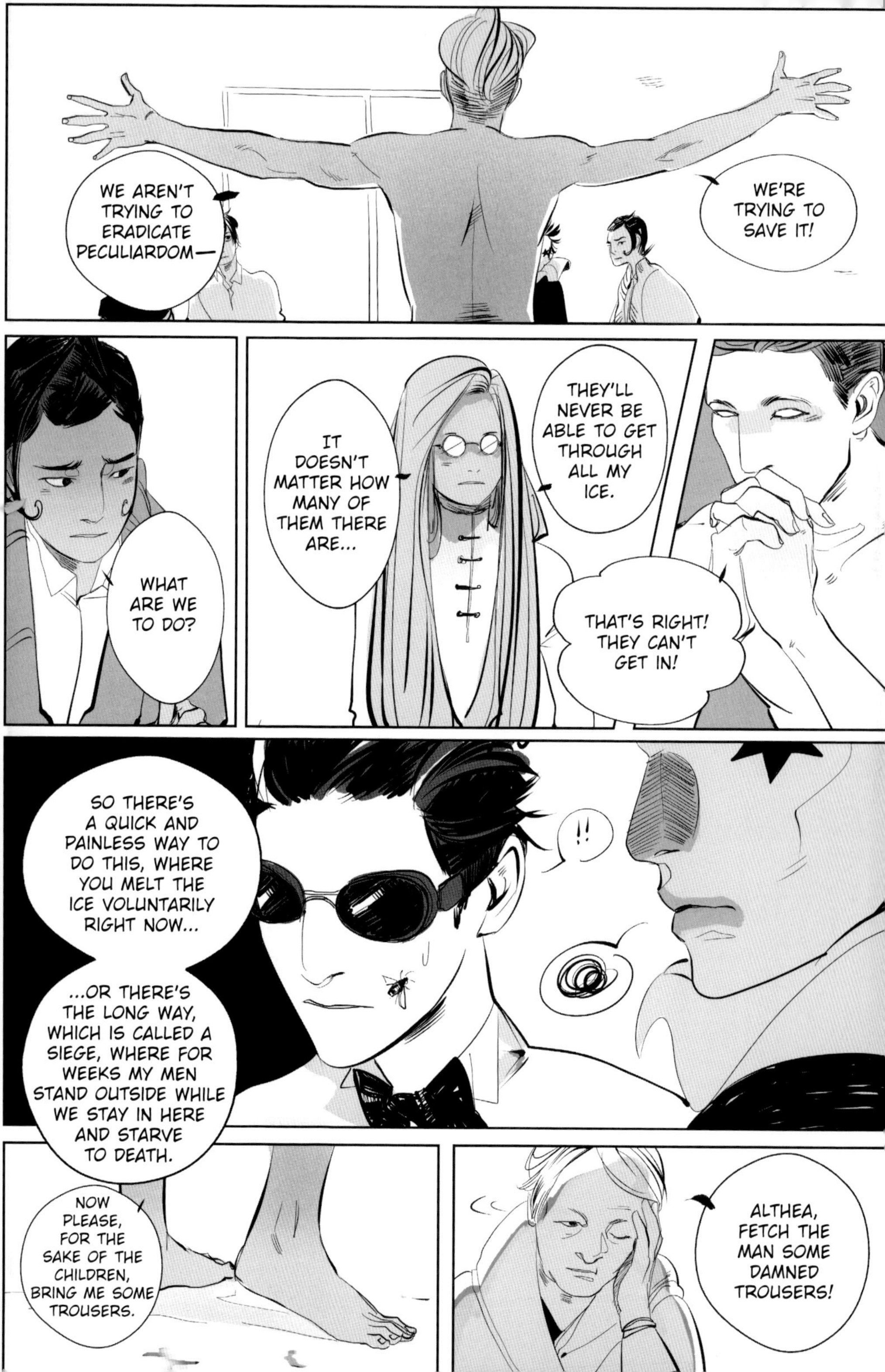
WE AREN'T TRYING TO ERADICATE PECULIARDOM—
WE'RE TRYING TO SAVE IT!
WHAT ARE WE TO DO?
IT DOESN'T MATTER HOW MANY OF THEM THERE ARE...
THEY'LL NEVER BE ABLE TO GET THROUGH ALL MY ICE.
THAT'S RIGHT! THEY CAN'T GET IN!
SO THERE'S A QUICK AND PAINLESS WAY TO DO THIS, WHERE YOU MELT THE ICE VOLUNTARILY RIGHT NOW...
...OR THERE'S THE LONG WAY, WHICH IS CALLED A SIEGE, WHERE FOR WEEKS MY MEN STAND OUTSIDE WHILE WE STAY IN HERE AND STARVE TO DEATH.
!!
NOW PLEASE, FOR THE SAKE OF THE CHILDREN, BRING ME SOME TROUSERS.
ALTHEA, FETCH THE MAN SOME DAMNED TROUSERS!

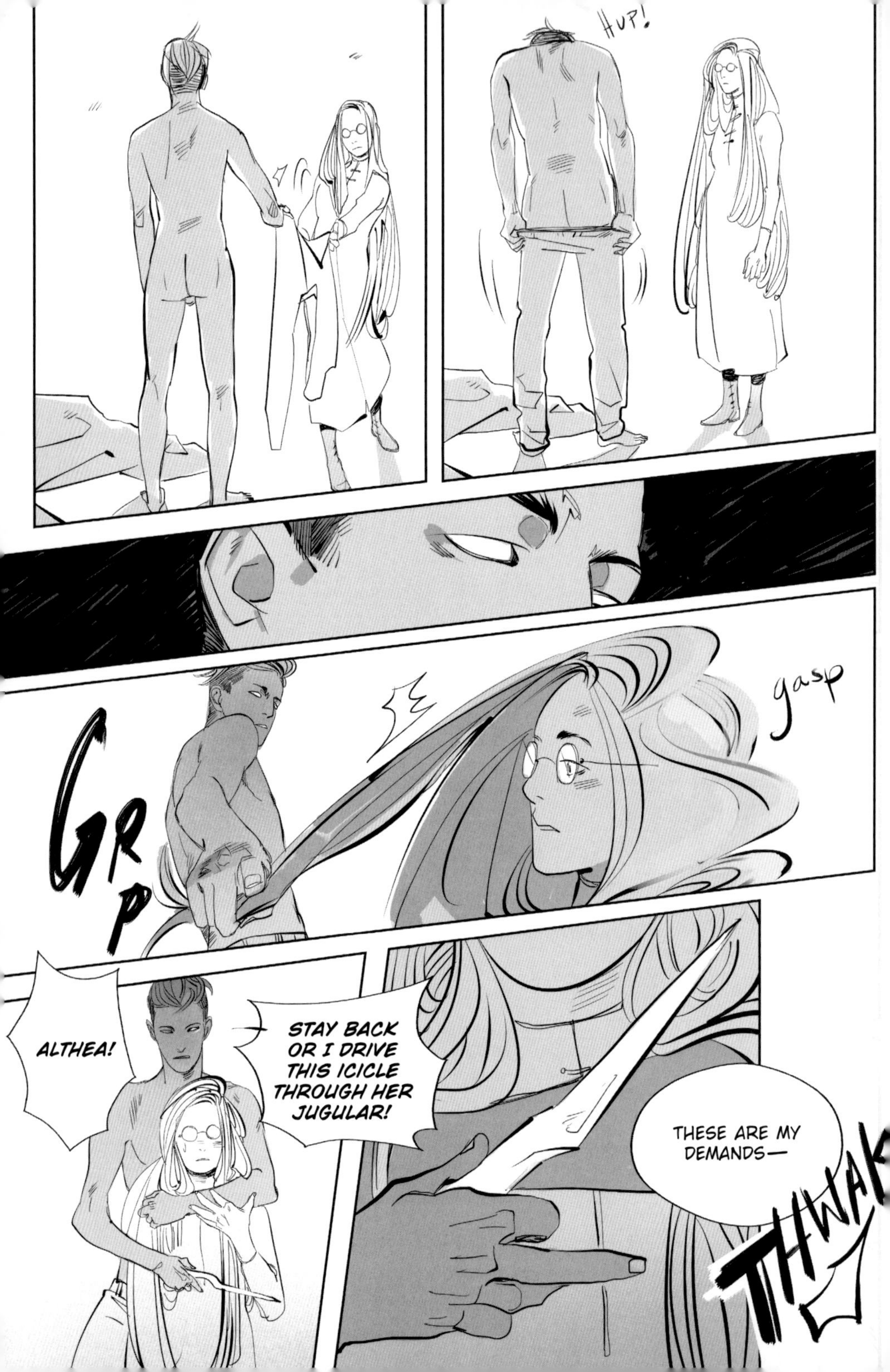
HUP!
GRP
gasp
ALTHEA!
STAY BACK OR I DRIVE THIS ICICLE THROUGH HER JUGULAR!
THESE ARE MY DEMANDS—
THWAK

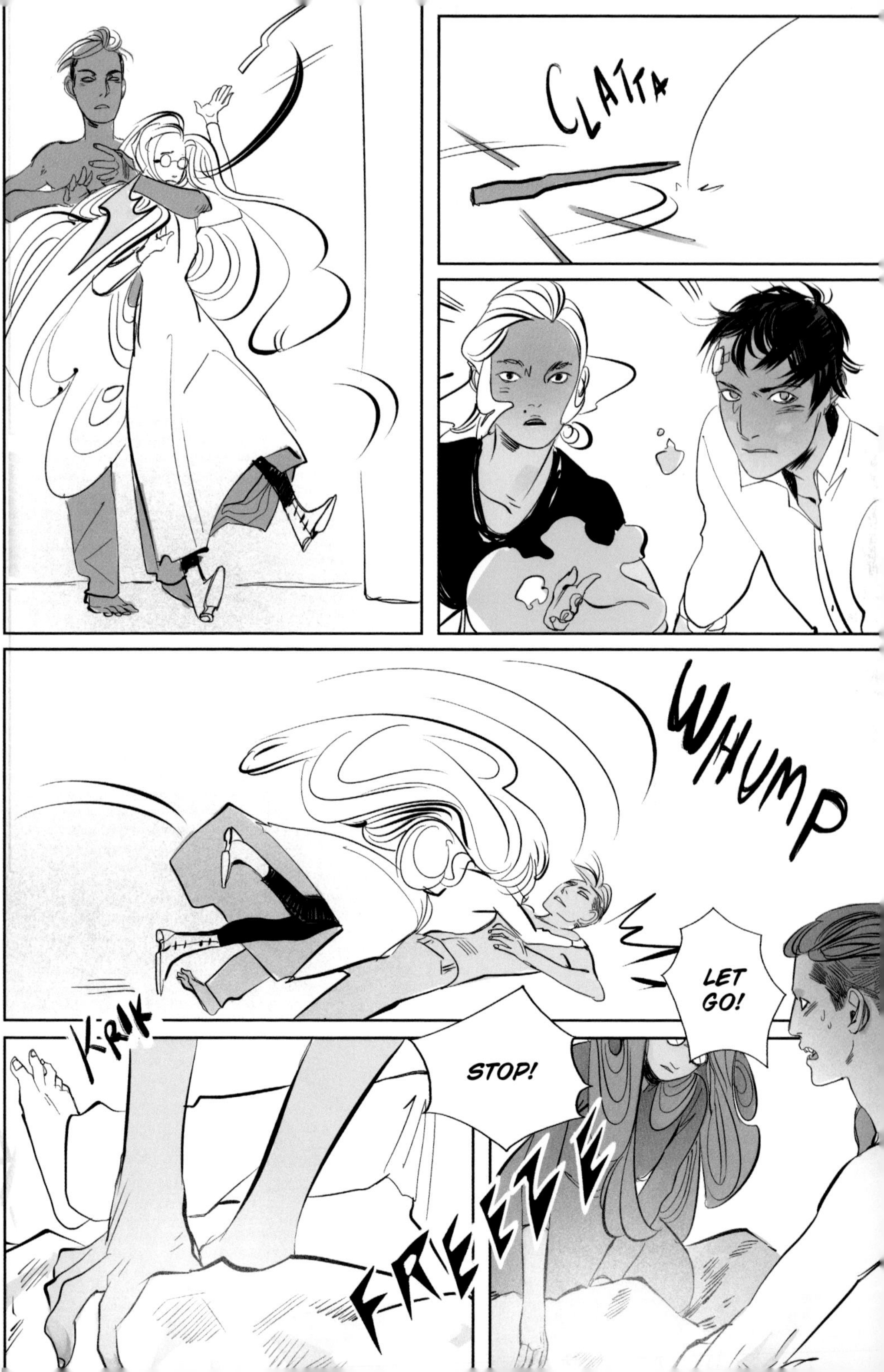
CLATTA
WHUMP
LET GO!
KRIK
STOP!
FREEZE

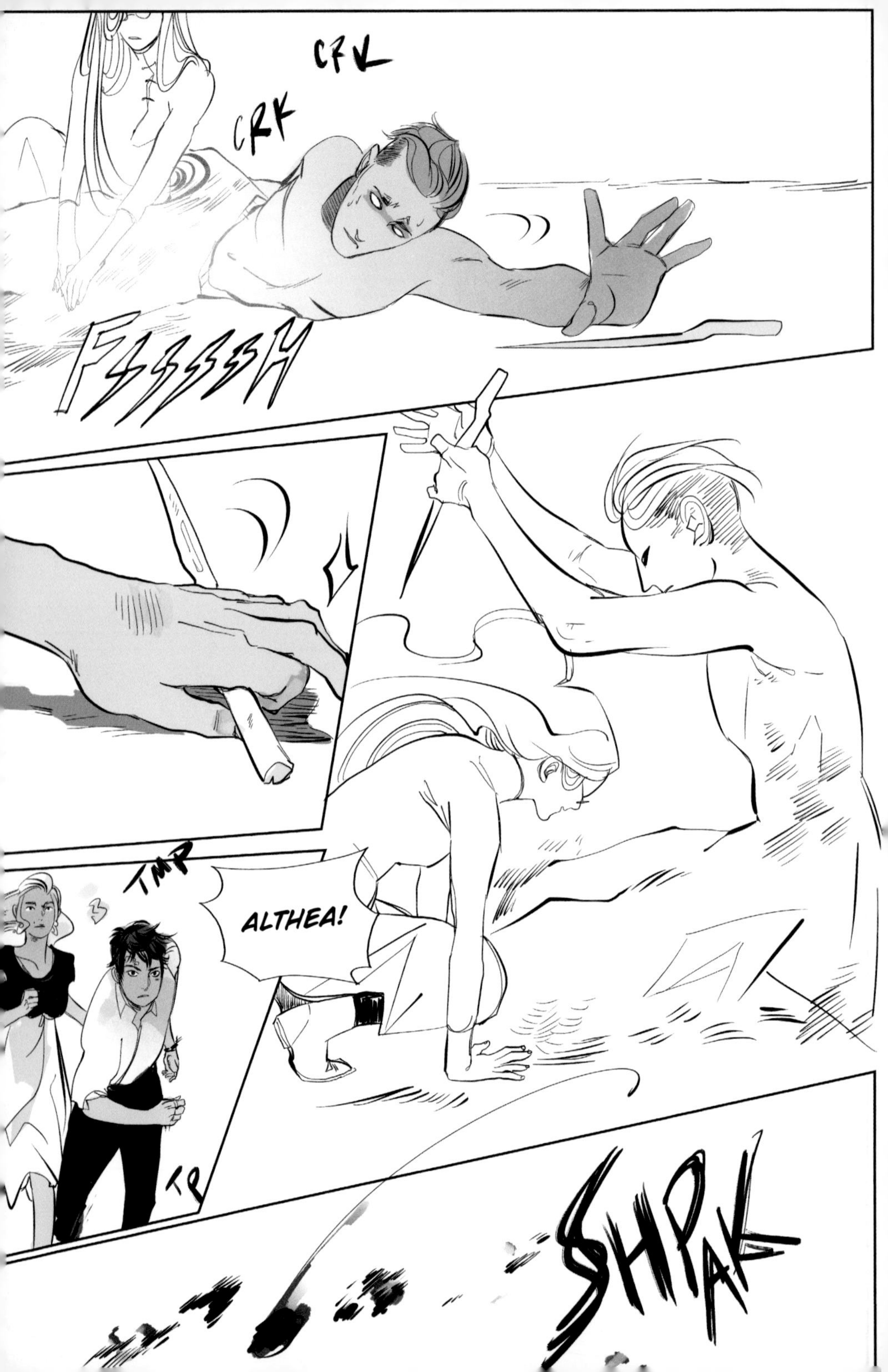
CRK
CRK
FSSSSH
TMP
ALTHEA!
TP
SHPAK

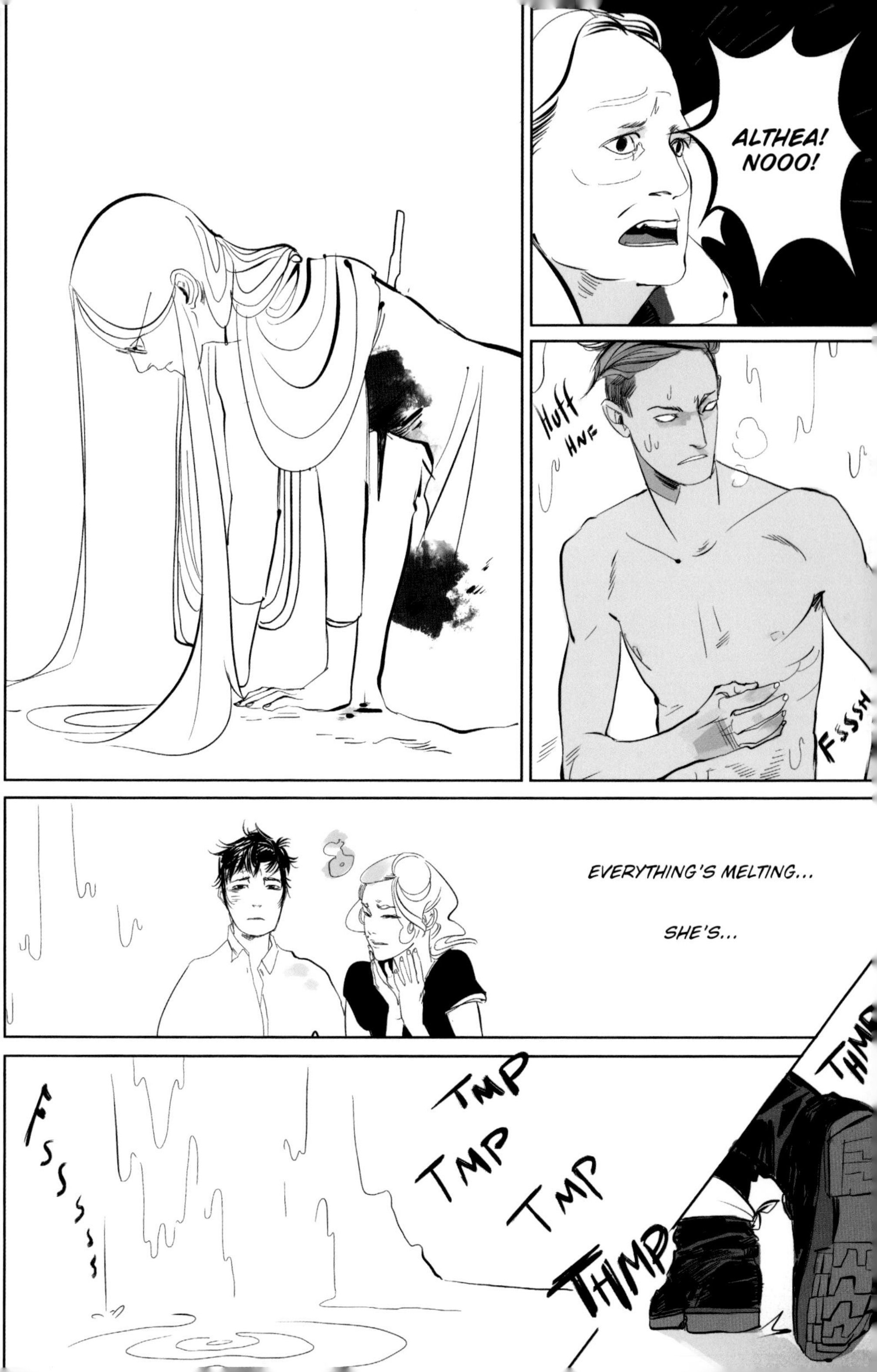
ALTHEA! NOOO!
HUFF
HNF
FSSSH
EVERYTHING'S MELTING...
SHE'S...
FSSSSS
TMP
TMP
TMP
THMP

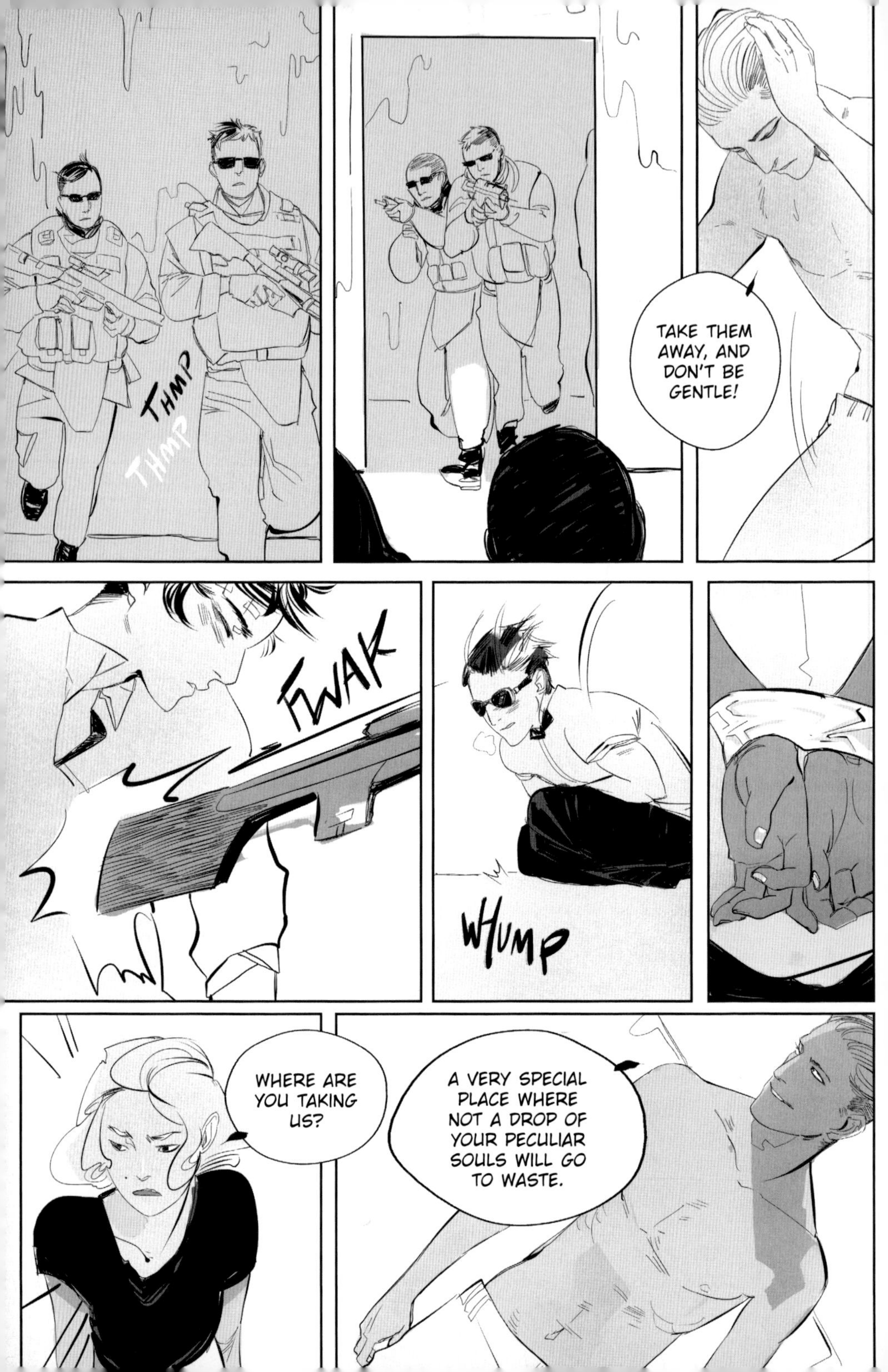
THMP
THMP
TAKE THEM AWAY, AND DON'T BE GENTLE!
FWAK
WHUMP
WHERE ARE YOU TAKING US?
A VERY SPECIAL PLACE WHERE NOT A DROP OF YOUR PECULIAR SOULS WILL GO TO WASTE.

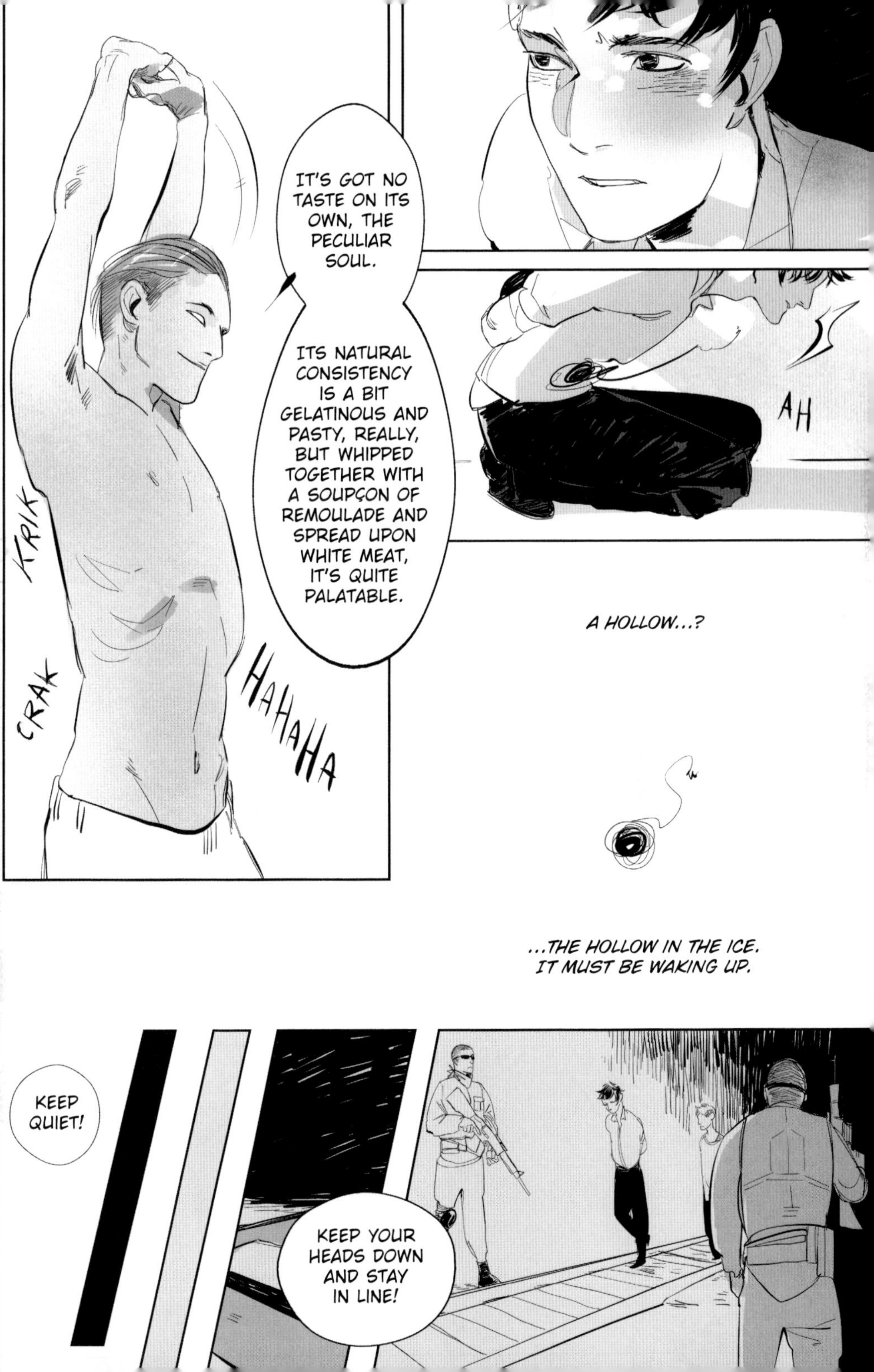
IT'S GOT NO TASTE ON ITS OWN, THE PECULIAR SOUL.
ITS NATURAL CONSISTENCY IS A BIT GELATINOUS AND PASTY, REALLY, BUT WHIPPED TOGETHER WITH A SOUPÇON OF REMOULADE AND SPREAD UPON WHITE MEAT, IT'S QUITE PALATABLE.
KRIK
CRAK
HAHAHAHA
AH
A HOLLOW...?
...THE HOLLOW IN THE ICE. IT MUST BE WAKING UP.
KEEP QUIET!
KEEP YOUR HEADS DOWN AND STAY IN LINE!

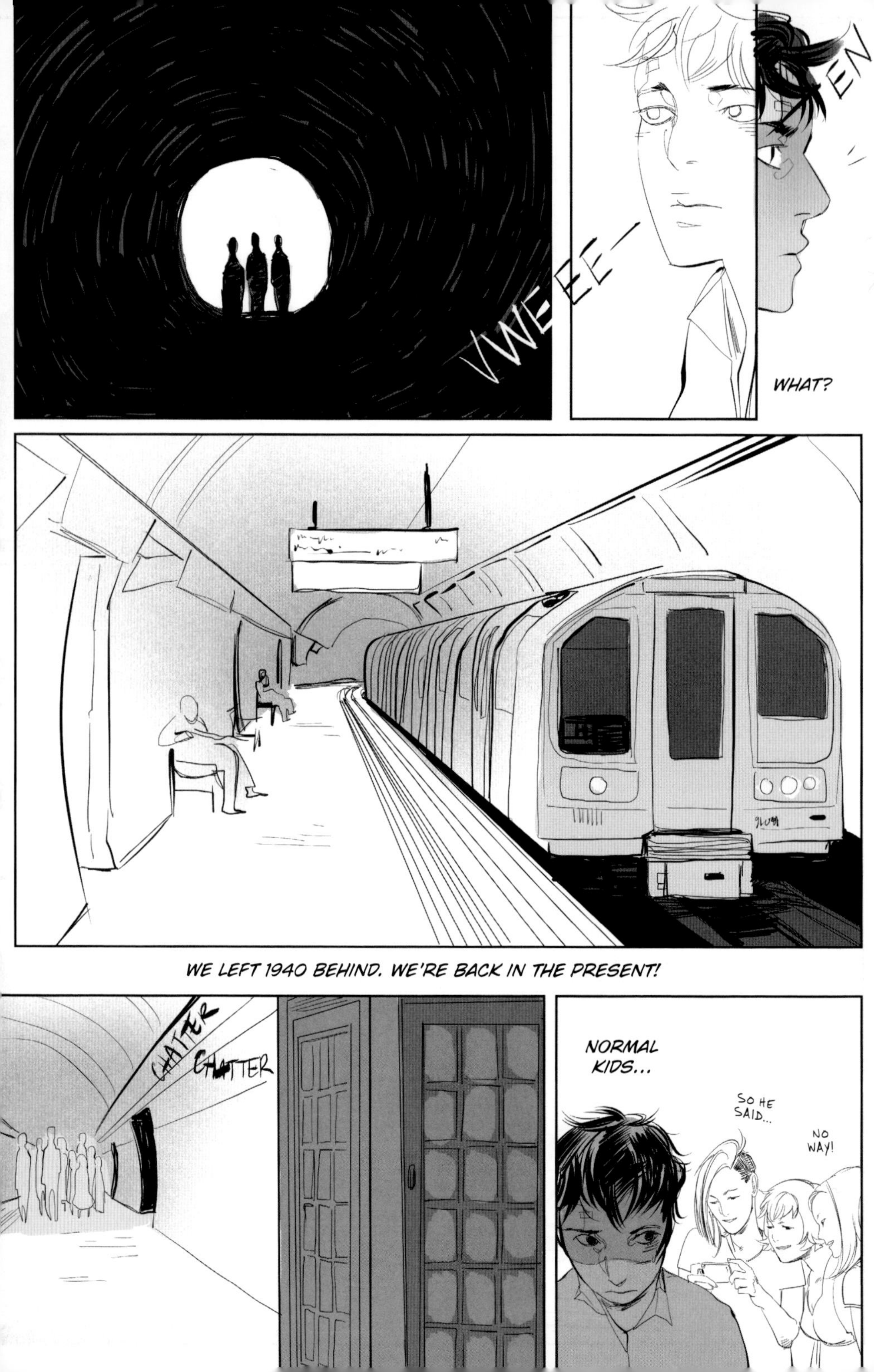
VWEEE—
EN
WHAT?
WE LEFT 1940 BEHIND. WE'RE BACK IN THE PRESENT!
CHATTER
CHATTER
NORMAL KIDS...
SO HE SAID...
NO WAY!

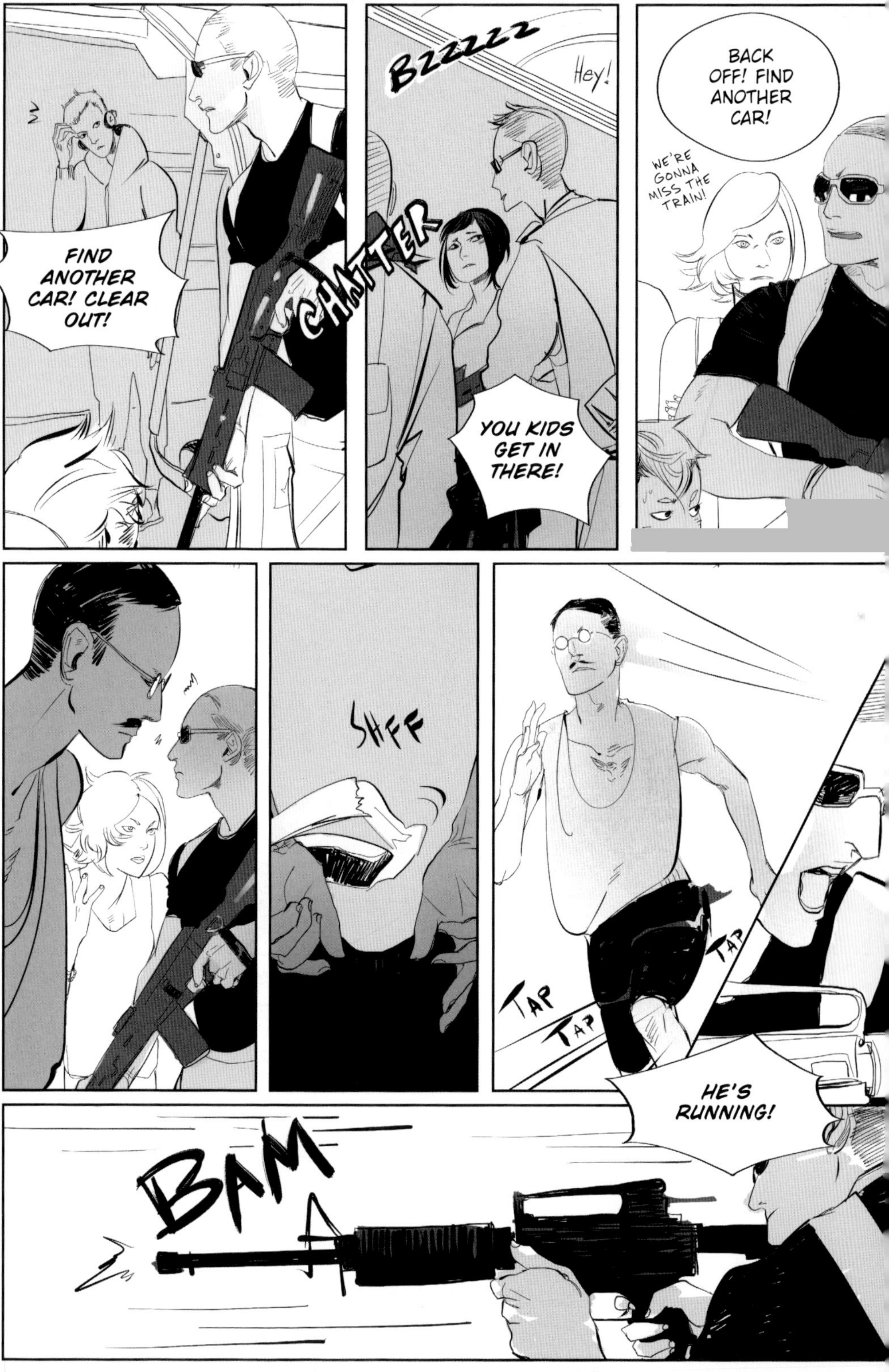
FIND ANOTHER CAR! CLEAR OUT!
Bzzzzz
Hey!
CHATTER
YOU KIDS GET IN THERE!
BACK OFF! FIND ANOTHER CAR!
WE'RE GONNA MISS THE TRAIN!
SHFF
TAP
TAP
TAP
HE'S RUNNING!
BAM

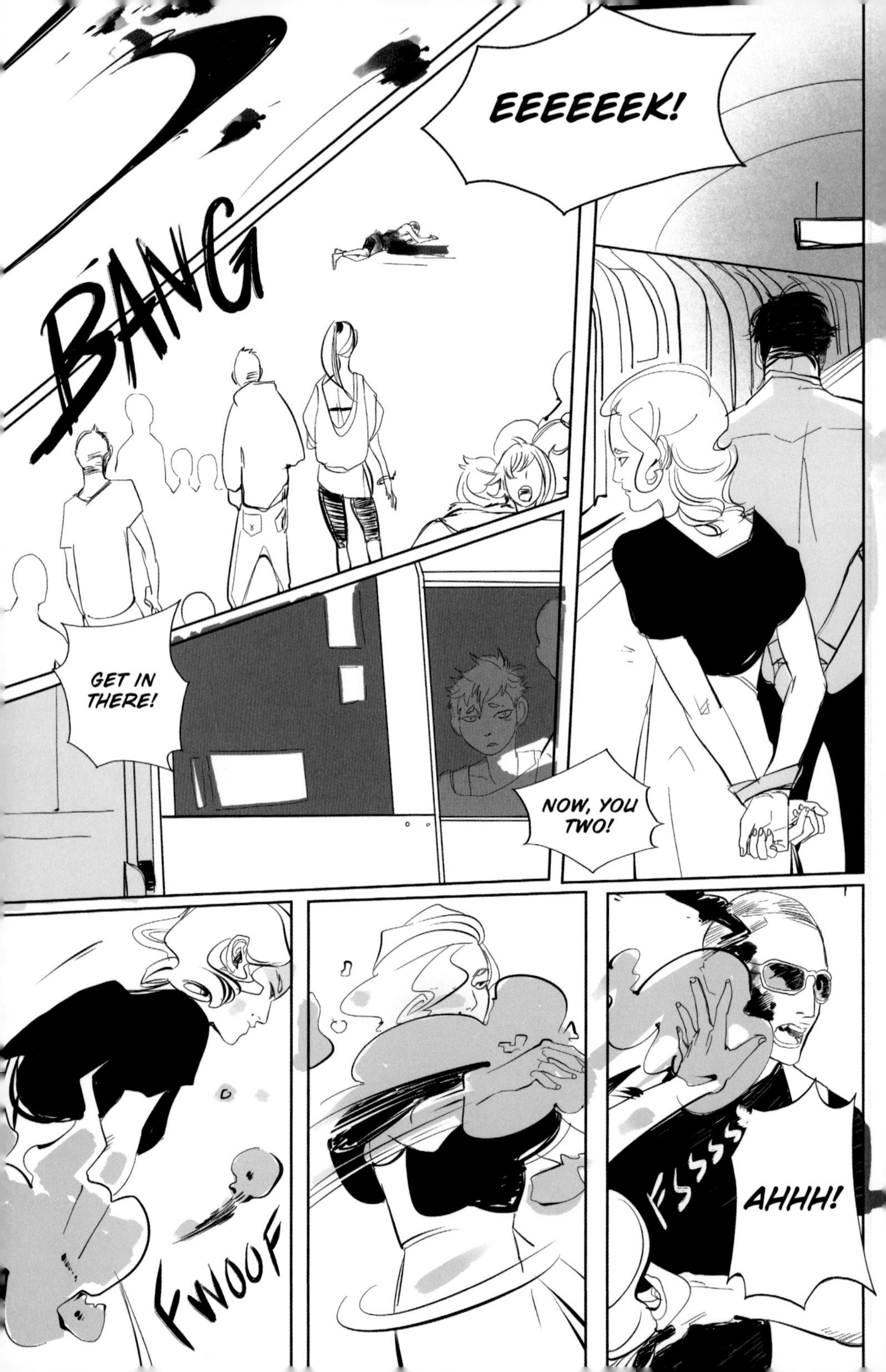
BANG
EEEEEEK!
GET IN THERE!
NOW, YOU TWO!
FWOOF
FSSSSS
AHHH!

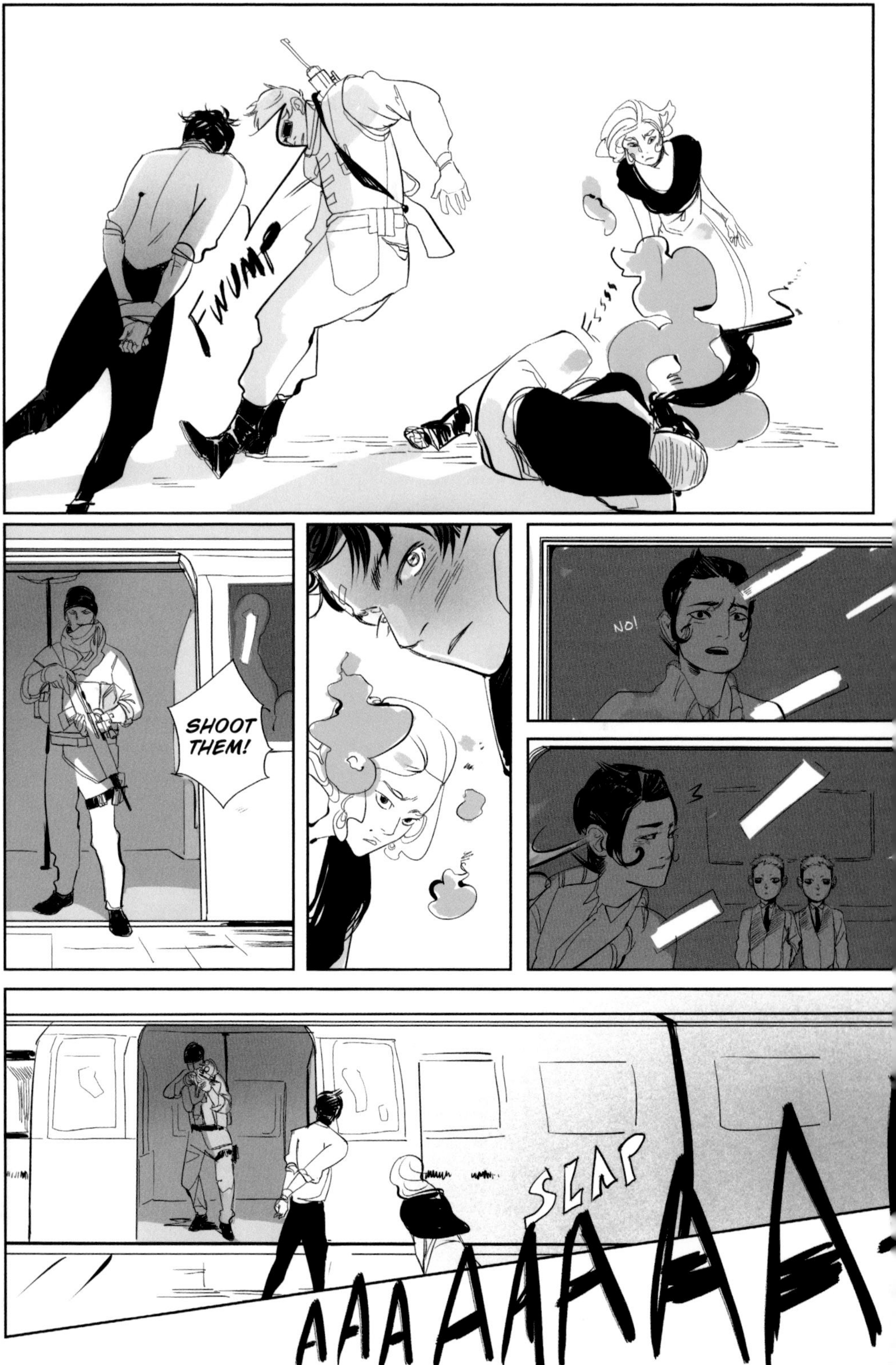
FWUMP
FSSSS
SHOOT THEM!
NO!
SLAP
AAAAAAAA

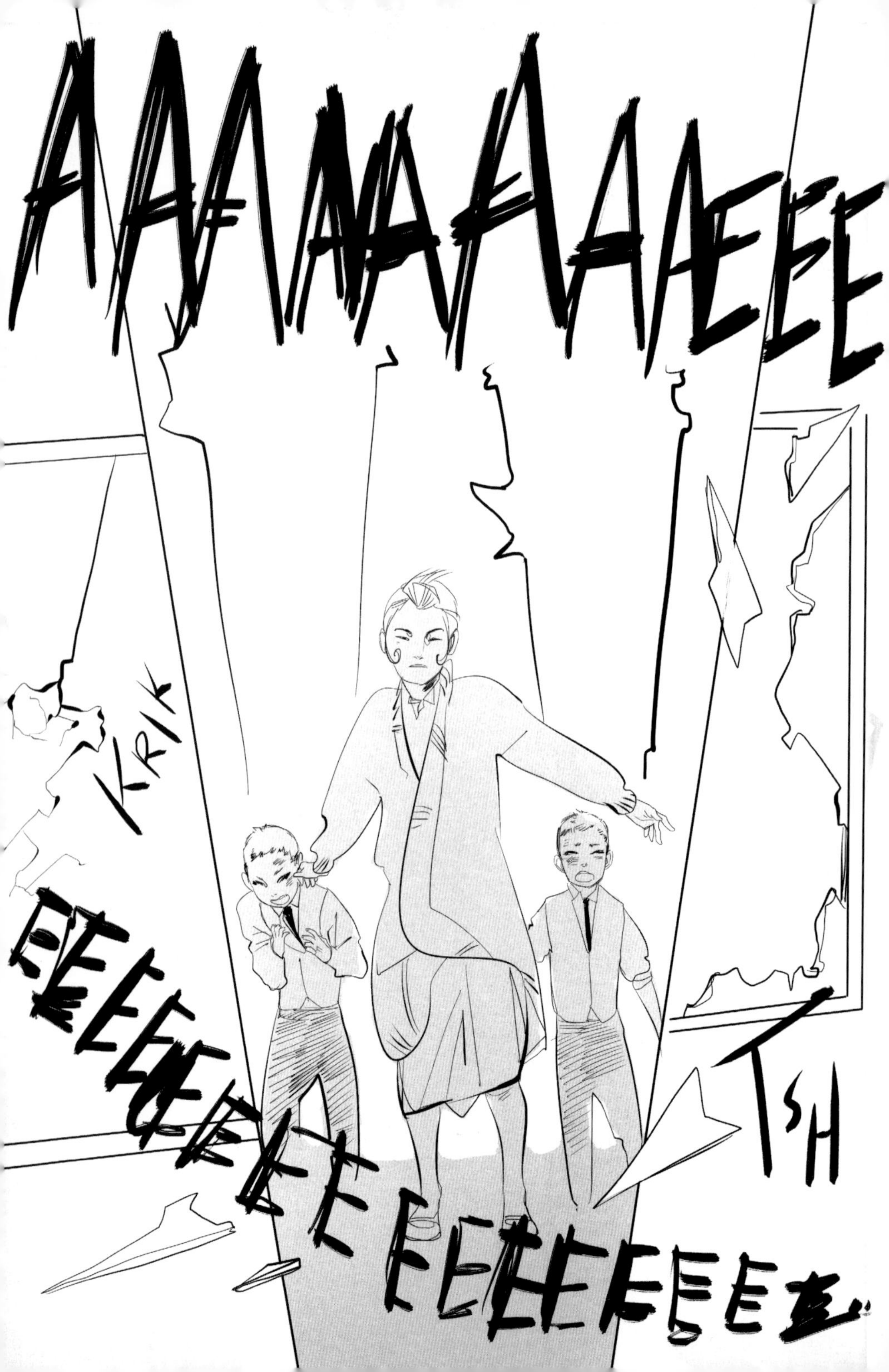
AAAAAAAAAEEE
KRIK
EEEEEEEEEEEEEEEEEE!
TSH

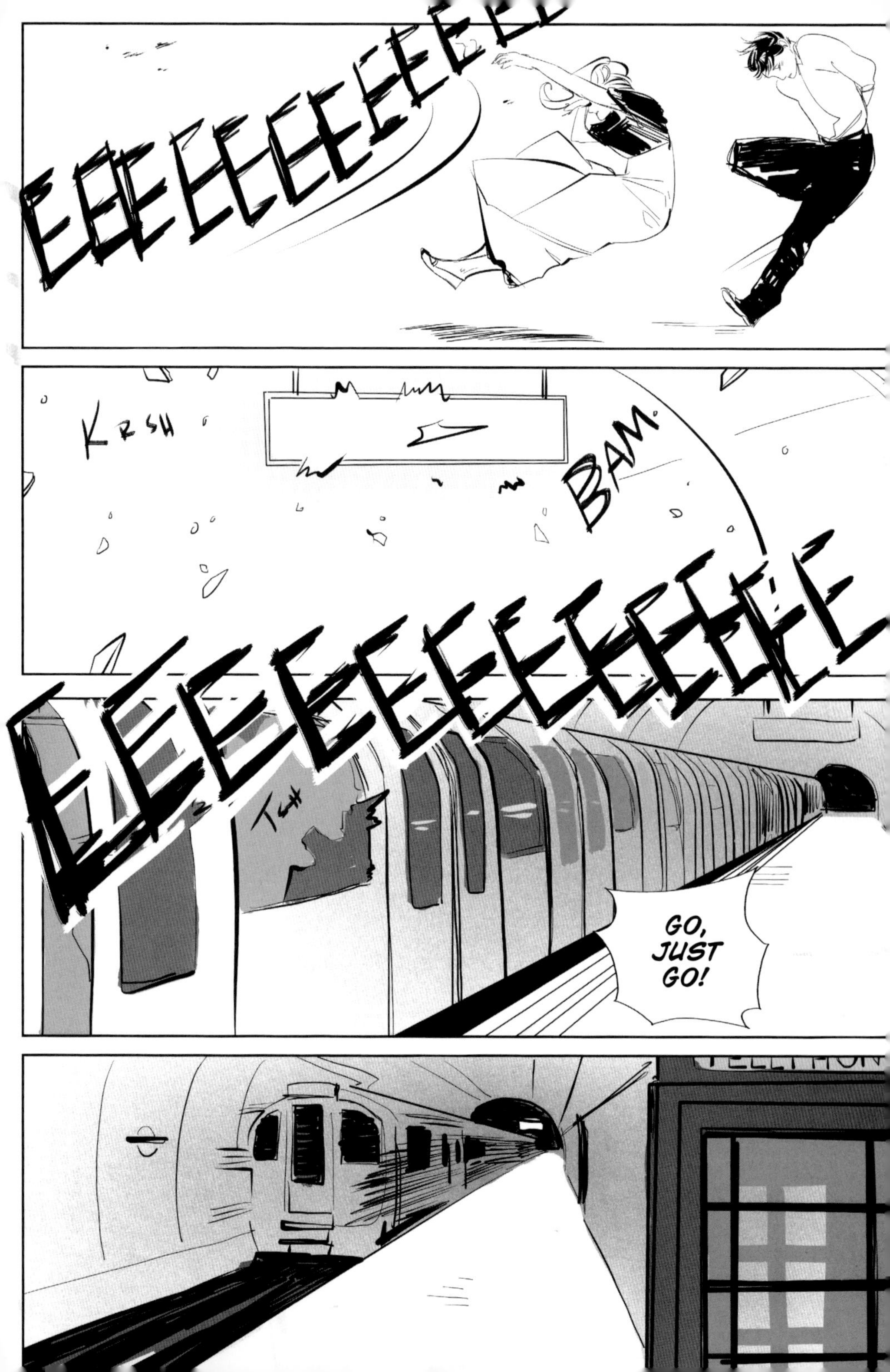
EEEEEEEEEEEEE
KRSH
BAM
EEEEEEEEEEEEEE
TCH
GO, JUST GO!

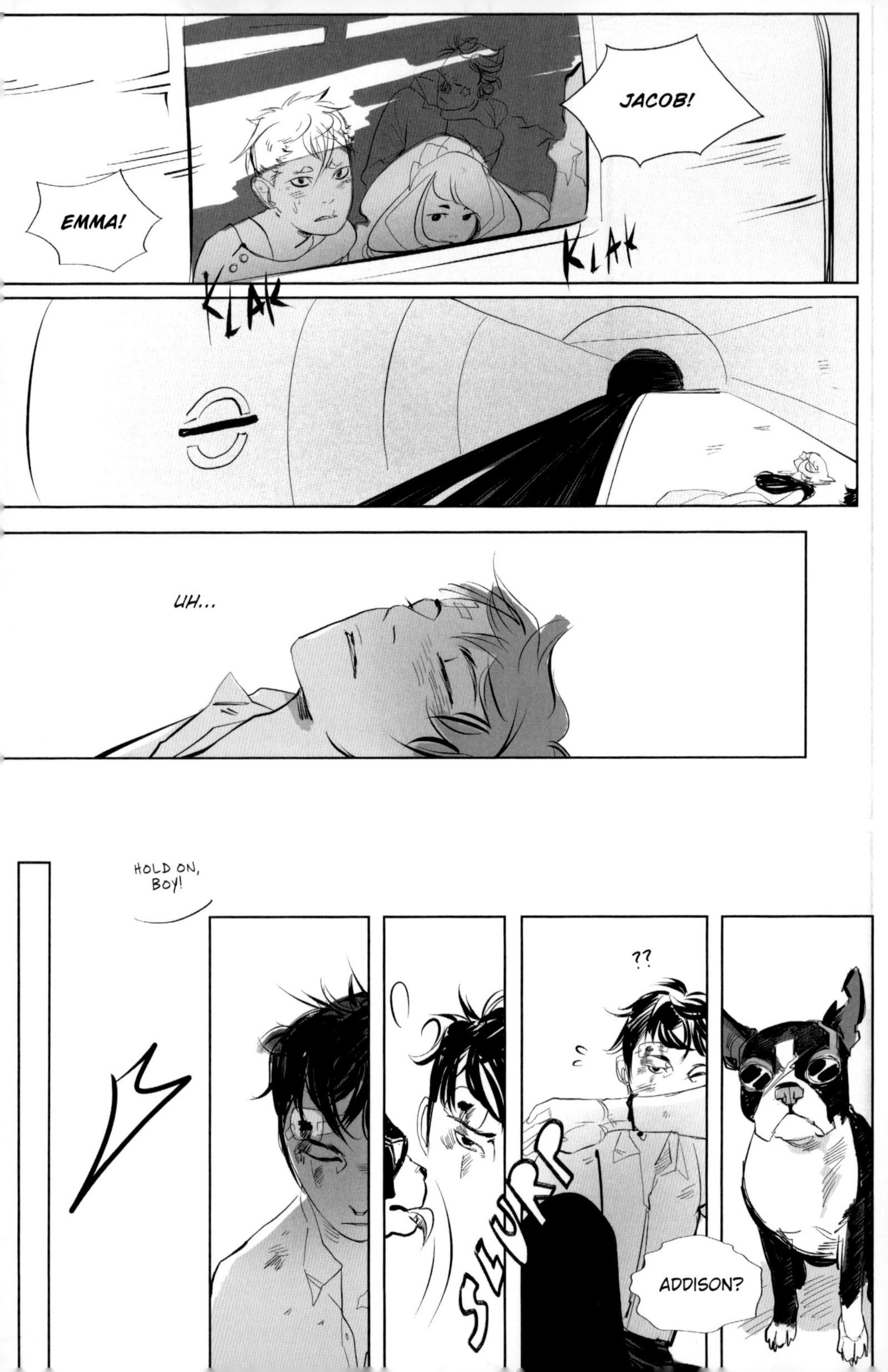
EMMA!
JACOB!
KLAK
KLAK
UH...
HOLD ON, BOY!
SLURP
??
ADDISON?

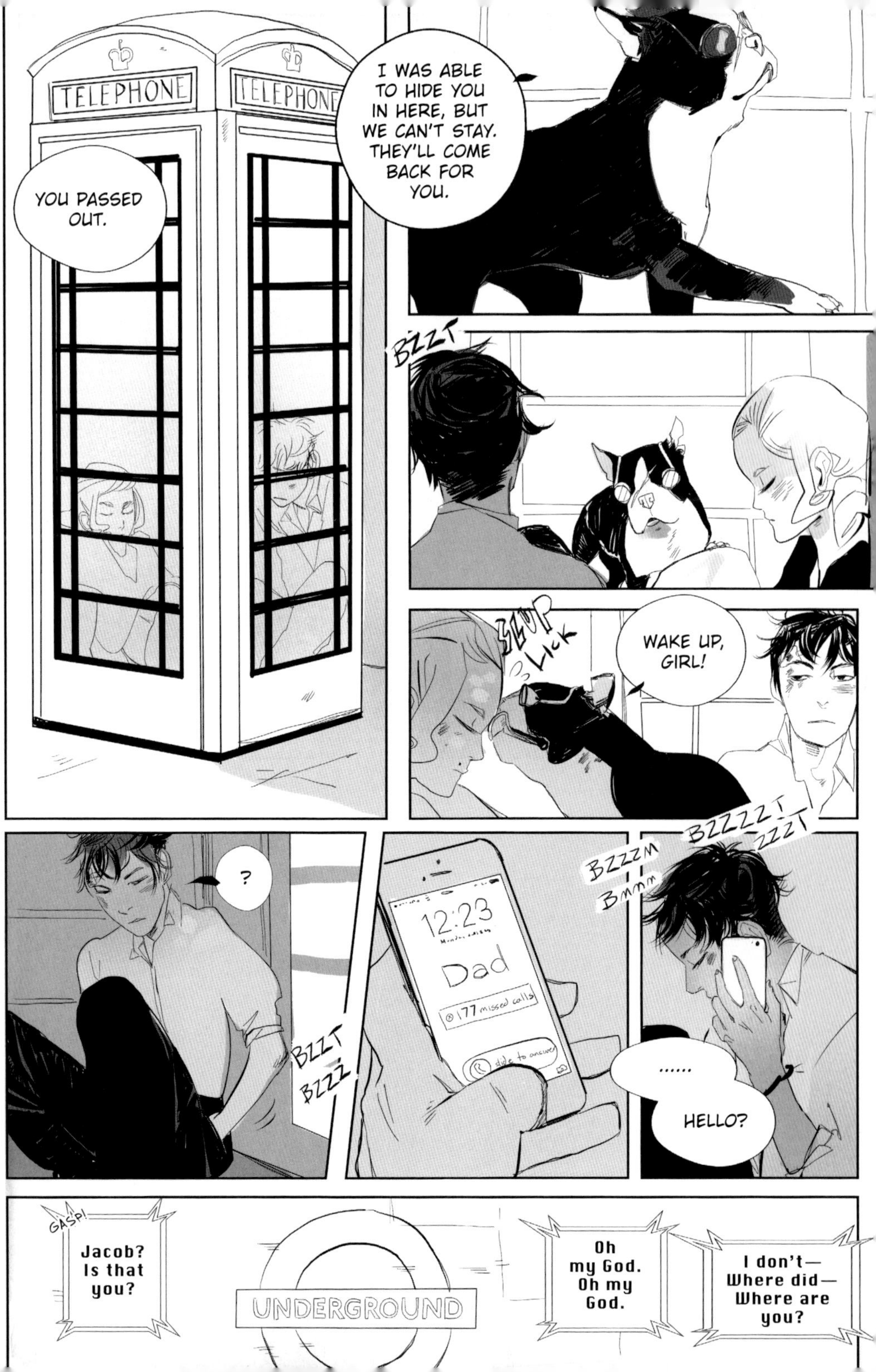
TELEPHONE
TELEPHONE
YOU PASSED OUT.
I WAS ABLE TO HIDE YOU IN HERE, BUT WE CAN'T STAY. THEY'LL COME BACK FOR YOU.
BZZT
LICK
WAKE UP, GIRL!
?
BZZT
BZZZ
12:23
Dad
177 missed calls
slide to answer
BZZZM
Bmmm
BZZZZT
ZZZT
......
HELLO?
GASP!
Jacob? Is that you?
UNDERGROUND
Oh my God. Oh my God.
I don't— Where did— Where are you?

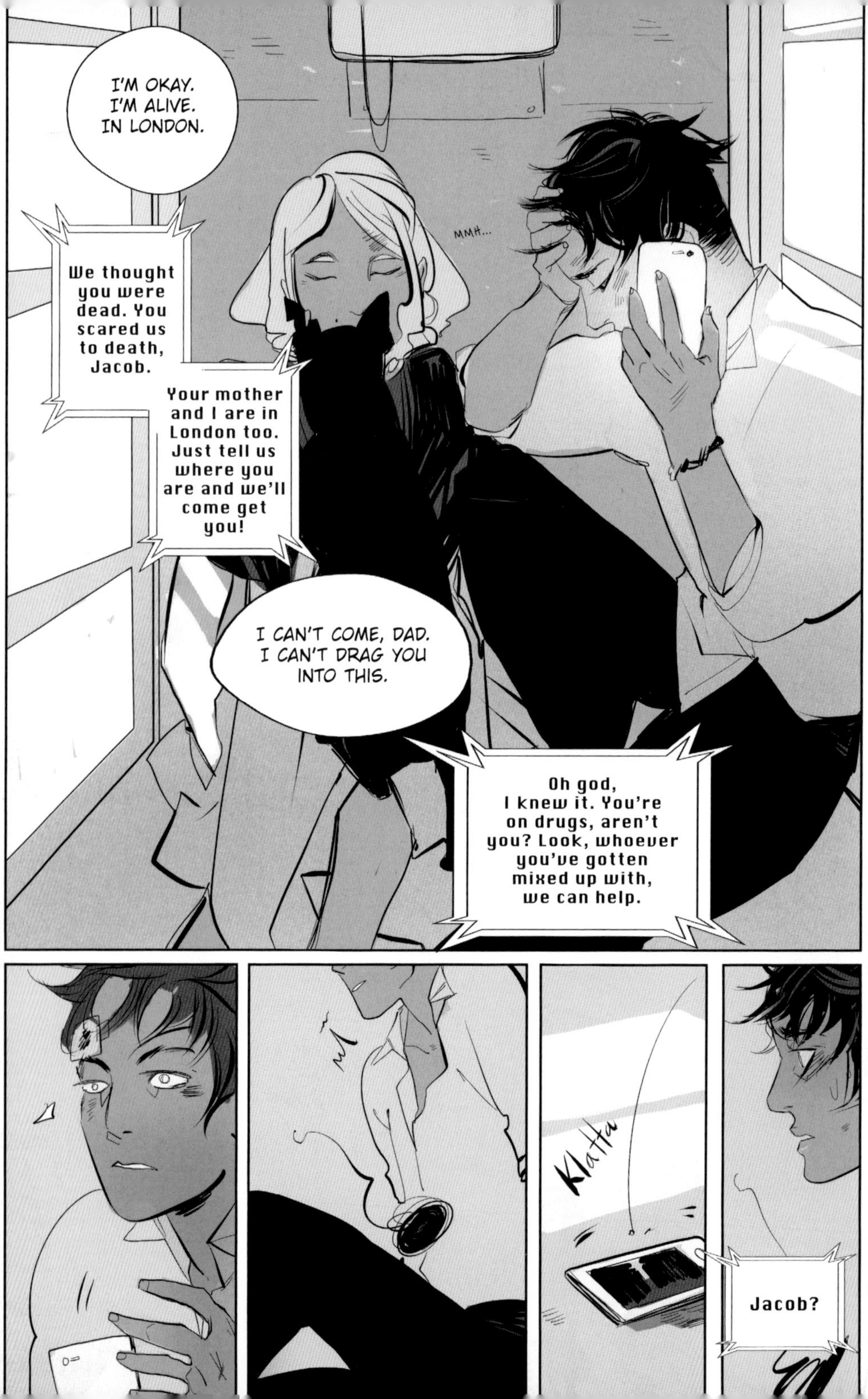
I'M OKAY. I'M ALIVE. IN LONDON.
We thought you were dead. You scared us to death, Jacob.
MMH...
Your mother and I are in London too. Just tell us where you are and we'll come get you!
I CAN'T COME, DAD. I CAN'T DRAG YOU INTO THIS.
Oh god, I knew it. You're on drugs, aren't you? Look, whoever you've gotten mixed up with, we can help.
Klatta
Jacob?

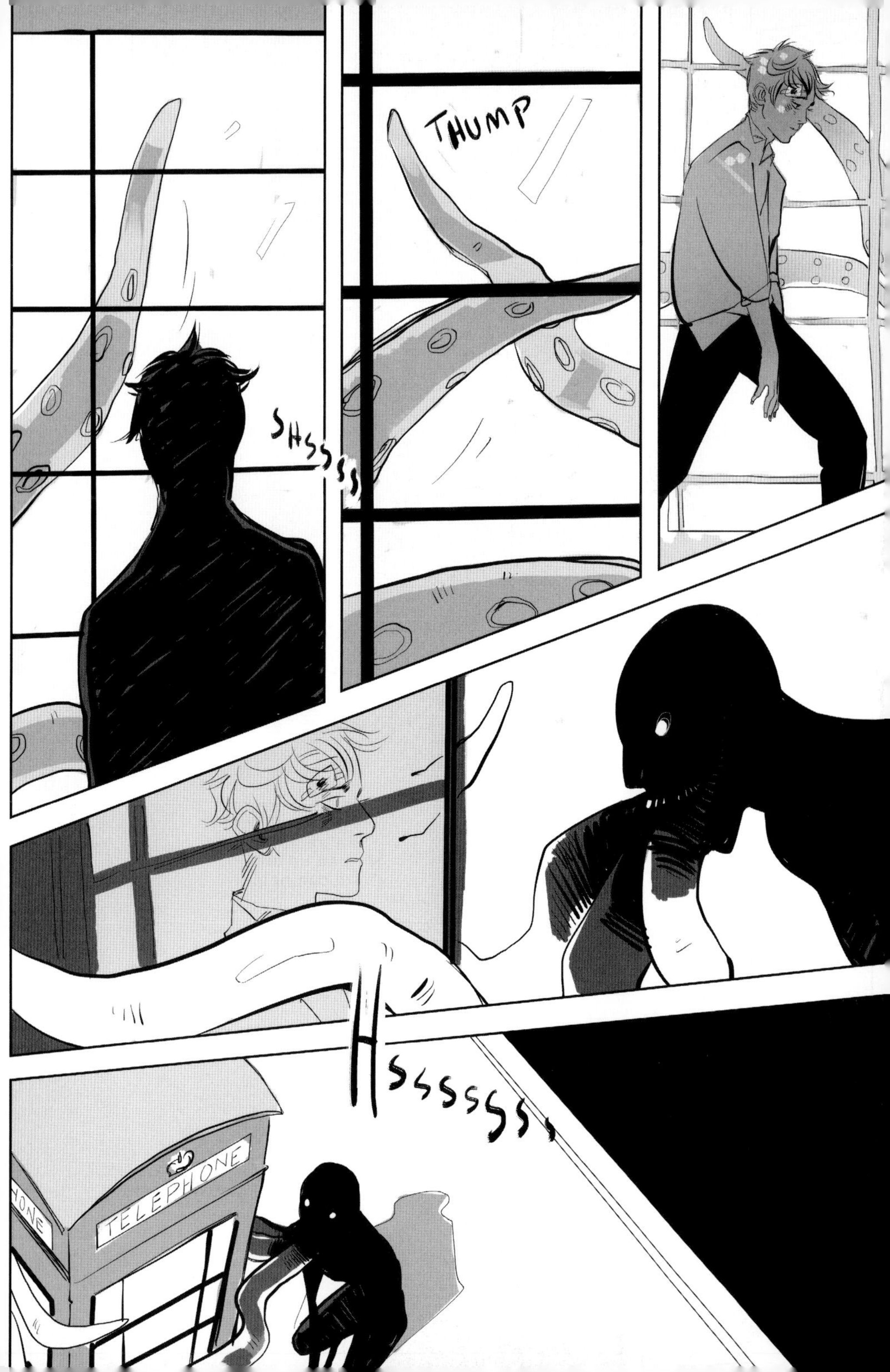
SHSSSSS
THUMP
HSSSSSSS,
TELEPHONE
TELEPHONE
HONE

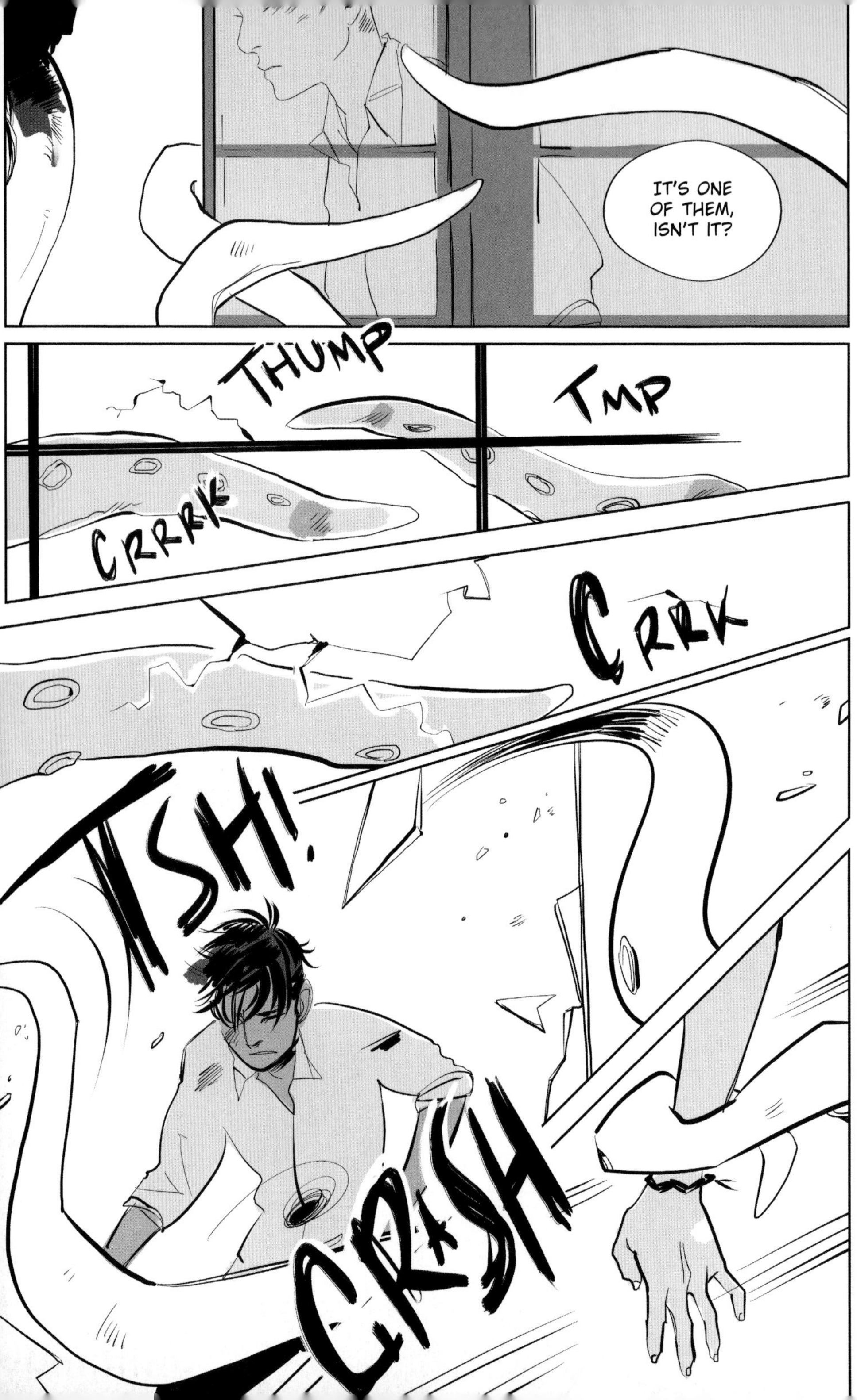
IT'S ONE OF THEM, ISN'T IT?
THUMP
TMP
CRRRK
CRRK
TSH!
CRASH

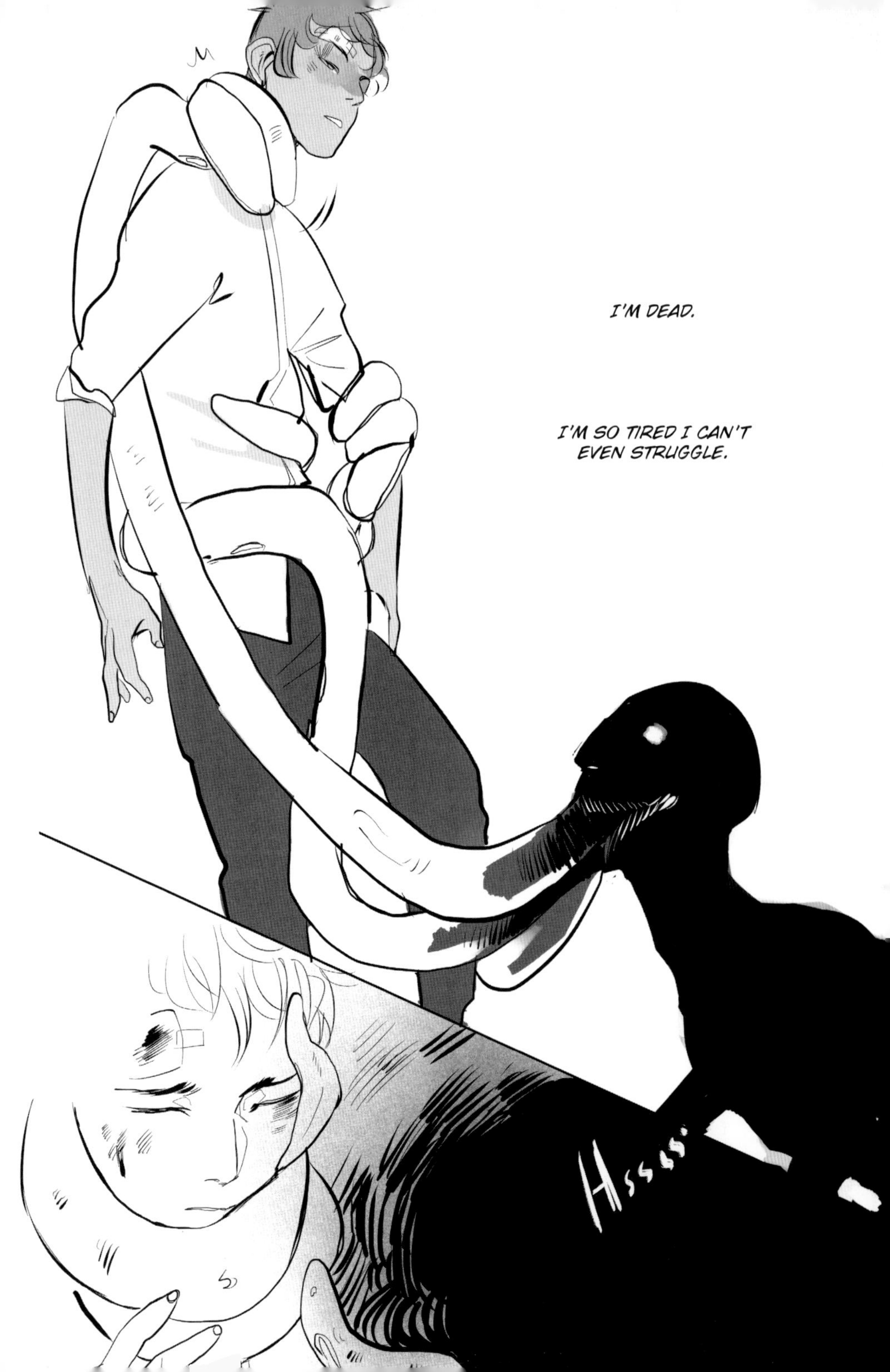
I'M DEAD.
I'M SO TIRED I CAN'T EVEN STRUGGLE.
Hssss

JACOB.

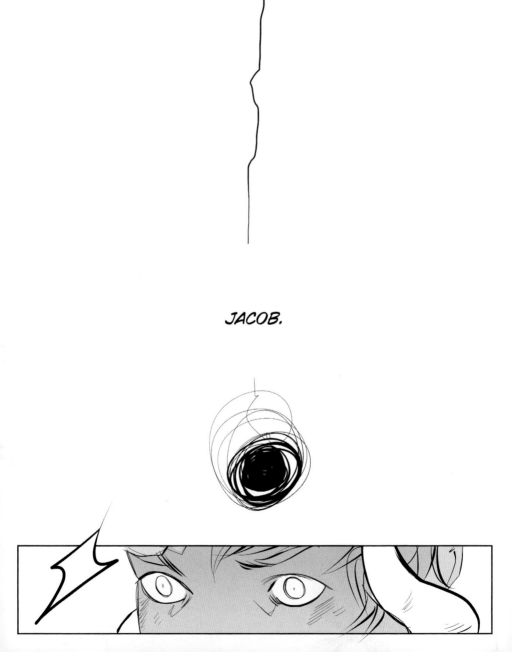

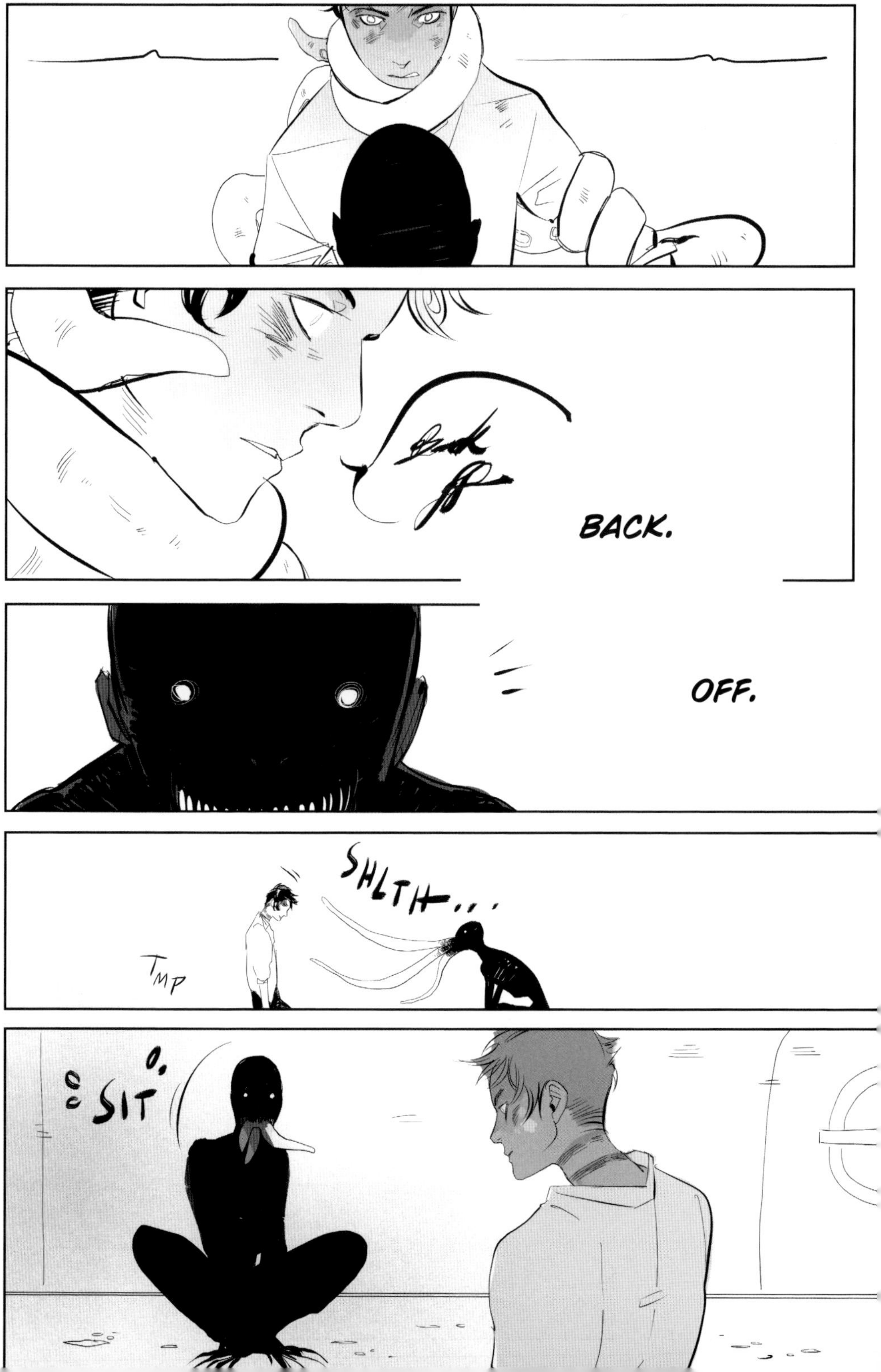
BACK.
OFF.
SHLTH...
TMP
SIT

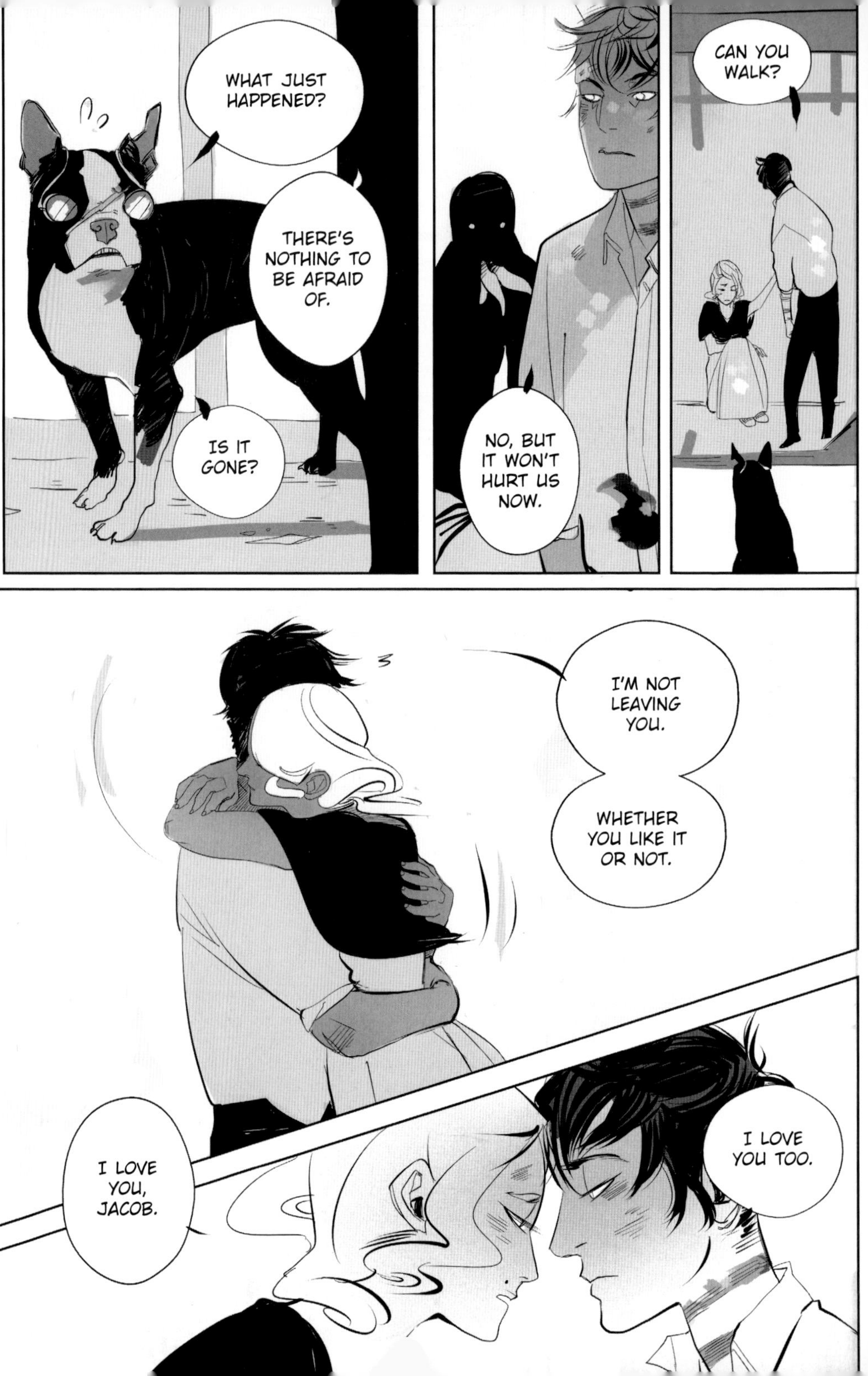
WHAT JUST HAPPENED?
THERE'S NOTHING TO BE AFRAID OF.
IS IT GONE?
NO, BUT IT WON'T HURT US NOW.
CAN YOU WALK?
I'M NOT LEAVING YOU.
WHETHER YOU LIKE IT OR NOT.
I LOVE YOU, JACOB.
I LOVE YOU TOO.